Additional praise for *A Companion to the Anthropology of Japan*

"Despite the magnitude of the task, Robertson has succeeded in this collection. Taken together, these 29 original chapters provide historical and theoretical grounding across a range of subjects. The diverse approaches taken here offer insight into a great variety of cultural aspects and social players, but articulate a 'Japan' that eludes any claims of homogeneity."
Steffi Richter, Universität Leipzig

"This *Companion* provides amazingly wide coverage on contemporary Japan. What's more, it challenges the very idea of anthropology in interesting ways. Although written by experts in the field, it will be of such great interest to students and others new to the field that it may well spark the imagination of the next Ruth Benedict in the making."
Kazue Muta, Osaka University

"*A Companion to the Anthropology of Japan* is a rich collection by Japanese and international researchers that demystifies Japanese culture and society. Challenging static and ahistorical perceptions of Japan, it ranges widely across space and time to provide an innovative and critical study of minorities, gender, culture, education, family, ritual, citizenship, and more."
Mark Selden, Binghamton and Cornell Universities

Blackwell Companions to Anthropology

Blackwell Companions to Anthropology offers a series of comprehensive syntheses of the traditional subdisciplines, primary subjects, and geographic areas of inquiry for the field. Taken together, the titles in the series represent both a contemporary survey of anthropology and a cutting-edge guide to the emerging research and intellectual trends in the field as a whole.

A Companion to the Anthropology of Japan

Edited by Jennifer Robertson

BLACKWELL PUBLISHING
350 Main Street, Malden, MA 02148–5020, USA
9600 Garsington Road, Oxford OX4 2DQ, UK
550 Swanston Street, Carlton, Victoria 3053, Australia

First published 2005
First published in paperback 2008 by Blackwell Publishing Ltd

1 2008

Library of Congress Cataloging-in-Publication Data

A companion to the anthropology of Japan / edited by Jennifer Robertson.
    p. cm. — (Blackwell companions to anthropology; 5)
    Includes bibliographical references and index.
    ISBN 978-0-631-22955-1 (hardcover : alk. paper)—ISBN 978-1-4051-8289-8 (pbk : alk. paper)
       1. Ethnology—Japan. 2. Japan—Social life and customs. I. Robertson, Jennifer Ellen. II. Series.

GN635.J2C65 2005
306′.0952—c22

2004022308

A catalogue record for this title is available from the British Library.

Set in 10/12.5 pt Galliard
by SPi Publisher Services, Pondicherry, India
Printed and bound in Singapore
by Markono Print Media Pte Ltd

For further information on
Blackwell Publishing, visit our website at
www.blackwellpublishing.com

Contents

Synopsis of Contents

Part I: Introduction

1 Introduction: Putting and Keeping Japan in Anthropology
Jennifer Robertson

Robertson explores the "ancestry" of (Anglophone) Japan anthropology from the 1930s through the early 1960s, a 30-year period when Japan was acknowledged in the discipline as an important site of and for anthropological knowledge and theory-making. She asks why, since then, "Japan" seems to have passed out of, and to have been passed over by, the anthropological mainstream, and suggests that the legacy of certain "ancestors" may be partly responsible. The question, "Where is 'Japan' in anthropological discourse today, and what are the significant contributions to social and cultural theory that Japan anthropologists have made since 1970, and are making today?" sets the stage for the essays that follow.

Part II: Cultures, Histories, and Identities

The essays in this section critically examine the processes of history- and culture-making along with identity formation, majority and minority alike.

2 The Imperial Past of Anthropology in Japan
Katsumi Nakao

Nakao argues that to explore the history of prewar ethnographic research is tantamount to remembering and confronting modern Japan's imperialist past. The apparent "historical amnesia" among anthropologists in Japan parallels the low level of historical consciousness of Japanese people in general about Japan's imperial past. Ethnographic research in the first half of the 20th century collectively helped to facilitate Japan's administration of its scattered Asian Pacific empire. As Nakao shows, Japanese anthropology of the imperial period – the late 19th century through

1945 – possessed a distinctive character that calls for wider recognition and analytical scrutiny.

3 Japanese Archaeology and Cultural Properties Management: Prewar Ideology and Postwar Legacies
Walter Edwards

Edwards explains how, as part of Japanese efforts at modernization, the adoption of Western academic disciplines in the late 19th century included the introduction of scientific archaeology. Early cultural properties management policies had a strong ideological component, in large part a consequence of the symbolic importance placed on the imperial institution, taken to be a source of pride for the nation in the modern world due to its "unique continuity from an ancient and divine origin." The legacy of the imperial household on archaeology today is investigated.

4 Feminism, Timelines, and History-Making
Tomomi Yamaguchi

Yamaguchi observes that in the mid-1990s, notable numbers of books on the history of the women's liberation movement (*ribu*) since the 1970s were published in Japan. Many, if not most, included a *nenpyō* (timeline): a chronological list of events, a style commonly used in Japanese historical writings. For feminist writers, the timeline is a vehicle for producing an alternative version of existing writings on the history of the *ribu* movement. Yamaguchi's analysis of *nenpyō*-writing offers a significant venue to examine the philosophy of time reflected in this particular mode of history-writing, and the contested discourses on the politics of history-writing in contemporary Japan.

5 Making Majority Culture
Roger Goodman

Goodman poses the rhetorical question, "Who are 'the Japanese'?" While there is evidence of attempts to construct ideas of Japanese ethnic identity that go back two millennia, most commentators point to the Meiji period (1868–1912) as when this process became particularly emphasized in Japan. Faced by both internal and external threats, the Meiji oligarchs developed a rich litany of symbols and rituals that helped to construct the ideas of Japaneseness that were disseminated through an education system constructed, in part, for that purpose. Scholarly research on Japanese ethnic identity together with popular notions of the superiority of Japanese culture came to the fore again in the 1980s as the Japanese economy went into overdrive. Goodman points out the presumption, in these dominant ideas of Japaneseness, that "culture" is static, timeless, and self-evident.

6 Political and Cultural Perspectives on "Insider" Minorities
Joshua Hotaka Roth

Roth reminds us that there are a variety of "insider" minorities in Japan – the Burakumin, Ainu, Okinawans, Nikkeijin, the disabled, and atomic bomb victims. These groups vary widely in size, history, consciousness as groups, and criteria for membership. Yet they have several characteristics in common that justifies their treatment together. They are all "insiders" in the sense that most other Japanese currently do not question their status as Japanese. Insider status does not, however, shield any of these groups from discrimination. Roth explores and compares the two major perspectives – cultural and political – that are used by social scientists in analyzing discrimination in Japan, and offers a synthesis.

7   Japan's Ethnic Minority: Koreans
Sonia Ryang

Ryang argues that studies of ethnic minorities in Japan lag behind in the overall scheme of the anthropology of Japan. Koreans in Japan, perhaps the best-explored group in light of this situation, still need to be looked at from multiple angles and dimensions in terms of analysis and interpretation. This has been done by Korean and Japanese writers in Japan, but the Anglophone literature on Koreans in Japan has many gaps. Ryang reminds us that the main purpose of studying Koreans in Japan is to understand their position in Japanese society as an indissoluble part of Japan itself, as well as to grasp their internal situation as "resident aliens."

8   Shifting Contours of Class and Status
Glenda S. Roberts

Roberts looks critically at the contours of class and status in Japan, focusing in particular on the rise of egalitarianism in the postwar era and the manifestations of social class through the lens of gender. She argues that we need more research on the ways in which gender and ethnicity inform social class practices. The contours of class and status in Japan appear to be shifting away from a large "middle-mass" toward a more polarized society, characterized by less job stability even for the middle classes, and increasing concern in the media over the uncertainties that accompany the current fluid situation.

9   The Anthropology of Japanese Corporate Management
Tomoko Hamada

Hamada notes that during the 1960s, Japan was often cited as a case in point to support or refute dominant Western theories of economic development and modernization, and the "Japanese style of management" was presented as a distinct cultural form. With the bursting of Japan's economic bubble in the early 1990s and the consequent continuing recession emerged a new research agenda to investigate the pathological aspects of corporate Japan. As Hamada shows, in the 21st century, the theme of "globalization" has been affixed to this agenda, where the global standard as the dominant Western norm is positioned against the reality of diverse adaptative mechanisms among and within contemporary capitalistic entities of unequal relations.

10 Fashioning Cultural Identity: Body and Dress
Ofra Goldstein-Gidoni

Goldstein-Gidoni explores the centrality of distinctions in dress in the construction of Japanese cultural identity. Modern Japanese wear both Western-style clothing (*yōfuku*) and Japanese-style attire (*wafuku*), although the latter is worn mainly on ceremonial occasions. She considers the dynamic process of the construction of gendered cultural identities in modern Japan through both a historic perspective and present-day ethnography, looking closely at the gendered effects created through clothing in the coming-of-age ceremony (*seijin shiki*). The sartorial politics of cultural identity in modern Japan consists of two separate but related aspects: the cultural construction of what is Japanese and what is Western, and the construction of "the traditional" and "the modern."

11 Genders and Sexualities
Sabine Frühstück

Frühstück identifies three main trends that have characterized anthropological studies on sex, gender, and sexuality in Japan. Studies on women as Other attempt to bring women's lives into view where previously this had not been pursued as a research objective in its own right. Gender studies since the late 1970s have been based on a feminist understanding of the sex-gender system as consisting of two distinct if intertwined categories of biological characteristics and sociocultural attributes. These studies have also overwhelmingly focused on women, but they more critically examine gender-formation processes in a variety of areas ranging from families to health and politics. A third, recent, trend suggests that genders and sexualities in Japan are even more ambivalent and ambiguous than previously acknowledged. These most recent analyses reconsider and interrogate the integration of women's and men's social and sexual experience.

Part III: Geographies and Boundaries, Spaces and Sentiments

The essays in this section explore the different degrees and configurations of the geographic and sentimental boundaries delineating Japaneseness.

12 On the "Nature" of Japanese Culture, or, Is There a Japanese Sense of Nature?
D. P. Martinez

Martinez observes that conventionally, "the Japanese" sense of nature is depicted as being both unique and homogenous: it is seen to be holistic and different from "the Western concept." She challenges this representation as one that falls back on the simplest forms of Othering and Orientalism. Yet, it must be noted, there is a widespread Orientalist assumption among many Japanese that their nature *is* somehow unique and that part of the experience of being Japanese includes the "unusual" experience of living on islands, with the threat of earthquakes, volcanic eruptions, and typhoons, and with four very clearly marked seasons. Martinez questions whether this is really the most accurate way to understand Japanese attitudes toward nature.

13   The Rural Imaginary: Landscape, Village, Tradition
Scott Schnell

Schnell writes that, although Japan has become a highly urbanized and cosmopolitan society, its culture is still perceived as being heavily rooted in the agrarian – and specifically rice paddy – traditions of its rural villages. The privileging of rice production as cultural exemplar, however, serves to both obscure and discredit a number of alternative traditions, such as those of mountain communities where the land is too rugged for growing rice. Many rural communities have turned to local tourism as a means of economic development, often reinforcing in the process the stereotypes about them. Schnell argues that rural residents are more knowledge-able about the metropolitan center than the center is about them, and that the flow of information from television and other nationally distributed mass media is unidirectional.

14   Tokyo's Third Rebuilding: New Twists on Old Patterns
Roman Cybriwsky

Cybriwsky reports on recent changes in Tokyo's built environment that are strikingly represented in four sites near the city's center: the commercial center of Shinjuku; the well-known redevelopment project named Yebisu Garden Place; a new urban district on fresh landfill named Daiba; and a redeveloped old residential neighbor-hood named Shioiri. Collectively, these are new landscapes that provide insight to current features of Japanese society. He offers a critical analysis of the four sites, and points to the various excesses that characterized the economic bubble of the 1980s and early 1990s, the disproportionate influence on the country of the construction industry, the peculiar and extraordinary desire of Japanese to show themselves as being "international" and world-wise, and the persistence of various old ways in modern Japanese life.

15   Japan's Global Village: A View from the World of Leisure
Joy Hendry

Hendry shows that leisure activities in contemporary Japan encompass an interest in "the global." She offers an interpretation of the significance of foreign country theme parks, some apparently foreign restaurants, and longer-standing architectural innovations, as well as influences in contemporary music. Recent trends in local tourism demonstrate the deep interest of Japanese people in many parts of the world beyond the United States, whose influence has dominated postwar Japanese perceptions of "abroad." The choice of restaurants, theme parks, and holiday loca-tions has recently been made in a spirit of greatly increased knowledge of the places in question, and Hendry attempts to show how this richer awareness may have affected aspects of daily life, internal attitudes to global issues, and sources of Japanese identity.

Part IV: Socialization, Assimilation, and Identification

The essays in this section introduce institutions, in the broadest sense, that both enable and inhibit personal and cultural agency.

16   Formal Caring Alternatives: Kindergartens and Day-Care Centers
Eyal Ben-Ari

Ben-Ari explores the role and rationale of the Japanese state in structuring the pre-school system, and shows that a focus on how children constantly question different structures of meaning is important. Japanese preschools enroll over 95 percent of Japanese children and are differentiated into kindergartens and day-care centers. Whereas kindergartens are educational institutions, day-care centers have a custodial role for children of working mothers. The main differences between preschools are based on class, government versus private institutions, and religious affiliation. The trend to smaller families has led to competition centered on attracting children on the basis of each institution's distinctive character.

17   Post-Compulsory Schooling and the Legacy of Imperialism
Brian J. McVeigh

McVeigh investigates how Japan's imperial legacy relates to its post-compulsory schooling system. Vestiges of imperialism and trans-war continuities are apparent in two ideological currents: "colonial Japan" and "superior Japan." In order to illustrate these currents, throughout his analysis of post-compulsory schooling McVeigh weaves five themes: (1) trans-war continuity of state structures; (2) an educatio-examination system driven by economic nationalism; (3) the myth of a "homogeneous" Japan; (4) confronting the wartime era; and (5) a patriarchal capitalist system. Such themes deeply implicate definitions of "Japaneseness" (political/citizenship, ethnocultural/heritage, or "racial"/perceived physical traits).

18   Theorizing the Cultural Importance of Play: Anthropological Approaches to Sports and Recreation
Elise Edwards

Edwards notes that, paralleling trends in the United States and Europe, the discipline of physical anthropology in Japan was a central force in the late 19th-century development of physical education programs and influenced the character of sporting practices. She provides a sense of the questions and interests that have fueled anthropological explorations of sport and recreation in Japan, and underscores the social scientific roots of modern athletics, highlights the political and ideological forces that have shaped investigations into the culture of sport past and present, and identifies the promising possibilities of recent studies and future projects.

19   Popular Entertainment and the Music Industry
Shuhei Hosokawa

Hosokawa presents "entertainment" as a vehicle for creation, recreation, and socialization that encompasses numerous issues, including cultural agency and collective sensibility. As a cultural institution, entertainment consists of production teams, products, and audiences. Hosokawa deals mainly with the cultural history of popular music since the Meiji period (1868–1912), and emphasizes the interplay of reproductive and audiovisual technologies, the entertainment industry and popular audiences.

20 There's More than *Manga*: Popular Nonfiction Books and Magazines
Laura Miller

Miller focuses on the past and present trends in Japanese nonfiction book and magazine publishing, and points out that the volume and breadth of print media in Japan offer scholars a rich resource for understanding contemporary cultural processes, especially shifts in the display and exercise of cultural authority. Print media practices and representations also have much to tell us about the formation of individuals into productive workers, national subjects, and gendered reproducers.

Part V: Body, Blood, Self, and Nation

The essays in this section highlight the confluence of the body, politics of "blood" – as a metaphor for kinship, family, and nationality – social reproduction, and nation-building.

21   Biopower: Blood, Kinship, and Eugenic Marriage
Jennifer Robertson

Robertson writes that in fin-de-siècle Japan, the ideal of "eugenic modernity," or the application of scientific concepts and methods as a means to constitute both the nation, its culture, and its constituent subjects (New Japanese), crystallized in the space of imperialism. The legacy and ramifications of early expressions of eugenic modernity remain salient today. Three of the main themes she explores are the application of eugenic principles to make connections between biology, kinship, and the plasticity of the human body; the scientific rationalization of historical stigmas; and the promotion of "pure-bloodedness" and "ethnic-national endogamy" as ideal modes of sexual and social reproduction.

22   The *Ie* (Family) in Global Perspective
Emiko Ochiai

Ochiai places the *ie* (household) in the context of global family history and attempts to answer some of the questions raised in previous discussions on the *ie* and the stem family, including the questions of whether the Japanese *ie* is a stem family, and whether it can be placed in the same category as a generalized European stem family. Her discussion focuses on regional diversity within Japan, and takes into consideration various aspects of the household system, including size and structure, the living arrangements of elderly members, marriage and fertility, and headship succession.

23   Constrained Person and Creative Agent: A Dying Student's Narrative of Self and Others
Susan Orpett Long

Long reviews some of the central interpretations of Japanese personhood and argues that we must explore the ways in which sex, gender, age, and social class shape and constrain the construction of "the self." Yet, through the narrative of defining who one is, broader social meaning is created and enacted as well. Excerpts from a series of conversations Long had with a dying 21-year-old college student demonstrate the ways in which the young woman drew on her personal relationships, her experiences of age, gender, and class, and especially her own illness experience to construct a narrative of personhood. In the process of creating an articulate and meaningful "self" for the anthropologist, the young woman also established a strong social agency, attempting to negotiate the levels of assistance and independence she desired, thereby influencing the behaviors and practices of those around her.

24   Nation, Citizenship, and Cinema
Aaron Gerow

Gerow notes that recent theorizations of the nation, both inside and outside Japan, have investigated the historical formation of the conception of the nation as an ancient, bordered entity containing citizens united by language, "blood," and culture, and have posited that the nation and its particular manifestation, the nation-state, are of recent origin. He reviews the recent work on theorizing the nation, particularly the scholarship that attempts to deconstruct "Japan," arguing that it is a historical entity exhibiting more differences than unity, defined by phenomena such as language that are really modern constructions. Gerow employs cinema as a discursive example to illustrate the problems and transformations experienced in creating the nation, as well as the paradoxes posed, in the process, by a globalized world system.

25   Culinary Culture and the Making of a National Cuisine
Katarzyna Cwiertka

Cwiertka sketches the culinary scene of contemporary Japan and provides insight into its historical development during the last century by identifying the forces that molded Japanese culinary culture into its present form. Food is not merely purchased in Japan's omnipresent supermarkets, convenience stores, vending machines, and restaurants, it is also a favorite souvenir and seasonal gift, and frequently appears in religious rituals. Moreover, many Japanese presume that foodways are a fundamental key to national character and that food reflects social attributes and cultural values. Food is also a regular feature of the Japanese mass entertainment. From cookery books, recipes, and restaurant reviews in newspapers and magazines to cooking shows and culinary documentaries on television, the entertainment value of food is enormous.

Part VI: Religion and Science, Beliefs and Bioethics

The essays in this section critically review scholarly and everyday practices with respect to religion, science, and biotechnology.

26   Historical, New, and "New" New Religions
Ian Reader

Reader writes that the complex structure of Japanese religion includes numerous sects of established Buddhism, Shinto, an ethnically oriented historical tradition, and numerous "new" religions. Japan is especially significant for anthropologists and sociologists of religion as a highly developed post-industrial society in which the various problems and vicissitudes of, and theoretical issues relating to, religion in modern societies are manifest, such as questions of secularization, the relationships of religion, state, and society, religious reactions to modernity and globalization, and so forth. Reader shows that Japan provides a vital comparative frame of reference to the post-industrialized Western world in such contexts – and often correctives of Western-derived theories.

27   Folk Religion and its Contemporary Issues
Noriko Kawahashi

Kawahashi considers the kinds of questions and issues salient today that must be considered when researching Japanese folk religion. She addresses these issues and discusses recent reassessments of folk religious terminology together with a consideration of the ways in which the field of folklore studies itself has been critically re-examined. Special emphasis is placed on gender-related issues in folk religion, the practice and the field of study.

28   Women Scientists and Gender Ideology
Sumiko Otsubo

Otsubo observes that modern Western science enjoys a popular image as universal, objective, value-neutral, and international, and that scientific research and development is conducted in a decidedly male-dominant environment. Science has perpetuated an androcentrically hierarchical view of sex and gender. She examines the careers of women scientists before, during, and after the Asia-Pacific War (1937–45), and reviews their education, family, employment, mentors, and social activism. Her aim is to illustrate the basic structure of Japanese scientific research and to analyze: female (Japanese) research subjects; the mechanism of constructing, deconstructing, and reconstructing gender stereotypes in scientific research; and the unintended impact of science in shaping gender perceptions.

29   Preserving Moral Order: Responses to Biomedical Technologies
Margaret Lock

Lock emphasizes that a consideration of the ways in which the body is represented and managed in health and illness provides insights into how subjectivity, self and other, mind and body, the individual and society, are commonly conceptualized in any given society. She employs ethnographic data from Japan, combined with an analysis of relevant texts in connection with death and dying, terminal care, organ transplants, and new reproductive technologies, to show how widely shared values and associated disputes are aired in connection with the subjective experience and management of these events and conditions. Lock underscores the utility of examining societal reactions to the body in health and illness as an indispensable lens for gaining insights about everyday life in contemporary Japan and the broader social and political forces that impinge on the lived experience of individuals.

Notes on Contributors

Eyal Ben-Ari is Professor, Department of Sociology and Anthropology, the Hebrew University of Jerusalem. He has carried out fieldwork in Japan (on white-collar suburbs, early childhood education, and the contemporary self-defense forces), Singapore (on the Japanese community), and Israel (on Jewish saint worship, the Israeli army, and United Nations peacekeeping forces). Among his recent publications are *Body Projects in Japanese Childcare: Culture, Organization and Emotions in a Preschool* (1997) and *Mastering Soldiers: Conflict, Emotions and the Enemy in an Israeli Military Unit* (1998).

Katarzyna Cwiertka is Post-Doctoral Researcher, Centre for Japanese and Korean Studies, Leiden University. Her primary research interests are Japanese culinary culture in contemporary and historical contexts, Japanese communities in Europe, and the globalization of Japanese cuisine. Cwiertka is the editor of *Asian Food: The Global and the Local* (2002), and her most recent publications are "Eating the World: Restaurant Culture in Early Twentieth Century Japan," *European Journal of East Asian Studies* (2003), and "Western Food and the Making of the Japanese Nation State," in M. Lien and B. Nerlich, eds, *The Politics of Food* (2004).

Roman Cybriwsky is Associate Dean, Temple University, Tokyo and Professor of Geography and Urban Studies, Temple University, Philadelphia. A specialist in urban social geography, he has written extensively about Tokyo's recent growth and development, including *Tokyo: The Shogun's City at the Twenty-First Century* (1998), as well as about various other cities such as Philadelphia, Singapore, and Jakarta. He is presently working on the urbanization of Batam Island in Indonesia and his fourth book about Tokyo.

Elise Edwards is Assistant Professor, Department of Anthropology, Butler University. Among her several articles is "From Boom to Bust? The Political and Cultural

Economies of Japanese Women's Soccer at the Turn of the 21st Century," in Fan Hong and J. A. Mangan, eds, *Kick Off a New Era: Women's Football in the World – Progress and Problems* (2003), and she is currently revising her dissertation,"The 'Ladies League': Gender, Politics, National Identity, and Professional Sports in Japan" (University of Michigan, 2003), for publication. Edwards continues to conduct research on soccer and sport in Japan, including corporate sport, and on sport and national identity construction in Japan in the 1990s and into the present. Now primarily a scholar of sport, Edwards once spent three seasons playing in Japan's Ladies League.

Walter Edwards is Professor and Chair, Japanese Language Course Department of Asian Studies, Tenri University. He authored *Modern Japan through its Weddings: Gender, Person, and Society in Ritual Portrayal* (1990). His current research interests focus on Japanese notions of identity and how these are linked with readings of its past, including its archaeological heritage. Edwards has written many articles on Japanese archaeology, introducing the results of Japanese archaeological research, and also examining how that research relates to contemporary views of the nation's cherished traditions.

Sabine Frühstück is Associate Professor of Modern Japanese Cultural Studies, Department of East Asian Languages and Cultural Studies, University of California, Santa Barbara. Her research interests include modern Japanese history and anthropology; theory and history of sexuality and gender; knowledge systems; colonial and postcolonial history; military–societal relations; violence; and mass culture. She is the author of *Colonizing Sex: Sexology and Social Control in Modern Japan* (2003) and co-editor (with Sepp Linhart) of *Japanese Culture Seen through its Leisure* (1998). She is currently completing a new book, "Avant-garde: The Army of the Future."

Aaron Gerow is Assistant Professor of Film Studies, Department of East Asian Languages and Literatures, Yale University. He has published widely in a variety of languages on early, wartime, and recent Japanese film, including articles for *Yuriika, Iris, Sekai, Eizōgaku, Iconics, Screening the Past, Image Forum, Eiga geijutsu*, and *Gendai shisō*. He is currently writing a book on Kitano Takeshi for the British Film Institute. Gerow has also worked as a coordinator at the Yamagata International Documentary Film Festival and continues to write reviews of recent Japanese films for the *Daily Yomiuri*.

Ofra Goldstein-Gidoni is Senior Lecturer, Department of East Asian Studies and Department of Sociology and Anthropology, Tel Aviv University. She is the author of *Packaged Japaneseness: Weddings, Business and Brides* (1997) and of numerous articles relating to Japanese weddings, professional housewives, gender, tradition in modern Japan, Israeli images of Japan, and globalization.

Roger Goodman is Nissan Professor of Modern Japanese Studies, Nissan Institute of Japanese Studies and Institute of Social and Cultural Anthropology, University of Oxford. His primary research interest is in Japanese educational and welfare institutions. Goodman has edited several books, including *Family and Social Policy in Japan* (2002), and is the author of *Japan's "International Youth"* (1990) and *Children of the Japanese State* (2000).

Tomoko Hamada is Professor and Chair, Department of Anthropology, The College of William and Mary. The primary focus of her research is the culture of complex organizations, ethnicity at work, and organizational cultures of multinationals. Her publications include *American Enterprise in Japan* (1991) and *Anthropological Perspectives on Organizational Culture* (co-edited with Willis Sibley) (1994). She is the editor of *Studies in Third World Societies*.

Joy Hendry is Professor of Social Anthropology and Director of the Europe Japan Research Centre, Oxford Brookes University, and a Senior Member of St Antony's College, Oxford. She has carried out fieldwork several times in various parts of Japan and has published extensively on her findings. Among her several books is *Understanding Japanese Society* (2nd edn, 1995). Hendry's recent research is concerned with cultural display in a global context, and her most recent book is *The Orient Strikes Back: A Global View of Cultural Display* (2002).

Shuhei Hosokawa is Associate Professor, International Research Center for Japanese Studies, Kyoto. He has published several books in Japanese on the aesthetics of recorded sound and Japanese-Brazilian music and film history. He has also co-edited (with Toru Mitsui) *Karaoke around the World* (1998) and has published articles in *Cultural Studies, Japanese Studies, The British Journal of Ethnomusicology*, and other journals. Hosokawa is currently working on a history of popular music in Japan from the mid-19th century to 1945.

Noriko Kawahashi is Associate Professor of Religion, Nagoya Institute of Technology. She has published extensively in English and Japanese on the subject of women and religion in Japan and Okinawa, including "Jizoku (Priests' Wives) in Soto Zen Buddhism: An Ambiguous Category" and "Seven Hindrances of Women? A Popular Discourse on Okinawan Women and Religion," both in *Japanese Journal of Religious Studies*, 1995 and 2000 respectively. Kawahashi was guest co-editor of the *Japanese Journal of Religious Studies* Fall 2003 special issue on "Feminism and Religion in Contemporary Japan." Her forthcoming book (in Japanese), co-authored with Masako Kuroki, is on postcolonial feminism and religion.

Margaret Lock is Marjorie Bronfman Professor in Social Studies in Medicine, Department of Social Studies of Medicine and the Department of Anthropology, McGill University. A medical anthropologist and author of over 150 articles, Lock's monographs include the award-winning books *Encounters with Aging: Mythologies of Menopause in Japan and North America* (1993) and *Twice Dead: Organ Transplants and the Reinvention of Death* (2002).

Susan Orpett Long is Professor of Anthropology, John Carroll University. She has conducted ethnographic research in Japan and in the United States in cultural and medical anthropology, gender, and bioethics. In addition to two edited volumes, her published work includes *Family Change and the Life Course in Japan* (1987), and she is completing "Final Days: Japanese Culture and Choice at the End of Life."

D. P. Martinez is Senior Lecturer in Anthropology, School of Oriental and African Studies, University of London. Along with numerous articles on tourism, religion, gender, and the mass media in Japan, she is the author of *Identity and Ritual in a Japanese Diving Village* (2004), co-editor of *Ceremony and Ritual in Japan* (1996), and editor of *The Worlds of Japanese Popular Culture* (1998).

Brian J. McVeigh is Adjunct Instructor, Department of East Asian Studies, University of Arizona, Tucson. Until very recently he was Chair, Cultural and Women's Studies Department, Tokyo Jogakkan University. He specializes in Japanese culture, gender, education, consumerism, and political as well as psychological anthropology. Chinese American culture is a current interest. Among his five books are *Nationalisms of Japan: Managing and Mystifying Identity* (2004) and *Wearing Ideology: State, Schooling, and Self-Presentation in Japan* (2000). He is now writing a book tentatively titled "The State Bearing Gifts: Deception, Dramatics, and Exchange in Modern Societies."

Laura Miller is Associate Professor of Anthropology, Loyola University, Chicago. Her research interests include linguistic ideology, interethnic communication, applied linguistics, folk models, popular culture, and gender representations in media and language. She recently published "Media Typifications and Hip *Bijin*," *U.S.–Japan Women's Journal* (2003) and "Mammary Mania in Japan," in *positions: east asia cultures critique* (2003), and is working on a book titled "Beauty Up: Selling and Consuming Body Aesthetics in Japan."

Katsumi Nakao is Professor of Anthropology, Department of Literature, Osaka City University. His main geographic areas of historical and anthropological research are mainland China, Hong Kong, and Taiwan. Widely published in Japanese, Nakao's main articles in English include "Japanese Colonial Policy and Anthropology in Manchuria," in Jan Bremen and Shimizu Akitoshi, eds, *Anthropology and Colonialism in Asia and Oceania* (1999) and "Political Structure and Social Change in a Chinese Village," *Asia Political and Economic Association* (1990). He is presently working on the legacy in the Japanese academy today of anthropological research conducted under the aegis of Japanese imperialism.

Emiko Ochiai is Associate Professor of Sociology, Faculty of Letters, Kyoto University. Her main research interests are family sociology and family history, and gender studies. Ochiai's current project, which combines family history and historical demography, involves an investigation of the Japanese family before modernization. Among her English publications are the award-winning *The Japanese Family System in Transition: A Sociological Analysis of Family Change in Postwar Japan* (1997), "The Reproductive Revolution at the End of the Tokugawa Period," in Hitomi Tonomura et al., eds, *Women and Class in Japanese History* (1999), and "Adoption as an Heirship Strategy under Demographic Constraints" (co-authored with Satomi Kurosu), *Journal of Family History* (1995).

Sumiko Otsubo is Assistant Professor of History, Metropolitan State University. Her research interests include Japanese science history, eugenics, and science and gender. Among her publications are "Feminists' Maternal Eugenics in Wartime Japan," *U.S.–Japan Women's Journal* (1999); "Engendering Eugenics: Feminists and Marriage Restriction Legislation in the 1920s," in Barbara Molony and Kathleen S. Uno, eds, *Gendering Modern Japanese History* (forthcoming); and "Between Two Worlds: Yamanouchi Shigeo and Eugenics in Early Twentieth Century Japan," *Annals of Science* (forthcoming).

Ian Reader is Professor of Religious Studies, Lancaster University. His research interests include the study of religion and religious phenomena in Japan, including pilgrimage and the relationship between religion and violence. His most recent books include *Religious Violence in Contemporary Japan: The Case of Aum Shinrikyo* (2000) and *Practically Religious: Worldly Benefits and the Common Religion of Japan* (co-authored with George J. Tanabe, 1998).

Glenda S. Roberts is Professor of Anthropology, Institute of Asia-Pacific Studies, Waseda University. She is the author of *Staying on the Line: Blue-Collar Women in Contemporary Japan* (1994) and co-editor of *Japan and Global Migration: Foreign Workers and the Advent of a Multicultural Society* (2000). Her interests include the gender politics of class and labor relations, working women in Japan, and globalization and migrant labor in Japan and China. She serves on the editorial board of *Social Science Journal Japan*.

Jennifer Robertson is Professor of Anthropology, University of Michigan. She has published many articles and book chapters on a wide spectrum of subjects ranging from the 17th century to the present. Her most recent research projects include Japanese colonial culture-making, eugenic modernity, war art, and comparative bio-ethics. Robertson is the author of *Native and Newcomer: Making and Unmaking a Japanese City* (1994 [1991]), *Takarazuka: Sexual Politics and Popular Culture in Modern Japan* (2001 [1998]; Japanese translation 2000), and editor of *Same-Sex Cultures and Sexualities: An Anthropological Reader* (2004). She also created and is general editor of the book series "Colonialisms" (University of California Press). She is finishing a new book, "Blood and Beauty: Eugenic Modernity and Empire in Japan."

Joshua Hotaka Roth is Associate Professor of Anthropology, Mount Holyoke College. His research interests include Japanese Brazilian ethnicity, images of Japan in the Brazilian context, and sports and ethnicity. His recent publications include *Brokered Homeland: Japanese Brazilian Migrants in Japan* (2002) and "Urashima Taro's Ambiguating Practices: The Significance of Overseas Voting Rights for Elderly Japanese Migrants to Brazil," in Jeffrey Lesser, ed., *Searching for Home Abroad* (2003).

Sonia Ryang is Associate Professor of Anthropology, Johns Hopkins University. She is the author of *Japan and National Anthropology: A Critique* (2004) and *North Koreans in Japan: Language, Ideology, and Identity* (1997), and the editor of *Koreans in Japan: Critical Voices from the Margin* (2000). She is currently conducting research into the historical interrelation between the emergence of Japan's national sovereignty and the 1923 massacre of Koreans in the aftermath of the Great Kanto earthquake, and writing a book on love under the title "Five Scenes of Love from Japan."

Scott Schnell is Associate Professor of Anthropology, University of Iowa. His research focuses on challenges to the concentration of power through the mobilization of localized identities, particularly in cases involving ritual and other forms of narrative and performance. The author of *The Rousing Drum* (1999), Schnell is currently working on a new book that combines anthropology with history and literature in evaluating a Japanese historical novel as both an important source of ethnographic data and a veiled form of political dissent.

Tomomi Yamaguchi is Post-Doctoral Fellow, Department of East Asian Languages and Civilizations, University of Chicago. Her research interests are in the cultural construction of gender, sexuality, and race/ethnicity in postwar Japan, and Japanese feminism. Yamaguchi is currently revising for publication her dissertation, "Feminism Fractured: An Ethnography of the Dissolution and Textual Reinvention of a Japanese Feminist Group" (University of Michigan, 2004), which examines the achievements of, and problems facing, late 20th-century Japanese feminism. Her recent publications include " 'Kekkon' no Teigi o Meguru Tatakai: America Massachusetts-shū no Dōseikon Hanketsu" (Fight on the Definition of "Marriage": The Massachusetts Gay Marriage Case), in *Onna-tachi no 21-seiki* (Women's 21st Century) (2004) and "Media kōgi 1976-nen ikō" (Media Protest after 1976) in Kōdō-suru Kai Kirokushū Henshū Iinkai, ed., *Kodo-suru onna-tachi ga hiraita michi: Mexico kara New York made* (The Road Cultivated by the Women of Action: From Mexico to New York) (1999).

PART I Introduction

CHAPTER **1**

Introduction: Putting and Keeping Japan in Anthropology

Jennifer Robertson

ANCESTORS, LEGACIES, AND ADUMBRATIONS

Thirty-five years ago, John Bennett (1970) remarked that social research on Japan "has not yet made significant contributions to social and cultural theory." Although Bennett's remark remains relevant, it is not quite accurate. The wartime ethnographies by Japan anthropology ancestors John Embree and Ruth Benedict entered the mainstream of (American) anthropology where "Japan" became a proving ground for debates about the pros and cons of National Character Studies and of the Culture and Personality school (Benedict 1946; Embree 1945).[1] Actually, Embree's earlier monograph, *Suye Mura: A Japanese Village* (1939), the progenitor of ethnographies of Japan, was part of a global series of comparative field studies on literate communities or villages – and the first on types of East Asian societies – orchestrated by social anthropologists (affiliated with Harvard University and the University of Chicago) Fay-Cooper Cole, A. R. Radcliffe-Brown, Robert Redfield, and Lloyd Warner (Embree 1939:ix–x, xvi–xvii).

Thus, as I have argued elsewhere, it was in the 1940s that "Japan" entered mainstream (Anglophone) anthropological debates (Robertson 1998). And, Japan – often paired with Turkey – was also very much part of the anthropological discourse of modernization theory in the 1950s and early 1960s (Bellah 1957; Ward and Rustow 1964).[2] Since the 1960s, and in keeping with Bennett's observation, "Japan" seems to have passed out of, and to have been passed over by, the anthropological mainstream. What happened? Could it be that only as, simultaneously, a militaristic imperial power – a threat to the United States and western Europe – and a nation of villages (epitomized by Suye) – a quintessential anthropological subject – did Japan attract the intellectual interests of anthropologists? Where is "Japan" in anthropological discourse today, and what are the "significant contributions to social and cultural theory" that Japan anthropologists have made since 1970, and are making today?

These questions address both the efforts made by Japan anthropologists to engage with social and cultural, and more recently critical, theories, and also the apparent disinterest in and ignorance of Japan of many anthropologists who, suffice it to say at this moment, should know better.[3]

It would appear that anthropologists in general do not regard Japan as a geographical "prestige zone"; that is, that – unlike Bali or Morocco or the Andes, or Oaxaca, Mexico – they do not regard Japan as a cultural area of choice and theoretical cachet. The existence of prestige zones has partly to do with the distance of anthropological theorizing from current affairs, and partly to do with the colonial history of Euro-American anthropology and the canonical emphasis since the 19th century on the cultures of peoples of color with a history of domination by "the West." (For largely the same reason western Europe – the "Old Europe" – and North America are still under-represented in anthropology.) Japan confounds the simple binarism informing the construction of anthropology's Other: it was never a colony of "the West," and in the first half of the 20th century Japan occupied the ambivalent position of an anti-colonial colonizer, although its ambiguity in this regard was overshadowed in the United States first by its status as absolute enemy and later by its unconditional surrender in 1945. Moreover, the discipline of anthropology in Japan was itself facilitated, if not motivated, by Japanese colonialism in Asian and Pacific Rim countries (see chapter 2 in this volume). The rhetorical question thus arises: Is Japan, like western Europe and the United States, somehow perceived as too much like "us" to be recognized and appreciated as a worthwhile subject of anthropological inquiry?

At this juncture, I would like to insert, in two parts, an excerpt from a review I wrote in 1995 (but which was published in 1998) about the place of Japan in American anthropology.[4] The excerpt compares the intellectual engagements and legacies of Japan anthropology's two renowned – especially in the United States – ancestors, Ruth Benedict and John Embree, and constitutes one response to the rhetorical question I raised at the end the previous paragraph.

> [*Gyokusai* was a] wartime expression coined by military ideologues to beautify self-sacrifice and mass deaths in combat.... *Gyokusai* literally means "jewel smashed." It was precisely such baroque expressions and drastic acts that occasioned the Office of War Information to commission Ruth Benedict to write *The Chrysanthemum and the Sword*, in which she attempted to "understand Japanese habits of thought and emotion and the patterns into which these habits fell.... The Japanese were the most alien enemy the United States had ever fought in an all-out struggle. In no other war with a major foe had it been necessary to take into account such exceedingly different habits of acting and thinking.... We had to understand their behavior in order to cope with it" (Benedict 1946:4, 1).
>
> Earlier, in 1943 ... Embree published *The Japanese* as part of the Smithsonian's War Background Studies series. This was followed by *The Japanese Nation* in 1945. Benedict cites the latter along with Embree's more well known ethnography, *Suye Mura, A Japanese Village*, published in 1939, but Embree himself is conspicuously absent from her acknowledgments in *The Chrysanthemum and the Sword*. Embree too directed his wartime studies toward better understanding and determining Japanese attitudes and

behavior, but whereas Benedict sought to explain "the Japanese" in terms of a timeless cultural profile fabricated from fragments of data, Embree, in *The Japanese Nation*, focused on providing a socio-historical and ethnographic "context for the interpretation of the behavior of Japanese and some basis for an understanding of future developments in Japan."

In a nutshell, Benedict's intellectual project was one of selective incorporation and containment, and Embree's one of linear unfolding. She collapsed past and present, and fused shreds and patches of data in formulating a unique and timeless janusian core (aka the "chrysanthemum" and the "sword") that was "the Japanese" cultural personality. He, on the other hand, acknowledged the effects of historical transformations and political ideologies in shaping particular configurations of individual and collective behavior without denying altogether the continuity of certain cultural patterns. Writing against national character studies, Embree historicized his portrayal of Japan and questioned the validity of using culture patterns which determine individual behavior within a social group as an "explanation" for national and international socio-economic-political developments.... [A] summary (even when accurate) of a nation's citizens' behavior traits... does not provide a magic explanation for a nation's aggressive warfare whether it be Japanese, British, American, or Russian (1950: 443).

I do not wish to simply cast Benedict as the "bad guy" and Embree as the "good guy" – the methods of both are equally problematic, although Benedict's work has occupied more mnemonic space in American anthropology. Rather, I have invoked Ancestors Benedict and Embree for two basic reasons. First, their work, but especially Benedict's, might usefully be regarded as constituting the historical – perhaps even obsessive – memory shaping the practice of Japan anthropology in the United States since the end of World War Two. Second, it is through their efforts that Japan first entered the mainstream of American anthropology as a contested discourse on, simultaneously, Japanese culture, ethnographic representation, and anthropological theory.... Japanese imperialist designs in Asia and the Pacific, and the attack on Pearl Harbor; the Axis Alliance; the internment of Japanese Americans; and the atomic bombing of Hiroshima and Nagasaki followed by the largely American occupation of Japan, were all events which helped to overdetermine the salience of Japan as a particularly rich and controversial site of and for anthropological inquiry in the 1940s. (Robertson 1998:300–301)

Let me reiterate the question: is Japan, like western Europe and the United States, somehow perceived as too much like "us" to be recognized and appreciated as a worthwhile subject of anthropological inquiry? In mulling over this question in 1995, I ventured the following response (the second part of the excerpt).

[I]t occurred to me that perhaps some – or many – people believe that there is nothing left to learn about Japan, or nothing really new and interesting – apart from gee-whiz factoids about rampant consumerism, such as the price in square centimeters of Ginza real estate, or the number of $500 musk melons sold at the Takano Fruit Parlor during the two annual gift-giving periods. Perhaps they believe that Ruth Benedict said it all: Namely, that despite their hi-tech veneer, the Japanese are a people unified in their confidence in hierarchy, whose public acts are regulated by shame, and who put a premium on cleanliness, education, and self-discipline. Ironically, Benedict never went to Japan nor did she know the language. Yet, she proceeded to construct "cultural regularities" from fragmentary data, including novels, movies, interviews with interned Japanese Americans, and the small and "lacking" (Embree 1947) – described by Benedict as "vast" – corpus of existing scholarly literature on Japan 1946: 6).[5] I do not wish to diminish Benedict's formidable anthropological skills and scholarly legacy, but by the same token, neither do I want to diminish the consequences of her work. In a sense, Benedict made getting to know Japan look too easy, and the Japan she profiled seemed all too knowable; once inscrutable, the Japanese were suddenly crystal clear.

Embree did not attempt to encapsulate Japanese cultural history within a formula, although he acknowledged the persistence of certain cultural practices and attitudes, and his books are certainly very formulaic in terms of their organization.[6] Although both Benedict and Embree constitute the braided memory of Japan anthropology, Benedict's bold bricolage has been far more influential in shaping people's image of Japan than has been either Embree's rather dry, methodical ethnography or his sharp critiques of national character studies.[7]

I believe that the easy and monolithic knowability of Japan construed from *The Chrysanthemum and the Sword* is fundamentally related to the double agenda of that book. A didactic book, *The Chrysanthemum and the Sword* was as much an attempt to explain a hitherto inscrutable Japan to a hostile American audience as it was an effort to evince and highlight American national character against the foil of Japan. Benedict's humane objective with her double agenda was to encourage Americans, dizzy from propaganda proclaiming the Japanese a "most alien enemy," to see Japanese as human too. To this end she positioned each people as the mirror image of the other. Benedict declared that "[t]he arc of life in Japan is plotted in opposite fashion to that in the United States": whereas Americans increase their freedom of choice during the course of their lives, "the Japanese rely on maximizing the restraints upon [them]" (1946:253–4, 254). In Benedict's mirror, the Japanese reliance on hierarchy is reflected back as the American faith in freedom (1946:43). Whereas "sensitivity about trifles" is virtuous behavior in Japan, it is recognized as "neurotic" and "adolescent" in the United States (1946:108) If the Japanese "play up suicide," Americans "play up crime" (1946:167). And whereas in Japan performance deteriorates under competition, in the United States competition stimulates performance, yielding socially desirable results (1946:153). These are but a few of the oppositional representations of "the Japanese" and "the Americans" developed by Benedict, who concluded that in Japanese life, "the contradictions, as they seem to us, are as deeply based in their view of life as our uniformities are in ours" (1946:197).

Like her colleague Clyde Kluckhohn, author of *Mirror for Man* (1949), Benedict used anthropology as a mirror held before us to allow and encourage a better understanding of ourselves through the study of others. But a mirror is not an inert device and can be deployed as an agent in the resolution of difference and opposition. In the bamboo mirror held before Americans, Japanese national character was rendered intelligible as American national character the other way around. The potential for solipsism should be obvious; the apparent wholeness of the mirrored image can deflect recognition of the need to learn more about Japan on terms relevant to the dynamic and intertwined histories of localities and subjective cultural formations and practices within that country. As Embree noted in his 1947 review of *The Chysanthemum and the Sword*, the only way to begin to really know the Japanese people, "is to accumulate comparative data on the basis of a series of field studies in different areas of the culture. . . . So far these are lacking for Japan" (1947:246).

Today, ethnographies based on fieldwork in Japan are certainly more plentiful than in 1947, but I will argue that anthropologists since then have in one way or another, continued to work both through and against a conventionalized conception of Japan as a mirror image of, or enantiomorphic with, the United States [and, more generically]. . . "the West." The ever growing anthropological literature on "the Japanese self," for example, both works to locate "indigenous" constructions of selfhood and to distinguish the Japanese from the American (or Western) self.[8] Similarly, and not surprisingly, "mirror" and "mask" are popular words in titles of books on Japan, and the objective of revealing, unmasking, or unwrapping the "real" Japan has motivated many a Japan scholar.[9]

One last factor to consider with respect to Benedict's central role in facilitating the knowability of "the Japanese" concerns the influence of *The Chrysanthemum and the Sword* in Japan, where it was published in translation in 1948. In their 1953 review of the critical reception of the book among Japanese scholars, John Bennett and Michio Nagai point out that,

> [i]t should be understood that the translation of *The Chrysanthemum and the Sword* has appeared in Japan during a period of intense national self-examination – a period during which Japanese intellectuals and writers have been studying the sources and meaning of Japanese history and character, in one of their perennial attempts to determine the most desirable course of Japan's development (1953: 404).

In more recent years, the Japanese social critic and philosopher Tamotsu Aoki (1991 [1990]) has suggested that *The Chrysanthemum and the Sword* "helped invent a new tradition for postwar Japan" (see also Doak 1996). Benedict's homogenizing and timeless portrait of "the Japanese" added momentum to the growing interest in "ethnic nationalism" in Japan, evident in the hundreds of ethnocentric *nihonjinron* – treatises on Japaneseness – published since the postwar period.[10] As I have argued elsewhere (Robertson 1997, 1998), the obsession today in Japan with cultural distinction mirrors a similar obsession with internationalization; in fact, the two obsessions can be understood as enantiomorphic: that is, the same impulse the other way around.[11]

My point in this digression on the reception in Japan of *The Chrysanthemum and the Sword* is to suggest that despite criticisms of Benedict's failure to discriminate among historical developments and "differing institutional contexts of data" (Bennett and Nagai 1953:408), Japanese culture critics were especially interested in her attempt to portray the whole or total structure (*zentai kōzō*) of Japanese culture – a goal which, Bennett and Nagai note, had been "common enough in certain branches of Japanese humanistic studies" (1953:406). In short, Benedict's bricolage – her totalizing ensemble of fragments – reinforced and was reinforced by similar efforts on the part of her Japanese counterparts, for whom the widest and thickest line of difference has been drawn between a unique Japan and the rest of the world (basically, "the West") as if both entities were internally coherent (cf. Tamotsu 1991 [1990]:31–32). Thus, ongoing Japanese attempts to locate cultural uniqueness mirror the attempts of non-Japanese anthropologists, among others, to unmask, unwrap, and to otherwise reveal the presumptive authentic core or essence of Japanese society. (Robertson 1998:304)

BRICOLAGE REDUX

Benedict's ahistorical and homogenizing portrait of "the Japanese" has been complicated over the past two decades by the proliferation in the number of both dominant and marginal sites, situations, and actors (including the ethnographer), in part due to theoretical attention in anthropology to such matters of late. Consequently, the archetypal peasant of Embree's *Suye Mura* is now many ethnographic subjects, including weekday white-collar worker and weekend farmer; local tourist attraction and custodian of the landscape of nostalgia; youth idol; migrant worker; dispensable day laborer in the automotive and nuclear energy industries; religious cultist; political activist; ethnic or sexual minority and resident "Other"; and victim of industrial pollution, to name some of the more conspicuous ones (Robertson 1998:310).

Nevertheless, some scholars have argued that Benedict's unitary if Janus-faced – in the sense of mutually antagonistic – portrait of "the Japanese" remains the backdrop in front of which these new actors have debuted and back into which they are reabsorbed. This was a charge which motivated the publication in 1988, and an expanded edition in 1997, of a volume titled *The Other Japan*, identified as a book "about the other side of the story"; a book about "the unresolved conflicts beneath the smooth surface of managed capitalism in Japan today" (Tsurumi 1988:3; Moore 1997).[12] The title of and rationale for this book alerts us to the Catch-22 confounding the matter of representation in Japan anthropology: it seems that cultural portraits contrary to the tenaciously normative template constructed by Benedict and subsequently reproduced can only always be "alternative" or "other" as opposed to unacknowledged facets of the complex, composite, and integrated whole of "Japanese culture." This crisis of representation, as it were, has as much to do with the dominant mythos *in* Japan of a homogenous society as it does with the perception *of* Japan as knowable in opposition to "the West," and more specifically, the United States (Robertson 1998:310–311).

One way to resolve this crisis is, figuratively speaking, to refabricate[13] the received and homogenous (and homogenizing) portrait of "the Japanese" in the multifaceted mode of a 100-headed Kannon (Bodhisattva of Compassion). This move is already evident, in part influenced by the newly and loudly audible voices of Koreans, Ainu, Okinawans, and all those who may have been, and in some cases continue to be, constructed as "other." They reside not below the "smooth surface" of Japan today but rather comprise an integral part of that surface, which in reality is exquisitely – and phenotypically and culturally – textured. All of Kannon's heads are different and differentiated, yet they all belong to the same body and collectively make up its integral, organic identity. In a similar sense, the 29 essays comprising this volume, introduced below, all contribute "talking heads" to the Japanese body (*kokutai*), and, moreover, each represents a different "talking head" of that academic body, Japan anthropology.

Ironically, especially in light of my earlier analysis, it is Benedict the Bricoleur who offers sage and useful advice on the method of refrabrication by way of her two-sided, albeit one-dimensional, portrait of "the Japanese." Although she used data drawn from a broad range of sources, from archives to interviews, her inability to read or speak Japanese, together with the fact that she had never been to Japan, coupled with her restrictively schematic theoretical framework, drastically circumscribed and de-limited her ethnographic portrait of Japan and the peoples living and working there. Today, the majority of (professional) non-Japanese ethnographers of Japan are fluent in Japanese and have spent a number of years living and working in that country. However, to avoid creating a paint-by-numbers portrait of Japan – even if the paints and outline are of Japanese manufacture – we need to pay attention to and address and redress, as opposed to simply conform to, current issues and developments in anthropology, the discipline, and to thicken, layer, texture, and complicate our representations of Japan and Japanese peoples (Robertson 1998:316).

The reading and speaking fluency of most Japan anthropologists in Japanese is best applied toward utilizing information from a diverse number of individuals and groups (who are not presumed a priori to represent "the Japanese" voice), as well as from a broad and deep range of Japanese texts. The relative dearth and narrow scope of the Japanese-language materials utilized in a significant proportion of ethnographies on Japan is dismaying, especially given the high premium placed in Japan, past and present, on writing and the generation of documents on every conceivable subject. Without sufficient efforts to broaden the range and scope of the Japanese-language materials utilized, patterns of Japanese culture canonized in the anglophone literature can be accorded, almost by default, the status of truisms which are then reproduced by successive generations of Japan anthropologists. It is not that these patterns and truisms are wrong or misleading per se, but that they should be subjected now and then to what is known colloquially as a "reality check."

If there is one gatekeeping concept that is unequivocally appropriate for Japan scholars to employ it ought to be "bibliophilia": the long cultural history of literacy and range and diversity of textual production in Japan are reasons compelling enough to demand (greater) attention to bibliography. In the context of bibliography, one type of "reality check" would involve exploring the multifarious ways in which topical issue, say organ transplantation, has been debated among sundry constituencies, as opposed to presenting unproblematically "the Japanese" position (Robertson 1998:307).[14] The merits of bricolage – less as a type of "cultural logic" (Lévi-Strauss 1962a, 1962b), and more as a method of tapping a heterogeneous repertoire of cultural resources – should be evident. Bricolage is both a demanding method and a method demanding a supple intellect, as one must draw and synthesize (fabricate) from the visual and the textual, the historical and the "now moment," the voiced and the silent (and silenced), the present and the absent (and disappeared), the ubiquitous and the scarce, the polemical and the nuanced, the actual and the potential, the animate and inanimate, and so on.

As I see it, bricolage, as simultaneously a theory of cultural resources and a method for tapping them, is a variant of the process of "condensation" developed by that consummate (if not recognized as such) ethnographer, Gertrude Stein. Stein scrutinized her (human) subjects until, over time, there emerged for her a repeating pattern to their words and actions. Her literary portraits (e.g., Stein 1959) were condensations of her subject's repeatings, an ethnographic technique quite the opposite of the "social scientific" process of ideal typing (Robertson 1994 [1991]:1). What I wrote in 1991 with respect to "condensation" versus "ideal typing" remains – from my observations traveling through the fields of anthropology – quite viable today.

> [Robert] Nisbet has likened ideal typing to sculpting. Like sculptors, social scientists, figuratively speaking, chip away at a block of marble in order to expose the Michelangelesque sculpture within. This method involves a priori knowledge of both the presence and the exact form of the ideal-type figure trapped inside: "the object, whether structure or personage, [is] stripped, so to speak, of all that is merely superficial and ephemeral, with only what is central and unifying left" (Nisbet 1977:71). Contrarily, the wholeness of Stein's subjects bespeaks the acquisitive – as opposed to reductive – nature of her mode of portraiture. She did not presume to know beforehand what was superficial and what was central. These are arbitrary criteria not isolable in any one individual or group.[15] Those features labeled either "superficial" or "central" exist in a flux of words and actions differently repeated over time and space by individuals or groups. (Robertson 1994 [1991]:1–2)

In her novels and essays on writing, Stein identifies what I perceive as the salient features of the ethnographic process: it is personal; it requires time and patience, for knowledge and understanding are acquired gradually; and it involves a struggle to convey critically that knowledge and understanding about a pluralistic world in flux through the relatively static medium of (English) words (Dubrick 1984:93; Robertson 1994 [1991]:2; see also Agar 1986:x).

By the same token, our attention must also be directed toward a sustained analysis of the history of intersections, past and present, of Japanese and Euro-American strategies of cultural critique. Knowledge of the socio-historical constructedness of cultural practices does not preclude either understanding or appreciating them or working within their parameters (cf. Bourdieu 1986:2, 4; Dubrick 1984:26). This practical knowledge, moreover, is crucial if an ethnographer is to avoid the reifications and spurious homogeneity that ideal typologizing . . . can promote (Robertson 1994 [1991]:2).

So, for example, instead of (or, at the very least, in addition to) clamping a "Freudian" interpretive framework onto current Japanese sexual and gendered practices, one might fruitfully look at the history of sexology in Japan, or at the history of Freudian theory in Japan, and its adaptations, transformations, and critiques there as well as in Europe and the United States. Many of us (Japan anthropologists) work to minimize or avoid the fallacious tendency of forcing Japanese cultural practices into "Western" analytical categories. But we must also strive to distinguish those practices from the dominant ideology operating in Japan at different historical moments.

Locating and historicizing theory in this way would help to temper and moderate a tendency I have observed in certain recent monographs on Japan (and in critiques of Japanese Studies) to use theory, sometimes in lieu of sufficient Japanese and other archival and empirical material, as a totalizing explanation, rather than as a reasonable conjecture resonant with specific historical circumstances, or as a guide for further investigations. Obviously, the mere invocation of, say, a theory of practice or of subjectivity is not a viable substitute for exploring and recording the everyday practices of actual subjects and their collective activities in particular geographical places and historical times. It is useful to remember that theories can only be developed and modified by engaging with an ever-expanding body of tangible, empirical information lest they lose their value as theories and become frozen as formulaic explanations (Vance 1985:18; Robertson 2001 [1998]:24).

Other factors instrumental in generating research that works to complicate the "received" portrait of Japan include extended periods of residence in Japan and regular long and short return visits. A familiarity with history, the product and process, is very important, and one must be constantly attentive to distinguishing it from "tradition." Also, attention to the historical vicissitudes of social and cultural formations is crucial, along with, ideally, a familiarity with a wide range of idea-generating literatures outside the purview of Japanese Studies.

I must also note in this context something that seems obvious to me, and that is that to be or to become a good bricoleur or a good ethnographer or anthropologist is unconnected to, and quite a separate matter from, one's ethnicity or nationality. I further distinguish in this regard between phenotypic Japaneseness and cultural Japaneseness; the two are not the same thing although they can overlap. The former refers to ancestry expressed as outward features stereotypically marked as "Japanese" regardless of one's culture or socialization; the latter to socialization and enculturation within a culture not necessarily connected to one's ancestry. Recently, phenotype has been privileged as a marker of "positionality," a "ready-to-wear" product of an identity politics that has been especially endemic to American universities.[16] Ironically, phenotype may not reveal but instead may actually camouflage and obscure one's unique and complex genetic, personal, and family history, even as it imparts, within a rigidly constructed identity politics, an illusion of self-conscious identity formation (Robertson 2002:788).[17] One of my points here is that confidence and effectiveness in exercising one's authorial "voice" ought not to lie in phenotype or genealogical claims or a childhood in Japan, but in the assiduous fieldwork and archival research necessary to generate historically resonant, thick descriptions and subtly evocative interpretations of people's lives in all their messy complexity. However, as someone who was raised in Japan, I would be the last person to dismiss the advantages to an ethnographer of the profound familiarity that long-term residence and socializing (and socialization) in a place can afford. In my experience, though, such familiarity is most effectively conveyed not by superficial claims to "insider" status and, by extension, to arcane insights, but in the thoughtful choice of an ethnographic subject and the caliber, subtlety, and resilience of research undertaken to elucidate it.

CONTENTS AND CONFIGURATIONS

In a way, this book is a study in bricolage even if the individual authors neither utilize that method nor claim to be bricoleurs. Over two years ago, when I was invited to organize and edit this volume, my idea was to treat the book as a whole as a nexus of intersecting forces, ideas, things, and events represented by the vectors formed from the thematic units and constituent chapters. As I wrote in my original proposal to Blackwell, the

> forces, ideas, things, and events accounted [in this volume] for are those that I perceive to be especially salient to Japan yet general enough to be the basis for both comparative research and contributions to anthropological theorizing. In addition to essays that demonstrate the salience of Japan as a place to undertake and generate innovative and exciting scholarship, the *Companion* also aims to make "Japan" in its many guises and dimensions more easily accessible to scholars unfamiliar with that country but interested in comparative research and information.

That said, the resultant edited volume is less a product of my ideas about Japan anthropology and more a portrait of Japan and the Japanese peoples, whose "repeatings" in a variety of historicized contexts are apprehended by and understood through a mix of theoretical and methodological approaches employed by the diverse and international group of contributors. I am very grateful to my colleagues who accepted the challenge of writing a concise yet comprehensive essay on their subject or area of expertise. Not everyone invited was able to contribute or to complete an essay for one reason or another. Nevertheless, the 29 essays comprising this volume represent the application of a heterogeneous repertoire of theories and methodologies to the study of Japan, the country, cultures, and peoples. The subjects explored, summarized below, are equally heterogeneous.

I have divided the chapters into six thematic units. I. Introduction; II. Cultures, Histories, and Identities; III. Geography and Boundaries, Spaces and Sentiments; IV. Socialization, Assimilation, and Identification; V. Body, Blood, Self, and Nation; and VI. Religion and Science, Beliefs and Bioethics. The first unit contains my introduction, in which I chart the legacies of Ruth Benedict and John Embree and propose ways in which to both critique and build on their work.[18] The subjects explored in the second unit critically examine the processes of history- and culture-making along with identity formation, majority and minority alike. Essays address the relationship between Japanese imperialism and colonialism and the development of anthropology in Japan (Katsumi Nakao); archaeology, ideology and the management of cultural properties (Walter Edwards); the ubiquity, in feminist and other texts, of timelines as a mode of history-making (Tomomi Yamaguchi); the construction and reproduction of majority culture (Roger Goodman); the formation and trans-formations of "insider" and "outsider" minorities (Joshua Hotaka Roth and Sonia Ryang); vicissitudes of class and status (Glenda Roberts); myths and realities of corporate culture (Tomoko Hamada); the sartorial fashioning of cultural identity (Ofra Goldstein-Gidoni); and the influence of nexuses of sex, gender, and sexualities on both Japan anthropology and Japanese national identity (Sabine Frühstück).

The third unit explores the different degrees and configurations of the geographic and sentimental boundaries delineating Japaneseness. The four constituent essays include a stereotype-bending analysis of the historical transformations of "nature" as a social construct (D. P. Martinez); a critical examination of the contradictory images and expectations of rural Japan (Scott Schnell); a discerning review of four newly built urban landscapes in Tokyo (Roman Cybriwsky); and a meditation on the celebration of Japanese manufactured foreignness, from restaurants to theme parks (Joy Hendry).

Institutions, in the broadest sense, that both enable and inhibit personal and cultural agency are introduced in the fourth unit. The five authors report on a broad range of interrelated subjects, including the role and rationale of the state in structuring preschools (Eyal Ben-Ari); the legacy of imperialism on post-compulsory education (Brian McVeigh); the place of sports and recreation in Japanese cultural history (Elise Edwards); the vicissitudes of popular musical entertainment and pat-terns of consumption (Shuhei Hosokawa); and the exercise of cultural authority and subject formation through popular nonfiction books and magazines (Laura Miller).

Unit V highlights the confluence of the body, politics of "blood" – as a metaphor for kinship and nationality – social reproduction, and nation-building. The constitu-ent essays explore the history of eugenics as one way in which scientific concepts and methods were applied to the joint project of culture-making and nation-building (Jennifer Robertson); the regional varieties of Japanese households and their global context (Emiko Ochiai); the construction of personhood through the embodied medium of a terminal illness (Susan Orpett Long); the historical formation and operations of a "Japanese" cinema that reveals and contests "glocalization" (Aaron Gerow); and the historical beginnings and contemporary features of a national cuisine (Katarzyna Cwiertka).

Comprising the sixth unit are essays that critically review scholarly and everyday practices with respect to religion, science, and biotechnology. The four authors perceptively investigate the tremendous variety of religious practices in Japan and importance of scholarship on Japanese religions as a corrective to Euro-American derived theories (Ian Reader); the most salient issues today in folk religion research, including terminology and gender ideologies (Noriko Kawahashi); the structure of scientific research through the optic of gender (Sumiko Otsubo); and the process through which social ethics and values of moral worth are shaped by, and shape, new biomedical technologies (Margaret Lock).

We, the contributors to this edited volume, neither claim to offer exhaustive coverage of things Japanese nor to promote our essays as the most determinative to date on a particular subject.[19] For scholars and readers unfamiliar with Japan as a country but interested in comparative research and information, our collective intent is to make empirical and interpretive information about "Japan" past and present (more) easily accessible. For anthropologists of Japan and elsewhere, our essays represent a nexus of theories, methodologies, and modes of cultural interpretation that not only yield a prismatic view of Japan and Japanese peoples, but also provide plenty of material for comparative scholarship. And, for ourselves and all our readers, we aim to complicate the understanding and appreciation of Japanese cultures, institutions, and social practices and their layered histories and complex genealogies.

ACKNOWLEDGMENTS

I was very pleased when Jane Huber, Blackwell's energetic, enterprising, and graciously patient anthropology editor, invited me to edit an anthology on Japan anthropology for Blackwell's *Companion* series, and it is to her that I owe the first of many grateful thanks. I also owe thanks to Emily Martin, an editorial assistant at Blackwell, from whose spirited efficiency I have greatly benefited, and to Janet Moth and Anna Oxbury for their conscientious and thorough copy-editing. I owe hearty and heartfelt thanks to the 27 contributors from around the world whose essays made this volume possible in the first place. I might note here that the list of contributors changed over the course of the two years it took to complete this edited volume. I regret that several who were invited to contribute were unable to do so, and I am very grateful to those scholars who, despite their own busy schedules, took up the baton.

NOTES

1   See Lowie (1945) for a portrait of German national character.
2   See also the five-volume series, Studies in the Modernization of Japan, published between 1965 and 1971 by Princeton University Press. For a critique of modernization as ideology, see Latham (2000).
3   Even those whose geographical areas of specialty were profoundly impacted by Japanese (cultural) imperialism have tended to overlook or ignore that history. Others, in conversations, have categorically dismissed Japan as "uninteresting," often exhibiting a disturbing tendency to invoke uninformed stereotypes about "the Japanese" as a rationale.

4   I feel that it is especially appropriate to draw at length from my 1998 publication on the place of Japan in American anthropology not only because what I wrote there remains relevant, but also because the very high price of the hardcover edited volume in which it appears seems to have precluded its wide circulation. I use "American" in reference to an institutional nexus rather than as an isolable thing or unique characteristic.

5   Embree described the state of the field somewhat differently in *Suye Mura*: "No social studies of Japanese village life have been published in English and very few in Japanese" (1939:xvii n.3).

6   It is instructive in this connection to compare the matter-of-fact table of contents in Embree's *The Japanese Nation*: Historical Background, Modern Economic Bases, Government Structure, Social Class System, Family and Household, Religion, etc., with Benedict's more evocative and psychological headings in *The Chrysanthemum and the Sword*: Taking One's Proper Station, Repaying One-In-Thousandth, Clearing One's Name, The Dilemma of Virtue, Self-Discipline, The Child Learns, etc.

7   *The Women of Suye Mura*, published by Robert J. Smith and Ella Lury Wiswell (the widow of John Embree) based on Wiswell's field notes of 1935–6, adds flesh to Embree's somewhat skeletal account of everyday life in *Suye-mura* (Wiswell and Smith [1982]).

8   In this connection, William W. Kelly has remarked that "Selfhood is a field of argument among multiple, competing, and shifting cultural representations, and the best of these recent studies underscore this. Where they have stressed the ideological construction and institutional nexus of self-expression, they succeed in problematizing the relation between cultural construct and social praxis. Where they remain cast in broad and ahistorical terms, they are dangerously essentialist and suspiciously Orientalist" (Kelly 1991:403).

9   Ian Buruma has capitalized on the salience of both tropes: his 1984 book *Japanese Mirror* was republished a year later under the title *Behind the Mask*. Joy Hendry (1993) writes of Japan as the epitome of "wrapping," which she describes as a "veritable cultural template" and a "cultural design."

10 For a thorough analysis of *nihonjinron*, see Befu (1993) and Goodman (chapter 5 in this volume). A recent dissertation on the fetishization of "women's language" in *nihonjinron* is Fair (1996).

11 See also Sonia Ryang's impassioned critique of Benedict's legacy (2004).

12 The journal *Bulletin of Concerned Asian Scholars* (*BCAS*), recently retitled *Critical Asian Studies*, is an excellent source for articles "that challenge the accepted formulas for understanding Asia, the world, and ourselves," as noted on the inside cover of every issue. *Ampo* and *positions: east asia cultures critique* are similarly oriented if differently conceptualized. Generally speaking, the former, along with *BCAS/Critical Asian Studies*, tends to deal more directly, empirically, and analytically with practices and policies of social, economic, and political consequence, while the latter tends to offer articles of a more "current" literary and critical theoretical bent.

13 "Fabricate" in the sense of a making that unites many parts into a whole.

14 In this connection, see Margaret Lock and Susan Long (chapters 29 and 23, respectively, in this volume). See also Hardacre (1994), Lock and Honde (1990), Lock (2002), and Ohnuki-Tierney (1994).

15 This sentence effectively dispatches superficial similarities between Benedict's bricolage and Stein's condensation.

16 Over the past two or three decades, persons representing a hitherto under-represented sex, gender, sexuality, ethnicity, disability, religion, socioeconomic status, and so forth, collectively and steadily have complicated, thankfully and for the better, the social texture of American institutions. Recently, however, buffeted by market forces, those same identity categories have been packaged as "ready-to-wear" consumables guaranteed to

clarify one's location or position within the undulating academic landscape (Robertson 2002:788).

17   See Robertson (2002) for the complete context and nuances of my argument. See Tirosh (2004) for a similar argument from a legal perspective.

18   It goes without saying that both Benedict and Embree, but especially Benedict, exerted an influence on Japan anthropology far outside the boundaries of the American university. In fact, the perceived dominance of American scholars, institutions, and publishers in the field of Japan anthropology has been a recurring topic of "discussion" at the annual, European-based Japan Anthropology Workshop (JAWS) meetings.

19   The constituent essays were submitted over period of two years and thus the most recent publications in a given field may not be acknowledged.

REFERENCES

Agar, M. 1986. Foreword. *In* Self, Sex, and Gender in Cross-Cultural Fieldwork. T. L. Whitehead and M.E. Conaway, eds. Urbana and Chicago: University of Illinois Press.

Befu, Harumi. 1993. Nationalism and *Nihonjinron*. *In* Cultural Nationalism in East Asia: Representation and Identity. Befu Harumi, ed. pp. 107–135. Institute of East Asian Studies, University of California.

Bellah, Robert. 1957. Tokugawa Religion: The Values of Pre-Industrial Japan. Glencoe, NY: The Free Press.

Benedict, Ruth. 1946. The Chrysanthemum and the Sword: Patterns of Japanese Culture. Cambridge, MA: Houghton Mifflin.

Bennett, John. 1970. Some Observations on Western Anthropological Research on Japan. *In* The Study of Japan in the Behavioral Sciences. Edward Norbeck and Susan Parman, eds. pp. 11–27. Rice University Studies 56.

Bennett, John, and Michio Nagai. 1953. The Japanese Critique of the Methodology of Benedict's *The Chrysanthemum and the Sword*. American Anthropologist 55:404–411.

Bourdieu, P. 1986. Outline of a Theory of Practice. Trans. R. Nice. Cambridge: Cambridge University Press.

Buruma, Ian. 1984. Japanese Mirror: Heroes and Villains of Japanese Culture. London: Jonathan Cape.

—— 1985. Behind the Mask: On Sexual Demons, Sacred Mothers, Transvestites, Gangsters and Other Japanese Cultural Heroes. New York: Meridian.

Doak, Kevin. 1996. Ethnic Nationalism and Romanticism in Early Twentieth-Century Japan. Journal of Japanese Studies 22(Winter):77–103.

Dubrick, R. 1984. The Structure of Obscurity: Gertrude Stein, Language, and Cubism. Urbana and Chicago: University of Illinois Press.

Embree, John. 1939. Suye Mura: A Japanese Village. Chicago: University of Chicago Press.

—— 1945. The Japanese Nation: A Social Survey. New York: Farrar & Rinehart.

—— 1947. Review of Benedict (1946). American Sociological Review 1(1):245–246.

—— 1950. A Note on Ethnocentrism in Anthropology. American Anthropologist 52(3): 430–432.

Fair, Janet Kay. 1996. Japanese Women's Language and the Ideology of Japanese Uniqueness. Ph.D. dissertation, University of Chicago.

Hardacre, Helen. 1994. Response of Buddhism and Shintō to the Issue of Brain Death and Organ Transplant. Cambridge Quarterly of Healthcare Ethics 3:585–601.

Hendry, Joy. 1993. Wrapping Culture: Politeness, Presentation and Power in Japan and Other Cultures. Oxford: Clarendon Press.

Kelly, William. 1991. Directions in the Anthropology of Contemporary Japan. Annual Review of Anthropology 20:395–431.

Latham, Michael. 2000. Modernization as Ideology: American Social Science and "Nation Building." Chapel Hill: University of North Carolina Press.

Lévi-Strauss, Claude. 1962a. La Pensée sauvage. Paris: Presses Universitaires de France.

—— 1962b. Le Totemisme aujourd'hui. Paris: Presses Universitaires de France.

Lock, Margaret. 2002. Twice Dead: Organ Transplants and the Reinvention of Death. Berkeley: University of California Press.

Lock, Margaret, and Christine Honde. 1990. Reaching Consensus about Death: Heart Transplants and Cultural Identity in Japan. In Social Science Perspectives on Medical Ethics. G. Weisz, ed. pp. 99–119. Dordrecht and Boston: Kluwer Academic Publishers.

Lowie, Robert. 1945. The German People: A Social Portrait to 1914. New York and Toronto: Farrar & Rinehart.

Moore, Joe, ed. 1997. The Other Japan: Conflict, Compromise, and Resistance Since 1945, new edn. Armonk, NY: M. E. Sharpe.

Nisbet, R. 1977. Sociology as an Art Form. London: Oxford University Press.

Ohnuki-Tierney, Emiko. 1994. Brain Death and Organ Transplantation: Cultural Bases of Medical Technology. Current Anthropology 35(3):233–254.

Robertson, Jennifer. 1994 [1991]. Native and Newcomer: Making and Remaking a Japanese City. Berkeley and Los Angeles: University of California Press.

—— 1997. Empire of Nostalgia: Rethinking Internationalization in Japan Today. Theory, Culture and Society 14(4):97–122.

—— 1998. When and Where Japan Enters: American Anthropology, 1945 to the Present. In Postwar Development of Japanese Studies. Helen Hardacre, ed. pp. 295–335. New York: E. J. Brill.

—— 2001 [1998]. Takarazuka: Sexual Politics and Popular Culture in Modern Japan. Berkeley and Los Angeles: University of California Press.

—— 2002. Reflexivity Redux: A Pithy Polemic on "Positionality." Anthropological Quarterly 75(4):755–762.

Ryang, Sonia. 2004. Chrysanthemum's Strange Life: Ruth Benedict in Postwar Japan. Japan Policy Research Institute, Occasional Paper 32(July). www.jpri.org.

Smith, Robert, and Ella Lury Wiswell. 1982. The Women of Suye Mura. Chicago: University of Chicago Press.

Stein, Gertrude. 1959. Picasso. Boston: Beacon Press.

Tamotsu, Aoki. 1991 [1990]. Nihon bunkaron no hen'yo (The Transformation of Treatises on Japanese Culture). Tokyo: Chūō Kōronsha.

Tirosh, Yofi. 2004. Adjudicating Appearance: Law, Culture and the Predicaments of Identity. Ph.D. dissertation, University of Michigan Law School, 280 pages.

Tsurumi, Patricia, ed. 1988. The Other Japan. Armonk, NY: M. E. Sharpe.

Vance, Carol. 1985. Pleasure and Danger: Toward a Politics of Sexuality. In Pleasure and Danger: Exploring Female Sexuality. Carol Vance, ed. pp. 1–27. Boston: Routledge & Kegan Paul.

Ward, Robert, and Dankwart Rustow. 1964. Political Modernization in Japan and Turkey. Princeton: Princeton University Press.

PART II Cultures, Histories, and Identities

CHAPTER 2

The Imperial Past of Anthropology in Japan

Katsumi Nakao

INTRODUCTION: THE POLITICS OF NAMING

In 1995 the Executive Committee of the Japanese Society of Ethnology (Nihon minzoku gakkai) proposed that the society's name be changed and distributed questionnaires on the subject to its members. The main reason for the name change was that several members had requested that the term "cultural anthropology" (*bunka jinruigaku*) be used rather than "ethnology" (*minzokugaku*). There were heated arguments concerning this proposal at the general meeting that year. Various opinions were aired about how to properly characterize ethnology and anthropology, how to assess the position of cultural anthropology in the university curriculum, and how to account for historical changes in the discipline since World War II. It was soon evident that the arguments about the proposal to change the society's name were connected to ideas about the identity of socio-cultural anthropologists in Japan.

The Japanese Society of Ethnology was founded in 1934. Between 1942 and 1945 it was called the Foundation Ethnology Association (Zaidanōjin minzokugaku kyō-kai). In 1964 it finally changed its name to the Japanese Society of Ethnology (Zaidanhōjin nihon minzokugaku kyōkai). After World War II, "ethnology" disappeared as an academic discipline and was most typically replaced with "cultural anthropology." This was largely due to the fact that "ethnology" had become a term associated with the wartime research carried out by Japanese cultural anthropologists working under the auspices of the National Museum of Ethnology (Kokuritsu minzoku hakubutsukan) in Osaka. After World War II, the University of Tokyo established a major in cultural anthropology in recognition of the popularity of the subject and as a result of the influence of developments in American cultural anthropology. During the immediate postwar period, "cultural anthropology" was critically referred to by conservatives as a discipline representing an "American style." Among intellectuals, however, "ethnology" was associated with the racial policies carried out by the imperialist Japanese state within the so-called Greater East Asia Co-Prosperity

Sphere (*daitōakyōeiken*). Furthermore, there was negative recognition of having cooperated in the war of aggression, and for the latter, the introduction of the term "cultural anthropology" effectively separated the "new" discipline from the wartime nuances of "ethnology" (Ishida 1972:16–17). It was in this rhetorical climate that cultural anthropology was established as a major at Tokyo universities and elsewhere.

At the general meeting of the Japanese Society of Ethnology in 1995, I voiced my opposition to the proposed name change. Changing the name of the society, I argued, would effectively erase the colonial history of Japanese ethnology before that history had been described in sufficient detail. I felt that it was important for us to remain conscious of the continuities in the discipline with Japan's imperial past, when ethnological studies were carried out in conjunction with Japanese colonial policies. Only a few publications describe the history of anthropology in Japan in detail. The formation of anthropology and ethnology in Japan was a process which coincided with efforts to build a strong nation-state, and the discipline was intertwined with such state apparatuses as the system of universal education, imported from Europe in the late 19th century. The acquisition of overseas colonies brought with it the responsibility of administering indigenous peoples and, consequently, anthropologists provided colonial administrators with information that facilitated the pacification and control of the diverse peoples within the growing empire. Although the Japanese Society of Ethnology was founded in 1934, ethnology was included as a subject in anthropology meetings well before then, along with physical anthropology and archaeology. As Japan's colonial empire expanded so too did the number of regions actively researched.

Taiwan was made a colony of Japan in 1895. In 1905 Japan extended its colonial reach to southern Sakhalin and the Liaodong peninsula in China. Korea was annexed in 1910, and nine years later, Micronesia was transferred from German to Japanese jurisdiction. The puppet state of Manchuria was established in 1932. By 1942, Japan controlled a vast Asian-Pacific region stretching from Indonesia to the Aleutian Islands, and Japanese ethnologists were dispatched to even the most remote islands.

Japanese anthropologists trained in the postwar period were strongly influenced by structural functionalism and structuralism. Consequently, they were not especially interested in or concerned with the historical background of ethnography and anthropology in Japan.[1] This also explains why they perceived cultural anthropology as a "new" discipline developed under American influence. In this chapter I will provide a brief overview of the history of anthropology and ethnology in Japan, and will characterize those features through comparisons drawn with the discipline as it is practiced in other countries.

THE IMPORTANCE OF ANTHROPOLOGY IN COLONIAL ADMINISTRATION

In 1886 *Tōkyō jinruigaku zasshi* (the Tokyo Anthropology Journal) was first published in Japan. As in Europe and the United States, anthropological and ethnological studies in Japan were initiated by interested amateurs and medical doctors who cooperated to produce said journal. The earliest articles were written by specialists, such as doctors, for whom physical anthropology was a second specialty, and also by archaeologists, historians, and amateur anthropologists. At this time, the "origins" of the Japanese people was a hotly debated topic, and the central question was whether or not the Ainu (see chapter 6 in this volume) were living vestiges of the earliest Japanese. Professor Koganei Yoshikiyo, for example, who was affiliated with the anatomy section of the medical department at the University of Tokyo, strongly supported the hypothesis that the "ancient Japanese were Ainu." Consequently, all the human bones that were excavated from kitchen middens were sent to him for analysis (University of Tokyo, Science Department 1990:3).

The first lectures in Japan on anthropology were delivered in the science department at Tokyo Imperial University, whose first professor was Tsuboi Shōgorō. Tsuboi, born in 1863, had read a report filed by Edward Morse, an American zoologist, on the Ōmori shell mounds in Tokyo which he had discovered and excavated in 1884 with assistance from that university. In 1884 Tsuboi established the Anthropology Meeting Association (Jinruigakkai) as an outgrowth of his studies in England with Edward Tylor from 1889 to 1892.[2] Upon his return to Japan, Tsuboi became a professor in the science department of the University of Tokyo where he taught anthropology – the very first lectures on anthropology in Japan.

Inō Kanori, a journalist at the time, participated in the Tokyo Anthropology Meeting Association and edited Tsuboi's lectures. His notebook was reprinted under the title, *Tsuboi no jinruigaku kōgi* (Tsuboi's Anthropology Lectures) (Inō 1995). According to Inō, Tsuboi's lectures focused on the anthropological thought of ancient Greek, Roman, and Egyptian scholars, and on trends in natural historical studies along with Darwinian evolutionist theory. The last chapter in Inō's notebook refers to the situation of the Anthropology Meeting Foundation in Britain at the end of the 19th century, and especially on the Foundation's investigation of aborigines in the British colonies. Significantly, Inō was inspired by Tsuboi's lectures to travel to Taiwan in order to conduct fieldwork among the aboriginal population there. Inō later researched Han Chinese social customs as well, and published the three-volume ethnography, *Taiwan bunkashi* (Taiwan Cultural History; 1928). He and his colleagues also wrote many articles on Taiwanese society and culture. I realized while perusing all of the articles published in The Journal of the Anthropological Society of Nippon (Tōkyō jinruigakkai zasshi), that 1895 – the year Japan won the Sino-Japanese War and colonized Taiwan – vividly marked a turning point in the content and orientation of Japanese anthropology.

Tashiro Yasusada was another ethnologist who served as a temporary administrator with the office of the governor general of Taiwan. Torii Ryūzō, of Tokyo Imperial University, published the results of his fieldwork during the early stages of the Japanese colonization of Taiwan in the journal noted above. His ethnography of Taiwanese aborigines was distinctive in utilizing photography as a methodological tool. His work included physical anthropological data as well as descriptions of cultural practices. Torii's monographs were translated and published in French (Torii 1910), indicating that the work of Japanese anthropologists was known outside of Japan. Yagi Shōtarō, regarded as Tsuboi Shōgorō's successor at Tokyo Imperial University, followed the precedent set by his predecessor and went to work for the governor general of Taiwan, who was responsible for organizing anthropological research projects. It is clear that anthropological studies of Taiwan began with Japanese research on Taiwanese aborigines.

In 1901 the Japanese authorities in Taiwan organized an office responsible for researching traditional customs, which marked a new stage in the anthropological research of the island. Information on land-use customs was needed by the Japanese colonial administrators in order to enact laws commensurate with Taiwanese traditions, and it was necessary that legal procedures be devised that were consonant with customary law. However, in order to understand the land-use system, Japanese administrators needed to be familiar not only with the Chinese and Taiwanese administrative systems but also with the systems of lineage, succession, and marriage.

The section head in charge of these ethnological investigations was Okamatsu Sanarō, a professor of law at Kyoto Imperial University. He had been to Germany and studied civil codes and primitive law under the instruction of Josef Kohler, who was one of a group of scholars who studied and compared the laws of primitive societies. Johann Jakob Bachofen, who wrote *Myth, Religion and Mother Right* (1967 [1861]), founded this group, and Albert Kohler, along with Hermann Post, kept it going. Okamatsu adapted German methods of investigation to the anthropological study of Taiwan; his first reports on land and kinship in Taiwan were published in English (Okamatsu 1902), and were quoted by Josef Kohler (Kohler and Wenger 1914). The basic data in Okamatsu's investigation was used in codifying a colonial legal system in Taiwan, thereby legitimizing Japan's governance (Nakao 2000:395).

To summarize, then, the methods used in the Japanese colonial research on Taiwan were informed by three major sources: German methodologies developed for the study of primitive law; British methodology employed in the study of colonized indigenous peoples; and the Chinese classics, the intensive and comparative study of which had been greatly developed in the Edo period (1603–1868). From its inception, *The Journal of the Anthropological Society of Nippon* included anthropology, ethnology, and archaeology under the rubric of general anthropology. However, the number of papers on physical anthropological factors, such as the characteristics of bone and blood samples that are usually grouped under the heading of "physical anthropology," increased remarkably from 1924 onwards.

A similar situation existed in Korea, which was colonized by Japan in 1910. Keijo Imperial University was founded there in 1927,[3] and anthropology courses were taught in the medical department. Not surprisingly, most of the staff specialized in physical anthropology and published a great many papers about Korean physical anthropology in the *Journal of the Anthropological Society of Nippon*.

Akiba Takashi and Suzuki Eitarō were sociologists in the department of law and literature at Keijo Imperial University, and Akamatsu Chijō was a scholar of religion there. Before being assigned to Keijo Imperial University, Akiba had studied anthropology in England with Edward Westermarck. Based at Tokyo Imperial University, Akamatsu studied religious psychology and sociology in France under the direction of Émile Durkheim. Akiba and Akamatsu conducted fieldwork together on religious anthropology and focused specifically on shamanism in Korea and Manchuria. They collected the songs of Korean shamans and published them in their jointly authored book, *Chōsen fūzoku no kenkyū* (The Study of Korean Shamanism), which included the original verses in Korean together with their Japanese translations (Akamatsu and Akiba 1937–38). Their co-authored study, *Manmō no shakai to bunka* (Ethnicity and Society in Manchuria and Mongolia) (Akamatsu and Akiba 1941), was an in-depth research report on the religion and society of the minority people of northeastern China. Izumi Seichi, who became a professor at the University of Tokyo, includes an interesting anecdote about the two in his autobiography. When Izumi met Akiba and confided his interest in studying anthropology, he was handed a copy of Malinowski's *Argonauts of the Western Pacific* (1922) with the warning that, "You can work on such a thing your entire life and it'll still be hard to get a job." Izumi read *Argonauts* and told Akiba that he still wanted to study anthropology, whereupon the senior scholar happily accepted him as a student (Izumi 1972: 211–212). Among other things, this anecdote shows Malinowski's influence among early Japanese anthropologists.

Those Japanese anthropologists who were based at Keijo Imperial University gradually expanded the area of their fieldwork from Korea to Manchuria, Mongolia, Thailand, and New Guinea. The physical anthropologists among them put together excellent collections of human bone specimens. After World War II, these same anthropologists returned to Japan where they obtained university teaching positions. They made a point of keeping in touch with each other. Izumi referred to the group as the "Keijo anthropology school" (Keijō Teikoku Daigaku Sōritsu 50 Shūnen Kinenshi Hensan Iinkai 1974:239–243).

What was the status of anthropology at other Japanese colonial universities? In 1928 Utsurikawa Nenozō, who had trained as an anthropologist under Roland B. Dixon at Harvard University, joined the literature and law faculty of Taihoku (Taipei) Imperial University in Taiwan, which included an Institute of Ethnology. As I noted earlier, the Japanese governor general of Taiwan supervised the survey of existing customs, and thus many anthropologists came to Taiwan to conduct research during the late 19th and early 20th centuries. Because the university was established 20 years after Taiwan became a Japanese colony, there was no relationship between the early colonial surveys and the ethnological research done at Taihoku Imperial University. In contrast, the social scientists at Keijo Imperial University cooperated from the outset with the colonial administrators in Korea, which was formally occupied by Japan in 1910. A study group organized at the Institute of Ethnology published the journal *Nanpōdozoku* (Ethnography of the Southern Regions), which focused on the aborigines of Taiwan and Southeast Asia.

Utsurikawa employed the genealogical method developed by William Rivers and began a research project on the oral history of Taiwanese aborigines. However, Utsurikawa was essentially an armchair anthropologist and his student, Mabuchi Tōichi, did the actual fieldwork. In 1935 they jointly published a research report titled *Taiwan takasagozoku keitōshozoku no kenkyū* (The Formosan Native Tribes: A Genealogical Study), which was widely praised. Mabuchi learned about ethnological theory and methods by reading the Anglophone ethnographies in Utsurikawa's office and through the actual practice of doing fieldwork among the aborigines.

Kanezaki Takeo, a specialist in physical anthropology, was in the medical department of Taihoku Imperial University. He assisted with the publication of *Minzoku taiwan* (Taiwan Folklore), a magazine that targeted amateurs and the general public rather than specialists. At that time the Japanese colonial administration in Taiwan was promoting the assimilation of Japanese culture; the journal indirectly criticized this policy by showcasing the "traditional" culture of Taiwan. As was to be expected, this resulted in a governmental inspection of the publication, but ultimately the authority of Kanezaki and Taihoku Imperial University insured its publication until the end of the war.

The motivation that led to the establishment of special courses in anthropology occurred not only in Japanese colonial universities but also at Tokyo Imperial University. There, Matsui Akira became Tsuboi's successor. Matsui conducted field-work in Micronesia soon after it became a Japanese colony and published his ethnography in English in 1918 (Matsui 1918). He died suddenly in 1926 at the age of 55. Hasebe Kotondo from Tohoku Imperial University was recruited in 1928 to succeed Matsui at Tokyo Imperial University. Hasebe, who had a medical degree, had studied physical anthropology in Germany. Like his German counterparts, he synthesized physical anthropology, archaeology, ancient history, and ethnographic studies. Hasebe eventually developed a special anthropology course in the science department. The course, which was first offered in April 1938, was designed to train specialists in anthropology for state-sponsored research on the ethnic minorities living in Japan's colonies, particularly Manchuria, Mongolia, and Siberia (Terada 1981:256–257).

When a department of anthropology was created at Tokyo Imperial University in April 1939, Hasebe was put in charge of the general theory of anthropology, somatology, and osteology, Suda was appointed to head ethnography, and Yahata Ichirō was assigned to teach prehistory. In addition to participating in seminars on these subjects, students were required to learn anthropological methods of participant observation and fieldwork, and to write a graduation thesis. Hasebe believed that anthropology students also needed some knowledge of basic medicine, and, accordingly, he made students attend lectures in the medical department. The physical anthropologists who were attached to the medical department had studied anthropology in Germany, and thus the influence of German anthropology was pronounced (Terada 1981:258).

Just as Germany became a model for nation-state-building activities in Japan, so scholarly societies in Japan, especially those in law and medicine, were strongly influenced by the German academy. Although physical anthropology followed the German model, cultural anthropology was strongly influenced by Tyler, Malinowski, and Rivers, and further modified by the Japanese to fit various colonial contexts. For example, because customary law prevailed among the native people colonized by Japan, Japanese law could not effectively be applied to them, and therefore Japanese jurists researched the laws and customs of the non-industrialized societies in the colonies. Henry Sumner Maine's *Ancient Law* (1861) was read by Japanese lawyers, and Malinowski's book on the family and primitive law was translated by jurists and read both as a popular European anthropological study and as a monograph for understanding Micronesian society, especially after 1918 when Micronesia became a trust territory of the League of Nations to be managed by Japan.

ANTHROPOLOGY AND MARXISM, NATURAL HISTORY AND RELIGIOUS STUDIES

What motivated the study of cultural anthropology and ethnology in the interwar period? There were three basic influences particular to Japan in this regard, as

THE IMPERIAL PAST OF ANTHROPOLOGY   25

illustrated by the biographies of interwar anthropologists: Marxism, natural history, and religious studies.

Marxism is concerned with direct political action. Even anthropologists not deeply concerned with political action such as Oka Masao and Mabuchi Tōichi read the classic texts of Marxism as ethnology majors. Their interest was related to the spread of socialist thought in Japan in the 1920s. The sudden success of the Russian Revolution made Marxism and socialism very popular among the younger generation of Japanese intellectuals. Marx's *Das Kapital* was published in Japanese in 1920, and the works of Engels, Lenin, and Kropotkin were also translated, further stimulating an interest in Marxist thought. High school and university students were especially interested in socialism, and many books on that subject were translated and published in affordable paperback editions. However, following the Maintenance of the Public Order Act in 1925, the socialist movement was brutally suppressed by the government and many intellectuals were arrested. Most were released if they declared that they had abandoned Marxism. These people were popularly referred to as *tenkō* or converts, and among them were several ethnologists and folklorists, including Yanagita Kunio.

Although Yanagita founded the field of Japanese folklore studies, he did not have a university post, and folklore was established as an independent area of research. Yanagita organized private study groups and conducted folklore research on his own. Some university students and local intellectuals who were interested in ethnography and local history, and who joined Yanagita's project were later arrested because of their activities in the socialist-leaning student movement (see Fukuda 1990; Tsurumi 1998).

Ishida Eiichirō became a famous anthropologist after World War II, and his biography is illustrative. He was born in Osaka in 1903 and participated in a study group on Marxism at his high school. In 1924, he entered the department of economics at Kyoto Imperial University and joined a social science study group that was part of a left-wing student organization. He also studied Russian under Nikolai Aleksandrovich Nevskii, a Russian who came to Japan in 1915 to pursue research on Japanese language and folklore, focusing on Okinawan, Miyako Island and Ainu folktales. Ishida learned about the Japanese folklore studies of Yanagita Kunio and Origuchi Nobuo from Nevskii. Ishida's hereditary status of baron did not prevent his arrest in 1926 under the Maintenance of Public Order Act. He was released but continued his involvement with the left-wing student association and, consequently, was rearrested and sent to prison from 1927 to 1934. He used his time in prison to develop a foundation in anthropology by reading Morgan's *Ancient Society* and Frazer's *Golden Bough*, which had been introduced to him by Nevskii.

Following his release from prison, Ishida participated in Yanagita's study group where he made the acquaintance of Oka Masao. In 1937 Ishida enrolled in Vienna University, where he studied ethno-history under Wilhelm Schmidt and wrote a doctoral dissertation on the cultural history of the horse and the origins of inner Asian nomadic culture. Upon his return to Japan in 1939, Ishida was employed part-time as a researcher for the East Asian Minorities Research Committee of the Imperial Japanese Academy, under whose auspices he explored, in 1941, the lineage of the Uilta (at that time called the Orokko). Ishida traveled to Inner Mongolia the following summer in order to conduct research on Chinese Muslims. From 1944 to 1945 he was the vice-chief of the Northwest Institute in Zhangjiakou, Mongolia.

Although he interacted with fieldworkers such as Imanishi Kinji and Umesao Tadao, Ishida himself did not do any fieldwork (Harayama and Morita 1986:74–75; Sugiyama 1988:313–315; Tsurumi 1998:171–186). He returned to Japan after World War II and found employment during the Allied occupation as an academic advisor to the Civil Information and Education Section of General Headquarters. In 1951 he was made a professor at the Institute of Oriental Culture, University of Tokyo, where he established a cultural anthropology curriculum and played an important role in anthropology education in the early postwar period.

Oka Masao was another anthropologist whose early studies of ethnology led to his influential role in postwar cultural anthropology. Oka was born in 1898 in the city of Matsumoto in Nagano Prefecture. He was a high school student when the Russian Revolution broke out in 1917 and this event sparked his interest in leftist ideology. He read some left-wing magazines, a book by Kropotkin, and some German books on Marxism. He also taught himself Russian, participated in the student-led democracy movement, and joined up with several college students who subscribed to Marxism. He also obtained a copy of Friedrich Engels' *The Origins of Family, Private Property and the State* (1844) and Lewis Henry Morgan's *Ancient Society* (1877). He developed an interest in ethnology and decided that he wanted to major in that subject.

In 1920 Oka registered for the sociology course in the Department of Literature at Tokyo Imperial University and attended the lectures on anthropology given by Torii Ryūzō. He read the ethnology "classics" – he was especially interested in Frazer's work – and wrote his graduation thesis on the element of magic in archaic societies. At one point during his studies, Oka visited Yanagita Kunio and asked him to write the preface to the Japanese translation of Frazer's books *The Magic Art* and *The Evolution of Kings*. However, knowing that the book contained some references to Japanese emperors, Yanagita opposed the publication of the translation. Nevertheless, Yanagita was pleased that students at the University of Tokyo were studying folklore, so he permitted Oka to attend his study group.

Among the books Oka read in laying a foundation in ethnology were Wilhelm Schmidt and Wilhelm Koppers' *Völker und Kulturen*, vol. 3, *Der Mensch alter Zeiten* (1924; the Japanese translation was published in 1944), W. H. R. Rivers' *The History of Melanesian Society* (1914), and Heinrich Shurtz's *Altersklassen und Männerbünde. Eine Darstellung der Grundformen der Gesellschaft* (Age Grades and Men's Associations: An Outline of the Foundation of Society; 1902). For a while he edited the magazine *Minzoku* (The Folk), which focused on ethnology and folklore, and later attended Vienna University from 1929 to 1933. There he wrote his Ph.D. thesis, *Kulturschichten in Alt-Japan* (Cultural Strata of Ancient Japan). Upon the completion of his studies, Oka was employed at Budapest University as a visiting lecturer from 1938 to 1940, after which he traveled to the Balkan peninsula, where he observed conflicts among the area's diverse ethnic groups. Although he was eager to understand the actual conditions of the various ethnic groups, Oka realized that it was impossible to understand, much less resolve, such problems on the basis of theories he had learned in Vienna. He thus began to question the "real world" relevance of the dominant ethno-historical theories (Oka 1963:346; 1981:678).

The "culture-sphere" theory of the Vienna School was based on the hypothesis that complex cultural areas established in the past have continued up to the present.

The major application of this theory was toward the reconstruction of cultural history. Culture-sphere theory called for the classification of ethnographic descriptions into individual cultural elements, which could then be reassembled. The Vienna School lost influence in anthropology departments the world over after World War II (Ōbayashi 1987:668), and Oka turned to British social anthropology which he viewed as more appropriate for the task of acquiring socially "useful" information.

Oka returned to Japan in 1940. A charismatic personality and skilled conversationalist, he was able to make connections with scholars, military authorities, and government officials. Through this network Oka was successful in orchestrating the establishment of an Institute of Ethnology in 1943. Oka was appointed director and oversaw its management until it was dismantled in September 1945. After the war, the Institute was criticized by right-wing scholars for having organized anthropologists to gather cultural information for wartime authorities. Oka temporarily abandoned academia and returned to Matsumoto. In 1948, however, he returned to scholarly work under the auspices of a symposium organized to explore the roots of Japanese culture, a topic popular among journalists at the time. The anthropologists Ishida Eiichirō, Egami Namio, and Yawata Ichirō participated in symposium, and the proceedings were published under the title, *Nihon minzoku no kigen* (The Origin of the Japanese Race) (Oka et al. 1958).

The 1948 symposium was based on the culture-sphere theory of the Vienna School as elaborated in Oka's doctoral dissertation; namely, the reconstruction of ancient Japanese culture was perceived as a way to discover the roots of Japanese culture within Asian culture. "Culture" here was broadly defined as a synthesis of archaeology, mythology, physical anthropology, and so forth. This conception of Japan's relationship to Asia emerged in the early 20th century; however, because Japanese mythology and religion were themes intrinsically connected to the emperor system, ancient Japanese culture was deemed a politically taboo subject during the wartime period. After 1945, this theme could be more freely discussed, although the exercise was sometimes criticized as an attempt to remake the Greater East Asia Co-Prosperity Sphere. In 1951 Oka was made a professor of social anthropology at Tokyo Metropolitan University, and later served as chair of the Japanese Ethnological Association. In spite of the greatly diminished influence globally of the Vienna School's "culture sphere" theory, it nevertheless remained popular among certain anthropologists in Japan, because the otherwise taboo imperial system could be analyzed under its auspices.

Ishida Eiichirō and Oka Masao had very different personalities but shared a similar background. Both were high school students during the Taisho period (1912–26), and the Russian Revolution sparked their interest in socialism. Both came in contact with Marxism by reading popular edited books on the subject or the German originals. This can also be said of Mabuchi Tōichi, who will be discussed later. The social sciences were imported into Japan along with Marxism, and historical materialism was adapted as a theory of social evolution during 1920s to 1930s. Ishida and Oka both also joined the student movement after the Russian Revolution. Whereas British anthropology developed under the influence of the theory of evolution, the development of anthropology in Japan was greatly influenced by Marxism and historical materialism, as explicated in works by Morgan and Engels. Social scientists were often under surveillance by the police because of their interest in Marxism. Although politically suspect, their investigative services were considered important, and they staffed the research section of the South Manchuria Railway Company.

Among those scholars who worked in Manchuria was Imanishi Kinji of Kyoto Imperial University,[4] who was at the center of a group interested in a natural-history approach to anthropology. Imanshi was one of the leaders of the Kyoto Exploration Geography Association at Kyoto Imperial University, basically a mountaineering club, whose members eventually developed an expertise in frontier exploration and ecology. When the Japanese army launched military invasions in 1938 from Manchukuo to Mongolia, Tokyo Imperial University dispatched an investigative team whose members were mostly natural scientists who had earlier conducted a large-scale investigation in Ruhe (now known as Chengde), north of Beijing. Imanishi opined that Kyoto Imperial University should organize a similar investigative team, and one was dispatched from the university in the summer of 1941 to the Japanese-controlled South Pacific island of Ponape. The original plan had been to go to New Guinea, but soon after the ship left port the war in the Pacific erupted, and the team's research destination was changed to Melanesia. Following the completion of their research there, the Kyoto team set out the following year on an expedition through the Dahsinganling mountains in Manchuria along the Russian border. There, Imanishi trained them in fieldwork methodology, report-writing, etc. Umesao Tadao, Kawakita Jirō, and Kira Tatsuo were among those on Imanishi's team; they later became professional anthropologists or naturalists and rose to the top of their fields.

Imanishi was appointed to direct the Northwest Institute established by the government of Mongolia in 1944. Pupils such as Umesao Tadao, who had trained with Imanishi at Kyoto University and in Manchuria, accompanied him there. He started his new assignment and did fieldwork in Inner Mongolia. Although his specialty was natural science, in 1959 Imanishi was appointed to be the first professor of social anthropology at the Human Sciences Institute for Research in Humanities at Kyoto University. Under Imanshi's leadership Kyoto University developed a unique course of study and research methodology bridging the natural and social sciences, as demonstrated in fieldwork conducted in Africa and the Himalayas.

Religious studies produced many anthropologists, including Furuno Kiyoto and Sugiura Kenichi, both of whom graduated from the Department of Literature, University of Tokyo, with a specialization in religion. The connection between anthropology and religious studies was forged in the early 20th century with the study of primitive religions. Established in 1905, the University of Tokyo religious studies course was influenced by European Oriental Studies, and religions other than Christianity were studied from a comparative, social-analytic viewpoint. Religious philosophy, Buddhism, Shintoism, and shamanism were included in the religious studies course (Fujii 1985:17–58). Furuno Kiyoto enrolled on the religious studies course at the University of Tokyo in 1923 and joined a "primitive religion" study group that had just been organized (Fujii 1985:47). He wrote his graduation thesis in French on Durkheim's theories of religion, and in 1930 translated into Japanese and published the French anthropologist's *Les Formes élémentaires de la vie religieuse* (1912). Sugiura was appointed the first professor of anthropology at the University of Tokyo largely on account of his background in comparative religious studies. The work of James Frazer and Émile Durkheim influenced those scholars pursuing a psychological approach to religious ritual, such as Uno Enkū. Uno, who was in

Europe from 1920 to 1923 and studied anthropology under Marcel Mauss, researched the rice crop rituals of Malaysia after returning to Japan (Ōyano 1982:87; Uno 1941). He later chaired the Japanese Ethnology Association.

WARTIME USES OF ETHNOLOGY: THE INSTITUTE OF ETHNOLOGY

In the late 1930s the Japanese government reorganized academic activities as part of its preparation for the possibility of a full-scale war. Information on the frontier districts of Japan's empire was urgently needed and ethnology was perceived as an important instrument in procuring it. As noted earlier, Oka Masao headed a group of ethnologists who requested that the Japanese government and the military author- ities establish a national research organization in their discipline, and in 1943 the state established the Institute of Ethnology. One of its first research activities was to take on an "ethnic files" project focusing on peoples under Japanese domination and to update them annually based on ethnographical fieldwork. Before the Institute was founded the East Asian Ethnic Groups Research Committee of the Imperial Japanese Academy had been in charge of planning the "ethnic files" project in the late 1930s. The purpose of the project was to research the circumstances of the 75 or so different ethnic groups living along the volatile border areas of Japan's Asian Pacific empire. Ethnographers with specialties in physical, linguistic, and cultural anthropology were commissioned by the Committee to conduct fieldwork throughout the empire on such topics as physiology and phenotype, economic activity, ecological habitats, social structure, religion, modes of entertainment, fashion, and language. Previous famil- iarity with a given ethnic group was desirable but not necessary. The Imperial Japanese Academy published four volumes of ethnographies on the Gilyak, Ainu, and Koreans. As a corollary of the ethnic files project, the academy published, in 1944, *Tōaminzoku meii* (The Dictionary of Ethnic Names in East Asia) (Teikoku Gakushiin 1944). This contained the names and locations of minority populations living in Southeast Asia, New Guinea, and Melanesia.

An obvious counterpart to the Japanese ethnic files project is the Human Relations Area Files (HRAF) project inaugurated in 1937 in the United States with a mandate to collect material from published ethnographies in order to construct a comparative cultural database that was global in scope. With the outbreak of World War II the collection of these data – especially data on Latin America and from areas under Japanese control – was promoted as a governmental project (Murdock 1982). Because information on New Guinea and Oceania was of particular strategic importance, the US government made use of Japanese ethnographies, employing (interned) Japanese Americans to translate them into English for use in the HRAF files. Both the American and the Japanese "ethnic files" projects directly connected the discipline of anthropology and its practitioners to the war and wartime strategizing.

While in Vienna, Oka witnessed Nazi Germany's annexation of Austria in 1939. He illustrated his arguments about the necessity for an Institute of Ethnology by pointing to the Nazi party's commitment to the study of folklore in establishing both the "traditions" of the "Aryan race" and the basis for German patriotism.

Oka wanted for Japan an ethnological institute like the one recently founded in Germany. Once founded, it was his hope that the existence of an institute would establish ethnology as an independent discipline in its own right, as opposed to a branch of general anthropology which included physical anthropology, as was the case at Tokyo Imperial University. Some professors, such as Hasebe Kotondo of Tokyo Imperial University, did not support the creation of a Institute of Ethnology. Hasebe worried that the framework of general anthropology would be undermined and that the interest of young anthropologists would shift to the sort of cultural anthropology developed by Oka. He was able to use his ties to military and governmental officials to brush aside such dissenting opinions (Nakao 1997:49).

Members of the Institute of Ethnology read textbooks on anthropology, such as Robert Lowie's *The History of Ethnological Theory* and Wilhelm Schmidt's *Handbuch der Methode der kulturhistorischen Ethnologie*. Ethnographies on India and Vietnam were also translated into Japanese, and the Association of Ethnology published Shirokogoroff's *A Tungus Dictionary* (Shirokogoroff 1944). A dictionary of Uighur was also being compiled by the Institute, but the war ended before it was published and the manuscript was confiscated by SCAP (Supreme Command Allied Powers) forces and subsequently "lost" (Takeuchi 1982:36).

The Institute of Ethnology organized fieldwork during the last couple of years of World War II, such as the research conducted by Makino Tatsumi on Hainan Island and by Iwamura Shinobu on Chinese Muslims. These were completed within the span of a few weeks. Japanese military authorities facilitated Iwamura's research on Chinese Muslims because they were preparing to cooperate with Muslims in blocking Russian aid to China. The Japanese army also intended to create a puppet government in Central Asia, and disseminated propaganda among Chinese Muslims that stressed the ethnic conflict between the Han Chinese and the Muslims, and asserted that the Communist Party would suppress Islam. Accordingly, the Institute of Ethnology commissioned ethnographic research into the cultural character of Islamic society and the role of the mosque as a social unit as part of the military's objective to manipulate and control China's Muslim minority. Four anthropologists from the Institute were dispatched to undertake this specific project under the direction of Ono Shinobu, an ethnographer in the research department of the South Manchuria Railway Company. Prior to departing, Ono developed questionnaires based on the examples in *Notes and Queries on Anthropology*, a British anthropology manual, which he translated into Chinese for use in the field. Data from respondents were recorded on notecards and published after the war under the name of Iwamura Shinobu (Iwamura 1949–50). Because most of the investigations of Chinese Muslims to date had focused on religious philosophy or history, Ono and Iwamura's ethnographic research is regarded as an unprecedented analysis of Muslim society in China.

However, their research has been criticized as inaccurate by the Chinese Muslim scholar, Zhang Chengzhi, who is noted for his study of Chinese Sufism. A friend of Zhang's father, who was one of the informants interviewed by Ono and Iwamura, claims that the Chinese Muslims had been coached by their peers as to what sorts of questions to expect and what sorts of answers to give. The fact that the Japanese army urged Muslims to cooperate with the Institute's research team heightened the suspicions of Muslim leaders, who were afraid that, perceiving potential danger, local imams would divulge more information than was wise. Muslim leaders therefore handpicked the respondents and instructed them to give only the most minimally necessary answers and to remain silent about important religious doctrines.

The concerns of Chinese Muslim leaders were related to the Japanese army's policy toward Islam in association with the Japanese government's attempts to create puppet governments in Manchuria and Mongolia under the auspices of China's royal family. Clearly, the creation of a puppet government in central Asia required that the Japanese army identify an Islamic leader whose influence extended beyond a local parish: Ma Zhenwu, the eighth-generation heir of the founder of Chinese Sufism, who at that time was in hiding in Bejing. Chinese Muslim leaders suspected the Japanese of conducting ethnographic field research as part of a broad effort to locate Ma Zhenwu (Nakao 2000:239–240).

Throughout the war the Japanese government organized a number of ethnographic teams to undertake field research in the newly occupied territories. Typical of this kind of research was the Ruhe project, noted earlier, organized in 1938 by Tokyo Imperial University. Egami Namio was one of the prominent anthropologists participating in these team projects. Naoe Hiroji, a specialist in Chinese folklore, was a member of the Shanxi Investigation Commission formed in 1942, and Izumi Seiichi participated in the 1942 New Guinea Investigation Commission.

CONCLUSION

Nakane Chie has defined cultural anthropology in Japan as a "new" discipline that was developed after World War II, and "ethnology" as the "old" discipline characteristic of the first half of the 20th century (Nakane 1974:57). However, can cultural anthropology and ethnology really be separated in this way? When cultural anthropology was being reconstructed in postwar Japan, ethnology was characterized as "European" and cultural anthropology as "American." As noted earlier, in Japan anthropology was developed in the late 19th century, when the country made the transition from an isolated feudal polity to an imperialistic nation-state. The acquisition of colonies called for a new knowledge of, and expertise in administering, culturally different societies; with no native models on which to rely, the Japanese turned to European anthropology. From the outset, an emphasis was placed on surveys through which to collect information that would facilitate the pacification and control of colonized peoples. The first such surveys were conducted only in areas directly under Japanese colonial administration. The outbreak of World War II prompted a significant shift in methodology, and surveys were initiated in newly occupied areas and regions in Asia and the Pacific speculated to be sites of future battlefields. Voluminous translations of local materials were also undertaken. The result was a tremendous advance in accumulated anthropological knowledge of the Asia Pacific region.

Japan's defeat in 1945 had a drastic effect on the development of anthropology in the Japanese academy. Whereas "ethnology" (*minzokugaku*) was the term in common use during the imperial period, "cultural anthropology" (*bunka jinruigaku*) and "social anthropology" (*shakai jinruigaku*) were the prevalent terms used after the war. As noted above in reference to Nakane Chie, this shift in terminology corresponded to a perceived break between wartime ethnology and postwar cultural anthropology. After the war, the link between anthropology and government policy was severed. Japan was stripped of its colonial possessions, and the country, under the umbrella of United States, adopted a new constitution that forbade the use of an offensive military force as an instrument of state policy. Although these developments alone would have fundamentally altered the focus of Japanese anthropological research, other circumstances played a significant role in reshaping the discipline. Japan's postwar economic success made more funds available for ethnographic research, including increasingly more fieldwork in developing regions with no particular ties to Japan. As a result, the monographs published by Japanese anthropologists today largely mirror those written by their American and European counterparts in terms of content and narrative structure, and Japanese anthropology has lost much of what once made it distinctive.

Nevertheless, it is simplistic to describe the vicissitudes of anthropology in Japan from its early years through the postwar period to the present as a simply a substitution of European-inspired ethnology with American-style cultural anthropology. Not only has the research material and theory of prewar ethnology deeply influenced the cultural anthropology of the postwar period, but prewar ethnographers have remained central actors in postwar academic circles. To explore the history of prewar ethnographic research is tantamount to remembering and confronting modern Japan's imperialistic past. The apparent "historical amnesia" among anthropologists in Japan parallels the low level of historical consciousness of Japanese people in general about Japanese imperialism.

Up until the 1960s, ethnographers from Europe conducted fieldwork in former European colonies, where research permission was easier to obtain and abundant written material was readily available. Even in postcolonial situations, those from each of the metropolitan countries had an obvious advantage in doing research in the former colonies. In contrast, colonial ties were deemed irrelevant to ethnographic studies by Japanese scholars after 1945, when Japan's defeat suddenly severed colonial connections, a condition widely emphasized by many Japanese scholars today. After the war, Japanese ethnographers embarked on fieldwork in any accessible locale without considering whether it used to be part of Japan's colonies and what that might mean in and for their work. Ironically, in a sense, resounding defeat in World War II freed postcolonial Japan from the yoke of colonial legacies. Herein lies a stark difference between Japan's anthropology and its counterparts in Europe and the United States. Historical disconnections from former colonies as such cannot be morally judged. Rather, colonial legacies should be criticized from the vantage point of the present. The emphasis, by postwar Japanese scholars including anthropologists, on Japan's disconnectness from its former empire has encouraged an amnesia regarding the role that they and their predecessors played in Japan's colonial expansion and its aftermath.

I have outlined the development of anthropology in Japan and have introduced the background and work of some Japan's better-known anthropologists active in the first half of the 20th century. Some were critical of the imperialist enterprise: Ishida, for example, opposed wartime trends in academia, but he could neither resist nor assert his opinion. He could only react by not cooperating. Ethnographic research in the first half of the 20th century collectively helped to facilitate Japan's administration of its scattered Asian Pacific empire. Japanese anthropology of the imperial period, the late 19th century through 1945, possesses a distinctive character that calls for wider recognition and analytical scrutiny.

NOTES

1 Of course, one could also argue that the desire to dissociate wartime from postwar academic practices was best served by structural functionalism and structuralism.
2 When Tsuboi realized that Tylor's lectures were drawn mainly from his books *Primitive Culture* (1871) and *Anthropology* (1881), which he had already read, he stopped going to the lectures and took up an intensive schedule of reading anthropology texts in the college library (Terada 1981:76).
3 The reason for the establishment of Keijo Imperial University was related to the independence movement of March 1, 1919. The Japanese governor general of Korea used the police and army to suppress independence activities. At the same time, the Japanese authorities did not allow Korean intellectuals to cooperate with the colonial government.
4 Moreover, mountaineering was an impetus to anthropology for some, including Izumi Seiichi at Keijo Imperial University.

REFERENCES

Akamatsu, Chijō, and Takashi Akiba. 1937–38. Chōsen fūzoku no kenkyū (Study on Korean Shamanism). Ōsakaya-shogō-shoten.
—— 1941. Manmō shominzoku no minzoku to shakai (Ethnic Groups and Culture in Manchuria and Mongolia). Ōsakaya-shoten.
Ayabe, Tsuneo, ed. 1988. Bunkajinruigaku gunzō, Nihon (Japanese Cultural Anthropologists). Tokyo: Academia.
British Association for the Advancement of Science ed. 1912. Notes and Queries on Anthropology. London: Royal Anthropological Institute.
Durkheim, Émile. 1912. Les Formes élémentaires de la vie religieuse. Paris.
Frazer J. G. 1911. The Magic Art and the Evolution of Kings. London: Macmillan.
Fuji, Kenji. 1985. Department Biographical Sketch Data of University of Tokyo Religious Studies (Taisho Era). *In* Nihon no shūkyō gakusetu (Religious Studies in Japan). Tokyo: University of Tokyo.
Fukuda, Ajio. 1990. Folklore Study and Marxism in Japan. Bulletin of the National Museum of Japanese History 27.
Harayama and Morita. 1986. Seihokukenkyūjo no omoide (Memory of West North Institute). Narashigaku 4:56–93.
Inō, Kanori. 1995. Jinruigaku hattatsushikō Tsuboi Shōgorō sensei kōjutsu (Outline of the Development of Anthropology Lecture Notes of Doctor Tsuboi Shōgorō). Tono Jomin University.
Ishida, Eiichirō. 1972. Ishida Eiichirō zensyū (Collected Works of Ishida Eiichirō), vol. 8. Tokyo: Chikuma Shobo.
Iwamura, Shinobu. 1949–50. Chūgoku kaikyō no kōzō (The Structure of Chinese Islam Society). Tokyo: Nihonhyōronsya.
Izumi, Seiichi. 1972. Haruna na yamayama (The Distant Mountains). Izumi Seiichi zenshū (Collected Works of Izumi Seiichi), vol. 7. Yomiuri Publishers.
Japan Society of Ethnology, ed. 1949. Gendai Amerika no shakaijinruigaku (The Social Anthropology of Contemporary America). Tokyo: Shokosyoin.

Keijō Teikoku Daigaku Sōritsu 50 Shūnen Kinenshi Hensan Iinkai. 1974. Konpeki harukanari (The Distance of Green). Tokyo: Keijo Imperial University Class Reunion.

Kohler, Josef, and Leopold Wenger. 1914. Allgemeine Rechtsgeschichte. Leipzig: Teubner.

Lowie, Robert H. 1937. The History of Ethnological Theory. London: George G. Harrap.

Mabuchi, Tōichi. 1988. Mabuchi Tōichi zenshū (Collected Works of Mabuchi Tōichi), supplement. Tokyo: Shakai-shisosha.

Matsui, Akira. 1918. Contribution to the Ethnography of Micronesia. Journal of the College of Science, Imperial University of Tokyo 40:art. 7.

Morse, Ronald. 1975. Personalities and Issues in Yanagita Kunio Studies. Japan Quarterly 22(3).

Murdock, P. ed. 1982. Outline of Cultural Materials. Human Relations Area Files project.

Nakane, Chie. 1974. Cultural Anthropology in Japan. Annual Review of Anthropology 3.

Nakao, Katsumi. 1997. Minzoku kenkyūjō no sōshiki to katsudō: senjichū no nihon mizokugaku (The Organization and Activities of the Institute of Ethnology). Japanese Journal of Ethnology 62(1).

—— 2000. Seihoku kenkyūjō no sosiki to katsudō (Organization and Activities of the Institute of the Northwest). In Shokuminchi jinruigaku no tenbō (The Perspective of Colonial Anthropology). K. Nakao, ed. Tokyo: Fūkyōsha.

Ōbayashi, Taryō. 1987. Cultural Sphere and Cultural Sphere Theory. Bunkajinruigaku jiten (Encyclopedia of Cultural Anthropology). Tokyo: Kobundo.

Oka, Masao. 1935. Dokuō ryōkoku ni okeru minzokugaku kenkyū (Folklore Studies in German and Austrian). In Nihonminzokugaku kenkyū (Study on Japanese Folklore). Kunio Yanagita, ed. Tokyo: Iwanami-shoten.

—— 1963. Oka Masao Writing Catalog. In Oka Masao Sixtieth Birthday Commemoration. Minzokugaku nōto (Notes on Ethnology). Tokyo: Heibonsha.

—— 1981. Oka Masao-shi danwa (Oka Masao's Talk). In Shibusawa Keizō, vol. 2: Shibusawa Keizō Denkihinsan Kankōkai, ed. pp. 664–668. Shibusawa Keizō denkihinsan Kankōkai.

—— et al., eds. 1958. Nihonminzoku no kigen (The Origin of Japanese). Tokyo: Heibonsha.

Okamatsu, Santaro. 1902. Provisional Report on Investigation of Law and Customs in the Island of Formosa. Kobe: Kobe Herald Office.

Ōyano, Fumiaki. 1982. Uno Enkū: no hito to gakumon (Unō Enkū: The Man and his Scholarship). In Nihon no shyūkyō gakusetsu. Tamaru Tokuzen, ed. Tokyo: Tokyo University Religious Class.

Shirokogoroff, S. M. 1944. A Tungus Dictionary: Tungus–Russian and Russian–Tungus, photogravured from the manuscripts. Tokyo: Minzokugaku Kyokai.

Sugiyama, Kōichi. 1988. Ishida ēichirō. In Bunkajinruigaku gunzō, nihon (Japanese Cultural Anthropologists). Ayabe Tsuneo, ed. pp. 312–331. Tokyo: Academia.

Takeuchi, Yoshinori. 1982. Uiguruzoku tono deai to omoide (Encounter and Memory with the Uighur). Ajia-africa shiryō tsūhō 20(4).

Teikoku Gakushiin. 1944. Tōaminzoku meii (The Dictionary of Ethnic Names in East Asia). Sanseidō.

Terada, Kazuo. 1981. Nihon no jinruigaku (Anthropology of Japan). Tokyo: Kadokawa-Shoten.

Torii, Ryūzō. 1910. Études anthropologiques: Les Aborigènes de Formose. Journal of the College of Science, Imperial University (Tokyo) 28:art. 6.

Tsurumi, Tarō. 1998. Yanagida Kunio to sono deshitachi (Yanagida Kunio and his Students). Kyoto: Jinbunsyōrin.

University of Tokyo Science Department 1990. Tōkyō daigaku rigakubu jinruigaku kyōshitsu 50 shūnen – kinen syuppanbutsu (Fiftieth Aniversary of the Establishment of the University of Tokyo Science Department Anthropology Classroom). Tokyo: University of Tokyo.

Uno, Enkū. 1941. Mareeshia no inasakugirei (Rice Ritual in Malaysia). Tokyo: Tōkyōbunko.

von Schmidt, Wilhelm. 1937. Mit Beitragen von Wilhelm Koppers, Handbuch der Methode der kulturhistorischen Ethnologie. Munster: Verlag der Aschendorffschen Verlagsbuchhandlung.

CHAPTER 3

Japanese Archaeology and Cultural Properties Management: Prewar Ideology and Postwar Legacies

Walter Edwards

ACADEMIC ARCHAEOLOGY AND CULTURAL PROPERTIES POLICY

After the Meiji Restoration of 1868, Japan embarked upon a program of modernization that witnessed the rapid implementation of new systems of government, defense, and education. Included in the latter were modern universities, where Euro-American academic instruction was offered in the natural sciences, medicine, jurisprudence, and the liberal arts. In time these developments also led to the introduction of academic archaeology, still a relatively new discipline in Europe and the United States.

As in Europe, a strong antiquarian interest had already emerged among educated Japanese in the 18th and 19th centuries. Stone tools, ancient bronzes and pottery, fossils, and other oddities were introduced in various books, and groups of collectors held regular meetings to exhibit and discuss these items. But such activities did not lead to the systematic study of antiquities or the sites which produced them (Bleed 1986; Ikawa-Smith 1982). Credit for the first scientific investigation of an archaeological site goes to Edward S. Morse, an American hired by the Meiji government to teach biology at Tokyo Imperial University in the late 1870s. Riding the train from Yokohama to Tokyo shortly after his arrival in 1877, Morse noticed shell deposits in a cut made through a low mound near Ōmori station. He immediately recognized this as a shell midden, a refuse heap made primarily of discarded shells at a site of human habitation. The remains at Ōmori date from approximately 3,500 B.P., when much of the shoreline along Tokyo Bay formed shallow inlets ideal for gathering clams and other shellfish. This stable and plentiful food resource supported large settlements, and over time the layers of cast-off shell accumulated to depths of a meter or more. Morse had helped investigate similar sites on the east coast of the United States, and in late 1877 he brought his university students to dig at Ōmori (Saitō 1974; Shiono 1983).

Two years later, prior to returning to America, Morse produced a handsome site report written in both English and Japanese, widely recognized as having set high standards for the field. He correctly labeled the site's residents as "prehistoric," thereby introducing to the Japanese the concept of prehistory. He also referred to the pottery as "cord-marked," after its decorative pattern made by rolling a cord across the surface before firing. The Japanese translation of the term *jōmon* became the name now applied to this type of pottery, as well as to the long period (ca. 10,500–400 B.C.E.) over which it was used. Some of the students who participated in the investigation at Ōmori later excavated another shell midden on their own, and the news of Morse's dig appears to have prompted other excavations to be conducted for academic reasons. But Morse's students went on to careers in their primary field of training, which was biology, not archaeology.

Other Europeans and Americans in late 19th-century Japan also took an active interest in its archaeological past. William Gowland, a technical advisor to the Japanese finance ministry from 1872 to 1888, made extensive surveys of monumental burial mounds built by chiefly elites during the Kofun period (250–600 C.E.), Japan's protohistoric era named after the native term for these tombs. But Gowland's investigations involved no participation from Japanese scholars, his results were not published until long after his return to England, and they appeared only in English. Hence his work had little impact in Japan (Shiraishi 1993).

Accordingly, it was Japanese who had studied abroad, rather than figures like Morse and Gowland, who helped establish Japanese archaeology as a discipline in its own right. Foremost among the first generation of Japanese archaeologists was Tsuboi Shōgorō. While still an undergraduate in the Faculty of Science at Tokyo Imperial University, Tsuboi led a group of students in forming the Anthropological Society of Tokyo in 1884. Their activities included exploring shell middens in the Tokyo area, where they soon discovered a type of pottery clearly different from the thicker-walled Jōmon. Made by early bearers of the wet-rice agricultural complex, who had built their residences atop an older shell midden, it took the name "Yayoi" from the Tokyo neighborhood where it was found. Later this was applied to the period spanning the introduction of the rice-growing way of life from the Asian mainland around 400 B.C.E., and the emergence of the chiefly tombs in the mid-third century C.E. (Ueno 1984).

As a graduate student, Tsuboi was sent in 1886 by his university to Tochigi Prefecture north of Tokyo, to excavate two burial mounds on land scheduled for conversion to a public park. Rather than focusing solely on the rich grave goods they contained, Tsuboi carefully observed the structure of the tombs and the manner in which such objects had been laid, proving well ahead of his time in his first real test as an excavator. Tsuboi investigated another group of tombs in Saitama Prefecture near Tokyo, and several *kofun* in Kyushu, before leaving at the end of the decade for three years' study in England. Upon his return he was soon made professor at Tokyo Imperial University and given a chair in anthropology. Although Tsuboi conducted another series of *kofun* investigations toward the end of his career, he spent more energy excavating shell middens, and attempting to establish the identity of the people who left them through ethnological and folklore studies. But his greatest contributions lay in fostering the growth of the Tokyo Anthropological Society, and in training influential students such as Torii Ryūzō, who pioneered ethnographic and archaeological studies in Japan's Asian colonies.

Another figure who studied abroad was Hamada Kōsaku. After majoring in history in his university days, Hamada shifted to archaeology thereafter. Hired by Kyoto Imperial University in 1909 to teach the nation's first lecture course in archaeology, he was soon sent to England, where he studied for three years under Sir Flinders Petrie. Working with vast amounts of data from Egypt, Petrie had developed the technique of seriation, of tracing out chronological relations through changes in artifacts. Hamada later introduced such advances to the analysis of materials unearthed from burial mounds, helping Kyoto Imperial University maintain a position of pre-eminence in Kofun period studies for more than four decades.

Hamada's return in 1916 was occasion for his university to upgrade its program to the level of department, a sign that academic archaeology had become established on a firm basis. Enough fieldwork, including both surveys and excavations, had already been conducted by the end of the previous century for general treatments like Yagi Sōsaburō's *Japanese Archaeology* to make their appearance. The journal of Tsuboi's old Tokyo Anthropological Society, which had long served as a major venue for archaeological reports, had yielded in 1910 to the more specialized *Journal of the Archaeological Society of Japan*. Hamada's first lecture course in archaeology at Kyoto was soon followed by one at Tokyo Imperial University in 1914. And, three years later, Hamada was promoted in rank to become Japan's first full professor of archaeology, just as the first half-century of its modern era was drawing to a close.

In terms of measures to protect cultural properties, Japan was in certain respects even ahead of many of its Euro-American counterparts. When the Old Shrines and Temples Preservation Law was passed in 1897, only England, France, Greece, and four other European nations had similar legislation in place (Tanaka 1982). Moreover, passage of that law capped a long program of surveys, conducted on a nationwide basis, to identify, catalog, and evaluate art items and ancient relics for which protection was needed. As early as May 1871, the government had announced a "Plan for the Preservation of Antiques and Old Properties," prompted by upheavals attending the Meiji Restoration. The nationalistic fervor which had returned power to the emperor strongly supported the native Shinto religion, while castigating Buddhism as having corrupted Japan's ancient indigenous culture. In the hectic days after the Restoration many Buddhist temples were literally torn down, and concern over the destruction of art treasures held by these institutions was high. Another incentive for the government's early initiative was the outflow of works of art to overseas markets. These included many Buddhist items; there had even been talk of selling the Kamakura Daibutsu, a bronze image of the seated Buddha 11.5 meters tall, simply for the value of the metal (Bunkazai Hogo Iinkai 1960:13).

The program of surveying and cataloging art treasures was overseen by the Museum Bureau, the government office in charge of planning and administering national museums, institutions that became central to cultural properties protection policies and activities. During the 1870s the bureau was headed by Machida Hisanari, a liberal-minded samurai who had studied for two years in England prior to the Restoration. Machida had visited the British Museum, and also attended the fourth World's Fair at Paris in 1867. On his return to Japan he attempted to create national museums infused with the same open and progressive spirit he had observed abroad. The Tokyo Imperial Museum was established in 1872 as the first of these institutions. In addition to his work of surveying and cataloging art objects, Machida also bought up newly discovered archaeological treasures on the museum's behalf, such as a spectacular gold crown and inscribed sword unearthed by local residents in 1873 from the Eta Funayama Tomb in Kyushu. The law covering the disposition of lost property, enacted in 1876, facilitated such acquisitions by recognizing the state's claim to items whose original ownership could not be established. The purpose of that measure was to provide museums with a means for collecting materials to illustrate the advances in handicrafts over the course of history, and promote thereby the people's achievements (Tanaka 1982).

Passed after more than 200,000 items of artistic or historic merit had thus been evaluated and cataloged, the Old Shrines and Temples Preservation Law of 1897 formalized procedures for the treatment of items selected for preservation as national treasures. Moreover, it incorporated a system of government grants, begun in 1879 and already numbering 539 nationwide by the time the new legislation was passed, that were provided to temples and shrines for the conservation of items thus pro-tected (Bunkazai Hogo Iinkai 1960:15, 23). But while an article in the law extended its coverage to places of scenic beauty and historic interest as well, that provision was seldom utilized, and the recipients of protection were largely objects in the care of religious institutions.

By the start of the 20th century, however, transformations in the landscape brought by modernization were clearly a threat to historic and natural monuments. Two societies for the preservation of such items, the Imperial Ancient Sites Survey Society and the Society for the Investigation and Preservation of Historic Sites and Aged Trees, were formed by men of prominent social standing in the century's first decade. Lobbying by such organizations resulted in a resolution in the House of Peers for conservation measures, eventually leading to the Law for the Preservation of Historic Sites, Places of Scenic Beauty, and Natural Monuments, passed in 1919. This was essentially an extension to natural, historic, and archaeo-logical sites of the same type of cataloging and protective measures already in place for temples, shrines, and works of art. Its enactment stimulated prefectural govern-ments from the 1920s on to conduct extensive surveys necessary to locate and identify such sites, leading in many cases to excavation in conjunction with conservation measures.

THE EFFECTS OF IMPERIAL IDEOLOGY ON PREWAR ARCHAEOLOGY

The attention which thus came to be focused on cultural properties in general, including archaeological sites and finds, also had a strong political component regarding materials of the Kofun period: the great burial mounds which gave that period its name had been pressed into service by the modern state. To see how this was so, we must look first at the historic significance of these monuments in their original context, and their treatment up through the Meiji period.

The late third century C.E. witnessed the emergence of a new type of burial facility, far larger in scale than any previously known and taking a keyhole-shaped outline as its standardized form. Appearing first in the central Yamato region (now Nara Prefecture), this new type of tomb spread outward, replacing the regional diversity in shape previously exhibited by Yayoi elite burials. By the end of the fourth century its distribution extended over most of the archipelago, strongly suggesting a process of political unification. During the fifth century the largest of these tombs reached lengths exceeding 400 meters. Clearly their occupants commanded enormous economic resources, and must be regarded as paramount rulers of a vast, though still preliterate, state. At some point in this murky period, known but obliquely through native chronicles recorded in the early eighth century, fragmentary accounts surviving in older Chinese sources, and the archaeological record, the ruling line bolstered its position of pre-eminence within the aristocratic elite through claims to divine descent. These were codified into an official genealogy in the late seventh century at a time when elite Japanese were rapidly adopting Buddhism, writing, and formal organs of state based on Chinese and Korean models. The genealogy was also "documented" by designating a tomb for each member of the ancestral line. This treatment was extended even to clearly mythical figures such as the first emperor Jimmu, held to be a direct descendant of the sun goddess herself. Provision for the upkeep of these tombs was made by the state, and public rites were regularly conducted at certain of them during the Nara (710–794) and Heian (794–1185) periods (Edwards 2000).

This system disintegrated during the turbulent centuries comprising Japan's medieval era (1185–1573), and the locations of most of the tombs formerly attributed to the earlier figures in the imperial genealogy were forgotten. Several attempts to re-establish the designations were made in the Edo period (1603–1868), the 260-year-long span of relative seclusion immediately preceding Japan's modernization. These efforts intensified in the mid-19th century, as the imperial institution was taken as rallying point against the foreign threat posed by European and American forces interested in opening up the country. An extensive program of identification and repairs was undertaken by the samurai government in the early 1860s (Edwards, 2003a, 2003b). Not long afterwards, as it became clear that the samurai could no longer retain political control, sovereign powers were returned to the emperor in 1867, and, in a relatively peaceful transition, a new government formed the following year.

The Meiji leaders were already convinced that the only way to deal with the Euro-American nation-states was to emulate them. Accordingly, they initiated the widespread reforms already mentioned, thus setting Japan squarely on the path toward modernization. But they retained an emphasis visible in the earlier anti-foreign sentiment, that the continuity and divine origin of the imperial line made Japan unique among, and superior to, other nations of the world. This focus on the unbroken continuity of the imperial line became the cornerstone for efforts to promote a sense of national pride. Directed both internally and toward the outside, its spirit is well exemplified by a statement in a manual for history teachers, published by the Ministry of Education in 1910:

> Although the nations of the world are great in number, no other country approaches ours in age, nor possesses as splendid a history. When it is said that China and Egypt are old, this means only that civilization developed very early in those regions, for the nations themselves have been constantly changing. In China, only 250 years have passed since the founding of the current Qing Dynasty...But in our land the Emperors have ruled in lineal succession, unbroken for ages eternal, from before the time knowable to human wisdom...(Kita 1910:1–2)

The phrase describing the imperial line as "unbroken for ages eternal," *bansei ikkei* (literally, "a line of ten thousand reigns," implying "for all eternity"), was used early on by the Meiji government to proclaim the unique nature of the Japanese monarchy in its diplomacy with the USA and European countries. The first major initiative in this regard was the Iwakura Mission to America and Europe (1871–73), which presented a letter to President Grant introducing the Meiji emperor with this term (Yamamuro 1994:136–137). By the mid-Meiji period this concept had become so central to state ideology that it was incorporated in key documents such as the 1889 Constitution, the first article of which declares: "The Empire of Japan shall be reigned over and governed by a line of Emperors unbroken for ages eternal."

Documenting the unbroken continuity of the ruling line thus became a priority that affected policies toward the ancient imperial tombs, and, by extension, materials of the Kofun period as a whole. When the identification program of the 1860s ended, the locations of 18 tombs of emperors remained undetermined. Designations of these began to be made by the Imperial Household Ministry in the 1870s, with the remaining ones decided collectively in 1889, in time for the promulgation of the Meiji Constitution. The concern was not merely to have the entire genealogy "documented" by physically embodying it in the mausolea, but also to assert its divine origin. This is shown by the designation in 1874 of "tombs" for the three generations linking Jimmu with the sun goddess Amaterasu. According to myth, Amaterasu dispatched her grandson, Ninigi no Mikoto, down from the Plain of Heaven so that her descendants would rule the Japanese islands in perpetuity. Alighting in the westernmost island of Kyushu, Ninigi's line remained there until his great-grandson Jimmu determined to journey east and quell Yamato, where he ascended the throne as the first earthly emperor. In deference perhaps to the dubious nature of the myth, none of the "tombs" designated for the three generations prior to Jimmu can be considered real tombs on archaeological grounds, but are rather natural features (two mountain tops and a cave).

Designations of imperial mausolea were not limited to the allegedly direct links between the Meiji emperor and the sun goddess. In addition to designations for emperors, tombs of ancient empresses and royal princes were designated in the first part of the Meiji period. Further, there are currently some 46 tombs treated by the Imperial Household Agency as *sankōchi*, sites possibly connected in some way with the imperial line. The naming of tombs in this category began around the time of the Meiji Constitution, and continued into the first decades of the 20th century. The political nature of these designations can also be seen in the care to select tombs in prefectures where no other imperial mausolea were located (Imai 1977).

Of all the mounded tombs in the country as whole, only a small fraction came to be designated as associated with the imperial line. But as long as the program of designations was still under way, the possibility that *any* mound might be regarded as associated with the imperial line affected the treatment of Kofun period materials as a whole. As early as 1874, the government issued to local administrators the following proclamation, admonishing against disturbing mounded tombs:

> With regard to ancient imperial tombs whose locations are as yet undetermined, in other words those still under investigation, when uncultivated lands in various districts are developed . . . for places which appear to be ancient mounds [*kofun*] . . . reckless digging is not to be permitted, and if such has already occurred, reports accompanied by drawings must be submitted to the Ministry of Education. (quoted in Saitō 1993:149)

The lack of precise definition of what constituted "reckless digging" casts doubt on the proclamation's efficacy. Moreover, it was common enough for local residents to uncover burial chambers in the course of agricultural work, or simply from curiosity piqued by the prospect of finding treasure, and remove any grave goods they found. But whereas such activities had been frowned upon by the authorities since the Edo period, the government's new directive certainly heightened the apprehension of local officials when such cases came to their attention. This is seen in the following example from Kagawa Prefecture, on the island of Shikoku.

Iwasakiyama kofun, a 49-meter-long keyhole-shaped tomb, was initially opened during the Edo period when a farmer went to cut down an old tree in 1809, and while digging up the roots came upon the stone burial chamber. After removing some beads and other items, he was ultimately investigated by a samurai official of the local domain, who confiscated a mirror and retained possession of it. In 1873 locals again opened the tomb, presumably in the hope of finding more valuables. The incident ultimately came to the attention of a local official for the new prefectural government, who sent a letter reporting it to his superiors. Accompanied by drawings and citing the earlier investigation, it notes that the mirror was still extant, and commented on the unusual nature of the tomb. "In any event it cannot be thought the tomb of a commoner," the official wrote, citing the presence of cinnabar – a reddish ore of mercury favored as a pigment in elaborate burials – which remained to a depth of several centimeters inside the stone coffin, itself a sign of the occupant's high status. Raising the possibility that it was a "divine tomb," meaning one associated with the imperial line, the official went on to note that locals had erected a small shrine above the tomb in face of such an ominous contingency and were conducting rituals there. But he feared that, with time, erosion would again expose the chamber, and warned of rumored plots to dig out grave goods once more (Kagawa Prefecture 1930).

The prospect of a tomb being regarded as "divine" was not always thought ominous by local personnel. Rather, in some cases such status was actually sought, as shown by the history of the Mae Futago *kofun* in Gunma Prefecture, north of Tokyo. This 92-meter keyhole tomb was opened in March 1878 by villagers who were chasing a badger, and, digging out the hole into which it had escaped, hit upon a stone chamber. The grave goods found inside included a gold earring, along with numerous beads, plus pieces of pottery, weaponry, and equestrian gear. The discovery soon came to the attention of the local authorities, and a report carefully inventoried the grave goods, sketching their positions as found within the chamber. The finds were then locked away in the storehouse of the village shrine for safe keeping (Gunma Prefecture 1929).

Later that same year some of the items were taken out and included among a display of local products on the occasion of an "imperial progress" conducted through the northern portion of Honshu. These excursions, six of which were made on a grand scale over the period from 1872 to 1885, were planned by the Meiji government as a means of remedying the neglect which befell the imperial institution during the Edo period, and fixing the current monarch more firmly in the popular imagination as head of the new nation-state. They were also taken as opportunities to let the emperor inspect noteworthy aspects of various regions in his realm (Fujitani 1996). The grave goods from Mae Futago did attract the attention of Iwakura Tomomi, one of the most influential ministers in the Meiji bureaucracy, who instructed that they be presented to the Imperial Household Ministry. A portion was thus submitted in February the following year, along with a claim about the identity of the tomb's occupant. Local traditions held it was the tomb of one of the sons of Sujin, tenth monarch in the official genealogy. The ancient chronicles relate that Sujin sent his son Toyoki Irihiko to be governor of the eastern sector, and named the latter as ancestor of the chiefs in the region forming modern Gunma Prefecture. The Imperial Household Ministry was not impressed enough to designate the mound as an imperial tomb, however, and returned the grave goods in March.

While in rare cases "reckless digging" by locals led to criminal proceedings, for the most part government policy toward the tombs did not prevent local residents from opening them up, as the above examples illustrate. Academics could not afford to be so lax in matters where the possibility of contravening imperial ideology was present. And while no archaeologist suffered the fate of historians Kume Kunitake or Kita Sadakichi, forced from their posts in 1892 and 1911 for statements held to be disrespectful to the imperial institution, there was at least one close encounter, experienced by Tsuboi Shōgorō. His investigations of tombs fall into two distinct periods, one from 1887 to 1890, and the other a decade later. The reason for the hiatus was recounted as follows by Torii Ryūzō, many years later:

> While still a graduate student, the Professor [Tsuboi] went to Kyushu and excavated a certain tomb, which caused him immediate trouble as it was one with ties to the Imperial Household Ministry. Tsuboi accordingly apologized profusely, tendering a written promise never to excavate again a tomb having such a connection, and the matter passed without consequence. But from that time on he would even turn visibly pale whenever Kofun period topics came up. (Torii 1932)

There were notable exceptions to the negative impact of imperial ideology on excavations of *kofun*. One was the investigation of the Saitobaru tomb group in Miyazaki Prefecture, the region in Kyushu where the imperial line is said in myth to have resided for three generations prior to Jimmu's journey east. The single most important group of mounded tombs in all of Kyushu, this underwent a series of excavations from 1912 to 1917 initiated by the prefecture's governor, in an unsuccessful attempt to "prove" a connection with the mythic account (Takehara 1984). For the most part, the importance attached to the imperial institution impeded *kofun* research. At a time when Japanese archaeologists were actively excavating shell middens, the vast majority of data on burial mounds obtained up to the 1919 Law for the Preservation of Historic Sites, Places of Scenic Beauty, and Natural Monuments came from sites opened up by local residents, or by accident during the construction of roads and railways. From the end of the 1920s surveys conducted by various prefectures to identify sites worthy of preservation under the new law produced a surge of information on the locations of archaeological sites, especially *kofun*. But the law reconfirmed the influence of imperial ideology over the excavation of mounded tombs, as it specified that permission to excavate any *kofun* surveyed must be granted by the Minister of Education *in consultation with* the Imperial Household Minister – a restriction not applied to other archaeological materials. Umehara Sueji of Kyoto Imperial University, who was very active in the surveys, complained in 1935 of the difficulties in investigating the keyhole tombs. Most of his survey work was limited to mapping the surfaces of the mounds, plus examining burial facilities that had previously been exposed. On the whole, scientific excavations of tombs up until 1945, the end of the Pacific War, especially those not discovered by chance, were exceedingly rare (Shiraishi 1993; Tsude 1986).

Imperial politics affected the treatment of cultural properties in other ways as well, particularly as imperial ideology strengthened over the period leading up to the Pacific War. The Tokyo Imperial Museum, inaugurated by the Ministry of Education in 1871 with Machida Hisanari's vision of an open institution similar to those of European nations, came under the administrative control of the Imperial Household Ministry in 1886. From that point on it was increasingly transformed into a private treasure house of the imperial family. By the time its name was formally changed to Tokyo Imperial Household Museum in 1900, it had already become so notoriously closed that it drew criticism in the Diet for its lack of concern to provide the larger society with access to its holdings (Tanaka 1982:768). Survey work to identify sites for preservation, begun in response to the 1919 law to protect natural and historic monuments, was also affected. In the 1930s, this took on a new focus under a succession of programs to designate "sacred sites" associated with various emperors. The most extensive of these linked 377 sites nationwide with the Meiji emperor, including many of the stopping points along the routes of his imperial progresses, accounting for nearly 40 percent of all historic sites designated by the central government up to the end of the war. More modest programs were conducted to identify sites associated with the mythic first Emperor Jimmu, and other members of the imperial genealogy. It is worth noting that these programs were not motivated by concerns over destruction of cultural properties or by academic interest, but solely by the ideological agenda of the state (Inada 1986).

Postwar Cultural Properties Policy

The emperor-centered ideology of the prewar period was grounded in a view of history privileging the position of the imperial line. Its claimed continuity from divine origins was taken as the source of the nation-state's inherent superiority over others and the reason its subjects owed the emperor utmost loyalty. As the country plunged into full-scale war after the outbreak of fighting with China in 1937, this ideology took on the additional claim that the sphere of imperial rule was destined to expand until it covered the entire earth. Monuments projecting this ideology both backwards and forwards in time were construction in locations throughout Japan (Edwards, 2003a, 2003b).

The discrediting of imperialist ideology following Japan's defeat in 1945 effectively dissolved the Japanese people's sense of national history. The emperor publicly renounced his claims to divinity in January 1946. Later that year, new history texts produced for elementary school use removed the mythic account of the nation's origins for the first time since the 1880s, replacing it with archaeological materials of the Jōmon period. People who had grown up believing "that the emperor was a god and we were the children of gods" suddenly found themselves groping for new understandings of their past and for different ways to define who and what they were. It did not take long before powerful new images emerged to fill this void. In keeping with the democratic ideals brought by the Allied occupation, and quickly embraced by the defeated nation, a magazine column shortly after the war's end called for a history focused not on elite institutions but on the common people, a history "of the nameless masses born and working in society, of what kind of livelihood they practiced" (Edwards 1991).

As if in answer to this call, archaeologists from five universities in Tokyo organized a joint excavation aimed at documenting the antiquity of the rice-growing way of life in Japan. This was the investigation of the Yayoi period site of Toro in Shizuoka, begun in the summer of 1947. Initially discovered during construction of a propeller factory in 1943, the site yielded large amounts of wooden implements in good states of preservation, unusual at the time, from its deep, waterlogged layers. More significantly, the postwar excavations uncovered a vast irrigation system, consisting of a main water channel 300 meters long flanked by paddies, their carefully maintained dikes held firmly in place by rows of wooden stakes driven deep into the soft earth. Nearby were the remains of eight dwellings and several storehouses for grain. The practice of rice cultivation in the Yayoi period had long been surmised from the presence of agricultural tools, and from impressions of rice grains and discoveries of charred rice in Yayoi pottery. But this was the first time that actual fields emerged, together with residential remains, documenting in concrete fashion a 2,000-year legacy as a nation of rice farmers.

The image of the harmonious, cooperative agricultural community as a wellspring of the national character had been a minor theme in prewar debates over Japanese identity, as seen in the studies of folklorist Yanagita Kunio (see chapter 13 in this volume). In the early postwar years this peaceful image gained in appeal precisely because of its contrast with the militarism of the recent past. The excavations at Toro reinforced this image through a fortuitous lack of weaponry and defensive facilities.

Writing shortly after the end of the first season's work, one of the excavators asked his readers to "imagine a party of men and women, farm tools in hand, heading by twos and threes along the banks [of the canal] on their way home from the fields . . . Do we not see a picture of the peaceful livelihood of the Toro villagers floating before our very eyes?" (Ōba 1948:63).

The Toro investigation, which thus symbolized the ideological change under which postwar archaeological work began, spearheaded an increase in excavations that came to be called an archaeological "boom." Contributing to this phenomenon were changes in laws covering cultural properties. Prewar legislation was superseded in 1950 by the Cultural Properties Protection Act, whose broader scope included "Sites of Archaeological Interest" as a new category for protective measures. By 1975, this had been expanded to cover the settings of historic buildings as well. And thanks to grassroots movements arising in response to threats of destruction of sites by development, the practice of having local Boards of Education conduct cultural properties surveys prior to development also became established policy. Today, when a survey determines that development will destroy archaeological features, the site in question must be excavated under standard procedures. In such cases the costs of excavation are borne by the agent, whether public or private, who initiates the development (Inada 1986).

These measures, coupled with the spurt in development which accompanied Japan's economic growth from the 1960s on, have fostered a tremendous increase in the amount of archaeological activity, albeit mostly in the nature of salvage work. The number of excavations conducted yearly more than doubled from 1955 to exceed 600 in 1965, jumping to nearly 3,000 just ten years later, and topping 10,000 in 1995. Numbers of cultural property management specialists have shown a similar increase, reaching the thousand mark by 1975 and 6,000 by 1995. It can safely be said that Japan is today one of the most thoroughly excavated countries in the modern world.

However, the sites designated as imperial tombs remain immune to this atmosphere of open archaeological inquiry. Those predating the Nara period, for which the designations are open to question, include the largest and most important tombs of the Kofun period. Access to these sites is vital to the study of Japan's ancient history, yet the Imperial Household Agency (downgraded from its prewar status as a ministry, but retaining much of its former autonomy within the government) has steadfastly denied requests that it allow open inspections of tombs under its care, despite claims that such sites are cultural properties of the Japanese people as a whole. The agency stresses their private aspect, arguing that these tombs are gravesites where religious rites propitiating the ancestors of the imperial family are conducted. Ironically, the same laws used to promote public over private interests in cases where important cultural properties are threatened by destruction, allowing the government to designate them as historic sites for preservation, give priority to the rights of the landowner where such threats are absent. As long as the Imperial Household Agency asserts its intention to maintain the sites as graves of the imperial family, there are no grounds for invoking the law. Controversy over the issue of access thus reflects the ambiguous status of the postwar emperor, as both public symbol of the Japanese nation and private individual (Edwards 2000).

Apart from this clear legacy of prewar ideology, we might ask whether contemporary Japanese archaeology can be seen as free of political constraints in its investigation of the past. In his consideration of links between postwar archaeology and Japanese identity, Fawcett (1996) suggests this is not the case. On the one hand, many Japanese archaeologists' presentations and interpretations of data are influenced by their *a priori* assumptions of the uniqueness and homogeneity of Japanese culture. Cultural differences among past populations thus tend to be downplayed, while links between contemporary Japanese and the prehistoric inhabitants of the archipelago are overemphasized. Fawcett also argues that political motivations characterize state-supported programs of preservation. The measures taken in the 1970s to preserve the Asuka region, located in the southern part of the Nara basin and the cultural and political center of the nation from the late sixth through the seventh centuries, are presented as such an example. By limiting development the state has turned the region into a romanticized embodiment of an idyllic past, the source of Japan's allegedly unique (and inherently superior) culture, while linking this image to the imperial institution by stressing the region's ties with ancient emperors.

I suggest these examples involve unconscious links between notions of identity and archaeology which may be impossible to exorcise. Tendencies to emphasize unity with past populations are an unavoidable by-product when archaeology is seen as an extension of history, and thus the study of one's own ancestors. As social actors, archaeologists are, moreover, caught up in the dominant mores of their times, as were the excavators at Toro. And the tendency will always be present for the state to support research which projects images of ancient society pleasing to contemporary values. The postwar study of administrative and political centers as a whole, of which Asuka forms but a part, is illustrative. In the 1950s and 1960s, under pressure from preservation movements, the government purchased the palace site at the eighth-century Nara capital and established there a national research institute which undertook the extensive excavation and research of archaeological remains. These efforts uncovered evidence of a vast complex of government offices, where state bureaucrats kept detailed records on tax payments, the movement of goods in from the regions, evaluations of the job performance of government personnel, and so forth. From the 1960s through the 1970s, researchers who had gained experience at the Nara palace site were sent out to help with the establishment of similar institutes and research programs at regional administrative centers such as Dazaifu in Kyushu (Tsuboi 1986). By 1980, such efforts had led to major excavations at over 30 sites, including the remains of state-supported temples as well as outlying government offices, which together may be seen as extensions of the centralized order into the countryside. While none of these facilities had been the object of excavation before the war, the image they projected of an elaborate and efficient bureaucracy bringing order to society was surely one the postwar state was more than happy to underwrite.

CONCLUSION

I have sketched the development of archaeology in Japan since its introduction just over one and a quarter centuries ago. Like many other innovations adapted after European and American institutions, it was soon brought into line with the particular contours of its new social context, and has subsequently evolved as that context itself has changed. And while archaeological research has been freed in this process from the most overt constraints imposed by specific political agendas, insofar as notions of the past and its meaning for the present are never innocent of their contemporary settings, we can only expect continued evolution in the future.

REFERENCES

Bleed, P. 1986. Almost Archaeology: Early Archaeological Interest in Japan. *In* Windows on the Japanese Past: Studies in Archaeology and Prehistory. R. J. Pearson, ed. pp. 57–67. Ann Arbor, MI: Center for Japanese Studies.

Bunkazai Hogo Iinkai, ed. 1960. Bunkazai hogo no ayumi (The Progress of Cultural Properties Preservation). Tokyo: Bunkazai Hogo Iinkai.

Edwards, Walter. 1991. Buried Discourse: The Toro Archaeological Site and Japanese National Identity in the Early Postwar Period. Journal of Japanese Studies 17:1–23.

—— 2000. Contested Access: The Imperial Tombs in the Postwar Period. Journal of Japanese Studies 26:371–392.

—— 2003a. Monuments to an Unbroken Line: The Imperial Tombs and the Emergence of Modern Japanese nationalism. *In* The Politics of Archaeology and Identity in a Global Context. S. Kane, ed. pp. 11–30. Boston: Archaeological Institute of America.

—— 2003b. Forging Tradition for a Holy War: The Hakkō ichiu Tower in Miyazaki and Japanese Wartime Ideology. Journal of Japanese Studies 29(2):289–324.

Fawcett, C. 1996. Archaeology and Japanese Identity. *In* Multicultural Japan: Palaeolithic to Postmodern. D. Denoon, M. Hudson, G. McCormack, and T. Morris-Suzuki, eds. pp. 60–77. Cambridge: Cambridge University Press.

Fujitani, T. 1996. Splendid Monarchy: Power and Pageantry in Modern Japan. Berkeley: University of California Press.

Gunma Prefecture, ed. 1929. Gunma-ken shiseki meishō tennen kinenbutsu chōsa hōkoku (Gunma Prefecture Historic Sites, Places of Scenic Beauty, and Natural Monuments Investigation Report), vol. 1. Maebashi: Gunma Prefecture.

Ikawa-Smith, F. 1982. Co-traditions in Japanese Archaeology. World Archaeology 13:296–309.

Imai, T. 1977. Meiji ikō ryōbo kettei no jittai to tokushitsu (The Actual Condition and Characteristics of Imperial Tomb Designations from the Meiji Period On). Rekishi hyōron 321:64–80.

Inada, T. 1986. Iseki no hōgo. (Archaeological Site Preservation). *In* Iwanami kōza Nihon kōkogaku (Iwanami Lecture Series, Japanese Archaeology), 7 vols; vol. 7: Gendai to kōkogaku (Archaeology and the Present). Kondō Y., series ed. pp. 71–132. Tokyo: Iwanami Shoten.

Kagawa Prefecture, ed. 1930. Kagawa-ken shiseki meishō tennen kinenbutsu chōsa hōkoku (Kagawa Prefecture Historic Sites, Places of Scenic Beauty, and Natural Monuments Investigation Report), vol. 5. Takamatsu: Kagawa Prefecture.

Kita, S. 1910. Kokushi no kyōiku (Japanese History Education). Tokyo: Sanseidō.

Ōba, I. 1948. Toro iseki kenkyū (Research on the Toro Site). Suwa: Ashikabi Shobō.

Saitō, T. 1974. Nihon kōkogakushi (History of Japanese Archaeology). Tokyo: Yoshikawa Kōbunkan.

—— 1993. Nihon kōkogakushi nenpyō (Chronology of Japanese Archaeological History). Tokyo: Gakuseisha.

Shiono, S. 1983. Ōmori kaizuka (Ōmori Shell Midden). *In* Nihon no iseki monogatari (Stories of Japanese Archaeological Sites), 10 vols; vol. 2: Jōmon jidai (Jōmon Period). Mori K., series ed. pp. 89–112. Tokyo: Shakai Shisōsha.

Shiraishi, T. 1993. Kofun jidai kenkyūshi (History of Research on the Kofun Period). *In* Kofun jidai no kenkyū (Research on the Kofun Period), 13 vols, vol. 1: Sōron/kenkyūshi (Comprehensive Treatises/History of Research). Ishino H. et al., eds. pp. 139–165. Tokyo: Yūzankaku.

Takehara, M. 1984. Saitobaru kofun gun (Saitobaru Tomb Group). *In* Nihon no iseki monogatari (Stories of Japanese Archaeological Sites), 10 vols; vol. 7: Kofun jidai 3 (nishi Nihon) (Kofun Period 3 [Western Japan]). Mori K., series ed. pp. 309–334.Tokyo: Shakai Shisōsha.

Tanaka, M. 1982. Iseki ibutsu ni kansuru hogo gensoku no kakuritsu katei (The Process of Establishing the Principles of Preservation Regarding Archaeological Sites and Artifacts). *In* Kōkogaku ronkō (Treatises in Archaeology). Kobayashi Yukio Hakase Koki Kinen Ronbunshū Kankō Iinkai, ed. pp. 765–783. Tokyo: Heibonsha.

Torii, R. 1932. Kofun no tatari (A *Kofun*'s Curse). Dorumen 1:4.

Tsuboi, K. 1986. Kodai tsuiseki: aru kōkogakuto no kaisō (In Pursuit of the Ancient: Recollections of a Student of Archaeology). Tokyo: Sōfūkan.

Tsude H. 1986. Nihon kōkogaku to shakai (Japanese Archaeology and Society). *In* Iwanami kōza Nihon kōkogaku (Iwanami Lecture Series, Japanese Archaeology), 7 vols, vol. 7: Gendai to kōkogaku (Archaeology and the Present). Kondō Y., series ed. pp. 31–70. Tokyo: Iwanami Shoten.

Ueno T. 1984 Yayoi-chō iseki (The Yayoi-chō Site). *In* Nihon no iseki monogatari (Stories of Japanese Archaeological Sites), 10 vols, vol. 3: Yayoi jidai 1 (higashi Nihon) (Yayoi Period 1 [Eastern Japan]). Mori K., series ed. pp. 81–104. Tokyo: Shakai Shisōsha.

Yamamuro S. 1994. Meiji kokka no seido to rinen (The Principles and Organization of the Meiji State). *In* Iwanami kōza nihon tsūshi (Iwanami Lecture Series Survey of Japanese History), 21 + 4 vols, vol. 17: Kindai 2 (Early Modern Period 2). Asao N. et al., eds. pp. 113–148. Tokyo: Iwanami Shoten.

CHAPTER 4

Feminism, Timelines, and History-Making

Tomomi Yamaguchi

INTRODUCTION

A *nenpyō* is a timeline of historical events and is commonly found in Japanese historical and history texts. I grew up in Japan, and the *nenpyō* "genre" was a ubiquitous part of my educational experience there. In my history classes, *nenpyō* had always been a required text that had to be within easy reach, and I had to memorize the dates and events listed in various *nenpyō* for my college entrance exams. Even outside of the classroom, many kinds of *nenpyō* are available in bookstores and on the internet. *Nenpyō* are so much a part of my everyday and academic life that I did not grasp the significance of rendering history as a timeline until my advisor[1] suggested that I include a chapter on *nenpyō* in my dissertation (Yamaguchi 2004).

For a couple of months toward the end of 1998, I spent most of my weekends and weekday evenings on the time-consuming task of *nenpyō*-making with two other women from a Tokyo-based feminist group, the Women's Action Group (Kōdō-suru Onna-tachi no Kai). The group was established in 1975, and I observed its dissolution during my three years of ethnographic fieldwork in Tokyo between 1996 and 1999. Following the breakup, I participated in the history-writing project initiated by one faction of the group, which eventually resulted in a book, published in 1999, which includes a long *nenpyō* of 32 pages (Kōdō-suru Kai Kirokushū Henshū Iinkai 1999).

In this short chapter I will examine the attempts of one faction of the Women's Action Group to represent the newly dissolved group's history through the construction of a long *nenpyō*. I will focus specifically on the group's strategies of timeline-making and, in addition to analyzing the metahistory of the genre, I will argue that the women of the Action Group appropriated the literary form of the "timeline" in an effort to assert their political relevance. By the same token, they sought to *re*present history in a way that would challenge existing narratives of Japanese feminism. Although a seemingly innocuous act, the group's effort to produce a linear depiction of Japanese feminist history was at its core a political act, a challenge to claims and positions of other feminist groups, and an attempt to assert the group's position in the past, present, and future of an important social movement.

HISTORY AS FLOW (*nagare*)

Usually, *nenpyō* appear in a chart-like format, divided into multiple columns. For instance, the Iwanami Japanese History Time Line (*iwanami nihonshi nenpyō*) is divided into three categories: "politics and economy," "society and culture," and "the world" (Rekishigaku Kenkyūkai 2001). The Gakken Japanese History Cartoon Timeline (*gakken nihonshi manga nenpyō*) for children has three columns: "major events in Japan," "flow of culture" and "major events in the world" (Tashiro 1992). By having multiple columns, history, in the sense of the "passed past," is divided into subsections that may interact but do not mix. In the prefaces and postscripts of most published *nenpyō*, the editors explain that multiple columns make it easier for readers to compare and contrast histories both geographically and topically. Multiple columns, they argue, provide a "three-dimensional" look at history by supplying different angles, and further contextualize the particular history of an event or thing.

 Nenpyō editors explain that the purpose of the genre is to grasp the *nagare*, or flow, of history. In fact, the word "flow" is frequently used in the titles for the columns featured in a timeline, such as "the *flow* of culture." Dictionary definitions of *nagare* reveal that in Japanese culture this word is used in many ways that, commonsensically, are associated with history. For instance, in the encyclopedic *kōjien*, *nagare* is defined as "gradual change or movement" (Shinmura 1998:1979). However, in an another dictionary produced by a rival publisher, *nagare* is defined even more explicitly as "history itself that continues moving without interruption," and "the future direction of things from the viewpoint of their rise and fall" (Yamada et al. 1989:950).

 Ugoki is another word typically encountered in *nenpyō* – although perhaps not as commonly as *nagare*. *Ugoki* refers to "purposeful changes or movements with the passage of time" (Shinmura 1998:229), or in reference to something that "cannot maintain an earlier state and begins to change into something new through the actions of some agent" (Yamada et al. 1989:100). Thus, as a euphemism for history, *ugoki* denotes an active, agent-informed process of change in contrast to the agentless *nagare* that "flows naturally" from one point to another, from one event to what follows it, without disruption. In the case of *nagare*, "things happen"; in the case of *ugoki*, "things are made to happen." Jennifer Robertson's discussion of the transitive verb *tsukuru* (to make, to build) versus the intransitive verb *naru* (to become, to evolve, to be) in the context of local and national efforts at *furusato-zukuri* (native place-making),[2] is instructive here:

> *Naru* brackets, deflects, and conceals intentionality: creation is presented as an irruption, an epiphany, a release of what is already there.
> *Naru* contrasts with *tsukuru* . . . a transitive verb that denotes intentional, purposeful action. . . . Unlike *naru*, *tsukuru* acknowledges that creation is a form of labor, a conscious construction. *Naru* elides or renders unproblematic the sociohistorical conditions

of production; things simply enter the realm of present actuality from somewhere in the past. (Robertson 1991:29–30)

I describe the use by Japanese feminists of *ugoki* in the next section.

In order to grasp the *nagare* of history, *nenpyō* editors argue, the "scientific" and "accurate" classification and organization of historical "facts" is necessary. Because of its chart-like format, a timeline *looks* objective and fact-based, much more so than other forms of written history. *Nenpyō* editors, including the women of the Action Group, share the notion that making a timeline is a very straightforward and objective process that does not involve any subjective evaluation of historical events or their contexts. I would argue, instead, that the Action Group and others turn to *nenpyō* because a timeline effectively masks the political and ideological biases informing its making, and presents a given history as truthful material evidence. However, because it is impossible to list all relevant historical events in timeline, *nenpyō*-makers have to choose which variables to include and which to exclude. Moreover, if a given timeline is divided into multiple columns, editors must decide how to divide history into different categories and under what logic to assign which variables to which column. These are the indisputable occasions where *nenpyō* editors' political and ideological biases come into play. The makers of timelines cannot but construct their own versions of *nagare*, despite their professed belief that "flow" is an inherent characteristic of history.

When I volunteered to join in the Action Group's *nenpyō*-making project, I thought my main job would be simply to enter dates and events into a computer file, whereupon the publisher would convert it into a handsome chart. Compared to the narrative portion of the book, in which writers related their personal experiences of feminist activism, timeline-making seemed to be a less complicated task. As it turned out, I was absolutely wrong about that. Originally, I thought producing a timeline would be a much more "objective" or "etic" method of representing the group's history. In fact, typing was only the beginning of the long and at times contentious process of *nenpyō*-making. And, rather than an "objective" or "scientific" collection of facts, the Action Group's *nenpyō* was a strongly political and ideologically informed piece of historical documentation.

STRATEGIES OF *NENPYŌ*-MAKING

A close examination of the various processes involved in the Action Group's timeline-making project highlights the kinds of political and ideological concerns that inform timeline construction more generally.

For the Action Group members, the first step of *nenpyō*-making was to collect data from various sources; the "accuracy" of the data, especially dates, was a key concern. Members expressed a bias toward written texts, rather than personal memory or oral testimony, as the most trustworthy sources. They scoured newsletters, books, pamphlets, fliers, opinion and complaint letters, handwritten notes taken during meetings, and timelines produced by themselves and other feminist groups, in search of important dates and illuminating events. Almost any printed source – even entrance examination prep books – was deemed worthy of investigation. In their view, the painstaking and comprehensive effort to parse data imbued the *nenpyō* with authority, and the "correctness" of the data would be indisputable. When there was conflicting information, members gave priority to those sources interpreted as "primary," which invariably were documents produced by the Action Group. So strong was the authority members gave to written documentation that if the details of a given event had not been chronicled, then it was not included the timeline. The following is a case in point.

One of the editorial board members, Sachiko (a pseudonym), wanted the first meeting of the Action Group she attended on April 18, 1975, to be recorded in the *nenpyō*. She argued that the meeting was significant because it marked the first time she had spoken publicly about her experience with domestic violence and had argued for the need for domestic violence shelters for women and children. It was also a watershed moment for the Action Group in its efforts to persuade the Tokyo Metropolitan Government to establish the first public domestic violence shelter in Japan. Despite Sachiko's insistence on the importance of the event, nobody on the editorial board remembered the gathering, and written "proof" of its occurrence could not be found. Other members told Sachiko that they could not include the item unless she could bring a written record as evidence of its veracity. It was only when Sachiko showed her colleagues a reference to the meeting in her private diary that her claim was accepted and the event included in the timeline. Despite the unquestionable subjectivity (and possibly dubious veracity) of a personal diary entry, what was crucial for the Action Group was that the event had been recorded *in writing* and was, therefore, accepted as a "primary" datum.

For the Action Group, the second step of *nenpyō*-making was to decide on the historical variables that would be included and in which column of the timeline they should be listed. Their timeline was divided into two columns: "records of group-related actions," and "social *ugoki*, or agentive change." Using *ugoki* rather than *nagare*, the Action Group members invoked an epistemology of history quite different from that informing the Japanese history timelines described earlier. For the group, history was not simply a matter of "things happening" but rather was constituted by events that represented proactive change. The Action Group's *nenpyō* assumed and asserted a dialectical relationship between the events in the "group-related" and "social change" columns. For example, one item in their "social change" column was the date and fact of the withdrawal of the governor of Tokyo from the judging panel for the 1990 Miss Tokyo contest.[3] His withdrawal was the direct result of the Action Group's and other feminist organizations' protests against the (still) ubiquitous "Miss" contests in Japan. These actions were enumerated in the "group-related activities" column of the timeline.

The vast majority of the events selected for the "group-related activities" column were actions targeted at the general public, such as public gatherings, protests, rallies, distribution of fliers, and press conferences. Internal group meetings tended not to be included, with the exception of those that had a big impact on the group's future, such as the 1985 summer camp where the future direction of the group was discussed, or meetings in 1996 where they decided to dissolve the group.

The model of history represented by the Action Group's timeline was a somewhat rigid, event-focused one. To be included in the timeline, an event must have a specific date and place of occurrence. Everyday routine and practical activities, situations that emerged or developed gradually over time, and references to people who worked on internal or non-public matters for the group were left out – unless they could be assigned a specific date and place of occurrence. Moreover, because of the timeline's format as lists or columns of dates and places, the actual events inevitably appear as if they were all of equal magnitude and the same level of significance. Realizing this, the Action Group – like all *nenpyō* editors – had to come up with an operative formula for selecting those events comprising the timeline. At the same time, however, *nenpyō* editors, feminists included, can enhance the importance of a particular event by including it in a timeline. For example, in the Action Group's timeline, the juxtaposition of entries for the great Hanshin earthquake of 1995, in which 6,000 people lost their lives, and a small concert held by feminists, visually imparts the effect that the two events were somehow of similar or equivalent social significance. Hence, the structural form of *nenpyō* is both shaped by and shapes the way its makers and readers visualize and comprehend "history."

As the title of the column "group-related actions" implies, activities by groups other than the Action Group were included in that column and feminism-related items were placed in the "social change" column. "Group-related actions" included references to groups that were regarded as "us"; that is, groups that were spawned by the Action Group and also various allied organizations. In the "social change" column, feminism-related events that were not "us" but that were assessed as matters with which the Action Group claimed an affinity, were included. By the same token, many feminism-related events and variables were excluded from the Action Group timeline. Among the more notable of the exclusions were events associated with both large-scale mainstream women's organizations, known generically as *fujin dantai*, and academic feminists. These deliberate omissions allude to the frosty relationship between these groups and the Action Group, and reflect the fact that the latter's *nenpyō* aimed to present a chronicle of Japanese feminism from the margins of society and from outside of the academy.

The juxtaposition of events in the different columns of a timeline ostensibly forms a single stream of history or *nagare* in more conventional *nenpyō*. Timelines created by political groups, such as the Women's Action Group, attempt to schematically represent the dialectical relationship between activism and social change. Such timelines tend to view history more in terms of *ugoki* than *nagare*. In the case of the Action Group, the deliberate use of *ugoki* also points to the group's identity as an activist group working to initiate concrete social transformations by staging events and activities aimed at the general public.

REPRESENTING EVENTS

The third step of *nenpyō*-making is to compose and edit the phrases necessary to describe an event. Owing to the limited space allowed by the timeline format, a very concise "caption" is required. The Action Group's *nenpyō* group spent a great deal of time and energy checking the format and style of writing, and the choice of words. It was also faced with the task of translating visual images into written text. For instance, the group lodged a protest against two posters circulated in 1991 by the AIDS Prevention Foundation backed by the Ministry of Health. The central image of one of the posters was a photographic image of a Japanese man in a business suit hiding his eyes with his passport. "Have a good trip, be careful about AIDS," read the caption. The other poster featured the image of a nude woman cocooned within a giant, transparent condom. Her hair was rendered long and dark, but her face was deliberately blurred. Insofar as Japanese men departing on sex tours to Southeast Asia were the target audience for the posters, it seems likely that the nude woman represented a generic Southeast Asian woman, identified implicitly as the source of the HIV contagion. According to the poster, she was not the one who needed protection; she victimized Japanese males. In attempting, in the short space allowed by the *nenpyō* format, simultaneously to describe the visual messages of the posters and to lodge its protest, the group came up with the phrase: "1991.11.26, sent a letter of protest against the posters of the AIDS Prevention Foundation because they would further the practice of [Japanese males] buying sex abroad and increase discrimination against women and AIDS patients."

The group understood its mission to be one of providing concise and comprehensive entries in its timeline as a political act against the government's and mass media's tendency to use vague and imprecise language when reporting on women's and sex-related issues. The women were extremely discerning about their vocabulary, including whether or not they should use quotations around certain words. For instance, the term "comfort woman" (*ianfu*) was always put in quotation marks, expressing their criticism of the term used to describe wartime sex slaves, which they viewed as inappropriately vague and euphemistic.

The Action Group's entry for a notorious case of sexual assault in 1994 is another good example of the *nenpyō* group's attempt to frame an event from a feminist viewpoint. The case in question involved a former Kyoto University professor, Yano Toru, who for years had made a practice of sexually assaulting his (female) secretaries. In its timeline, the Action Group described Yano's activities as "rape" (*reipu*)[4] whereas other *nenpyō* by feminists and scholars only used the term "sexual harassment" (*sekushuaru harasumento* or *sekuhara*).[5] The Action Group's timeline also includes an entry for the "guilty" verdict against Yano, in part to provide evidence to its readers that feminist activism had succeeded in helping to win the case for the victims. Other feminist *nenpyō* did not mention the outcome of Yano's trial, and one *nenpyō* by academic historians gave only a very vague description of the case without mentioning the offender's name.[6] The different types of timeline entries for the Yano case show how different editors made, or did not make, links between the practice of sexual violence and the efforts of feminist activists to prosecute such behavior. Because of the limited space for explaining the contexts of a historical event, *nenpyō* editors must distill its "essence" into a few words. In a timeline entry then, a given word or term carries much more weight than it might in a longer narrative account. Therefore, the *nenpyō* part of the Action Group's book project was much more time-consuming and deliberative than was the drafting of the prose narrative part.

The Action Group felt that the *nenpyō* was the "hook" that would enhance the sales potential of the book. Its members were not alone in thinking this way: most of the reviews of the book appearing in major newspapers and various newsletters referred to the Action Group's *nenpyō* as "having an important archival [*shiryōteki*] value." By invoking the word "archive," the reviewers underscored the popular and dominant image of timelines as repositories of "primary data." However, as I have argued, *nenpyō* are not simply collections of "raw," or unprocessed, politically neutral facts. They are carefully constructed, juxtaposed, and orchestrated distillations of events, and part of a project of history-making and remembering that is, depending on the editors, either politically charged or politically undercharged.

NOTES

This chapter was first presented under the title "Feminism as Chronology: The Place of Timelines (*Nenpyō*) in Women's History" at the Association for Asian Studies (AAS) Annual Meeting 2003, "Tropics of History: Genealogical Forces and Fictions in East Asia" panel. See also Edwards (2003) and Robertson (2003) for relevant and related discussions of history-making in Japan.

1   Jennifer Robertson.
2   See chapter 13 in this volume.
3   The Miss Tokyo contest was first held in 1966, and has been held every year until today. The event is funded by Tokyo-based newspaper and television companies, and backed by the Tokyo Metropolitan Government. The winners are supposed to take a PR role in various events by the Tokyo Metropolitan Government for a year. In 1990 the Action Group staged a major protest by having some members apply for the contest to demonstrate their opposition, and the protest gained major coverage in newspapers and popular magazines. It was one of many feminist protests against beauty contests, especially the ones sponsored by local governments, from the late 1980s to the early 1990s; see Yunomae (1996:107–108) and Kaya (1995:388–389) for a brief description of the Action Group's protest against the Miss Tokyo contest. See also Robertson (1991:58–62) for links between the suburban "Miss" contests and the Miss Tokyo contest.
4   The word *reipu* is a loanword from the English "rape." The Japanese word for "rape" is usually *gōkan*. Among the *nenpyō* editors, there was a discussion on which word to use, and they chose *reipu* instead of *gōkan* because of the problematic *kanji* used for *gōkan*; that is, the *kanji* for *kan* is the combination of three *kanji* characters that mean "woman." The group considered the bad connotations of *kanji* for women as the expression of a culture of discrimination against women, thus the choice became to avoid the *kanji* and write *kan* in *hiragana*, or use the loanword *reipu*. In the end, for ease of understanding, the group chose *reipu*. This is one of the many instances in which the women of the Action Group were extremely concerned about the minute details of the connotations of words and characters in the *nenpyō*-making process.
5   The notion of "sexual harassment" was introduced and spread rapidly in Japan in 1989, when the country's first sexual harassment lawsuit was filed in Fukuoka district court. In the beginning, the Japanese phrase *seiteki iyagarase* was used to express the notion, but feminists soon chose to use the English phrase as they felt that the Japanese word *iyagarase* was a broad and vague notion, and did not necessarily contain the same sense of the seriousness of an action as "harassment." In the media coverage the word was then shortened into *sekuhara*, and the shortened word lost the original connotation of seriousness. Often used in sensational contexts in the media, the word *seku hara* won a "New Word Prize" in the annual Vogue Word Award contest in 1989 (Tsunoda 2001:68).
6   The *nenpyō* by the Women's Action Group has the longest description of the incident:

1994.3.18, A former professor of Kyoto University, Yano Toru, who has been accused of rape [*reipu*], files a lawsuit against the Minister of Education and a female professor at the same university who supported the victim. 3/27/1997, Kyoto District Court admits the claim of the female supporter and rejects Yano's claim . . . Yano's actions are recognized as rape [*reipu*] and sexual harassment [*sekuhara*]. 4.1, Yano's wife files an additional lawsuit against the female victim (Kōdō-suru Kai Kirokushū Henshū Iinkai 1999:xxvii).

The *nenyō* by a large-scale mainstream women's organization, the League of Women Voters of Japan, has the description: "1993.12.17, Kyoto University Professor Yano Toru quits the university after he was publicly accused of committing sexual harassment [*sekuhara*]. Later, the professor files a lawsuit requesting the invalidation of his resignation and compensation for defamation of character" (Nihon Fujin Yūkensha Dōmei 1995:45). The *nenpyō* by scholars of women's studies has: "1993.12.17, A newspaper reports accusations for committing sexual harassment [*sekushuaru harasumento*] against Kyoto University Professor Yano Toru by the secretaries at his office. Yano quits his university position at first, but then files a lawsuit requesting the invalidation of his resignation, and sues one of the victims for defamation of character" (Inoue and Morohashi 1995:278) Compared to the Action Group's *nenpyō*, these *nenpyō* by mainstream and academic feminists are centered around actions initiated by Yano. *Nenpyō* edited by academic historians (including both male and female scholars; it is unclear whether or not they are feminists) has the least detailed explanation. It says: "1993.12, A female secretary of a Kyoto University professor files a human rights claim with the Kyoto Bar Association. (Kyoto University Sexual Harassment Incident/Kyōdai Sekushuaru Harasumento Jiken)" (Onna-to Otoko no Jikū Henshū Iinkai 1998:356). In this description, the offender's actions remain invisible, and it is not clear why the secretary filed the claim and what happened afterwards.

REFERENCES

Edwards, Elise. 2003. Claiming the Game: The "Ancient" Game of *Kemari* and Japanese Claims to Modern Soccer. Presented for the panel organized by Jennifer Robertson, "Tropics of History: Genealogical Forces and Fictions in East Asia," Association for Asian Studies Annual Meetings, New York, March 28.

Inoue, Teruko, and Taiki Morohashi. 1995. Sengo joseishi nenpyō (Post-War Women's History *Nenpyō*). *In* Josei no data book (Women's Data Book), 2nd edn. Teruko Inoue and Yumiko Ehara, eds. pp. 216–283. Tokyo: Yūhikaku.

Kaya, Emiko. 1995. Mitsui Mariko: An Avowed Feminist Assemblywoman. *In* Japanese Women: New Feminist Perspectives on the Past, Present and Future. Kumiko Fujimura-Fanselow and Atsuko Kameda, eds. pp. 384–392. New York: The Feminist Press.

Kōdō-suru Kai Kirokushū Henshū Iinkai ed. 1999. Kōdō-suru onna-tachi ga hiraita michi Mexico kara New York (The Road Cultivated by the Women of Action: From Mexico to New York). Tokyo: Miraisha.

Nihon Fujin Yūkensha Dōmei. 1995. Nihon fujin yūkensha dōmei nenpyō, 1990–1995 (League of Women Voters Japan *Nenpyō*, 1990–1995). Tokyo: Nihon Fuijn Yūkensha Dōmei.

Onna to Otoko no Jikū Henshū Iinkai ed. 1998. Nenpyō onna to otoko no nihonshi (*Nenpyō* Japanese History of Women and Men). Tokyo: Fujiwara Shoten.

Rekishigaku Kenkyūkai, ed. 2001. Nihonshi nenpyō (Japanese History *Nenpyō*), 4th edn. Tokyo: Iwanami Shoten.

Robertson, Jennifer. 1991. Native and Newcomer: Making and Remaking of a Japanese City. Berkeley and Los Angeles: University of California Press.

——2003. Eugenical Phantasms: Embellishments and Erasures in Japanese Science History. Presented for the panel organized by Jennifer Robertson, "Tropics of History: Genealogical Forces and Fictions in East Asia," Association for Asian Studies Annual Meetings, New York, March 28.

Shinmura, Izuru ed. 1998. Kōjien, 5th edn. Tokyo: Iwanami Shoten.

Tashiro, Osamu ed. 1992. Nihonshi manga nenpyō (Japanese History: Cartoon *Nenpyō*). Tokyo: Gakushu Kenkyusha (Gakken).

Tsunoda, Yukiko. 2001. Seisabetsu to bōryoku (Violence and Gender Discrimination). Tokyo: Yūhikaku.

Yamada, Tadao, Kyosuke Kindaichi, Takeshi Shibata, and Akio Yamada. 1989. Shinmeikai kokugo jiten (Shinmeikai Japanese Dictionary). 4th edn. Tokyo: Sanseido.

Yamaguchi, Tomomi. 2004. Feminism Fractured: An Ethnography of the Dissolution and Textual Reinvention of a Japanese Feminist Group. Ph.D. dissertation, Department of Anthropology, University of Michigan.

Yunomae, Tomoko. 1996. Commodified Sex: Japan's Pornographic Culture. *In* Voices from the Japanese Women's Movement. AMPO-Japan Asia Quarterly Review, ed. pp. 101–110. Armonk, NY, and London: M. E. Sharpe.

CHAPTER 5 Making Majority Culture

Roger Goodman

"Who are the Japanese?" became the question that dominated the study of Japan in the 1980s. As the Japanese economy expanded and looked set to become the largest in the world by the end of the century, the government, under the direction of then prime minister, Nakasone Yasuhiro, established and generously funded the International Research Center for Japanese Studies (known popularly as Nichibunken) in Kyoto to look at the origins and development of what constituted Japanese culture. The publication of works about what constituted the key characteristics of Japanese society and culture flourished and, rather than being categorized by disciplinary background, were increasingly shelved in bookshops under the generic heading of *nihonjinron* (literally, "theories about the Japanese people"). Some of the authors of these works, such as the psychologist Doi Takeo and the anthropologist Nakane Chie, found that they had written best-sellers which went into many editions. Towards the end of the decade a powerful critique of this genre also appeared – most notably in the work of sociologists of Japan such as Yoshio Sugimoto and Ross Mouer and the anthropologist Harumi Befu – which suggested that, rather than critically exploring theories of Japanese culture, the *nihonjinron* literature actually contributed to its mystification. This chapter explores this tension between the analysis and mystification of Japanese culture in the light of mainstream work on the anthropology of ethnicity and nationalism.

Marcus Banks (1996), in his introductory textbook on ethnicity, suggests that it is useful to think of the field divided into two main camps revolving around the presumed reasons for the existence of ethnic identity. On the one hand, he identifies the "primordialists" who perceive ethnicity as an innate aspect of human identity: "it is a given, requiring description rather than explanation" (1996:39). On the other hand, he describes what he calls the "instrumentalists," who "hold that ethnicity is an artefact, created by individuals or groups to bring together a group of people for some common purpose." While Banks emphasizes that these are extreme positions and most anthropologists can see common ground between them, they – like most extreme positions – provide useful reference points for understanding the study of ethnicity in any society, and perhaps particularly so in a country like Japan where, as we shall see, the debate has become increasingly politicized.

If we follow Banks' division, we will see that the *nihonjinron* literature is essentially "primordialist" in its view of Japanese culture and ethnicity. Its emphasis is on finding continuities between contemporary Japanese social values and so-called "traditional" practices and in explaining both in terms of Japanese geography, topography, and agriculture. A book published by Nippon Steel in 1984 – published in both Japanese and English so as to enable Japanese employees of the company to explain to foreigners in English how Japan works – very neatly summarizes many of these ideas. Under the general heading of "culture" it summarizes "The Japanese Character" in terms of the following categories: the avoidance of friction between people; a propensity to work hard; conformity and concern about what others will think; awareness of hierarchy and an emphasis on vertical relations; the belief that man should live in harmony with, and not try to conquer, nature (1984:322–325). The development of each of these cultural characteristics is described in terms of Japanese "historical" practices, and an examination of just a couple of these standard descriptions will help us to understand better those who critique them.

The avoidance of friction, for example, is normally summed up in terms of the single word *wa*, generally translated as "harmony." Mature individuals in Japan are expected to maintain a sense of *wa* between them and all others at all times whether they agree with those others or not. Those who do not do so are dubbed *meiwaku* (a nuisance) and considered socially immature. Underlying this idea is the strong belief that the group is more important than the individual, and maturity – *contra* the idea in the West – is the awareness that one cannot do anything by oneself. The Nippon Steel volume (1984:326–329) explains the development of this group consciousness in terms of Japan's method of wet-paddy rice cultivation, which historically made it necessary for people to work in groups and develop a system of joint cooperation: "The people in the area had to band together in the planting and harvesting of the rice, and it was also necessary for these groups to institute some system among themselves for allocating the water to the paddy. All this instilled in the agricultural workers a consciousness of belonging to their localized farming communities." These ideas of group consciousness, the explanation adds, were reinforced by a number of other factors, including: Japan's "homogeneity" and "long period of isolation from the rest of the world"; the introduction of Confucianism from China which emphasized the concept of belonging to either a "family" or, among the warrior (*samurai*) class, to a "clan"; and, in the contemporary period, the modern employee's sense of belonging to a company because of its features of lifetime employment, seniority-based promotion, and company-based welfare.

In related vein, the Japanese propensity to work hard is explained in terms of Japan's subsistence economy, topography, and history (Nippon Steel 1984:325): "The small scale of the land has severely restricted the use of oxen and horses, so the ratio of human effort has been high…Shirking of work has usually meant reduced harvests…In feudal times, land taxes (in kind) and tenancy rates were high, and farmers working their small plots of land needed to increase their harvests." Again, it is argued, this cultural ethos was reinforced by more modern historical experience: the Meiji Restoration swept away the old class system and replaced it with a meritocratic education system which meant that those with ability could be socially mobile, as long as they applied themselves with sufficient effort.

As we shall see, the above types of explanations are problematic. It is, though, a little harsh to pick out in isolation quotations from the Nippon Steel publication since – like other introductory accounts of Japanese society put out by Japanese companies (see Yoshino 1992:ch. 8) – it draws from a wide literature. This literature covers a wide range of disciplines – for example, linguistics, biology, history, sociology, psychology, neurophysiology, sociology, anthropology, religious studies, geography – of widely varying levels of scholarship (see, for example, Miller's [1982] excoriating review of a number of such works, including the Japanese version of Tsunoda's book [English translation, 1985]). While many books have been extremely broad in their approach, the works which have perhaps become best known, certainly outside Japan, have been those which have attempted to summarize the essence of Japanese society in just a single concept, two examples of which are Nakane Chie's theory of Japan as a vertically oriented society (*tateshakai*) and Doi Takeo's view of it as based on *amae* (normally translated as dependency). In many ways, these two theories are complementary.

Nakane's book – published in English in the early 1970s as *Japanese Society* (1970) but drawing on working published in Japanese during the 1960s – is generally seen as the best expression of how the twin values of groupism and hierarchy operate in Japanese society. Indeed, the book was considered by the Japanese Foreign Ministry in the early 1970s to be such a good explanation that it gave many copies away free to foreigners interested in Japan.

Nakane's argument is based around an analytical distinction between what she calls frame (*ba*) and attribute (*shikaku*). The former refers to the context or group within which a person is situated, the latter to the individual qualifications which they possess. Nakane argues that in Japan a person's sense of identity comes more from their frame than their personal attributes, whereas in the West it is the other way around. To use her own example: a Japanese person is likely on meeting someone to tell them to which company, university, or institution he or she belongs (Mitsui, Mitsubishi . . .), while in the West, a person is more likely to say what job it is that he or she actually does (chauffeur, quality control engineer . . .). In Japan, Nakane argues, individuals get their sense of identity and status from their companies, which "explains" why they work so hard for them. Indeed, according to Nakane, the Japanese word *kaisha* is better translated as "my company" than simply as "company," since Japanese employees see their company as an extended family rather than simply as an employer. Rather like the "traditional" Japanese family (a concept we will come to later), people make a major distinction between those inside and outside the company, a distinction which, to some extent, determines not only their everyday treatment of others but also their whole moral universe. Loyalty to the company is given high status and the threat of ostracism from it remains a powerful sanction. Groups such as companies are, in short, self-contained, and individuals have both a very strong sense of a group's "history" and of their responsibility to those who will be members of the group in the future.

It is within companies, however, that Nakane's well-known concept of *tateshakai* can be most clearly observed, since she argues that, within companies, as within all groups in Japan, relations can only be understood hierarchically operating around *oyabun* (parent part) and *kobun* (child part) dyads. She represents (1970:43) this diagrammatically in the form of an "inverted V" with A at the apex and B and C in inferior positions to A. The crucial point is that the vertical relationship that both B and C have with A is far more important than the horizontal relationship they have with each other; they are expected to follow and show loyalty to A in return for benevolent support. As Nakane goes on to argue, the A–B–C "inverted V" is likely to be only part of a much more elaborated system where B and C will act as superiors to – and will exchange benevolence from for loyalty towards – others. The important point that Nakane makes about this elaborated "inverted V" structure is not only that vertical relationships remain more important than horizontal ones, but also that there is no way to bypass intermediary vertical relationships. G cannot have a direct relationship with A without going through C. A, however, remains the ultimate *oyabun* for the whole group and, as with the head of the family, will take responsibility for all the actions of all the members of the group. There are many examples in the Japanese corporate world of heads of corporate groups resigning to take responsibility of the actions of those in their organizations for which they could not possibly have been directly responsible, although in many of these cases, it should be noted, the individual's reward for "doing the right thing" is that they will often resurface fairly soon afterwards in another related, and almost equivalent, position.

There is no limit to the size of groups which operate on the dyadic, vertical system described by Nakane – new members can join at the bottom of the system indefinitely. Nakane suggests that it is the model, if not the practice, for social relations in virtually all large organizations. She gives examples of its operation not only in Japanese companies, but also religious organizations, universities, and traditional Japanese arts groups. Moreover, not only do the same principles apply to relations within groups but also to relations between groups. Japanese corporations, for example, are made up of a large number of small companies which are tied into *oyabun* and *kobun* relationships where the "junior partner" will do the best to supply whatever is required by the "senior partner" in return for the knowledge that it will continue to receive orders from the "parent" company whatever the broader economic situation.

Doi Takeo's (1971, 1973) concept of *amae* can in many ways be seen as the "psychological glue" which holds together Nakane's sociological model. Doi suggests that *amae* is not easy to translate into English because no cultural equivalent exists. Most translations involve some variation of the English word "dependency" but while this carries a negative connotation in English, *amae* carries a positive one in Japanese. Doi argues that the idea that individuals should presume upon, and seek indulgence from, a superior, however defined, is seen as both natural and healthy in a Japanese context in the sense that it means that people recognize the extent to which they rely on others in order to achieve anything in life. Not to recognize this – and hence not to presume upon seniors – is seen as much more problematic.

The power in the arguments of both Nakane and Doi comes from the fact that both can summarize in simple, understandable terms behavioral traits that are widely recognizable to many Japanese from a wide variety of contexts. This is reinforced by their ability to "explain" how the cultural values that underlie these traits developed. Doi relates the development of *amae* to the early socialization experiences of young children in Japan. As has been well documented, while an American mother is socially expected to separate a new child from herself and get it to "stand on its own two feet" as early as possible, a Japanese mother is much more likely to make it dependent on her (Caudill and Weinstein 1986). Scholarship on Japanese childrearing has documented in detail the degree to which Japanese parents develop this sense of dependency though practices such as co-sleeping and co-bathing and a greater reliance on physical contact (often called "skinship") and anticipation of the needs of their children.

Nakane's explanation for the origins of *tateshakai* can probably be traced to both her own background and her training in British social anthropology (she did her doctoral thesis at the London School of Economics). Having grown up in China and done research in India, she contrasted Japanese social organization with those societies rather than with some putative "West" with which, as we shall see, most scholars compared Japan at that period. At the same time, she was clearly influenced by the focus of British social anthropology on kinship, and in particular on the idea that the kinship system of a society provides the basic idiom for talking about other forms of social relations. The basic idiom in Japan, Nakane argued, is the *ie* system. The *ie* system was the standard kinship structure for the elite, samurai class in the Tokugawa period and, through the process dubbed by Befu (1981:50) as "samuraization," it was disseminated down through the rest of the society during the Meiji period as the feudal class system was dismantled. Much has been written about how the *ie* operates both in theory and in practice (see chapter 22 in this volume), but as far as Nakane's model is concerned the following are the crucial elements:

1   Certain roles and positions – for example head, successor – are only defined in the context of the *ie*. Hence an *ie* is distinct from a "family" (*kazoku*), where genealogy rather than position is paramount, and the actual residence (*setai*) in which members live. It is best thought of as a "corporate group" and indeed many *ie* were established around particular occupations.
2   It is a corporate body which has its own status, assets, career, and goals.
3   It has an existence over and above its immediate membership but includes both predecessors and successors. The main role of the current membership is to pass it on to the next generation in the best possible state out of respect for those who came before, even if this means adoption from outside the *ie*. Whatever happens, continuity must be ensured.
4   The *ie* as an institution has always had priority over the individuals who constitute it. There is a very strong distinction – expressed linguistically and symbolically – between those who are inside the *ie* (*uchi*) and those who are outside it (*soto*); those who marry out are no longer considered members, while those who move into the *ie* must learn its ways of doing things.
5   All individuals in the *ie* are in some kind of hierarchical relationship to each other; no two are ever equal. This ranking is based on criteria such as age, gender, and whether someone was born into, or moved into, the *ie*. All members of the *ie* are expected to show loyalty to the head of the *ie*, who is expected to demonstrate benevolent leadership in return.
6   Those younger sons who move out of the *ie* on marriage may either take up the headship of the *ie* of their bride or set up their own *ie* which is linked with their

natal *ie* in a *oyabun–kobun* relationship in what is known as a *dōzoku* (extended family) system.

It is not difficult to see from the above list how Nakane makes the connection between the idiom of the *ie* kinship model and the development of relations in contemporary institutions, just as it is easy to see how the early socialization practices in Japan lead to the development of *amae* as described by Doi. Indeed, in much of what they wrote Nakane and Doi were expressing ideas that were becoming increasingly common in the growing literature in the 1970s about Japanese management and corporate culture. Many authors at the time were keen to address the question of why Japan was developing so fast economically compared to other societies which had been at the same stage of economic development in the 1950s. There seemed to be a connection between Japanese culture and its extraordinary economic growth. Japan, some suggested, had developed a form of capitalism that was qualitatively different from Western capitalism. It exhibited consensus, harmony, affective relationships, hierarchy, and groupism that were distinct from ideas of individualism, class conflict, and putative egalitarianism. This was best exemplified in the so-called three jewels (*sanshu no jingi*) of the Japanese employment system – lifetime employment, seniority promotion, and company unionism – which in turn produced a loyal workforce with a strong sense of identification with their company. As outlined in the genre of literature on the Japanese company which appeared in the 1970s and 1980s, the roots of much of this system were to be found in feudal Japan, in particular in the organization of the household. Indeed, one rather surprising 1980s bestseller was the reissue in 1982 of Miyamoto Musashi's 17th-century samurai classic, *The Book of Five Rings*, with the new subtitle, "The Real Art of Japanese Management." Underlying the general argument in this genre of literature is the suggestion that it is best to think of the *ie* kinship system – at least as it existed in the prewar period – as an occupational group, and of the Japanese company as based on (fictive) kinship. The thesis generally takes it for granted (see, for example, Murakami, Kumon, and Sato 1979) that the modern Japanese company emerged from the already existing occupational structure of the feudal *ie*.

In many ways, the *nihonjinron* theses of Nakane, Doi, and others offer very useful, occasionally brilliant, insights into the workings of contemporary Japanese society and during much of the 1970s they constituted cornerstones of what the sociologists Mouer and Sugimoto (1986) later called "The Great Tradition" – by which they meant the collective theories of uniformity and consensus in Japanese society. Indeed, it was only in the 1980s that critics began to seriously question whether theories such as these were problematic.

The criticisms of the *nihonjinron* literature in the 1980s were both general and particular. On the general side was the fact that the literature largely generated models of Japanese society in opposition to the values of some monolithic, homogenous entity known as "the West." Figure 5.1 gives a good overview of nine of the best known Japanese–Western dyads which were developed in this context, most of which have been touched upon in the above discussion.

In the same vein of criticism was the questioning of the idea that Japanese society was itself homogenous and monolithic and hence all the values on the right-hand side of the figure were shared by all Japanese and, at the same time, all Japanese insti-

"Western" values	"Japanese" values
1. RACIAL HETEROGENEITY (*jinshū no konketsu*)	RACIAL HOMOGENEITY (*tan'itsu minzoku*)
2. COMPETITIVE CONFLICT (*meiwaku*)	HARMONY (*wa*)
3. INDIVIDUALISM (*kojinshugi*)	GROUPISM (*shūdanshugi*)
4. EGALITARIAN, HORIZONTAL TIES (*yoko*)	VERTICAL, HIERARCHICAL TIES (*tate*)
5. UNIVERSALISTIC ETHICS (*kochokuteki genri*)	PARTICULARISTIC ETHICS (*jōkyō ronri*)
6. SENSE OF RIGHTS (*kenri*)	SENSE OF DUTY (*gimu*)
7. LOGICAL/RATIONAL (*goriteki*)	AMBIVALENT/EMOTIONAL (*kanjōteki*)
8. INDEPENDENCE (*dokuritsu*)	DEPENDENCE (*amae*)
9. CONTRACTUALISM (*keiyaku*)	"KINTRACTUALISM" (*en'yaku*)

Figure 5.1   Nine Major Japan–West Dyads Developed in the *Nihonjinron* Literature

tutions were, to some extent, based on these values. The highly structured nature of the models appeared to determine how people would live their lives and to leave little room for individual agency in either Japan or in the supposedly monolithic "West." We will return to this question of structure versus agency later.

The second major critique of the *nihonjinron* literature was – perhaps surprisingly in the light of the apparently historical basis of Nakane Chie's work given above – that it was essentialist and ahistorical. Essentialism is the charge that the analyst works on the assumption that certain cultural features have always been present in any society and his or her job is simply to find and record these essentialist features and to document how they have continued virtually unchanged over centuries. As we saw earlier in Banks' description of work on ethnicity, those who take an "instrumentalist" view of society (who constitute the large majority of contemporary anthropologists) see it as socially constructed.

The third critique of the *nihonjinron* work – alluded to by Mouer and Sugimoto's description of the "The Great Tradition" – is that it worked on the assumption that Japanese society was harmonious and stable, a view of society which is generally described, in the anthropological and sociological literature, as "functionalism" and which is often associated with the work of the 19th-century scholar Émile Durkheim. Functionalism sees society as an organic whole – it often uses analogies with biology – with each of the constituent parts being in some form of balance, just as the parts of a body work to maintain both each other and the body as a whole. It is taken for granted that the way in which the constituent parts operate is for the good of the society as a whole, and also that the normal state of a society is harmonious; social conflict is seen as aberrant. Functionalism was the dominant discourse in both sociology and social anthropology in the immediate postwar period – probably reflecting the search of nations for some form of stability after the end of the war itself – and in many ways descriptions of Japan in such terms were consonant with social scientific descriptions of other industrial and pre-industrial societies at the time.

In the 1960s, however, functionalism came under sustained attack from a number of sources. The critiques were based on its philosophical, historical, and political assumptions. At the philosophical level, scholars questioned whether societies could have "needs" in the sense that a human body has "needs." At the historical level, even if society can be shown to have "needs," to show how those "needs" are met necessitates a detailed historical and causal analysis and is not something which can just be taken for granted. At the political level, scholars began to ask in whose interest it was that society should be seen as naturally stable and consensual. These new ways of thinking which developed in opposition to functionalism – some of which might be described as neo-Marxist, others of which can be seen as developments of the ideas of Max Weber about human agency – came to affect the way that some scholars began to view the *nihonjinron* rhetoric in the 1980s.

At one level, the easiest critiques of the *nihonjinron* material were at the level of historical accuracy. Japanese history is replete with example of paternalistic neglect and absence of loyalty. This has perhaps, ironically, been best recorded in the case of early Meiji factory management, where conditions could best be described, in British terms, as "Dickensian" (see Hane 1982). Indeed, there is considerable historical evidence to show how the idea of the Japanese company-as-family was deliberately developed in order to counteract the labor mobility that early factory conditions led to. In the 1890s, employers found themselves facing severe labor shortages and to confront this they began to introduce better conditions for workers. In particular, they offered free housing, food, and *okeiko* (training in the traditional arts needed to improve marriage prospects) to female workers; young girls had been the main source of labor in the textile industry, which had been Japan's earliest industrial development in the Meiji period, and many had suffered severe abuse.

When new industries – metalworking and engineering – which involved the employment of an increasingly skilled male labor force came to the fore at the turn of the century, employers made the shift from daily wages to offering career prospects, seniority promotion in return for loyalty, welfare schemes, and bonuses, all as a means of keeping workers. In the case of both female and male workers – though particularly in the case of the latter – employers developed a new rhetoric to legitimate and justify their employment practices. This rhetoric drew heavily on the idea of the company-as-family, as a form of occupational grouping that arose naturally out of feudal (Tokugawa) "tradition" (see Clark 1979). There is indeed considerable evidence to suggest that the efforts of employers to have the Japanese company viewed as a family have been repeated many times over the past hundred years. Kinzley (1991) outlines the details of the Kyōchōkai (Harmonization Society) which in 1919, with government sponsorship, did much to "reinvent" the rhetoric of "natural" management–employee cooperation in Japan; Crawcour (1973) describes the work of the Zensanren (the All-Japan Producers' Union) in responding to increasing union strength in the late 1920s and 1930s. It was in the course of this campaign, Crawcour says, that the "traditional" spirit of Japanese labor relations took shape as orthodox doctrine. And once again, in the immediate postwar period, faced by increasingly left-wing union agitation, the Japanese government, together with the American occupation authorities (facing the prospect of the Cold War) acted to encourage the growth of company unions in order to serve the interests of the company as a whole and not only its workers. In each example, the discourse called on the structure of the traditional Japanese household (*ie*) as the model for industrial relations in the Japanese company, and in each case it was what Kinzley (drawing on Hobsbawm and Ranger 1983) has termed the "reinvention of tradition." It was this reinvented tradition that Western commentators, suddenly alerted to Japan's new economic strength, "discovered" in the 1980s, almost exactly a hundred years after it first appeared.

At the philosophical level, there is considerable ethnographic material to show that, while there may be powerful social ideologies of consensus and harmony in a society, individuals do not lose their agency to accept or ignore these ideologies. As Befu (1990) showed in his use of the Weberian concept of social exchange, individuals in Japan in the 1980s were well aware of the social rewards that can come from compliance with the general consensus in society. The fact that workers did not organize against management during much of the 1970s and the 1980s was not due to any innate sense of social harmony but because of awareness that the interests of the company in a growth economy were also their own interests (plus the fact that the wage differentials between workers and management were much less than among other OECD countries). Ben-Ari (1990) indeed gave a good example of how workers with lifetime employment security in large companies (who constitute only about 25 percent of the total Japanese labor force) symbolically represented their solidarity in the annual *shuntō* (spring offensive) without needing to resort to actual strike action.

Perhaps the strongest critique of the *nihonjinron* literature, however, was the fact that there was considerable ethnographic evidence to show that, despite the ideology of homogeneity and of company-as-family that was central to its ideas, there was in fact considerable diversity in Japan by region, by gender, by occupation, by ethnic identity, and by social class. Indeed, examination of these areas suggests that there was not only diversity but also considerable stratification which ideologies of homogeneity, at best, ignored and, at worst, could be accused of helping to mask and disguise. Those who led this political critique of *nihonjinron* views of Japanese society asked where these ideas came from and whose interests they served. The sociology of knowledge of the *nihonjinron* became an increasingly complex literature in its own right. At its basis, however, was the assumption that "culture" is not a given in any society but is socially constructed and manipulated by particular groups with the economic and political power to do so, and that those who draw on "natural" features of a society to explain its "culture" are often, even subconsciously, part of the process of disguising the "constructed" nature of that society. One good example of this type of approach could be seen in the critique of Nakane's *Japanese Society* by two neo-Marxist sociologists, Hata Hiromi and Wendy Smith (1983).

Hata and Smith critiqued Nakane's English-language version of her book (which they pointed out was different in significant details from its Japanese original, *Tate-shakai no ningen kankei* [1967]) on some of the ethnographic, methodological, and theoretical points outlined above: it ignored contrary evidence, it was premised on the assumption that Japanese society was homogenous and monolithic, and it took it for granted that Japanese society had always been, and would always remain, the same (the basis of the concept of the "utopian society" which they mention in the title of their article). They added to these critiques, however, an extra twist. They suggested that Nakane's work – and by implication other works in the *nihonjinron* genre – was best understood as a form of ideology which, rather than explaining Japanese behavior, actually served to reinforce, legitimate and, in some circumstances, possibly create it. It doing so, it was acting on behalf of the state and its organs, particularly big business, in very much the same way as the Meiji state had developed the idea of all Japanese being part of one family under the Meiji emperor, to whom ultimate loyalty was owed in return for the benevolence which he bestowed (see Gluck 1985). Hata and Smith suggested a number a number of ways in which Nakane's book might serve the interests of big business. They pointed out, for example, that the idea that workers were "naturally" tied into vertical *oyabun–kobun* relationships meant that they were ultimately under the control of their bosses and that it was difficult for them to conceive of making horizontal links that might lead to a powerful counter to the designs of those bosses. This tendency was exacerbated in that vertical ties, as far as the individual worker was concerned, only extended to their immediate boss, and hence it was even harder for them to see who was really controlling them. The idea that the company was one large family undermined further the development of opposition between the owners of business (who controlled the means of production) and their workers, and the loyalty that was demanded by *oyabun* of *kobun* often meant that a worker's primary affiliation was with their company rather than with their own family. Indeed, workers who regularly left work to go home at the first opportunity were tagged with the pejorative label of *maihōmuizumu* ("my-homeism") from the 1960s. Later empirical work by the sociologist Yoshino Kosaku (1992) to some extent supported the idea that business leaders were one of the groups in Japan which most supported the dissemination of the tenets of the *nihonjinron*, and he argued that it was no coincidence that a company like Nippon Steel should produce the book, *Nippon: The Land and its People*, discussed earlier.

Hata and Smith imply that Nakane assumed that there was a natural consistency in society between norms and behavior and failed in her work to distinguish between ideology and practice. An article by the Marxist sociologist Kawamura Nozomu (1980), however, takes their argument one stage further in suggesting that Nakane's work is part of active Japanese state propaganda and involves active collusion between the government, leading academic institutions such as the universities of Tokyo and Kyoto, and leading publishers such as Iwanami Shoten and Kōdansha Shuppansha. Kawamura sees Nakane and Doi's work fitting into a genre of literature – supported and propagated by the Japanese state and that has emphasized elements of Japanese uniqueness – that goes back to the beginning of Japan's development of ultra-nationalistic ideologies in the 1930s. The anthropologist Aoki Tamotsu (1990) provides a much more detailed, but in broad terms similar, account in his review of postwar *nihonjinron* literature. There is indeed an argument for suggesting that this process can be directly traced back to the Meiji samuraization period, with the liberal period of the late 1910s and the 1920s being seen as the exception (see Tipton and Clark 2000). Tanaka (1993) can even see similarities in Japan's earliest recorded history, though at that period it was China which acted as the foil for developing concepts of Japanese cultural differences, a role which has been played by the "West" since the 1860s.

The above account has concentrated on books from the 1970s and 1980s for the simple reason that this was the height of the *nihonjinron* literature as scholars inside and outside Japan sought to make sense of its astonishing economic growth. The economic recession of the 1990s saw an obvious reduction in such books, though it is significant that many of the features which were used in the 1980s to "explain" Japan's success are now used to "explain" its economic, political, and structural problems (Harootunian 2001:723). What does the *nihonjinron* literature, however, add to our understanding of the construction of "ethnic identity" with which we began this chapter?

On the one hand, the *nihonjinron* literature reflects a process which can probably be seen in all nation-states, which is the use of history in order to construct and legitimate a sense of a commonly shared culture. As many anthropologists have argued, the manner in which interest groups struggle over, select, and present their "history" tells us as much about the ever-changing present as it does about the supposedly unchanging past. In some ways what is most distinctive about the Japanese case is not that such a process occurs, but that, as a result of Japan's having been on the losing side in the World War II, its occurrence should still be so closely monitored. As Peter Cave (2003) points out, it is conspicuous that the way in which Japan teaches about its colonial past is much more heavily criticized, both internally and externally, than is the way in which England teaches about its own colonial history.

We might also argue that there is not much difference between the manner in which national identity is constructed in Japan and how it is constructed in other modern nation-states. As Edward Said (1979), in his classic work on Orientalism, pointed out, the imperialist nations in the West constructed an image of themselves in opposition to a negatively caricatured and stereotyped East. In the same way, the manner in which a resurgent Japan in the 1980s conflated and negatively evaluated so-called Western values could be termed a form of "Occidentalism," and the increasingly positive evaluation given to Japanese values by Western nations at the same time as "reverse Orientalism" (Moeran 1989; see also Sakai 2001, on what he calls "the historical role of the West and Asia binary"). If we continue this analogy to its logical conclusion, then the current positive evaluation of Western "values" in Japan could be termed "reverse occidentalism."[1]

What, of course, is unique in the case of each country is the material each can draw on to construct its sense of national identity. Generally, making "majority culture" means downplaying "minority culture," and the existence of (by the standards of some European countries) substantial minority groups – Ainu, Burakumin, Japanese Koreans and Okinawans – continues to be minimized (see chapters 6 and 7 in this volume). Further, the absence of references to Japan's Asian neighbors in the *nihonjinron* literature is conspicuous and can be seen, in some ways, as a throwback to the early Meiji ideology of taking Japan out of Asia (*datsua-ron*) and setting it in the context of the leading Western nations of the period. What is significant, of course, is that in making their comparisons with a monolithic West, the *nihonjinron* authors concentrate on demonstrating how different Japan is from it. In the light of this, a sociology of knowledge that examined the *nihonjinron* literature of the 1970s and 1980s in terms of an attempt to reassert a sense of national identity after the "imposed" Americanization of Japan after World War II might lead to some interesting conclusions.

Finally, of course, the symbols that powerful groups in a nation-state can draw on in order to construct a sense of uniqueness are culturally specific even if they share generic features. For example, a National Identity Office that was set up in the 1980s in Thailand drew on the Thai language, its king, and Buddhism as symbols around which to construct a shared sense of Thai-ness in what might be considered a very ethnically diverse society, just as elites within Japan have drawn on its own language, emperor, and Shintoism in order to construct an idea of Japanese-ness at various periods since the Meiji Restoration. Shared rituals and ceremonies are also an effective, if culturally specific, means of constructing a sense of "natural" unity among a population. Finally, as we have seen, every society has its own chest of historical "facts" on which it can draw not only to "explain" common links and shared values between people but also to "construct" and "legitimate" those links and values. There are few people in most societies who know enough about the real origins of these shared symbols, rituals, and histories to be able to challenge their authenticity. To return to Banks' distinction between "primordial" and "instrumental" views of ethnicity, the case of the *nihonjinron* example in Japan suggests that, even if ethnic identity can be shown to have been constructed instrumentally, it is still experienced by most of those at whom it is directed as primordial.

ACKNOWLEDGMENTS

I should like to thank both David Gellner and Lola Martinez for their helpful comments in constructing the argument of this chapter.

NOTE

1   Editor's note: In Robertson 2001 [1998], chapter 3, I make a different argument about Japanese Orientalism, and point out the theoretical and methodological problems with a definition of colonialism/imperialism based on a binarist division of West and East, North and South, colonizer and colonized.

REFERENCES

Aoki, Tamotsu. 1990. "Nihonbunkaron" no hen'yō: sengo nihon no bunka to identity (The Transformation of "Theories of Japanese Culture": Culture and Identity in Postwar Japan). Tokyo: Chūō Kōronsha.
Banks, Marcus. 1996. Ethnicity: Anthropological Constructions. London: Routledge.
Befu, Harumi. 1981. Japan: An Anthropological Introduction. Tokyo: Tuttle.
——1990. Four Models of Japanese Society and their Relevance to Conflict. *In* Japanese Models of Conflict Resolution. S. N. Eisenstadt and Eyal Ben-Ari, eds. pp. 213–238. London and New York: Kegan Paul International.
Ben-Ari, Eyal. 1990. Ritual Strikes, Ceremonial Slowdowns: Some Thoughts on the Management of Conflict in Large Japanese Enterprises. *In* Japanese Models of Conflict Resolution. S. N. Eisenstadt and Eyal Ben-Ari, eds. pp. 94–124. London and New York: Kegan Paul International.

Caudill, William, and Helen Weinstein. 1986. Maternal Care and Infant Behavior in Japan and America. *In* Japanese Culture and Behavior: Selected Readings, revised edn. Takie Sugiyama Lebra and William P. Lebra, eds. pp. 201–246. Honolulu: University of Hawaii Press.

Cave, Peter. 2003. Teaching the History of Empire in Japan and England. International Journal of Educational Research 37:623–641.

Clark, Rodney. 1979. The Japanese Company. New Haven and London: Yale University Press.

Crawcour, E. S. 1973. The Japanese Employment System. Journal of Japanese Studies 4(2):225–245.

Doi, Takeo. 1971. Amae no kōzō (The Structure of Dependency). Tokyo: Kōbundo.

—— 1973. The Anatomy of Dependence. Trans. John Bester. Tokyo: Kōdansha International.

Gluck, Carol. 1985. Japan's Modern Myths: Ideology in the Late Meiji Period. Princeton: Princeton University Press.

Hane, Mikiso. 1982. Peasants, Rebels and Outcastes: The Underside of Modern Japan. New York: Pantheon Books.

Harootunian, Harry. 2001. Japan's Long Postwar: The Trick of Memory and the Ruse of History. The South Atlantic Quarterly 99(4):715–739.

Hata, Hiromi, and Wendy A. Smith 1983. Nakane's "Japanese Society" as Utopian Thought. Journal of Contemporary Asia 13(3):361–388.

Hendry, Joy. 1981. Marriage in Changing Japan. London: Croom Helm.

Hobsbawm, Eric, and Terence Ranger, eds. 1983. The Invention of Tradition. Cambridge: Cambridge University Press.

Kawamura, Nozomu. 1982. The Historical Background of Arguments Emphasizing the Uniqueness of Japanese Society. *In* Japanese Society: Reappraisals and New Directions. Theme issue. Sociological Analysis 5(6):44–62.

Kinzley, W. Dean. 1991. Industrial Harmony in Modern Japan: The Invention of a Tradition. London: Routledge.

Miyamoto, Musashi. 1982. The Book of Five Rings: The Real Art of Japanese Management. Toronto: Bantam Books.

Moeran, Brian. 1989. Language and Popular Culture in Japan. Manchester: Manchester University Press.

Mouer, Ross, and Sugimoto, Yoshio. 1986. Images of Japanese Society: A Study in the Structure of Social Reality. London: Kegan Paul International.

Murakami, Yasusuke, Kumon, Shunpei, and Sato, Seizaburō. 1979. Bunmei toshite no ie-shakai (The *Ie* Society as a Pattern of Civilization). Tokyo: Chūō Kōronsha.

Nakane, Chie. 1967. Tate shakai no ningen kankei: tan'itsu shakai no riron (Human Relations in a Vertical Society: A Theory of a Unified Society). Tokyo: Kōdansha.

—— 1970. Japanese Society. Harmondsworth: Penguin Books.

Nippon Steel Corporation, Personnel Development Division. 1984. Nippon: The Land and its People. Tokyo: Gakuseisha.

Robertson, Jennifer. 2001[1998]. Takarazuka: Sexual Politics and Popular Culture in Modern Japan. Berkeley: University of California Press.

Said, Edward. 1979. Orientalism. New York: Vintage Books.

Sakai, Naoki. 2001. "You Asians": On the Historical Role of the West and Asia Binary. The South Atlantic Quarterly 99(4):789–817.

Tanaka, Stefan. 1993. Japan's Orient: Rendering Pasts into History. Berkeley and London: University of California Press.

Tipton, Elise K., and John Clark, eds. 2000. Being Modern in Japan: Culture and Society from the 1910s to 1930s. Reading: Craftsman House and the Australian Humanities Research Foundation.

Yoshino, Kosaku. 1992. Cultural Nationalism in Contemporary Japan: A Sociological Enquiry. London: Routledge.

SUGGESTED READING

Some key texts on theories of Japanese society (*nihonjinron*) in English

Ben-Dasan, Isaiah. 1982. The Japanese and the Jews. Tokyo: Weatherhill.
Suzuki, Daisetz T. 1973. Zen and Japanese Culture. Princeton: Princeton University Press.
Tsunoda, Tadanobu. 1985. The Japanese Brain: Uniqueness and Universality. Trans. Oiwa Yoshinori. Tokyo: Taishukan.
Watsuji, Tetsuro. 1963. A Climate. Tokyo: Japan Information Centre.

Some key discussions of the *nihonjinron* literature

Befu Harumi. 2001. Hegemony of Homogeneity. Melbourne: Trans Pacific Press.
Dale, Peter. 1986. The Myth of Japanese Uniqueness. London: Croom Helm.
Johnson, Sheila K. 1975. American Attitudes towards Japan, 1941–1975. Washington: AEI-Hoover Policy Study 15.
Kreiner, Josef, and Hans Dieter Olschleger, eds. 1996. Japanese Culture and Society: Models of Interpretation. Tokyo: Siebold Institute.
Littlewood, Ian. 1996. The Idea of Japan: Western Images, Western Myths. London: Secker & Warburg.
Miller, Roy Andrew. 1982. Japan's Modern Myth: The Language and Beyond. Tokyo: Weatherhill.
Oguma, Eiji. 2002. A Genealogy of Japanese Self-Images. Melbourne: Trans-Pacific Press.
Wilkinson, Endymion. 1983. Japan Versus Europe: A History of Misunderstanding. Harmondsworth: Penguin.

Political and Cultural Perspectives on "Insider" Minorities

CHAPTER **6**

Joshua Hotaka Roth

This chapter looks specifically at "insider minorities," those whose difference is of a sort that currently does not deny their Japanese-ness in the eyes of other Japanese, as opposed to the "outsider" minorities discussed by Sonia Ryang (chapter 7 in this volume), who are considered foreign despite their residence within Japan. Most surveys of minorities in Japan have focused on ethnic minorities, such as the indigenous Ainu and the Okinawans, with the Burakumin the only non-ethnic group to be included (see De Vos and Wagatsuma 1995; Ohnuki-Tierney 1998; Weiner 1997). There are several reasons to cast the net somewhat more broadly. Ethnic minorities, together with the Burakumin, account for only 4 to 6 percent of the Japanese population (De Vos and Wagatsuma 1995:272), a figure which does not deter many Japanese, most famously former prime minister, Nakasone, from claiming Japan to be a homogeneous society. Edward Fowler writes that in order to be able to recognize the range of difference that exists in Japan, "we must effect a change in our hermeneutic register. . . . We cannot think simply in terms of ethnicity as the basis for social heterogeneity. . . . We must also think in terms of class and even of caste" (1993:217; see also Fowler 1996, and chapter 8 in this volume). Although for reasons of space this chapter will not include a discussion of Japanese day laborers,[1] it will survey three non-ethnic or "insider" minorities: the Burakumin descendants of former outcaste groups, the disabled, and atomic bomb victims (*hibakusha*), in addition to the Ainu, Okinawans, and Nikkeijin (overseas Japanese) migrants to Japan.

Another reason to consider this diverse set of minorities together lies in the fact that they share experiences of stigmatization and discrimination. In some cases, discrimination may literally throw various minorities together spatially as they are marginalized in certain urban or rural districts. In a Burakumin neighborhood of

Kyoto, for example, reside a large number of disabled people who are not Burakumin (Caron 1999:436). Undocumented foreign workers can often be found in neighborhoods populated by Japanese day laborers (Ventura 1992). In other cases, some Japanese may actually mix the identities of various minorities, as in the following examples of harassing telephone calls made to a Buraku Liberation League office:

> "You people are *chonko* [a term of abuse derived from Chosen-jin (Korean) – similar to "Jap" for "Japanese"], aren't you?" or "Aren't you guys *buraku-min*?" or "You're Koreans. Go and check in at the municipal office" or "Do you want me to find you a good mental doctor?" (Mihashi 1987:S23)

Japanese confusion about these various minority groups is not peculiar to the current moment. In the 18th and 19th centuries, some Japanese had speculated that Burakumin had originated from groups of captured Ainu (Ooms 1996:297) or of Chinese refugees "who had lived in the wild and eaten animal and bird meat" (1996:305). Although there is little evidence to support the notion of the Korean or Chinese origins of the Burakumin (Hudson 1999), Burakumin, Koreans, Chinese, and the mentally ill have been conflated at times in the popular imagination. At least at one level, this calls for an integrated analysis.

Two major perspectives – cultural and political – are relevant for analyzing Japanese minorities. The cultural perspective posits that the concepts of purity (*hare*) and pollution (*kegare*) that derive from Buddhist and Shinto traditions, and the related understanding of strangers (*tanin, ijin*) that derive from folk traditions have shaped Japanese understandings of difference. According to this perspective, these concepts comprise a cultural baseline that has been relatively fixed throughout Japanese history. Minority groups, most notably the Burakumin, have been discriminated against because they fall within a culturally defined category of the polluting.

The political perspective encompasses a more dynamic politics underlying supposedly fixed cultural principles. This perspective emphasizes the historical and political processes of minority group formation. Thus, proponents of this perspective might emphasize how things considered either polluting or pure in one historical context have lost or gained such associations over time under specific circumstances often involving the workings of state power and other political and economic interests.

This chapter examines the Burakumin, *hibakusha*, the disabled, Nikkeijin, Ainu, and Okinawans from the cultural and political perspectives. Despite the significant differences among these groups, I suggest that all of them have suffered similar patterns of discrimination based on the cultural frameworks of the majority Japanese. It also indicates that the politicized quality of minority identification in the 20th century was not a completely new phenomenon that only developed in the context of the modern nation-state, but that boundaries between groups were created and negotiated through the political manipulation of cultural frameworks from much earlier times.

BURAKUMIN

The Burakumin (literally, hamlet people) minority does not have any racial or linguistic characteristics that mark them off from the "mainstream" Japanese population.

Scholars have most often applied the cultural perspective of purity and pollution to explain the Burakumin. The Burakumin traditionally have worked as tanners, butchers, undertakers, cleaners of latrines, caretakers of the sick, and in other occupations which were considered polluting because of their association with death and bodily excretions. Ohnuki-Tierney writes that "Burakumin were specialists in impurity, who spare[d] others from dealing with the inevitable problems of pollution and dirt. In the process, they became identified with impurity itself" (1984:45). During the Tokugawa period Burakumin were generally located at the edges of villages. Ohnuki-Tierney suggests that conceptions of purity and pollution were given spatial coordinates; things located on peripheries correlated with pollution, while things located in centers correlated with purity. Burakumin residence at the margins of towns was just one indication of a wider principle (1984:21–27).

The cultural perspective provides a powerful analysis for a range of purity and pollution beliefs and practices. Death was not uniquely polluting, but one instance of a class of things that were so considered because of their position at a threshold, or margin, between realms. Leather workers were situated at the threshold between the living and the dead. Itinerant performers such as monkey trainers (Ohnuki-Tierney 1987) and ritual puppeteers (Law 1997) were associated with pollution because they were outsiders, "non-residents" of local villages (Law 1997:78–79; Ohnuki-Tierney, 1998:37), who were thought to come from an unknown, dangerous, and polluted external world. Itinerants shared with leather workers and outcaste peoples of diverse occupations a function in mediating between symbolic realms.

As mediators between symbolic realms, outcaste groups included not just undertakers but those who delivered children. They included not just those who cleaned latrines, but those who cleaned temple grounds. Japanese conceptions of pollution (*kegare*) therefore must be seen in terms quite distinct from modern notions of hygiene (see Douglas 1966). The term most often translated as purity, *hare*, literally means bright, clear, or pure, and can be defined more generally as "that which enhances life and is creative" (Law 1997:60). Pollution, or *kegare*, is "that which undoes life and leads to death and destruction" (1997:61), and yet it also contains within it generative powers (see Yamaguchi 1977:154; Yoshida 1981:44). In the Kojiki and Nihongi, the eighth-century chronicles of the gods and early kings (Japan's creation myths), various bodily excretions and body parts that are considered polluting have powerfully generative powers when handled in ritually proper ways (Law 1997:65).

While the purity/pollution framework provides a powerful analytic tool, scholars writing from the political perspective reject ahistorical notions of a deep structure of Japanese thought. Herman Ooms argues that the idiom of purity and pollution was applied situationally rather than universally, even in premodern Japan (1996:ch. 6). Ooms writes that the application of the pollution concept "could be customary (but custom is flexible), institutional (but institutions change), or situational (and therefore contestable)" (1996:275). He describes a case in which local authorities in one province conveniently ignored the pollution concept, intervening on behalf of Burakumin (then commonly referred to as Kawata, literally "leather worker") under their jurisdiction in a conflict with non-Burakumin peasants from a neighboring region (1996:257–261).

Ooms also notes that, during the period of internecine warfare in the 16th century, Kawata were located at the center of castle towns because of the importance of leather workers for the manufacture of weapons and armor, and that they and their work were not stigmatized as they were later on (Ooms 1996:279; see also Ninomiya 1933). Prejudice grew during the Tokugawa period, a time of relative political stability, and was accompanied by the relocation of Burakumin to the peripheries of towns and villages (Ooms 1996:281) and the increasing usage of the disparaging term *eta* (literally, "defilement abundant") to refer to them (Ooms 1996:282). Ooms contends that the concept of pollution was open to manipulation by parties interested in enforcing or establishing a social, economic, and political hierarchy.

Ian Neary presents a picture of the gradual politicization of Burakumin identity in the 20th century that suggests that the cultural perspective is appropriate for understanding the construction of Burakumin at an earlier time, while a political perspective is more appropriate for analyzing the modern situation. But even in the Tokugawa period, Kawata did not necessarily accept the negative labels applied to them (Ooms 1996:248). While 19th-century nativist scholars concocted theories of *eta* descent from captured Ainu or from shipwrecked Chinese, Kawata elites kept records of their genealogies suggesting descent from "the Japanese mythical figure Somin-shorai, a poor man who had become wealthy because he had lent his humble abode to a god," or later to divine figures such as Hakusan or Ebisu, or from the Minamoto shogun (1996:307). Clearly, the purity/pollution complex existed in competition or juxtaposition with a variety of other cultural categories that allowed Kawata to construct positive mytho-histories for themselves.

In the late 19th century, the Meiji government renamed Burakumin "new commoners" (*shin heimin*), as opposed to just "commoners," and in so doing indexed and maintained the stigmatized status to which they had been yoked during the Tokugawa period. The government's system of household registration (*koseki*) made it possible to trace individuals to their hometowns and that of their forebears, making it easy to identify Burakumin. Thus, modern government policy has helped shape the category of Burakumin, shackling those who had long since ceased to practice what had been considered polluting occupations to an identity they may not have wanted to retain.

Social conditions and the influence of radical foreign ideas in the early 20th century stimulated a social movement, centered around the group Suiheisha, that consciously rejected the cultural underpinnings of discrimination (Neary 1989:51). In the postwar period, Burakumin concerned with fighting discrimination formed the Burakumin Liberation League and developed a political strategy of publicly denouncing those who expressed prejudice toward them. Denunciations were effective in extracting apologies and greater care in the use of discriminatory language, and they motivated other minority groups and women to follow their example (Takaki 1992). Such social movements could help these groups forge positive self-identities. Frank Upham argues, however, that the tactic of denunciation fails to develop an understanding of rights to cultural difference, and assumes only the right to be treated the same as other Japanese. He suggests that formal legislation or litigation could be a more fruitful avenue toward such a goal (Upham 1987:118–123).

HIBAKUSHA

Hibakusha (atomic bomb victims) are another minority group, who, like Burakumin, are not distinguishable from other Japanese by either phenotypic or linguistic characteristics. The category of *hibakusha* often refers just to those people who were either killed or who suffered medical problems as a result of the atomic bombs that the United States dropped on Hiroshima and Nagasaki. Early estimates of the numbers killed in these two cities were roughly 70,000 in Hiroshima and 25,000 in Nagasaki. Later calculations place the numbers more in the range of 140,000 in Hiroshima and 70,000 in Nagasaki (see Committee for the Compilation of Materials on Damage Caused by the Atomic Bombs in Hiroshima and Nagasaki 1981:364; Dower 1998:ix).

Most died at the time the bombs were dropped and in the weeks and months following, but many died in the following decades of diseases related to radiation exposure. Until the 1980s, residents of these cities have had a higher rate of leukemia than Japanese of other cities, and women who were pregnant at the time of the bombing gave birth to children who suffered mental retardation and other disabilities. Others have survived without medical problems but were scarred by the trauma of fleeing through streets filled with burnt corpses, and have lived with the constant fear of disease arising from radiation exposure. Since 1957, the Japanese government has extended special medical services to *hibakusha*, and in the process defined *hibakusha* as those who were within 4 kilometers of ground zero at the time of the explosion, those who came within 2 kilometers of the center within three days of the explosion, and those who were *in utero* when their mothers were exposed (Dower 1998:ix). A broader definition of *hibakusha* would include all of those who have been affected by the bombs in some way. Thus, people who have suffered discrimination as a result of their association with Hiroshima could also be considered *hibakusha*. Women from Hiroshima and Nagasaki have had trouble finding marriage partners because of fears that their children would have birth defects (Chujo 1986:26–46). Some Japanese Americans who were in these two cities when the bombs were dropped later hid their experience when back in the US for fear of being denied health insurance (Sodei 1998:91).

Some *hibakusha* have taken it upon themselves to be as visible as possible. They have done so as participants in various Japanese peace movements that center around the sites of Hiroshima and Nagasaki. Such activists hope that, by helping educate others about the horrors of atomic war, they may help prevent it from ever occurring again. Some quieter victims of the bomb complain, however, that discrimination against them has been exacerbated by the exaggeration of radiation sickness as a result of peace movement activities (Chujo 1986). The Hiroshima peace movement has been characterized as vocal and angry in contrast to the more quiet and meditative quality of Nagasaki's, and this may be reflected in the relative abundance of *hibakusha* literature produced in the former city (see Treat 1995:310–317). The characteristics of these two cities may actually represent the two alternative approaches of visibility and invisibility available to all *hibakusha*. Some who choose invisibility consider the category of *hibakusha* as something created and imposed from the outside and have not embraced it as an identity.

Can the cultural perspectives on the stranger and purity and pollution help explain the discrimination that *hibakusha* have faced in Japan? In what way do *hibakusha* occupy a threshold? The stigma attached to *hibakusha* could stem from their contamination by an external agent – bombs produced and dropped by Americans. Such an analysis would overstretch the usefulness of the cultural perspective, however, for we must distinguish between strangers, i.e. people from the outside, and objects or ideas. The Japanese have always been engaged in the trade of goods and the exchange of ideas. Outside influences have shaped every aspect of Japanese culture. Thus the atomic bomb's foreign origin cannot explain the stigma attached to *hibakusha*. Rather, this stigma may derive in part from the position *hibakusha* occupy on the threshold between life and death, as well as that between health and illness.

The stigma of radiation sickness also taints the descendants of those who survived the bombing. Families frequently use private detective services to look into the backgrounds of prospective marriage partners to expose *hibakusha* and other invisible insider minorities (see Hayashida 1975). If a detective working for a prospective groom's family discovered that a prospective bride's father or mother was in Hiroshima at the time the bomb dropped, marriage plans might be shelved. The same could happen if the detective discovered that the other family had relatives who lived in Buraku neighborhoods, had a Korean background, or had a history of disabilities and mental illnesses. The transmission of this stigma to second- and third-generation *hibakusha* involves the racialization of this category, a process stimulated in part by the import of European and American eugenics discourse since the late 19th century (see Weiner 1994). Eugenics laws in 1940 during World War II, as well as in 1948 in the early postwar era, mandated sterilization for certain hereditary diseases, mental illness, or retardation (Matsubara 1998:194–195), and various infectious diseases such as tuberculosis, venereal diseases, and leprosy, which were thought, in Lamarkian fashion, to be hereditable (Otsubo and Bartholemew 1998:547–548; see also Robertson 2002, and chapter 21 in this volume).

PEOPLE WITH DISABILITIES

People with physical disabilities (*shintai shogaisha*) and mental illnesses (*seishin shogaisha*) may also be considered insider minorities. Although the category of the disabled is very broad, covering many people who may not share any sense of common identity, others may perceive various disparate individuals and groups as all being of a kind. Japanese may conceive of certain disabled as occupying a threshold between realms. Itinerant blind *shamisen* performers of Tsugaru (see De Ferranti 2000) exemplify the association between disability, itinerancy, and marginality. Blindness and other physical and mental conditions were also attributed to special powers of communication with the transcendental realm. Thus, in certain parts of Japan, they were employed as mediums.

The Japanese government in the late 1980s recognized only about 3 percent of the national population as suffering from any form of disability, a much smaller figure than in most other industrialized countries. The United Kingdom and the Netherlands both recognized roughly 10 percent of their populations, Belgium 12.5 percent, Poland 14 percent, and Sweden as much as 34.8 percent (Mogi 1992:440).

The Japanese government has slowly started to increase services for the disabled, but many groups have yet to be recognized. Greater visibility on the part of the disabled is crucial in order to gain recognition and access to services, as well as to achieve more positive self-identities. People with disabilities number in the millions and comprise such a wide range of conditions and degrees of debility that they should be considered as a category more than a group. Those who share a specific type of condition, such as the deaf or the blind, have formed groups that have pressured the government for greater services. Some groups, such as the Osaka Association of Families of the Mentally Disabled, have also protested the use of discriminatory language by print and broadcast media (Gottleib 1998:163, see also Takaki 1992) and have pushed news agencies to devise lists of words to avoid.

While increased visibility can potentially foster positive identities for the disabled minority, for some it may just involve a shift from attempts to hide their disabilities to efforts to overcome and erase them. As David Engle has said in relation to special educational programs for the disabled in the US, the parents of disabled children often demand such programs in the hope that special treatment could maximize the potential that their children achieve "normalcy" (Engle 1993:140–141). The identity of the disabled minority appears by nature contingent, but it is no more so than that of ethnic minorities, some of whose members have striven for a similar invisibility via passing or assimilation into the "mainstream."[2]

NIKKEIJIN

Nikkeijin (literally, "sun-line people," referring to people of Japanese ancestry who have resided all or much of their lives outside of Japan) are concentrated mostly in the Americas. Brazil has the largest Nikkeijin population at over 1.2 million (Centro de Estudos Nipo-Brasileiro 1990). There are substantial populations in the US and Peru, and a smaller number in Bolivia, Mexico, Paraguay, and Argentina. The emigration to Hawaii and the west coast migration to Brazil started in 1908 when the US made it more difficult to enter the country, and the bulk of prewar migration to Brazil took place after 1924 when the US more completely closed the door to Japanese migrants. Over decades, migrants and their children adapted to the Brazilian context even while fashioning a strong ethnic Japanese identity (Lesser 1999; Maeyama 1996, 1997).

In the late 1980s, the economic boom in Japan and the economic bust in Brazil compelled Nikkeijin to take advantage of preferred visas statuses that the Japanese government made available to them in 1990. Since then, hundreds of thousands of Nikkeijin have gone to work in Japan, and by 2000 more than 250,000 were residing there, concentrated in the industrial belt between Nagoya and Tokyo. More than three-quarters of these were from Brazil, and most of the rest from Peru (see Watanabe 1995).

Some suggest that the Japanese may have viewed second- and third-generation Nikkeijin from Brazil as having brought with them the pollution they acquired from living outside of Japan for most of their lives (see Tsuda 1998:337–345). The pollution of place sullied the purity of race – even for those Nikkeijin who were not of mixed ancestry. Takeyuki Tsuda notes, however, that Nikkeijin from Brazil and other developing countries were more gravely tainted than were those from the US, who, although "outside," were more positively associated with modernity. In addition, Nikkeijin were tainted by their association with manual labor (Tsuda 1998:323–330). The majority of the over 250,000 Nikkeijin working in Japan in the late 1990s were employed in manufacturing and electronics factories, food-processing, and unskilled service work (see recent ethnographies by Linger 2001; Roth 2002; the collection of essays by Yamashita 2001; and the 2003 edited volume by Lesser).

In addition to bringing pollution from the outside, Nikkeijin occupied a conceptual threshold in that they were often thought to be ethnically Japanese and yet were culturally very different. Fulfilling only certain of the criteria used to define who was Japanese, Nikkeijin seemed to occupy the margin between Japanese and Other. Moreover, they also had some of the positive generative attributes of polluting substances. Without the presence of Nikkeijin workers in the industrial belt spanning Nagoya to Tokyo, many small manufacturers would have been forced to close shop.

From the late 1980s through the 1990s, Nikkeijin gradually moved from the status of a preferred group to a stigmatized one, suggesting that the purity/pollution complex could shift or be manipulated with changing contexts. Initially, the Japanese government and businesses welcomed Nikkeijin as a preferred alternative to foreign migrants who were not ethnically Japanese. The onset of recession and decrease in demand for Nikkeijin led some Japanese to label Nikkeijin irresponsible or undependable workers, which we may interpret as transformations of the pollution metaphor. If Nikkeijin evinced certain qualities that could be interpreted as irresponsible, these were more a result of their status as temporary brokered or contract workers rather than a cultural predisposition, but Japanese managers and bureaucrats preferred the reverse explanation, which justified the marginal status of Nikkeijin in terms of their irresponsibility (see Roth 2002).

AINU

Unlike most of the other "insider minorities" discussed above, the Ainu had a distinctive language, clothing, material culture, social organization, and phenotypic features that set them apart from mainland Japanese. Some Japanese archaeologists consider the Ainu to preserve essences of a Jomon-period (10,000–300 B.C.E.) heritage (Howell 1996:174–175; see also Hudson 1999; McCormack 1996:277). The Ainu today reside primarily in the large northern island of Hokkaido. They were pushed to the northern extremes of the archipelago by the arrival of subsequent waves of settlers who brought rice-paddy agriculture from the Asian continent starting in the third century B.C.E. Although often depicted as remnants of the Jomon era, what is known as Ainu culture today developed through complex interactions with "four main archaeological cultures over different periods of time – the Epi-Jomon (250 B.C.E.–700 C.E.), the Okhotsk (600–1000 C.E.), the Satsumon (700–1200 C.E.), and the later Japanese" (Walker 2001:20).

The Ainu and Okinawans occupy the northern and southern extremes of the Japanese archipelago. From the perspective of the Japanese metropole in Edo or Kyoto during the Tokugawa period (1603–1868), the Emishi and Ryukyuans (as the indigenous groups at the northern and southern extremes of the Japanese archipelago were called at the time) constituted the "barbarian fringe." Because they were not fully controlled, the "barbarians" posed a threat to the center. However, through their payments of tribute, they simultaneously ensured the center's political prestige and economic status. Japanese leaders had developed this understanding of interstate tribute trade relationships with a civilized center and barbarian fringe (*ka'i*) from a Chinese model. Despite its Chinese origins, the model resonates at state-level political organization with the stranger paradigm discussed above in relation to village-level organization.

Nevertheless, as we have seen with other groups, the boundaries between these groups were not always as fixed as they seemed. Ainu cultural differences were clearly recognized during the 17th century, and yet the boundaries between them and Japanese were permeable. Brett Walker writes that some of the Japanese leading families in the contact zone with Ainu may have been descended in part from the Emishi (Walker 2001:26). He also shows that ethnic affiliation did not always determine interactions and alliances. Even Shakushain's War (1669), which led to much stronger Japanese control over the Ainu and is most often interpreted as having been a conflict along ethnic lines, started out involving fighting between Ainu groups, with some sympathetic locally residing Japanese supporting one Ainu faction and other Ainu supporting Japanese troops who later moved to establish control over the region (2001:48–72).

David Howell suggests that the ethnic boundaries between Ainu and Japanese became more and more institutionalized during the Tokugawa period. From the Tokugawa Shogunate's perspective, the northern Matsumae domain, which bordered on the Ainu lands of Ezochi (currently Hokkaido Prefecture), had legitimacy only in its function as intermediary with the Ainu. Thus, the Matsumae were scrupulous to maintain, and to some extent create, the Ainu as a distinct group in relation to which the Japanese (Wajin) were defined. As Howell puts it, "the Japanese in Hokkaido could allow neither the assimilation nor the extermination of the Ainu population because, quite simply, if there were no Ainu, the Matsumae house would have no formal reason to exist" (Howell 1994:85). Certain markers of difference such as language, clothing, and hairstyle were prescribed for Ainu. Such markers, however, were carefully chosen so that they did not interfere with the increasing dependency of Ainu on Japanese commodities and their incorporation into commercial fishing enterprises (1994:86–87).

The outsider minority status of Ainu shifted toward that of insider minorities with the Meiji period (1868–1912) establishment of the modern Japanese nation state and the urgency of clearly defining territorial borders in the face of Russian expansion. Tessa Morris-Suzuki argues that the Ainu, who had been conceived as existing spatially on the margins of Japan, were later formally incorporated into the territory of the nation-state by the more clearly drawn national borders established by the Meiji government. Even as they were spatially incorporated, however, Ainu were conceived as temporally Other, e.g. as prehistoric Japanese (Morris-Suzuki 1998:3–34). Separated primarily in a temporal dimension, the Ainu were the target of numerous assimilation programs that would raise their level of civilization. Most of these programs succeeded in further decimating an already fragile culture without assimilating Ainu into the Japanese mainstream. These programs only further impoverished and stigmatized the Ainu minority (Siddle 1996:51–75; Takagi 1993).

In some sense, however, the incorporation of the Ainu within the boundaries of the modern nation involved the domestication of Ainu difference from that of an absolute Other to one of regional variant (Howell 1996:178). Many contemporary Ainu, however, provide a multicultural twist to the understanding of "Japanese." Kayano Shigeru claims the label of Japanese as much for the Ainu as for their Wajin (mainland Japanese) neighbors and objects to the common opposition between "Japanese" and "Ainu." By using the term "Wajin" he positions mainland Japanese as one ethnicity among various within the Japanese nation (Kayano 1994). It is one part of a larger project to deconstruct the "majority" created during the era of the modern nation-state, and accompanies the Ainu revitalization that has gathered force since the 1970s (Siddle 1996:162–189).

OKINAWANS

The status of the Ryukyu Islands (of which Okinawa is the largest) and their inhabitants shifted in much the same way as did that of Ezochi (Ainu lands) as the Tokugawa shogunate gave way to the Meiji era of modern state-building. In both cases, what had been categorized as foreign lands on the margins of Japan were formally brought within the boundaries of the Japanese state. Okinawans, like the Ainu, were considered a primitive people, yet they had simultaneously enjoyed a somewhat higher status as members of the Kingdom of Ryukyu until 1872, when an imperial edict proclaimed the creation of the Domain of Ryukyu, taking the first step toward formal annexation and the creation of Okinawa as a prefecture in 1879 (Smits 1999:145).

Okinawans were not immediately subject to assimilation programs, however. Japanese policies in Okinawa initially mirrored those later adopted in other Japanese colonies. Prefectural assembly elections were established there in 1909, 19 years after they were in other parts of Japan. National assembly elections were established in 1912, 22 years later. "Universal" conscription was extended to Okinawa in 1898, 25 years later than other parts of Japan. Initially, Okinawans were even discouraged from assimilation through the explicit policy of "preserving old customs" (*kyūkan hozon*) (Smits 1999:144–149).

It was not long, however, before the modern Japanese nation-state moved toward an assimilation policy. Japanese schools constructed on Okinawa in the 1880s were the first step. The Japanese victory in the Sino-Japanese War (1895) motivated many Okinawan intellectuals thereafter to justify active assimilation to Japanese linguistic and cultural standards. Ota Chofu, known as Okinawa's Fukuzawa Yukichi, recommended Okinawans mimic the Japanese even in the way they sneezed (Kano 1997:4). Certain intellectuals, such as historian Higashionna Kanjun and linguist/ folklorist Iha Fuyu, explained Okinawan difference as the result of unnatural policies of the Tokugawa period (Smits 1999:149–155). After the Japanese failed to establish a direct trading relationship with the Ming government in 1615, the Ryukyu Kingdom's tribute–trade relationship with China became an important means for the Japanese to trade indirectly with China. In order for the Ryukyus to maintain their relationship with China, however, it was important that Japanese control of the

Ryukyus be surreptitious following its conquest by the Satsuma domain in 1609. The Japanese thus forbade Ryukyu islanders from wearing Japanese hair or clothing styles, and from taking Japanese names. Over time, Chinese cultural influences in Ryukyuan court life became fairly pronounced (1999:15–49).

While early 20th-century intellectuals constructed Okinawa as liberated from the effects of Tokugawa era policies and returning to its more natural relationship with Japan, by the 1920s, in the face of an increasingly oppressive assimilationist project, some began to question how liberating Meiji policy was. Okinawan writers such as Kushi Fusako and Yamanokuchi Baku were much more critical of Japanese discrimination against Okinawans and were sympathetic to the shared plight of Ainu and of Koreans, to whom the Japanese government had by that time imposed imperial subjecthood (Kano 1997:5). Writing in the 1930s, they moved toward a more positive embrace of Okinawan culture, a direction that was encouraged in the late 1940s and the 1950s when Okinawa was transferred to American military rule (1997:7).

American military rule itself soon stimulated the organization of a "return movement" (*fukki undō*), which once again revived idealistic constructions of Japan as an ancestral land for Okinawans. Okinawans' embrace of Japan in the 1960s while they were still under US rule, as well as after reversion to Japan in 1972, differed in significance from that of Meiji era intellectuals, however, in that the 1972 return was actively willed and brought about by Okinawans, whereas the positions of earlier writers constituted *post facto* justifications of forcible annexation and assimilation. The continued presence of American military bases which occupy so much of Okinawan land 30 years after reversion to Japan, however, has made clear Japanese government complicity with American military exigency, and led to an Okinawan re-evaluation of their relationship with Japan (Hein 2001). Since the late 1980s, Okinawans have protested the obligatory display of the Japanese flag at public events (Field 1993:33–106), and have launched a campaign to teach about the mass murders of local residents committed by Japanese soldiers during the battle of Okinawa at the end of World War II (Figal 2001). Concurrent with the growing critique of Japan, Okinawans have developed a much more positive appreciation of their own distinctive culture, both within Okinawa and in the diaspora spread across Hawaii, Peru, Brazil, and other parts of the Americas (Mori 2003; Nakasone 2002; Ota 1997; Roberson 2001).

CONCLUSION

The insider minorities treated in this chapter vary widely in size, history, consciousness as groups, and criteria for membership. Estimates of size range in the tens of thousands for Ainu, in the hundreds of thousands for Okinawans, Nikkeijin, and *hibakusha*, and in the millions for the disabled and Burakumin. Since the late 1980s some groups have migrated to Japan in numbers large enough to constitute a group there, such as the Nikkeijin, or the *hibakusha* who came into being when the atomic bombs were dropped on Hiroshima and Nagasaki in 1945. Others, such as the disabled, are only now organizing as a group even if disabled people or subgroups have existed throughout Japanese history. The history of the Burakumin can be traced back much further, as can that of the Ainu and Okinawans. Some scholars argue that none of these groups, however, can be said to have existed as a "minority" in the modern sense until the development of the modern nation-state and creation of a much clearer concept of a "majority" (Gladney 1998). Others, however, have argued that recognizing an Other precedes the definition of the Self (see Ishida 1998a, 1998b) and that, in the case of Japan, this process was already well under way during the Tokugawa period (Toby 1984, 1986).

Despite the diversity of these groups, it would be mistaken to assume rigid boundaries between them. There are Koreans, Burakumin, and Nikkeijin among the *hibakusha* (Kogawa 1981; Sodei 1998; Yoneyama 1999). There are Okinawans and Burakumin among the Nikkeijin (Mori 2003; Nakasone 2002). There are members of all these groups who are disabled. Some groups may reside side by side (Burakumin and the disabled), while others are separated by great distances (Ainu and Okinawans). Even in the latter case, however, knowledge of common experiences of discrimination can generate a sense of solidarity. In Okinawa there is a memorial to Ainu soldiers who, while serving in the Japanese army during the battle of Okinawa, tried to protect Okinawan residents from the violence of other Japanese soldiers (Figal 2001).

The discrimination that all these groups have faced justifies an investigation into the conceptual frameworks that have served to stigmatize them. This chapter has examined the related frameworks of the stranger and purity/pollution, which are most often discussed in relation to the Burakumin, but which may provide insight into Japanese perceptions of other minority groups as well. Terms such as irresponsibility (applied to Nikkeijin workers), barbarism (applied to the Ainu and to some extent to Okinawans), disease (applied to *hibakusha*), and deformity or debility (applied to the disabled), may function as transformations of pollution in specific contexts. Like Burakumin, many of the other minority groups can be conceptualized as positioned on thresholds between realms of life and death, health and illness, inside and outside.

Historical accounts reveal the political contingency of systems of classification. What appears to be the immutable status of a given minority at one point in time can shift with changed circumstances. The flexibility in the classification of the Ainu and Okinawans in the modern period casts doubt on the importance of the cultural perspectives. Such an objection, however, depends upon the assumption that culture is fully logical, consistent, and integrated.

Concepts do not have to be applied consistently at all times in order to be considered important aspects of Japanese culture. A culture should be seen as a loosely interlocking sets of practices and associations rather than a logical structure implanted in the minds of all of its members. Micaela di Leonardo suggests thinking in terms of a toolbox of cultural resources which can be accessed at opportune moments (di Leonardo 1984). Although the cultural horizons of certain individuals may be broader than those of others (see Hannerz 1989; Mathews 2000), no one has complete freedom to interpret as they choose. The stranger and the purity/pollution complexes may not be applied consistently at all times, yet we may consider them integral parts of a circumscribed Japanese cultural toolbox.

As with the case of purity/pollution, the racial framework has been subject to politically opportunistic manipulation. The differences in the internal logics of these frameworks may not lead to completely different consequences. For example, the importance of purification rites in Japan suggests that pollution is not a permanent condition, and holds open the possibility that minority individuals or groups can move out of the status of pollution. Nevertheless, many Japanese, long before the advent of modern race thinking, considered Burakumin pollution to pass from one generation to the next. Conversely, race thinking involves the notion that evolutionary development only occurs over very long time spans. Nevertheless, racially minded bureaucrats in the late 19th and early 20th centuries devised policies to assimilate minority groups within a generation or two when it was convenient to do so (Weiner 1994:31–32). This new framework has not replaced that of purity/pollution, but operates alongside it.

Denunciations, litigation, and international pressure can help combat discrimination in Japan and transform the frameworks that consign groups to inferior status or dismiss them altogether (Upham 1987). In 1986 the Japanese prime minister, Yasuhiro Nakasone, could make a statement claiming that the Japanese constituted a homogenous, "monoracial" nation (*tan'itsu minzoku*). The Japanese government did not even recognize the Ainu as an indigenous people until 1997; the impetus for recognition came when the head of the Ainu Association of Hokkaido, Chiichi Nomura, was invited to address the General Assembly of the United Nations in 1993 to celebrate the Year of the World's Indigenous Peoples (Dietz 1999: 362–364). Additionally, recognition was spurred on by the decision in a suit by Ainu against the central government over a dam constructed on Ainu lands. In his ruling, the presiding judge wrote that the Ainu fit the internationally accepted definition of an indigenous group and that the Japanese government had acted illegally in constructing a dam that adversely affected Ainu cultural practices (Dietz 1999:362; Kaizawa 1999:355–358). While the legal forum can be manipulated by dominant groups for their own purposes, it has also proven to be available to minority actors to protest injustices committed against them.

ACKNOWLEDGMENTS

I should like to thank Beth Notar, Michelle Bigenho, Miriam Fujita, and Jennifer Robertson for feedback on drafts of this chapter.

NOTES

1 See Fowler (1996) and Gill (2001) for recent Anglophone studies of day laborers.
2 Editor's note: 1983–92 was the United Nations Decade of Disabled Persons. The following year, 1993, the Japanese government promulgated a Basic Law for Persons with Disabilities which stipulates that disabled but functional members of society must comprise at last 1.6 percent of the workforce of companies having 63 or more employees. However, there is no substantial provision for penalizing companies that ignore the law: a token fine ($US500 per month) is levied for each unfilled position. Many companies choose to pay rather than hire a disabled person: in 1978 alone, the government collected $188 million in fines. The bigger the company, the lower the rate of compliance. This is despite the fact that the Japanese government provides incentives for the employment of

disabled persons, such as covering the first six months of salary and covering all costs associated with renovating space to allow for wheelchair access. In 1986 a political party, the Zatsumin-to ("Miscellaneous Persons Party"), was formed to address the rights of disabled and other marginalized persons. The party was an alliance of the physically disabled, and lesbians and gays. In 1995 the Japanese government formally adopted the Government Action Plan for Persons with Disabilities, a long-term policy with a budget around $80 billion targeted at rehabilitation and the normalization of everyday life. The plan also sought to improve the safety of and quality of life for disabled persons, to improve their ability to achieve a self-sufficient social life, and to establish a barrier-free society. In 1999 one of the most popular books published in Japan – it sold 1 million copies in the first six months – was Ototake Hirotada's *Gotai fumanzoku* (Nobody's Perfect; Kodansha), an autobiography by a profoundly disabled high school boy.

REFERENCES

Caron, Bruce. 1999. On the Downtown Side of Japan's Old Capital. Public Culture 11(3):433–439.

Centro de Estudos Nipo-Brasileiro. 1990. Pesquisa da população de descendentes de japonêses residentes no Brasil (Survey of the Population of Japanese Descendants Resident in Brazil). São Paulo: Centro de Estudos Nipo-Brasileiros.

Chujo, Kazuo. 1986. Genbaku to sabetsu (The Atomic Bomb and Discrimination). Tokyo: Asahi Shimbunsha.

Committee for the Compilation of Materials on Damage Caused by the Atomic Bombs in Hiroshima and Nagasaki. 1981. Hiroshima and Nagasaki. E. Ishikawa and D. L. Swain, trans. New York: Basic Books.

De Ferranti, Hugh. 2000. The Spirit of Tsugaru. Yearbook for Traditional Music 32:186–189.

De Vos, George A., and Hiroshi Wagatsuma. 1995. Cultural Identity and Minority Status in Japan. *In* Ethnic Identity. L. Romanucci-Ross and G. De Vos, eds. Walnut Creek, CA: Alta Mira Press.

di Leonardo, Micaela. 1984. The Varieties of Ethnic Experience. Ithaca, NY: Cornell University Press.

Dietz, Kelly L. 1999. Ainu in the International Arena. *In* Ainu: Spirit of a Northern People. W. W. Fitzhugh and C. O. Dubreuil, eds. Washington, DC: National Museum of Natural History, Smithsonian Institution.

Douglas, Mary. 1966. Purity and Danger. London: Routledge & Kegan Paul.

Dower, John W. 1998. Foreword. *In* Were We the Enemy? Rinjiro Sodei. Boulder, CO: Westview Press.

Engle, David. 1993. Law in the Domains of Everyday Life. *In* Law in Everyday Life. A. Sarat and T. Kearns, eds. Ann Arbor: University of Michigan Press.

Field, Norma. 1993. In the Realm of a Dying Emperor. New York: Vintage Books.

Figal, Gerald. 2001. Waging Peace on Okinawa. Critical Asian Studies 33(1):37–69.

Fowler, Edward. 1993. Minorities in a "Homogeneous" State. *In* What Is a Rim? A. Dirlik, ed. Boulder, CO: Westview Press.

—— 1996. San'ya Blues. Ithaca: Cornell University Press.

Gill, Tom. 2001. Men of Uncertainty: The Social Organization of Day Laborers in Contemporary Japan. New York: State University of New York Press.

Gladney, Dru. 1998. Making Majorities. Stanford: Stanford University Press.

Gottlieb, Nannette. 1998. Discriminatory Language in Japan. Asian Studies Review 22(2):157–173.

Hannerz, Ulf. 1989. Culture between Center and Periphery. Ethos 54(3–4):200–216.

Hayashida, Cullen T. 1975. The *Koshinjo* and *Tanteisha*. Journal of Asian and African Studies 10(3–4):198–208.

Hein, Laura. 2001. Introduction. Critical Asian Studies 33(1):31–36.

Howell, David L. 1994. Ainu Ethnicity and the Boundaries of the Early Modern Japanese State. Past and Present 142:69–93.

—— 1996. Ethnicity and Culture in Contemporary Japan. Journal of Contemporary History 31:171–190.

Hudson, Mark J. 1999. Ruins of Identity. Honolulu: University of Hawaii Press.

Ishida, Takeshi. 1998a. "Dōka" seisaku to kizutsukerareta kannen toshite no "nihon" (jo) ("Assimilation" Policy and the Developing Concept of "Japan," part 1). Shiso 892:47–75.

—— 1998b. "Dōka" seisaku to kizutsukerareta kannen toshite no "nihon" (ge) ("Assimilation" Policy and the Developing Concept of "Japan," part 2). Shisō 893: 141–174.

Kaizawa, Koichi. 1999. Shishirimuka: A Saru River Tale. *In* Ainu: Spirit of a Northern People. W. W. Fitzhugh and C. O. Dubreuil, eds. Washington, DC: National Museum of Natural History, Smithsonian Institution.

Kano, Masanao. 1997. Okinawa no keiken (The Okinawan Experience). Rekishigaku kenkyu 10:2–35.

Kayano, Shigeru. 1994. Our Land Was a Forest. K. Selden and L. Selden, trans. Boulder, CO: Westview Press.

Kogawa, Joy. 1981. Obasan. Toronto: Lester & Orpen Dennys.

Law, Jane Marie. 1997. Puppets of Nostalgia. Princeton: Princeton University Press.

Lesser, Jeffrey. 1999. Negotiating National Identity. Durham, NC: Duke University Press.

—— ed. 2003. Searching for Home Abroad. Durham, NC: Duke University Press.

Linger, Daniel T. 2001. No One Home. Stanford: Stanford University Press.

Maeyama, Takashi. 1996. Esunishitei to burajiru nikkeijin (Ethnicity and Japanese Brazilians). Tokyo: Ochanomizu Shobō.

—— 1997. Iho ni "nihon" o matsuru (Worshiping Japan from Abroad). Tokyo: Ochanomizu Shobō.

Mathews, Gordon. 2000. Global Culture/Individual Identity. London: Routledge.

Matsubara, Yoko. 1998. The Enactment of Japan's Sterilization Laws in the 1940s. Historia Scientiarum 8(2):187–201.

McCormack, Gavan. 1996. Kokusaika. *In* Multicultural Japan. D. Denoon et al., eds. Cambridge: Cambridge University Press.

Mihashi, Osamu. 1987. The Symbolism of Social Discrimination. Current Anthropology 28(4):S19–S29.

Mogi, Toshihiko. 1992. The Disabled in Society. Japan Quarterly 39(4):440–448.

Mori, Koichi. 2003. Identity Transformation among Okinawans and their Descendants in Brazil. *In* Searching for Home Abroad. J. Lesser, ed. Durham, NC: Duke University Press.

Morris-Suzuki, Tessa. 1998. Re-inventing Japan. Armonk, NY: M. E. Sharpe.

Nakasone, Ronald Y. 2002. Okinawan Diaspora. Honolulu: University of Hawaii Press.

Neary, Ian. 1989. Political Protest and Social Control in Prewar Japan. Manchester: Manchester University Press.

Ninomiya, Shigeaki. 1933. An Inquiry Regarding the Origin, Development, and Present Situation of the Eta in Relation to the History of Social Classes in Japan. Transactions of the Asiatic Society of Japan. 2nd ser., 10:47–152.

Ohnuki-Tierney, Emiko. 1984. Illness and Culture in Contemporary Japan. Cambridge: Cambridge University Press.

—— 1987. Monkey as Mirror. Princeton: Princeton University Press.

Ohnuki-Tierney, Emiko. 1998. A Conceptual Model for the Historical Relationship between the Self and the Internal and External Others. *In* Making Majorities. D. Gladney, ed. Stanford: Stanford University Press.

Ooms, Herman. 1996. Tokugawa Village Practice. Berkeley: University of California Press.

Ota, Yoshinobu. 1997. Appropriating Media, Resisting Power. *In* Between Resistance and Revolution. R. G. Fox and O. Starn, eds. New Brunswick: Rutgers University Press.

Otsubo, Sumiko, and James R. Bartholomew. 1998. Eugenics in Japan. Science in Context 11(3–4):545–565.

Roberson, James. 2001. Uchinaa pop. Critical Asian Studies 33(2):211–242.

Robertson, Jennifer. 2002. Blood Talks: Eugenic Modernity and the Creation of New Japanese. History and Anthropology 13(3):191–216.

Roth, Joshua H. 2002. Brokered Homeland. Ithaca: Cornell University Press.

Siddle, Richard. 1996. Race, Resistance and the Ainu of Japan. London: Routledge.

Smits, Gregory. 1999. Visions of Ryukyu. Honolulu: University of Hawaii Press.

Sodei, Rinjiro. 1998. Were We the Enemy? ed. J. Junkerman. Boulder, CO: Westview Press.

Takagi, Hiroshi. 1993. Fashizumuki, ainu minzoku no dokaron (Debates Concerning the Assimilation of the Ainu during the Fascist Period). *In* Bunka to fashizumu (Culture and Fascism). S. Akazawa and K. Kitagawa, eds. Tokyo: Nihon Keizai Hyoronsha.

Takaki, Masayuki. 1992. Sabetsu yogo no kiso chishiki (Basic Facts about Discriminatory Language). Tokyo: Doyo Bijitsusha.

Toby, Ronald. 1984. State and Diplomacy in Early Modern Japan. Princeton: Princeton University Press.

—— 1986. Carnival of the Aliens. Monumenta Nipponica 41(4):415–456.

Treat, John Whittier. 1995. Writing Ground Zero. Chicago: University of Chicago Press.

Tsuda, Takeyuki. 1998. The Stigma of Ethnic Difference. Journal of Japanese Studies 24(2):317–358.

Upham, Frank. 1987. Law and Social Change in Postwar Japan. Cambridge, MA: Harvard University Press.

Ventura, Rey. 1992. Underground in Japan. London: Jonathan Cape.

Walker, Brett. 2001. The Conquest of Ainu Lands. Berkeley: University of California Press.

Watanabe, Masako, ed. 1995. Kyōdō kenkyū dekasegi nikkei burajirujin (Collaborative Research on Japanese Brazilian Migrant Workers). Tokyo: Akashi Shoten.

Weiner, Michael. 1994. Race and Migration in Imperial Japan. London: Routledge.

—— ed. 1997. Japan's Minorities. London: Routledge.

Yamaguchi, Masao. 1977. Kingship, Theatricality, and Marginal Reality in Japan. *In* Text and Context. R. K. Jain, ed. Philadelphia: Institute for the Study of Human Issues.

Yamashita, Karen. 2001. Circle K Cycles. Minneapolis: Coffee House Press.

Yoneyama, Lisa. 1999. Hiroshima Traces. Berkeley: University of California Press.

Yoshida, Teigo. 1981. The Stranger as God. Ethnology 20(2):87–99.

CHAPTER 7

Japan's Ethnic Minority: Koreans

Sonia Ryang

THE BACKGROUND

Lately, titles of academic books on Japan include references to multiculturalism and multiethnicity, ostensibly to emphasize that Japanese society is no longer homogeneous (e.g. Lie 2001; Maher and Macdonald 1995; Weiner 1997). The once deafening discourse on Japanese cultural uniqueness, together with the discourse of homogeneity so dominant in Japan during the 1970s and 1980s, is significantly lower in tone. Japan was never and is not homogeneous; this was true even before, and it is certainly true after its empire-building in Asia from the late 19th century through the mid-20th century. The homogeneity discourse in Japan of the 1970s and 1980s is a historical product of the postwar Japanese self-representation, engineered by the government itself, and avidly supported by lay and intellectual writers.

The Japanese government is willfully oblivious to its colonial and imperial oppression in Asia prior to 1945. What is less known is the status of the former colonial immigrants, subjects who came or were brought to Japan during the imperial period, such as Koreans and Chinese, who continue to live in Japan. From the government's point of view, an insistence on Japan's racial homogeneity erases these immigrants and colonial and wartime reparation for them. Yet, what troubles serious scholars of ethnic minorities in Japan is the uncanny coincidence between the government's version of homogeneity accompanied by its amnesiac treatment of the past, and the relative inattention to Japan's minorities among the mainstream scholars of Japan.

In this chapter I focus on Koreans in Japan, although Japan's ethnic minorities would include Chinese residents who are also the former colonial subjects, and other foreign residents including temporary guest workers from Brazil, Chile, Iran, India, Pakistan, Indonesia, Sri Lanka, the Philippines, etc., and the so-called new-comers from China and Korea. According to the Ministry of Justice statistics, for 2000, foreign nationals totaled 1,686,444 persons. Koreans numbered 635,269 (37.7 percent), Chinese 335,575 (19.9 percent), and Brazilians 254,394 (15.1 percent), for example (www.moj.go.jp). Until very recently, however, "ethnic minority" in

Japan referred predominantly to Koreans who came to Japan during the colonial period (1910–45) and settled in Japan, and their descendants. It is only in the 1990s that Japan's foreign residents began to increase at average rate of a little over 60,000 persons a year; during the 1980s the yearly increase was less than 30,000 (www.moj. go.jp).

What distinguishes Koreans in Japan, and more precisely Korean old-comers in Japan, from the rest of the recent labor immigrants, including Korean new-comers, is complex yet clear. "Old-comer" Koreans were colonial migrants who moved from the periphery of the empire to the imperial metropolis, where they lived as sub-human subordinates to the ruling race. When Japanese colonial rule ended in August 1945, there were 2.4 million Koreans in Japan (Wagner 1951). The majority repatriated as soon as the war was over, but about 600,000 remained in Japan for various reasons: some had established their livelihood in Japan, and others were students, for example. Those Koreans who elected to stay in Japan found themselves stranded there due to the partition of their homeland (1945); the rise of mutually antagonistic regimes in the peninsula (1948); an insecure politico-economic situation; and the eventual civil (and international) war (1950–53) that made the partition more or less permanent. The subsequent Cold War that polarized Asia and the world deeply affected the everyday lives of Koreans who remained in Japan after World War II. A review of their postwar historical background is in order.

As soon as the war was over, Koreans in Japan were split between the supporters of North Korea and those of South Korea. Although more than 98 percent of the first-generation Koreans in Japan traced their place of origin in the provinces in today's South Korea, the postwar atmosphere of leftist revival and anti-Japanese nationalism strongly manifested among Koreans in Japan drove the majority of them to support the northern government which was then under the Soviets. An agreement reached just before the end of World War II between the Allied powers, Soviet Union, and China placed the part of Korea north of the 38th parallel under the Soviet Union, and the southern part under the American military government. At the time, this arrangement was understood as a temporary one (for details, see Cumings 1981).

The American military government preserved the colonial administrative structure, including the colonial bureaucracy. The economy was in chaos in the south, and a general atmosphere of terror prevailed. Anxious to return to their homeland, yet dissatisfied about the way things had turned out in the south, the originally southern Koreans rallied around the Sovietized north under a leadership that was able to claim authentically anti-Japanese roots, represented by the former anti-colonial guerrilla fighters, including the 33-year-old Kim Il Sung. The fresh, untainted appearance of the north, relatively free from foreign intervention, appealed to Koreans in Japan. Their support for the north would soon be reinforced by the socioeconomic reforms introduced by the northern regime, including the land redistribution among peasants, the nationalization of the ownership of heavy industry, and a gender equality law. Meanwhile the south, in contrast, was experiencing socioeconomic collapse and rising rates of inflation, and political instability. Moreover the American military government often took harsh measures against Koreans. Because of the widely held understanding that the partition was a temporary arrangement, a great many Koreans in Japan hoped that a unified Korea would take the form of the northern regime. In short, their support for the north was based more on nationalism than on communism.

Needless to say, not all followed the north. Whereas the north-supporters were identified with the leftist Choryōn (an abbreviation of what is in English the League of Koreans in Japan; hereafter the League), the south-supporters joined Mindan (the Association of Koreans Remaining in Japan). During the postwar period, the League and Mindan both had the character of interim organizations; each assumed that all Koreans in Japan would eventually return to Korea, and each defined its role to facilitate that end. The Korean War, however, changed this. Mindan sent volunteers to the front in Korea as a warring party, which infuriated the supporters of North Korea as a fratricidal act, making it impossible for any dialogue between these two opposing camps to happen in a foreseeable future.

By the time the Korean War began, the League had been suppressed by the Supreme Commander, Allied Powers, in 1949; its public support for North Korea became a problem for the US occupation authorities, especially after the reversion of the occupation policy in 1947. After the suppression, the north-supporters joined the Japanese Communist Party en masse and reorganized themselves as Minjōn (the Democratic Front), now placed directly under the supervision of the party. Under the party's direction, they engaged with subversive campaigns against the war and the Japanese authorities, which made them even more vulnerable in the face of amassing surveillance by the authorities against leftist Koreans.

The north-supporters and south-supporters shared a strong antipathy toward the Japanese. It needs to be borne in mind that they were predominantly first-generation Koreans who had just been emancipated from colonial rule. As is the case elsewhere, the former colonial subject often becomes truly anti-colonial after the fact. These Koreans were no exception: they detested anything that embodied the colonial past.

The bloody atrocities and fratricide committed by both sides during the Korean War divided Koreans living both on the peninsula and in Japan permanently into mutually hostile groups. Their hostility toward each other was so deep that even their shared antipathy toward the Japanese and common local origins in southern Korea failed to open any dialog between them. Koreans in Japan thus offered themselves as the willing parties in the Cold War polarization that reshaped their political orientation from that of a decolonized people to that of a people divided by iron curtains. This transformation took place within a decade of national independence. The lack of communication between north- and south-supporters outlasted the Cold War in Europe. At least for the period that the first generation constituted the main cast of actors in expatriate politics, the clear division of Koreans in Japan was the mirror image of the peninsula itself.

Koreans lived in Japan as a population with no civil status. This fact is crucial to keep in mind when studying about Koreans in Japan. It presents a situation quite different from that of other ethnic minorities studied by anthropologists. When World War II ended, Japan was placed under Allied occupation. Both the Japanese government and occupation authorities assumed that the solution for non-Japanese residents such as Koreans and Chinese, that is, former colonial immigrants, was repatriation. It needs to be emphasized that for the majority of Koreans also, repatriation was the only solution: they did not see an alternative possibility of living in Japan, due mainly to strong anti-Japanese, nationalistic sentiment. Moreover, a great many Koreans lost their livelihood with the end of the war, since they had either been brought to Japan by force for wartime home-front production or come to Japan looking for better job opportunities related to the wartime economy. As stated above, in a few years, the number of Koreans remaining in Japan was down to around 600,000.

The civil status of those Koreans who remained in Japan was precarious and unclear from the outset. Prior to the collapse of the empire, as far as Japanese domestic law was concerned, they were Japanese nationals. For example, Korean male taxpayers in Japan could vote and be elected to political offices. However, their colonial status was clearly marked by way of household registry. All the registers that originated in the colonies had to be kept in the colonies, i.e. outlands or *gaichi*, while all the Japanese registers that originated in Japan proper, i.e. inland or *naichi*, were kept in Japan; moving the *gaichi* register to *naichi* was prohibited by law and vice versa. When the war was over, the Japanese government relied on the *naichi* registry to determine who was included in the category of the Japanese. Of course this led to some unexpected mishaps by classifying Japanese women who were married to Korean men in Korea as non-Japanese and Koreans who were adopted into Japanese house-holds as Japanese – but these were only few in number. In a way, this arrangement of relying on the *gaichi/naichi* distinction is an unusual practice for the Japanese government, considering the *jus sanguinus* tradition of Japanese law in determining nationality. For Koreans in Japan, this principle worked as a definite exclusion from Japanese civil status.

On the agreement of the San Francisco Treaty between Japan and the US in 1952, all Koreans in Japan finally lost Japanese nationality completely and were now placed under the Alien Registration Law. The Japanese government unilaterally imposed this measure on them, and no option for Japanese nationality was made available, except for the already established procedure for naturalization. This kind of one-sided forfeiture of nationality was unprecedented and not followed by any major ex-imperialist metropolitan states in their postcolonial settlement: when the African colonies of the European nations became independent in the 1960s, nationality was decided in such a way to minimize the possibility of producing stateless people. In the 1952 case above, all Koreans in Japan became completely stateless, since Japan did not have any diplomatic relations with either regime of the Korean peninsula. It was only in 1965 that Japan and South Korea entered into diplomatic relations, when, by a treaty, the Japanese government recognized South Korean nationality. This had a grave political impact on the Cold War-torn expatriate community of Koreans.

Since they had joined the Japanese Communist Party because of the suppression of the League, Korean leftists were frustrated. The party at that time held to a belief in East Asian simultaneous revolution. The logic of this forced Koreans to serve the Japanese revolution first. Nationalists among Korean members insisted on going their separate way in order to directly contribute to a Korean revolution. After months of heated discussion in 1955, Korean leftists dissolved Minjōn, severed their tie with the Japanese Communist Party, and organized Chongryun, the general association of Korean residents in Japan. Chongryun declared that Koreans in Japan were North Korea's overseas citizens and therefore would not wage an anti-Japanese campaign and would abide by Japanese law. It firmly endorsed its leadership as North Korea and its enemy as the South Korean "puppet clique" and its US "overlord." By taking this stance, Chongryun successfully placed itself outside the intervention of the Japanese government, and this enabled it to concentrate on expanding ethnic education, now designed to educate Korean children in Japan to become North Korea's future generation.

This was not totally an ideological fallacy; prior to 1965, North Korea expressed concern over Koreans remaining in Japan, while South Korea ignored them. North Korea opened the repatriation route for Koreans in Japan in 1959 and began sending education aid from 1957. It was later said that North Korea at that time needed a labor force because of its enormous human losses in the Korean War. At any rate, a total of about 90,000 Koreans "repatriated" to North Korea between 1959 and the early 1970s; here "repatriation" is not quite the right word, since, as has been mentioned, the majority of the returnees did not originally come from the north. The repatriation was a one-way journey, since there were (and still are) no diplomatic relations between North Korea and Japan.

The 1965 deal between Japan and South Korea changed the balance of power. Because the treaty offered permanent residence only to those Koreans who opted to apply for South Korean nationality, Chongryun began losing its affiliates who still had their families in South Korea and wanted to visit them and their hometown. From the Japanese government's point of view, typical of the colonialist strategy, the 1965 treaty was a divide-and-rule policy: the treaty made it a practical condition that Koreans who supported North Korea would remain stateless, while Koreans who supported South Korea would be given fuller rights in Japan. At the same time, Koreans in Japan were by this time useful offshore pawns for both Koreas in their Cold War politics.

It was only in the early 1980s that, regardless of their nationality, Koreans obtained permanent residence in Japan. Having ratified the International Covenants on Human Rights in 1979 and joined the UN Refugee Convention in 1982, the Japanese government was forced to reform the treatment of Koreans in Japan. Permanent residence came with the makeshift travel document that enabled Koreans in Japan to travel outside Japan for the first time in 35 years, since the end of World War II. Since the early 1980s many reforms have been enacted regarding the Alien Registration Law, including the abolition of fingerprinting upon registration and allowing a longer period of leave from Japan, with a re-entry permit.

Now, at the beginning of the twenty-first century, many things have changed in terms of the everyday lives of Koreans in Japan. Their living standard is much higher, their educational level much better, and the general social awareness among the Japanese regarding the minorities, though still lagging behind the international standard, has improved tremendously. At the same time, culturally, Koreans in Japan have become very much Japanized now that a fourth or even fifth generation is being born in Japan. With the easing tension between North and South Korea, reflecting the end of the Cold War elsewhere, Koreans in Japan, who used to be divided into opposing camps, entrenched in the division of their homeland, are now seeing their future away from Korea itself, rooted in Japanese culture and society, no matter how marked the discrimination against them might be. The majority of the younger generation speaks only Japanese and has never been to Korea or does not wish to live there. No longer is the repatriation of all Koreans a future goal for Koreans in Japan; no longer is the reunification of the homeland their utopia.

RESEARCH TRENDS

It is important to register that only now are studies on Koreans in Japan becoming popular among Euro-American scholars of Japan. This means that those scholars who have recently taken up the subject would have a very different understanding of the situation of Koreans, as their life in Japan has improved greatly, and scholars need to be aware of the economic and political history of the Korean community in Japan.

Not many anthropologists – either Japanese or Euro-American – have participated in the study of Koreans in Japan. In Japan, it is historians and sociologists who have traditionally researched in this subject area, while Japanese anthropologists have studied overseas and taken a more politically unproblematic topic for their subject. So, for example, while historians studied Japan's colonial rule in Korea, economic extortion, and political persecution, anthropologists studied shamanism and kinship; while sociologists combined studies of Koreans in Japan with Burakumin studies, anthropologists ignored them. Anthropologists studied Okinawan kinship, but not the systematic oppression and exploitation of the islands by the central government; they studied Cheju island shamanism in Korea, but not the 1949 anti-American uprising on the island and the subsequent exodus of refugees to Japan.

Even among Japanese sociologists it was only in the 1980s that the voices of Korean informants became a central point of research. Fukuoka Yasunori's work on the identity of young Koreans in Japan is pioneering (Fukuoka and Tsujiyama 1991a, 1991b; Fukuoka 1993). It has contributed to portraying the diverse lifestyles that the younger generation of Koreans has adopted, breaking away from the models that their parents' and grandparents' generations presented. But the problem that Fukuoka's work has created is to simplify the classification of Koreans in Japan into a set of finite types, including the homeland orientation, the naturalization orientation, the individualist, and the assimilationist (Fukuoka 1993; see also Fukuoka 2000). Although it is true that elements of these types have their origins in the debate among Koreans in Japan over the issue of how they should associate themselves with the homeland – represented by Kang Sang-jung and Yang T'ae-ho (Kang 1991a, 1991b; Yang 1991a, 1991b) and introduced in English in Norma Field's seminal article (1993) – the corpus of Korean authors and scholars in Japan does resist this kind of typology.

But, in their turn, some Korean authors in Japan write from overly personalized (and often irresponsible) and fragmented positions (e.g. Kaneshiro 2000; Kyō 1987; Lee 1997; Yu 1995). It is regrettable that those writings that treat the issues of Koreans in Japan from a position that is removed from the collective past are the ones that are becoming increasingly popular among both Japanese readers and Western researchers, on the basis of a postmodern reinterpretation of a "heavy" ethnic past and movement from that toward a personalized zone: such an approach must ultimately misrepresent the true situation, considering that there is continuing structural discrimination against Koreans and other minorities in Japan. At least it needs to be said that any individual Korean writer writing about their personal world, fictionally or nonfictionally, has to be considered with reference to the collective concerns, no matter how general they might be, of Koreans in Japan as a whole, since the ethnic Korean subject (if you like) has not become (and perhaps will not become for some time) a bourgeois individual subject with inner autonomy and freedom of choice: their freedom is much too constrained by the government-engineered system of exclusion, and their autonomy too hampered by the negative self-image caused by the ongoing ethnic stereotyping and stigmatization in Japan.

Ethnographic works on Koreans in Japan did not appear until the mid-1990s. Harajiri Hideki's fieldwork-oriented studies of Koreans in Japan can be seen as a major contribution by a Japanese scholar in this field (Harajiri 1997, 1998). Of course, there are many biographical and autobiographical novels by Korean authors, which offer a great deal of ethnographic insight into the community (e.g., Gen 2000; Kin 1986; Ri 1972; Yi 1993). Also, there is a wealth of research combining life-histories, testimonials, local history, and archival investigation carried out by Korean researchers in Japan (e.g. Kim 1985; Pak 1992). In the academic and political portrayals of Koreans in Japan, the terminology has posited a considerable problem, and it continues to do so. Reflecting that in the alien registration *kankoku* meant the Republic of Korea, those Koreans in Japan who have South Korean nationality are called *zainichi kankokujin*, and the rest of Koreans whose alien registration simply states *chōsen*, Korea, are called *zainichi chōsenjin*. But the divide between the two is not clear. Those who have South Korean nationality may be educated in Chongryun schools and may identify themselves as *zainichi chōsenjin* (see Ryang 1997). As a result, the Japanese media have sometimes resorted to a non-offensive term for everybody, such as *zainichi korian*. Currently, the term *zainichi* (literally, "existing in Japan"), having no connotations of Korea or Korean, is often used to denote Koreans in Japan. In my view, this terminology is not free from problems: why say "existing in Japan" when they are excluded from many opportunities and rights that the Japanese enjoy? Nevertheless, this term has attained a certain currency to denote, without offending anyone, Koreans in Japan.

It was only in the late 1990s that serious ethnographic studies on Koreans in Japan written in English began to appear. The reason why it took Western anthropologists of Japan so long to begin studying Koreans in Japan is complex, but it definitely concerns the way in which Japan has captured the attention of anthropology in the West. Ever since *The Chrysanthemum and the Sword* (Benedict 1946), postwar discourses on Japanese culture and society have taken a predominantly holistic approach that presumed a homogeneous national character. Although not all anthropologists were dominated by holism, the influence was significant enough to mask exceptions, deviations, and transgressions from the eyes of researchers. Koreans in Japan are one great deviation and transgression, or even violation, vis-à-vis the concept of Japanese racial homogeneity and Japanese cultural uniqueness.

Today many anthropologists of Japan study Koreans and other minorities in Japan. What has lately attracted our attention is the widespread use of "multi" before adjectives such as "ethnic" and "cultural" and defining the name "Japan." Many books now introduce the reader to a new Japan that anthropologists did not know before and these tend to be written on the basis of interviews and fieldwork if not necessarily always written by anthropologists (e.g. Suzuki and Oiwa 1996). Ethnographies and other books solely on Koreans in Japan are also available today, as against in the past when the 1980 volume by Changsoo Lee and George De Vos remained the only source (Lee and De Vos 1980; see Ryang 1997 and 2000).

The recent ethnographic trend of introducing Koreans into the scene of Japanese studies presents a few problems. On the one hand, the study of the ethnic identity of Koreans leads to an inward-looking exploration of the community and often fails to connect the issue of Koreans in Japan with the overall state politics of the Japanese government. In this regard a mere denunciation of ethnic discrimination will not do, either, since it simply highlights the sufferings of Koreans as a minority without delivering an analysis of the mechanisms – both systematic and psychological, political and personal – of racial discrimination and oppression. Moreover, an excessive emphasis on the poverty and structural oppression that Koreans suffer has in the past presented this community as dehumanized and lacking in self-esteem. This approach loses the sight of agency and subjecthood among Koreans in Japan.

At the other end of the spectrum there is a trend that ultimately neutralizes the political nature of the oppression and discrimination that Koreans in Japan are subjected to by reducing the difficulties that they face to the level of a personal issue. Some of the increasing number of writings on Koreans' use of ethnic names which suggest that this has to be seen as a personal decision and not in the context of the political constraints imposed on the expatriate community by the Cold War, represent one such trend: often based on interviews with adolescent informants, this type of study, though very important, creates a vacuum-like space of individual freedom of choice which gives a false picture in light of legal and civil restrictions that every Korean individual is subjected to within the Japanese state structure.

While it may be true that studies on Koreans in Japan can posit a counter-discourse vis-à-vis holistic studies of Japanese culture, a narrowly focused ethnography of Koreans in Japan can also create a different form of holism, representing them as a single people and thereby reifying their diverse political and cultural orientations – as diverse as those of the Japanese mainstream population. As I have said, the long-lasting Cold War-inspired division created a deep divide between Koreans with different political allegiances, while the generation gap between the old and the young created a vertical chasm cutting across the community, and often the family. In addition, a deep-seated Confucian ethic that first-generation Koreans implanted in the younger generation manifests itself in the form of a confrontation between younger Korean males and females.

Furthermore, those who grew up in a more "Japanized" environment are undoubtedly in a different position, both emotionally and practically, from those whose upbringing was more immersed in the Korean neighborhood, ethnic education, and other important daily paraphernalia such as food, festivals, rituals, religion, names, language, tone of voice, smell, and life's small conventions. It is therefore dangerous to present Koreans in Japan as one people, as a simple appendix to Japanese homogeneity. Any ready-made typology defies the complexity and flexibility of division, alliance, and re-alliance among Koreans in Japan today.

RECENT DEBATES: A CASE STUDY

In this section, in order to highlight the debates that are going on among Koreans in Japan and which reflect the differentiated and often irreconcilable positions of individual Korean thinkers, I shall look at two recent works by Korean scholars in Japan.

Suh Kyung Sik is the younger brother of Suh Sung and Suh Jun Sik, the two Korean former students from Japan who were accused of being North Korean spies and jailed for more than a decade, from the 1970s through the 1980s, under the South Korean dictatorship. In his recent publication *Bundan o ikiru: "zainichi" o koete* (Living through [National] Division: Beyond "Zainichi"), Suh proposes that Koreans in Japan need to see themselves as existing in continuity with their nation, i.e. Korea. This does not mean that his position is identifiable with the position proposing to join the homeland; Suh's position is to emphasize the national subjecthood of Koreans in Japan, which is free from a territorialized concept of the nation (1997:ch. 3). From this, Suh suggests a "nation-in-diaspora" of Koreans in the world. According to him, Koreans must recognize that their ontological security is subject to the nation-state politics involving Japan and the two Koreas and beyond. This does not mean that Suh is concerned with immediate and practical matters regarding issues of nationality or citizenship. In his analysis, the Korean nation does not have to be territorially confined in Korea, but can exist in the world. While the Korean homeland has a distinct meaning for Koreans in diaspora, this does not mean that everybody must go back and live there. Rather, he is interested in ethos, sentiment, and inner quest as historical subjects that Koreans in Japan must ontologically define for themselves. Here he brings in the notion of the nation – if not a practical national belonging – as a conceptual base of his proposition.

The other author I wish to discuss is Chung Daekyun. Chung also has an interesting personal relationship with South Korea, where he lived and taught as a college professor for more than a decade. Chung's proposition is the mirror image of Suh's. Chung suggests that all Koreans in Japan must become absorbed in Japanese society, live as members of the Japanese cultural community, and abandon the unrealistic tie with their homeland, which has already been eroding for some time. In fact, according to Chung, Koreans in Japan are already culturally full members of Japanese society and therefore there is no need to insist on special status (2001). If, suggests Chung, they are not happy with the way Japanese naturalization law is set up, they need to direct their efforts at reforming this law and demand Japanese nationality by some alternative method. Chung also concerns himself not so much with practicality – for example he has nothing to suggest in terms of an alternative method of obtaining Japanese nationality other than naturalization – but more with the basic attitude of Koreans in Japan toward Japanese society (see below).

What is new in my view in the case of both writers is that neither falls into a clear-cut right/left classification that has so pervasively influenced the way Koreans classified themselves. Suh's idea of a "nation in diaspora" can be criticized by more orthodox nationalists as idealistic and blurring the focus of loyalty that should be directed to the homeland only. Chung's stance will be open to wider criticism, both nationalist and otherwise, on a charge of pro-Japanese defeatism, but he does not make himself readily available to this charge as he directs his argument against the widely shared sentiment that Koreans in Japan today are different from Koreans in Korea in all practical senses. Since they are already so similar to mainstream Japanese society, why choose victimhood or celebrate the culture of the victim?

In a crucial point, however, these authors are completely divided: this concerns the notion of the nation, or nationhood. According to Chung:

Are Korean second- and third-generation parents prepared to answer when their children ask them why they are not Japanese, although they were born in Japan? For those parents...South Korea is not the land toward which they have the sense of belonging...Despite this reality, why do they retain South Korean nationality? To have South Korean nationality means to share a destiny with South Korea. Although our status in Japan was decided by the Japanese and South Korean governments, how can we explain the fact that we identify our destiny with a country which we do not even feel we belong to?...

So, what could be the solution? I propose that Koreans in Japan switch the belonging itself that fits their identity. In other words, we should obtain Japanese nationality and live as a full member of this [Japanese] society. If necessary, we should insist on the freedom of choice of the nationality and criticize the [current] naturalization procedure and its shortcomings. Obtaining Japanese nationality is also helpful for Koreans in Japan in creating an equal relationship with Koreans in Korea. (Chung 2001:4–5; my translation)

As can be seen, Chung bases his proposition on the assumption that one's national/ethnic identity has to coincide with one's legal nationality. This assumption is itself ideological – it stands on the premise that nationality defines identity. In other words, the nationality that one is born with *must* reflect a set of characteristics (like "blood" in biological determinism), the sense of belonging, and loyalty to that nation. Only those who possess the national characteristics of a nation are members of that nation; conversely, those who possess these characteristics must have that nation's nationality. The construal of these characteristics is, however, largely arbitrary and politically predetermined, based on the nationalist myth.

Chung's ideas are not new: they correspond with the traditional Japanese government's position toward Koreans in Japan: "Be naturalized; if not, go back to Korea." They also correspond in principle to the traditional Korean attitude toward Japanese nationality: "Don't be naturalized; if you do, you'll become Japanese to the core." In other words, both firmly rest on the idea that legal nationality reflects one's essence, ethnic roots, and identity. What is new, however, is his writing position: whereas the existing discourses on the pros and cons of naturalization posited Koreans and Japanese as opposing parties, Chung posits Koreans in Japan and Koreans in Korea as the opposing sides.

His denial of South Korea being a home for Koreans in Japan is the main framework for suggesting that Koreans in Japan firmly root themselves in Japan and legitimize their existence in Japan by adopting Japanese nationality. The interesting thing about Chung is that he does not necessarily suggest that Koreans be naturalized within the confines of the existing naturalization law. He is, rather, suggesting this as a concept: he alludes to the fact that the existing naturalization law is not satisfactory and one should criticize it, in order to improve the chances for Koreans in Japan to be naturalized easily. His more important emphasis throughout the book is how much Koreans in Japan are different from Koreans in Korea, a fact he believes he can testify to on the basis of his 14-year experience of having lived there. In this vein of thought, Koreans in Korea – no matter what they turn out to be, reflecting the historical transformation of their own society – always represent the "Korean nation," and those who do not behave like them do not belong to that nation.

Suh's ideas also contain nationhood at their core, though in a very different form. Suh suggests that Koreans belong to the Korean nation no matter where they are and, by implication, which legal nationality they have, because of residence, place of birth, and other personal factors. His notion of the nation is conceived expansively, deterritorialized, and transnational. Since Koreans are one of the most dispersed nations in the world and, particularly, because their Korean homeland is still divided into halves, Suh emphatically suggests that Koreans – no matter where they are – must discover their imagined Korean homeland, be connected with it, and construct strong emotional and moral ties with it.

Suh encourages his Korean readers to look beyond the narrow confines of Japan and find the way to be Korean regardless of where one is in the global landscape. Understandably, Suh is highly interested in the Jewish diaspora, the Holocaust, the work of Primo Levi, subaltern studies, Fanon's anti-colonial nationalism, and the history of slavery, and tries to synthesize the case of Koreans in Japan in close connection with other persecuted and divided peoples in the world. In this sense, Suh is very new; he goes several steps further beyond the myopic Japan–Korea or Korea–Korea oppositions of existing views.

WHAT FUTURE NOW?

What the difference in opinion as seen in Chung and Suh can suggest in terms of possible further anthropological studies of Koreans in Japan is immense. Chung and Suh point to the reality where no holism can work. Koreans in Japan are not a simple appendix to Japanese homogeneity. Rather, we must take our point of departure from the supposition that Koreans in Japan are diverse people, replete with subtle and sometimes more acute differences. We have known this for some time, but what is new is that the confrontation and internal division among Koreans in Japan are now multiple, not just north/south or nationalist/assimilationist. Multifaceted debates subtly align people through various nodes in an unpredictable and non-partisan way. This does not, however, mean that all we therefore need to do is to look at individualized opinions and personal worlds: such a "personalization" or "individuation" of a group of people who are known to be oppressed and discriminated against would bring about a conservative turn, as it would reduce the collective suffering and history of persecution to matters of personal difference and individual sentiment.

There certainly are real, concrete issues that we need to address politically regarding the situation that Koreans in Japan continue to face there, including civil rights, political franchise, ethnic discrimination, unresolved postwar reparation, and proper education of the Japanese with regard to their nation's past deeds in Asia. Anthropologists must pay attention to both collective and personal issues, guarding themselves against the possibility both of turning the study of Koreans in Japan into voyeurism or dilettantism and of rendering their everyday life into an overly politicized sphere thereby forgetting intricate human aspects of a community that has been torn apart by the Cold War. In order for such a study to emerge, the researcher must first be critically familiar with Japanese society – the way in which certain foreigners are disenfranchised from social activities – and then with the history and changing everyday lives in the Korean community. Occasionally, I receive an inquiry from prospective professional anthropologists about the possibility of studying Koreans in Japan. To my disappointment, many are interested in Koreans in Japan mainly because they see a marketing niche in such research, as it would offer a glimpse of an unusual, unfamiliar, and hidden enclave of Japanese society. Voyeurism or sensationalism cannot be a good basis for studying Koreans, or any minority.

Having said this, there are great many topics to explore in this sub-field. Koreans in Japan can offer a set of topics that takes us beyond anthropological studies of Japan by necessitating the comparative discussion of themes such as micro power relations within an ethnic community, as in the cases of labor aristocracies, the intersections between ethnicity/race and gender, the feminisms of color, and generational differences within a community. Internal to the Korean community, there still remain a number of issues that require serious attention. These include language and the linguistic practice of partial bilinguality, ideological commitment to the homeland and its transformation, and the tension between regional identities attached to the Japanese locality and their coexistence with the wider, collective memory of horror and violence under Japanese colonial rule, while there is a wide range of social groups within the community that require critical and close anthropological study, including Korean children who attend Japanese schools, Koreans who intermarry Japanese and raise bicultural children, families that are directly influenced by the history of the peninsula, involving family dispersion and reunion, women whose voices are not heard enough due to male dominance, adolescents who are going through growing pains that come with the further twist of being a Korean in Japan, small business owners who employ the so-called newcomers from South Korea as well as foreign laborers, intellectuals who are actively making their voices heard in the Japanese milieu, first-generation Koreans and their life histories involving personal experience through colonial and postcolonial periods, and the human flow between the peninsula and Japan including shamans, pedlars, and tourists. (Needless to say, studying Koreans in Japan requires both fluent Japanese and adequate Korean, particularly studying the old generation.)

Most importantly, studies of Koreans in Japan can offer a point from which more critical views of Japanese society and Japanese studies can be formed. Already many Japanese and Korean researchers in Japan are trying to go beyond the Japan/Korea dichotomy and extend their critiques toward studies of identities, both majority and minority, especially in such fields as education, sociology, and history. Western anthropological studies of Koreans in Japan (participated in by both Western and non-Western anthropologists) can make an important contribution to this, by connecting studies of Koreans in Japan to the mainstream debates found in Western academe.

REFERENCES

Benedict, Ruth. 1946. The Chrysanthemum and the Sword. Boston: Houghton Mifflin.
Chung, Daekyun. 2001. Zainichi kankokujin no shūen (The End of Koreans in Japan). Tokyo: Bungei Shunjusha.
Cumings, Bruce. 1981. The Origins of the Korean War, vol. 1: Liberation and the Emergence of Separate Regimes 1945–1948. Princeton: Princeton University Press.

Field, Norma. 1993. Beyond Envy, Boredom, and Suffering: Towards an Emancipatory Politics for Resident Koreans and Other Japanese. positions 1(3):640–670.

Fukuoka, Yasunori. 1993. Zainichi kankoku chōsenjin: wakai sedai no aidentiti (Koreans in Japan: The Identities of the Young Generation). Tokyo: Chūōkōronsha.

—— 2000. The Lives of Young Koreans in Japan. Melbourne: Pacific Press.

Fukuoka, Yasunori, and Tsujiyama, Yukiko. 1991a. Hontō no watashi o motomete (In Search of True Self). Tokyo: Shinkansha.

—— 1991b. Dōka to ika no hazama de (Between Assimilation and Differentiation). Tokyo: Shinkansha.

Gen, Getsu. 2000. Kage no sumika (Where the Shadows Reside). Tokyo: Bungei Shunjusha.

Harajiri, Hideki. 1997. Nihon teijū korian no nichijō to seikatsu: bunkajinruigakuteki apurōchi (Daily Lives and Livelihood of Koreans Permanently Living in Japan: An Anthropological Approach). Tokyo: Akashi Shoten.

—— 1998. Zainichi to shite no korian (Koreans in Japan as Zainichi). Tokyo: Kōdansha.

Iinuma, Jirō, ed. 1991. Zainichi kankoku chōsenjin: sono nihonshakai ni okeru sonzaikachi (Koreans in Japan: Their Existential Value in Japanese Society). Osaka: Kaifūsha.

Kaneshiro, Kazuki. 2000. Go (Gō). Tokyo: Kōdansha.

Kang, Sang-jung. 1991a. "Zainichi" no genzai to mirai no aida (Between Present and Future of "Zainichi"). In Zainichi kankoku chōsnejin: sono nihonshakai ni okeru sonzaikachi (Koreans in Japan: Their Existential Value in Japanese society). Iinuma Jirō, ed. pp. 249–261. Osaka: Kaifūsha.

—— 1991b. Hōhō to shiteno "zainichi" – Yang T'ae-ho shi no hanron ni kotaeru ("Zainichi" as a Method – In Response to Mr. Yang T'ae-ho's Critique). In Zainichi kankoku chōsnejin: sono nihonshakai ni okeru sonzaikachi (Koreans in Japan: Their Existential Value in Japanese Society). Iinuma Jirō, ed. pp. 275–287. Osaka: Kaifūsha.

Kim, Ch'an-jōng. 1985. Ihōjinwa kimigayomaru ni notte (Strangers Arrived on Board Kimigayomaru). Tokyo: Iwanami Shoten.

Kin, Kakuei. 1986. Kin Kakuei sakuhin shūsei (Kin Kakuei: Collected Works). Tokyo: Sakuhinsha.

Kyō, Nobuko. 1987. Goku futsū no zainichi kankokujin (An Ordinary South Korean in Japan). Tokyo: Asahi Shinbunsha.

Lee, Changsoo, and George De Vos, eds. 1980. Koreans in Japan: Ethnic Conflict and Accommodation. Berkeley: University of California Press.

Lee, Seijaku. 1997. Zainichi kankokujin sansei no mune no uchi (Inner Thoughts of a Third-Generation Korean in Japan). Tokyo: Sōshisha.

Lie, John. 2001. Multiethnic Japan. Cambridge, MA: Harvard University Press.

Maher, John, and Gaynor Macdonald, eds. 1995. Diversity in Japanese Language and Culture. London: Kegan Paul International.

Pak, Kyōng-sik. 1992. Zainichi chōsenjin, kyōseirenkō, minzokumondai (Koreans in Japan, Forced Labor Recruitment, and the National Question). Tokyo: Sanichi Shobō.

Ri, Kaisei. 1972. Kinuta o utsu onna (The Woman Who Fulled Clothes). Tokyo: Bungei Shunjusha.

Ryang, Sonia. 1997. North Koreans in Japan: Language, Ideology, and Identity. Boulder, CO: Westview.

—— ed. 2000. Koreans in Japan: Critical Voices from the Margin. London: Routledge.

Suh, Kyung Sik. 1997. Bundan o ikiru: "zainichi" o koete (Living through the [National] Division: Beyond "Zainichi"). Tokyo: Kage Shobō.

Suzuki, David, and Oiwa, Keibo. 1996. The Japan We Never Knew. Toronto: Stoddart.

Wagner, Edward W. 1951. The Korean Minority in Japan: 1904–1950. New York: Institute of Pacific Relations.

Weiner, Michael, ed. 1997. Japan's Minorities: The Illusion of Homogeneity. London: Routledge.

Yang, T'ae-ho. 1991a. Jijitsu to shiteno "zainichi" – kang sang-jung shi e no gimon ("Zainichi" as a Fact – Question for Mr. Kang Sang-jung). *In* Zainichi kankoku chōsnejin: sono nihonshakai ni okeru sonzaikachi (Koreans in Japan: Their Existential Value in Japanese Society). Iinuma Jirō, ed. pp. 263–273. Osaka: Kaifūsha.

—— 1991b. Kyōzon, kyōsei, kyōkan – kang sang-jung shi e no gimon (II) (Existing Together, Living Together, Feeling Together – Question for Mr. Kang Sang-jung (II)). *In* Zainichi kankoku chōsnejin: sono nihonshakai ni okeru sonzaikachi (Koreans in Japan: Their Existential Value in Japanese Society). Iinuma Jirō, ed. pp. 289–301. Osaka: Kaifūsha.

Yi, Yang-ji. 1993. Yi yang-ji zenshū (Collected Works of Yi Yang-ji). Tokyo: Kōdansha.

Yu, Miri. 1995. Kazoku no hyōhon (Family Specimen). Tokyo: Asahi Shinbunsha.

SUGGESTED READING

Hamamoto, Mariko. 1995. Hitowa ikanishite mizukaraga umare sodatta basho de ihōjin tariuruka – zainichi chōsenjin no nanori no mondai (How Can a Person be a Foreigner in his Birthplace? The Question of Self-Naming of Koreans in Japan). *In* Shakaikihan – tabū to hōshō (Social Norms: Taboo and Reward). Nakauchi Toshio, Nagashima Nobuhiro et al., eds. pp. 86–111. Tokyo: Fujiwara Shoten.

Kashiwazaki, Chikako. 2000. To Be Korean Without Korean Nationality: Claim to Korean Identity by Japanese Nationality Holders. Korean and Korean American Studies Bulletin 11(1):48–70.

Kim, T'ae-yōng. 1999. Aidentiti poritikusu o koete (Beyond Identity Politics). Tokyo: Sekai Shisōsha.

Ko, Sōn-hui. 1995. Shin kankokujin no teijūka: enerugisshuna gunzō (Settling Residential Pattern of New Koreans: An Energetic Image). *In* Teijūka suru gaikokujin (Settling Foreigners). Komai Hiroshi, ed. pp. 227–254. Tokyo: Akashi Shoten.

Kuraishi, Ichirō. 1996. Rekishi no nakano "zainichi chōsenjin aidentiti": raifu histori kara no ichi kōsatsu ("Korean Identity in Japan" in History: A Study from Life Histories). Soshioroji (Sociology) 41:51–67.

—— 2000. Kyōiku jissen kiroku ni okeru shihaiteki katari no tassei kijo: zainichi chōsenjin kyōiku no jissenkiroku no tekisutobunseki (Order of the Emergence of Dominant Discourse in the Documentation in Educational Practice: The Analysis of Documents in Educational Practice of Koreans in Japan). Soshioroji (Sociology) 45:73–91.

Miyauchi, Hiroshi. 1999. Watashiwa anatagata no koto o donoyōni yobeba yoinodarōka? Zainichi kankoku chōsenjin? Zainichi chōsenjin? Zainichi korian? Soretomo? (How Do I Address You? Koreans in Japan? Zainichi Koreans? Or What?). Korian mainoriti kenkyū (Korean Minority Studies) 3:5–28.

Pak, Il. 1999. "Zainichi" to iu ikikata (A Lifestyle Called "Zainichi"). Tokyo: Kōdansha.

Ryang, Sonia. 1998a. Nationalist Inclusion or Emancipatory Identity? North Korean Women in Japan. Women's Studies International Forum 21(6):581–597.

—— 1998b. Inscribed (Men's) Bodies, Silent (Women's) Words: Rethinking Colonial Displacement of Koreans in Japan. Bulletin of Concerned Asian Scholars 30(4):3–15.

—— 2001. Diaspora and Beyond: There Is No Home for Koreans in Japan. Review of Korean Studies 4(2):55–86.

Taira, Naoki, Kawamoto, Hitomi, Shin, Yōng-gūn, and Nakamura, Toshiya. 1995. Zainichi chōsenjin seinen ni miru minzokuteki aidentiti no jōkyō ni yoru shifuto ni tsuite (Situational

Shifting of Ethnic Identity Seen Among Korean Youths in Japan). Kyōiku shinrigaku kenkyū (Japanese Journal of Educational Psychology) 43:380–391.

Takeda, Seiji. 1996. Zainichi to taikōshugi (*Zainichi* and Confrontationism). *In* Iwanamikōza gendai shakaigaku 24: minzoku, kokka, esunishiti (Iwanami's Contemporary Sociology Series 24: Nation, State, Ethnicity). Inoue Shun, Ueno Chizuko, Ōsawa Masayuki, Mita Sōsuke, and Yoshimi Shunya, eds. pp. 103–115. Tokyo: Iwanami Shoten.

Takenoshita, Hirohisa. 1999. Tabunka kyōiku to esunishiti: zainichi kankoku chōsenjin shūjūchiku o jirei ni (Multicultural Education and Ethnicity: With the Example of Korean Residential Areas). Shakaigaku hyōron (Japanese Sociological Review) 49:531–548.

Tani, Tomio. 1995. Zainichi kankoku chōsenjin shakai no genzai: chiiki shakai ni shōten o atete (The Present State of Korean Society in Japan: With Particular Focus on Local Communities). *In* Teijūka suru gaikokujin (Settling Foreigners). Komai Hiroshi, ed. pp. 132–161. Tokyo: Akashi Shoten.

Shifting Contours of Class and Status

CHAPTER **8**

Glenda S. Roberts

Japanese people often characterize Japan as a "classless" society, wherein the majority of people identify themselves as *chūryū*, or mid-stream. From a distance, they most certainly look so. With high per capita incomes, social welfare "safety nets" such as unemployment insurance, pension systems, a national health insurance system, and long-term care insurance for the infirm elderly, the populace seems comfortable. Urban housing is mixed; there are no "gated communities" for wealthier residents. Life spans are the longest in the world, and no-cost public schooling is available to all through junior high school, with the vast majority of youngsters now continuing on through high school and many beyond, to tertiary education. Public education at the university level, too, is set at "affordable" levels, though entrance is highly competitive. High-quality public day-care centers with trained personnel provide childcare on a sliding-scale fee basis, so that families of low income or without income can access day care free of charge. Subsidies are also provided for all children up to the age of 6, and school lunches are subsidized for income-qualifying residents. Many a visitor to urban Japan, noting the well-dressed commuters crowding the trains and subways, has commented to me on the affluence of the population. One scholar of public policy in Japan, in her recent assessment of Japan's postwar poverty alleviation strategies, notes, "The net result has been a relatively egalitarian contemporary society and a broad array of welfare-state policies" (Milly 1999).

In fact, in the span of time since the Meiji Restoration in 1868, Japan's government declared itself free of class restrictions (which had been quite real, even codified: warriors, farmers, craftsmen, merchants, and the underclass) and eventually achieved a society that, at least on the surface, seems quite free of "class conflict," wherein there is social mobility. None of this was accidental, however, nor was it a sudden coup. And many scholars, perhaps especially since the end of the "high growth period," have been pointing out that social class and status remain salient issues in contemporary society.

While there have been attempts (Steven 1983, for instance) to understand Japanese society according to a strictly Marxist class analysis, it seems more useful to employ an approach that views the society through the lenses of social capital, after Bourdieu, and to recognize Japanese social classes as "social fields" rather than groups "mobilized for struggle" (Clammer 1997). Indeed, as Gordon (1998) argues, most elements of struggle between labor and management seem to have disappeared or been silenced as labor made deals for higher wages and benefits during the 1960s in return for a highly cooperative stance on other workplace issues, such as hours or job content. If we look at class in terms of social fields whereby people are distinguished depending on their possession of cultural capital – knowledge and competence of how to function in the society – and social capital – social networks at one's disposal to facilitate one's goals – then we can certainly talk about the existence of classes in Japan. Moreover, we can discuss what sorts of issues various authors see as formative of practices in class distinctions in Japan, including education, employment, lifestyles, consumption, and notions of self and identity. Even with the "social field" approach, however, many authors caution us against considering class as a unitary phenomenon: for instance, "middle-class" or "mid-stream" is composed of people in various different statuses who will differ along several lines of occupational prestige, education, income, assets, living style, and power (Clammer 1997; Ishida 1993; Sugimoto 1997).

This chapter will introduce the reader to the salience of class in Japan, beginning with a discussion of class distinctions in the Meiji and Taisho eras, of which we are informed by both historians and anthropologists, and wherein we see the beginnings of a "middle class," to the postwar period, where the "mid-stream consciousness" becomes increasingly strong, economic inequalities ease, and an egalitarian consciousness is promulgated. While the urban "salaryman"/"professional housewife" motif is taken up as the boilerplate gender role model for the nation, I will demonstrate through my own research with blue-collar women workers in the 1980s (Roberts 1994), white-collar women bankers in 2000 (Roberts 2004), and senior citizens in government-sponsored work projects (Roberts 1996), that there is a good deal of variation in what people consider important in life and how they go about setting and achieving their goals, much of this related to class.

Some believe that social classes are becoming more entrenched than they had been in the years of high economic growth, that Japan is becoming a society where one has to be born into a well-off family in order to be set for life, and that it is no longer a society where if one tries one will succeed (*yareba nantoka naru*), but one where even if one tries, it is of no use (*yatte mo shikata ga nai*) (Satō 2000). The latter critique has surfaced in recent years, during the prolonged recession after the economic "bubble period" of the 1980s and early 1990s. I will comment on that critique later in this chapter.

Prewar Modern Japan

As the historian Andrew Gordon relates, "Only a minority identified themselves as participants in middle-class life in [pre-World War II] Japan" (2002:110). Those who did identify themselves as such did not necessarily do so out of a sense of financial superiority over the lower classes – because, indeed, the incomes of many salaried employees in the 1920s scarcely differed from those of manual workers. In fact, salaried men of the day were referred to as "Western clothes paupers." Rather, Gordon notes, the distinction lay in "cultural style or social identity and background – especially educational background – as much or more than it was a distinction grounded in wage levels" (2002:115). Furthermore, the laborers saw the distinction similarly. Their major union refused to affiliate with that of the *sarariiman*, those workers of the fledgling middle class whose salaries were paid in monthly, rather than daily, wages (2002:116). From the early 20th century onward, what distinguished the class structure was that education rather than inherited status became the linchpin for access to middle-class occupations, and the middle-class lifestyle itself became defined by a variety of consumer goods and pursuits not previously available (2002:116). Hence began the middle-class anxiety over achievement in education, notes Gordon, that continues to this day. I shall argue later in this chapter that working-class people in contemporary society exhibit far less anxiety over the educational rat race.

Certainly historians and anthropologists alike have demonstrated that Meiji, Taisho, and early Showa attitudes of the more educated populace toward the working class, and especially toward working-class women, were not very complimentary. According to anthropologist Tamanoi Mariko, from the Meiji period (1868–1912) in villages and small towns, it became fairly commonplace for ordinary families to hire young (as young as 5 years old) live-in child-minders, called *komori*, to care for the children while the parents made a living. These child-minders, drawn from the ranks of both girls and boys at first but later only girls, came from impoverished families and were often hired as indentured servants. It was not the households of the emerging middle class who employed them, because they regarded *komori* as untrained, violent, ill-mannered, promiscuous, and crude. They were not status symbols but necessary for the maintenance of the household economy; they had little education and could not be compared with the nannies of European households of the time (Tamanoi 1998). Through song, with lyrics full of complaint against their mistreatment and harsh existence, *komori* "retrieved their subjectivities from the middle-class discourse on their language and behavior," in the face of the state's attempts to educate them and inculcate them with middle-class values of propriety (Tamanoi 1998:82–83).

Factory workers fared not much better in terms of the respect the educated population gave them for their labors. As Japan industrialized during the Meiji period, women were called upon to fill the ranks of workers, particularly in the light manufacturing sector of the textile mills. At first these jobs were performed by the daughters of wealthy samurai who were extolled for their virtues in building the state economy. By the end of the century, however, women of lower social status filled these jobs. These were mostly rural women, including some married women. Unmarried women lived in the mill dormitories in tuberculosis-breeding unsanitary conditions, and suffered from long hours of work and harsh treatment. As with the child-minders, factory women were disparaged by the media and social reformers alike as lacking in morals, unhygienic, and crude. Tamanoi writes that a major social reformer of the period, Hosoi Wakizō, described the factory women as having a retarded culture and "who have more or less the psychology of uncivilized savages" (Tamanoi 1998:97).

As the ideology of the "good wife, wise mother" gained momentum as the favored gender paradigm of Japan in the 20th century, Hosoi believed that factory women should cease to work in factories after marriage, lest they "destroy" their family lives

(Tamanoi 1998:99). This is remarkably similar to the comments of the president of the owner of a large lingerie firm some six decades later (see Roberts 1994). Hence even a labor reformer such as Hosoi did not approve of women's work outside the home after marriage. Tamanoi notes that both male unionists and social reformers failed to take factory women seriously, disparaging them as emotional and unable to be organized. Women's own actions belied such opinions, as they organized Japan's first labor strike at the Amamiya Silk Mill in Kōfu in 1886 (Tamanoi 1998:98), and, like the child-minders, composed songs documenting their difficult lives as well as demonstrating their pride as major producers for the nation. They continued to work in the mills, the mines, and in middle-class households as housemaids until the postwar era (Hunter 1995).

In contrast with factory women, rural women of the early 20th century were portrayed in the media and in scholarly publications to be true repositories of Japanese "tradition," selflessly devoting themselves to their families and to the nation by their honest and virtuous labor. Toward the end of the war, they were also recruited to work in munitions factories, stores, and train stations, as men increasingly went to the front. Furthermore, from the 1930s they were sent as "continental brides" (*tairiku no hanayome*) to wed Japanese men who had settled in Manchuria as agents of Japanese colonialism. Nationalist discourses represented rural women as superior producers of children. The government urged them to "propagate and multiply," and they complied (Tamanoi 1998:163). Importantly, Tamanoi notes that Japanese scholarly and governmental romanticism regarding rural women's virtues was misplaced. Rural women worked so hard not because of some mystical power inherent in country women, emanating from their identity as Japanese, but for survival (1998:177).

THE POSTWAR ERA AND INCREASING EGALITARIANISM

In his book documenting the struggles of Japan's workers from the Meiji period through the postwar era, Kumazawa Makoto compares and contrasts the lower-class workers of the early 20th century to the workers of today:

> The workers of eighty years ago had no social security whatsoever, and could not hope to advance in this fashion. Moreover, under a hierarchical regime of labor management lacking even a nominal commitment to equality or fairness, they could not claim any pride in being a factory worker... "Workers" and "paupers" may have been differentiated conceptually in Japan by the start of this century, but in the reality of lived existence the two terms were basically synonymous. The social world of the urban lower class embraced so many different elements that one cannot call it simply a worker society. (Kumazawa 1996:32).

According to Kumazawa, a main difference between prewar and postwar workers was the transformation in the wage system. In the prewar period, the *nenkou* wage system, established from the 1920s to 1930s, was based on seniority and merit. Through this system, workers gained some long-term social security. Although there was some path of advancement even for those with only an elementary school education, Kumazawa notes that from today's standpoint this system seems "rigidly hierarchical and status bound" (Kumazawa 1996:37). During the postwar period, workers demanded a much less hierarchical system, whereby all employees received almost automatic pay raises based on seniority. They fought to have status-based labels that separated staff from production employees removed, and to have the monthly wage system apply to blue- and white-collar workers alike. Moreover, they made equal access to company welfare facilities another of their demands (1996:49). Workers were more successful in having the status-based distinctions removed and less so in achieving automatic pay increases by seniority. In the late 1960s, wage rates linked to job classes were replaced with merit- and ability-based wage evaluations, but the labor unions welcomed this shift (1996:52). Workers also resisted employers' perceived right to dismiss those workers whom they judged lacking in ability or dedication, and the unions engaged in "anti-dismissal struggles" (1996:53). Eventually they prevailed against dismissal at the cost of concessions on other issues, such as control over job content or other quality of life issues. Wages made big gains throughout the period of high economic growth (1955–75), however, and the material aspects of people's lives greatly improved.

Blue-collar workers' living standards rose to middle-class levels, with blue-collar workers purchasing not only durable consumer goods and fashionable clothing, but also cameras and domestic vacations, homes, and even a college education for their children. Hence, by the end of the high-growth era, most workers felt they had joined the "mid-stream" of Japanese society, as did farmers, who for the most part had abandoned full-time farming in favor of factory work or office work during the week, shifting to weekend and holiday farming plus relying on wives and parents to carry out the bulk of farm labor during the year. Whereas agricultural workers made up 40 percent of all workers in 1955, their share had fallen to 20 percent in 1965, and 5.3 percent in 1997 (Ishida 2001; Japan Institute of Labour 2000:24). On the other hand, the skilled working class grew from 9 percent in 1955 to 17 percent in 1965, and 20 percent in 1985 (Ishida 2001:592).

Had workers really joined the mid-stream? Had the Japanese, in the short span of three decades after World War II, really achieved a meritocracy wherein any child who tried could be upwardly mobile? This interesting question has engaged many. Ishida Hiroshi, in his ground-breaking work on social mobility (1993), uses the 1970s scholarly debates on this topic as a springboard for his own quantitative study. According to Ishida, in the 1970s three prominent social scientists began the debate over the nature of class in postwar Japan: Murakami Yasusuke, Kishimoto Shigenobu, and Tominaga Kenichi (Ishida 1993:18–20). Ishida himself, a sociologist, analyzed the Social Stratification and Mobility (SSM) national survey of 1975 to try to definitively answer remaining questions about the nature and extent of social mobility. Could Japan really be labeled a homogeneous society? Or did seeming homogeneity in lifestyles and consumption patterns simply mask fundamental differences in assets, indicating a bipolar split between workers and capitalists? Or would "diversity" better be understood as "status inconsistent," whereby a person might have high status on some scales (such as education), but low status on others (such as income)?

Ishida found that the amount of family property and other assets makes a larger difference in matriculation to college in Japan than in Great Britain or the US. This, he notes, supports the claims that cram schools and private tutors, which are quite expensive, are essential to prepare a child for the college entrance examinations. His research confirmed firm size as a significant source of status differentiation among the Japanese, supporting the "dual-structure hypothesis" that sees firm size as an important characteristic in the stratification of workers in Japan, with those in large firms receiving higher wages, more benefits, and better working conditions than those in medium- to small-sized firms (the latter of which are in the majority). Moreover, in contrast to America, in Japan firm size was more important a distinction than skill level (Ishida 1993). He also found "class is far more important than education and occupational status in explaining inequality in income, home owner- ship and stock investment" both in Japan and the United States (1993:237). Furthermore, Ishida found that one's class position in Japanese society influences the extent to which one's educational credentials increase one's financial standing. All in all, Ishida found Japanese society to be fairly similar in class structure to American society: it is partially characterized by "bipolarization" in status, wherein the em- ployer class is at the top of status hierarchies and the manual worker occupies the bottom rung. In Japan, a large proportion of people (47 percent of the male labor force) are "status inconsistent," such as professionals and managers, who have achieved high status in education but who are lower on home ownership (1993:259). In sum, Ishida notes that "the Japanese class structure is characterized by a combination of polarization and inconsistency of status characteristics with a further differentiation among employees by firm size" (1993:259).

Thomas Rohlen, an anthropologist who carried out a major study in the late 1970s on high school education in Japan, found that social class had much to do with where students end up in school, as success in competition to attend the elite public and private universities is tied to success in entrance to elite private or college-preparatory- oriented high schools. Preparation for the entrance exams to such schools to some extent rests on a child's socioeconomic background and the parents' ability to pay for the extra cram school tutorials necessary for their child to prepare well for the entrance examinations. Moreover, financial backing alone is insufficient, as success also almost always requires the presence of a parent – the mother – at home who will coddle, cajole, shepherd, and support the student through this grueling process. In his qualitative comparative study of high schools in Kobe, Rohlen found that the higher the rank of school attended, the more likely were the children to come from homes where their mothers were full-time homemakers, and they were also likely to have rooms of their own in which to study. Furthermore, their fathers were likely to have tertiary levels of education and be employed in white-collar jobs (Rohlen 1979:130).

The "exam hell" that sorts students and channels a young person's future has not receded in the years since Rohlen did his study. In April of 2002 the Ministry of Education, as part of its strategy to make the education system less stressful for children (*yutori kyōiku*), did away with Saturday half-day classes, which had been held every other weekend. In their weekly television series, *Kurosu appu gendai* (Close-up on Contemporary Issues), the Japanese public television channel NHK reported on protests by some parents of public junior high school children in Tokyo who could not afford to send their children to cram schools but who felt that this reduction in classroom hours would cause their children to be less competitive in high school and college entrance exams.

But do all people in Japan care so much about the quality of schools their children enter, or the size and fame of the firm where they eventually gain employment? Or is this mainly a preoccupation of the more elite in society to begin with? One cannot but read accounts of education in Japan, such as those by Rohlen, or Okano and Tsuchiya (1999), Ryang (1997), Slater (2003), or Yoder (2002), without realizing that social class as well as ethnicity (whether of indigenous populations such as the Ainu, or permanent resident non-Japanese ethnic populations such as the *zainichi* Koreans or Chinese, as well as minority ethnically Japanese former outcaste group, the Buraku-min), are highly significant factors influencing educational opportunities and out-comes (see chapters 6 and 7 in this volume). In particular, Robert Yoder (2002), through a longitudinal (spanning almost 20 years and three surveys) qualitative study of two urban neighborhoods in the greater Tokyo metropolitan area, illustrates the very different outcomes in delinquent behaviors, adult occupations, and family formation patterns, for youths in a working-class neighborhood and a bedtown community of the well-off. As the educational system will be dealt with in other chapters in this book (see chapters 16 and 17), I will not dwell on it further here.

My own research on gender and work in contemporary Japan has brought me into contact with people from many different backgrounds. They hold a variety of statuses in Japanese society. Some are junior high school or high school graduates, while others are university-educated, some at the most elite levels. Some work in factories, others in firms as managers or owners; some are entertainers, others, educators; still others are full-time, highly educated homemakers. Over the years interacting with this wide variety of people, I can only conclude that there are significant differences among them, often in their aspirations about what the future should hold for their children, but also in their pastimes and their orientations toward the world. It should not come as a surprise that there is a "mid-stream" consciousness among most Japanese, but that there are also significant differences among them in terms of lifestyles and values.

To answer my question above, not all people are concerned with getting their children into prestigious institutions of higher education, nor do they necessarily feel like failures for working at the local restaurant or dry cleaner's. There are plenty of families where winning a bet on the horses or coming out lucky at the *pachinko* parlor are sources of great pleasure and signs of success. In my research on work projects for retirees (Roberts 1996), I recall one older couple who lived in the "low town" or "downtown" neighborhood of *shitamachi* in Tokyo, telling me how pleased they were that their eldest son had not excelled in school and had decided to forgo college. Rather, he lived with them, married, and carried on the family business, an industrial knitting shop that occupied a small room within their home. They were happy living and working with their son and daughter-in-law, with whom they were in daily and close contact. Their social status as owners of a very small knitting firm may not be considered as high as that of a managerial-class worker in a large corporation, but they seemed comfortable with who they were, they were respected members of the local government's Silver Talent Center and hence active in their local community, and highly satisfied with their family situation, wherein the eldest son would inherit and continue their business. In a similar vein, in his ethnography of blue-collar workers in a small firm in Kanagawa, James Roberson (1998) has done much to illustrate differences in life-course trajectories, attitudes toward work, diversity in lifestyles, family interactions, and the hobbies or interests of the workers he studied in contrast to the ways workers are generally portrayed in the academic literature on *sarariiman*, the male white-collar office workers.

In the Japan of the "post-bubble" recession, when jobs for construction workers have grown more and more scarce, those who have perhaps suffered the most are the aging day laborers, who occupy the bottom rung of the construction industry's hierarchy. Ethnographic work by Brett deBary (1988), Edward Fowler (1996), and Carolyn Stevens (1997) on day laborers and the volunteers supporting them contributes a great deal to our understanding of the social services provided to these men and the interrelationships between the service providers and the day laborers themselves. This anthropology of the margins elucidates how mainstream society operates while it clarifies the diverse values people at the margins hold. Day laborers, at the lowest level of the labor hierarchy, certainly stand at the margins of society. Thomas Gill (2001), through his ethnography of the inhabitants of Kotobukicho, the day laborer's district of Yokohama, has revealed the intricacies of lives of men who are neither salaried employees nor "pillars of the household," belonging to neither company nor family. In a society where "belongingness" is held in high esteem (Lebra 1976), these men are held in low esteem. The men themselves, however, gain certain freedoms in their marginality and simultaneously have positive as well as negative sentiments in regard to their lifestyles. Gill reports mainstream attitudes toward these men as ranging from envy at their freedom from responsibility to disgust, expressed in violence toward homeless men. Since the bursting of the economic "bubble," the number of homeless residents in urban areas of Japan has also increased greatly. Anthropologists have carried out ethnographic work on homelessness in Japanese society (see Margolis 2002), and one expects this work will also expand our understanding of the phenomena of homelessness in OECD countries. Such research, one hopes, may also inform policy.

Other work by anthropologists which has enriched our understanding of social class in urban Japan is that of Bestor (1989), who studied an urban old-middle-class neighborhood in Tokyo. Bestor found class indeed to be a dynamic and salient feature of life in the district he researched, and he deftly portrays the grappling for power in a shifting field among the subcultures of the merchant "old middle class," the newer salaried employee class, and young laborers from outside the neighborhood. Bestor illustrates how the old middle class sought to legitimate its bid for continuing power in the community by manipulating the idioms of traditionalism and stressing the values of localism and community participation with the knowledge that these criteria of "good citizenship" could not be claimed by the "new middle class" despite its numerical dominance. For the old-timers, the social worth of a man and his prestige was measured not by mainstream values such as higher education or employment in a prestigious firm, but by explicitly local values that may not be recognized outside of the district.

Owners of small and medium-sized businesses, though they may be less well educated than the salarymen or professional class, own property, operate a significant proportion of businesses in Japan and wield clout in local politics. Whether and how they will retain their special status as deregulation and pressure against protectionism open markets are important topics for anthropologists to investigate. Owners of small factories have also been among the first since the 1980s to hire undocumented migrant workers and to use "trainees" as a labor force when Japanese youths began to shun manual work. How they view and treat foreign workers in their midst is another important topic to be investigated, as it heralds Japan's as yet tentative discourse on multiculturality (see Douglass and Roberts 2000). Studies by Douglass and Roberts (2000), Lie (2000), Pollack (2000), Roth (2002), and Tsuda (2003) suggest that many Japanese people are uneasy living and working among peoples from other countries, including Brazilians (and others) of Japanese descent. As the current low birth rate threatens labor shortages in the years ahead, it is likely that Japan will need to rely on foreign labor if it is to sustain production levels. Class will be a salient issue in future research on how migrants adjust and are (or are not) integrated into life in Japan. I expect anthropologists in and of Japan to make important contributions to the anthropology of migration. Let us turn now to another contested lifestyle: the blue-collar woman who stays on the line as a regular employee.

GENDER AND SOCIAL CLASS

I would now like to bring in some reflections from my research on blue-collar women in the 1980s, by way of explaining some differences I see in what one might term "class cultures" in Japan. One twofold aspect of social class that is not informed by large surveys such as the SSM utilized by Ishida above, is that of sex and gender (see chapter 11 in this volume for definitions of these terms). The SSM's subjects are males only. How do sex, gender, and social class interact in Japan? As di Leonardo (1991) points out, analyses of social class that ignore sex and gender, race and ethnicity, are sorely lacking in explanatory value. My own work has focused mainly on gender ideology and work in contemporary Japan, especially with respect to female employment, and it is to this topic that I shall now turn.

   According to the economist Nancy Folbre, "structures of constraint" "locate individuals in different positions in terms of asset distributions, political rules, social norms, and personal preferences" (Folbre 1994:5). Gender and class are two of the structures of constraint that Folbre identifies in her work, the others being age, sexuality, nation, and race. In Japan, we can certainly distinguish patterns through which gender and social class operate to encourage male and female individuals to adopt certain lifestyles and to constrain them from adopting others. In Japan, the "good wife/wise mother" model of female domesticity was conceived and promoted universally in Japan during the Meiji period, along with the ideal of conjugal monogamy (see chapters 21 and 22 in this volume). This model has reigned since then as the dominant paradigm for proper middle-class female behavior, and it dovetailed perfectly with what became known in the 1960s as the "Japanese system of management," which is characterized by family welfare-ism, lifetime employment for (male) core employees, and the seniority-based wage. Under this basically sexist and starkly gendered system of management, core jobs are allocated to men, and peripheral jobs are taken up by women, whose job tenure is expected to be brief as women's main roles continue to be perceived as overseeing the social reproduction of the household, and caring for the young and for older generations. It goes without saying that the "core" jobs held by men could not exist without the social reproductive functions carried out at home by women. Neither could men's jobs be protected as the "core" without corporations using women as the flexible periphery of "part-time" workers, some 30 percent of whom work in insecure jobs at full-time hours for no benefits and half the pay of regular employees (Nagase 2002). Furthermore, this system, which is labeled the "male breadwinner model" by sociologists in the United States and Europe, is well supported in Japan by underlying social policy, such as the tax structure that encourages married women to work only in peripheral statuses rather than as regular employees (Osawa 2002).[1]

The flip side of the "good wife, wise mother" model, of course, is that men are still expected to be the main providers for their households. That this sex–gender paradigm remains dominant can be almost palpably felt in the recent social uproar over young men who, rather than taking full-time regular jobs after college, enter part-time contingent jobs as so-called *furiitaa*, a Japanese neologism that combine "free" with the German word *Arbeit* (work). The social angst is particularly directed at young men; young women who fail to enter regular work after college, although also called *furiitaa*, are not so chastised. Indeed, my students at Waseda University inform me that a young woman seeking to fill in the blanks of her employment history can simply enter *kaji tetsudai* (helping out with housework at home), as no questions will likely be asked. Woe betide the young man who decides to follow his heart to join a rock band and work as a part-time grocer rather than buckle down and take a steady job as a salesman. He certainly could not fill in his employment blanks with *kaji tetsudai* or the like. My point is that the sex–gender system constrains both females and males, although in different ways and with different social ramifications. One could even imagine the married woman who holds a full-time corporate position as occupying a position structurally similar to that of a man who decides to walk away from his white-collar job and take up organic farming: both are anomalies in the dominant "Japanese system."

I noted above that the "salaryman/professional housewife" model of the sexual and gendered division of labor is typical of the middle classes in particular. What about the working classes? Did this model spread as thoroughly among all social classes? Does it affect all people to the same extent and in the same ways? The answers to these questions are multifaceted. First, one must remember that the model itself was invented during the Meiji period and took some time to spread to the lower classes (see Smith and Wiswell 1982; Tamanoi 1998). In the postwar period the central government enshrined this sex–gender model in the tax code, by putting a threshold on the amount of tax-free income a homemaker can earn without a tax penalty. Furthermore, this model has been utilized on a very wide scale throughout industry in Japan, discouraging women and men from choosing alternate work/life patterns (Brinton 1993; Kondo 1990; Ogasawara 1998; Roberts 1994; Rosenberger 1991). No matter what one's social class position, the dominant sex–gender paradigm affects one's options and outcomes. Class does matter, though. Lebra (1990) demonstrated that upper-class women in the early part of the last century did not subscribe to the nurturing mother mandate of the "good wife, wise mother" paradigm, but hired surrogates to perform this role instead. Bernstein's (1983) ethnography of a farm woman's life in the 1970s dispels any doubt that postwar Japanese farm women led lives consumed by their wifely and motherly duties alone; physically demanding farm production took up most of the farm wife's day, with household management and childrearing filling in any remaining moments. In her study of farm women of the late 1980s, Tamanoi reminds us that this lifestyle of hard labor continues – only now the farm women are also doing industrial piecework at home, as many working-class urban housewives did before "part-timer" jobs became available in the 1970s, and they still do if they cannot leave their homes to work.

The "good wife, wise mother" paradigm of the Meiji period has had a lot of staying power in postwar Japan. When I began my doctoral research in the early 1980s, I wanted to discover how married blue-collar women regarded this paradigm given their inability to fit the mold of the stay-at-home wife and mother. The results of this research are detailed elsewhere (Roberts 1994, 1996). Here, I would like to make some comparisons between how the blue-collar women see themselves in relation to this ideal, and how upper-middle-class women, both homemakers and working professionals, position themselves within it, especially with respect to their attitudes toward childrearing and education, work schedules and time with family, and the division of labor at home.

The factory where I studied blue-collar women workers was part of "Azumi" (a pseudonym), a large, world-renowned company. While most companies at this time did not encourage women lacking high-level skills to remain at work after marriage and childrearing, this company employed a sizeable number of married women as full-time, "regular" employees. Many of the production workers of my acquaintance were resisting the mainstream sex–gender paradigm by insisting on remaining in their full-time jobs as regular employees in a large company; sometimes this meant resisting their husbands as well, who reluctantly "allowed" their wives to work "only so long as nothing slips at home." These women challenged cultural norms that classify women's main role as housewives and mothers and their monetary contributions to the household as supplementary. They also challenged both implicit company policies and explicit, publicly voiced opinions of top managers that favor women workers' early retirement at marriage or upon the birth of the first child.

Some of my co-workers had begun their jobs after junior high school or high school and had stayed through marriage, pregnancy, and childbearing and -rearing. Others entered after their children were of school-age, but they had entered as regular employees because the company, a major producer of lingerie and leisurewear, was expanding and needed employees who could be relied upon to do overtime.[2] My co-workers felt fortunate to have jobs as regulars when most women of their age cohort could only find jobs as irregular-status *paato* (part-time) (Roberts 1994). Indeed, they were right. The second year of my research I interviewed many *paato* factory workers who regretted that they could not find a job as a regular employee.[3] Most of my co-workers shared the desire to keep their jobs, and a few of them are still at Azumi, years later.

Several co-workers emphasized that it is a waste of resources to have a woman at home when she could be out working. They also were well aware that while *paato* employment was available, it would be foolish to trade a stable, well-paying but exacting job at Azumi for a *paato* job that offered more flexibility but vastly reduced income and benefits.[4] They voiced pity for full-time housewives, since the ones they knew had to operate within one salary alone. While the literature on Japanese professional homemakers often cites their control of their spouses' paychecks as a sign of their considerable authority in the domestic realm, this authority becomes a burden when the paycheck barely meets ordinary household expenditures.[5]

My co-workers used words such as "dark," "shut-in," and "depressing" when commenting on full-time homemakers.[6] Although for the most part they did not disparage full-time homemakers, few of them longed to trade places.[7] In sum, married co-workers at Azumi remained because they felt that, in so doing, they could consistently provide their families with a much higher standard of living than if they pursued any of the other alternatives. Years of working for a large and famous company had also given them pride in their accomplishments, though they were not without criticism of the way the firm treated them.

Two of the main duties of the "professional housewife" are childrearing and attention to education of the children. Of course, full-time working women are not able to fulfill these duties themselves, but must use surrogates of some kind. The working-class women I knew were much more relaxed about both childrearing and education, and quite happy to leave childrearing to grandparents and day-care professionals, and education to the public school system. Although I did hear comments disapproving of day care, they all came from those without children or from women who had raised their children themselves until they were school-aged, before they returned to the workforce. I did hear complaints from those who relied on grandparents for childcare: they said the grandparents spoiled the children.

Women who remained at Azumi through pregnancy and childbirth relied on a combination of public day care, after-school childcare programs, and relatives to assist them in childrearing from the end of pregnancy leave through elementary school. While it is commonplace now for Japanese children to attend some form of preschool from the age of 3 or 4, day care for infants goes against the cultural norm that babies need their mother's special care to develop properly (see also chapter 16 in this volume). Although there are public day-care centers for infants, the demand for them far exceeds their availability, and thus working mothers must plan far in advance to secure reliable sources of childcare. Working-class mothers who had made use of public day care had nothing but praise for their caregivers. Far from worrying that their children were being inadequately prepared for life ahead, they were confident that the centers were providing them good care.

What we can glean from such attitudes above is respect for day-care personnel as being perfectly qualified, even more qualified than the mothers themselves, for raising children. In contrast, I have never heard (or heard about) an upper-middle-class mother commenting that she felt that full-time day-care personnel were more expert than she in the basic care and training of her child. Sharon Hayes, in her study of working-class and professional-class mothers in the United States (Hayes 1996), also found "working-class and poor mothers seem to be more likely than their middle- and upper-middle-class counterparts to believe that other people know more about childrearing than they do . . . By contrast, no professional-class mothers describe their children's paid care-givers as more competent and knowledgeable than themselves" (Hayes 1996:92). While there are undoubtedly cultural differences between working-class women in the United States and those in Japan, this may be one area where attitudes are similar, although further research is needed to substantiate this.

As regular employees, my co-workers could not spend a lot of time with their families, beyond weekends and the occasional holiday. During busy periods they were obliged to work overtime. If a child became feverish and needed to be sent home from day care or school, it was difficult for Azumi women to leave the floor to go home. Many women stated that, in such cases, they would ask relatives to watch the sick child. A few had husbands whose workplace offered more flexibility than Azumi did, so the husband would take time off. Mothers could only occasionally get the time off to attend their children's school events, so their own mother or their husband's mother would go in their place when possible. It was also difficult for working mothers to attend PTA meetings, which took place during the day, another indication of the institutionalized nature of the professional housewife model.

How does the experience of working-class mothers differ from that of professional working mothers? The latter have similar constraints, except that they are very likely to be married to men with equally constrained or even tighter work schedules. Furthermore, most of the factory women I knew had less overtime on a regular basis than did the professional women, for whom overtime was unpaid but regularly expected. In that sense, it was in some ways easier for working mothers to keep working in blue-collar jobs than in white-collar professional jobs. Since 1992, Japanese companies have been asked to implement the Childcare Leave Law, which gives either parent leave from work for up to a year after a baby's birth. I am currently researching how professional women and men utilize this leave, but it is also essential to ask how working-class women and men (including those in low-level service industry jobs) regard and make use of it. In the mid-1990s a (female) labor union representative remarked to me that she thought such leave would sap women's desire to return to work, and that maternity leave alone (14 weeks) was plenty of time off. Many of the professional women I have interviewed have said that a year is really too long to be gone, not because they lose their desire to work, but because they will not be able to keep up with changes in workplace technology and business strategies.

How much did my co-workers stress educational goals for their children? What sorts of futures did they envision for them? While no one I knew at the factory was preparing her children for elite government or business careers, some supported their children through sports-oriented high schools, two-year technical colleges, or four-year universities, and some of these children have entered white-collar jobs. Several women mentioned they were paying for cram school lessons for their children. While they had neither the time nor the educational background to tutor their own children, they took great pride in their children's accomplishments.

Social class differentially affects women's strategies and options with regard to work, and this in turn affects their children's futures. Highly educated women from upper-middle income brackets face both strong incentives to work, given their career aspirations, and strong disincentives to do so, especially if they have children to "groom" for similarly high social status – or families who believe that the children should be so groomed. It is this social class from where come the so-called *kyōiku mama*, or "education mamas," who prepare their children from an early age to pass the entrance exams to reputable schools.

Japanese mothers' worries about children's education seem to be class-sensitive and seem to start fairly early. In interviews with career-women bankers and other professionals in Tokyo in the late 1990s, I occasionally heard women express fears that if their children attended the full-time day-care programs sponsored by the Ministry of Health, Labor and Welfare instead of the part-time kindergarten programs sponsored by the Ministry of Education, they would not get the academic leg up they needed to begin first grade. Such women sometimes relied on their relatives for childcare so that the grandparents could take the child back and forth from a half-day, private kindergarten program. They also voiced concerns over their abilities to shepherd their children through the time-consuming process of preparing for various entrance examinations.

In 1994 I had the opportunity to put my daughter into an elite kindergarten in the suburbs of Tokyo for a summer program. The director noted that there was only one other working mother among all the kindergartners enrolled, and her mother-in-law was responsible for the child's activities. He had doubts about how I would manage on the days when the children were sent home at 11.30 a.m., and was disappointed that I would not be able to join the mothers' chorale, which met in the morning. When I went to pick up my daughter after her first day at school, I was struck at the sight of all the other mothers waiting outside the doors of the school, chatting with each other. Dressed to the nines, they looked fit to grace the covers of *Katei gahō* (Household Pictorial). Their lifestyles matched their wardrobes. Well educated, married to professionals, business magnates, and stars of the film and television world, many of these women were sophisticated consumers of international culture. They dedicated a good deal of their time to their children, supervising their play groups, taking them on outings, and staying up late at night to help their older children study for exams. One of the women, a full-time homemaker, with a kindergartner and an elementary-age child enrolled in said school, remarked to me that she was throwing all her energies into preparing the best meals she possibly could for her family, as she saw this as the most important thing she could do for them. This was a far cry from the directions in which the less well off blue-collar working women I knew were investing their energies. For them, neither gourmet nor health food was on the agenda, and the local Seven-Eleven provided the standard snack fare for their children. Their rationales were similar, though: both invested their energies from the desire to support their children to the greatest possible extent.

The mothers of children in this elite private kindergarten invested considerable capital in their children's education from a very early stage, not only in the form of the cost of the schooling and other cultural and academic lessons, outings, and trips, but in the process of pursuing the role of "professional homemaker" with zeal. Such expenditure of their time and energy, however, leaves these women very vulnerable in the event of a divorce. Blue-collar women's ideas on divorce have likely relaxed since I first heard their views in the early 1980s, but at that time several middle-aged women told me that because the wife/mother is always blamed as the cause for a divorce, a woman should only divorce as a last resort. The divorce rate in Japan has risen in the last decade and, at 2.27 per 1,000 couples, is presently on par with those of France, Germany, and Sweden (Curtin 2002). Aside from social approbation, which seems to be waning, what all but independently wealthy women must face is the downturn in their finances in addition to their own and their children's loss of social status after divorce. Since divorce settlements for wives are notoriously low in Japan – not to mention the fact that few ex-husbands assume any responsibility for supporting their children[8] – and because women and older workers are discriminated against in the job market, a significant drop in living standard after divorce is likely. J. S. Curtin has found that, in the 1990s, lone-mother families were on average among the poorest in Japan, and that this was largely due to fathers' failure to comply with child-support directives. He also found that, despite Japan's lone mothers exhibiting a high rate of employment in comparison with lone mothers in other industrialized countries, their low wage levels keep them in poverty (Curtin 2000, 2002). As Osawa (2002) reminds us, the government supports the salaryman/ homemaker couple, and not a single or divorced woman who is maintaining a household and supporting a child or children on her own. What is needed is ethnographic research on how social class positions affect the perception, status, and livelihoods of single or divorced female heads of household.

How did the factory women I knew manage what Hochschild (1989) refers to as the "second shift"? Working full-time at Azumi without the cooperation of one's spouse was no easy task. Some women were able to negotiate cooperation from their spouses over a number of years, while others, especially the younger women, expected and received cooperation in childcare and housework from their husbands, unless their mothers-in-law were able and willing to assist. My younger women co-workers were aware of the dominant gender ideology deeming husbands incompetent in household management and childcare, but resisted capitulating to it.

What about the case of married professional women in regular employment who have children? How do these women experience the constraints and freedoms of the dominant gender paradigm? Although I cannot do this question justice in this chapter, my current research on the work–life balance among highly educated women in a large corporation in Tokyo allows me to make a few observations (Roberts 2004). One is that, for most of these women, their job commitment is grounded largely in the challenges of the position and their authority in the workplace, rather than in economic need – although some women who purchased homes during the "bubble period" of the economy had to work in order to pay their mortgages; they had no option. Second, like Azumi women, these women tend to rely to a great degree on family members for childcare. They also make use of private and government day-care centers. One important difference between professional and blue-collar working women is that, because the former are married to high-income-earning spouses, they cannot declare their employment to be necessary for the sake of their children's well-being. Unlike the blue-collar women I knew, these women had high educational attainments, sometimes because their own professional-homemaker mothers had pushed them from their teenage years to pursue a career path instead of falling into the role of a full-time homemaker.

In terms of sharing the household and caretaking duties with husbands, professional women were in a tighter spot than their factory-worker counterparts, as the husbands of most worked at white-collar jobs in large firms with heavy overtime commitments for (male) core employees. Although most of the women I interviewed were dissatisfied with this sexual and social division of labor, in which their spouses helped out only on weekends or perhaps dropped off the baby at day care on a weekday, and were aware of alternative models, most felt it that was futile for them to try to fight the status quo. On the other hand, they were in some sense beneficiaries of flexible work arrangements such as the corporate childcare leave policy, which allowed employees up to one year of leave to care for a new infant. While the policy itself was sex-blind, no male has yet to take advantage of it. This phenomenon is by no means specific to Japan. It is much easier for American women to leave work early for a child's needs than it is for a man (see e.g. Perlow 1997). Childcare leave notwith-standing, it seems to be more difficult for professional women in certain corporate jobs to continue working than for women in blue-collar jobs on account of the high levels of overtime work expected of them. Even if a company has flexible work arrangements, many professional women feel that they cannot take advantage of these for ever, noting that it takes 18 years to raise a child, and older children too need a lot of parental attention.

Since I first studied Azumi in 1983, it has increasingly shifted production offshore, downsized domestic operations, and hired part-time production workers to replace regular-status workers who have retired or quit. Yet many women there wish to remain in their jobs throughout marriage and childrearing. In a 1994 survey of 235 Azumi women workers nationwide, Yamamoto found that unmarried production workers were the most likely of any category of woman worker at Azumi (including manager/specialty worker/designer, sales worker and office worker) to want to continue at Azumi after marriage.[9] Will they be able to do so? More to the point, can they continue as regular workers? The Japanese economy has not yet recovered from the recession following the "bubble period," and unemployment is at an all-time high. Researchers have recently pointed out the trends for companies to down-size their core employees and hire more peripheral employees, such as dispatch workers, temps, and part-time employees, to replace them (Weathers 2001). Further-more, firms are steadily going offshore in search of cheaper labor. The opportunities for regular employment in blue-collar or even low-level service industry work – even for men – may be shrinking as companies try to save costs. More research needs to be done on what working-class people see as their future under these circumstances.

A New Class Society?

In 2000 the popular magazines *Bungei shunjū* and *Chūōkōron* both ran articles on the increasing class-based nature of Japanese society. *Bungei shunjū*'s piece was written from the perspective of the elite, well-paid salaryman who had followed all the correct social rules only to find they no longer protected him. The article constructed a discourse of "winners" versus "losers." The former were internationally savvy and entrepreneurial self-made men, and the latter equally hard-working but hapless men who had unwittingly cast their lot with firms that failed to meet the global competi-tion. These are not stories of the little man who ekes out a living in a small family business, but of the endangered upper-middle-class male who suddenly find the rules have changed and the door has slammed shut, with house loans looming and tuition fees to be paid. What are the rules? They are that elite education will lead to a respected position in a stable firm, where every man of the same age receives approximately the same salary, where effort is appreciated over achievement, and where the generalist can expect to spend his entire career at the same company. The *Bungei shunjū* article blames the economic malaise on the "dog-eat-dog" era of global standards, wherein "winners" and "losers" become differentiated. They report that many firms are changing their salary schemes to reflect achievement over seniority. They conclude that "the days are over when the company would protect the individual. The equality of result that supported Japanese society is fading away" (*Bungei shunjū* 2000:102). As evidence for an increasingly stratified society, the editors note that an increasing number of entrants to the most elite national university, the University of Tokyo, hail from private and national junior and senior high schools rather than from local public institutions.

These *Bungei shunjū* editors end their piece by arguing that the majority of Japanese people do not believe in rewarding achievement as much as rewarding effort. This was gleaned from the 1995 SSM survey. They ask whether Japan can find a middle way between the "traditional" Japanese model and what they perceive to be the "American," winner-take-all model. Looming over this discussion of malaise and bifurcation are the very real problems associated with a rapidly aging society, a declining birth rate (see Roberts 2002), and the threat of increasing tax burdens on the working population to cover pensions, national health, and long-term care insurance. In the United States this discourse would be about the illusion of the American Dream, and the odds against making it, but in Japan it is about a loss of security; the loss of a sure thing. It is arguably a largely middle- and upper-middle-class anxiety, as workers in small firms have never experienced the so-called traditional Japanese model of employment stability.[10] A social class perspective on the effects of the recession and capital flight offshore might better clarify the range of "winners" and "losers" in this new situation.

NOTES

1   Editor's note: The OECD released a report in early November 2003 that strongly criticized Japanese companies for their "incomprehensible [sex] and age-related barriers that keep skilled and experienced women from returning to work [after bearing children] of the same level as before they left." The report cites companies' "inefficient us of the labor force" and calls "unnecessary" the tax and pension system, which "rewards" women for remaining the lowest income earners in a household (Wijers-Hasegawa 2003:2).

2   I was told by managers that unlike many industries that can be almost totally mechanized, the clothing industry needs the eyesight and hands of humans to sew and inspect delicate materials such as silk and lace. This company was intent on keeping if not increasing its market share and fine reputation, and it was very concerned about maintaining quality. If the company wanted to expand, it needed to hire more people. The years of expansion ended after the oil crises of the 1970s, and the 1980s saw an increasing shift of production to less expensive rural areas of Japan as well as offshore in Southeast Asia and China.

3   Kaye Broadbent has written extensively, based on participant observation fieldwork, on the topic of female *paato* employees in the supermarket industry. She includes updates of the 1990s on part-timers' legal status, and their tenuous relationship with enterprise unionism. See Broadbent 2000, 2001.

4   An editorial in the *Japan Times*, "Same Pay for the Same Work," notes that the average hourly wage for regular workers in 2001 was ¥2,778, whereas for part-time workers it was ¥1.026 (*JT* December 7, 2002, p. 18).

5   Along these lines, one of my co-workers, a married woman in her late fifties whose husband worked for a driving school, remarked that her husband was fond of drinking beer, consuming a not insignificant amount of the household budget in this manner. She was trying to find a way to curb his habit, as she felt that after they retired she could not balance the budget if he kept it up.

6   This probably speaks to the conditions of the average apartment affordable to single-earner blue-collar workers.

7   Women who had entered the company after a period of staying home to raise their children did voice worries over the effect of their absence from home on the children's well-being.

8   Editor's note: The current (2003) prime minister, Koizumi Junichirō, is a case in point. After fathering two children, he divorced his pregnant wife at the urging of his (male) secretary in order to concentrate on his rising political career, and has had virtually no contact of any kind with his own children and former wife. Koizumi's behavior is considered par for the course, and has not been a negative factor in his political career.

9   Of the 73 production workers surveyed, 55 (75.3 percent) indicated they desired to continue working after marriage. Although 89.3 percent (n = 25) of the 28 women in the manager/specialty worker/designer category came in at the top on this question, in a subsequent question which queried how they planned to continue working after marriage, a lower percentage of women in the manager/specialty worker/designer group planned to return to Azumi after maternity leave than did those in the production worker sample. Fifty-three percent (n = 30) of the production workers sampled indicated they would prefer to return to the present job after maternity leave ended. Forty percent (n = 10) of 25 managers, specialty workers, and designers, 27.1 percent (n = 13) of 48 office workers, and 31.6 percent (n = 12) of the sales personnel chose this pattern (Yamamoto 1994:71).

10 In 1999, 48.1 percent of workers were employed in firms of fewer than 30 employees (Japan Institute of Labour 2000:27).

REFERENCES

Bernstein, Gail. 1983. Haruko's World. Stanford: Stanford University Press.

Bestor, Theodore. 1989. Neighborhood Tokyo. Stanford: Stanford University Press.

Brinton, Mary C. 1993. Women of the Economic Miracle: Gender and Work in Postwar Japan. Berkeley: University of California Press.

Broadbent, Kaye. 2000. Shortchanged? Part-Time Workers in Japan. Japanese Studies 21(3):293–304.

——2001. Power in the Union? Part-Time Workers and Enterprise Unionism in Japan. International Journal of Manpower 22(4):318–332.

Bungei shunjū. 2000. Shōgeki repōto amerika gata jyakuniku kyōshoku wo yurusu no ka: shin kaisō shakai nippon (Japan: The New Class Society: Will We Adopt the Dog-Eat-Dog American Style? Shock Report). Bungei shunju May:94–107.

Clammer, John. 1997. Contemporary Japan: A Sociology of Consumption. Oxford: Blackwell.

Curtin, J. Sean. 2000. Lone Mother Poverty in Japan: An Analysis of Social Trends in the 1990s. The Annual Report of the Regional Research Institute, Asahikawa University, No. 23, December:43–74.

——2002. Trends in Single-Parent Welfare Policy. Paper presented at the EASH 2002 4th International Conference: East Asian Social Welfare Policies, St. Catherine Women's College, Hojo, Japan, September 27–29.

deBary, Brett. 1998. San'ya: Japan's Internal Colony. In The Other Japan: Postwar Realities. E. Patricia Tsurumi, ed. pp. 112–118. Armonk, NY, and London: M. E. Sharpe.

di Leonardo, Micaela. 1991. Gender at the Crossroads of Knowledge: Feminist Anthropology in the Postmodern Era. Los Angeles: University of California Press.

Douglass, Mike, and Glenda S. Roberts. 2000. Japan in a Global Age of Migration. *In* Japan and Global Migration: Foreign Workers and the Advent of a Multicultural Society. Mike Douglas and Glenda S. Roberts, eds. pp. 3–37. London and New York: Routledge.

Folbre, Nancy. 1994. Who Pays for the Kids? Gender and the Structures of Constraint. London and New York: Routledge.

Fowler, Edward. 1996. San'ya Blues: Laboring Life in Contemporary Tokyo. Ithaca, NY: Cornell University Press.

Gill, Thomas P. 2001. Men of Uncertainty: The Social Organization of Day Laborers in Contemporary Japan. Albany: State University of New York Press.

Gordon, Andrew. 2002. The Short Happy Life of the Japanese Middle Class. *In* Social Contracts Under Stress: The Middle Classes of America, Europe, and Japan at the Turn of the Century. Olivier Zunz, Leonard Schoppa, and Nobuhiro Hiwatari, eds. pp. 108–129. New York: Russell Sage.

—— 1998. The Wages of Affluence: Labor and Management in Postwar Japan. Cambridge, MA: Harvard University Press.

Hamabata, Matthews. 1991. Crested Kimono: Power and Love in a Japanese Business Family. Ithaca, NY: Cornell University Press.

Hayes, Susan. 1996. The Cultural Contradictions of Motherhood. New Haven and London: Yale University Press.

Hochschild, Arlie. 1989. The Second Shift: Working Parents and the Revolution at Home. New York: Viking.

Hunter, Janet, ed. 1995. Japanese Working Women. London and New York: Routledge.

Ishida, Hiroshi. 1993. Social Mobility in Contemporary Japan. Stanford: Stanford University Press.

—— 2001. Industrialization, Class Structure, and Social Mobility in Postwar Japan. British Journal of Sociology 52(4):579–604.

Japan Institute of Labor. 2000. Japanese Working Life Profile 2000: Labour Statistics. Tokyo: The Japan Institute of Labour.

Kondo, Dorinne. 1990. Crafting Selves: Power, Gender, and Discourses of Identity in a Japanese Workplace. Chicago and London: University of Chicago Press.

Kumazawa, Makoto. 1996. Portraits of the Japanese Workplace: Labor Movements, Workers, and Managers. Boulder, CO: Westview Press.

Lebra, Takie S. 1976. Japanese Patterns of Behavior. Honolulu: University of Hawaii Press.

—— 1990. The Socialization of Aristocratic Children by Commoners: Recalled Experiences of the Hereditary Elite in Modern Japan. Cultural Anthropology 5(1):78–100.

—— 1993. Above the Clouds: Status Culture of the Modern Japanese Nobility. Berkeley: University of California Press.

Lie, John. 2000. The Discourse of Japaneseness. *In* Japan and Global Migration: Foreign Workers and the Advent of a Multicultural Society. Mike Douglass and Glenda S. Roberts, eds. pp. 70–90. London and New York: Routledge.

Margolis, Abby. 2002. Samurai Beneath Blue Tarps: Doing Homelessness, Rejecting Marginality and Preserving Nation in Ueno Park. Ph.D. dissertation, University of Pittsburgh.

Milly, Deborah J. 1999. Poverty, Equality, and Growth: The Politics of Economic Need in Postwar Japan. Cambridge, MA: Harvard University Press.

Nagase, Nobuko. 2002. Wife Allowance and Tax Exemption behind Low Wages for Part-Time Workers. Japan Labor Bulletin 41(9):8–10.

Ogasawara, Yuko. 1998. Office Ladies and Salaried Men: Power, Gender and Work in Japanese Companies. Berkeley: University of California Press.

Okano, Kaori, and Mamoru Tsuchiya. 1999. Education in Contemporary Japan: Inequality and Diversity. Cambridge: Cambridge University Press.

Osawa, Mari. 1994. Bye-bye Corporate Warriors: The Formation of a Corporate-Centered Society and Gender Biased Social Policies in Japan. Tokyo: University of Tokyo Institute of Social Science Occasional Papers in Labor Problems and Social Policy 18.

——2002. Twelve Million Full-Time Housewives: The Gender Consequences of Japan's Postwar Social Contract. *In* Social Contracts Under Stress: the Middle Classes of America, Europe and Japan at the Turn of the Century. Olivier Zunz, Leonard Schoppa, and Nobuhiro Hiwatari, eds. New York: Russell Sage Foundation.

Perlow, Leslie. 1997. Finding Time. Ithaca, NY: Cornell University Press.

Pollack, David. 2000. Aliens, Gangsters and Myth in Kon Satoshi's World Apartment Horror. *In* Japan and Global Migration: Foreign Workers and the Advent of a Multicultural Society. Mike Douglass and Glenda S. Roberts, eds. pp. 153–175. London and New York: Routledge.

Roberson, James. 1998. Japanese Working Class Lives: An Ethnographic Study of Factory Workers. London and New York: Routledge.

Roberts, G. S. 1994. Staying on the Line: Blue-Collar Women in Contemporary Japan. Honolulu: University of Hawaii Press.

——1996. Between Policy and Practice: Silver Human Resource Centers as Viewed from the Inside. Journal of Aging and Social Policy 8(2/3):115–132.

——2002. Pinning Hopes on Angels: Reflections from an Aging Japan's Urban Landscape. *In* Family and Social Policy in Japan. Roger Goodman, ed. pp. 54–91. Cambridge: Cambridge University Press.

——2003. Balancing Life and Work: Whose Work? Whose Life? Whose Balance? In Challenges for Japan, Third Shibusawa International Seminar on Japanese Studies. Gill Latz, ed. pp. 75–109. Tokyo: International House of Japan.

——2004. Globalization and Work/Life Balance: Gendered Implications of New Initiatives at a US Multinational in Japan. *In* Equity in the Workplace: Gendering Policy Analysis. Heidi Gottfried and Laura Reese, eds. pp. 294–314. New York: Lexington Books.

Rohlen, Thomas P. 1979. Japan's High Schools. Berkeley: University of California Press.

Rosenberger, Nancy. 1991. Gender and the Japanese State: Pension Benefits Creating Difference. Anthropology Quarterly 64(4):178–193.

Roth, Joshua H. 2002. Brokered Homeland: Japanese Brazilian Migrants in Japan. Ithaca: Cornell University Press.

Ryang, Sonya. 1997. North Koreans in Japan: Language, Ideology, and Identity. Boulder, CO: Westview.

Satō Toshiki. 2000. Fubyōdō shakai nihon: sayōnara sōchūryū (Japan, the Unequal Society: Farewell to the Mass Mainstream). Tokyo: Chūkō Shinsho.

Slater, David. 2003. Class Culture: Pedagogy and Politics in a Japanese Working-Class High School in Tokyo. Ph.D. dissertation, University of Chicago.

Smith, Robert J., and Ella Wiswell. 1982. The Women of Suye-Mura. Chicago: University of Chicago Press.

Steven, Rob. 1983. Classes in Contemporary Japan. Cambridge: Cambridge University Press.

Stevens, Caroline. 1997. On the Margins of Japanese Society: Volunteers and the Welfare of the Urban Underclass. London: Routledge.

Sugimoto, Yoshio. 1997. An Introduction to Japanese Society. Cambridge: Cambridge University Press.

Tamanoi, Mariko. 1998. Under the Shadow of Nationalism: The Politics and Poetics of Rural Japanese Women. Honolulu: University of Hawaii Press.

Tsuda, Takeyuki. 2003. Strangers in the Ethnic Homeland: Migrant Nationalism and the Making of Japan's New Immigrant Minority. New York: Columbia University Press.

Weathers, Charles. 2001. Changing White-Collar Workplaces and Female Temporary Workers in Japan. Social Science Japan Journal 4(2):201–218.

Wijers-Hasegawa, Yumi. 2003. Improve Job Situation for Women, Firms Told. Japan Times, November 5, p. 2.

Yamamoto, Saeko. 1994. Contemporary Japanese Women's Views toward Marriage and Work: A Questionnaire Survey. MA thesis, University of Hawaii Department of Asian Studies.

Yoder, Robert. 2002. Youth Deviant Behavior, Conflict, and Later Consequences: Comparison of Working and Middle-class Communities in Japan. Unpublished MS; paper given at the Association of Asian Studies Conference, Washington, DC, April 2002.

SUGGESTED READING

Kelly, William. 2002. At the Limits of the New Middle-Class Japan: Beyond Mainstream Consciousness. *In* Social Contracts Under Stress: The Middle Classes of America, Europe, and Japan at the Turn of the Century. Olivier Zunz, Leonard Schoppa, and Nobuhiro Hirowatari, eds. pp. 232–254. New York: Russell Sage.

Turner, Christina. 1995. Japanese Workers in Protest: An Ethnography of Consciousness and Experience. Berkeley: University of California Press.

9 The Anthropology of Japanese Corporate Management

Tomoko Hamada

INTRODUCTION

This chapter (re)traces four decades of anthropological research on Japanese management and connects the study of corporate Japan to theoretical developments in the social sciences. During the 1960s, Japan was often cited as a case in point to support or refute dominant Western theories of economic development and modernization. To add a spark to the dispute about the universality of Western industrial models, the "Japanese style of management" was presented as a distinct cultural form. The highly controversial *nihonjinron* (theories of Japanese-ness) debate[1] and the rise of the total quality management (TQM) movement in the 1980–1990s urged a critical assessment of Western organization theories, corporate culture research methodology, and theories of cross-cultural technological transfer. The last section of this chapter focuses on the current implications of globalization on the future of the Japanese corporate structure.

STUDYING JAPANESE CORPORATIONS

Japanese industry and work relations became subjects of study by many social scientists after World War II. Abbeglen's work (1953) was a pioneer study of the structure of the Japanese company. Abbeglen identified two distinct characteristics of Japanese management: the system of lifelong employment, and the seniority principle. De Vos (1965, 1976) described the high achievement motivation and role commitment of the Japanese, which he claimed were nurtured in the socialization process. Doi (1962, 1973) analyzed the psychological concept of *amae*, a term which refers to the dependence or nurturance needs of the Japanese. He argued that, unlike "Westerners," who are encouraged to be self-sustaining and independent, "the Japanese" are allowed or encouraged to be psychologically dependent on family members, friends, or business associates. The psychology of *amae*, or the presumption of others' indulgence, Doi argued, encourages Japanese conformity to the group. People who support one another due to *amae* communicate easily on a warm personal level and tend to develop a sense of belonging to the group. According to Doi, *amae* is one of the key factors for creating company familism and a strong sense of loyalty to the Japanese worker by the company. *Amae* was a useful but limited tool for explaining complex behaviors of the Japanese in formal business organizations, where other environmental and structural factors are also in effect. In addition to his homogenizing allusions to the behavior of "Westerners," Doi's theory lacked an explanation of other aspects of *amae*, such as the psychology of those who are depended upon by others, and who extend their support and assistance to fulfill the dependency needs of others.

The anthropologist Nakane (1969, 1971, 1978) introduced another theory based on the vertical relationship of Japanese organization members. Much of Nakane's work was influenced by a sociologist, Kawashima (1950, 1957) and his work on familism in the *ie*, or traditional household, and its application to modern organizational settings. *Ie* refers to the social relationships of the members of a Japanese household before World War II, where each individual was expected to act according to his or her relative social position in a superior–inferior status hierarchy. Kawashima (and Nakane) believed that many aspects of contemporary Japanese behavior could be explained by analyzing this cultural tradition (see chapter 22 in this volume).

The so-called groupism (*shudan-shugi*) model was slowly developed to explain the cultural characteristics of the Japanese corporate structure. Individuals carry behavioral principles developed in their socialization process into corporate settings and conform to the group norms either due to *amae* or the cultural tradition of the *ie* system (see chapter 16 in this volume). Groupism and familism were treated as independent variables in order to explicate organizational features such as lifelong employment and seniority-based wages and promotions. Vogel (1979) praised Japanese groupism as contributing to their economic prosperity and social stability, and Drucker (1973) pointed out the capacity for the Japanese to work for a distant goal in such an environment. The structural characteristics of the Japanese company were extensively discussed by many social scientists during the period when Japanese economy was expanding at a remarkable pace (e.g., Abbeglen 1953; Ballon 1972; Clark 1979; Cole 1971a, 1971b; Dore 1973; Hazama 1963, 1964, and 1974; Iwata 1977, 1978; Marsh and Mannari 1976; and Yoshino 1976).

The following table shows the stereotypical characteristics of the Japanese company compared with those of the generalized Western corporation, as noted by the Japan specialists cited in this chapter. One can observe the construction of an overly simplified model of the Japanese style of management emerging from such dichotomous comparisons (see also chapter 5 in this volume).

The model in Table 9.1 has often been called the groupism model; it was put forward originally by Abbeglen, Doi, Iwata, Kawashima, and Vogel who presented a Japanese model in contrast to a Western individualism model. Hamaguchi (1977) expanded the concept of Japanese situational values (i.e., values conditioned by the immediate status relationship between individuals), which had been described by

Table 9.1 Stereotypical binary comparison of Western and Japanese management systems

	Western system	Japanese system
The concept of the company	Place for work	Ideally a community
Employment	Contractual: job- and position-oriented	Permanent: company-oriented
Labor mobility	Higher	Lower
Recruitment	Emphasize specific skills Immediate capability	General background Long-term potential
Unit function	Individual as a unit	Group as a unit
Task assignment	Given to an individual by mutual choice and negotiation	Given to a group/ individual works as a part of a team
Career development	Functional and professional track Expertise valued	Broad and general within one company Experience valued
Reward system	Merit and performance/ bottom lines	Seniority, but merit not ignored
Job description	Clearly defined	Flexible
Responsibility	Individual accountability	Group responsibility
Authority	Specifically defined Formally delegated	Implicitly defined Informally delegated
Position and individual power	Formal position defines the power	Personal attributes influence the power – must be earned
Leadership	Ideal of a dynamic leadership Personal initiative	Managing consensus Sensitivity to group harmony
Communication	Explicit, detailed, and written filing and documentation	Implicit, informal, oral Mutual trust stressed Tacit communication and shared understanding
Retirement	Legal age	No legally fixed age, but customarily 55–60
Employee loyalty	Job-, work unit-, and people-oriented	Company-based

Ruth Benedict (1946; see chapter 1 in this volume), and applied them to the organizing principle of Japanese firms. Iwata (1977, 1978) argued that cultural tradition was a crucial element that created and developed the style of Japanese management. Hazama (1974) and Tsuda (1976, 1977) also stressed the importance of culture in the Japanese management system.

By the end of the 1970s, the influence of Japanese culture on organizational structure had become a hot issue among scholars. Many argued against the culturalists' explanation. For instance, Marsh and Mannari (1976) stressed that the social organizational variables (such as seniority increments and lifelong employment) that were considered distinctly Japanese had less causal impact on economic performance than did more universal variables, such as employee status and job satisfaction. They pointed out that the cultural variations between Japanese and Western firms were not so great or important as earlier writers had averred. Likewise, Azumi (1978), Johnson (1977a, 1977b), Johnson and Ouchi (1974), and Ouchi and Jaeger (1977) demonstrated the existence of a very wide variation within each culture, and argued that national cultural differences are not powerful enough to override internal variations. Azumi reported that a comparison of 12 matched samples of business organizations in Japan, Britain, and Sweden revealed little between-country variation on all structural dimensions except the number of ranks. Lincoln et al. (1978) found little correlation between structural characteristics and the number of Japanese nationals and Japanese Americans in their survey of 54 Japanese business firms in southern California.

Social scientists such as Cole (1967, 1971a, 1971b, 1972, 1976), Kamei (1978), Koike (1979, 1988), LeVine et al. (1973), Noda (1975), and Tanaka (1979) also stressed the importance of the economic rationality of the Japanese style of management instead of Japanese cultural tradition. Taira (1970) argued that the development of permanent employment and seniority increments had been deliberately created by profit-maximizing entrepreneurs because these practices had been economically rational and feasible. They also attacked the culturalists by critiquing their static views of culture. For example, sociologist Cole's findings on the Japanese blue-collar workers revealed rapid structural changes of labor management and the weakening of the workers' commitment to the company due to the shift in economic conditions (Cole 1972, 1976). Austin (1976) described how the Japanese system was not as stable as previously described and how Japan was a paradox of progress.

Thus, a wave of scholarly debates emerged on the cultural specificity or universality of the Japanese style of management, which led to dispute among social scientists on the issue of the future convergence or divergence of managerial practices across national borders. For example, Tsurumi (1976) argued that, in view of the increasing internationalization of Japanese business, the Japanese management system would be forced to conform to managerial ideologies prevalent in Western countries, and would eventually converge with a Western style of management. An English social scientist, Dore (1973), on the other hand, presented the "latecomer" theory in order to explain the difference between the Japanese and British styles of labor management. Arguing against the groupism model, Dore concluded that, as a latecomer in industrialization, Japan could leap ahead of older industrialized nations and create more advanced forms of managerial practice. According to Dore, the growing similarities between the Japanese and Western systems would come from the adoption elsewhere of the Japanese model of labor management with its more flexible occupational roles, greater worker participation in the decision-making process, and broader responsibility of management that emphasizes the well-being of the workers.

Yoshino (1968, 1975, 1976) was the first scholar to address the Japanese style of decision-making. He described both positive and negative aspects of the *ringi* system, where a number of individuals are involved in group decision-making and assume group responsibility for the issue concerned. *Ringi*, which literally means "rotating discussion," is a style of decision-making where a proposal is written in a *ringi-sho* (a particular form for decision-making) which is passed around for the approval of all organizational units concerned. The number of participants in the *ringi* system is greater than in the Western decision-making system. The practice of *ringi* has been cited as evidence of the low degree of centralized authority and decision-making power in the Japanese company.

Azumi's (1978) quantitative analysis of Japanese and Western firms, however, refuted the assumption that the Japanese would be low in the official hierarchy of authority and in job specialization. Lincoln et al.'s (1978) quantitative research supported Azumi's findings. They did not find any significant correlation between the centralization of decision-making and the Japanese-ness of a firm, judged by the number of Japanese in Japanese-owned firms in California. These quantitative studies on the decision-making process concluded that there was little difference in the style of decision-making or communication flow between Japanese and Western firms. Thus, such research tended to deny the existence of cultural effects on organizational decision-making style. Most of this quantitative organization research, however, focused on formal structure; the actual content of the ongoing decision-making process was rarely studied. Consequently, cross-cultural comparisons of systems involved categorizing the forms and styles of decision-making, rather than identifying the reasons behind a particular decision or its content. The most important issue overlooked in such comparisons was not the way in which the Japanese make decisions, but the reasons why they make particular decisions. To summarize, Table 9.2 shows three major "schools" of thought about the relationship between management structure and the culture of management.

While many scholars reassessed the simple cultural model of the Japanese corporate practice, Befu (1977) presented a theory of social exchange as an alternative to the groupism model, in order to explain the Japanese organizational principle. His work was compatible with T. Lebra's (1975) analyses of reciprocity in Japanese situations.

The debate on conversion/diversion continued throughout the 1980s and 1990s. Cultural traditionalists who advocated the groupism versus individualism model tended to emphasize what appeared to be the unchanging rather the changing aspects of the Japanese system. However, many changes or transformations had already taken place and were happening when scholars focused on cultural tradition in the 1980s.

Another significant aspect of this conversion–diversion debate is the appropriation of the Japanese culture model by members of the Japanese corporate business elite themselves. As Japan entered the period known as the "bubble economy," the corporate familism and groupism acquired a new status. As the Japanese economy rapidly moved to the world center-stage, management began to recognize that the *ie* ideology was an effective tool for justifying their corporate philosophy and quelling any criticism that might pose a threat to their managerial practices. In the late 1980s and early 1990s, *ie* ideology – that of organizational continuity over time, or "the reproduction of its structure over time" – was creatively adopted by the Japanese business elite, which often invoked it to contrast it with "individual-based" social control mechanisms. Nationalist scholars such as Eto Jun helped popularize this image by stating that, while the self had become fragmented in Europe and America, the Japanese had retained a firm identity because of their integration into the larger social group (Eto 1993).

During this same period, not only Japanese management scientists but also top Japanese firms such as Toshiba and Nippon Steel were eager to explain Japan and the Japanese people to the outside world. For example, in 1982 Nippon Steel

Table 9.2 Theoretical models of corporate structure and culture

Names of schools	Major advocates	Points of discussion
Groupism vs. individualism model	Abbeglen, Hazama, Iwata, Nakane, Tsuda, Vogel	Corporate structural differences between Japanese and Western firms can be explained by cultural factors
Universalism Economic rationality school	Azumi, Johnson, Lincoln et al., March and Mannari, Ouchi et al.	National differences are not significant. Structural differences can be explained by economic rationality
Conversion-Westernization school	Tsurumi	Japan becomes more Westernized because of corporate globalization
Conversion-Japanization school	Dore	Western corporations become more like the Japanese model
Conversion-culture resistance school	Yoshino	Japanese model must change but cultural resistance will make this difficult

Corporation's division of human resource development published an English-language book titled *Japan: The Land and its People*, which has sold more than half a million copies, mostly among business people, and is now in its fourth edition. The videotaped version of the book won awards from the Ministry of Foreign Affairs. The company has shipped the 12-volume videos and 10-volume audiotapes to more than 50,000 firms, schools, and organizations globally. Nippon Steel and other international firms are acutely aware of the likelihood of misunderstanding and friction arising between Japan and other countries. Therefore, Nippon Steel argued, "from now on, it will be imperative for the Japanese not only to know more about foreign countries but also to take every possible opportunity to assist people everywhere to obtain a broader and deeper understanding of Japan" (1982:12). Yoshino Kosaku, who analyzed the content of this and other books popular among business people, concluded that Japanese businesses had applied cultural relativism to explain the Japanese way of thinking. "Cultural relativistic thinking as applied to the Japanese context has resulted in the assertion of Japanese uniqueness because of the Japanese conscious attempt to challenge the assumption that the Western ways are the 'universal' ways, and to emphasize that the Japanese ways should equally be respected in the community of world cultures" (Yoshino 1992:179–180).

It is still common for Japanese businessmen to attempt to explain the Japanese style of management as characteristic of Japan's "unique" culture. They often use the *ie* metaphor to explain basic organizational principles. Such cultural explanations neglect the fact that many frictions in labor management are economic or class-based and have little to do with culture per se. In addition, and perhaps more important, such explanations neglect the fact that the historical experiences of most Japanese are extremely varied. Far from being unitary or monolithic, contemporary Japanese culture contains many more "foreign" elements than it consciously excludes. The more Japanese discuss the image of a "unique" Japanese society in terms of the prototypical Japanese household, the more they enter the realm of fantasy.

The *ie*, or household, became a collective symbol around which Japanese business elites rallied to identify and organize themselves in opposition to the so-called West. But the ideological base of the corporate *ie* is actually anti-family. During the last several decades, Japanese masculinity has become more and more directly linked to corporate employment. The centralizing principle of corporate familism has excluded women, while highly centralized and rapidly globalizing firms have incorporated more and more Japanese males into wage- and salary-based employment. Today 80 percent of Japan's labor force consists of waged and salaried workers.

It is important to note that, until the 1970s, the word *sarariiman* (salaried man, or "salaryman") conjured up a rather drab occupation and low socioeconomic status: the sons of the unpropertied classes who labored in drab urban buildings and received salaries that were determined by their companies. A new image of company men emerged only in the late 1970s and early 1980s, when the Japanese economic structure underwent a transformation, impelling gradual changes in both the occupation and the socioeconomic level of the salaryman. This era was also marked by frequent usage of the *ie* metaphor in analyzing the benefits of the so-called Japanese style of management. By then Japan's most significant economic activity had shifted to corporatons, while the numbers of farmers, fishermen, craftsmen, and small business proprietors steadily declined. As the occupation of salaryman absorbed more and more Japanese men, leaders of male-dominated work organizations began to provide their employees with corporate ideology for a "home-like" totalizing social environment. In official corporate familism, the gender role for Japanese males was always clear: Japanese men should find jobs and work hard for the company. They should be the sole wage-earners of the Japanese household. A Japanese husband could work as long and as hard as he wished at his job because his wife raised the children, looked after the house and attended to his daily needs with a high degree of competence. In other words, men utilized their wives as caretakers so that they themselves could perform at full capacity in the corporate world.

During the era of Japanese economic expansion in the 1960s, the original stereotype of corporate automatons became woefully inadequate as some companies began to establish salaries based on individual abilities rather than on seniority. A new word, *bijinesuman* ("businessman"), became prevalent to describe a respectable number of those who worked as pillars of large Japanese corporations. However, the pitiful salaryman images continued to appeal to ordinary workers, who related to and were comforted by them. Like the cartoon character Dilbert, who exemplifies marginalized masculinity in contemporary corporate America, the bumbling, bone lazy, rank-and-file office worker called *hira-shain* became a stock figure of comedy in the Japanese mass media, TV home drama, and *manga* (comic books).

Some social scientists (e.g., Koike 1994) argued for the merits of this sexual division of labor in production-reproduction, pointing out that it helped to foster the relatively long-term attachment of (male) employees to firms, and enabled firms to invest in long-term human capital formation. They asserted that, with the corporate evaluation and reward systems based on skill and competence development over many years, Japanese (male) employees were motivated to learn and upgrade their skills. The contribution of this human resource strategy was regarded as a definite advantage of large Japanese manufacturing firms.

Only a small number of workers enjoyed the benefits of lifelong employment and long-term career paths in Japanese companies during the period of Japan's economic expansion. Those who were at the center of the business elite were the full-time "regular-status" employees, mostly university-educated males who worked for large corporations. The significant number of workers who were excluded from this privileged core did not enjoy the benefit of job security or long-term career development. Even in large firms many workers were classified as "non-regular" or "contingent" workers. These workers were hired not for the long term, but for non-regular employment characterized by such conditions as a shorter work period, fixed-term or temporary contracts, or an employment relationship with a third party. The Japanese dual-employment structure consisting of core businessmen and periphery workers has also been connected to the sex–gender system, as I elaborate below.

SEX- AND GENDER-BASED DISCRIMINATION

The system of lifetime employment, the seniority system, and the bureaucratic, tightly knit nature of industrial policy have served as barriers to women's entry into management in Japan. While women provide over 49 percent of the workforce of Japan, they number only 8 percent of its managers, having increased from 6 percent a decade ago. Although the Equal Employment Opportunity Act of 1986,[2] combined with the 1980s bubble economy, did facilitate an increase in career opportunities for some women, the economic recession of the 1990s in conjunction with changing attitudes of female workers seemed to diversify both the status and strategies of female workers. We need to revise the earlier representations of Japanese female workers provided by such scholars as Brinton (1989, 1993), McLendon (1983), Pharr (1981), Rohlen (1974), and Smith (1978). These earlier representations or models stressed the transient and auxiliary functions of Japan's female labor force. They portrayed women as starting to work in a company upon graduation from school, resigning from their company on marriage or childbirth, and then, once their children had grown up, rejoining the labor force as part-time workers. The most prominent protagonist in this stereotypical scenario was the so-called "office lady" or "OL." These office ladies have been portrayed as the workers who are exploited as temporary, and therefore less expensive, labor, cast out at a marriageable age for a new, younger crop of female school graduates.

Today, corporations are experiencing more office automation and financial pressures to reduce human resource costs. In the past decade, the number of contingent workers who do not hold regular full-time employee status has almost doubled. While several types of contingent workers exist (e.g., temporary workers hired directly by the employer or its subcontractors), contingent workers are increasingly hired through temporary-help agencies. Legally, such workers are not employees of the employer at whose location they work, but of the agency through which they are hired.[3]

In addition, there is also a large and diverse category of self-employed individuals. Overall 90 percent of contingent workers hired through temporary-help agencies are female. The exodus of young Japanese women from Japanese corporations to work only as temporaries despite its negative effects demonstrates their changing attitude toward corporate careers.

Another noticeable change in the labor mobility of Japanese women today is their exodus from Japan in search of overseas job markets, and to international organizations and multinational corporations. Finally, an important aspect of Japanese women's changing attitude toward production and reproduction is found in the nation's declining birth rate, which is now at a historical low of 1.2 children per (married) woman (see chapter 21 in this volume).

CHANGES IN REPRODUCTION

Japanese women are no longer willing to shoulder total responsibility for family, children, and eldercare. Young men are also expressing a desire for a life outside of their careers. In the official *ie* ideology, the greatest contribution women could make was through the birthing and raising of children. As Nakane (1971) explained in *Japanese Society*, the primary family relationship in Japan is the mother–child unit, "to which the husband (father) attaches.... The core of the Japanese family, ancient and modern, is the parent–child relationship, not that between husband and wife" (Nakane 1971:127–128). Many social scientists have since pointed out that there is a high degree of emotional autonomy in Japanese conjugal relationships. Samuel Coleman (1983) found that the Japanese couples he studied had difficulties discussing which method of birth control to use because conjugal sexuality, like emotional intimacy, is de-emphasized. Social scientists who have invoked *amae* to theorize about the child's emotional dependence on the mother also note that the recent dramatic decline in the birth rate has actually prolonged and made more intense the parenting by the Japanese mother and more protracted the period of dependency by the child.

However, the latest research findings also indicate that the image of the self-sacrificing, nurturing mother may no longer fit a majority of young mothers now in the middle of their childbearing years. My own research on young mothers in their twenties and thirties indicates that this new generation does not necessarily subscribe to the belief that *kodomo ga ikigai* (my child is my *raison d'être*) or *kodomo wa jibun no bunshin* (my child is my *alter ego*) (Hamada 1997).

The psychologist Kashiwagi Keiko observed that young mothers expressed frustration and anxiety over childrearing by stating *kodomo wa futan* (children are burdensome) or *kodomo kara kaihōsaretai* (I want to be free from children), and that the ratio of negative feelings toward childrearing was actually higher if the mothers were full-time housewives (Kashiwagi 1994). This sense of frustration among full-time housewives may match recent employment trends: Japanese women now make up 40 percent of the labor force and more than half of all married women work.

For full-time mothers, having children has narrowed their freedom and they yearn for "self-actualization beyond maternity" (*ikuji igai ni jibun no nōryoku o nobashi-tai*). A cross-cultural study of women in Japan and Brazil conducted by Hanasawa Seiichi (1982) found that Japanese mothers lag behind Brazilian mothers in terms of their maternal identification with their offspring. The "new" mother in Japan is not necessarily a woman who devotes her life to her child (or children) but rather is someone who seeks her own personal satisfaction, often outside the household. As soon as her children enter kindergarten, many so-called *yan-mama* (young mothers) leave their small urban apartments and return to the workplace in order to satisfy their emotional, social, intellectual, and material needs.

Of course, the cost of housing and their children's education are two of the main reasons middle-aged women give for returning to work. They make up the fastest-growing segment of the workforce, although it remains the case that the vast majority of Japanese women were and still are largely blocked from seeking careers in large Japanese firms. These middle-aged women manage to find mostly minimum-wage jobs, for example as lunch-delivery persons, supermarket cashiers, or part-time factory workers, in Japan's sex- and gender-based dual-employment structure. Those who are financially better off enjoy their free time as consumers. They go to restaurants, concerts, theaters, department stores, shopping malls, hot springs spas, cultural centers, karaoke clubs and even on overseas shopping tours, while their husbands work to support their affluent lifestyle.

Meguro Yoriko (1987) found that the sense of independence is stronger among Japanese females than males. In her cross-cultural analysis of American and Japanese mother–infant interaction patterns, she concluded that educational background, rather than nationality and culture, explains differences in mother–infant interaction. The classic (or stereotyped) image of the Japanese mother's close bond with her infant, as reified in *amae* theory, needs to be revised.

Degrees of emotional commitment to children or childrearing differ rather widely among women, and between women and men, regardless of whether they are Japanese or American. Kashiwagi and Wakamatsu (1994) found a growing disjuncture between Japanese fathers' traditional concept of parenthood and Japanese mothers' shifting attitudes toward childrearing. Kashiwagi's previously mentioned study also found that those who tend to believe *kodomo ga ikigai* or *kodomo wa jibun no bunshin* tend to be Japanese fathers, not mothers. Thus, we are seeing a clear difference in both sex and gender, and ideal and real perceptions of the ideal household. Traditional and hitherto unproblematized images of Japanese nurturance in terms of maternity and paternity must be re-examined.

The 1995 census revealed that as Japan grays – and Japan is the fastest-"graying" society in the world – people are staying unmarried longer, living alone more, and having fewer children. The latest population statistics show that those who are in the 65-and-older age group grew to 18.3 million or 14.5 percent of the population, while the 15-and-younger age group declined to 20.1 million or 15.9 percent of the population. The Japanese government has long promoted the desirability of home care for the elderly, but it now realizes that such an approach is not going to meet the needs of the rapidly aging population. The number of those over 65 is predicted to reach over 22 percent of the population by the year 2011, and over 28 percent by 2025 (Kurosu 2003).

Currently about two-thirds of those who need around-the-clock care are looked after by women, mainly daughters-in-law; the rest are in hospitals and nursing homes. *Oi no michi, onna no michi* (Old Age Road, Women's Road), a column in the daily newspaper *Yomiuri shinbun* which debuted in 1984, portrays various situations in which old people with dementia are being looked after at home, mostly by daughters-in-law. Increasingly, however, housewives do not want to take care of their aging parents-in-law.

While feminism is seldom, if ever, cited as the reason behind the growing number of Japanese women in the workplace or the crisis in caring for the elderly, many of the women I interviewed are currently engaged in what I call "active forms of with-drawal" within the areas over which they have personal control (Hamada 1997). These forms of female noncompliance include such things as not cooking special dishes to accommodate the tastes of parents-in-law or not fixing dinner for a husband who comes home late; refusing to accompany husbands to new job locations; and refusing to clean up the house for them. As more and more women work outside the household for wages, some women are refusing, in addition, to take care of their aging in-laws (a majority of whom are also women) and are demanding "burden-sharing" from their husbands.

Japanese women have the longest life expectancy of any people in the world. They can now expect to live to over 81 years of age, quite a change from the prewar days, when most women died by the age of 50. In those days, the average woman had five children and unending household chores. Her youngest child entered school when she was about 42, and she herself died some eight years later. Today, by the time a Japanese woman is 35 or 40, she has become "free" of childrearing tasks because, typically, she has had only one child, and she has another 40 years to live. The latest (2000) census statistics also reveal that 69 percent of Japanese men and over 54 per-cent of women in the 25–29 age group are still single, the highest rate in the history of the census. The number of people living alone in Japan rose about 27 percent between 1990 and 2000, to nearly 13 million.

In my interviews with Japanese housewives, they seemed quite willing to re-examine the myth of the *ie* household and their traditional sex and gender roles. Some are seeking new ways to reconceptualize marital and parental relationships. Another statistic that points to the changing moral standards of the Japanese family is the tenfold increase in alcohol consumption among young people compared to 11 years ago. While the legal drinking age in Japan is 20, the law does not require entertainment establishments or liquor stores to "card" customers. In addition, Japan is the only country in the world where alcoholic drinks can be obtained from (ubiquitous) vending machines. There are more than 200,000 vending machines selling alcoholic beverages in Japan. Since the 1970s, the number of female drinkers has risen substantially as the alcoholic beverage industry has targeted the rising disposable income of women and their increased freedom. The phenomenon of the "kitchen-drinking" syndrome has spread among middle-aged housewives who drink alone at home (Tanaka 1995). Today the ratio of female to male drinkers has reached the European level of 1 woman to 1.4 men (Hughes 1995). As the new economic, social, and sex-gender realities sink in, absent fathers have begun to look back fondly to their homes and children. The Japanese are weaving multiple images of work, family, and household. What is irrefutably clear is that the idealized Japanese *ie* is gone for ever.

CHANGING PATTERNS OF YOUTH EMPLOYMENT: FREETER AND NEET

During the 1980s, a new type of worker, termed "freeter," emerged in Japan. "Freeter" is a contraction of "free *Arbeiter*" and implies a serial part-time worker who only holds part-time jobs or who moves from one job to another. A freeter has no intention of settling down to a serious career, and spends most of his or her time pursuing other interests or just enjoying freedom. According to Kosugi, many young people reject the constraints of being a *sarariiman* in a corporate society and become freeters (Kosugi 2002).

Besides the psychological reasons given by Kosugi and others, there are economic reasons behind the recent increase in freeters. Today the part-time job market is much larger than it was 20 years ago. The declining chance of coming across a permanent job to which a young person can commit themselves undermines their commitment to the job in which they are currently engaged, and results in a rash of unemployment and job-switching. Young part-timers become dependent upon their parents, creating the so-called "parasite singles" phenomenon (Yamada 1999). The emergence of parasite singles is a direct consequence of a substantial decline in labor demand for young people and of structural changes in the corporate environment, as well as of the psycho-social characteristics of today's youth. In 2004 a new term, NEET (No Education, Employment or Training) came into use to describe young individuals (Nakamura 2004). Unlike freeters, NEET youths are unwilling to take any job. Experts believe that about 400,000 people aged between 15 and 24 were NEET youth in 2003, five times the figure in 1997 (Nakamura 2004). The rise of NEET youths has become a social issue in Japan, similar to the ones experienced by some European nations since the late 1990s, with these nations having undergone changes in their industrial and employment structures.

ORGANIZATIONAL CULTURE AND TOTAL QUALITY MANAGEMENT

Earlier, I discussed how the influence of Japanese culture on corporate structure became a controversial issue among social scientists in the last decade. The rise and fall of the Japanese style of management created several important theoretical questions in cross-cultural management research. For example, do universally applicable structural variables determine people's behavior in organizations, or do national, racial, or ethnic-cultural conditioning influence organizational activities? An increasing number of organizational scientists attacked the universality myth in transnational organizational research (see Osigweh 1989 for a review) as the interfaces between the Western and non-Western cultures became an important area of scientific inquiry (Adler 1983a, 1983b, 1986).

Within the discipline of anthropology, research on North American work organizations began to flourish in the 1980s. The now well-known "organization culture" movement started when American society was faced with international competition, particularly from Japan. The debate on culture and industrial organization began to define the distinct specialization of organizational anthropology as a field of study. In 1982 interest in corporate culture suddenly exploded with the publication of popular works such as Dean and Kennedy's *Corporate Cultures* and Peters and Waterman's *In Search of Excellence*. The impact of their messages spawned research exploring the relationship between culture and productivity. At that time, many American manufacturers faced a major challenge in making sense of the novel exogenous threat from Japan, in such key industries as automobiles, steel, office machinery, machine tools, and electronics. Something akin to a social movement arose in response to Japan's quality management ideology, and TQM dominated managerial discourse for almost two decades.

TQM had its origins as a practitioner-led movement in Japan without much academic involvement, and it continued in that mode when it was adopted by American industries. A pervasive theme in the TQM literature has been the importance of employee involvement in continuous process improvement. Several key features characterized the American TQM movement in the 1980s and early 1990s: a process orientation; an emphasis on the centrality of production processes in contrast to characteristics of products; a focus on the customer as the final arbiter of quality; an emphasis on the systematic application of tools to evaluate and improve work processes; and an insistence on the principle that managers at all levels take responsibility for quality improvement. Although a number of TQM advocates touted the benefits of creating such an organizational culture, there were few attempts to measure its existence empirically and to assess its impact on organizational performance (Cole and Scott 2000). The TQM movement, however, did bring about major changes in the meaning of quality for many people, from corporate leaders to workers, and from customers to clients. In Hamada (2000) I suggested that the idea of quality continues to evolve. Today, in Japanese firms, the concept of "quality" is increasingly associated with attention to the environment.

The rise and fall of the TQM movement in America during the 1980s and 1990s greatly influenced US production. American managers constructed new social meanings of quality and made sense of the suddenly competitive environment as they came to grips with the new model of industrial quality management. For the first several years, the conditions for effective learning were not met. While Japan's economic threat forced managers to think deeply about appropriate corporate strategies, many entrenched institutional factors in American firms worked against the recognition of quality as a competitive factor and against learning effective responses to this challenge. However, in the process, they recognized that programs based on individual improvement were not sufficient, and they began to create system-based approaches to prevention and process improvement. According to Easton and Jarrell (2000), almost all of the key concepts of total quality management persist today, including process concepts, systematic improvement, employee involvement, empowerment, teamwork, customer focus, supplier integration, emphasis on metrics, and cycle-time reduction. TQM was instrumental in legitimizing the already existing team-based management approaches. Combining the ideas of process management and a general orientation toward employee empowerment led to more self-managed work teams and company-wide involvement in quality orientation.

Partly because of their experiences with TQM (Deming 1986), managers, consultants, and scholars have increasingly recognized the value of considering organizational activities in terms of processes rather than functions. In the past, the physical design of manufacturing and service processes were in the domain of industrial engineering, operations research, and operations management, while the original TQM movement grew out of the field of statistics (Deming 1986; Shewhart 1939). At the same time, re-engineering has its roots in information technology and computer science. In contrast, organizational scholars have primarily studied the behavioral aspects of change. Therefore, there was a clear need for an interdisciplinary theory of process improvement that could integrate the physical structure of improvement with an understanding of human decision-making in organizations. Today, organization scientists stress the mutual, recursive links among technological artifacts, physical layouts, organizational structure, and the mental models of organizational actors and their behaviors. These are interconnected with explicit feedback processes that create organizational dynamics.

JAPAN'S RECESSION ECONOMY IN THE 1990S AND NEW MANAGERIAL RHETORIC OF GLOBALIZATION IN THE 2000S

Japan's real estate soared to its highest level in 1988, and its stock market peaked in 1989. Then, in February 1991, the bubble burst. By 1992, the Nikkei stock index had dropped by more than 40 percent of its 1989 value. The bursting of Japan's economic bubble in 1992 precipitated a recession which in turn occasioned a new agenda for organizational research, namely, an investigation of the pathological aspects of corporate Japan. The core problem of the 1990s Japanese recession was the proliferation of non-performing loans made by banks and financial institutions. As stocks and land prices fell, land developers and companies failed to make payments on their loans. It was also widely believed that banks had extended more loans to poor performers – a practice called "evergreening" – in order to make it appear that those performers were paying off their interest. As the banks themselves became unprofitable, they restricted lending, thus creating more bankruptcies. Small and medium-sized firms were badly hit by the credit crunches. More firms collapsed, and the unemployment rate began to climb. This was also a time when many corruption scandals were sensationalized in the mass media, and public confidence in corporate Japan decreased rapidly. Corporate governance and business ethics became new areas of study.

   A major restructuring took place in Japan's financial sector during 2001–2004. Many city banks and financial institutions merged, in part to absorb the losses and to re-establish the sector. It was at this time that the *zaibatsu*-style[4] holding company, dismantled during the occupation period, became restored as a legal entity. Banks were newly allowed to offer a wide range of financial services. During this period, several mega-mergers took place. In the early 2000s, Fuji Bank, Industrial Bank of Japan, and Dai-ichi Kangyo Bank fused into a trillion-dollar superbank named Mizuho. Tokai Bank, Sanwa Bank, and Toyo Trust & Banking merged to create United Financial of Japan or UFJ Holdings Inc. Sumitomo and Sakura banks joined to create a superbank called Sumitomo Mitsui Banking Corporation (SMB). Tokyo and Mitsubishi banks merged to form the Tokyo-Mitsubishi Bank, which later joined the Mitsubishi Trust and Banking to form Mitsubishi Tokyo Financial Group Inc.

In 2004 there were four mega-banks in Japan: Mizuho, UFJ, Sumitomo-Mitsui, and Mitsubishi-Tokyo. In the summer of 2004, Mitsubishi Tokyo Financial Group together with UFJ Holdings Inc. announced their merger plan to create the largest bank in the world, with some $1.7 trillion in assets, outstripping the country's leader, Mizuho Financial Group, and the global leader, Citigroup Inc. Major restructuring is also under way in financial institutions and insurance companies.

In tandem with intensifying globalization, critical discussions of so-called "Japanese-style" employment relations by the management began in the early 1990s, when top business leaders themselves began to express their doubts about their feasibility and validity. In December 1991, for instance, Keizai Doyukai (the Japanese Association of Corporate Executives), a major forum of top business executives, wrote a report on corporate governance titled *Oopun shisutemu e mukete no kigyō kakushin* (Corporate Innovation Toward an Open System) (Keizai Doyukai 1991). That same year, Morita Akio, then vice-president of Japan's powerful Keidanren (Japan Federation of Economic Organizations) and the chairman of Sony, also wrote a stinging criticism of Japanese-style management in the monthly magazine *Bungei shunjū*. (Morita 1991) The Morita paper was followed by a rebuttal by Nikkeiren (the Japanese Employers Federation) in 1992, which was in turn followed by a remark by Hiraiwa Gaishi (then president of Keidanren) supporting many of the points raised by Morita. Whereas the executives of the largest Japanese companies emphasized the need for structural reforms in Japanese corporate governance, the first shift in managerial rhetoric concerned, in keeping with precedent, the welfare of employees.

A content analysis of the public announcements issued by three major employee associations and in the annual reports of the top 20 major corporations over the last five years reveals that the typical Japanese company is discarding its long-held ideology of "the company as the family" and "the commitment of the corporation to employee job security." These slogans are being dropped from official corporate documents. Today, managerial rhetoric emphasizes market orientation and cost-effectiveness in light of global competition. *The Declaration for the 21st Century*, written by Keizai Doyukai at the end of 1999 used the word "market" 33 times, while the word "community" appeared only eight times. This declaration stated that the market should be the most important point of reference for a corporation's governance of its member companies.

Similarly, the most recent annual reports produced by many of the major corporations state that a given company must "improve" its employment practices in order to strengthen its market competitiveness. Previously taboo words such as "restructuring," "rationalizing," and "human cost reduction" appear quite often in these reports, strengthening the impression that Japanese management may have forgotten its previously avowed obligations to the welfare of employees. Also stressed were independence and choice of employment, in the sense that there should be opportunities to cast off the worker's "excessive dependence on the company and becoming independent" (Keizai Doyukai 2001).

Structurally such a managerial rhetoric is translated into the inauguration of a more rigorous, merit-based pay system and the demise of the seniority-based wage system. Now the majority of corporate executives agree that the seniority-based wage system is dead. Linking the wage and salary system more closely to merit not only provides an incentive to individual workers, it also clarifies the relationship of the pay scale to labor market value. Nikkeiren is encouraging more labor mobility, flexibility, specialization, and diversity. It complains that Japan's labor market has been highly regulated, and that regulatory reform is urgently needed. A major complaint is about the lack of flexibility in hiring temporary workers for, currently, there are limits on the length of an employment contract for such workers. There have also been prohibitions on the dispatch of health-care personnel from manpower agencies to health-related companies. Employers argue that such restrictions should be lifted. Many Japanese companies are now overstaffed, and employees are getting older. Containing total labor costs has become an urgent matter if a company wishes to maintain its competitiveness. Management is also feeling competition from other Asian firms enjoying labor cost advantages.

Thus, according to the discourse of top Japanese management, it appears that the Japanese employment system is outmoded and no longer functioning well in light of global economic competition. Moreover, it seems clear that the Japanese employment system and corporate governance are or should be approaching the Western idea of an economic system driven by the market and investors. At the present time, only the largest and most export-oriented and efficient corporations in Japan are discussing such transformations. Unfortunately, the rest of the corporate sector is deeply rooted in the "traditional" system and, consequently, is economically "ineffective."

The emphasis of Euro-American corporations on creating good returns for investors has never really existed in Japan. Consider layoffs, for example. In the United States, management regards layoffs as a standard procedure when a company no longer has enough work for its workers. However, in Japan, until quite recently, when a company had a few months of poor sales it tended to absorb the losses rather than lay people off. The company tried to protect its full-time workers by finding different work for them to do and new products for them to produce, rather than firing them outright. In recent years, however, even large Japanese firms have experienced serious financial troubles. They have adopted various strategies to reduce the labor costs and/or to "reform" the employment structure. Many firms have transferred idle workers to affiliates, thereby shifting the financial burden of labor costs from the parent company to subcontractors and affiliates; the salaries of individual employees are substantially reduced in the process. What the company is doing in this case is creating both a small core of employees who benefit from long-term employment and a large group of peripheral workers who have neither guaranteed job security nor fringe benefits, and who often make substantially less than full-time employees. The hiring of temporaries and female workers is considered a desirable cost-saving strategy.

Recently Japanese companies have begun to include more legal contractual terms in the hiring process. For example, employees in their early fifties who have not yet been promoted to an executive rank are asked if they would like to take early retirement. If they do not, they will be put into a newly created contractual position with a reduced salary until their mandatory retirement at 60. This strategy effectively reduces the number of new hires while rationalizing the presence of the older and more expensive sector of the employees; it also reduces and even eliminates bonuses and fringe benefits.

In Japan, major manufacturers organized on the basis of the conventional vertical *keiretsu* system continue to operate a wide array of businesses. This is because these firms attach greater importance to both worker benefits and the local governments where their plants are located than to stockholders. As a result, these companies experience low profitability in comparison to their foreign counterparts.

In order for Japanese makers to compete with powerful overseas companies, most scholars agree that a major change in the structure of their business is necessary: Firms must nurture core businesses that will lead to future growth, and sell or dismantle unprofitable or inefficient ones. Only companies that are able to implement a rigorous and impartial procedure of "selection and concentration" will survive the next couple of years. Companies are only just beginning to understand the dangers of maintaining large inventories and are beginning to scale back. In this new corporate reality, businessmen are increasingly subject to demotion and firing, making wage labor an unstable source of masculine identity and human dignity. In addition, starting in the late 1980s the *shinjinrui*, or "new breed," of young businessmen began to defy the doctrine of self-sacrifice that suggested they were nothing more than latter-day kamikaze pilots in business suits. They refused to sacrifice family and self for the corporate bottom line, and began to question the traditional premium on blind loyalty to the company and the self-sacrificing work ethic of their elders. They became less concerned with their jobs and promotions and more involved with their hobbies and/or families. The recession in the 1990s provoked doubts about corporate familism among even the staunchest "corporate warriors."

The mass media reports have made much of Japan's current record high rate of unemployment (5.5 percent). Historically, however, the unemployment rate has been much higher. The perception that the Japanese economy is doing badly is much greater abroad than it is inside Japan. Although the Japanese people may complain about the inability of the government to rescue the economy, they still pride themselves on living in what is obviously one of the most affluent countries in the world. Certain manufacturing sectors are doing very well, the country has a strong account surplus, and many Japanese firms lead technologically in key areas such as optics, office machinery, computerized control systems, wireless technology, and robotics. In other words, the current unemployment statistics belie the very real successes of the Japanese economy, where sales of mobile phones or leisure travel packages are booming.

According to Befu et al. (2000) and Befu and Guichard-Anguis (2002), since the late 1980s the term "globalization" has displaced "internationalization," a popular word in the 1970s and 1980s. Globalization is now commonly invoked in the Japanese media, and used frequently by such public figures as Ohmae Kenichi (Ohmae 1995, 1999), who wrote a number of books on Japan's economic globalization. The Japanese leadership, top management, and politicians, in the late 1990s and the early 2000s, often emphasized the negative side of globalization, stating that the Japanese economy suffered due to foreign competition. Because Japan was perceived abroad as having economic difficulties due to global competition, the United States and European nations became less critical of Japanese corporate practices. This contrasts with the 1980s, when Japan was perceived as an economic juggernaut, inviting fierce criticism from Euro-America. In reality, Japan's trade became far stronger in the 2000s, and Japanese companies accelerated their foreign investments, particularly in Asia, which targeted advanced Euro-American markets. Today America has the largest trade deficit in history. And yet the American media no longer focus on the trade imbalance issue. Among other things, the Bush administration's "war against terror" has put a new twist on the American government's agenda for the Japanese in emphasizing friendly alliances with its trade and military partners.

JAPAN'S TRADE PATTERNS

In 1998 Japan enjoyed the highest trade surpluses in its history at ¥13.99 trillion, and while the surplus went down to ¥10.71 trillion in 2001 (¥51.65 trillion in exports, and ¥40.93 trillion in imports) Japan continues to have a very favorable trade surplus. Broken down by country, both exports and imports to and from the United States increased dramatically during the last decade. This is an important time for anthropologists to examine the relationship between managerial discourse, global geopolitics, and international trade and investment. In focusing on Japan's trade patterns, I have observed highly internationalized segments in the hard industries, particularly in the advanced electronics sector. For example, the manufacture of laser diodes is a very capital-intensive process involving highly proprietary production processes. Industrial robotics is another such area, as is the manufacture of machine tools, advanced electronic components, and the materials that go into those components. All of these require enormously sophisticated resources. Great Britain used to be the leader in industrial machinery production until the United States took over the lead up to the 1970s. Since then, Japan, Germany, Switzerland, and a few smaller countries have assumed the leadership in manufacturing industrial machinery. As the United States moved toward the so-called New Economy in the 1980s and 1990s, it abandoned many of the industries that had previously placed American firms in direct competition with their Japanese counterparts, such as textiles, machine tools, optics, photography, watches, printing machines, and consumer electronics. Consequently there are now fewer trade disputes between the two nations.

Despite the economic recession in Japan, it is also noteworthy that overall corporate R&D continued to rise during the 1990s. In 1997, Japan filed 9.4 percent of patents worldwide, followed by the US (5.2 percent) and Germany (4.3 percent). In 1997 the United States held a total of 1,113,000 patents worldwide. Japan held 871,000 and Germany, 337,000. Japan's achievements in corporate R&D are concentrated in such fields as solid-state technologies, optics, semiconductor manufacturing systems, and robotics. To compete successfully in the most sophisticated forms of manufacturing, particularly electronics, requires an enormous amount of capital per worker and proprietary expertise.

Japan has a trade surplus with most countries except for China and certain nation-states in the Middle East, due to Japan's overwhelming (80 percent) dependence on oil imported from China. In 2002 Japanese exports to China were worth $31 billion, while Japanese imports from China were worth $58 billion. China is now the second largest market for Japanese exports after the United States, and China exports a major share of textile and agricultural products to Japan. With respect to consumer electronics, China's advance into Japan has just begun, and it is still too early to discuss whether the Chinese will one day come to dominate the Japanese consumer electrics market. It is noteworthy, though, that the Chinese have begun to shift their strategy from one of protecting their own domestic market share to one of expansion into overseas markets. Chinese manufacturers are moving aggressively into Japanese markets. Leading the pack is the Haier Group, China's largest consumer electronics firm, which has entered into a comprehensive alliance with Sanyo. These Chinese–Japanese coalitions are partly motivated by the Chinese fear that they will be unable to survive if they rely on the Chinese or Asian markets alone. Since the mid-1990s, Chinese manufacturers have dominated the Chinese market, which was once nearly monopolized by Japanese appliance-makers. The saturation of the Chinese consumer market has occasioned cutthroat competition in recent years, and many Chinese manufacturers have begun turning their eyes to overseas markets.

GLOBALIZATION AND FOREIGN MANAGEMENT: THE CASE OF THE AUTO INDUSTRY

In this highly dynamic setting, globalization has become a reality, especially for those Japanese industries that face intense foreign competition. The automobile industry is a case in point. Automobile manufacturing is now totally global and, in a sense, the world has become a single market for any and every automobile maker, making domestic automobile industry concerns indistinguishable from international issues. Auto market competition has intensified, partly because of the entry of new participants, excess inventories, new inspection standards, the development of new sales channels, and advancing technology. Profit margins are shrinking while price competition is becoming very intense. Retailers must respond by seeking low-cost products, attractive models, and innovative ways to entice customers.

Traditionally, Japanese automobile makers belonged to the Japan Automobile Manufacturers Association (JAMA). By 2002, only about 11 or 12 manufacturers were members of JAMA; today only a few JAMA members have 100 percent Japanese capital. There is little distinction between domestic and international affairs because of the global-level restructuring of automobile makers. Toyota and Honda are still 100 percent Japanese-owned. However, Toyota has entered into several alliances with General Motors, and signed agreements to share parts with Volkswagen. Toyota is not interested in acquiring a foreign automobile maker because the firm sees a danger of potential cultural clashes. The firm recognizes that it is very difficult to proceed, much less succeed, with different corporate cultures. Therefore, instead of forming international mergers and joint ventures, Toyota has forged links with Japanese companies such as Daihatsu and Yamaha.

Daimler and Chrysler merged to form DaimlerChrysler, the world's fourth-largest auto maker after GM, Toyota, and Ford. DaimlerChrysler later acquired a stake in Mitsubishi Motors, from which it distanced itself in 2004. The new global environment dictates that manufacturer–supplier relationships can no longer be measured in terms of corporate nationalities and reciprocal trade flows. With respect to the supply of auto parts, mergers and joint ventures are increasing, and foreign companies are playing a role through direct investment, marketing, and technological exchange with Japanese firms. However, it remains the case that the car manufacturer in Japan is more likely to rely on local suppliers, be they foreign or domestically owned, since the local supplier is better able to meet the requirements of modern management technology, which include inventory control, rapid delivery, and interface with the manufacturer.

In 1997 the Ford Motor Company bought a controlling stake in the Matsuda (Mazda) Motor Corporation, replaced Matsuda's president, Wada Yoshihiro, and brought in Mark Fields to head the company. Fields graduated from Rutgers University in 1983 with a degree in economics and graduated from Harvard School of Business in 1989 with an MBA. He joined Ford in 1989 and has served in a variety of positions. Prior to his appointment in Japan, he was managing director of Ford Argentina, SA. From 2000 to 2002 Fields led Mazda through a significant transformation (Ford Japan 2002).

The globalization of personnel at Nissan Motors was more dramatic than at Mazda. In July 1999, when Renault SA of France bought a 36.8 percent stake in Nissan for $5.4 billion, the Japanese auto maker had shown its seventh loss in eight years to the tune of $571 million. While the arrival that year of a Brazilian of Lebanese descent, Carlos Ghosn, as Nissan's new president was initially feared by employees, his strategies for overhauling the management of Nissan were positively evaluated. Ghosn's management approach differed in many ways from the "traditional" Nissan style of management. For example, early in his tenure at Nissan, Ghosn decided to reduce the number of suppliers and chose global suppliers on the basis of quality and cost, rather than sticking to affiliated (*keiretsu*) companies out of the loyalty. Ghosn also set up teams of workers to draw ideas from the younger ranks, another drastic departure from the hierarchical, seniority-based decision-making patterns of Japan's (pre-globalized) corporate world. Executive meetings orchestrated by Ghosn were conducted in English. Junior executives and members, for the first time, could express their candid opinions and critiques of past actions, as the English language allowed them to bypass the hierarchical, sex- and gender-inflected, "polite" and status-sensitive Japanese language. His approach to management includes traditional techniques, such as stressing transparency in all business dealings; utilizing a cross-functional team approach; benchmarking for cost containment; and sparking innovation by breaking hierarchical barriers (Magee 2003).

By 2002 Nissan had closed three Japanese plants, and the company's production capacity in Japan had dropped to 1.65 million units from 2 million. It slashed 14 percent of its workforce worldwide, leveling off at 127,000 employees by the fiscal year beginning April 1, 2002. Of the 21,000 jobs cut over the three-year restructuring, about 16,500 were in Japan, 2,400 in Europe, and 1,400 in the United States. Nissan offices in New York and Washington were closed. Although the size of Nissan's job cuts in Japan was unprecedented, they were not unusual in the global auto industry: Ford, for example, announced in March 2002 its intention to eliminate 35,000 jobs. However, compared to the almost perfunctory layoff strategies of American firms, Nissan's restructuring method was similar to that used by other Japanese companies. Instead of laying off people outright, as American auto makers tended to do, Nissan's cuts came through attrition, an increase in part-time and flexitime schedules, the hiring of contractual workers, and spin-offs and early retirements. Nissan decreased its cost base vigorously, resulting in cumulative purchasing cost reductions of 18 percent within a year.

As a result of this belt-tightening, just a year after its "near death" experience Nissan began to revive, at least in terms of the bottom-line numbers. In October 2001, the second year of its restructuring, Nissan reported a third consecutive half-year of record profits, with an operating income expected to be ¥187 billion ($1.56 billion), a jump of 39 percent from the previous year, and an operating margin of 6.2 percent. Ghosn also reported that Nissan had reduced its consolidated net automotive debt by ¥149 billion ($1.24 billion) within six months to ¥804 billion ($6.70 billion) and expected its net income after taxes be 64 percent higher.

While the jury is still out on the ultimate success of Nissan's revival, the fact that Carlos Ghosn slashed costs and personnel, and revived the half-dead Nissan in less than a year surprised everyone in Japan. Ghosn's approach served as a wake-up call for many Japanese executives who seemed unable or unwilling to change the status quo, although the corporate bottom-line number had been deteriorating badly. That Ghosn kept his promise to turn the company around in one year was widely recognized and appreciated. In February 2002 Renault raised its stake in Nissan to 44 percent. That same year, Nissan also entered into a joint agreement with the hugely successful cellphone company NTT Do-Co-Mo, to study mobile multimedia. To add a crown of laurels to Ghosn's head, Nissan's Altima received the American car of the year award. Until earlier this year, Ghosn was one of the most popular business leaders in Japan, irrespective of nationality, although the future of Nissan is still uncertain.

THE LANGUAGE OF GLOBAL BUSINESS

In the previous section I discussed the roles of two successful foreign executives in changing the mindset of Japanese managers. Until quite recently, foreign heads of big Japanese corporations were unheard of, and this makes the Nissan recovery story even more remarkable as he applied his Western management methods to turn the company around effectively. While the number of foreign executives is very small,[5] the impact of foreign management such as Nissan cannot be underestimated because many Japanese companies are searching for more efficient ways of running business in an intensifying international competition.

I will now consider the role of English as the lingua franca for business. One interesting aspect of the Nissan recovery story is the fact the new Chief Operating Officer, who could not speak Japanese, insisted that all board meetings and important business meetings be conducted in English. The company doubled its financial support for those taking English lessons. Within the corporate culture of Nissan, the ability to speak English became an important job qualification for managers. It has been said repeatedly that a major obstacle for Japanese globalization is the English language. However, in recent years an increasing number of Japanese businessmen and women speak English proficiently enough to conduct international business.

In January 2001 the Recruit Company[6] conducted a questionnaire survey of 13,000 company employees in Tokyo and found that, while the Japanese still have a long way to go in business English, an increasing number of younger employees think that they are overcoming this linguistic barrier. The survey, which asks for informants' self-perceptions of their English language competence, revealed that

22.9 percent of those between the ages of 35 and 39 years said that they can converse in English well enough, and nearly 6 percent said that they could conduct business in English. However, among those between the ages of 55 and 59, only 12.6 percent claimed to be able to converse in English and less than 4 percent said they were able to conduct business in English. In general, those "thirty-somethings" who say that they can speak business English are likely to be junior managers working on the frontiers of international business.

Japanese companies used to rely on English specialists who worked in international or overseas departments to negotiate international issues. However, the significance of global competition has motivated companies to nurture and support the advancement of those employees who can conduct business in English. The demand for competence in English is increasing in a wide range of business activities, from computer graphics, technological transfer, and marketing to executive decision-making.

TOEIC (Test of English for International Communication) is a widely used English proficiency test developed by the Educational Testing Service (USA) in 1979 and published by its subsidiary, the Chauncey Group International. Taken by over 2 million people per year, it is an English language proficiency test targeted at the workplace. In February 2001, TOEIC conducted a survey of 763 large Japanese corporations concerning their needs regarding business English and found that 13.8 percent of the firms already required TOEIC as a condition of corporate hiring, while 40.1 percent responded that they planned to make it a requirement in the future, and 42.5 percent do not plan to take the candidate's ability in English into consideration when hiring.

CONCLUSION

I have traced the four decades of research on and theoretical discussions about Japanese management. The "Japanese style of management" was originally presented as a distinct, if not "unique," cultural form, with a direct connection to the highly controversial *nihonjinron* (theories of Japaneseness) debates. The rise and fall of the total quality control management (TQM) movement in the 1980s and 1990s added another motive to the critical assessment of Euro-American organization theories, corporate culture research methodology, and theories of cross-cultural technological transfer. Finally, I have discussed the implications and significance of globalization for the future of Japanese corporate structures, together with the matter of employee welfare, including gender discrimination, the rise of contingent workers, and youth unemployment in Japan. During the decade-old economic recession, many Japanese firms suffered from poor financial results, deteriorating market conditions, and intensified international competition. In addition, corporate mergers and acquisitions by foreign firms, particularly in the automobile and finance sectors, have fundamentally affected inter-corporate relations and organizational cultures. Many large Japanese firms have revised their managerial ideology from the "company-as-the-community" to belt-tightening globalization in recent years, and they have cited intense market competition as the main reason for eliminating the seniority rule and other aspects of the traditional Japanese employment system. Today, in describing globalization, people give multiple descriptions and explanations of the capitalistic conditions in their own highly internationalized work lives.

It is ironic that the necessity for a new market orientation is understood by the most efficient corporations in Japan. As they cut off the excess labor, these most efficient corporations in automobiles, consumer electronics, optics, semi-conductors, and so forth now employ little more than 10 percent of all workers. Those corporations in notoriously "backward" firms in traditional industries such as construction are very slow to follow their lead. Japanese construction firms alone retain about 10 percent of the total Japanese labor force. Besides the dual employment structures of the smaller core and larger periphery workers, I see another dual industrial structure emerging in Japanese corporate practices. This dual structure is characterized by, on the one hand, a small core of highly competitive multinationals that have implemented globalization policies and, on the other, a majority of more traditional companies that remain "very Japanese" and economically inefficient. When one examines the process and emergent structures of globalization, the systems of "traditional" corporate Japan are increasingly differentiated and checkered, and parallel the increasingly unequal distribution and division of capital, resources, and labor in the world as a whole.

NOTES

1   *Nihonjinron* means "theory of, or debate on, the Japanese people."
2   The Equal Employment Opportunity Law (EEOL) came into effect in 1986. The law contained provisions that companies must voluntarily endeavor to not discriminate in recruiting, hiring, assignments, and promotion. The law also had provisions to prohibit discrimination in retirement, dismissal, fringe benefits, and training. However, the law included no provision to penalize companies for non-compliance. In 1997 the Japanese Diet passed revisions to several laws, including the EEOL, the Labor Standards Law, and other related laws, in order to guarantee employment equality and to improve work opportunities for female workers. When these revisions came into effect in April 1999 they effectively abolished legal provisions protecting women employees, which means they are now exposed to the same working conditions as men. With these revisions, the supporters of protective measures for women (and men) effectively lost to those who support equality. The 1997 revisions not only abolish restrictions on overtime, late-night work, and holiday work, they also make mandatory the EEOL anti-discrimination provisions related to recruiting, hiring, assignments, and promotion, which previously employers only needed to make voluntary efforts to comply with. Enforcement provisions in the new revisions appear very weak, with the only penalty being that violators may have their names made public. The new laws also contain some *positive action* (similar to "affirmative action" in U.S.) provisions for companies to take measures to encourage improvements in women's employment.
3   Over the past decade, those workers who prefer to work on a contingency basis refer to themselves as "freeters" (*furiitā*), a neologism constructed from the English word "free" (*furii*) and the German word *Arbeiter* (*arubaitā*).
4   The *zaibatsu* (literally "financial cliques") means the diversified family enterprise that rose to prominence during the Meiji era (1868–1912). The Meiji government granted these family-owned companies a privileged financial position by providing them with subsidies and tax concessions in order to accelerate Japan's strategic economic development. Some of

the most important *zaibatsus* were Mitsui, Mitsubishi, Konoike (Hitachi), Sumitomo, and Yasuda, Suzuki, Okura, and Furuta. They maintained close relations with the major political parties and pooled their resources to form the banking and industrial combines of modern Japan. Japan before World War II was dominated by four large *zaibatsus*: Mitsubishi, Mitsui, Sumitomo, and Yasuda After Japan's surrender (1945), the Allied occupying force began breaking up *zaibatsu* monopolies to enhance competition. However, in 1948 the Allied forces realized that they needed a strong Japan to fight the Korean War and communism in general, and they stopped weakening the Japanese economy. Consequently few large companies were actually broken up, and in the amendments to anti-trust laws in the aftermath, many became re-established. This time, companies grouped round the banks that were then allowed to hold shares in other companies. Several old *zaibatsus* re-emerged as *keiretsu* (literally "groups of companies"). Mitsui, Mitsubishi, Sumitomo and other *keiretsu* groups mobilized Japan's subsequent rise as a global business power.

5   In 2002 there were a total of 64.14 million Japanese employees of Japanese businesses, of which 3.79 million were corporate board members. This means about 6 percent of all employees were executives. Of the 600,000 foreigners working in Japan, 40,000 were board members (6.7 percent). In other words, fewer than 1 percent of all executives in Japan were non-Japanese.

6   Incorporated in 1963, the Recruit Company is a large information-industry company dealing mainly in human resources. It publishes a wide range of popular magazines such as *B-ing* (employment), *AB-Road* (travel) and *Keiko to Manabu* (learning). Recruit has annual sales of approximately ¥300 billion and an operating income of approximately ¥100 billion. Total circulation of Recruit's information magazines is approximately 7 million.

REFERENCES

Abbeglen, James. 1953. Japanese Factory: Aspects of its Social Organization. Glencoe: Free Press.

Adler, Nancy J. 1983a. Cross-Cultural Management Research: The Ostrich and the Trend. Academy of Management Review 8(2):226–232.

—— 1983b. Organizational Development in a Multicultural Environment. Journal of Applied Behavioral Science 19(3):350–365.

—— 1986. International Dimensions of Organizational Behavior: Boston: Kent Publishing.

Austin, Lewis, ed. 1976. Japan, the Paradox of Progress. New Haven: Yale University Press.

Azumi, Koya. 1978. Japanese Organization: Are They Really So Different? Paper Presented at the Colloquium. Center for Japanese and Korean Studies, University of California, Berkeley. February 22.

Ballon, Robert J. 1972. Foreign Competition in Japan: Human Resource Strategies. Tokyo: Sophia University Press.

Befu, Harumi, ed. 1977. Cultural Nationalism in East Asia: Representation and Identity. Institute of East Asian Studies, Berkeley: University of California Press.

Befu, Harumi, J. S. Eades, and Tom Gill. 2000. Globalization and Social Change in Contemporary Japan. New York: International Specialized Book Service.

Befu, Harumi, and Sylvie Guichard-Anguis. 2002. Globalizing Japan. New York: Routledge.

Benedict, Ruth. 1946. The Chrysanthemum and the Sword. Boston: Houghton Mifflin.

Brinton, Mary. 1989. Gender Stratification in Contemporary Urban Japan. American Sociological Review 54:549–564.

Brinton, Mary. 1993. Women and the Economic Miracle: Gender and Work in Postwar Japan. Berkeley: University of California Press.

Clark, Rodney. 1979. The Japanese Company. New Haven: Yale University Press.

Cole, Robert E. 1967. Japanese Blue Collar Worker: A Participant Observation Study. Ph.D. dissertation, University of Illinois.

——— 1971a. Japanese Blue Collar: The Changing Tradition. Berkeley: University of California Press.

——— 1971b. Permanent Employment and Tradition in Japan. Economic Development and Cultural Change 20(October):47–70.

——— 1972. Permanent Employment and Tradition in Japan. Industrial and Labor Relations Review 26(October):615–630.

——— 1976. Changing Labor Force Characteristics and their Impact on Japanese Industrial Relations. In Japan, the Paradox of Progress. L. Austin, ed. pp. 165–214. New Haven: Yale University Press.

Cole, Robert E., and W. Richard Scott, eds. 2000. The Quality Management and Organization Theory. Thousand Oaks, CA: Sage Publications.

Coleman, Samuel. 1983. Family Planning in Japanese Society: Traditional Birth Control in a Modern Urban Culture. Princeton: Princeton University Press.

Deal, Terrence E., and Allen A. Kennedy. 1982. Corporate Cultures: The Rites and Rituals of Corporate Life. Reading, MA: Addison-Wesley.

Deming, W. Edward. 1986. Out of Crisis. Cambridge: Massachusetts Institute of Technology Press.

DeVos, George. 1965. Achievement Orientation, Social Self Identity and Japanese Economic Growth. Asian Survey 5(12):555–589.

——— ed. 1976. Socialization for Achievement: Essays on the Cultural Psychology of the Japanese. Berkeley: University of California Press.

Doi, Takeo. 1962. Amae: A Key Concept for Understanding Japanese Personality. In Japanese Culture: Its Development and Characteristics. R. K. Smith and R. K. Beardsley, eds. pp. 132–139. Chicago: Aldine.

——— 1973. The Japanese Patterns of Communication and the Concept of Amae. The Quarterly Journal of Speech 56(2):180–5.

Dore, Ronald P. 1973. British Factory–Japanese Factory: The Origin of National Diversity in Industrial Relations. London: George Allen & Unwin.

Drucker, Peter. 1973. Management: Tasks, Responsibilities and Practices. New York: Harper & Row.

Easton, George S., and Sherry L. Jarrell. 2000. Patterns in the Deployment of Total Quality Management: An Analysis of 44 Leading Companies. In The Quality Movement and Organization Theory. Robert E. Cole and Richard Scott, eds. pp. 89–130. Thousand Oaks, CA: Sage Publications.

Eto, Jun. 1993. Seijuku to soshitsu: haha no hokai (Maturity and Loss: The Collapse of Mother). Tokyo: Kodansha.

Ford Japan, Inc. 2002. Annual Report. www.ford.co.jp.

Hamada, Tomoko. 1997. Absent Father, Feminine Son, Selfish Mother, Disobedient Daughter: Revisiting the Japanese Ie Household. Japan Policy Research Institute Working Paper Series No. 33:1–6. San Diego: Japan Policy Research Institute.

——— 2000. Quality as a Cultural Concept: Messages and Meta-messages. In The Quality Movement and Organization Theory. Robert E. Cole and W. Richard Scott, eds. pp. 295–314. Thousand Oaks, CA: Sage Publications.

Hamaguchi, Eshun. 1977. Nihon rashisa no sai-hakken (Rediscovery of Japanese-ness). Tokyo: Nihon Keizai Shinbun-sha.

Hanasawa, Seiichi. 1982. Bosei ishiki no hikaku bunkateki kenkyū: nihon to burajiru fujin tono hikaku (Comparative Study of Maternal Consciousness: Comparison of Japanese and Brazilian Women). Nihondaigaku Jinbun-kagaku Kenkyūjo Kiyō 26:34–52.

Hazama, Hiroshi. 1963. Nihonteki keiei no keifu (Genealogy of Japanese Style Management). Tokyo: Nihon Keizai Shinbun-sha.

—— 1964. Nihon rōmu kanri-shi kenkyū (Study of the History of Japanese Labor Management). Tokyo: Daiamondo-sha.

—— 1974. Nihon-teki keiei; shūdan-shugi no kōzai (Japanese Style of Management: Merits and Demerits of Groupism). Tokyo: Nihon Keizai Shinbun-sha.

Hughes, Henry J. 1995. Alcohol Use: Snow, Social Life and Customs. Japan Quarterly 42:67–74.

Iwata, Ryushi. 1977. Nihonteki keiei no hensei genri (Organizational Principle of the Japanese Management). Tokyo: Bunshin-do.

—— 1978. Gendai nihon no keiei fūdo (Climate of Management in Contemporary Japan). Tokyo: Nihon Keizai Shingun-sha.

Johnson, Richard T. 1977a. Are the Japanese Managers Really Better? Journal of American Chamber of Commerce in Japan. February:55–57.

—— 1977b. Communication and Decision Making: A Cross-Cultural Study of Japanese and American Companies in the United States and Japan. Research Paper, Stanford Graduate School of Business. Polo Alto, CA: Stanford University.

Johnson, Richard T, and William G. Ouchi. 1974. Made in America (Under Japanese Management). Harvard Business Review 525(September–October):61–69.

Kamei, Masao. 1978. Nenko shingin taisei minaoso (Reconsider the Seniority-Based Wage System). Asahi Shinbun. February 12.

Kashiwagi, Keiko. 1994. Seisa no yurai: Hatten shinrigaku no tachiba kara (Sexual Differences: From the Position of Developmental Psychology). Jendaa Raiburarii Shakai-kagaku 2:274–298.

Kashiwagi, Keiko, and Wakamatsu, Motoko. 1994. Oya to narukoto ni yoru jinkaku-hattatsu: shōgai hatten-teki shitenkara oya o kenkyūsuru kokoromi (Development of Personality by Becoming a Parent: Experiment to Study Parents from the Perspective of Life-Course Development). Hatten-shinri-gaku kenkyū (5):72–83.

Kawashima, Takeyoshi. 1950. Nihon shakai no kasokuteki kōsei (The Familistic Composition of Japanese Society). Tokyo: Nihon Hyōronsha.

—— 1957. Ideorogii to shiteno kasoku-seido (The Family System as an Ideology). Tokyo: Iwatani Shoten.

Keizai Doyukai. 1991. Ōpun shisutemu e mukete no kigyō kakushin (Enterprise Innovation toward an Open System). Tokyo: Keizai Doyukai.

—— 2001. The Beginning of the Year Message. Tokyo: Keizai Doyukai.

Koike, Kazuo. 1979. Kotoshi no seisaku kadai: chūko nen sō no koyō tasaku o (Policy Issue for This Year: Employment Policy for Middle-Aged and Older Workers). Nihon keizai shinbun. January 9.

—— 1988. Understanding Industrial Relations in Modern Japan. New York: St. Martin's Press.

—— 1994. Nihon no koyō shisutemu: sono fuhensei to tsuyomi (Japanese Employment System: Its Universality and Strengths). Tokyo: Toyo Keizai Shinpo.

Kosugi, Reiko, ed. 2002. Jiyū no daisho-furiitā: gendai wakamono no shokugyō ishiki to kōdō ("Freeters" and the Cost of Freedom: Occupational Consciousness and Action of Contemporary Youth). Tokyo: Nihon Rōdō Kenkyū Kikō.

Kurosu, Masashi, ed. 2003. Japan Almanac 2004. Tokyo: Asahi Shinbun.

Lebra, Takie Sugyama. 1975. An Alternative Approach to Reciprocity. American Anthropologist 77(3):550–565.

LeVine, Solomon, with Kazuo Okochi and Bernard Karsh, eds. 1973. Workers and Employers in Japan: The Japanese Employment Relations System. Princeton: Princeton University Press.

Lincoln, James R., with Hon Olson and Mitsuyo Hanada. 1978. Cultural Effect on Organizational Structure: The Case of Japanese Firms in the United States. American Sociological Review 43(December):829–847.

Magee, David. 2003. Turnaround: How Carlos Ghosn Rescued Nissan. New York: Harper Business.

Marsh, Robert M., and Hiroshi Mannari. 1976. Modernization and the Japanese Factory. Princeton: Princeton University Press.

McLendon, James. 1983. The Office: Way Station or Blind Alley? In Work and Life Course in Japan. David W. Plath, ed. pp. 156–182. Albany, NY: State University of New York Press.

Meguro, Yoriko. 1987. Kojinka suru kazoku (Individualizing Family). Tokyo: Keiso Shobō.

Morita, Akio. 1991. Nihonteki keiei seido (The Japanese-Style Employment System). Bungei shunjū (72):148–165

National Institute for Social Development and Demography, Ministry of Health and Welfare, Japanese Government. 2003. Life Expectancy at Zero Years Old. In Impacts of Population Aging on Economic and Social Factors. Tokyo: Ministry of Health and Welfare.

Nakamura, Akemi. 2004. No Education, No Employment, No Training: Being NEET Is Not So Neat for the Nation's Youth. Japan Times June 19.

Nakane, Chie. 1969. Kazoku no kōzō: shakaijinruigakuteki bunseki (The Structure of the Family: A Social Anthropological Analysis). Tokyo: Tokyo daigaku tooyoo bunka.

——— 1971. Japanese Society. Berkeley: University of California Press.

——— 1978. Tateshakai no rikigaku (The Dynamics of the Vertical Society). Tokyo: Kodansha.

Nippon Steel Corporation. 1982. Japan: The Land and its People. Tokyo: Gakuseisha.

Noda, Kazuo. 1975. Nihon no keiei (Japanese Management). Tokyo: Diamondosha.

Ohmae, Kenichi. 1995. The Evolving Global Economy: Making Sense of the New World Order. Boston: Harvard Business School.

——— 1999. The Borderless World: Power and Strategy in the Interlinked Economy. New York: HarperBusiness.

Osigweh, Chimezie A. B., ed. 1989. Organizational Science Abroad: Constraints and Perspectives. New York: Plenum.

Ouchi, William K., and Alfred M. Jaeger. 1977. Type Z Organization: A Better Match for a Mobile Society. Research Paper 314. Palo Alto: Graduate School of Business Stanford University.

Peters, T. J., and R. H. Waterman, Jr. 1982. In Search of Excellence: Lessons from America's Best-Run Companies. New York: Harper & Row.

Pharr, Susan. 1981. Political Women in Japan: The Search for a Place in Political Life. Berkeley: University of California Press.

Rohlen, Thomas P. 1974. For Harmony and Strength: Japanese White-Collar Organization in Anthropological Perspective. Berkeley: University of California Press.

Shewhart, Walter A. 1939. Statistical Method from the Viewpoint of Quality Control. Washington, DC: Graduate School of the Department of Agriculture.

Smith, Robert John. 1978. Kurusu: The Price of Progress in a Japanese Village, 1951–1975. Stanford: Stanford University Press.

Taira, Koji. 1970. Economic Development and the Labor Market in Japan. New York: Columbia University Press.

Tanaka, Hirohide. 1979. Genryōkeiei wa tenkanki ni aruka? (Is Rationalization at a Turning Point?). Nihon keizai shinbun. January 22.

Tanaka, Yukiko. 1995. Contemporary Portraits of Japanese Women. Westport CT: Praeger.

Tsuda, Masumi. 1976. Nihon-teki keiei no yōgo (Defending Japanese-Style Management). Tokyo: Tōyō Keizai Shinpō sha.

—— 1977. Nihon-teki keiei no ronri (Principles of Japanese-Style Management). Tokyo: Chuo Keizai-sha.

Tsurumi, Yoshi. 1976. The Japanese Are Coming. Cambridge, MA: Ballinger.

Vogel, Ezra. 1979. Japan as Number One: Lessons for America. Cambridge, MA: Harvard University Press.

Yamada, Masahiro. 1999. Parasaito shinguru no jidai (Days of the Parasite Single). Tokyo: Chikuma-shobo.

Yomiuri shinbun. 1984. Oino michi onna no michi. December 3.

Yoshino, Kosaku. 1992. Cultural Nationalism in Contemporary Japan: A Sociological Enquiry. New York: Routledge.

Yoshino, Michael. 1968. Japan's Managerial System: Tradition and Innovation. Cambridge, MA: MIT Press.

—— 1975. Emerging Japanese Multinational Enterprises. *In* Modern Japanese Organization and Decision Making. E. Vogel, ed. pp.146–166. Berkeley: University of California Press.

—— 1976. Japan's Multinational Enterprises. Cambridge, MA: Harvard University Press.

CHAPTER 10 Fashioning Cultural Identity: Body and Dress

Ofra Goldstein-Gidoni

INTRODUCTION

Modern Japanese wear Western clothing (*yōfuku*). Japanese attire (*wafuku*) that is clearly distinguished from Western attire is worn mainly on ceremonial occasions especially in life-cycle events, such as weddings, funerals, and the coming-of-age ceremony (*seijin shiki*) celebrated at the age of 20. On all these occasions it is predominantly women who put on the kimono while men appear in what is considered formal Western attire. I suggest that we should regard this gendered distinction in dress as part of a much more general and complex process of the construction of cultural identity in modern Japan. The distinctions between the "Western" and the "Japanese," the "modern" and the "traditional," lie at the heart of this process.

The striking symbolic distinction between the sexes can be well observed in the difference in dress on significant formal occasions, especially in life-cycle events. While men wear rational, "active" Western suits, women are encouraged to put on the kimono. This is more than a question of fashion or taste: the kimono that is wrapped around the female body has become a national symbol of traditionality, and so perfectly completes the image of Japaneseness, which is opposed to Westernness. Wrapped in this symbol of traditional Japaneseness, the Japanese woman herself has gained a symbolic role, as her kimono-clad image has become one of the "eternal" images of Japanese uniqueness.

As the kimono has become so separated from everyday life in contemporary Japan, kimono dressing itself has become the esoteric knowledge of a few. These are women who have achieved their expertise through special kimono schools offering courses to modern women who lack familiarity with the kimono and kimono-dressing. The involvement of such expert hands in producing the right kimono appearance has created a complicated process aimed at achieving a well-packaged "symbolic" form of the female body.

In modern Japan, the kimono has gained the role of an active player in the process of molding the female body not only into a cylindrical form, but in fact also into a specific cultural pattern. Since the Meiji era (1868–1912), with the state's declared official aim of building a rational modern nation, the role of women in the new Japan was clearly and officially defined as benefiting the nation by being wives and mothers. The preoccupation of the new nation with women's proper role has remade them as representations. However, this has not been in the sexual sense that is usually implied in feminist writing, but in the sense of models of tradition and the maintenance of the precious household (*ie*). The proper role of women, which has been defined since the Meiji period by the slogan "good wife, wise mother" (*ryōsai kenbo*), is clearly opposed to the role of men, who are regarded as models for action and rational enlightenment.

This is in no way to argue that women in contemporary Japan are restricted only to traditional roles. Their involvement in wage labor is high and steadily increasing (Brinton 1993; Molony 1995), and their intimacy with the West has been growing (Kelsky 2001). The important point is that the construction of modern Japanese identity has involved inventing distinct cultural roles for men and women. This chapter will look at this dynamic process of the construction of gendered cultural identities in modern Japan through a historic perspective, by looking closely at such processes mainly in the Meiji period, and through an elaborated ethnographic example from contemporary Japan: the role of dress in the construction of gendered distinctions in the coming-of-age ceremony.[1]

GENDERED DRESS REGULATIONS AND MODERN INVENTIONS IN THE MEIJI PERIOD

When modern Japanese refer to Japanese attire (*wafuku*), they refer to *kimono*. Literally, the word kimono simply denotes something to wear; however, while in premodern Japan it included various styles of everyday as well as festive clothing (Yanagida 1957:11), in modern Japan only one mode has remained. The modern kimono stems from the decorative festive clothing worn by the elite on special occasions (Dalby 1993:139). The shift to a single-mode kimono was coupled with the almost total neglect, as well as delegitimization, of the many traditional work kimonos, especially those of rural men and women (Segawa 1948:89). My argument is that it is certainly not accidental that the invention of the modern kimono took place in the Meiji period. It is related to the intense effort of the Meiji government to build a modern, "rational" nation, modeled on a Western ideal. In dress, this effort was seen in the massive promotion by the new centralist government of Western attire, mainly for men, as well as in the overt involvement of the government in cultivating a single, native, so-called "traditional" kimono, as distinct from the modern, Western, one.

A massive "invention of traditions" has been related to processes of nation-building in Europe (Hobsbawm 1983) as well as in Japan (Vlastos 1998). As in other areas of the world, the field of national costume offers a creative arena for invention and deliberate change. While governmental intervention in people's dress and appearance was not new in Japan, in premodern Japan it related mainly to class distinctions. In the Meiji period, when Western rationalization was the declared goal of the government and when the cultural distinction between the Western (*yō*) and the Japanese (*wa*) was created, new regulations related primarily to Western–Japanese/male–female distinctions.

The regulations regarding formal dress were abundant and naturally related mainly to men, who were regarded as the formal public representatives of both family and state. One example of the novelties of the time was the November 1872 proclamation of the chancellery that the Western morning suit (*mōningu*) would substitute for the formal Japanese attire worn by noblemen at court. This has remained the formal wear for men since. Grooms used to wear it side by side with their kimono-clad brides throughout the Taishō (1912–25) and a large part of the Shōwa (1926–89) periods (Goldstein-Gidoni 1997:138) and wedding guests still wear these suits, considered old-fashioned in the West, on these occasions.

While Japanese men of the Meiji period gradually changed to Western clothing, the most notable innovation for men was cropped hair. But not all men were quick to part with their samurai-style topknots and sidelocks. The government's resolve was firm, with fines for men who did not follow the new fashion and certificates of merit given to village mayors who successfully promoted the haircut in their jurisdictions. A verse that appeared in a magazine of 1871 perfectly conveys the symbolic aspect of this new Western style:

> If you tap a shaven and topknotted head you will hear the sound of retrogression; if you tap an unshaven head you will hear the sound of the Restoration; but if you tap a close-cropped head of hair you will hear the sound of culture and enlightenment. (quoted in Yanagida 1957:28)

During that same period, some Tokyo women found it stylish to cut their hair short like men. However, public as well as governmental opposition soon appeared. The following comment from one of the leading magazines of March 1872 is especially illuminating: "Recently in the city we have seen women with close-cropped hair. Such is not the Japanese custom and furthermore nothing of the sort is seen among the women of the West. The sight of this ugly fashion is unbearable" (quoted in Yanagida 1957:29). The Tokyo government's reaction was swift. In April of the same year it proclaimed a strict ban on short haircuts for women.

This illuminating example of governmental intervention in fashioning the male and female bodies can be seen as sending distinct symbolic messages to Japanese women and men. The message for women was to become repositories of the past and of traditional values. This kind of role has been identified in other rapidly changing societies as bestowed on women by men, who tend to translate their fear of change into attempts to prevent changes in women's roles. Whereas Japanese women gained the role of models of tradition and representations of unique Japanese beauty and form, at the same time, the symbolic message sent to men was that of conferring on them the role of carriers of rational enlightenment.

THE KIMONO TAKES ON THE SYMBOLIC ROLE OF (MAINLY FEMALE) NATIVE DRESS

The invention of the kimono as a feminine and national dress in modern Japan has been coupled with a larger discourse on the allegedly "natural" relationship between the kimono and the Japanese people. Writers like Kiyoyuki Higuchi (1974) find a complete fit between the kimono and Japan's climate, as well as its people's mentality and body type. More generally, the kimono takes on a role in the intensive discourse on Japanese uniqueness, the vast literature usually referred to under the rubric of *nihonjinron* (discourse on being Japanese) (see Dale 1986).

In this literature, the uniqueness of the Japanese heart and spirit is typically distinguished from the West. Norio Yamanaka, a distinguished figure in the world of the kimono, writes in a quasi-academic publication, "At the mention of kimono, our minds immediately tend to make a distinction between Japanese and Western styles of clothing" (Yamanaka 1986:9). This is not a distinction in clothing alone. Yamanaka says that, in order to understand the role of the kimono in Japanese culture, it is important to understand the West as having a *suru bunka*, a culture that does things, whereas Japan has a *naru bunka*, a culture in which things become (Yamanaka 1986:7). Yamanaka explains Western culture as calculated and having utilitarian goals, whereas Japanese culture prizes love, admires beauty, respects courtesy, and fosters harmony with nature. This harmony, regarded by the Japanese as a unique characteristic of their culture, is directly related to their love of the kimono. These attributes are deeply incorporated in the popular image of the kimono. For example, the distinction between a culture which does and one in which things become was expressed in an interview between the female owner of a large kimono school and a kimono expert. When asked whether wearing the kimono feels constraining and uncomfortable, she replied that it gives a feeling that a "non-Japanese cannot understand."

> There is a great difference [between Western and Japanese attire]. When I wear Western dress like today, I [come to] have a feeling of activity and moving [*katsudō teki ni narimasu*]; kimono, on the other hand gives one a feeling of calmness [*yuttari to*] and an urge to quit work. Life now is very busy in Japan, but when one wears kimono it gives her the opposite feeling.

Like Yamanaka and others, the kimono expert sees the difference in clothing as a basic cultural distinction between the Japanese and the Western. The West not only plays a role as a distinguishing category, but also as the Significant Other. As explained by another kimono expert: "After the war many things entered [Japan] from America....Because of this, it became necessary to save something Japanese, and thus kimono has gradually become a national costume [*minzoku ishō*]."

Kimono has indeed become one of the main symbols of Japan and Japaneseness both inside and outside Japan. Nevertheless, it is important to note that this so-called national costume has been reproduced mainly for women. Thus, while the kimono gained a significant role in the internal cultural discourse about Japanese uniqueness, there were some early voices, especially those of women, who rejected this direction. This critical voices of women choosing to dress in the kimono instead of adopting a

Western style of dressing was typically related to the same characteristics as those praised by the contemporary kimono expert quoted above. The beauty of the kimono is found in immobility and calm gestures, as in those of the tea ceremony; Western attire encourages movement. This Japanese beauty has confining attributes, as a woman writer commented in the journal *Bunka seikatsu* (Cultural Life) in 1924 (Saga 1924). In the article, she calls on Japanese women to adopt a Western way of dressing in order to "liberate [their] body movements from the traditionally restrictive and non-movement-prone kimono." She argues that, especially considering the period of rebuilding the nation after the devastating earthquake in the Tokyo area in 1923, when the country demanded a joint effort from women, women should adopt Western-style dressing in order to free their minds from "childishly receiving the standard of beauty from others." In these "others," she included not only most esthetic critics but also Japanese men in general, as well Western visitors to Japan. This writer encourages women to adopt Western-style attire, which is related to a "freedom of choice," in order to "raise their own consciousness."

Japanese women, especially in postwar Japan, certainly adopted a Western way of dressing in their everyday life. Nevertheless, in the symbolic domain, the kimono is still linked both to the Japanese spirit in general and, more specifically, to the ideal of eternal Japanese female beauty. This is certainly evident in the language of kimono entrepreneurs. Slogans such as "The beauty of kimono is the heart of Japanese people" (*kimono no utsukushisa wa nihonjin no kokoro desu*) are very common in popular kimono magazines. Kimono entrepreneurs also always emphasize the natural "longing" (*akogare*) any Japanese girl orwoman has (or should have) to don a kimono. These kinds of advertisements are especially numerous in the months before January 15, the coming-of-age day.

THE COMING-OF-AGE CEREMONY

Since World War II the coming-of-age day has been a national holiday. Celebrated on January 15, schools, municipalities, and other social institutions hold public ceremonies called *seijin shiki* (the coming-of-age ceremony) symbolizing the attainment of legal majority of men and women who will reach the age of 20 in the course of that year. However, it seems that in recent years participation in the ceremony itself has certainly not been the main focus of the day; it is the attire, and especially the expensive kimono, worn by the female participants. Most of the girls questioned regarded the event mainly in terms of a social gathering and as an opportunity to be seen (or displayed). The nature of the event was clearly described by the mother of a celebrating girl:

> The day itself is mainly a kind of a reunion, meeting friends one hasn't seen for a long time. It does not have so much the meaning of becoming an adult. For the girls it is an opportunity to show off. Since it is not compulsory, it seems that those who cannot afford *furisode* [a kimono with swinging sleeves – the proper kimono for the occasion] do not come.

Indeed, an elaborate kimono has come to play a crucial role in the coming-of-age ceremony. In light of the decreasing number of women wearing the kimono for other ceremonial occasions such as weddings and funerals (mainly due to the economic recession), its recent increasing popularity for the coming-of-age ceremony is especially illuminating.

Boys and girls both dress up for the occasion. However, whereas great effort and money are invested in producing the perfect woman in kimono, men are formally required to don a Western suit, which they will use later for job interviews and when going to work. This distinction between Western attire for boys and Japanese attire for girls has become a significant attribute of the occasion to the extent that girls who cannot afford the costume that will make them the proper model of Japanese femininity prefer to avoid the ceremony altogether.

Japanese etiquette and rules of formality require the proper dress, with great attention to detail. For example, while men must don a white tie when attending a wedding, a black tie with the same black suit is appropriate for a funeral. Other rules apply to the dress of women on similar occasions. Such strict rules of formality imply that, on occasions such as weddings and funerals, most attendants of the same gender dress very similarly.

Gender distinctions can be observed through ceremonial dress well before the coming-of-age ceremony, in earlier life-cycle events, for example, in the *miyamairi* ceremony, in which newborn babies are presented for the first time to the local deity, and in the 7-5-3 (*shichi-go-san*), a day of celebration on 15 November when children aged 3, 5, and 7 are dressed in fine clothes and taken to visit shrines. All these occasions not only require special attire, but also mark clear distinctions between the dress of boys and girls in color and symbolic utterances such as a black kimono with house crests for baby boys and an uncrested kimono for girls in their first presentation to the local deity (see Omachi et al. 1962:240).

The coming-of-age ceremony is considered in modern Japan as one of the life-cycle rituals (*kankon sōsai*) that the Japanese are keen to perform properly. However, despite the importance attributed to formality, contemporary Japanese consider themselves ignorant in such matters. This presumed ignorance is perpetuated by so-called experts, including mutual assistance organizations for ceremonial occasions (*kankon sōsai gojokai*). The latter were established after World War II to assist poor Japanese with such compulsory ceremonies and have since then become savings organizations for such occasions. Other important sources of information and guidance on proper etiquette in formal occasions are instructive books and manuals; e.g., the bestseller, "Introduction to Ceremonial Occasions" (*Shin kankon sōsai nyūmon*; Shiotsuki 1991).

Experts leave little room for personal preferences in terms of dress and total appearance in the case of the coming-of-age ceremony. While suggesting an expensive kimono for girls, to be used later for other ceremonial occasions, Shiotsuki (1991:36) recommends suits for boys. "There is no doubt," she writes, "that the dark blue suit will be useful as everyday attire later on." While boys are excused from severe formality, such permissiveness is out of the question in the case of girls. Shiotsuki (1991:36) exempts the boys from following the formal rules of etiquette according to which they should wear a morning suit (*mōningu*), which is worn on other formal occasions such as weddings. With girls, the experts are very particular concerning dress and general appearance, which includes hair setting, hair decorations, and the proper way to wear a shawl.

This expert advice is instructive with regard to distinctions between young women and young men. Advising boys to purchase a suit that can be used later for the job interviews that are an inseparable part of the life of the Japanese salaryman, the expert reproduces their male role as models for instrumental action. On the other hand, although most Japanese girls will also be university or college graduates and will go to job interviews in Western attire, this dress is not regarded as their formal attire. On the formal occasion that represents their entry into adult society they should symbolically adopt a "traditional Japanese" appearance.

PRODUCING THE PERFECT JAPANESE FEMALE FORM

So complicated is the total appearance required from girls for the coming-of-age ceremony that they need experts to aid them in achieving the desirable image. These experts include kimono shops, department stores, wedding parlors, beauty salons, photo studios, and other producers of various traditional Japanese accessories considered appropriate when donning the kimono. Their role in producing the proper female model is twofold: they provide the proper items and necessary services, and also their expertise, which is considered essential for those Japanese eager to perform properly. Japanese women regard their own ignorance of the "secrets" of kimono dressing as an embarrassing flaw in proper etiquette and femininity. Mothers who send their daughters to kimono school as part of their bridal preparation are attempting to correct this flaw. But for the mothers who did not attend such schools, the alternative is to rely on experts (*kitsuke no hito*) to dress their daughters and themselves on the rare ceremonial occasions that require a kimono.

Mothers play a significant role in preparing their daughters for the coming-of-age ceremony. In fact, most girls, when asked for their motivation for donning a constraining kimono and participating in the ceremony, answered, "Because my mother wanted me to," or "I couldn't resist my mother's will." Japanese mothers are generally involved in the lives of their sons and daughters even when they reach matrimonial age. Mothers of the postwar generation also regard their daughters' opportunity to don the kimono, which they themselves lacked in the harsh economic times of their youth, as too important to forsake. Mothers are responsible for making all the arrangements for the ceremony, and they are advised to make their appointments early in the year, since beauty shops in charge of dressing the girls soon become over-booked. At the Cinderella beauty shop located in a commercial wedding parlor in a large city in western Japan where I conducted my fieldwork working as a part-time dresser, mothers booked their daughters for dressing as long as a year in advance of the ceremony.

Booking an appointment at the beauty shop is not the first step in the preparation process. First, the mother has to convince her daughter to wear a kimono for the occasion. The alternative of putting on Western dress has become inconceivable. While more and more girls consent, or even find this "once in a lifetime" opportunity for donning a kimono appealing, there are those who refuse to participate. Financial considerations seem to be one reason for this. While parents regard the high cost of up to ¥1,000,000 (about $10,000) for purchasing a kimono as a kind of a social must, some "modern" girls prefer to spend the money differently. Other girls of this "new breed of humans" (*shinjinrui*) – a derogatory term used by social critics and by older people to describe a young generation which has become removed from traditional Japanese values – take an even more critical stance. These are mainly wealthy and well-educated university students, who find this custom old-fashioned and repulsive because it is an ostentation of the lower middle classes. This negative attitude nevertheless does not usually prevent the girls from participating. Evoking the ideology of *nihonjinron*, an owner of a kimono school gave a simplistic explanation for this generation gap:

> For the parents it is their desire. From the day a girl is born they have the desire to dress her in *furisode* when she becomes 20 in the *seijin shiki*, take her picture, and send it to relatives as custom requires. In some cases, the mother herself also wore a *furisode* she received from her mother in her *seijin shiki*. This is still left. Deep in their heart, the Japanese still have kimono as a latent image, as their greatest longing [*akogare*]. This is a proof of that [longing], I think, though it is usually not said. This is why they want to dress their daughter. They work hard for this. There are, though, some cases in which the girl says that it would be enough to rent a kimono and that she would prefer a small car instead.

The kimono expert continued her well-informed observations emphasizing not only the parents' so-called natural longing for a sense of Japaneseness, but also the aspects of conspicuous display:

> Everything together [the total cost of kimono and other preparations and photographs] reaches the average of ¥1,000,000. In this sum it is possible to buy a small car. The girl wants this [the car] but for the parents it is like a proof [*akashi*]. If they have the possibility of dressing their daughter in a ¥1,000,000 kimono it is proof that they have worked hard all their lives and can afford it. It is the result of their life work. If they don't dress her it is as if they couldn't reach this stage. They are watched by the people around. It is a display for the neighborhood. While other girls in the neighborhood wear *furisode* in their *seijinshiki* and only their daughter doesn't, they are ashamed. This kind of feeling has been left. But the girls do not always understand their parents' feelings and they say they would prefer a car.

Having the economic means to dress one's daughter in an expensive kimono for her coming-of-age ceremony is considered important for the public image of the modern Japanese household. This nuclear family household has emerged in Japan mainly since the 1960s, with the emergence of the new middle class and the archetype of the Japanese salaryman (Vogel 1963). Its well being is maintained by the mutual efforts of the salaryman as breadwinner and his wife as homemaker. Japanese society in general and Japanese women in particular attach high value to the role of the "professional housewife" (Vogel 1978). She is the one responsible for managing the household, including its budget, and taking care of and educating the children.

While the feminine model is opposed to the rational male model, mothers are very rational with regard to household finances. The mothers of coming-of-age girls who cannot afford the expense of a ¥1,000,000 kimono do not hesitate to look for cheaper ways to dress their daughters in the desired costume. The obvious alternative is to rent instead of purchasing it. More prudent mothers find that the cheapest way is not to rent through ordinary kimono shops but rather through one of the mutual assistance organizations for ceremonial occasions which offer kimonos at very reasonable prices to their members. These organizations are well aware of the recent tendency of the Japanese to economize due to the recession. Thus, as compared to the "bubble days" of the late 1980s and early 1990s, they increasingly are promoting kimono rental for the coming-of-age day.

The morning of the coming-of-age day is a very busy one for 20-year-old girls and their mothers. It is also hectic for those involved in producing the proper appearance and for those in charge of manufacturing their replicas or representations. At the beauty shop, the employees are summoned to work at 4.30 a.m. to be ready for the first girls, scheduled for 5 a.m. Photo studio workers arrive at 6 a.m. Extra part-time staff are necessary for the task of preparing 120 girls in a few hours. The beauty shop employs as many as 30 part-time beauticians and kimono dressers for the day, many more than the average number of women employed on busy wedding days. Each of the workers knows her responsibility for the day (as rehearsed) and has her assigned room. The two rooms usually used for dressing female wedding guests are arranged differently for the day. A larger room is used for dressing and a smaller one for getting undressed and for putting on the special underwear necessary for the kimono (*hadajuban*). In the larger room, eight to ten pairs of dressers occupy the two mirrored sides. The beauty shop assigns as many women as possible to setting hair and doing make-up, which are the most time-consuming chores. The beauticians occupy the beauty salon and additional available space. Another group of four women struggles against time in the room usually used for dressing the groom and male guests at weddings in order to make up the queuing girls. There is no fixed sequence: the girl may begin in either of the rooms, and the procedure is decided more on the basis of convenience and the length of the queue than on any other consideration. Each of the girls holds a piece of paper, detailing the different sections of preparation and accessories needed, with which she moves between the different rooms. In each room an employee adds the necessary fee. When fully ready in her kimono with her hair set and her face made up, the girl goes back to the beauty shop, where she pays the accumulated fees for the total form. This amount, averaging about ¥20,000, depends mainly on the various kimono and hair accessories the dressers managed to promote as "indispensable" for a perfect appearance.

KIMONO DRESSING AS SHAPING THE JAPANESE MODEL OF BEAUTY AND FEMININITY

Kimono dressing can best be described as a series of correcting, binding, and packaging. Hendry (1993:73–74) writes, "Japanese kimonos, perhaps more than any other garments, are literally 'wrapped' around the body, sometimes in several layers, like the gifts, and they are secured in place by sashes, with a wide obi to complete the human parcel." The girls being produced by the experts for the coming-of-age ceremony can indeed be seen as "parcels" or as packaged products of the vast industry involved in the reproduction of their feminine Japanese image. Western attire is usually adapted to the female body; not so the kimono, where the woman's body is made to fit an ideal cylindrical shape. The modern art of kimono dressing has developed this aim to an extreme.

Dressing a woman in a kimono requires "correction" (*hosei*), which refers to padding the body with gauze and towels to make it fit the ideal feminine form. If she is thin, the woman will be padded out with an extra towel; if fat, her breasts will be flattened. If, alas, she has any fault such as a low shoulder this must also be perfectly "corrected." After the body has been padded, special undergarments are carefully wrapped around it, tied with cloth cords, and then fixed with an elastic belt. The kimono is wrapped over them and then folded and bound in the same way. After each layer has been bound, a final binding completes the wrapping: the binding of the *obi*. The latter should not only be done firmly to keep the whole "parcel" tightly fixed, but also beautifully, in a way that the pattern on the *obi* will be most obvious. The exquisite kimono bindings are prepared in advance to save time in the demanding schedule of the day and to be as perfect as possible. Attention is also given to rules of etiquette as well as art in modern kimono dressing. These require a single kind of tie for married women's kimonos, while allowing a proliferation of shapes (carrying names such as "butterflies and "flowers") for the kimono of the unmarried woman.

The kimono invites the plausible feminist reaction to clothing as restricting the female body, and therefore a device for the subordination of women. It suggests parallels with such fashions as the those of the Victorian era, which included several layers of clothing and constraining elements such as the corset. The kimono has indeed been described as restricting the Japanese woman's movement and as making her defenseless as well as rigidly disciplined. The kimono does constrain the female body. The vocabulary used by the dressers – including holding out (*gambaru*) and endurance (*gaman*) – illustrates this. Notions of patience and endurance have been regarded as part of femininity training in Japan. The ability to stay put and tidy when wearing a kimono has always been considered as part of this kind of socialization for girls (Lebra 1984:42–45). The dressers at the beauty shop ignore young women's complaints about constraining ties, while they may take into account the same complaints made by older women. As if fulfilling their own role in training Japanese girls for proper female roles, the dressers, as experts of feminine knowledge, frequently remind the girls (at times quite severely) that they should know how to hold out and endure suffering.

A "constraining-oppression" analysis should be used with caution in the Japanese case, as in other similar cases, in order not to oversimplify the explanation for the oppression of women. The Japanese case must take into account the fact that notions of endurance and patience are characteristic of Japanese society in general. Taking into account that notions such as *gaman* and *ganbaru* were defined as keywords in Japanese culture (Moeran 1984) we must admit that, while being an appealing explanation, the constraining argument is not satisfactory. The alternative interpretation offered here is embedded in the symbolic aspects of kimono and kimono dressing. The way kimono dressers themselves explain how body correction creates the right Japanese ambiance confirms this point: "the correction [*hosei*] is used so that the woman's appearance will give the impression that she is gentle and open-hearted." In other words, the female body is not just constrained; more significantly, it is molded into a ready-made pattern, which is the model Japanese woman.

"Good Wife, Wise Mother": The Cultivation of Form

A kimono school owner summarized the experience of donning a kimono in the following words:

> When you wear kimono it reaches your feelings, it enlarges your mind and makes you calm; even if you want to run you cannot. You have to move in a natural way. So, if the feelings become calm so are your thoughts. Even if something bad is done to you, you do not react immediately, you think first before you act. A Japanese woman like this guarded the Japanese household [*ie*]. I would like the young women to be a little like this.

For the kimono expert, the kimono is much more than a constraint on the body; it has a mental influence and its ultimate role is to cultivate the perfect Japanese woman. This owner of one of the largest kimono schools, with branches all over Japan teaching about 30,000 students, indicated her expectations for the women who were taking courses for their bridal preparation. She hoped, she said, that the education they acquired at her school would help them to be "good wives and wise mothers" (*ryōsai kenbo*).

A characterization of the Japanese woman as "good wife, wise mother" emerged in Japan at the end of the 19th century. The term has since been promoted vigorously by male politicians who define women as domestic managers of households and nurturers of children. The concept has pervaded Japanese society and has come to constitute the official discourse of women in Japan (Uno 1993). Paradoxically, although this concept was initially taken from the Western model of the ideal Christian woman of the 19th century, it is now viewed as traditionally Japanese. The kimono school owner, who regards herself as an educator of women, said that being a good (Japanese) wife and wise mother "is a traditional Japanese pattern. . . . This is the splendid woman that guarded the Japanese household [*ie*] over the years".

The art of kimono dressing was not considered part of bridal training in prewar Japan since wearing a kimono was an integral part of everyday life. However, in modern Japan, as the kimono has become increasingly separated from everyday life and associated almost exclusively with special occasions, it has gradually found its place beside the refined arts of the tea ceremony and flower arrangement. A young unmarried woman, who like many other modern women took evening kimono classes after work, found it hard to explain why she was investing money and time in this pursuit. Finally she said, "You know, the kimono is a Japanese thing, like the tea ceremony and flower arrangement, that any Japanese girl should know [even though it] is something that one does not use every day." The explanation of an experienced kimono teacher supports the connection between knowing the secrets of kimono dressing and proper Japanese femininity. As she said, "A woman who does not practice such things [as the tea ceremony, flower arrangement, and kimono] is considered no good." Most Japanese women do not take courses in traditional Japanese arts in order to achieve any mastery of them. They take the courses in order to internalize proper manners and comportment through the arts. The study of manners is part of the curriculum of kimono schools, and the kimono, like similar feminine pursuits, is considered to be a perfect way to cultivate modesty, elegance, tidiness, and courtesy.

The emphasis on cultivation of form and on appearance related to Japanese women partly explains the significance given to the coming-of-age photograph. It often seems that, as in the case of weddings, the production of the formal representation of the model girl in a kimono overshadows the event itself (see Goldstein-Gidoni 1997:73–77). For several months before January 15, the Japanese media, including local and national newspapers and women's magazines, carry advertisements for the coming-of-age ceremony. The ads, always with a picture of a kimono-clad young woman, usually emphasize the "natural" longing (*akogare*) girls have to don a kimono. Sentences such as "Every female longs for a beautiful and charming kimono appearance" (*utsukushiku, adeyakana kimono sugata wa josei no akogare*) or "Any female would yearn for a graceful manner in dress" (*shittori toshita kikonashi wa, josei nara dare mo ga akogaremasu yo ne*) are frequently used in many published materials. It is important to note that the advertisements do not refer to the civic event or the ideal of becoming an adult as much as to the "ceremonial (bright) appearance [*hare sugata*]" that the girl must leave an image of for the future ("Aren't you going to leave a memory of your ceremonial appearance?").

The professional studio photograph of a daughter's coming-of-age ceremony takes on some specific purposes. Young women are likely to choose January 15 to pose for portraits that will be shown to potential marriage partners in a matchmaking (*miai*) procedure. It is also customary to send photographs to relatives who have sent congratulatory gifts (*o-iwai*) for the occasion of the daughter's coming of age. The Japanese attach great importance to what they call *seken*, meaning a reference group (Inoue 1977). Responsibility for maintaining the right image for others, or of the *sekentei* (the honorable appearance as viewed by the surrounding world), falls mainly upon the housewife. A mother of a 20-year-old girl, highly aware of her responsibility for maintaining her household *sekentei*, told me of the efforts it took her to convince her daughter to put on a kimono that she had bought for her. The girl consented only on condition that she would be taken by car directly to the beauty shop and from there directly to the photo studio. Going to the civic ceremony or even walking in the streets was totally out of the question. However, for her mother this solution was satisfactory since it saved her from the embarrassment she would have faced if photographs of the kimono-clad daughter had not been sent to thank all the congratulating relatives.

There seems to be an almost "natural" link between Japanese women and *form*. This can be observed through their occupation in esthetic pursuits such as flower-arranging and kimono, tasks that a kimono expert defined as "things that fit into form" (*kata ni hamatta mono*), which are in fact "meaningless things" (*nani-mo-nai koto*). Moreover, it seems that the exaggerated occupation in the cultivation of form can end in the woman herself becoming a form and a model. Freezing the perfect female image in a frame as in the coming-of-age portraits is related to the way in which Japanese women has been made into models of Japaneseness. Robins-Mowry (1983:xviv) has elegantly described it:

> The world gently placed this living, breathing woman into the glass box used throughout
> Japan to encase all treasured kimono-clad and artistically hand-wrought dolls. She was

entrapped in the legends of her own perfection – a likeness that harmonized with those perpetuated symbols of Japan: cherry blossom and Mount Fuji.

CONCLUSION

The kimono-clad Japanese woman has become a symbol in modern Japan. Like cherry blossom and Mount Fuji, it is one of the best-known symbols of Japan as a nation. I have shown that the process by which the kimono and the women who put it on have become symbols of tradition in modern Japan has been deliberate. There was first direct state involvement in the crucial Meiji period and then the role of kimono experts and entrepreneurs in producing this model of traditional Japanese femininity, which is clearly distinct from the model of Western rationality imposed on Japanese men.

This analysis has not focused on the actual position of women in contemporary Japan, but rather has investigated their culturally constructed position. Producing Japanese women as models of traditional Japaneseness should be understood against the background of more general processes of the construction of Japanese modern cultural identity. Processes of self-definition tend to intensify the sense of self by dramatizing the difference from and opposition to the Other; in the Japanese case, the distinction between the "Japanese" and the "Western" has been pervasive and diffused through all spheres of Japanese life. Using historic and ethnographic perspectives I have offered here a glance at the gendered symbolic aspects of these significant cultural distinctions.

NOTE

1   Fieldwork was conducted from 1989 to 1991 in a wedding parlor's beauty shop. I also participated in kimono classes and conducted interviews with kimono experts and practitioners. Additional data were collected in a two-month visit in 1997.

REFERENCES

Brinton, Mary C. 1993. Women and the Economic Miracle: Gender and Work in Postwar Japan. Berkeley: University of California Press.

Dalby, Lisa. 1993. Kimono: Fashioning Culture. New Haven and London: Yale University Press.

Dale, Peter. 1986. The Myth of Japanese Uniqueness. London: Croom Helm.

Goldstein-Gidoni, Ofra. 1997. Packaged Japaneseness: Weddings, Business and Brides. Honolulu: Hawaii University Press.

Hendry, Joy. 1993. Wrapping Culture: Politeness, Presentation, and Power in Japan and Other Societies. Oxford: Clarendon Press.

Higuchi, Kiyoyuki. 1974. Umeboshi to nihontō (Pickled Plums and Japanese Swords). Tokyo: Non-Book.

Hobsbawm, Eric. 1983. Mass-Producing Traditions: Europe 1870–1914. In The Invention of Tradition. Eric Hobsbawm and Terence Ranger, eds. pp. 263–309. Cambridge: Cambridge University Press.

Inoue, Tadashi. 1977. Sekentei no kōzō (The Structure of *Seken*). Tokyo: Nihon Hōsō Shuppan Kyōkai.

Kelsky, Karen. 2001. Women on the Verge: Japanese Women, Western Dreams. Durham and London: Duke University Press.

Lebra, Takie, Sugiyama. 1984. Japanese Women: Constraint and Fulfillment. Honolulu: University of Hawaii Press.

Moeran, Brian. 1984. Individual, Group and *Seishin*: Japan's Internal Cultural Debate. Man 19(2):252–266.

Molony, Barbara. 1995. Japan's Equal Employment Opportunity Law and the Changing Discourse on Gender. Signs 20(21):268–302.

Omachi, Takuzō et al. 1962. Nihon minzokugaku taikei (An Outline of Japanese Folklore). Tokyo: Heinonsha.

Robins-Mowry, Dorothy. 1983. The Hidden Sun: Women of Modern Japan. Boulder, CO: Westview Press.

Saga, Fusako. 1924. Nihon fujin no yōsō ni tsuite (On Western-Style Attire for Japanese Women). Bunka seikatsu March:22–25.

Segawa, Kiyoko. 1948. Kimono. Tokyo: Rokuninsha.

Shiotsuki, Yaeko. 1991. Shin kankon sōsai nyūmon (A New Introduction to Ceremonial Occasions). Tokyo: Kobunsha.

Uno, S. Kathleen. 1993. The Death of Good Wife, Wise Mother. *In* Postwar Japan as History. Andrew Gordon, ed. pp. 293–321. Berkeley: University of California Press.

Vlastos, Stephen, ed. 1998. Mirror of Modernity: Invented Traditions of Modern Japan. Berkeley: University of California Press.

Vogel, Ezra F. 1963. Japan's New Middle Class: The Salary Man and his Family in a Tokyo Suburb. Berkeley: University of California Press.

Vogel, Suzanne E. 1978. Professional Housewife: The Career of Urban Middle Class Japanese Women. Japan Interpreter 12(1):16–43.

Yamanaka, Norio. 1986. The Book of Kimono. Tokyo: Kodansha.

Yanagida, Kunio. 1957. Japanese Manners and Customs in the Meiji Era. Charles S. Terry, trans. Tokyo: Obunsha.

CHAPTER 11 Genders and Sexualities

Sabine Frühstück

Around 1900, scholars of ethnology and folklore were fascinated by Japan's abundant artifacts of fertility and potency as well as its sexual rites and customs. Jurists and other visitors noted with astonishment, excitement, and perhaps pleasure their "discovery" of Japan's prostitution quarters, while ethnologists and medical doctors began to compile books on "the erotic" in Japan. Since then, studies of sexual practices, rites and customs, gender, women's status, nudity, and sexuality in Japan have crystallized, diversified, and eventually branched out in several distinct yet overlapping directions. This chapter traces some of these branches of an anthropology of genders and sexualities in Japan since the first attempts at capturing what was around 1900 referred to as the "Japanese sex life." I will show that today's inquiries into sexualities in Japan have a history (even if its authors are not always aware of it) that includes the approaches of sexual ethnology, women's studies, and gender studies.

Several features complicate the story of these four types of anthropological studies, namely, studies of gender and sexuality are perhaps more interdisciplinary and transdisciplinary than most types of scholarly inquiries. They draw from a number of academic and non-academic fields, including history and the social sciences as well as women's, feminist, and – more recently – gay and lesbian organizations' debates and publications. Moreover, the meanings of analytical categories such as sex, gender, femininity, feminism, manhood, masculinity, and so forth have changed significantly since the early days of the anthropology of Japan. These categories have also been constantly appropriated in different ways by different groups of people, including scholars, journalists, activists, and many others. Finally, "gender" and "sexuality" are intimately entangled with power, and so interest in the relations of sex, gender, and sexuality has rarely been far from attempts at changing these very relations. New approaches to the analysis of sex, gender, and sexuality have gone hand in hand with certain styles of engagement with normative scientific and/or sexual practices and attitudes.

SEXUAL ETHNOLOGY AND THE ESCAPE FROM WESTERN PURITANISM

In fin-de-siècle Japan, books on the "Japanese sex life" by Japanese scholars were often driven by a nostalgic sense of a more harmonious and less self-conscious past and – at the onslaught of modernization – a supposed need to enshrine "tradition" in a scholarly form. Western scholars often framed their books as critiques of Western (European) puritanism and hypocrisy concerning sexual matters when they drew a picture of the "Japanese sex life" that seemed open-minded and unprejudiced by comparison. Dr. Friedrich Solomon Krauss, for example, agreed with other folklorists and ethnologists of East Asia that "the Occidental looks at Japan through Occidental glasses: He sees moral degeneration where there is in naked reality nothing but unmediated joy of life and irrepressible joy for sexual matters combined with a lack of any kind of hypocrisy" (Krauss 1911 [1907]:10).

On the one hand, praise for attitudes toward sexual matters in Japan was often directed at the restrictive sexual order at home in Europe or the United States. On the other, critics of sexual matters in Japan were occasionally put in place by prominent intellectuals. Nitobe Inazō, for example, wrote in a book on *Unser Vaterland Japan* (Our Fatherland Japan) in 1906 that "It is a general perception of foreign tourists (many of whom are *learned gentlemen* [my emphasis]) that Japanese life lacks morality just as its flowers lack a scent. What a sad confession of the moral and intellectual imagination of these tourists themselves!" (quoted in Krauss 1911 [1907]:13).

In 1907 Dr. Friedrich Solomon Krauss, a pioneer of sexual ethnology who had traveled from Vienna to Tokyo to collect material for a book on Japan's "sex life," published *Das Geschlechtsleben in Glauben, Sitte, Brauch und Gewohnheitsrecht der Japaner* (The Sex Life in Beliefs, Morals, Customs, and Common Law of the Japanese). It appeared as a supplement to *Anthropophyteia: Jahrbücher für folkloris-tische Erhebungen und Forschungen zur Entwicklungsgeschichte der geschlechtlichen Moral* (Anthropophyteia: Yearbooks for Folkloristic Surveys and Research on the History of the Development of Sexual Morals). Krauss was the editor of *Anthropo-phyteia*. Among other leading personalities from the world of science and medicine, Dr. Franz Boas, Dr. Albert Neisser, and Dr. Sigmund Freud served on the editorial board. In contrast to earlier works by Japanese and other scholars, Krauss included not only a description of the cults of male and female genitalia but also long chapters about previous works on Japanese phallicism, the beauty of Japanese women, the status of women, the meaning of menstrual blood, the "third sex" (homosexuals), pregnancy and birth, marriage practices, prostitution, erotic pictures, and several other phenomena he classified as sexual.

Krauss was eager to promote his sexual ethnology and claimed that the evaluation of a people by examining its military and its economic or literary successes was insufficient. As the development and progress of *men* depended entirely on the flourishing of *women*, the foremost goal of the folklorist, he declared, was to increase knowledge about the status of women in a culture. "Sexual activity," in his view, had to be at the core of any analysis of cultural development and progress (Krauss 1911 [1907]:1). Full-page photographs of stone phalluses, rather explicit erotic woodblock prints, and a long chapter on attitudes toward "homosexual love," in which he claimed that "the old attitude of the samurai continues to live on in quiet and its main carrier still is the military" (Krauss 1911 [1907]:161) – even in a book that was explicitly restricted to a specialist readership, these had to be justified. Hence, in the preface to the first edition Krauss stated that recognizing phenomena "unbeautified and uncorrected, in their undisguised reality" before searching for explanations or for higher causes was the most important, if not the only guiding principle for a true ethnology and anthropology, as for any true scientific inquiry (Krauss 1911 [1907]: preface to the first edition).

In 1895 the University of Chicago Press had published a 34-page dissertation by Edmund Buckley, *Phallicism in Japan*, ironically at a time when the Japanese state had begun to prohibit phallus-related rituals as backward and uncivilized. There had been other authors, including William George Aston and W. E. Griffis, who had touched upon phallicism in their works, but Buckley's was the first "serious study of any branch of phallicism to be presented to a university" (Goodland 1931:91). *Phallicism in Japan* apparently traveled to Japan but was only read by university professors in the fields of religious studies, anthropology, and archaeology. Only when Deguchi Yonekichi, the Japanese pioneer of sexual ethnology, published a translation of Buckley's work in the Japanese Journal of Anthropology (*Jinruigaku zasshi*) did phallicism and sexual ethnology become a field of research in Japan as well. Deguchi Yonekichi completed his own book on phallicism, titled *Nihon seishokki sūhai ryakusetsu* (An Outline of Phallic Worship in Japan), in 1917 and published it in 1920. According to ethnologist Kawamura Kunimitsu (1999:5–7), Deguchi's wonderfully rich account was based not only on the study of documents but also on conversations with locals all over Japan, at a time when "fieldwork" had not yet been established as a method of anthropological inquiry (Kawamura 1999:3–32).

Within a few decades, the study of sexual practices and attitudes changed radically under the influence of an emerging sexual science whose representatives included Richard von Krafft-Ebing in Austria, Havelock Ellis in England, Magnus Hirschfeld in Germany, Yamamoto Senji and Yasuda Tokutarō in Japan, and Alfred Kinsey in the United States. This new kind of sexology did not strive to simply document "undisguised reality," as Krauss had thought he had done, but pursued a complex political agenda as well. Dr. Magnus Hirschfeld, director of the Institut für Eugenik und Sexualwissenschaft in Berlin, a reader of Krauss' *The Sex Life*, and a deeply impressed visitor to Japan, declared in 1933 that no two countries or peoples in the world had identical sex institutions. In Hirschfeld's view, this dissimilarity was not based on differences in sex tendencies, which, taken as a whole, he considered absolutely alike in all peoples and races. A uniform solution of sex and love morality, Hirschfeld thought, could be based only on findings of biological and sociological sex research. At a time when homosexuality was a crime according to German law, Hirschfeld hoped that an objective scientific study of mankind and of sex would prepare the way for a complete realization of human sexual rights. He also hoped to find some clues in Japan, where sex and sexuality seemed to be dealt with so differently, and where homosexuality was not prohibited by law (Hirschfeld 1935 [1933]:xviii–xix).

By the beginning of the 1930s when Hirschfeld visited Japan, a handful of Japanese sexologists were discussing the results of their sex research, of the kind Hirschfeld had been promoting, in major physiological, smaller sexological, and general-audience mass-marketed women's and health journals and magazines

(Frühstück 2000). However, even though Hirschfeld met with important figures of the academic world in Tokyo and Osaka, it does not seem that he came into close contact with Japan's sex researchers. They too had been marginalized by their academic peers, in part because of the object of their research and in part because of their political engagement in support of birth control, the legalization of abortion, and the reform of gender relations (Robertson 1999:22–24).

The works I have discussed so far are impressive in scope and accuracy even by today's anthropological standards, but they were printed in small numbers and circulated in relatively closed circles of specialists in ethnology, folklore, history, medicine, sexual science, and eugenics. To be sure, Euro-American works were translated and discussed in Japan, but the same was hardly true the other way around. Other books affected Western images of Japan much more, far into the 20th century. Authors such as Joseph E. de Becker (1905 [1899]), a specialist in international law who spent most of his life in Japan and wrote several books on the Japanese legal system, a certain Trésmin-Trémolières (1910 [1905]), whose identity remains obscure, and George Riley Scott (1943) directed the ethnological, male, Western gaze at a different arena of sexual conduct. The prostitution quarters of Tokyo – a "nightless city" for de Becker and the "Japanese city of love" for Trésmin-Trémolières – were condemned for their existence as well as praised for the exotic beauty of their *geisha*, the cleanliness of their establishments, and the seemingly well-treated and comparatively healthy female prostitutes.

The emerging abolition movement in Japan proved them wrong on all counts, of course. From 1912 onwards, members of the Purity Society (Kakuseikai), an organization that fought for the abolition of prostitution, denounced both rural fathers for selling their daughters to brothels and the state for tolerating, if not supporting, the practice. They demanded better health services for prostitutes and ways out of the "water trade" for them. Abolitionists initially debated the question of how to do away with prostitution; later, when that seemed impossible, they argued over how to better regulate the prostitutes in order to protect the health of Japan's men. By 1940, even most critics of the prostitution system agreed that it was better, or even necessary, to sacrifice what seemed to them a small number of women in order to keep the social order intact, protect "decent" women from male sexual violence, and to keep up soldiers' morale in the "homeland" and on the front.

Despite the abundance of anthropological research on sexual matters in Japan available at the time, in Europe and America the popular image of the gracious *geisha* as both an image of *the* Japanese woman and of a (traditional, almost lost) Japanese culture proved resistant to newer, more diverse, and more realistic pictures. I will turn to these subjects in the next section.

WOMEN'S STUDIES AND THE END OF THE UNIVERSAL "MAN"

The era from the 1910s to the 1930s was characterized not only by a boom of phallicism studies and a new kind of social scientific sex research, as noted above, but also by heated debates about women's roles in Japanese society. In contrast to similar discussions at the end of the 19th century, these debates were to a significant extent carried by women. They shared an interest in a diverse set of problems, including questions of love, motherhood, sexual freedom, birth control, and women's suffrage. Their views ranged from those of conservative feminists like Yamada Waka and Hiratsuka Raichō, who promoted the valorization of motherhood in order to improve the status of women, to more radical feminists like Yamakawa Kikue, Yosano Akiko, and Yasuda Satsuki, who insisted on a woman's right to abortion and birth control. For all their differences, however, sexuality in these women's everyday lives clearly had been more a domain of restriction, repression, and danger than a domain of exploration, pleasure, and agency.

Hence, much like their Western sisters, many of these early feminists pursued asexuality as an option for respectable women and used the concept of female passionlessness and male sexual restraint to challenge male prerogatives. The representatives of this first wave of Japanese feminism developed their ideas in debates with and over "Western" feminism, but grappled for an autonomous cultural synthesis of the concepts of autonomy, emancipation, and equality for women in Japanese culture and society. In a debate on motherhood protection, for example, Yosano Akiko brushed off what she perceived as Western feminism. She could not agree to the demand of some members of the Western women's movement that women should ask for special protection by the state in the time of pregnancy or birth (Kōnai 1984:85). Motherhood protection policies, she believed, would further undermine women's independence by acknowledging their value as mothers only.

Returning to the development of the anthropology of sex and gender in early 20th-century Japan, it was the exploitation of women in industrialization that first prompted quasi-anthropological studies of women as a special group. *The Sad Story of Women Workers* (Hosoi 1996 [1925]), for example, describes the pitiful living and working conditions of young female migrant workers. The book's author, Hosoi Wakizō, was a former textile worker and trade-union activist. Perhaps following the zeitgeist of the 1920s that practically burst with sex talk and script, Hosoi designated a whole chapter to the "psychology of female factory workers," in which he matter-of-factly wrote about these young women's sexual desires. As common features of factory workers' psychological make-up, he described their attitudes toward love, morals, and virginity, as well as instances of lesbianism, masturbation, jealousy, and other features of these women's sexual psychology.

Lacking similar reports, the sturdy peasant women and their migrant daughters studied by Hosoi and the feminist writers and intellectuals mentioned above, all of whom contributed to the survival of their household as well as to Japanese modernization, were widely ignored in the European and Anglo-American anthropology of Japan at the time. Ella Lury Wiswell was the first American exception. She was not an anthropologist by training but accompanied her husband John Embree and assisted him in his research in 1935–36, a few years before Japan's attack on Pearl Harbor would create a very different kind of interest in the study of Japanese culture. It remains unknown whether Wiswell had in mind the *geisha* image when she embarked on Japan's shores, whether she secretly, if unknowingly, bonded with the outspoken Japanese feminists of her time, or whether she sympathized with the exploited women in Japan's factories. Most likely, she did not know much about any of these worlds when she began taking notes of whatever exciting event was happening in the small village of Suye Mura in Kumamoto Prefecture, Kyūshū.

In contrast to her husband's and other anthropologists' claims, Wiswell (Smith and Wiswell 1982:149–175) found that women in Suye Mura were quite independent when it came to marriage, divorce, and sexual matters. We have conflicting accounts about how well Wiswell spoke Japanese, but she did not seem to read the language and thus had little if any access to any of the Japanese anthropology I have discussed above. Had Wiswell's study been published immediately instead of in 1982, this chapter would most probably look quite different. A classic of the anthropology of women ever since its publication, *The Women of Suye Mura* grants a short chapter to sexual matters and constitutes the first ethnographic study in English to focus on the everyday lives of rural women in Japan.

The "community studies" approach – portraits of Japanese women as a whole by studying one woman or a small community of women and their immediate environment – have been with us ever since. Gail Bernstein's *Haruko's World: A Japanese Farm Woman and her Community* (1983), for example, is based on research in a village in Ehime Prefecture in 1974–75. As a "portrait of contemporary rural Japanese women viewed primarily through the eyes of one woman," Bernstein's book describes these women's work and their family life as well as their feelings, problems, and aspirations – topics that Bernstein felt were often neglected in conventional village studies. "To observe the lives of farm women today," Bernstein suggests, "is to recapture something of Japan's past, but it is also to record the great changes overtaking rural Japan" (1983:xi). The book is a three-part richly nuanced description of how she as a scholar approached her subject, the life in the farm family she stayed with, and broader issues the farm community dealt with. Like a good novel, it leaves the reader amused, edified, and sorry when the final page is reached. One of the great merits of the "women's portrait" kind of studies is that they give a voice to comparatively "ordinary" and rarely heard women. They also put in perspective, if only implicitly, mainstream descriptions that still nonchalantly regard middle-class, white-collar, male employees of large corporations as the whole of Japanese society.

However, these studies also have their less satisfactory sides: one is no wiser about what Japanese and other anthropologists have to say about the subject. Bernstein – much like her predecessors as well as many anthropologists of Japan and particularly those who write "books on women" to this day – does not integrate Japanese scholarship on the subject. Nor is she interested in confronting mainstream anthropology with her findings. Hence, her book is – like many women's studies books – an "addendum" to the existing anthropology of rural Japan rather than provocative and creatively disruptive of the order of things anthropological in the Japan field.

Since the 1980s, female anthropologists have infiltrated the field which had analyzed almost exclusively spheres that were implicitly and unquestioned marked as "male," claiming a gradually expanding space for the anthropology of Japanese women, and in the process changing some of the discipline's written and unwritten rules. Useful and necessary as these descriptive accounts of the lives of rural and urban women, farmers, workers, and housewives are, they have tended to imply a situation in which society had need of particular sorts of acculturated persons, who were rather uncomplicatedly female and male. Gender identity was perceived as culturally constructed, but it was regarded in the end as little more than a self-evident outcome of sexual differentiation.

When these studies first became more than an aberration from anthropological writing on Japan, the anthropology of women turned the tide and began to cast doubt on the essential and universal "man" which was the subject and paradigmatic object of nonfeminist anthropology. Important studies emerged, ranging from Takie Sugiyama Lebra's pathbreaking work that follows a lifecycle approach (Lebra 1984), analyses of the lives of housewives (A. Imamura 1987; LeBlanc 1999) and gainfully employed women (Rosenberger 2001; Tanaka 1995), to studies of women with rather unusual lives such as those of *geisha* (Dalby 1983) or of priestesses of Okinawa (Sered 1999). More recent works attempt to reintegrate men and grant more discussion to relationships between women and men. "Women's studies" have become theoretically more sophisticated, but they still tend to fail at, or are simply not interested in, a critical examination of their research objects' sexual and gender identities. These studies also assume that marriage is of central importance to and a quasi-natural element of women's lives, while their heterosexuality is presented as a given, as is their ethnic homogeneity.

Karen Kelsky's book, *Women on the Verge: Japanese Women, Western Dreams* (2001), tells a quite different story. The subject is the "narratives of internationalism which some Japanese women use to justify their shift of loyalty from what they call a backward and 'oppressive' Japan to what they see as an exhilarating and 'liberating' foreign realm" (Kelsky 2001:3). The book is also, however, the first feminist study of Japan's eroticization of the West and in a way the present-day reverse of the West's (non-feminist) eroticization of Japan which I briefly discussed at the beginning of this chapter.

The number and variety of Japanese women's studies is too vast to describe even selectively here. Suffice it to say that *Nihon joseigaku nenpō* (the Yearbook of Japanese Women's Studies), published by the Women's Studies Society of Japan, and the *Nichibei josei jānaru* and its English supplement *US–Japan Women's Journal*, published by the Center for Intercultural Studies and Education at Josai University, reflect a phenomenally productive field. The *Nichibei josei jānaru/US–Japan Women's Journal*'s pursuit of the international exchange of interdisciplinary feminist articles, reports on a wide range of women's issues, men's studies, and statistical information on the status of women is exemplary of the much-needed comparative study of women's issues. Its agenda also points to the interconnections within the anthropology of Japan between women's studies and gender studies, the subject of the next section.

GENDER STUDIES AND THE TRANSGRESSION OF "WOMAN"

Gender studies have introduced an analytically useful distinction between "sex" as a signifier of biological characteristics and "gender" as a marker of sociocultural attributes. With respect to Japan, while these studies also focus overwhelmingly on women, they more critically examine gender-formation processes in areas ranging from the division of labor; institutions that reproduce gender norms, such as families, enterprises, and social welfare settings; female and male identities and self-concepts in their interaction; and social and cultural representations including images of femininity and masculinity.

Based on the erosion of the assumption of an essential sameness among women, the related doubts of the usefulness of analysis that has essential, universal "woman" as its subject or object, and of female gender roles as the quasi-natural outcome of sexual differentiation since the late 1970s, anthropologists of Japan during the past 20 years or so have established the notion that sexual and gender identities are interconnected in rather complicated ways, are constantly negotiated, and are much more malleable than their predecessors had dared to think. The shift from studies that add important perspectives on the female half of the population to "gender studies" that problematize gender roles, identities, and politics more centrally is an important one. The category of "woman" is no longer the "other" in society, but a crucial nexus of politics, the nation-state, technology, and women's (and, to a lesser extent, men's) everyday lives. In 1994 Ōsawa Mari – until a few years ago the only female sociologist at the Institute of Social Science of the University of Tokyo – called for a "gender revolution" in Japan's social science. In 1996, the government-sponsored Council for Gender Equality announced that this century was "significant in that equality between men and women has become accepted as a universal value" and claimed that "in Japan the construction of the social framework has taken place to materialize that concept for the first time in human history" (Council for Gender Equality 1996:1).

Subsequently, Ōsawa, Ueno Chizuko, Ehara Yumiko (1995, 1998, 2000), and other feminist Japanese sociologists and anthropologists have paved the way for an increasing number of publications that focus on mechanisms of gender inequality at the workplace, the commercialization of sex, the interrelations between women, violence and the nation, and gender questions concerning new reproductive technologies. A remarkable number of volumes in English also point toward future, more extensive and diverse, work in this area by scholars based in the United States. The defining parameters of "femininity" and "womanhood" are questioned by these scholars, and women have emerged in ever-increasing numbers as full-time white-collar workers (S. Buckley 1997; Fujimura-Fanselow and Kameda 1995; A. Imamura 1996; Kondo 1990; Lo 1990; Ogasawara 1998; Roberts 1994; Saso 1990; Skov and Moeran 1995).

As a double-sided category, "gender" in these works functions as a system of classification of persons into gendered positions and as a category that legitimizes existing hierarchies between these positions as "natural." In order to disrupt its potential for the legitimization and stabilization of social inequality, approaches to gender imply several methodological consequences. As anthropologists have shown, a gender approach cannot limit itself to women but must research women and men as well as interactions and exchanges between different social spheres, aiming for an integrative perspective. Feminist anthropologists have realized, for example, that the choice to study only the household (and housewives), leaving the study of the workplace (and men's primary social spheres) to others to investigate, as many women's studies did, not only overestimates women's social strength in Japan but also reinforces gender role stereotyping. The establishment of the theoretical and analytical notion of the "sex/gender system" also has allowed for recent anthropological, historical, and sociological work on masculinity, men's bodies, men's lives, and problems of manhood in contemporary Japan.

The majority of the older generation of (male) Anglo-American anthropologists have accepted women's studies as an addition to the anthropology of Japan by women without letting it influence their own, usually gender-blind work. But a small portion of younger-generation scholars have turned to that complex interplay of questions following both Japanese feminists as well as the very few male scholars of gender studies (Inoue et al. 1995; Itō 1996). The first such collection of essays in English is *Men and Masculinities in Contemporary Japan: Dislocating the Salaryman Doxa*, co-edited by James Roberson and Suzuki Nobue (2002). Contributions on transgender practices, male beauty work, popular culture, the marriage market, the new "family man," working-class masculinity, day laborers, domestic violence, gay men, and fatherhood and work successfully make the point that not every Japanese man is an ideal-type salaryman, imagined or constructed, and not every Japanese man even strives to be like an ideal-type salaryman. One can only hope that the presently very slim body of works which examine notions of manhood and masculinity from the perspective of gender and history will not only broaden our understanding of the variety of Japanese men but also challenge "conventional" notions of manliness supposedly embodied in the salaryman. Remembering the "diversity approach" in 1980s women's studies especially, one must admit that we still know next to nothing about the gender of policemen, soldiers, yakuza, scientists, and many other social groups which are associated with a supposedly conventional manliness that the above-mentioned authors intend to challenge.

In addition, the quest for an integrated approach is also valid for relating gender to other categories of social inequality, such as social stratification and ethnicity (Honda 2000 [1993]; Keyso 2000; Nihon Joseigaku Kenkyūkai 1994). Despite their particular relevancy in Japan, where media and popular consensus stress ethnic homogeneity, and where consensus for "traditional" gender roles is demanded in the name of "Japanese culture" or true "Japaneseness," both sets of problems still are sorely understudied.

SEXUALITY STUDIES

Perhaps because biological and sociological sex research in Japan was marginalized during the 1920s, repressed during the 1930s and 1940s, kept at a low profile during the 1950s, and for the most part shunned by the academy until the 1980s, anthropological studies of Japan's "sexual culture" only caught up and reconnected with the sexual ethnology of the fin de siècle very recently. It was not until the 1990s that Japanese as well as Euro-American scholars rediscovered that sphere of inquiry and began to question the kinds of Japanese "sexual knowledge" that had been created primarily between the late 19th and the early 20th centuries. This trend, however, is by no means a return to the sexual ethnology of Deguchi Yonekichi or the sexology of Yamamoto Senji from almost a hundred years ago.

Rather, the trend toward sexuality studies was inspired by several developments within and outside the discipline of anthropology. Histories of premodern and early modern Japan and elsewhere created a space for sexuality studies in present-day Japan. A new interest in the body in anthropology, history, philosophy, and other disciplines (Inoue Shun and Tominaga 1991; Moerman and Nomura 1990) triggered a diversification of anthropological studies and a shift toward queer study-type analyses, focusing on the lives of homosexual men and women, bodily concerns including reproductive practices (Coleman 1983; Hardacre 1997; Lock 1993), the politics of physical beauty (Miller 1998; Robertson 2001), and attempts at grasping the meanings of sexual imagery in media and art (Allison 2000 [1996]; Napier 2000). In addition, the advent of HIV and AIDS not only caused a largely media-generated panic in Japan (Treat 1994) but also highlighted the lack of a systematic and inclusive sex education (Imamura et al. 1990; Kawahara 1996; Nishigaito 1993). Finally, the emergence of a gay/lesbian/queer movement in Japan prompted a growing number of coming-out essays and novels – reminiscent of the same development in early women's studies – ranging from Fushimi Noriaki's *Puraibēto gei raifu: posuto renai-ron* (Private Gay Life: After Love Discussions; 1991), to Itō Satoru's tearful *Otoko futarigurashi* (Living as a Male Couple; 1993), and Kakefuda Hiroko's *Rezubian de aru to iu koto* (The Meaning of Being a Lesbian; 1992). Besides these highly personal accounts of being a gay man or a lesbian woman in Japan, anthropological studies on these respective communities include Wim Lunsing's *Beyond Common Sense: Sexuality and Gender in Contemporary Japan* (2001) and Mark McLelland's more media-centered *Male Homosexuality in Modern Japan: Cultural Myths and Social Realities* (2000).

In most general terms, the existing sexuality studies question the previously implicit, normative and exclusive prioritization of heterosexuality. Against the backdrop of American-style identity politics which tend to idealize a singular and whole self and to presuppose an "individual oneness" (Lunsing 2001:17–18), it is not surprising that anthropologists of sexuality in Japan continue to grapple with what is often perceived as Japanese "multiple selves." These anthropologists are not always aware that historically, in Japan and elsewhere, "sexual practices have not presumed a specific sexual orientation or identity, although today, some lesbian and gay activists and homophobic critics alike tend to fuse the two" (Robertson 1998 [2001]:174). One curious effect of the emphases in recent sexuality studies is that we now know more about homosexual lives than we know about heterosexual (and supposedly mainstream) lifestyles. There also seem to be more scholars engaged in the examination of sex, gender, and sexuality in representations of popular culture, especially comics, animation, and film, than there are students of the appropriations of a sex/gender system in "real lives."

While there is not a single available monograph in English on, for example, the pornography and/or prostitution industry in Japan (Fukushima and Nakano 1995), we have fine examinations of representations of sexuality – including "pornographic" ones – in Japanese animated films (Napier 2000). While we still know next to nothing about incest in Japanese society (Ikeda 1991), its representations in Japanese comics and other popular media have been tackled (Allison 2000 [1996]). Whereas we have a number of detailed studies about the wartime system of sexual slavery, we still almost entirely lack a thorough examination of "military prostitution" in present-day Japan.

The examination of what had been implicitly considered "marginal" identities in earlier anthropological research is fruitful and important, but it does not absolve us from the necessity of critical studies about "normative" sexuality. An integrated analysis that focuses on gender and sexuality, women and men remains necessary in order to understand the workings of the sex/gender system, and in order to overcome a fragmentation of the field reminiscent of the position of early women's studies at the margins of anthropology several decades ago. To speak about sexuality means to speak about society, its gender relations in particular and its power relations more generally. Hence, even though dichotomies between men and women, heterosexuality and homosexuality, are empirically false, we cannot afford to dismiss them as irrelevant as long as they structure Japanese (as well as our) lives and consciousness. In perhaps the most challenging anthropology of sexuality in Japan to date, *Takarazuka: Sexual Politics and Popular Culture in Modern Japan*, Jennifer Robertson makes a crucial point about the plasticity of genders and sexualities. It is the "composite character of gender," Robertson writes, that makes it fundamentally ambivalent and ambiguous. It is capable of fluctuating between or being assigned to more than one referent or category and thus is capable of being read or understood in more than one way. Such an excessive semiosis reflects an epistemology of *both/and* rather than *either/or* (Robertson 1998 [2001]:40).

CONCLUSION

Over the past hundred years, the anthropology of genders and sexualities in Japan in both Japanese and English has undergone important changes. In addition to the formation of the four overlapping branches discussed above, other transformations have affected the anthropology of gender and sexuality as well as the anthropology of Japan more generally. One has to do with language, the other with processes associated with "globalization."

Up to the 1970s most anthropologists did their fieldwork with the help of an interpreter and spoke Japanese only rudimentarily or not at all. In recent decades, it seems to me that more anthropologists speak and read Japanese well enough to conduct research on their own. Another language-related flaw seems to be lessening as well. Many early American anthropologists of Japan hardly looked at what their Japanese colleagues (let alone colleagues from other linguistic communities) wrote on the phenomena they studied. Even though many anthropologists' bibliographies of Japanese-language sources and secondary material are still shockingly thin, this neglect of "indigenous" scholarship, especially in a highly bibliophile culture with an enormous output of scholarly publications like Japan, appears to be less tolerated today.

The effects of "globalization" are closely connected to linguistic requirements. Today, Japan-related scholarship in and outside Japan seems to be more a consequence of two-way interactions than has been the case in previous decades. Japanese ethnographies of female factory workers, as well as the writings of the early 20th-century feminists and of the sexologists, remained unknown to Anglo-American anthropologists until historians and historically oriented anthropologists rediscovered them. In contrast, the acceleration of interactions between scholars from different cultural communities and the physical exchange of students and scholars across geographic, cultural, and linguistic boundaries necessitate and further the speaking of the same language, both linguistically and in terms of the subjects these scholars recognize as worth talking about and researching. Interactive and integrative efforts that are also historically informed will, in the end, not simply allow us to better understand how Japanese women and men live and think about sexuality, but will provide us with opportunities to come up with better problems to analyze than those with which we have started.

ACKNOWLEDGMENTS

Research for this chapter was supported by a Japanese Ministry of Education Monbusho scholarship. I am grateful to Jennifer Robertson and Elise Edwards for comments on earlier drafts.

REFERENCES

Allison, Anne. 2000 [1996]. Permitted and Prohibited Desires: Mothers, Comics, and Censorship in Japan. Berkeley: University of California Press.

Becker, Joseph E. de. 1905 [1899]. The Nightless City, or The History of the Yoshiwara Yūkaku. Yokohama and London: no publisher given.

Bernstein, Gail. 1983. Haruko's World: A Japanese Farm Woman and her Community. Berkeley: University of California Press.

Buckley, Edmund. 1895. Phallicism in Japan. Chicago: University of Chicago Press.

Buckley, Sandra, ed. 1997. Broken Silence: Voices of Japanese Feminism. Berkeley and Los Angeles: University of California Press.

Coleman, Samuel. 1983. Family Planning in Japanese Society: Traditional Birth Control in a Modern Urban Culture. Princeton: Princeton University Press.

Council for Gender Equality. 1996. Vision of Gender Equality: Creating New Values for the 21st Century. Tokyo: Council for Gender Equality.

Dalby, Liza Crichfield. 1983. Geisha. Berkeley and Los Angeles: University of California Press.

Ehara, Yumiko. ed. 1995. Sei no shōhinka (The Commodification of Sex). Tokyo: Keisō Shobō.

——1998. Josei, bōryoku, nēshon (Women, Violence, Nation). Tokyo: Keisō Shobō.

——2000. Seishoku gijutsu to jendā (Reproductive Technologies and Gender). Tokyo: Keisō Shobō.

Frühstück, Sabine. 2000. Managing the Truth of Sex in Imperial Japan. Journal of Asian Studies 59(2):332–358.

Fujimura-Fanselow, Kumiko, and Atsuko Kameda. 1995. Japanese Women: New Feminist Perspectives on the Past, Present, and Future. New York: Feminist Press.

Fukushima, Mizuho, and Nakano Rie. 1995. Kau otoko. Kawanai otoko (Men Who Buy. Men Who Don't Buy). Tokyo: Gendai Shokan.

Furukawa, Makoto. 1996. Dōseiai no hikaku shakaigaku: rezubian gei sutadīzu no tenkai to danshoku gainen (A Comparative Social Study of Homosexuality: The Evolution of Lesbian and Gay Studies and the Notion of Sodomy). In Sei no shakaigaku (Sociology of Sex). Inoue Shōichi et al., eds. pp. 113–130. Tokyo: Iwanami Shoten.

Fushimi, Noriaki. 1991. Puraibēto gei raifu: posuto renai-ron (Private Gay Life: After Love Discussions). Tokyo: Gakuyō Shobō.

——1995. Kuia paradaisu (Queer Paradise). Tokyo: Shōheisha.

Goodland, Roger. 1931. A Bibliography of Sex Rites and Customs. London: Routledge & Sons.

Hardacre, Helen. 1997. Marketing the Menacing Fetus in Japan. Berkeley and Los Angeles: University of California Press.

Hirschfeld, Magnus. 1935 [1933]. Men and Women: The World Journey of a Sexologist. O. P. Green, trans. New York: G. P. Putnam's Sons.

Honda, Katsuichi. 2000 [1993]. Harukor: An Ainu Woman's Tale. Kyoko Selden, trans. Berkeley: University of California Press.

Hosoi, Wakizō. 1996 [1925]. Jokō aishi (The Sad Story of Women Workers). Tokyo: Iwanami Shoten.

Ikeda, Yoshiko. 1991. Nanji waga ko o okasu nakare: nihon no kinshinkan to seiteki gyakutai (Thou Shalt Not Rape Thine Own Child: Intimacy and Sexual Abuse in Japan). Tokyo: Kobundō.

Imamura, Anne. 1987. Urban Japanese Housewives: At Home and in the Community. Honolulu: University of Hawaii Press.

——ed. 1996. Re-imagining Japanese Women. Berkeley and Los Angeles: University of California Press.

Imamura, Naomi, Unno, Yūki, and Ishimaru, Kumiko, eds. 1990. Moa ripōto now (More Report Now). Tokyo: Shūeisha.

Inoue, Shun, and Tominaga, Shigeki, eds. 1991. Soshioroji 36(1): Shakai to shintai (Sociology: Special Issue on Society and the Body).

Inoue, Teruko, et al. eds. 1995. Danseigaku (Men's Studies). Tokyo: Iwanami Shoten.

Itō, Kimio. 1996. Danseigaku nyūmon (Introduction to Men's Studies). Tokyo: Sakuhinsha.

Itō, Satoru. 1993. Otoko futari gurashi: boku no gei puraido senden (Living as a Male Couple: My Gay Pride Propagation). Tokyo: Futarō Jirōsha.

Kakefuda, Hiroko. 1992. Rezubian de aru to iu koto (The Meaning of Being a Lesbian). Tokyo: Kawade Shobō Shinsha.

Kawahara, Yukari. 1996. Politics, Pedagogy, and Sexuality: Sex Education in Japanese Secondary Schools, Ph.D. dissertation, Yale University.

Kawamura, Kunimitsu. 1999. Sei no minzoku kenkyū o megutte (Towards a Folklore Studies Approach to Sexuality). In Sei no minzoku sōsho (Folklore Studies of Sex Series). Kawamura Kunimitsu, ed. pp. 3–32. Tokyo: Bensei Shuppan.

Kelsky, Karen. 2001. Women on the Verge: Japanese Women, Western Dreams. Durham, NC, and London: Duke University Press.

Keyso, Ruth Ann. 2000. Women of Okinawa: Nine Voices from a Garrison Island. Ithaca: Cornell University Press.

Kimoto, Itaru. 1976. Onanī to nihonjin (Masturbation and the Japanese). Tokyo: Intanaru Kabushikigaisha Shuppanbu.

Kōnai, Nobuko. 1984. Shiryō bosei hogo ronsō (Material on the Motherhood Protection Debate). Tokyo: Ronsō Shirīzu 1.

Kondo, Dorinne. 1990. Crafting Selves: Power, Gender and Discourses of Identity in a Japanese Workplace. Chicago: University of Chicago Press.

Krauss, Friedrich S. 1911 [1907]. Das Geschlechtsleben in Glauben, Sitte, Brauch und Gewohnheitsrecht der Japaner. Beiwerke zum Studium der Anthropophyteia: Jahrbücher für folkloristische Erhebungen und Forschungen zur Entwicklungsgeschichte der geschlechtlichen Moral, vol. 2, ed. Friedrich S. Krauss. Leipzig: Ethnologischer Verlag.

LeBlanc, Robin. 1999. Bicycle Citizens: The Political World of the Japanese Housewife. Berkeley and Los Angeles: University of California Press.

Lebra, Takie Sugiyama. 1984. Japanese Women: Constraint and Fulfillment. Honolulu: University of Hawaii Press.

Lo, Jeannie. 1990. Office Ladies, Factory Women: Life and Work at a Japanese Company. Armonk, NY: M. E. Sharpe.

Lock, Margaret. 1993. Encounters with Aging: Mythologies of Menopause in Japan and North America. Berkeley and Los Angeles: University of California Press.

Lunsing, Wim. 2001. Beyond Common Sense: Sexuality and Gender in Contemporary Japan. London and New York: Kegan Paul.

McLelland, Mark. 2000. Male Homosexuality in Modern Japan: Cultural Myths and Social Realities. Surrey: Curzon Press.

Miller, Laura. 1998. "Bad Girls": Representations of Unsuitable, Unfit, and Unsatisfactory Women in Magazines. US–Japan Women's Journal (English supplement 15):31–51.

Moerman, Michael, and Nomura Masaichi, eds. 1990. Senri Ethnological Studies 27. Ōsaka: National Museum of Ethnology.

Napier, Susan. 2000. Anime: From Akira to Princess Mononoke. New York: Palgrave.

National Women's Education Center. 1997. Status of Women as Seen in Statistics. Tokyo: National Women's Education Center.

Nihon Joseigaku Kenkyūkai. 1994. Nihon joseigaku nenpō 15 (Annual Report of Japanese Women's Studies). Kyoto: Nihon Joseigaku Kenkyūkai.

Nishigaito, Masaru. 1993. Seikyōiku wa ima (Sex Education Today). Tokyo: Iwanami Shoten.

Office of Gender Equality. 1996. The Present Status of Women and Measures: Fifth Report on the Implementation of the New National Plan of Action toward the Year 2000. Tokyo: Office of Gender Equality.

Ogasawara, Yuko. 1998. Office Ladies and Salaried Men: Power, Gender, and Work in Japanese Companies. Berkeley and Los Angeles: University of California Press.

Ōsawa, Mari. 1994. The Gender Revolution in Social Science. Social Science Japan 2:1–3.

Roberson, James E., and Suzuki Nobue, eds. 2002. Men and Masculinities in Contemporary Japan: Dislocating the Salaryman Doxa. London: Routledge.

Roberts, Glenda. 1994. Staying on the Line: Blue-Collar Women in Contemporary Japan. Berkeley and Los Angeles: University of California Press.

Robertson, Jennifer. 1998 [2001]. Takarazuka: Sexual Politics and Popular Culture in Modern Japan. Berkeley: University of California Press.

—— 1999. Dying to Tell: Sexuality and Suicide in Imperial Japan. Signs: Journal of Women in Culture and Society 25(1):1–35.

—— 2001. Japan's First Cyborg? Miss Nippon, Eugenics and Wartime Technologies of Beauty, Body and Blood. Body & Society 7(1):1–34.

Rosenberger, Nancy. 2001. Gambling with Virtue: Japanese Women and the Search for Self in a Changing Nation. Honolulu: University of Hawaii Press.

Saso, Mary. 1990. Women in the Japanese Workplace. London: Hilary Shipman.

Scott, George Riley. 1943. Far Eastern Sex Life: An Anthropological, Ethnological, and Sociological Study of the Love Relations, Marriage Rites, and Home Life of the Oriental People. London: Gerald G. Swan.

Sered, Susan Starr. 1999. Women of the Sacred Groves: Divine Priestesses of Okinawa. Oxford and New York: Oxford University Press.

Skov, Lise, and Brian Moeran. 1995. Women, Media and Consumption in Japan. Surrey, UK: Curzon Press.

Smith, Robert, and Ella Lury Wiswell. 1982. The Women of Suye Mura. Chicago: Chicago University Press.

Tanaka, Yukiko. 1995. Contemporary Portraits of Japanese Women. Westport, CT: Praeger Press.

Treat, John Whittier. 1994. AIDS Panic in Japan, or How to Have a Sabbatical in an Epidemic. positions: east asia cultures critique 2(3):629–679.

Trésmin-Trémolières. 1910 [1905]. Yoshiwara: Die Liebesstadt der Japaner. Sexualpsycholo-
gische Bibliothek, ser. 1, vol. 4). Bruno Sklarek, trans.. Berlin: L. Marous.

SUGGESTED READING

Books

Allison, Anne. 1994. Nightwork: Sexuality, Pleasure and Corporate Masculinity in a Tokyo
    Hostess Club. Chicago: Chicago University Press.
Asayama, Shinichi. 1957. Sei no kiroku (Records of Sexuality). Osaka: Rokugetsusha.
Bornoff, Nicholas. 1991. Pink Samurai: The Pursuit and Politics of Sex in Japan. London:
    Grafton Books.
Bumiller, Elisabeth. 1995. Secrets of Mariko: A Year in the Life of a Japanese Woman and her
    Family. New York: Times Books.
Ishikawa, Hiroyoshi, Saitō, Shigeo, and Wagatsuma, Hiroshi. 1984. Nihonjin no sei (Sexuality
    of the Japanese). Tokyo: Bungei Shunjū.
Lebra, Joyce, Joy Paulson, and Elisabeth Powers. 1978 [1976]. Women in Changing Japan.
    Stanford: Stanford University Press.
Matsumoto, Seiichi, ed. 1996. Sexuality and Human Bonding. Proceedings of the XIIth World
    Congress of Sexology. Amsterdam: Elsevier.
Morley, Patricia. 1999. The Mountain Is Moving: Japanese Women's Lives. New York: New
    York University Press.
Ogawa, Naohiro, and Robert D. Retherford. 1991. Prospects of Increased Contraceptive Pill
    Use in Japan. Studies in Family Planning 22(6):378–383.
Ōishi, Toshihiro. 1995. Sekando kamingu auto: dōseiaisha toshite eizu totomo ni ikiru (The
    Second Coming Out: Living with AIDS as a Homosexual). Tokyo: Asahi Shuppansha.
Stratz, C. H. 1902. Die Körperformen in Kunst und Leben der Japaner. Stuttgart: F. Enke.
Yashima, Masami, ed. 1997. Dansei dōseiaisha no raifu hisutorī (Life Histories of Homosexual
    Men). Tokyo: Gakubunsha.

Periodicals

Femirōgu. Edited by Femirōgu-kai, a group of feminists working in several disciplines of the
    humanities and social sciences based in Kyoto.
Kuia sutadīzu. Edited by Kuia Sutadīzu Henshū Iinkai, Tokyo.
Nichi-bei josei jānaru and its English supplement US–Japan Women's Journal. Published by
    Josai University, Japan.
Josei hakusho. Edited by Nihon Fujin Dantai Rengōkai; contains statistical data on women in all
    realms of life.
Takarajima bessatsu. Published by Takarajima-sha, Tokyo. Among the issues of particular
    interest here are Stories of Women Who Love Women (64), The Pervert Comes (146), The
    Massive Advance of Obscenity (174), and Fifty Years of Sex Media (240).

PART **III** Geographies and Boundaries, Spaces and Sentiments

12 On the "Nature" of Japanese Culture, or, Is There a Japanese Sense of Nature?

D. P. Martinez

Conventionally, the "Japanese" sense of nature is depicted as being both unique and homogeneous: it is seen to be holistic and different from the "Western" concept of nature. Examples of this are numerous, but are often similar to a pæan by Brecher found in his recent book on the subject:

> In Japan, nature has always been viewed as essentially good and as a principal fountain-head of liberation, be it spiritual or corporeal. By becoming one with the self and accepting subordination to the oneness of Creation the individual can live in intimacy with the natural world. (Brecher 2000:80)

Such poetic assertions are then followed by a seeming paradox: why, then, do the Japanese have such a poor record of caring for their environment? This echoes, obviously, the famous opening of Benedict's *The Chrysanthemum and the Sword*, one of the key texts in establishing the discourse of Japanese Otherness:

> The Japanese are, to the highest degree, both aggressive and unaggressive, both militar-istic and aesthetic, both insolent and polite, rigid and adaptable, submissive and resentful of being pushed around, loyal and treacherous, brave and timid, conservative and hospitable to new ways. (Benedict 1946:2; see also Robertson's introduction to this volume)

Both assertions, that the Japanese know how to live in harmony with nature and that they have concreted over and polluted that very same nature, erase diachronic and synchronic differences. Historically, we can find a variety of attitudes toward nature in Japan[1] and, important for the modern case as well, these differences were often based on class differences – by this I mean class in its Marxist sense: a particular relationship to the means of production.

In this chapter, I would like to challenge the standard representation of Japan as a holistic society, as one that falls back on the simplest form of othering: depictions of Native Americans, Pygmies, Alaskan natives, Amerindians, and others, also include holistic constructions of nature without also noting that these more "natural beings" are often the most efficient and, by some people's standards, the most callous exploiters of nature's bounties. Yet, it must be noted, this sort of othering corresponds to a widespread assumption amongst many Japanese that *their* nature *is* somehow unique and that part of the experience of being Japanese includes the "unusual" experience of living on islands, with the threat of earthquakes, volcanic eruptions, typhoons, and four very clearly marked seasons, and that this experience has formed a particular Japanese character (cf. Watsuji 1972).[2] But is this really the most accurate way to understand Japanese attitudes toward nature? If we look at the Japanese relationship with the natural not only as a social construct, but also as a construct that has varied over time and region, and differed according to class, we might solve the puzzling dichotomy that represents the Japanese as being very sensitive to nature, but somehow also totally insensitive to the environment (cf. Asquith and Kalland 1997).

One of the starting points for discussions of the difference in attitudes toward nature in Japan and "the West" is to deconstruct the term *shizen*, an imported Chinese term made up of characters that are often translated as: oneself (*shi, ji*) and "to decree," "if so, in that case," "due, proper, reasonable, respectable, justifiable" (*zen, nen*). The Chinese word from which it originates, *ziran*, initially designated a state of being that was "opposed to the will and the designs of the self (*wo*) and therefore associated with non-action (*wu wei*)" (Berque 1997:137). This state represented an opposition to that which was culture, and eventually the term came to be extended to that which was "distinct from humanity and of . . . human nature" (Berque 1997:137). The term was extended to include what might be called the environment, and it arrived in Japan with Buddhism in the sixth to eighth centuries. *Shizen*'s long entry in the *Kodansha Encyclopaedia of the Japanese Language* gives meanings that include the "natural" world, the universe, all things of heaven and earth, the material world, that which is "fresh" and without artifice, and, in opposition to the experience of freedom and duty that is culture, it connotes a world of casual necessity.

Few writers note, as does Berque (1997), that in its "foreign roots" and various usages, *shizen* rather resembles the English term "nature"; although Berque is correct to argue that the large overlap does not mean that all meanings of both words are mutually translatable. Both English and Japanese have other terms that are applied to aspects of "nature" – environment, ecosystem, ecology, and climate being a few such terms in English. In general, however, the fact that the Japanese word includes the character for "self" is then contrasted with a Euro-American post-Darwinian and post-Freudian notion of nature as something which is the object of human activity and must be "conquered": a concept whose roots are seen to lie in Cartesian notions of the mind/body dualism and Platonic notions of nature as something outside that needs to be understood. Again, few of these definitions look at the etymology of the term nature itself – a linguistic analysis of which produces a similar confusion to the Japanese term *shizen*, a point which Asquith and Kalland (1997:8) have neatly made. "Nature" is not just the ecological world outside us, as used in English (and a discussion of the relevant terms in other Indo-European languages would take too long to go into here), but is also "what we are": the nature of being human, a quality, like *shizen*, of the self. More importantly, however, analyses of terms and their meanings are not, for an anthropologist, to be understood without reference to human actions: to deconstruct *shizen*, to argue that this imported word tells us something about how the Japanese have, over centuries, understood and lived with nature, is a fallacy of the highest order.

The first point to make is that despite claims, here and there in the world, for people's ability to live "closer" to nature or to be alienated from it, the fact remains that whatever the natural world is, it is always experienced by human beings as part of the social. There is no "raw" nature, to paraphrase Lévi-Strauss; humans are always "cooking" it. Moments of unmediated experience in the natural world are highly prized and there is plenty of work on Japan which insists that the Japanese are able to do this because of some Buddhist- or Shinto-induced sensitivity:[3] but first the person having the experience must do it in a place they define as "nature" and one person's nature might well be someone else's culture. Moreover, Zen Buddhist ideas, as they relate to esthetics and the practice of certain arts, are often posited as a blanket ideology for all of Japanese Buddhism by outsiders; they have also been used to inform post-Meiji ideas about Japanese arts by the Japanese themselves (Pincus 1996). Yet, in the Japanese case as elsewhere in the Buddhist world, the doctrine of Buddhism argues that the world of appearances is illusory: the only "pure" experience is one in which the self and the world are forgotten. Such Buddhist ideology does not mean the self should get lost in the natural, but that it should transcend it, as it is non-existent and impermanent anyway.[4] There is, then, a difference between a Platonic notion that the "truth is out there" somewhere, while we live in the shadows searching for it and a Buddhist notion that it is all illusion and that human transcendence is to become part of nothingness rather than to continue suffering the illusion of being. Yet in both conceptions of the world we can only know what we experience and, by experiencing it, we transform it into socialized understanding.

What, then, of Shinto, the native religion of Japan, that is so often noted as being at the root of a Japanese ability to live with nature, rather than trying to conquer it? As an ancient animistic tradition, Shinto was created as an organized religion in opposition to Buddhism's importation to Japan in the sixth to eighth centuries C.E. Some of its concepts might well be pre-historical, but are now filtered through an interaction with Taoism, Confucianism, and Buddhism that is centuries old. It must also be understood that, over the centuries, Shinto religious practices have always been at the mercy of politics; no more so than today when they have been relegated to the arena of cultural nationalism (cf. Yoshino 1992). The idea of folk Shinto practices (cf. Tsurumi n.d.(a)), which are closer to a Japanese spirit are often reconstructed from the practices of fishing and farming communities,[5] and generally tied to the nostalgia for the *furusato* (hometown) that is seen to be located somewhere in the countryside (Robertson 1991; Vlastos 1998).

What has been best studied of this strand of religious thinking in Japan is in relation to the term *kami*, a concept that encompasses both anthropomorphic beings, and the power/spirit that can imbue rocks, mountains, trees, places, people momentarily, actions, etc. (cf. Herbert 1967). To translate *kami* as god, in a Judaeo-Christian sense, does not work for these other manifestations of the concept. Yet, whatever a *kami* is, as Yamaguchi (1991) has pointed out, it is always best expressed in something made (*tsukuru*): that is, that while some *kami* seem to represent the very forces of nature itself, the representation of, the offerings to, and the very beingness of these forces are to be found in made/manufactured objects. Thus we know that a rock is *kami* because it has been wrapped in folded white paper hung on twisted straw rope (Hendry 1993). We find the more anthropomorphic *kami* such as Amaterasu represented by jewels or mirrors or a sword (the *shintai*), secreted behind the doors at the back of altars, wrapped by the architectural design of Shinto shrines themselves. Sometimes there is no *shintai* hidden away, and the very place – the shrine and its paths and garden – act as the very embodiment of the *kami*'s presence, bringing us close to the concept of the simulacrum. And even offerings to *kami*, argues Yamaguchi, should be paradoxically fresh, of nature, and yet made into mimetic objects that will "associate something in immediate view with the primordial things of the distant past" (Yamaguchi 1991:64).

In short, while traditionally the Japanese have not used a vocabulary of conquering nature, as it is assumed "the West" does, it has always had a vocabulary that reveals an attitude to nature as something which must be worked on to be acceptable, something that is acted on, trimmed, shaped, appeased even, but never truly experienced in its raw form. That is, the highest form of Japanese nature is estheticized and best expressed in various forms of art. It is no surprise, then, that when Japanese writers write about nature, their books are invariably tied to art or literature.[6] Yet even that generalization can only stand so far – for while it can be argued that farmers shaped the rice paddies and fields, that charcoal burners and woodcutters shaped the "wild" forests of Japan, and that the *yamabushi* (mountain priests) and Shinto and Buddhist priests dealt with what could not be totally controlled – developing rites of appeasement and containment – all humans do suffer from powerful natural events in the raw: violent storms and earthquakes, for example. No society that I know of, not even those in the Euro-American world, has come up with a way to control these events: to argue that the Japanese have some superior handle on coexisting with such imminent disasters is to ignore the lives of Italians who live near Mount Etna, Alpine dwellers who live with the threat of avalanches, North American midwesterners who live with the threat of tornadoes, coastal dwellers living with the threat of hurricanes, and the many regions of the world where earthquakes are common events. Is there something holistic and Buddhist about these people's ability to pick up the pieces and rebuild their homes?

It has been suggested by Asquith and Kalland (1997) that the Japanese perceive nature on a continuum from bound to unbound: from that which they can shape to that which cannot be controlled. I would like to build on this idea to argue that the Japanese experience of nature is never a single experience: that the experience of nature for urban dwellers in Japan has more in common with the experiences of urban dwellers throughout the industrialized, developed world than it does with, in the example given below, the experience of fishermen. Moreover, there are elements of political and economic expediency, national mythmaking and class differences that must be taken into account when talking about nature in Japan. Thus, despite the cultural differences in how a bound nature might be shaped, or interacted with (*bonsai* versus the ubiquitous English lawn), people in towns experience a nature that is created by the form of the city itself: by its parks, gardens, access to places to grow one's own flowers or vegetables, and so on. In this I am taking some of Berque's (1995) ideas in a different direction, for while he has written about how the city can shape such experiences, he still lays emphasis on some pan-Japanese relationship with nature that makes these experiences somehow different from those of Euro-Americans. While I would not disagree with the idea that nature in an urban environment might be valued somewhat differently from society to society, I also think that urban nature anywhere is bound nature, and its presence in the urban indicates a certain attitude that assumes nature can be managed and that modern decisions about its management are made often by politicians.[7] Thus a mélange of rural practices, esthetic ideals and a reconstruction of things Japanese by politicians is used, vis-à-vis Japan's cultural nationalism, to articulate Japanese difference from "the West" (Gluck 1985). However, the homogenous national discourse deconstructs if we look at particular examples; in order to make this point clearly I will turn now to a very specific empirical example.

On Fishing, Technology, and Ritual

One of the disconcerting aspects of working as a maritime anthropologist in the era of cultural relativism and deconstruction is that the material on fisherfolk around the world so often throws up important similarities. From types of nets used and the way in which knowledge and skills are transmitted to the way in which modern methods are incorporated into traditional fishing techniques and the position of women in fishing villages: the similarities are often more numerous than the cultural differences in fishing societies. The most frequently encountered similarity is embodied in the simple statement that fishermen are more superstitious than other people. If by superstitious it is meant that they engage in more ritual activity and worry more about luck then others, then this statement is very true. However, "superstitious" rarely means that fishermen are above using modern technology.

During fieldwork and later visits (1984–86, 1987, 1991) to Kuzaki-chō, a ward of Toba City in Mie Prefecture, Japan, I was witness to the changes in local discourses related to nature – in this case, the weather and the sea itself. The peninsula of which Kuzaki was part, Shima hantō, was part of one of the first national parks established in postwar Japan; thus, while shielded from some of the effects of industrialization, the men and women of Kuzaki were keen to talk to me about what had changed in the 20th century and to discuss the benefits and limitations of modern life. I was also frequently told that, despite a very rich and active ritual life in the village, many other ritual practices had died out – particularly those related to fishing – because fishing was becoming an increasingly unimportant economic activity. In order to understand this, it is useful to describe how the village's remaining 25 fishing families dealt with the weather.

All Kuzaki fishermen listened to television and radio weather reports as many times a day as possible, sometimes switching between television channels to see if another weatherman had a different forecast. Yet these same men also spent time watching the sky and sea – science was not considered totally reliable in predicting what might happen in nature. Many afternoons were spent at Kuzaki's fishing cooperative waiting for the head of the cooperative to approve the departure of the village flotilla for an evening's prawn fishing. If the sky was clear and the sea calm, but the cooperative head hesitated because of weather reports that predicted a rapid change, then those afternoons were spent in increasingly acrimonious discussions. Rebellion would be in the air: clouds would be studied and analyzed, the phase of the moon taken into account, the type of waves observed; the tide would be considered; ancient grandparents would be consulted to see if on other days in other years such weather had ever turned; women who were known to have some sort of sense about the weather would be hailed as they made their way across the docks; and the cooperative head would be urged to ring, yet again, the coastguard weather service. It was not that the fishermen did not believe that the weather at sea could change rapidly – they were acutely aware of the fact that men died at sea even in what seemed the calmest of conditions – but the question would be whether the timescale of the weather report was seen as accurate: would the change in weather happen later than predicted, giving enough time to come back with fishing done? Would the change be so drastic? Would the storm even reach the coasts? After all, would argue the men who had sailed on Japan's huge global fishing fleets, their offshore fishing did not take them very far out to sea. These were seen to be important points and, before Kuzaki fishing was so tightly organized by the cooperative in the 1920s and again in the 1950s, choosing what to do would have been left to individual fishermen. Ironically, the opposite situation was more bearable: if stormy weather was supposed to improve and the cooperative allowed fishermen to head out to sea, individual men could decide not to set out – that was permissible and even prudent. But nothing was worse than to lose a day's income because the weather forecasts were wrong by several hours, or even a day or two: that was deeply resented. In such a situation a man could feel lucky and argue that his experience told him it would be all right to fish, but this counted for nothing at the cooperative.

It was this increasing dependence on science that led some men to say to me, rather bitterly, that skill no longer counted for anything in fishing. In the past, they would say, it was a man's knowledge of the shore, his previous experience of the weather and the seasons, and his luck that made all the difference. In the 1980s it was weather reports, sonar, and modern equipment that made all the difference. "Any idiot can fish these days" one friend told me frequently – a statement that shocked other maritime experts when they encountered it in my Ph.D. thesis. "Any idiot can fish, he just needs the money for the latest equipment," he would continue. Yet, in spite of such cynical statements, the same man spent a great deal of time worrying about his luck and looking for ways to improve it. Thus there seemed to be an interesting view on the limitations of science: it made it possible for "any idiot" to be able to take up fishing, but science could not make the fish run or keep you safe at sea – that took luck. There was no clearer example of that for the fishermen of Kuzaki than the failure of the seeding of *kuruma ebi* (prawns) after a few years' initial success.

The prawns, spawned in fishing farms, had been seeded into the waters around Shima peninsula to add to a natural increase in the prawn population that occurred in 1975, and for a few years there had been good money to be made from *kuruma ebi* fishing; but the hoped-for natural reproduction and increase of the prawns in the sea did not seem to be happening. By 1987 the Kuzaki cooperative had decided it was not worth the expense of buying in more cultivated prawns – increased cuttlefish catches seemed to make up the financial difference, so why pay out to seed prawns that would eventually disappear again?

The same thing had happened, but more quickly I was told, with *awabi* (abalone): the artificially grown abalone never seemed to survive in the ocean nor did it thrive and grow to a large size in tanks. The problem was different in each case according to the fishermen. Prawns could not survive in water polluted by the increased levels of sewage from tourist hotels and this was not helped by the overuse of bait by amateur line fishermen: the bait fell to the sea floor and helped create harmful algae infestations. Abalone, on the other hand, needs rough rocks to cling to, safe dark places to hide in, and a spacious habitat in order to grow to a large size: no tank could provide that. While these local fishermen were very concerned about conserving their environment and acquiesced, despite grumbling, in the cooperative's rules to prevent overfishing, they saw themselves in a no-win situation. Battling the larger industrial forces that had polluted the sea almost beyond, if not beyond, repair was something they did through their local and national politicians – and even once, in 1984, by sending older fishermen to visit Prime Minister Nakasone with a large, live lobster and a plea about environmental policy – but to little avail. In such cases neither science nor nature was seen to be able to cope with the worst effects of modernization, and fishing was definitely seen to be a dying way of life.

Yet, hand in hand with this pessimism and very clear understanding of what was happening to the environment, the fishermen and diving women also had another level of discourse about their work: skill and experience might count for less in the 1980s, but were still valued despite angry statements to the contrary. And necessary to have along with these individual qualities was the need for good fortune or luck. That is to say that no fisherman or diving woman ignored the many large and small rituals that accompanied their work – not even the men who relied the most on technology. This point was brought home to me when a friend finally bought the fishing boat of his dreams: this boat was larger, had a more powerful motor, sonar, a built-in toilet, an onboard refrigerator and cost ¥5 million (about $50,000). When I asked him why he had spent so much money after having told me many times that fishing wasn't worth it, he replied that it was for the tourists, who were where the money was. Just as prawns had appeared to naturally increase in 1975 and had led to fishermen making lots of money, in 1985 the increase in domestic tourists who came to Kuzaki not just for the food and scenery (cf. Martinez 1989) but to try their hand at fishing were seen to be a moneymaking opportunity. Yet even a boat purchased for such a prosaic venture needed to be properly launched. And a few days after it arrived in Kuzaki the boat was purified in a ritual that many claimed was very ancient indeed.

First, the new boat had to be decorated with *hata* (flags) which had the characters for *dairyō* (large catch) printed on them. Ideally each household which was related to the owners of the new boat had to provide one of these flags. Then the boat was launched from the harbor, and on board there had to be as many children as possible, for children bring good luck (so do foreigners, it was said). If possible, I was told, a longhaired woman should also come along to represent the *fukunokami* (the *kami* of good fortune). Also included were friends from the fisherman's *dōkyūsei* (age grade). Heading left from the beach toward the open sea, just outside the harbor, the boat should circle round three times to the left. That is, around to the port, the side for pulling in fish. The first turn was for *dairyō* (large catches), the second for safety, and the third turn was for the *fukunokami*. At the end, offerings of *azukigohan* (rice with adzuke beans), *kenchin*[8] salad which was eaten on various other ritual occasions such as weddings, and sake were made to the deity of the sea from the bow. These offerings were then made again off the port side, and then off the stern. No offerings were made off starboard: the fishermen said that "nothing important happens on that side."

When the boat returned to the harbor, a crowd gathered and the boat owner threw gifts of *sechi mochi*,[9] coins, fruit, and sweets to the waiting villagers. These gifts represent the wealth of a good catch, which must be shared with others. This was explained as "a fisherman has to give in order that the deities reward him with good luck. He must share his luck with others." This is a theme that recurred during the New Year ceremonies in Kuzaki when household boats were cleaned and decorated and their owners had to throw large catches of sweets and fruit to the women and children waiting on the dock. After the rituals at sea, the household held a banquet on the harbor by the new boat.

The ideal of sharing good fortune was a strong one: any fisherman who had had a good catch was expected to thrown an impromptu party on the dock the next day during net cleaning; any women and children present would be given sweets and the men sake. Any fish that a lucky household kept also had to be shared: some was left as an offering on household and village shrines, some given away to poor kin who might not often have fresh fish to eat. Such rituals were not limited to a new boat's launching or to New Year celebrations either. Each year, at the start of the abalone diving season, the sea itself was ritually blessed, while women divers prepared themselves for the season by drinking *amacha*, a diuretic tea that purified them internally. All equipment, for fishing or diving, was constantly cleaned, checked, and decorated with amulets or good luck symbols; and every female diver made the monthly climb up Kuzaki's sacred mountain, Sengen, to leave offerings for the sea god and to pray for good health and safety at sea for themselves and their family. No village Buddhist festival occurred without offerings being left to the Shinto sea deities, and no Shinto festival happened without offerings being made at the Buddhist temple. While older villagers lamented the loss of certain practices – the yearly pilgrimage to a nearby shrine whose deity was famous for protecting boats; the attendance of festivals outside Kuzaki in other villages – the fact remained that the people of Kuzaki, compared with their urban counterparts, spent more time in ritual activity. Festivals to celebrate the presence of the deity, which in more urban areas had been reduced to cultural expressions of Japaneseness or to being seen as expressions of community solidarity (Bestor 1988; Robertson 1987), were taken rather more seriously in Kuzaki.

Yet it would be wrong, even for a small community like that of Kuzaki, to write of a uniform experience of belief. One thing that became clear in my two years in the village was that men who had left fishing and moved into other sorts of occupations had a different attitude toward rituals. One such man, when I first arrived in the village, took me to see Kuzaki's Shinto shrine, where the sun goddess Amaterasu is enshrined, and offered to open the inner sanctum for me to look at – something I do not think a fisherman would ever have dared do. And even amongst the most dedicated believers it was not unknown for ritual practices to be done lightheartedly:

mankind might well be at the mercy of the *kami*, but it did not mean that the rituals done for them had to be devoid of gossip, jokes, and teasing the foreigner. Other personal practices and beliefs, as in urban areas, appeared to depend on the individual: illness, worrying about passing exams, being concerned about fertility, taking care of the dead – adherence to these rituals in Kuzaki seemed to be premised on the same principles as they might be elsewhere in Japan (cf. Reader and Tanabe 1998): need, personal preference, and concern for the opinions of others. When it came to rituals for diving and fishing, however, no one stinted: "It's my livelihood," said one woman to me; "I don't take chances with that."

It would be easy to attribute these practices to a less modern way of life, but such a position just would not hold true for the fishermen I knew: they were intimate with modern technology and lived very modern lives, owning the same sorts of houses and consumer goods as most Japanese (see also Kelly 1992). Divisions in belief, as nebulous as that is to measure, did appear to be occurring depending on occupation; that is, non-fishermen were not as observant in Kuzaki as were fishermen. And the wives of such men were often more outspoken about religion as well. "We do it because the grandparents expect us to," explained one young wife to me as she hurriedly decorated the *butsudan* at the very last minute for O-bon. Women who dived and whose husbands fished said very different things about the need to worship: the *kami* might be unpredictable – you could pray and they might or might not answer – but if you did not pray, then the consequences could be quite bad. When I took to trying to dive in the summer of 1984, I was urged to pray to the *kami*: they would not mind that I was a foreigner, I was told. It was a fisherman who tried to explain the "why" of this to me:

> Diving is dangerous you know. You can get caught in the rocks swimming along a narrowing crevice; you can stick your hand into a hole to feel for *awabi* and be stung by a puffer fish, or bitten by an eel. No matter how skilled [*jōzu*] you are or how much experience you have, it is dangerous and you can't be afraid [*kowai*] or you'll never be any good. No diver who is fearful can ever be any good.

I think he was also talking about fishing. The point of his statement is valid for both: you cannot ever really control or make accurate predictions about nature in any of its manifestations: the weather, puffer fish, eels, the reproduction of prawns, the spread of dangerous red algae, or the growth cycle of abalone. While skill, experience, and consulting others, even the use of modern equipment, can help, in the end no one can really control all the factors. For that reason, as one man laughingly told me one day: "We pray. If the *kami* give to us, good; if they don't, well we won't make offerings. But we pray."

Nor were humans considered to be infallible, so rituals for safety at sea were still very important. This attitude was very different from that of urban dwellers who relied mainly on weather reports for their information (normally to decide what to wear), and whose ritual life was less active and more aimed at praying for success at work and/or school. The contrast between these two attitudes could be seen when the urbanites came to holiday at the seaside: fishermen and divers were very critical of what they saw as an urban inability to take care of the environment, and this included cleaning up beaches after they had spent the day sunbathing, as well as larger concerns about industry and polluting the sea itself. Urban visitors to the seaside valued the fresh seafood and some would come to fish or swim, but they generally ventured outside as little as possible.

All these types of activity in nature lead us to a very different analysis than is usually offered in relation to Japanese nature in the urban environment or in the arts: in these cases nature is seen to be incorporated or depicted in such a way that a Japanese sensitivity to and identification with the natural is assumed. Fishermen could also make such claims: urging me to go see the first cherry blossom in the village; showing their bonsai collections to me; contrasting the shape of a Japanese woman in a kimono to the "unnatural" look of a woman in Western dress. This discourse of a unique Japanese experience of nature coexisted with their disdain for urban Japanese who were seen to be so careless about nature. The existence of these two different yet analogous tropes could well reduce a researcher to writing, yet again, about the dichotomy in Japanese attitudes toward nature, but if we introduce the ideas of class difference as a measure, in some part, of different relationships with the environment – we might well come up with a solution to this problematic opposition.

ON THE CAPITALIST EXPERIENCE OF NATURE

In a polemic against *nihonjinron* depictions of Japan as unique, the economist and journalist Ben-Ami (1997) has argued that Japan's drive to modernize made it no different from other capitalist countries in the western hemisphere. While Dore (2000) and others might well argue that we could find different structures of profit-making and -sharing even in Western countries, much of Ben-Ami's argument is valid. The spirit of capitalism, as Weber described it, is the essential idea that moneymaking is important and beneficial: however Japanese companies choose to spend it, they still need to make a profit. And throughout the industrialized world, profit-making and caring for the environment have long been at odds. The famous cleaning up of the US/Canadian Great Lakes, for example, considered to be so polluted that they were nearly dead in the late 1960s and early 1970s, was accomplished more by moving industry to countries where pollution laws had not become so strict and where workers would work for less money anyway than by the rapid enactment of strict anti-pollution laws. The air of Chicago's south side is much cleaner in the 21st century than it was in the 20th, but unemployment and poverty are also markedly higher: the great steel mills of the area are almost all closed down. Even today, the United States' national imagery of wilderness, of "purple mountains' majesty" and "fruited plains," is at odds with its reluctance to sign the Kyoto Agreement on Global Climate Change (Kageyama 2000). It should be no paradox, then, that having accepted the challenge to industrialize during the Meiji Restoration, and having striven to succeed in a global business world, Japanese industrialists have shown a similar callousness toward the environment.

For some writers, such as Brecher quoted at the outset, this similarity is puzzling: given that the Japanese have such a close relationship to nature, how could they allow their companies to so harm it? Such an approach does not take into account Japan's national vision since the Meiji Restoration in 1868: the drive to modernize was a much more powerful discourse than that of any dissenting voices. The promise of a better life for a large portion of the peasantry and town dwellers could also not be ignored as being attractive, particularly in the aftermath of World War II. It became a source of national pride and national priority that all Japanese take part in building up, yet again, a healthy industrial Japan. Such a vision included competing with more expensive Euro-American products and production techniques: the capitalist leaders of Japan, as in some parts of Southeast Asia and the Pacific today, were able to achieve this by paying employees less and by ignoring any impact their industries might be having on the environment.[10] The difference, as Tsurumi (n.d.(b), part III) has noted in an analysis of the famous Minamata mercury poisoning cases, is not in the priorities of industry, but in people's power to make industry accountable.[11] In the US, litigation against polluting companies can be enough to bring about change; in Japan, a society where going to court is a last resort, not a first one (cf. Feldman 2000), it can take 30 years even to get to court.

Yet, someone like Brecher might ask, why did not industrial processes get remade when they arrived in Japan, as so much else has been over the centuries? The Japanese, after all, are not only sensitive to the beauties of nature, but use this sensitivity as part of their esthetics and describe it as key to the experience of what it is to be Japanese. Moreover, the Japanese recycle and can conserve more fiercely than most modern societies; how is it that they will allow their companies to deforest Indonesia? And, while noting that Greenpeace and Friends of the Earth have branches in Japan, let us not mention whaling.

First of all, as previously suggested, the class differences between experiences of and attitudes towards nature are varied in Japan. As long ago as the 11th century the courtier Sei Shōnagon noted how much tougher life was for diving women, who worked at the mercy of nature (Morris 1967). She was thankful for the tranquil and beautiful life she led at court, where divers and the sea were the subjects of wistful poems, and cherry blossom viewing and firefly chasing were much more rewarding experiences of nature. While these latter pursuits have now become part of the construction of a modern Japanese identity, with cherry blossom viewing a national event, the divide between urban dwellers and others, as shown in the example of fishermen above, remains. The divide is no longer between a small aristocratic elite and a large peasantry, but between an urban middle and working class and a shrinking (less than 10 percent) rural-based population. And it is not a divide, as I have noted, between technocrats and artisans, as much as a divide between people whose experience of nature is limited to that of a sprawling urban environment interspersed with occasional visits to the shrinking "real" Japan and the people who occupy that endangered space.

For urban dwellers, beautiful nature is often the cultivated pine tree on a rocky shore (when they can find a bit of rocky shore) and, despite claims to the importance of oneness with nature, seeing the tree is enough – only *innaka* (country) folk might still worship the tree. Japan is, as many surveys prove year after year, not a religious country, or at least, not religious in any Judaeo-Christian or even "primitive" way (cf. Reader 1990). That is to say that Shinto has been elevated to the sphere of cultural practice and not religious worship. Parts of green Japan are maintained because they are too mountainous to farm or establish factories on: they can be seen as part of "wild" nature, and it is important that they be available for domestic tourism (Moon 1997). The important difference here is between the esthetic experience of nature in what Asquith and Kalland would call its "bound" form and the actual experience of dealing with nature in its more "unbound" form – fishermen appreciate the pine trees and forests as well, but wonder if wild boars might not come charging out at them from the latter. And while the sea is beautiful to contemplate, and in the 1980s most Japanese preferred to do that, rarely swimming in it, it is fishermen and diving women who know it for the very dangerous place it is. Thus, for the urban dweller, as long as they are recycling and there exist some nature parks and "wilderness" to gaze upon (cf. Urry 1990), it is easy to imagine that all is right with Japanese nature – a situation that politicians and manufacturers encourage. Such examples could be taken from other industrialized nations; in fact, the historian Simon Schama has recently made a similar point in his BBC series about industrializing 19th-century Britain. In contrast, for many fishermen, a dwindling population both in Japan and around the world, nothing could be more wrong with the environment and the biggest problem, from their point of view, is urban complacency. This last is, of course, a generalization, for some urban dwellers do get involved in environmentalist movements (cf. Knight 1997), and housewives are demanding pesticide-free milk and food for their children in Japan as elsewhere. But, to use a Marxist term, the alienation of the urban worker from their environment is generally quite complete and "nature" has become only a place to visit. This is, sad to say, a typical experience of urban life in all industrialized capitalist countries, and Japan is no exception.

In conclusion, then, I am arguing that, while the Japanese experience of nature can, in some part, be conceived of as having a different history and does perhaps make use of different tropes for nature's place in humankind's existence, we should not mistake a once elite discourse about the esthetics of experiencing nature for the pragmatics of living within nature. All human societies have to cope with the natural environment: describing it, attempting to shape it, or submitting to it when necessary. The ideology of being in nature, as some would have it for the Japanese, does not preclude the possibility of trying to bind it up: in fact the most beautiful examples of Japan's "working with nature" are often the most culturally bound examples of nature as culture. It could be argued that the elite practice of bringing the natural under the control of esthetic ideals is precisely what makes it possible, in some part, for many Japanese to ignore the destruction of theirs and others' environments: as long as one beautiful pine tree and interesting rock formation are wrapped as if sacred, who worries if the coast around them is covered in concrete? It is not a dichotomy of both living in harmony with nature and yet somehow not caring about its destruction; what we see in some modern Japanese attitudes toward nature is the resolution of this dichotomy: nature as an esthetic can always be maintained, no matter what the state of the water or the air might be. Yet, for fishermen, farmers and some urban dwellers in Japan, this is not good enough and it is they who might, ultimately, make a difference.

NOTES

1   A recent attempt to look at such differences, in the light of gender ideology in Japan, is Rosenberger's chapter in Asquith and Kalland (1997).

2   Watsuji's seminal work, *Fūdo*, translated as *On Climatology*, was written as a philosophical treatise, and in response to Watsuji's time in Europe studying philosophy with Heidegger. In the main Watsuji's book is an attempt to construct a contrasting model of being – this is never stressed enough – in response to the German philosopher's ideas. While Watsuji was critical of Heidegger's approach, he followed the German's anti-Cartesian line, a fact Berque (1998) examines in an insightful article. It is Befu (1997), however, who looks at Watsuji's nationalistic agenda.

3   Many writers on nature in Japan refer to a paper by Schmithausen (1991a), in which he argues that the Japanese inserted into imported Buddhism the doctrine of the sentience of plants and trees. These references ignore Schmithausen's next article, "The Problem of the Sentience of Plants in Earliest Buddhism" (1991b), in which he discusses how the concept can be found in original Buddhist texts; so the question becomes more "Why did other Buddhist societies drop it?", rather than "Why did the Japanese insert it?"

4   This is a simplistic summing up of various strands of Buddhist doctrine, but it will suffice to stand against the view held by some Westerners that Buddhism is all about being one with nature. For an important analysis of how Western views of Japanese Buddhism were shaped by Suzuki's work with, yet again, Heidegger see Sharf (1995).

5   This practice amongst Japanese social scientists of looking for "real" Japanese beliefs and practices in the margins of a modern/modernizing society was pioneered by the work of Yanagita Kunio (1981 [1950]) as well as of Miyata (1983), and can still be seen in such works as *Animizu no sekai* (Murataki 1997). Kawada (1993) and Ivy (1995) have both described and critiqued this sort of nationalistic mythmaking, which is, of course, a process all nation-states go through.

6   There are endless examples of this. A few are Anesaki (1933), Hirakawa and Tsuruta (1994), and Kawazoe (1957).

7   An edited book which manages to combine Orientalist views of Japan's relationship with nature with hard facts on the changes to its environment over the last century is Golany et al.'s *Japanese Urban Environment* (1998).

8   According to the villagers, the three ingredients of this salad – rice, fish, and vegetables – represent the three sources of Japan's wealth: the fields, the sea, and the mountains.

9   The same sort of huge *mochi* (rice cake) is used in Kuzaki weddings, as well as on other ritual occasions. *Sechi* seems to be a dialect word to refer to this type of pink and white *mochi*.

10   The practice of reshaping the environment was not necessarily new in Japan either. Walker (2001) looks at the damage to Ainu ecology that followed Japan's conquest of the north between 1590 and 1800, thus locating a disdain for the environment of others in a pre-industrial Japan. For a more recent example, the profits to be made from creating golf courses in Japan, despite the environmental destruction this causes, is another case of how a Japanese reshaping of the landscape can create problems; ironically in this case because the fertilizers and pesticides needed to create a perfect green lawn poison the water sources.

11   The villagers of Minamata, mostly fishermen, became ill from what was finally diagnosed as mercury poisoning. The nearby chemical plant was polluting the sea and the mercury was accumulating in the fish that they caught and ate. The victims of this "disease," with symptoms somewhat like those of BSE, took almost 20 years to get compensation. The case is now well documented in the literature on Japan (see George 2001; Ishimura 1990; Smith and Smith 1975).

REFERENCES

Anesaki, Masaharu. 1933. Art, Life and Nature in Japan. Boston: Marshall Jones.

Asquith, Pamela J., and Arne Kalland. 1997. Japanese Perceptions of Nature: Ideals and Illusions. *In* Japanese Images of Nature: Cultural Perspectives. Pamela J. Asquith and Arne Kalland, eds. pp. 1–35. London: Curzon.

Befu, Harumi. 1997. Watsuji Tetsurō's Ecological Approach: Its Philosophical Foundation. *In* Japanese Images of Nature: Cultural Perspectives. Pamela J. Asquith and Arne Kalland, eds. pp. 106–120. London: Curzon.

Ben-Ami, Daniel. 1997. Is Japan Different? *In* Cultural Difference, Media Memories. Phil Hammond, ed. pp. 3–24. London: Cassell.

Benedict, Ruth. 1946. The Chrysanthemum and the Sword: Patterns of Japanese Culture. New York: New American Library.

Berque, Augustin. 1995. The Rituals of Urbanity: Temporal Forms and Spatial Forms in Japanese and French Cities. *In* Ceremony and Ritual in Japan. Jan van Bremen and D. P. Martinez, eds. pp. 246–258. London: Routledge.

——1997. Japan: Nature, Artifice and Japanese Culture. Ros Schwartz, trans. Yelvertoft Manor, Northamptonshire: Pilkington Press.

——1998. The Question of Space: From Heidegger to Watsuji. *In* Interpreting Japanese Society, 2nd edn. Joy Hendry, ed. pp. 57–67. London: Routledge.

Bestor, T. 1988. Neighborhood Tokyo. Stanford, CA: Stanford University Press.

Brecher, W. Puck. 2000. An Investigation of Japan's Relationship to Nature and Environment. Lewiston, NY: Edwin Mellen Press.

Dore, Ronald P. 2000. Stock Market Capitalism: Welfare Capitalism, Japan and Germany versus the Anglo-Saxons. Oxford: Oxford University Press.

Feldman, Eric A. 2000. The Ritual of Rites in Japan. Cambridge: Cambridge University Press.

George, Timothy S. 2001. Minamata: Pollution and the Struggle for Democracy in Postwar Japan. Cambridge, MA: Harvard University Press.

Gluck, Carol. 1985. Japan's Modern Myths. Princeton: Princeton University Press.

Golany, Gideon S., Hanaki Keisuke, and Koide Osamu, eds. 1998. Japanese Urban Environment. Oxford: Elsevier Science.

Hendry, Joy. 1993. Wrapping Culture: Politeness, Presentation and Power in Japan and Other Societies. Oxford: Clarendon Press.

Herbert, Jean. 1967. Shinto, the Fountainhead of Japan. London: George Allen & Unwin.

Hirakawa, Sukehiro, and Tsuruta, Kin'ya hen. 1994. Animizumu o yomu: nihon bungaku shizen, seimei, jiko (Reading Animism: Nature, Life, and Self in Japanese Literature). Tokyo: Shinyosha.

Ishimura, Michiko. 1990. Paradise in the Sea of Sorrows. Tokyo: Yamaguchi.

Ivy, Marilyn. 1995. Discourses of the Vanishing. Chicago: University of Chicago Press.

Kageyama, Takashi. 2000. Style Differences at International Negotiations: A Comparison between Japan and the United States. Case Study of the International Negotiations on Global Climate Change. Cambridge, MA: Program on US–Japan Relations, Harvard University.

Kawada, Minoru. 1993. The Origin of Ethnography in Japan: Yanagita Kunio and his Times. London: Kegan Paul International.

Kawazoe, K. 1957. Nihon shizen shugi no bungaku (Japanese Naturalistic Literature). Tokyo: Shimada shoten.

Kelly, William W. 1992. Tractors, Television, and Telephones: Reach Out and Touch Someone in Rural Japan. *In* Remade in Japan. Joseph J. Tobin, ed. pp. 77–88. New Haven, CT: Yale University Press.

Knight, John. 1997. The Soil as Teacher: Natural Farming in a Mountain Village. *In* Japanese Images of Nature: Cultural Perspectives. Pamela J. Asquith and Arne Kalland, eds. pp. 236–256. London: Curzon.

Martinez, D. P. 1989. Tourism and the Ama: The Search for a "Real" Japan. *In* Unwrapping Japanese Society. Eyal Ben-Ari et al., eds. pp. 97–116. Manchester: Manchester University Press.

Miyata, Noboru. 1983. Onna no reiryoku to ie no kami (Womn's Spiritual Power and Household Deities). Kyoto: Jinbonshoin.

Moon, Okpyo. 1997. Marketing Nature in Rural Japan. *In* Japanese Images of Nature: Cultural Perspectives. Pamela J. Asquith and Arne Kalland, eds. pp. 221–235. London: Curzon.

Morris, Ivan, ed. and trans. 1967. The Pillow Book of Sei Shōnagon. Harmondsworth: Penguin.

Murataki, Seiichi. 1997. Animizu no sekai (The World of Animism). Tokyo: Yoshikawa Kobunkan.

Pincus, Leslie. 1996. Authenticating Culture in Imperial Japan. Berkeley: University of California Press.

Reader, Ian. 1990. Religion in Contemporary Japan. Basingstoke: Macmillan.

Reader, Ian, and George Tanabe. 1998. Practically Religious, Worldly Benefits and the Common Religion of Japan. Honolulu: University of Hawaii Press.

Robertson, Jennifer. 1987. A Dialectic of Native and Newcomer: The Kodaira Citizens' Festival in Suburban Tokyo. Anthropological Quarterly 60(3):124–136.

—— 1991. Native and Newcomer: Making and Remaking a Japanese City. Berkeley: University of California Press.

Rosenberger, Nancy. 1997. Interpretations of Nature and the Legitimation of Gender Differences: "Natural" Links in the Japanese Social Field. *In* Japanese Images of Nature: Cultural Perspectives. Pamela J. Asquith and Arne Kalland, eds. pp. 145–165. London: Curzon.

Schmithausen, Lambert. 1991a. Buddhism and Nature. *In* Proceedings of an International Symposium on the Occasion of EXPO 1990. Tokyo: International Institute for Buddhist Studies.

—— 1991b. The Problem of the Sentience of Plants in Earliest Buddhism. Studia Philologica Buddhica Monograph Series VI. Tokyo: International Institute for Buddhist Studies.

Sharf, Robert H. 1995. The Zen of Japanese Nationalism. *In* Curators of the Buddha. Donald S. Lopez, Jr., ed. pp. 107–160. Chicago: University of Chicago Press.

Smith, W. E., and Aileen M. Smith. 1975. Minamata. London: Chatto & Windus.

Tsurumi, Kazuko. n.d.(a). Aspects of Endogenous Development in Modern Japan. Part II: Religious Beliefs: State Shintoism vs. Folk Belief. Tokyo: Sophia University, Institute of International Relations, Research papers.

—— (b). part III Man, nature and technology: a case of Minamata. Tokyo: Sophia University, Institute of International Relations, Research papers.

Urry, John. 1990. The Tourist Gaze: Leisure and Travel in Contemporary Societies. London: Sage.

Vlastos, S., ed. 1998. Mirror of Modernity: Invented Traditions of Modern Japan. Berkeley: University of California Press.

Walker, Brett L. 2001. The Conquest of Ainu Lands: Ecology and Culture in Japanese Expansion, 1590–1800. Berkeley: University of California Press.

Watsuji, Tetsuro. 1972. Fūdo: ningengakuteki kōsatsu (On Climatology: A Philosophical Study). Tokyo: Monbusho.

Yamaguchi, Masao. 1991. The Poetics of Exhibition in Japanese Culture. *In* Exhibiting Cultures. Ivan Karp and Steven D. Lavine, eds. pp. 56–67. Washington, DC, and London: Smithsonian Institution Press.

Yanagita, Kunio, ed. 1981 [1950]. Kaisan no seikatsu no kenkyū. Tokyo: Kokuji kankōkai.

Yoshino, Kosaku. 1992. Cultural Nationalism in Contemporary Japan: A Sociological Enquiry. London: Routledge.

13 The Rural Imaginary: Landscape, Village, Tradition

Scott Schnell

Agrarian images seem out of place in the highly urbanized and cosmopolitan society Japan has become. When the subject of Japan is broached these days, one is far more likely to think of bullet trains and robotics, the fashion industry, *anime*, and popular music idols than rustic villagers in sedge hats bent over a flooded rice paddy. In fact, the rural population in Japan has been steadily decreasing for several decades, and the challenge of how to stem the flow of young people to the cities or to lure new residents to take their places is heavy on the minds of local administrators.

If rural areas are in such decline, why should they warrant more than a cursory glance by students of contemporary Japan? One could argue that the Japanese government's decentralization policies hinge on the revitalization of rural communities; that frustration with traffic congestion and cramped living conditions has led thousands of urban residents back to the countryside in search of a more satisfying lifestyle (the so-called "u-turn phenomenon"); that increasing concerns about air, food, and water quality and their effect on human health have led to a recognition of urban–rural linkages as the key to a more sustainable future (Knight 1994; Moen 1997; Moon 1997). Moreover, as an anthropologist who has conducted fieldwork for several years in Japan's mountainous interior, I can attest that many rural communities are alive and well, and deserve our continuing attention as interesting, dynamic places. In this chapter, however, I will confine my discussion to the significance of rural Japan as an abiding source not only of natural and human resources, but of symbolic ones as well. Whatever the actual case may be, Japan's cultural identity is *perceived* as being heavily rooted in the agrarian traditions of its rural areas. This in itself makes them important.

Many theorists have sought to demonstrate how the institutional structures of the past live on in the present (Nakamaki 1992; Nakane 1970; Umesao 1984, 1989). Indeed, Japan's distinctive historical experience is a major element in *nihonjinron* assertions. The more compelling issue, however, relates to strategic uses of the past for present purposes. The past, in other words, is commonly reconfigured in response to present needs. Thus tradition must be seen not simply as a static holdover from former times, but as an ongoing conceptual project – one that figures prominently in contemporary social and political agendas. Tradition, then, is qualified less by the passage of time than by the gravity of shared perception. Of course, historical precedent adds legitimacy and appeal to tradition, but this can be asserted retrospectively through creative theorizing.

Certainly, the topic of "invented tradition" has been widely addressed, with illuminating results (see, for example, Hobsbawm and Ranger 1983; Ivy 1995; Vlastos 1998). My objection to the concept, however, is that it seems to imply that some traditions are genuine while others are spurious and deceptive. The actual process of tradition-making is far more ambiguous. Quite frequently it *can* be demonstrated that certain institutions or activities have been of long duration. This does not mean, however, that they have always been interpreted the same way or have held the same significance. Furthermore, even if a particular custom has been handed down unaltered from long ago, it may have been practiced or observed by only a tiny minority of the people in question and thus cannot be taken as broadly representative. "Tradition" is rarely the product of either careful preservation or pure invention. Rather, it is a matter of reconciling past with present through the mediation of value-laden symbols, thereby rationalizing a favored agenda.

Take, for example, what is surely considered one of the most traditional of Japanese institutions, the *ie*, or "stem family" household. Once the mainstay of rural society, the patriarchal, multi-generation, ancestor-worshiping *ie* now seems destined to fade from the rural landscape along with the oxen and mulberry trees. Young women are so averse to marrying into traditional farm households that a serious bride shortage now exists in many parts of the countryside. Desperate households have resorted to recruiting "mail-order" brides from less economically advantaged areas in China, Korea, and Southeast Asia. And what of the eldest son, destined to succeed his father as head of the household? At one time considered fortunate by virtue of his rank in the birth order, he is now more likely to be pitied than admired. He remains stuck in his natal village while his siblings run off to fulfill their dreams of higher education, salaried employment, and more stimulating social opportunities in the cities.

The problem is magnified by the many challenges facing Japanese agriculture. The Japanese government has been protecting its farmers for decades with subsidies and import restrictions, but because the scale of their holdings is so limited it is virtually impossible for any particular household to support itself through agriculture alone. For the vast majority of farming households, most income derives from outside employment. As the eldest son matures, he typically finds a job at an office or factory nearby. Farming has thus become a part-time enterprise conducted on weekends or in the evenings after work, perhaps given over entirely to aging grandparents. Many households are dying out through lack of an heir, or yielding to development pressures to sell their land.

To say that the *ie* is fading away, however, is not entirely accurate. In a sense it has survived the transition to an urban-industrial context by serving as an organizational blueprint for other social groups, most notably the modern business corporation (see chapter 9 in this volume). As Rohlen (1974), Kondo (1990), and others have indicated, skillful managers promote the notion of "company as family" among their employees. Once this conceptual leap has been achieved, other ideological elements can be called into play: the company as the primary object of loyalty and locus of identity formation; filial piety expressed as respect and obedience to managers and senior employees; reverence to "the ancestors" in the guise of company founders and former executives; and, perhaps most importantly, a pervasive conviction that the needs of the collective take precedence over those of the individual.

The analogy may be extended beyond the household to the community level. The arrangement of work groups in an office layout, with the desks pushed together and facing inward toward one another, calls to mind the famous village dictum *mukō sangen, ryō donari* ("the three houses opposite, and the ones next door on either side"), indicating the households having the closest ties of mutual support with one's own. And the structural relationship between a major company and its subsidiaries is reminiscent of the *dōzoku*, the hierarchical pattern of genealogically related households (main household and subordinate branches) that is so prominent a feature in some parts of Japan, particularly the northeast.

How should these urbanized evocations of the traditional household be seen? Are they tenacious holdovers from the past, or elements of a clever administrative strategy that serves the interests of managing executives? Steven's description of the relationship between a large rural political network and the local population might just as easily be applied to a modern business corporation, its subsidiaries and employees: "[b]ecause all the organisations in this network...take on the identical form of the traditional household, exploitation is made to look like *benevolence*, contradictory interests appear *harmonious*, and the submission of the exploited takes on the form of *obedience* and *loyalty*" (Steven 1983:119). Note that the aforementioned office layout is conducive not only to easy interaction among fellow employees, but to mutual surveillance as well.

The suggestion of vested interest makes "tradition" far more compelling than the term at first implies. Who has the power to manipulate tradition, and for what purpose? These are the questions Sugimoto (1997:12–13) raises by drawing our attention to certain privileged and influential minorities which he refers to as "core subcultures," examples being "the management subculture in the occupational dimension, the large corporation subculture in the firm-size dimension, the male subculture in the gender dimension, and the Tokyo subculture in the regional dimension." Through their control of the educational system and mass media, these elite subcultures are able to present their own values, ideals, and priorities as representative of the nation as a whole.

In this vein, it is useful to note that the *ie* was originally an institution of the premodern samurai class, which comprised less than 7 percent of the total population. The *ie* was important to the samurai as a way of maintaining their hereditary privileges and passing on their wealth. While a few peasants were able to acquire enough wealth and property to achieve pseudo-samurai status, most members of the peasant class had little wealth or property to maintain, their rights to the land being granted at the discretion of their feudal overlords. For them, maintaining an *ie* of the type described above was simply out of the question, both practically and economically. Obviously, the peasants occupied households of some type, but they did not follow the same structural pattern, gender roles, or rules of succession as did the elite samurai (see

Bachnik 1983, Befu 1968, M. Ema 1943, and Muto 1985 for examples of various exceptions to the "norm").

The four-tiered class system (samurai, peasant, artisan, merchant) was abolished shortly after the Meiji Restoration of 1868. The new leaders, however, being themselves of samurai descent, naturally drew upon their own ideals and values in pursuing their reforms. The Meiji Civil Code, debated for years but finally promulgated in 1898, established the samurai-style *ie* as the basic social unit. Every citizen was required to register as a member of an *ie*, and every *ie* was to be represented by a patriarchal head who held legal authority over the other members. The Civil Code also established male primogeniture (succession by the eldest son) as the preferred pattern of succession. The eldest son's siblings eventually had to leave – his sisters marrying into other households, his younger brothers perhaps seeking employment in the burgeoning towns and cities.

The new Meiji leaders were thereby able to impose their own ideals and conventions on the entire population. In fact, practically all of what the general public outside of Japan now perceives as being quintessentially Japanese – patriarchal authority, male primogeniture, arranged marriages, submissive and subservient women, fanatical loyalty to lord or emperor, the martial arts, Zen-inspired austerity, haiku, ink painting, the tea ceremony, and, of course, the *ie* system itself, were products of the samurai tradition and had little or nothing to do with the majority of the Japanese people until well into the modern era. As Ueno Chizuko and others before her have pointed out, "democratization meant not the 'commoner-ization' of the samurai class but the 'samuraization' of the commoners." Interestingly, however, Ueno also acknowledges a "push–pull" dynamic, with many "commoners" eagerly embracing the changes as a means for achieving upward social mobility: "When social change abolishes a hierarchy, it is always the lower class that wants to escape the imposed class distinction in habits and behaviors. Thus the *ie* system, modeled on the patrilineal family system of the samurai household, was established by Meiji family law" (1987:S79).

There is one notable exception, however, where the favored images have emanated not from the top but from somewhere in the middle – where "commoner-ization" seems to have prevailed, in other words. This relates to the cultural significance attached to growing rice, which is widely considered the staple grain and a "key metaphor" in Japanese culture (Nakane 1970; Ohnuki-Tierney 1993). More than any other occupational activity, it is irrigated rice cultivation that is seen as conveying the distinctive elements of a Japanese social ethos.

In traditional rice-growing communities, the irrigation system was central. Water, which supplied the plants with most of their nutrients, was siphoned off rivers or channeled down from the mountains using an intricate system of ditches and weirs. In the spring, when the fields had been plowed and harrowed and the dikes between them repaired, the irrigation channels were opened and the water let in. The water then trickled from one paddy to the next through notches in the dikes, filling each paddy in a stepwise manner until all had been flooded. Owners of contiguous paddies were thus obliged by the flow of water to coordinate their efforts.

The saturated surface soil was churned and paddled into an even layer of soft mud covered by a few inches of standing water. Then the transplanting work began. Seedlings that had been grown in tightly packed nursery beds were now inserted into the mud at regular intervals. This allowed the roots to expand, anchoring the plants in the soil and absorbing nutrients for their growth and maturation. The integrative nature of the irrigation system, combined with the extra labor required at particularly busy times like transplanting and harvest, made it virtually impossible for any single household to act independently; each maintained reciprocal ties with other households in order to subsist.

Here again, a traditional pattern appears to have survived the transition to an urban-industrial society. This heritage of interdependence is routinely cited in explaining the Japanese propensity for group behavior – so prominent a feature in organizational settings. And as with the *ie* model, the notion of rice-growing villages as cultural exemplar coincides nicely with the needs of administrators, as it encourages individuals to put the interests of the collective ahead of their own. It also appeals to the nation's rice farmers who, despite their dwindling numbers, still maintain a prominent voice in electoral politics.

The privileged status of rice cultivation is further reinforced through myth and ritual. According to the Japanese creation myth, knowledge of growing rice originated with the sun goddess Amaterasu, and was entrusted to her grandson Ninigi when he was sent down from the heavens to establish an earthly government. As the myth unfolds, Ninigi first alights on Mount Takachiho in southern Kyushu. Later, his own great-grandson battles his way east along the Inland Sea, eventually establishing himself as the first Emperor Jimmu in what is now the vicinity of Osaka. The territory he occupies is referred to in the narrative as *mizuhō no kuni*, the land blessed with abundant rice. All subsequent emperors derive from this (mythological) single line of descent, and during an emperor's coronation he supposedly becomes the living embodiment of Ninigi, the "god of the ripened rice plant." Even today the emperor conducts an annual fertility ritual in the spring, transplanting some rice seedlings in a special paddy within his palace grounds to ensure a successful growing season for the entire nation.

Realistically speaking, however, the vast majority of the Japanese people get no closer to the nation's rice paddies than passing by them in a speeding car or train. The question thus arises once again: is contemporary Japanese groupishness merely a cultural survival from a bygone era? Or have rice cultivation and the cooperative images it evokes been strategically woven into an explanatory narrative, projecting contemporary values into the past to enhance their validity?

One problem with presenting rice cultivation as the cultural prototype is that over 80 percent of Japan's surface area is comprised of mountains, where the slopes are too steep to make rice cultivation feasible. Yet it is clear from the archaeological evidence that the mountainous areas were populated for thousands of years before agriculture was introduced. The people who occupied these areas maintained their own traditions, which were more suited to the forested landscape that encompassed and sustained them.

Consider, for example, an alternative image from the mountainous Hida region of central Japan, where I have been conducting fieldwork for many years. Though located in the very heart of the archipelago, Hida has historically been rather isolated due to its distance from major population centers, the rugged terrain, and heavy snow accumulation. Furthermore, in a political economy based on rice production, mountainous areas like Hida were at a distinct disadvantage. Most of the local residents made their living as hunters, timber cutters, charcoal producers, and swidden cultivators, none of which was held in particularly high esteem from the "mainstream" point of view.

Hida is mentioned briefly in the *Nihon shoki*, or "Chronicles of Japan" (720 C.E.), an interesting blend of myth and history written from the perspective of the imperial court. After a detailed account of the creation story, it proceeds to record various achievements of the early emperors. A brief passage relates that, during the reign of Emperor Nintoku (313–399 C.E.), there existed in the province of Hida an unusual character referred to as Ryōmen Sukuna – literally "Two-Faced Demon." As the name implies, he purportedly had two faces, oriented in opposite directions but joined to a single head and torso. Each face, moreover, was served by its own set of appendages. With two pairs of arms he displayed great skill with weapons, which he used to threaten and plunder the people. The Sukuna refused to comply with imperial directives, whereupon the emperor, during the 65th year of his reign (377 C.E.), dispatched one of his generals to vanquish the creature (see Aston 1886:298). This episode is thought to represent the Hida region being drawn under the authority of the newly emerging Yamato state (Ōno 1983:108).

The *Chronicles* were, of course, written with the aim of legitimizing imperial authority. The military campaign is thus described as an act of liberation, freeing the people of Hida from an evil despot. Local folk legends, however, relate a different point of view. They describe the Sukuna as a wise and benevolent leader who died defending his people from an invasive foreign power. The two faces represent both a strong and a compassionate side to his personality. Indeed, a famous local wood carving of Ryōmen Sukuna shows his face on one side with a menacing snarl, the hands grasping a bow and arrow, while the other side shows a peaceful and calm demeanor, the hands clasped in front of the chest in a gesture of devotion reminiscent of the Buddhist goddess Kannon. And while the "official" account in the *Chronicles* describes the Sukuna as wielding two swords, local images invariably show him holding an ax, an unmistakable allusion to the forested mountains that were his realm.

In short, the local legends suggest an alternative cultural identity and underlying opposition to outside control. This theme is repeated throughout Hida's history, which is punctuated by various acts of rebellion. Perhaps the most notable occurred during the second year of the Meiji period – the very dawn of the modern era.

The Tokugawa regime had ruled for well over 200 years through feudal ties of loyalty and obligation, but never represented the kind of strong, centralized authority associated with the modern nation-state. "Japan" was at the time divided into more than 250 semi-autonomous domains, each administered by a resident feudal lord. Hida, however, with its vast timber and mineral reserves, was one of the few provincial areas directly controlled by the Tokugawa from their locus in Edo (now Tokyo). Thus the people of Hida were accustomed to a certain degree of autonomy due to their geographical isolation and the absence of the kind of domineering samurai normally employed by resident feudal lords.

When the Meiji leadership took over in 1868, they immediately set about establishing a strong, centralized government that could unify the people and stand up to the encroachment of Western colonialism. In Japan, as elsewhere, national identity was not a "given"; it had to be actively created and maintained. Nationalist ideologues began to propagate the notion of state Shinto in an attempt to draw people's allegiances away from their local areas and toward the all-encompassing figure of the emperor. Not everyone welcomed the new order. Later that same year, the government sent Umemura Hayami, an idealistic but inexperienced young samurai, to serve as Hida's first governor. With little prior knowledge of the local people or their distinctive lifestyles, Umemura embarked on a program of bold but draconian socioeconomic and political reforms. Consequently the people of Hida rebelled, smashing and burning Umemura's administrative offices and attacking his supporters. In a climactic skirmish with angry rebels, Umemura himself was shot, and later died in prison pending an official inquiry into his abusive policies.

This incident is little known outside the Hida region, which seems unusual in light of its scale and level of violence. Japanese historians, if they address the incident at all, treat it in the manner of a standard peasant uprising directed at unpopular rice distribution policies and an increase in the land tax. The peasants themselves are portrayed as being ignorant and resistant to change, not understanding the progressive reforms the young governor was trying to implement. Local sources, however, reveal much more to the story: the peasants were reacting against Umemura's attempt to regulate not only their economy, but even the most intimate aspects of their daily lives, including cherished social institutions, religious beliefs and practices – even sexual behavior. These were the major factors that led them to rebel (see S. Ema 1997 [1949]). The entire incident may thus be seen as a clash involving two distinctive cultures, that of a local mountain-dwelling peasantry versus that of the centralized bureaucratic elite.

Labeling the rebellious peasants as ignorant or backward is a convenient way of avoiding the real issue, namely, that they had legitimate concerns about the nature and pace of the changes being foisted upon them. This technique has been employed all over the globe throughout the modern era for the purpose of dismissing anyone who stands in the way of state ambitions. The Meiji Restoration is widely portrayed as a time of progress, whereby Japan emerged from the darkness of feudalism through the institution of (as the reign name Meiji implies) "enlightened government." Incidents such as the Umemura rebellion pose an embarrassing challenge to this optimistic vision, and an interesting counterpoint to the rhetoric of unified nationalism. This perhaps explains its absence from standard historical accounts.

Nevertheless, local areas had to comply with state directives under threat of penalty and, perhaps even more threatening, serious loss of face. The pressure to conform was particularly intense among young people, who may have been led by the educational system to view their parents' lives as hopelessly old-fashioned and crude. This situation is poignantly illustrated in Natsume Sōseki's novel *Kokoro*, which is set at the end of the Meiji period. At one point the narrator, a young man originally from the countryside who has recently graduated from a university in Tokyo, returns to his natal village when his father falls ill. Throughout the visit he is very condescending to his parents and their neighbors, noting shortly after his arrival that "I began at last to dislike my father's naive provincialism" (Natsume 1957 [1914]:82). His mother, he observes, is quite ignorant about medical matters, "[a]s is commonly the case with women who live among woods and fields far from cities." (1957 [1914]:83). When talk turns to inviting the neighbors for a dinner party to celebrate his graduation, he confesses the following:

> I hated the kind of guests that came to a country dinner party. They came with one end in view, which was to eat and drink, and they were the sort of people that waited eagerly for any event which might provide a break in the monotony of their lives.... But I could hardly say to my parents, "Don't invite those rowdy boors here." (1957 [1914]:86)

The young man's father, though, offers the most telling observation on the social impact of uniform educational policies:

> "You know," he once said to me, "There are advantages and disadvantages in having one's children educated. You take the trouble to give them an education and, when they are through with their studies, they go away and never come home. Why, you can almost say that education is a means of separating children from their parents." (1957 [1914]:95)

Nagatsuka Takashi provides a more sympathetic look at late Meiji village life in his novel *Tsuchi* (The Soil). Among other things, this novel depicts socioeconomic relations within the village, particularly between the small owner and tenant cultivators and the wealthy landlord household referred to as "East Neighbor." Though hardly egalitarian in its relations with the rest of the community, the landlord household nevertheless stands in stark contrast to the detached arrogance of centralized bureaucrats. As Ann Waswo observes in the introduction to her English translation (Nagatsuka 1989 [1910]:xii):

> it is clear that East Neighbor's family remains "of the village" and involved, directly and indirectly, in its affairs. Precisely because they are relatively affluent and possess knowledge of the wider world, they are part of the cement that holds the community together.... The other villagers respect them and value the services they provide.

Nevertheless, among the less affluent villagers life was harsh, especially in light of the economic and technological developments that were transforming agriculture at the time. As Nagatsuka explains in the novel:

> It was no longer possible to obtain free compost from the forests as they had always done in the past. Now the forests were privately owned, and one had to pay to collect leaves or cut green grass....As the forests became depleted, all sorts of artificial fertilizers appeared in the countryside. But once again only those with money could make use of them. Poor farmers were caught up in a vicious circle. Lacking fertilizer they were unable to grow much more than they owed their landlords in rents. So they had to find other work in order to obtain the food they needed. But when they found such work they fell behind in weeding and cultivating their own fields. If they missed even a few days during the hot, wet summer the weeds would shoot up and stifle the growth of their crops. That alone was sufficient to reduce yields. It was just as if they had uprooted the crops before they had matured and eaten them. (1989 [1910]:47–48)

Waswo notes that Sōseki himself had written the introduction to the 1912 edition of Nagatsuka's novel. In it he is quite frank about his disdain for village life (Nagatsuka 1989 [1910]:xvi). Quoting Sōseki:

> Those who read *The Soil* will feel themselves dragged into the mud. That is certainly how I felt....When my daughters are older and talk of going to concerts and plays...I will

give them *The Soil* to read. No doubt they will complain and ask for some more entertaining romantic novels instead. But I will tell them to read it . . . [precisely] because it is painful to do so. I will advise them to persevere in reading it . . . to learn about the world, so that something of the dark, dreadful shadows of life will be [impressed] upon their character. (Bracketed words in Waswo's version)

Clearly, Sōseki is using Nagatsuka's account to underscore the advantages of the modernization, to which he and other urban intellectuals were so deeply committed. It is ironic, therefore, that the harsh living conditions and inequalities described in *The Soil* were largely engendered by "progressive" reforms, such as the introduction of a fixed annual land tax, private ownership of forested mountain lands once held in common, and the promotion of new technologies that were beyond the means of less affluent cultivators.

Waswo goes on to relate how this same novel has been reinterpreted over the years: as a Marxist critique of exploitative social relations during the 1920s and 1930s; as a call for communal solidarity and resolve during the war years; and, interestingly, as a vision of a lost utopia in the late 1970s. Citing one reader's reaction from the latter period, Waswo explains: "The villagers lived in harmony with a bountiful nature; they ate safe, uncontaminated food; old people were well cared for by the community, in contrast to rural Japan today, where the suicide rate among the elderly surpasses that of urban Japan" (Nagatsuka 1989 [1910]:xvii). Here the "dark, dreadful shadows" have become shining emblems of virtue, a striking demonstration of people's ability to mobilize images of the past in pursuing new agendas.

How was such a turnaround effected? Part of the answer lies in the influence of the Japanese ethnographer Yanagita Kunio (1872–1962) through his establishment and promotion of folklore studies. Midway through his career, during the late 1920s, Yanagita turned from an interest in fantastic tales and regional peculiarities toward an effort to discover a unifying essence for the Japanese people. This led him to articulate the concept of *jōmin*, or the "ordinary folk," whom he saw as being typified "by ancestor worship, rice cultivation, and a fixed domicile" (Figal 1999:173; Harootunian, in Vlastos 1998). These, to him, were the defining elements of a distinctive Japanese identity. Yanagita's work found great appeal among nationalist ideologues attempting to unite the diverse regions and peoples of Japan under a single imperial umbrella. He had seen in ancestor worship the roots of a cult of reverence for the emperor, and the images of diligence and cooperation conveyed by rice-cultivating villages were conducive to a broader emphasis on service to the nation. Conveniently left out of this scenario were the hunters, timber cutters, and swidden (*yakihata*) cultivators who populated the mountains at higher elevations, not to mention the residents of the many fishing villages lining the coast.

The notion of rice cultivation as cultural exemplar has been adopted and refined by a number of influential theorists, and Befu (2001:17–20) includes it as one of the major and recurring elements of *nihonjinron* conjecture. One of its leading advocates was philosopher-historian Watsuji Tetsurō (1889–1960), who adhered to a kind of environmental determinism in explaining the evolution of Japanese culture. More specifically, its location within the "monsoon belt" lying along the eastern coast of the Asian continent made the Japanese landscape particularly conducive to rice cultivation. In fact the moist, tropical air of the monsoon, combined with cold air flowing in from the continent, has given rise to some of Japan's most distinctive cultural features (Watsuji 1935). Befu (2001:18) provides an example:

> According to Watsuji, the open architecture of Japanese homes, which are adapted to humidity and heat, was necessitated by the monsoon climate. This open style of architecture in turn relates to the absence of privacy in Japan and even to the denial of individual rights and promotion of collective orientation.

Influential anthropologist Ishida Eiichirō (1903–68) elaborated on Watsuji's ideas in attempting to distinguish Japan and other East Asian nations from the West. Japanese society, having developed within the context of irrigated rice cultivation, took the form of closely knit, insular communities that were firmly rooted in place. Western society, on the other hand, originally developed out of the pastoralist subsistence economies of the Middle East, which explains its penchant for mobility and independence (Ishida 1969).

Though highly speculative and overly simplistic, such explanations have enjoyed unusual popularity. Even today, when people engage in discussing the basic differences between Japan and "the West," the image of "group-oriented rice farmers or company men versus the independent cowboy" distinction is almost invariably recounted. The very simplicity of the image partly explains its appeal, for it accounts for both the perceived groupishness and insularity of Japanese society on the one hand, and the selfish and intrusive nature of "the West" on the other. But it persists mainly because it is *useful* in justifying attitudes that have already become institutionalized and naturalized in schools, companies, and countless other organizations. Like all *nihonjinron* assertions, the rice cultivation model is the result of reasoning retrospectively from a present condition, making the condition itself appear natural or inevitable.

If some influential ethnologists have been guilty of promoting such stereotypes, however, others have endeavored to break them down. Folklorist Akamatsu Keisuke (1909–99) was particularly opposed to Yanagita's *jōmin* concept, claiming that it implied a uniformity that did not exist. It also encouraged discrimination against people who did not fit the standard image. Akamatsu subsequently declared his own interest in the *hijōmin* ("*un*ordinary folk"), devoting his research not only to those who had been marginalized but also to the kinds of topic that other folklorists had long been avoiding, such as the somewhat more relaxed sexual attitudes among rural villagers, or ethnic discrimination in towns and cities (Akamatsu 1986, 1991, 1995). Though largely avoided at their initial publication, many of Akamatsu's works have recently appeared in new editions and have attracted considerable interest and acclaim.

Other scholars have contested the primacy of the "mainstream" rice-based culture itself. Tsuboi Hirofumi (1929–88) persistently argued that dry-field cultivation was at one time equally important, if not more so. Though rice came to predominate in the coastal areas through a combination of political favor and economic policy decisions, a variety of crops continued to be grown in swidden or permanent dry-field plots at higher elevations. These included cereal grains as well as root crops and tubers. Tsuboi (1979, 1982) focused in particular on the cultivation of *imo*, a category of food plant that includes potatoes, taro, and yams. Based on these distinctive subsistence patterns, Tsuboi divided the cultural landscape of Japan into two broad categories: the lowlands (*sato*, meaning literally "village" or "hamlet"), typified by the standard rice-cultivating tradition, and the uplands (*yama*, or mountains), which included not only dry-field cultivation but hunting and logging as well. Of course, fishing villagers and merchants added to the diverse array of landscape categories. Tsuboi underscored the fact that the people who occupied these various niches were *interacting* with one another through complex exchange relationships, each providing what the others did not have (see also Kalland 1995). This suggests a much more dynamic model of social and economic activity in rural areas than is acknowledged by the dominant and naturalized model of paddy cultivation.

Most adamant in his opposition to conventional (and misleading) images of rural Japan has been Amino Yoshihiko, a revisionist historian heavily influenced by historical ethnography. Amino (1996) insists that the focus on rice cultivation as a defining element of Japanese culture derives from a misunderstanding of the term *hyakushō*, which is generally equated with the rice-farming peasantry. He claims that *hyakushō*, written with characters meaning "many names," originally included a variety of non-agricultural occupations such as hunting, timber-cutting, mining, fishing, and shipping. It also applied to dry-field cultivators who grew various grains, vegetables, and fruit. "In the everyday lives of the people, rice had no particular significance. Therefore [he concludes] the common view that Japan was an agricultural society based on paddy fields and rice must be seen as a fabrication, completely at odds with reality" (1996:237).

Cultural diversity exists not only between regions and occupations, but within them as well. Once while visiting the home of a Hida farmer, who happened also to be a Shinto priest, I noticed on his bookshelves the entire collected works of Origuchi Shinobu (1887–1953), whose prominence as a folklorist is second only to that of Yanagita. I asked my host what he thought of Origuchi's work, to which he replied, "Well, he conducted thorough research and gained deep understanding of the places where he worked, but he did not recognize that the neighboring village might be completely different." Motioning around us to his own community, he continued: "Even this tiny hamlet is divided into three contingents, and each has different ways of doing things."

These various sources underscore the point that the Japanese countryside is not a cultural monolith. The variations, however, have yet to be fully addressed. This is due in part to the sense of uniformity that Yanagita's term *jōmin* inspired among cultural ideologues. But it also relates to the difficulty of recovering data about people who were not considered particularly noteworthy by the literary elite. This is what makes the work of Akamatsu and others so important.

Diversity often implies competing interests, which in turn raise doubts about another hallmark of rural society, its alleged commitment to harmony and cooperation. Anyone who spends a significant amount of time living in a rural community will soon recognize that, although on the surface things seem placid, tensions and animosities seethe underneath. This is not to disparage the residents of such communities; the truly admirable achievement is how well they are able to hold their animosities in check, allowing the antagonists to peacefully coexist. Tensions are given free rein, however, on certain prescribed occasions or celebrations, such as a drinking bout or – one of my own special interests – a local Shinto shrine festival.

Kelly (1990:71) nicely captures the rationale underlying such events in his description of the Ōgi-sai in Kurokawa, a village in northeastern Japan. "This is a festival to invoke, entertain, and supplicate the tutelary god of the shrine and of its parishioners; the god is called upon to descend from its mountain abode, commune with parishioners, and bestow good fortune on their lives and livelihoods." The entertainment in this case centers on the local claim to fame: an amateur yet highly accomplished form of *nō* theater. Though ostensibly offered on the deity's behalf, the performances involve competition among the various members of two rival guilds. Kelly notes that, during the requisite feasting, the participants evoke little sense of a religious experience: "the focus of feast talk, well lubricated with sacred rice-wine, is less communion with the god than comparison with one's fellow performers.... Feast talk is artistic talk, incessant appraisals of one's family, friends, and foes" (1990:74).

Moreover, the performances themselves are hardly timeless and unchanging, as official descriptions lead outsiders to believe. In reality, this festival, like similar events all over Japan, has had to accommodate the various symptoms of modern society – busy work schedules, demographic changes, the higher cost of living – as well as the needs and expectations of tourists from the city. This leads Kelly to consider what he describes as the "cultural politics of heritage." To the performers, the festival is a contest for prestige and position; to tourists, *nō* aficionados, and the media, it is a celebration of the Japanese national heritage. Thus the local people find themselves ironically cast as authentic embodiments of tradition, even though their daily lives "are in many respects indistinguishable from those of the Tokyo tourists" (1990:70).

This relates to a more general dilemma involving the Japanese countryside and the way it is perceived by central bureaucrats and the urban public at large. As the backward and declining "boondocks," it must be drawn into contemporary society, presumably through economic development, educational reforms, and infrastructural improvements. But as the repository of Japan's distinctive cultural heritage it must be carefully preserved for future generations. "The festival expresses this fundamental tension of being drawn in while being held apart. It is an arena where the forms of inclusion and exclusion are contested and negotiated" (Kelly 1990:70; Robertson 1987).

My own research (Schnell 1999) has taken a historical approach in attempting to examine these articulations across national, regional, and local boundaries. The setting is a small agricultural and commercial town called Furukawa, located in the Hida region alluded to previously. The annual shrine festival, celebrated after the snow melts away in early spring, showcases an interesting ritualized event in which a large drum is placed on a huge rectangular platform made of overlapping beams and borne at night through the narrow streets in a rowdy procession. Meanwhile, teams of young men bearing smaller drums of their own rush out from the alleys and attack the platform as it passes through their respective neighborhoods. The platform is guarded by burly defenders, so the procession becomes a running battle that continues into the early morning hours.

In every sense a "tradition," the drum ritual is the result of an ongoing evolutionary process. It originated as an innocuous preliminary to the other events, which were performed in honor of the local guardian deity. Shortly after the Meiji Restoration, however, it began to expand, both in scale and level of intensity, eventually assuming center stage as the festival's defining element. I have related the transformation to dramatic social, political, and economic changes that were inundating the community at the same time. The drum ritual came to enact a scenario in which local residents band together in challenging authority. Through its performance, the spirit of resistance that motivated the Umemura rebellion and other historical incidents has been celebrated, perpetuated – even exercised, on several occasions escalating into politically motivated violence. One of the most famous examples occurred in 1929, when the massive drum platform was employed like a battering ram to crash into the local police station, which at that time was the local agent of an increasingly militaristic and oppressive central government. Scores of bystanders took this as their cue to pelt the station building with rocks, an act that was surely premeditated. The festival, with its massing of people, consumption of alcohol, and atmosphere of temporary license, offered one of the few opportunities available to local residents for publicly airing their grievances. The tradition continues to change in response to changing needs. Foremost in people's minds at present are not the predations of some callous landlord or abusive administrator, but the growth and vitality of the local economy. The festival is now being packaged as a tourist attraction, a compelling evocation of *furusato*, one's "native place."

Most contemporary Japanese were born in urban areas and have no personal experience of growing up in a rural village. For them, *furusato* has come to refer not to a specific location but rather a pervasive, nostalgia-driven ideal – one that represents whatever is felt to be lacking in contemporary industrialized society (see Robertson 1988, 1991, 1997, 1998). Surely this relates to one of the great ironies of the modern era: we yearn for the intimacy and simplicity of the past while investing ourselves ever more heavily in the trajectories of "progress" that destroyed them. The rural landscape thus becomes a kind of pilgrimage destination, with thousands of huddled city dwellers setting out into the countryside on weekends and vacations in search of reaffirming doses of *furusato*.

Robertson (1995), Ivy (1995), and Creighton (1997) have all described how the railroad companies helped to promote a sort of home-grown "orientalism" by marketing the countryside as an exotic landscape of adventure and discovery – an elaborate backdrop for staging one's own personal experiences. Furukawa, with its boisterous festival, quaint streets, and newly constructed folk museum complex, has been a willing partner and major beneficiary in such campaigns. By the same token, however, local residents are obliged to assume the role of entertainment and service providers, catering to tourist expectations and thereby reinforcing preconceived stereotypes. As Kelly (1990:65) suggests, communities like this one are "caught between having a past and being a past."

A recent development epitomizes this tendency. Furukawa was chosen as the setting for the morning NHK serial drama *Sakura*, which aired every weekday in 15-minute segments for a period of six months (April through September) in 2002. The plot revolves around the title character, an irrepressibly optimistic young Japanese American woman from Hawaii, who travels to Japan to discover her roots and ends up working as an English-teaching assistant at a middle school in Takayama (the Hida region's major city). Dissatisfied with the unmarried teachers' boarding house, Sakura opts for more culturally evocative lodgings and negotiates a home-stay arrangement in nearby Furukawa. The home is a traditional *ie*, whose primary occupation in this case is not agriculture but candle-making. The house itself replicates an actual *ie* that has been making candles in Furukawa for six generations. The characters in the program, however, are purely fictional. While most of the filming was done on a set built in Tokyo, some stock footage and authenticating sequences were shot in front of the actual house and at other locations in and around Furukawa.

The popularity of the television program has brought hordes of tourists to Furukawa in search of "Sakura's house." On a visit there in the summer of 2002, I was surprised one Sunday morning to witness a steady stream of tourist buses careening into town and disgorging their passengers to roam about the streets. Not surprisingly, I later found a throng of people gathered in the narrow street in front of the original house itself, some taking photographs and others attempting to buy candles as souvenirs. The current head of the household sat in his customary workplace, just inside the entryway and off to the left, busily fashioning handmade candles and greeting the tourists. There was a signboard propped in the doorway leading to the interior of the house where the family lives. The sign asked visitors to please not enter, this being an actual family's home. The current head explained to me that before they put up the sign, people had sometimes wandered freely through the door and into the living area as if the entire house were on display, perhaps expecting to catch a glimpse of Sakura or members of her host family. He added that visitors often greet him as "Numata-san," the name of his fictional counterpart in the television series.

Though they are often viewed with condescension, it could easily be argued that rural residents are far more knowledgeable about the urban center than the center is about them. After all, television, newspapers, and other forms of mass media emanate only from the major cities; the flow of information is unidirectional. Thus the people of Furukawa found great amusement in critiquing the Sakura program, from the actors' attempts at rendering the local dialect to the outlandish domestic situations and confusion of geographical references. While purportedly "about" the Hida region, the program was more a projection of urban attitudes and perceptions onto a generic rural background, yet another example of coopted images. It is ironic that visitors came to bask in the environs of fictional characters rather than to interact with and learn about the actual living residents.

Many of my friends in Furukawa lament that because of the crowds and traffic it no longer seems like the idyllic little town they have always known and loved. Indeed, every time I return there I am astonished by the changes that have taken place in the interim. The most recent include the construction of two large hotels and a spacious new bus terminal adjacent to the rail station, as well as an access tunnel through the mountains to connect with a nearby highway. While some residents have benefited economically from these changes, others clearly have not. The hotels draw business away from the more traditional, family-run *ryokan*. And while new highways and tunnels make Furukawa more accessible to the outside, they also make the outside more accessible to local residents. People are driving farther afield to do their shopping and socializing, with the result that many shops and services not directly related to the tourist industry are closing down.

But the changes do not stop there. The towns and villages of Hida, whose territories were originally defined by natural watershed boundaries, will soon be lumped together to form three new administrative districts. These, in fact, will be the largest such districts in the entire country in terms of surface area. This will mean more centralized educational and administrative facilities, and undoubtedly will result in the further erosion of local identities. Similar amalgamations (*gappei*) are being promoted all over rural Japan in an effort to streamline local administrative services and costs. In a sense, the perception of the countryside as being culturally uniform has become a self-fulfilling prophecy, as blanket policies are imposed by central bureaucrats upon a vast and varied landscape.

If the people of Hida were apprehensive about the amalgamation, why did they acquiesce? One reason is that, while they were offered nominal opportunities to air their reservations, they were never actually allowed to vote on the issue. The decision was made for them by local politicians, who were subjected to heavy carrot-and-stick incentives by the central government, which promised economic assistance for going along with the restructuring and threatened the withholding of funds for refusing to do so. Local administrators, facing a rapidly aging population that will require extensive health-care services and dwindling enrolment in remote village schools that are costly to maintain, saw little recourse but to comply. Many felt that the government was simply too powerful to oppose, and that the changes were probably inevitable.

But there is a more fundamental problem in interpreting the lack of opposition as implicit consent. In a society like Japan's where harmony and cooperation have been relentlessly promoted as fundamental principles of social interaction, it is often difficult to pose a direct challenge to the authorities. As mentioned earlier, there is also an inherent fear of being ridiculed as old-fashioned or backward for standing in the way of "progress." Thus when people feel compelled to express their opposition, they are likely to do so through less direct means, such as in the form of festivals that "spontaneously" escalate into violence, or in invoking vague fears of upsetting the ancestral spirits. If we do not learn to recognize the underlying anxieties inherent in such expressions, we will likely dismiss them as eccentric or superstitious, further justifying the implementation of "reforms."

REFERENCES

Akamatsu, Keisuke. 1986. Hijōmin no minzoku bunka: seikatsu minzoku to sabetsu muka-shibanashi (Folk Culture of the Unordinary Folk: Everyday Folk Customs and Tales of Discrimination). Tokyo: Akashi Shoten.

——1991. Hijōmin no seiminzoku (Sexual Folk Customs of the Unordinary Folk). Tokyo: Akashi Shoten.

Akamatsu, Keisuke. 1995. Sabetsu no minzokugaku (The Folkloric Study of Discrimination). Tokyo: Akashi Shoten.

Amino, Yoshihiko. 1996. Emperor, Rice, and Commoners. *In* Multicultural Japan. Donald Denoon, Mark Hudson, Gavan McCormack, and Tessa Morris-Suzuki, eds. pp. 235–244. Cambridge: Cambridge University Press.

Aston, W. G., trans. 1886. Nihongi: Chronicles of Japan from the Earliest Times to A.D. 697. London: Kegan Paul, French, Trubner & Co.

Bachnik, Jane M. 1983. Recruitment Strategies for Household Succession: Rethinking Japan-ese Household Organization. Man 18:160–182.

Befu, Harumi. 1968. Origin of Large Households and Duolocal Residence in Central Japan. American Anthropologist 70:309–319.

Befu, Harumi. 2001. Hegemony of Homogeneity: An Anthropological Analysis of *Nihonjin-ron*. Melbourne: Trans Pacific Press.

Creighton, Millie. 1997. Consuming Rural Japan: The Marketing of Tradition and Nostalgia in the Japanese Travel Industry. Ethnology 36:239–254.

Ema, Mieko. 1943. Shirakawa-mura no daikazoku (The Great Family System of Shirakawa Village). Tokyo: Mikuni Shobō.

Ema, Shū. 1997 [1949]. Yama no tami (The Mountain Folk). Tokyo: Shunjūsha.

Figal, Gerald A. 1999. Civilization and Monsters: Spirits of Modernity in Meiji Japan. Durham, NC: Duke University Press.

Hobsbawm, Eric, and Terence Ranger, eds. 1983. The Invention of Tradition. Cambridge: Cambridge University Press.

Ishida, Eiichirō. 1969. Nihon bunkaron (Theory of Japanese Culture). Tokyo: Chikuma Shobō.

Ivy, Marilyn. 1995. Discourses of the Vanishing: Modernity, Phantasm, Japan. Chicago: University of Chicago Press.

Kalland, Arne. 1995. Fishing Villages in Tokugawa Japan. Honolulu: University of Hawaii Press.

Kelly, William W. 1990. Japanese No-Noh: The Crosstalk of Public Culture in a Rural Festivity. Public Culture 2:65–81.

Knight, John. 1994. Rural Revitalization in Japan. Asian Survey 34:634–646.

Kondo, Dorinne. 1990. Crafting Selves: Power, Gender, and Discourses of Identity in a Japanese Workplace. Chicago: University of Chicago Press.

Moen, Darrell G. 1997. The Japanese Organic Farming Movement: Consumers and Farmers United. Bulletin of Concerned Asian Scholars 29(3):14–22.

Moon, Okpyo. 1997. Marketing Nature in Rural Japan. *In* Japanese Images of Nature: Cultural Perspectives. Pamela J. Asquith and Arne Kalland, eds. pp. 221–235. London: Curzon Press.

Muto, Atsuko. 1985. Miyagi-ken m-gun k-chō ni okeru "ane katoku" ni tsuite (Elder Daughter Inheritance in K Township, M County, Miyagi Prefecture). Minzokugaku-kenkyū 50:27–51.

Nagatsuka, Takashi. 1989 [1910]. The Soil: A Portrait of Village Life in Meiji Japan. Ann Waswo, trans. New York: Routledge.

Nakamaki, Hirochika. 1992. Mukashi daimyō, ima kaisha: kigyō to shūkyō (Once it was the Feudal Lord, Now It's the Company: Enterprise and Religion). Tokyo: Tankōsha.

Nakane, Chie. 1970. Japanese Society. Berkeley: University of California Press.

Natsume, Sōseki. 1957 [1914]. Kokoro (Heart). Edwin McClellan, trans. Chicago: Regnery Publishing.

Ohnuki-Tierney, Emiko. 1993. Rice as Self: Japanese Identities Through Time. Princeton, NJ: Princeton University Press.

Ōno, Masao. 1983. Hida no kuni shoshi (A Short History of Hida Province). *In* Hidaji no bunkaten (Cultural Exhibit of the Hida Road). Chūnichi Shinbun Honsha, ed. pp. 108–110. Nagoya: Matsuzakaya Honten.

Robertson, Jennifer. 1987. A Dialectic of Native and Newcomer: The Kodaira Citizens' Festival in Suburban Tokyo. Anthropological Quarterly 60(3):124–136.

—— 1988. Furusato Japan: The Culture and Politics of Nostalgia. Politics, Culture, and Society 1:494–518.

—— 1991. Native and Newcomer: Making and Unmaking a Japanese City. Berkeley: University of California Press.

—— 1995. Hegemonic Nostalgia, Tourism, and Nation-Making in Japan. *In* Japanese Civilization in the Modern World IX: Tourism. Tadao Umesao, Harumi Befu, and Shuzo

Ishimori, eds. pp. 89–103. Senri Ethnological Series, 38. Osaka: National Museum of Ethnology.

—— 1997. Empire of Nostalgia: Rethinking "Internationalization" in Japan Today. Theory, Culture and Society 14(4):97–122.

—— 1998. It Takes a Village: Internationalization and Nostalgia in Postwar Japan. *In* Mirror of Modernity: Invented Traditions in Modern Japan. Stephen Vlastos, ed. pp. 209–239 and nn. 611–623. Berkeley: University of California Press.

Rohlen, Thomas P. 1974. For Harmony and Strength: Japanese White-Collar Organization in Anthropological Perspective. Berkeley: University of California Press.

Schnell, Scott. 1999. The Rousing Drum: Ritual Practice in a Japanese Community. Honolulu: University of Hawaii Press.

Steven, Rob. 1983. Classes in Contemporary Japan. Cambridge: Cambridge University Press.

Sugimoto, Yoshio. 1997. An Introduction to Japanese Society. Cambridge: Cambridge University Press.

Tsuboi, Hirofumi. 1979. Imo to nihonjin: minzoku bunkaron no kadai (The Potato and the Japanese: A Problem in Folk Cultural Theory). Tokyo: Miraisha.

—— 1982. Ine o eranda nihonjin: minzokuteki shikō no sekai (The Japanese Who Chose Rice: The Realm of Folkloristic Thought). Tokyo: Miraisha.

Ueno, Chizuko. 1987. The Position of Japanese Women Reconsidered. Current Anthropology 28:S75–S84.

Umesao, Tadao. 1984. Keynote Address: Japanese Civilization in the Modern World. *In* Japanese Civilization in the Modern World: Life and Society. Tadao Umesao, Harumi Befu, and Josef Kreiner, eds. pp. 1–15. Senri Ethnological Series 16. Osaka: National Museum of Ethnology.

—— 1989. Keynote Address: The Methodology of the Comparative Study of Civilization. *In* Japanese Civilization in the Modern World IV: Economic Institutions. Tadao Umesao, Mark W. Fruin, and Nobuyuki Hata, eds. pp. 1–11. Senri Ethnological Series 26. Osaka: National Museum of Ethnology.

Vlastos, Steven, ed. 1998. Mirror of Modernity: Invented Traditions of Modern Japan. Berkeley: University of California Press.

Watsuji, Tetsurō. 1935. Fudo: ningengakuteki kōsatsu (Climate and Culture: A Humanistic Analysis). Tokyo: Iwanami Shoten.

14 Tokyo's Third Rebuilding: New Twists on Old Patterns

Roman Cybriwsky

Tokyo has many distinctions among the world's cities, including the fact that it is the planet's largest or almost-largest city, depending on definition and data source, one of its most expensive cities in terms of price of land and cost of living, and one of only three so-called "World Cities" in terms of its global economic influence according to the well-known thesis by Saskia Sassen (1991). Furthermore, Tokyo is known as being exceptionally crowded, particularly on rush hour trains and subways, for its tightly packed housing and small spaces, and perhaps for its remarkable efficiency in areas ranging from the transit system to community policing to trash collection. Less famous but also unrivaled is Tokyo's unusual geography, in which city limits (i.e., the territory within Tokyo Metropolitan Government and under the jurisdiction of Tokyo's governor) include not just the crowded central city and many of its suburbs, but also a wild, heavily forested mountainous area to the west of the urban center and chains of tiny Pacific islands with coral reefs and fine beaches stretching for more than 1,000 miles to the south to tropical climes (Cybriwsky 1998).

A third distinction, tied to the main focus of this chapter, is the extraordinary instability of Tokyo's built environment. All through its history, from when it was but a small castle town in the 15th and 16th centuries to modern times, it has continually been destroyed, most typically by fire, and subsequently rebuilt. In just the last century alone there were three destructions and rebuildings. No other city in the world, much less one so large and important, has been so ephemeral in physical form, and no other older city, much less one so historically significant, is so new in built environment and so completely lacking in old neighborhoods and historic buildings. As one tours Tokyo or gazes across the landscape from a high point, say the observation deck of Tokyo Tower, one is struck that here is a city where the overwhelming majority of buildings are recently built, that they are generally similar to each other, and that historic character is absent, at least superficially. In fact, visitors to the city from abroad have complained that they cannot see "Japan" or the great traditions of Japan in art and architecture in Tokyo, and that the city is instead a mishmash of ordinary buildings of no particular heritage, peppered with familiar uses such as the popular coffee shop beginning with S and the cholesterol capital with golden arches.

What are the three destructions and rebuildings of Tokyo in the last century? The first two are well known to anyone who knows the least bit about the city's history: the first was in 1923 as a result of the great Kantō earthquake and ensuing fires, while the second was the result of US air raids against the city in 1945 in the closing campaign of World War II. The third is a little less obvious, although its impact on the form of the city was much greater: the tearing down of the city that took place during the economic boom times of the 1970s and 1980s and the reconstruction that followed. This time, instead of disaster, the agent of change was profit for the real-estate industry, as well as urban improvement by the forces of city planning and redevelopment. Instead of the hurried rebuilding after 1923 and 1945, when the goal was to get the city operating again and reconstruction followed old lines, the most recent reconstruction was more calculated. It was designed to maximize land rent and/or to house Tokyo's masses more efficiently, and produced a radically different form for the city – one emphasizing high-rises instead of the low-slung profile of the past. We see this change in the title of historian Edward Seidensticker's book about the city's more recent developments: *Tokyo Rising* (1990).

This chapter takes a critical look at the Tokyo cityscape that was created by this third rebuilding. It is an appropriate topic for anthropologists, following the tradition in the discipline of studying built environments to gain insights about their inhabitants. But instead of excavating the ruins of an ancient city to learn about a people of the past, as anthropologists and archeologists often do, the focus here is on a cityscape of today to see something about contemporary society. The premise is that the built environment can be a faithful mirror of social or cultural values, and should be analyzed for insights into such aspects as economic and political relationships, relationships to natural environment, and national self-image. In our case, we will see that the landscape of Japan's capital reflects, among other things, the excesses of the nation during the economic bubble, the great power over the landscape of the so-called Japanese "construction state," and Japan's peculiar and extraordinary desire to show itself as being "international" and worldly-wise. We will also see that Tokyo's new landscape borrows liberally from cityscapes and landmarks around the world, resulting in a somewhat confusing mix of cultural traditions and architectural styles that, at least in new commercial districts, is coming to be Japan's new vernacular. Finally, we will see that there are historical precedents in Tokyo for rebuilding the city in a way that is both showy and international-looking, such that Tokyo's third rebuilding of the 20th century can be thought of as a case of new twists on old patterns.

Four Places in Central Tokyo

I will focus here on profiles of four places in Tokyo that collectively represent the new urban landscape. All are redevelopment or new development projects in one of the

23 central wards of the city, and are quite large in scale. The first three are very well known in Tokyo, attracting huge crowds of people on weekdays and weekends alike. The first is Shinjuku, a commercial center at a major rail–subway commuter interchange 5 or 6 kilometers to the west of city's principal business node. It is a large area of many sub-districts and land uses, and contains some of Tokyo's largest and showiest high-rise redevelopment projects, including "City Hall," which we will look at with extra measure. The second is Yebisu Garden Place, a large mixed-use redevelopment project on an old industrial site also on the central city's west side. It is a prototypical "island within a city," being self-contained with a wide range of land uses and standing apart in architecture from the surrounding neighborhood. The third is Daiba, a new mixed-use district (commercial, residential, recreation) developed since the 1980s south of the city center on a new island reclaimed from Tokyo Bay. The fourth place is Shioiri, a newly redeveloped residential district in a working-class zone northeast of the center, on the site of an old-style residential area of the same name. Somewhat isolated from the main flow of Tokyo, it is not widely known but now looks like much of the rest of the city. I shall describe each of these places in turn and then pull together common themes that reflect on critical aspects of Japan today.

Shinjuku

Shinjuku has a long history as a transportation junction and commercial center, but grew especially quickly in the 20th century to become a major rival to the city's original business district in the general area of Tokyo station, Nihonbashi, Marunouchi, and Ginza. One great spurt of growth came after the 1923 earthquake, when many businesses relocated there to safer ground, as well as to be near areas of emerging urban expansion. A second spurt is tied to urban planning efforts in the 1960s, when a decision was made to decentralize Tokyo's commercial functions, taking pressure off the overcrowded and expensive core, and to develop alternative commercial centers (*fukutoshin*) at key transportation nodes ringing the center. Shinjuku became the biggest of 20 or so such districts, in many ways eclipsing the old core itself. Its passenger station is Tokyo's busiest place (and maybe the busiest place in the world!), while the district itself ranks first in Tokyo (and maybe the world) in retail sales, numbers of bars and restaurants, as well as other possible measures, including Tokyo's all-important sex industry. The Shinjuku office towers are Tokyo's tallest buildings, so its skyline often stands for the economic power of Tokyo or Japan, much as the Manhattan skyline is an acknowledged symbol of the economic power of New York City or the United States.

There are so many things to say about Shinjuku that a book could be written about the place. However, there is a special story to tell about its principal cluster of high-rises, an area on the west side of Shinjuku station that is variously referred to as New Shinjuku City Center (Shin Toshin Shinjuku), West Shinjuku, or simply West Exit. The centerpiece is the 107-hectare site of an old water treatment facility that was redeveloped from 1960 into a carefully laid out arrangement of office towers and international hotels interspersed with straight, wide streets, sheltered pedestrian concourses, and various combinations of public plazas, enclosed shopping malls, fountains and sculptures, and landscapers' greenery. The first tower to be completed was the Keiō Plaza Hotel in 1971, with various other buildings opening later in the 1970s and 1980s, into the 1990s. The newest high-rises, often taller and more distinctive in form than those of the first generation, are on surrounding blocks, as redevelopment is ongoing and the office tower sub-district is expanded.

What is perhaps most remarkable about this area is the extent to which it is compared in Tokyo to New York's Manhattan. It does not matter that Nishi Shinjuku is no bigger than a few Manhattan blocks; it *is* Tokyo's answer to the skyline of its principal rival metropolis abroad. In Popham's words, written even before many of Shinjuku's most prominent buildings were built, Shinjuku is "the embodiment of [Tokyo's] Manhattan fantasies" (Popham 1985:101–102). The skyline of the district is represented often in Japanese film and television as the setting for big-city detective adventures and other dramas, and the backdrop for commercial advertising for various "urban-sophisticated" consumer products such as cigarettes, whiskey, and luxury automobiles. This is similar to the way in which the more famous profile of New York is often represented in America and other countries, and has resulted in Shinjuku's becoming what is almost certainly the most widely recognized urban scene in Japan. Imitation of New York is sometimes direct. I have a Christmas card illustrating the Shinjuku skyline on a quiet snowy night, Santa and his reindeer in the sky above, and the unmistakable reflection of the Statue of Liberty on the glass skin of one of the high-rises! So, too, I have a key chain that says "Tokyo Megalop-olis" and shows a montage of Tokyo's landmarks and the profile of New York's Chrysler building. What is more, there is a waterfall/fountain in Shinjuku's "Central Park" (Chūō Kōen) called Niagara Falls. Several blocks away, at the south exit of Shinjuku station, is a huge new shopping center named, you guessed it, Times Square.

Emulation of foreign cityscapes or landmarks is most extreme with respect to Nishi Shinjuku's (and Tokyo's) tallest building, Tokyo Metropolitan Government head-quarters. Called *tochō* or simply City Hall, it opened in 1991, replacing the over-crowded and exceptionally unimpressive offices of city administration that had stood in Marunouchi in the CBD. Relocation to Shinjuku had been a pet project of Suzuki Shunichi, Tokyo's enormously powerful governor between 1979 and 1995, and is in itself a telling indicator of the growing importance of this district. The design, by Tange Kenzō (b. 1913), the same architect who designed the outmoded City Hall (and who, therefore, had been given a rare chance to redeem himself, and whose career can be said to outlast his buildings), was intended to make the new City Hall not only the number 1 landmark in Nishi Shinjuku but also a major symbol of Tokyo itself, both nationally and internationally, eclipsing Tokyo Tower in this role. According to promotional literature touting its state-of-the-art, high-technology construction, the new City Hall is intended to launch Tokyo "toward the 21st century and beyond" (Tokyo Metropolitan Government 1993:74). When it opened, Governor Suzuki described the complex as "a gift for the metropolis' citizens of the 21st century" (Tabata 1991:18; see also Kenzo Tange Associates 1991–93).

The specific site of City Hall overlooks "Central Park" and faces the city's sprawling western suburbs. It consists of three buildings: two massive office sky-scrapers with distinctive shape and texture, and a lower, semi-circular "Assembly Building" that opens on to a grand public plaza. The taller tower, the so-called

Number One Building, rises to 243 meters and is the tallest building in the city; the Number Two Building is 163 meters high and also ranks among Tokyo's giants. The architectural details are fascinating, intending to convey Tokyo as both a traditional city (early Edo, Tokyo's name before 1868) and a city of "international stature as a world leader" (Kenzo Tange Associates 1991–93:31). At street level and below, there are aspects of the project that recall Edo Castle: stone facing that resembles the castle's walls, a kind of moat, and traditional Japanese greenscaping. This contrasts with the public plaza, called Tomin Hiroba, or Citizens' Plaza, which Tange has said was meant to evoke the Vatican's St. Peter's Square. However, instead of depicting saints and former popes, the semi-circular pantheon of statues is of nude or semi-nude young women. It has, therefore, been the subject of occasional protest by women and their supporters, as well as the focus of a very thoughtful scholarly critique of Tokyo's public art (Shimizu 1994). Further architectural contrast is with the façades of the towers above: they are meant to suggest the circuitry of a modern computer and the shapes of specific international landmarks. The Number One Building, for example, has a twin-towers configuration above the 150 meters level that Tange has explained as an echo of Notre Dame cathedral in Paris.

Because of the project's great size and visibility, as well as a price tag reported to be as high as ¥157 billion, critics have said that City Hall is either Tange's monument to himself or a monument to Suzuki, or both, and that it is a symbolic return to Edo Castle, the imposing center of power around which the city was originally founded. Unkind nicknames that have applied to the complex are "Tax Tower," referring to the high cost, and "Tower of Bubble," a label applied by Kurosawa Kishō, a prominent architect who was once a student of Tange's, to refer to the extraordinary buoyant economy that enabled construction (Tabata 1991:18). Indeed, all of the showy office district on Nishi Shinjuku, as well as projects in the vicinity such as the Times Square complex, where the shopping mall rises over 14 stories, reflect Tokyo's protean character and love for new construction.

Yebisu Garden Place

If the tall buildings of Shinjuku are meant to either rival or recall New York, then Yebisu Garden Place (also written as Ebisu Garden Place) is an echo of France or Paris. Located not far from Shinjuku in an upscale residential district at the boundaries of Meguro, Minato, and Shibuya Wards, it is a megastructure redevelopment project on the site of an old Sapporo brewery complex. With the land too valuable for just making beer, it was converted in the early 1990s to a sprawling mixed-use development that features, among other things, an office tower, a major international hotel, a department store and shopping center, lots of restaurants, a museum about photography, a beer garden, and, hooray, a museum about beer. All this is around a large central courtyard with an overarching roof that combines the feel of being outdoors with the benefits of climate control. The feeling of France comes mostly from the project centerpiece, a more or less faithful reproduction of a historic chateau. There are also French restaurants and cafés with "outdoor" seating, as well as sculptures, signposts, and other landscaping with a European flavor. Particularly on Sundays, Japan's main day of rest and shopping, Yebisu Garden Place is crowded with people enjoying the atmosphere. Musicians, magicians, and other street performers add to the pleasure. Some visitors choose to pose for pictures in front of the chateau, which will give the illusion that they have been abroad.

The success of Yebisu Garden Place as an alternative to Japan (or simply to the crowded conditions of Tokyo) depends also on its physical separation from the city. Although it is in the midst of a densely built-up (and generally well-regarded) neighborhood, it stands totally apart by design, so much so that high walls and steep slopes mark some of its edges. Other edges are formed by the backsides of the project's buildings, with main entryways opening toward the interior central courtyard rather than the outside. The insular feel also comes from the physical means of access. As anywhere else in Tokyo, most visitors would arrive by train or subway, but because the project is not immediately adjacent to such a station they are conveyed the last 400 meters by a specially constructed enclosed moving walkway. Once they get on the "Yebisu Sky Walk" at Ebisu station, people are moved in narrow files for about five minutes through an enclosed, climate-controlled tube that eventually deposits them at an inviting entryway with photogenic qualities. U-turns or turnoffs are discouraged by the design, while anticipation of what lies ahead is heightened by measured breaks in the walkway and little right-angle jogs that conceal the ultimate destination until the last stretch. All along the short journey, arriving customers pass colorful posters and backlit advertisements for shops, restaurants and other facilities that lie ahead. They are vetted by security personnel, who sometimes greet new arrivals at the walkway's start or watch through surveillance cameras as they glide toward the entry.

There are obvious parallels between design features of Yebisu Garden Place and those of Disneyland-type theme parks. In both cases there is a sharp break with the outside world and architectural devices such as anticipation-building approaches that heighten the feeling that one is in a different or special place. Both are also designed to make customers feel relaxed and comfortable, to encourage people to linger and spend money. Finally, both are extraordinarily safe and sanitary environments. At Yebisu Garden Place, security comes from a bevy of uniformed and non-uniformed guards and ubiquitous surveillance cameras, while the cleanliness is thanks to an army of men and women workers in lime-green jump suits who silently scrape, scrub, sweep, mop, and polish amidst the crowds of customers. The granite-faced walls are so shiny that they could be mirrors.

Daiba

Daiba (aka Odaiba) is a beachfront development on a new island in Tokyo Bay not far from the center of the city. Access is even more dramatic than that to Yebisu, as most visitors arrive via the Yurikamome line, a new monorail from central Tokyo across the high Rainbow Bridge, Tokyo's answer to the Golden Gate Bridge. There are sweeping views of the Tokyo skyline that one leaves behind and the futuristic urban scene ahead called Tokyo Teleport Town or the Waterfront Subcenter, of which Daiba is a part. Other visitors come by automobile on an expressway that crosses the same bridge, or from a different direction via tunnel under the bay. What they find at Daiba is still another escape from both the routines and the look of Tokyo. The focus is a new sandy beach that was laid down in an L-shape at the foot of the bridge and the gleaming new resortscape behind it. There are large shopping malls and entertainment complexes, dozens of bars and restaurants, hotels, office buildings and clusters of high-rise apartment and condominium buildings. On the upper floors of Island Mall is Little Hong Kong, a replica back street with Cantonese restaurants and Hong Kong souvenirs. A little further on are still more shopping malls, including one named Venus Fort where the streets and statuary resemble a Las Vegas version of Italy. Also, there are other high-tech entertainment centers, new conventional and exhibition halls, an amusement park, public swimming pool and tennis courts, and Telecom Center, an "intelligent" office building shaped like Le Grand Arc in La Défense in Paris. Perhaps the most striking sight is a large replica Statue of Liberty on a high pedestal near the Daiba beach. However, unlike her counterpart near New York, this lady has her back to the bay and the city, and holds her torch in the direction of the shoppers in Daiba's malls.

The waters of Tokyo Bay are not recommended for swimming, so except for some courageous windsurfers in wetsuits only a few wade in from the beach. However, during good weather the beach itself and walkways along it are crowded with Tokyoites enjoying the sun and the relative fresh air and quiet. The shopping malls and entertainment centers like Mega Web and the Joypolis video arcade are also crowded, especially on weekends and holidays when great throngs descend on the scene. Street musicians and other outdoor entertainment add to the festive atmosphere, as do the many boats for drinking parties, the Mississippi River steamboat that takes visitors on short cruises, and what is reputedly the world's largest Ferris wheel. The district is especially popular for dating. At sunset and after dark the Daiba waterfront is lined with couples evenly spaced along the sitting area, many of them in close embrace.

Thus, Daiba is a waterfront festival zone *par excellence*, offering countless diversions in a theme-park-like setting. We might call it "Santa Monica Land" or "Waikiki Land," or something after one of the resort towns in Australia's Queensland. The place also suggests famous big-city redevelopment projects like Baltimore's Inner Harbor and Canary Wharf in London. Whereas in many other cities such areas have been made from once derelict warehouse and industrial zones, in Tokyo the approach has been to build something totally new on new land, and to import a beach to boot. The fact that Daiba is only minutes away by rail from the center of the city and easily accessible by car (a rare feature in Tokyo) adds to the success. The residential buildings on the island are also popular, particularly if they are close to the rail stations and shopping for daily needs. The commute to downtown Tokyo is quick and easy, while at the same time there is a sharp break in landscape between the city of work and where one lives.

Development plans for Tokyo's waterfront have been even more ambitious than what is seen at Daiba. The waterfront area actually consists of several large new islands in various stages of completion, as well as sizeable extensions to the shoreline of Tokyo Bay, where there has been considerable construction for some time. One specific plan, linked to the same Tokyo decentralization concept that gave rise to Shinjuku, has called for a residential population of 63,000 and the workforce population is 109,000 – large enough to be considered a major extension of the city into the bay. There were also plans for a major world's fair on one of the new islands, although that particular idea and several other construction projects have fallen victim to the weak economy and taxpayer rebellions about subsidies for real-estate development. Consequently, still another type of landscape at the waterfront, in addition to the successful Daiba development, is new vacant land and undeveloped spaces in an otherwise very crowded city.

Shioiri

If Shinjuku suggests Manhattan, Yebisu Paris, and Daiba an American or Australian beach resort, then Shioiri is no place at all. The sad thing is that it had been a fine neighborhood with distinctive qualities before redevelopment, and that a decade of demolition and reconstruction in the 1990s produced nothing more than just another cluster of ordinary high-rise apartments, albeit for many more people than were housed in the old neighborhood. What makes the place different from countless other high-rise residences is that buildings in the center of the new Shioiri are colored pink, presumably to make the area cheery. There are also some concessions to local history: reuse of the area's toponymy; mosaics with historic scenes on the walls of the supermarket; no destruction of the old temple and its surrounding trees. Otherwise, everything in old Shioiri was chainsawed, bulldozed, and hauled away, possibly for Tokyo Bay landfill, and the topography was regraded. Residents and shopkeepers were given cash for their properties and priority for new apartments and commercial sites. Several thousand new people from elsewhere in Arakawa Ward and all over Tokyo came to settle, attracted by the newness and competitive rents in a housing project with public subsidies. Many of them are families with young children, a type of household being recruited by Arakawa and other wards on the blue-collar side of Tokyo to balance age structure and reinvigorate local economies.

The old Shioiri was a place that I had once considered to be one of my secrets about Tokyo. Even though it is generally near the center of Tokyo, the site is an out-of-the-way place, being a long walk from the nearest train station, on the far side of a long stretch of railyards and industries, and tucked within a sharp bend of the Sumida river. Paul Waley and Sugiura Noriyuki, two geographers who are experts on Tokyo, took me there in 1985 when I was beginning my professional interest in the city, and told me that I should get to know Shioiri to learn about Tokyo's past and present (see Waley 1984). I've been returning ever since, sometimes bringing friends who were visiting me to show them an alternative side of Tokyo. The appeal was to see one of the last vestiges in Tokyo of an old-style urban landscape and way of life. It was a tightly packed "urban village," of small wooden houses with tile roofs along narrow, crooked streets, small family-owned shops, and potted greenery double- and triple-stacked beside every building. The temple and its small grounds was a spatial focus. Neighbors also got together at the *sento*, the local bathhouse. There was a lot of outdoor activity as well. It seemed like everyone knew everyone else and that the community was exceptionally close-knit. I stood out when I visited, and was remembered by locals as the foreigner who had visited before whenever I returned.

Unfortunately, Tokyo's high-risers, including Tange Kenzō personally, also found Shioiri. For them, it was land used inefficiently in a crowded and expensive city, and housing that was substandard because it was drafty, not air-conditioned, and lacking in conveniences such as private baths and showers. The neighborhood was also said to be hazardous in terms of earthquake fires. And so this old section of Tokyo was modernized to make it better and safer, and to make room for more people. The neighborhood's original residents did not have much say in the changes, as demolition was imposed on them. Most of the locals are still around, living in better dwellings, but behind closed doors with air conditioning, cable TV, and private facilities instead of with their neighbors. For them neighborhood is gone, and the new place, now called River Park Shioiri, is like a move to a distant city.

The same change is happening in countless other places in Tokyo: communities of single homes are giving way to high-rise residences and multi-unit apartment-condominium structures called *manshon*. Just a bit upriver from Shioiri, also in Arakawa Ward, close to the sewage works, is another planned new high-rise residential area, one exceptionally densely developed. It houses many thousands on land where hundreds once lived and replaces traditional neighborhood life in old houses on narrow lanes with the faceless relations of a giant new complex of like buildings. In this particular project the architects' gesture toward making the place distinctive is having lots of freestanding Ionic columns all about and a narrow moat, just 1 meter across, at its edges. For some reason all these places, like River Park Shioiri, have names in English, written in Roman letters. Whoever it was who named this second place may have been part of a quiet resistance: its name is "Acrocity."

DISCUSSION: COMMON THEMES

So, here we have three famous places in Tokyo that attract the crowds, as well as a fourth new place, an ordinary residential district little different in appearance from countless other new residential developments. What things in common do we see in these four examples of Tokyo's third rebuilding and what do they tell us about contemporary Japan?

First and most obvious is that all four developments, as well as many other construction projects in the city of which these four are examples, are new, large in scale, and emphasize high-rises. This contrasts sharply with the low-slung, smaller-footprint profile of traditional Tokyo, and represents a significant change in the look of the city. Furthermore, there is an extra measure of pizzazz, such as an exaggerated international look for the three famous projects and the pink tone to the center of Shioiri, as well as a certain reliance on big-name architects to give each new project instant cachet. Cachet also derives from fancy-sounding foreign names given to the projects or individual structures, and/or from imitations of famous foreign places or landmarks. Other new construction projects in this vein are Tokyo Opera City, an oversized high-rise building and commercial complex with Tokyo's outstanding new National Theater near Shinjuku, and Tama Center, the main commercial district of a large, planned western suburb, where the main street is called Parutenon-dōri (Parthenon Street) and the visual focus is a stylized representation of the Parthenon on an artificial hill at the end of the street. Another important commonality is that all four developments stand apart by design from their respective surroundings and are "islands in the city" (or "cities within the city") with little or no articulation with the wider districts they occupy. In the case of Daiba, the "island" analogy is literal.

There is nothing particularly "Japanese" about urban development with these characteristics. Cities in other countries have similar building trends, so much so that some writers have lamented the lack of regional or cultural distinctiveness in new urban landscape and complain that, more and more, cities around the world, especially their commercial cores, look alike (Cybriwsky and Ford 2001; Ford 1994: 268–275). In his introduction to a landmark collection of social critiques about urban design trends, particularly in New York and other American cities, Michael Sorkin identified at least three physical characteristics that seem to hold as well for Tokyo: (1) "dissipation of all stable relations to local physical and cultural geography [and] the loosening of ties to any specific place"; (2) an "obsession with 'security,' with rising levels of manipulation and surveillance over [the] citizenry"; and (3) new emphasis on architecture of "simulation" in cities, giving cities, or parts thereof, some of the key characteristics of theme parks (Sorkin 1992:xiii–xv).

If anything can be said to be distinctively Japanese about the look of Tokyo's new developments, it is, ironically, the extent of copying of foreign (Western) landmarks and architectural styles, and application of Western-language names to buildings and other construction, as opposed to Japanese toponymy. These are patterns that date back to Meiji Japan (1868–1912), when the country emerged from a long period of enforced isolation under the Tokugawa shoguns and completed crash courses in modernization and internationalization. Tokyo assumed the special role as Japan's principal pupil, becoming the locus of a vastly disproportionate amount of the newness. As national capital it concentrated Japan's foreigners and foreign influences, in part to protect the rest of Japan from unwanted changes, and constructed for itself new series of landmarks to show to the world and to the Japanese alike that the nation was a fast learner, capable of achieving whatever others had achieved. Along with its newly created companion city of Yokohama, Tokyo became a showcase of new fashions and activities, as well as of grand buildings and entire districts with new architecture and foreign themes (Barr 1968; Sabin 2002; Seidensticker 1983; Tokyo Metropolitan Government 1993).

Two of the principal early landmarks in this vein were the Tsukiji Hoterukan and the Rokumeikan. The first was a large hotel completed in 1868 just across from a newly designated settlement for foreigners in the Tsukiji district at Tokyo Bay. It was a striking brick building which combined curious Western accretions on a traditional Japanese timber-frame base, reflecting Japan's awkward first encounters with the outside world. The word *hoterukan* itself was a strange new blend: the first syllables correspond to the Japanese pronunciation of "hotel," while *kan* is based on the Japanese for "inn." Unfortunately, the building had an unusually short life, as a great fire that swept through central Tokyo in 1872 and destroyed it. The Rokumeikan was completed in 1883. Located in Hibiya near the new government district, it was the work of English architect Josiah Conder, who was brought to Japan for the task at the request of the Ministry of Technology. Like its predecessor, it too was an elaborate hotel and gathering place with unusual, hybrid design. It was covered with stucco and combined Moorish, Mediterranean, and northern European styles. Its purpose was to be a place where cosmopolitan Japanese of the new era could mix with foreigners. During its heyday in the mid- and late 1880s, the Rokumeikan hosted countless elegant balls, formal dinners, musical performances, charity bazaars, and other Western-style "high society" events.

The famous district of Ginza is a prime example of an entire section of the city that was redeveloped in a foreign style. Originally the site of the shogun's silver mint and later one of the city's premier geisha districts, it bore the brunt of the 1872 fire and needed to be rebuilt. As an experiment to make the city safer, the reconstruction was done in brick, a first for Japan, after a plan by English architect Thomas Waters, and the district came to be called the Ginza Brick Quarter (Ginza renga gai). By the time work was completed, there were more than 1,000 brick buildings, many of which were two-story structures with colonnades and balconies. So, too, there were sidewalks, gaslights along the streets, and rows of planted willows. There were also quite a few problems with the construction, not the least of which was that buildings were poorly suited to the local climate and became excessively damp, so it took quite a while before the area became popular as a restaurant and shopping paradise.

A second European-looking district in Meiji Tokyo was the so-called Mitsubishi Londontown. Developed around the turn of the century on what was once a military parade ground and army barracks next to the Imperial Palace, it became Tokyo's premier office district after the opening of Tokyo station in 1914. The principal designer was once again Josiah Conder, and, as the name suggests, the district was an imitation of the English capital. Its main features were four-story, red-brick buildings that were vaguely reminiscent of Victorian Kensington, and a grid pattern of wide streets. It also took a while to catch on, but it eventually capitalized on its centrality and became pre-eminent.

There were other examples of Western building and landmarks in Tokyo in the decades that followed, not the least of which was Tokyo Tower, Tokyo's answer to the Eiffel Tower, completed in 1959. Thus, a pattern of Tokyo as "international city" with the look and landmarks of other places had been set. I argue that at Daiba, Yebisu, and "Tokyo's Manhattan" the pattern continues today, and that the "third rebuilding of Tokyo" is, therefore, not quite as great a break in local history and geography as it might initially seem.

Still another collection of thoughts about the four new developments is that, both individually and collectively, they reflect the enormous activity of the construction industry in Japan. The country has been described internally as *doken kokka*, a "construction state," in which vastly disproportionate power resides with top bureaucrats in the Ministry of Construction, their political allies in the National Diet, and the country's biggest construction companies, and where much of the economy is in construction and related industries. The result is a landscape, not just in the big cities but also in the remote corners of the country, of many new (and often large-scale) public works such as highways, bridges, tunnels, flood-control projects, landslide-control projects, museums, concert halls, and convention facilities, and of private works built with government largesse, whether they are needed or not (Kerr 2001:13–50). The culture of the times and apparent guiding principle of the Ministry of Construction is to build and keep building, with the corollary being that construction gets ever grander and more elaborate. As the biggest city and national capital, Tokyo represents the apex of this pattern. The nation's largest developers and construction companies are headquartered there, and it is there that they have erected some of their greatest monuments.

The case of Shioiri is a particularly poignant story with respect to the angle of the construction state in Tokyo. While building and rebuilding is endemic in the city, Shioiri seemed immune because of its remoteness. Yet, the city's builders were able to find the neighborhood and see that it had lots of land and many old houses, where "progress" could be brought. Shioiri residents protested the changes, citing immense satisfaction with their quieter, community-based life in the city, but to no avail, as the neighborhood was formally tagged as a concentration of substandard housing and a risk for flooding. In this way what had existed for decades was bulldozed, the land covered with new topsoil so that remaining traces would be buried, and the site made to look like so many other ordinary places in Tokyo.

Thus, one overarching conclusion about the new cityscape at Shioiri and the other study sites is that Tokyo is undergoing a conscious break from past patterns of land use and a deliberate change in the look of the city. Indeed, this is the claim of much of the publicity about these and similar redevelopment projects in Tokyo which emphasizes Tokyo's modernization and improved comfort for both living and business. This is seen especially clearly in the straightforward advertising campaigns of the Mori Corporation, one of the world's biggest land developers, headquartered in central Tokyo. The company has built well over a hundred high-rise office and residential towers, mostly at an advancing edge of the Central Business District in Minato Ward on the accumulated sites of older single homes, and, probably more than any other real-estate firm or land development company, represents the changes under way in the city. In its advertising it promotes itself with the slogan "We Design Tokyo." Moreover, the Mori Corporation has advertised its giant redevelopment projects such as Ark Hills, Roppongi Hills, and Moto-Azabu Hills as being "Where Tokyo Is Headed." Likewise, promoters of the new construction projects on islands reclaimed from Tokyo Bay have argued that their various exhibition facilities, office buildings, international hotels, and other new buildings are necessary to propel Tokyo through the 21st century, keeping the city competitive with Shanghai, Singapore, Hong Kong, and other business-aggressive urban centers in Pacific Asia that are also undergoing major redevelopment.

However, we can also say the exact opposite about these physical characteristics, and argue that they are best understood as contemporary manifestations of land use and lifestyle patterns that are long embedded in the city's history. That is, we can say that, while the projects themselves are new they actually represent aspects of Tokyo that have been around for some time, and that design details such as extra pizzazz, similarities to foreign landmarks and use of foreign names also have historical antecedents. In this regard, instead of signaling new directions for urban development in Tokyo and new modes of urban living, the high-rises of Shinjuku, the seemingly non-Japanese landscapes of Yebisu and Daiba, and even the new apartment blocks of Shioiri, among other recent developments, are all just new twists on old patterns.

REFERENCES

Barr, P. 1968. The Deer Cry Pavilion: A Story of Westerners in Japan. New York: Harcourt, Brace & World.

Cybriwsky, Roman. 1998. Tokyo: The Shogun's City at the Twenty-First Century. Chichester and New York: Wiley & Sons.

Cybriwsky, R., and L. R. Ford. 2001. Jakarta. Cities. The International Journal of Urban Policy and Planning 18(3):199–210.

Ford, L. R. 1994. Cities and Buildings: Skyscrapers, Skid Rows, and Suburbs. Baltimore: Johns Hopkins University Press.

Kenzo Tange Associates. 1991–93. The New Tokyo City Hall Complex. The Japan Architect 3:16–43.

Kerr, Alex. 2001. Dogs and Demons: Tales from the Dark Side of Japan. New York: Hill & Wang.

Popham, Peter. 1985. Tokyo: The City at the End of the World. Tokyo: Kodansha International.

Sabin, Burritt. 2002. A Historical Guide to Yokohama: Sketches of the Twice-Risen Phoenix. Yokohama: Yurindo.

Sassen, Saskia. 1991. The Global City: New York, London, Tokyo. Princeton, NJ: Princeton University Press.

Seidensticker, Edward. 1983. Low City, High City: Tokyo from Edo to the Earthquake. Rutland, VT and Tokyo: Charles E. Tuttle.

—— 1990. Tokyo Rising: The City since the Great Earthquake. New York: Alfred A. Knopf.

Shimizu, Aoi. 1994. Sexism in Tokyo's New Public Art: Results from Field Research and Opinion Surveys. Unpublished MA thesis, Temple University, USA.

Sorkin, Michael, ed. 1992. Variations on a Theme Park: The New American City and the End of Public Space. New York: Hill & Wang.

Tabata, M. 1991. Symbol of the Capital City. The Japan Times, April 10:18.

Tokyo Metropolitan Government. 1993. Tokyo: The Making of a Metropolis. Tokyo: TMG Municipal Library No. 27.

Waley, Paul. 1984. Tokyo Now and Then: An Explorer's Guide. New York and Tokyo: Weatherhill.

15 Japan's Global
Village: A View
from the World
of Leisure

Joy Hendry

Japan has been introducing ideas and artifacts from the outside world for as long
as there are records, and there have been periods of great interest in these alien
curiosities and periods of rejection as rulers of the time sought to consolidate
an internal identity. Japanese people have also traveled abroad to study, to do
business, to carry elements of Japanese culture to that same outside world, and
then quite often to return to live in Japan again. In the last century and a half,
successive Japanese governments have made extraordinary inroads into an international community of capitalist countries, dominated first by major European states,
then by the United States of America, and recently more accepting of other Asian
powers. Some Japanese individuals became involved in the communist world that for
a period represented its opposition, and a not insignificant part of the Japanese
government still represents this alternative view. Japan may legitimately claim a strong
role in the so-called global village the world has become, but how does that village
look from the perspective of ordinary Japanese people living at home? And how
global is the village?

In this chapter I will describe and analyze some examples of an interest in the global
in contemporary Japan, not from the point of view of the professional who travels
abroad, but from the perspective of ordinary people who may have little opportunity
for direct experience. I will take as my focus leisure activities rather than the economic
and political arenas more often chosen when global issues are discussed. I will
consider first the foreign country theme parks that appeared in various parts of
Japan in the late 1980s and 1990s, admire the creativity of the replicas on offer,
and examine local versions of authenticity underpinning them. I will then go on to
examine samples of apparently foreign restaurants that became a positive boom at the
turn of the century, and will look, too, at foreign motifs in the architecture of other
leisure facilities, such as love hotels and pensions. At the same time, I will cast a
backward glance over some longer-standing culinary and architectural innovation.

I will then briefly review some foreign influences in sport and contemporary popular music in Japan, and the knock-on effect on the appearance of young people. I will note, too, some recent trends in tourism and foreign travel, particularly a broadening of interest in locations other than the United States and Europe for cultural content as well as for pure hedonistic frolicking. There would appear to have been a genuine opening up in the world of leisure to an interest in many parts of the world other than the United States, whose influence has dominated Japanese perceptions of "abroad" for several decades. While this may in some ways seem paradoxical, in that globalization is often thought to be synonymous with Americanization, I would like to argue that it could instead represent a genuine degree of sophistication in Japanese attitudes to the world beyond its shores. The choice of restaurants, theme parks, and holiday locations has in recent years been made in a spirit of greatly increased knowledge of the places in question, and thus can be shown to demonstrate a greater awareness of the wider world.

Within Japan, then, are these examples of foreign culture much as they are found elsewhere, in their host countries or in any number of other countries of adoption? And is their adoption thus contributing to the development of a homogenous sort of world where the same kinds of food, play, and other entertainment can be found just about anywhere? I will address this question by examining ethnographic cases for signs of global characteristics, on the one hand, or, on the other, for local interpretations. I will assess the extent to which we find what may be called "glocalization" (global + local) in our Japanese examples, and a thorough Japanization of the international influence. I will also attempt to see how changes in interest in the wider world may have affected, or otherwise, aspects of daily life, internal attitudes to global issues, and sources of Japanese identity.

FOREIGN VILLAGES IN JAPAN

"Foreign villages," or *gaikokumura*, belong to a category of public places that are known in Japanese as *tēma pāku*, derived from the English "theme parks," which attaches to them for a native speaker an immediate source of scorn and triviality. The terms have been used literally for parks with themes, in this case foreign country themes, but for foreign visitors, and those Japanese who have lived or studied abroad, they are associated mainly with the further English connotation of fun and playfulness, of rides and escapism. They are thus often largely ignored by the people who could best judge their accuracy, and in a study I made of the parks (Hendry 2000), I was surprised to find that many of them could boast exceedingly accurate representations of the foreign countries in question. They boast literal copies of some of the "best bits" of foreign countries, but at the same time they are highly creative and offer interesting local versions of authenticity.

The parks comprise a large number of more or less sophisticated reproductions of chosen aspects of different foreign countries – usually individual countries, though some parks combine several, perhaps on a continuing theme. One of the most famous examples is named Huis ten Bosch, after a remarkable reproduction of the palace of the queen of the Netherlands, and it forms part of an enormous complex of Dutch buildings, streets, squares, and canals in northern Kyushu. It was also said by the constructors to be a design for future living and boasts an impressive underground network of services and facilities, including almost total recycling of wastewater on this area of reclaimed land. A tour of these backstage facilities explains that Dutch technology, or "know-how," has been combined with Japanese creativity to make for a completely new concept (cf. Robertson 1997).

Another large and popular one is Parque España, on the Ise peninsula, divided into reproductions of Spanish city, country, and seaside surroundings on regional themes that represent Madrid, Andalucia, Málaga, and Barcelona. A smaller, but remarkably accurately reproduced, park is Glücks Königreich in Hokkaido, where buildings associated with the lives of those famous purveyors of fairytales, the Grimm brothers, lived and worked. Yet another chose a Scandinavian theme that celebrated the life and work of Hans Christian Andersen.

In Hokkaido, too, one of the early parks set out to depict the Canadian houses and scenery that formed the background to the stories of a popular fictitious young lady named Anne of Green Gables. A visitor could immerse themselves for a day in sites of the activities they had read about in the stories and read about her creator's life inside the reproduced house of the title. On the shores of a beautiful lake in Tōhoku, on the other hand, visitors could imagine themselves in the Swiss meadows of another famous young character, Heidi, and gaze from her reproduced bedroom window onto a local mountain said to resemble the Matterhorn. Here they could also take classes in the woodcarving skills that occupied some of her grandfather's time. In the south of the Bōsō peninsula, only a little over two hours from Tokyo, any number of Shakespearean stories are explained and illustrated with life-size alabaster statues set out in a reproduction of New Place, home of the Bard in the latter part of his life.

Some parks provide a veritable journey of learning for the visitor to experience. A large one located in Shikoku offers an Oriental Trip that, evidently following in the boom of European parks, starts from Greece. A boat journey through a small, whitewashed village leads visitors into a giant escalator port that whisks them magically into an unspecified Middle Eastern location complete with golden domes and kasbahs. From here, a few steps lead to a "1st-century Nepalese temple," a remarkable if somewhat sanitized version of the original Swayambunath, located just outside Kathmandu. Other sections featured a 12th/13th-century Thai temple, said to epitomize the Angkor dynasty, a Thai water market, a series of Chinese restaurants, and a small Himalayan mountain to be climbed in order to reach a reproduced Bhutanese building. The last journey features "real Himalayan rocks" on the way, Hindu prayer wheels to spin on arrival, and a series of shrines inside the building where incense could be offered to a variety of Hindu deities. The view is also spectacular.

All of these parks provide gifts and souvenirs from the countries in question, food to buy on the premises or to take home, music, concerts and live shows – in short, plenty of fun, and all on the same general theme. There are often museums displaying objects from the area, craftspeople demonstrating skills that were developed there, and some of the parks even have hotels for an overnight stay. The parks also usually have rides of one sort or another. In reproduced Holland, for example, there are boat trips on the canals and bicycles for hire. In Spain, there is a whole "fiesta" area with large swings and merry-go-rounds set in Gaudí decor. In Glücks Königreich, there are children's rides themed on the Grimms' stories, and Canadian World's theme of wide-open nature was suitably low-tech, with a pony and trap and a hanging-log xylophone. This last park, like some later ones, has not ridden successfully through the economic recession of the 1990s, but for a while it provided work in the wake of the closing of the local mining industry.

Others have emphasized a philanthropic touch, though many of these parks sought to reproduce the extraordinary success of Tokyo Disneyland, which could for a while boast a greater turnover than the two original Disney parks in the US (Awata and Takanarita 1987). It seems to have been interpreted locally as a kind of short, imaginary trip to America, however, so the other parks offered alternative destinations, unfortunately never to do even half as well. There was concern for a while about this importation of American fun to Japan, and Tokyo Disneyland became a second set of Black Ships[1] in the eyes of some commentators, though the year it opened – 1983 – also became known as the First Year of Leisure (*rēja gannen*: Notoji 1990). Aviad Raz's anthropological study of Tokyo Disneyland came down heavily on the side of its clear modification in the Japanese context, however, and he chose his book title, *Riding the Black Ships*, to illustrate his comment that, if Disneyland is a Black Ship, then "the Japanese are riding it" (Raz 1999).

This is but one more example of an interesting aspect of Japan's acquisition of foreign culture in that it combines a high degree of skill in copying both form and technological support, but eventually produces innovative and often more successful versions of the chosen model. Examples abound in the industrial production of motor vehicles, electronic goods, and communications such as mobile telephones. A recent anthropological study by Rupert Cox (2002) on the Zen arts in Japan has examined in detail some of the reasons why copying is not only finely tuned as a mode of learning in Japan but is also still highly evaluated by its practitioners. The Japanese parks illustrate these skills again and again, and though they are all committed totally to the fun of a day out, there is undoubtedly a high level of learning taking place, even if only at a subliminal level. Foreigners may laugh at these reproductions of their homes, and postmodernists may deem them pastiche versions of reality, but some interesting local versions of authenticity may also be discerned. In the Shakespeare Park described above, the birthplace of the playwright has been reproduced, not as it stands 300 years old in Stratford-upon-Avon, but as far as possible as it was in the 16th century when the young William lived in it. It is thus described as a more authentic representation of the time than the "real" one that may be visited in England!

The developers of *gaikokumura* import foreign culture in quite an awesome abundance of architectural splendor and cultural creativity, but they also take over its presentation. In some of the parks, craftspeople from the country came over to construct, or reconstruct their buildings; in others, residents of the particular countries appear in the shows and demonstrate their native skills. They are keenly controlled by Japanese organizers, however, and the Spanish performers complained that they were allowed none of their usual spontaneity, while the Dutch cheesemakers had to throw away the vats of cheese they produced, for their methods did not meet local health regulations. In a Russian park in Niigata Prefecture it was possible, as one might expect, to eat beef Stroganoff, but it was served as a "set," with rice, soup, and pickles, and when I inquired into the nationality of the chef I was told he was Japanese, "for the food needed to be adapted to the Japanese palate."

EATING OUT IN A GLOBALIZED JAPAN

This is a general characteristic of foreign fare in Japanese restaurants – indeed probably of foreign fare in most countries – but some of the most popular dishes in Japan today are adaptations of food brought in from outside. *Karēraisu* ("curry-rice"), for example, is available in many types of general eating places, at a low price, with a standard, predictable flavor. Noodles, on the other hand, originally introduced from China and a staple ingredient of menus advertised as "Chinese cooking," are available in a great variety of different Japanese versions. Some have become regional specialities, so that a visitor to Okinawa is urged not to return without having sampled a local dish of noodles, and another variety has become so characteristically Japanese that it is sold around the world in a well-known chain of Japanese "fast-food" restaurants. Even the strongly flavored Korean *kimchi* has been selling well in Japan recently.

American cooking in the shape of hamburgers and other kinds of "fast food" has been widely accepted in Japan too, although, according to Ohnuki-Tierney's (1997) research, McDonald's is seen as a place for "snacks" rather than for a whole meal. The problem, her informants explain, is that bread is not really a "filling" enough substitute for the usual staple of rice to form a satisfying meal (1997:164). A rival Japanese food chain known as Mos Burger introduced rice burgers, where the outer layers of the sandwich are made from "bun-shaped wedges of pressed rice" (1997:166), and these became popular among university students. In fact, bread is widely consumed in Japan for breakfast, where very thick slices of toast seem to have become acceptable standard fare to be served with coffee in hotels and cafés.

Bread was introduced to Japan in the 16th century by the Portuguese; in fact, it was a kind of soft cake known as *kasutera* (*castella*) now a speciality associated with Nagasaki and other parts of Kyushu where the Portuguese influence was greatest. The use of bread spread widely in the latter part of the 19th century, when varieties of it were introduced again, and European ideas were adopted into home cooking in the early 20th century, along with the idea of a housewife devoting herself lovingly to a new kind of nuclear family (Cwiertka 1998). Cwiertka's examples of dishes that included European touches are heavily adapted to a Japanese palate again, however, and a new aspect of eating foreign fare in the late 20th and early 21st centuries would appear to be a drive for some of the "real thing." The *gaikokumura* very often advertise themselves as places where *genuine* Dutch, Spanish, or German food and drink may be purchased, and Merry White has carried out fieldwork in Italy with Japanese chefs, housewives, and others who wanted to acquire "authentic" Italian culinary skills (see chapter 25 in this volume).

In early 2002 I carried out a small, personal survey in a few eating places that claimed to be French. There has been an influx of new national cuisines on offer in recent years, but the French restaurant has come to hold a cachet all its own in turn-of-the-century Japan. Actually, I tried out my first taste of Japanese–French cuisine in Huis ten Bosch some years earlier in a food hall way ahead of its time that offered individual restaurants from various countries, just as the shopping center outside called itself a World Bazaar. I had chosen the French one partly because it exuded an air of elegant calm, a welcome contrast to the noisy bustle of the theme park outside.

The food I consumed was not memorable. It was tasty enough, if a little sparse, but it was served on the most beautiful plates, with chunky silver cutlery, all laid out exquisitely on white damask tablecloths. The waiters were smartly dressed and extremely polite, and the experience remains in my mind as an oasis of space in a busy day.

Other French restaurants I tried had different atmospheres, as indeed might restaurants in France, but they invariably served the food on delicate plates, each item being arranged attractively to offset its color and texture, although the taste was not universally top quality. In one case, on a weekday night in a provincial city, two Japanese friends and I were the only customers, and our waitress seemed also to be rushing into the kitchen to arrange each pre-prepared dish before she served it to us. In another, in a respectable area of Tokyo, where the menu was written up in particularly impressive French, and the food was more than acceptable, I ventured to ask about the chef, who could be seen in the kitchen beyond the eating area and looked very Japanese. "Had he perhaps trained in France?" I tried. "Oh yes," the waitress replied enthusiastically, "he spent two years in Italy." My face must have registered some surprise at her answer, for she added quickly, "and he went to France too."

My best example, however, was an expensive place where I did not really have the time or resources to sample the food, but the building is a well-known local land-mark. Part of an upmarket Tokyo shopping center that also boasts a (German-style?) "Beer Garden" and a (Prague-inspired?) Marionette Clock that has dolls march out and back on the quarter-hour, it is a reasonably impressive reproduction French *shato* (*château*). Spatially separated quite effectively from the crowded public areas, it also had a smartly uniformed concierge stationed at the entrance, so I decided to ask if this place might actually have a real French chef. He was again most polite and deferential, and he managed to make his answer seem just what one should expect if one were educated to appreciate this kind of establishment, but the substance was as follows: there were two chefs (of course), one of whom was Japanese (of course), and the other half French (at last) and half Thai (oops, silly me!).

Thai food is also popular in Japan at the start of the 21st century, as is a range of other Asian varieties of cooking, and a fashionable restaurant in a smart part of Tokyo that I visited on the same trip offered very acceptable versions of Thai, Indonesian, and Vietnamese dishes.[2] The decor was again designed to recreate a local feel, large potted plants offering a tropical surround, and the overhead fans a cool retreat from the heat outside. In fact, the front of the shop had used a bamboo curtain so effectively to create an attractive seating area that it was only after choosing a spot that we noticed how near we were to the passing Tokyo traffic. This restaurant is one of a series that shares an advertisement offering "Global Dining" with La Bohème Café, which I happened to visit the following day. There too the decor had been carefully designed to reflect the speciality of the title of the place, and a genuine attempt seemed again to have been made to offer a total experience reflecting the part of the world on offer.

These places of "global" entertainment have in fact been very successful in the last few years, belying the evidence elsewhere of a severe economic recession. Their creator, Hasegawa Kozo, has become well known for his rejection of some older ideas about the length of time it takes to train a chef, and the need to charge exorbitant prices for special foods. He has thus managed to create a chain of successful eating places offering a range of international ambiences that are popular with the public and therefore well attended. It might be necessary to wait a few minutes to be seated, but the food appeals to the taste buds of the sophisticated global diner and the prices are suited to the diminishing resources of the local population.

With dining, then, as with the theme parks, concessions may be being made for the local palate – and purse – after all, the aim is as always to please the customer; but there is considerable evidence of an effort to offer a broader global experience. In the case of restaurants, the food will certainly have inspired the venture, but the foreign reproduction is rarely limited to the culinary. French menus are also only the icing on the cake of a genuine attempt to create a little French bistro, a Southeast Asian dining hall, or whatever the model may be. The walls are almost invariably decorated with posters of local scenery, the serving staff dressed in appropriate costumes, and in many cases the whole space has been rebuilt to give the customer the effect of being "wrapped" in a foreign building as they taste the foreign fare (cf. Hendry 1993). The total effect may be far from a perfect reproduction of the country in question, but in copying the model, the creative imagination of Japanese entrepreneurs again offers a new and, almost incidentally, sometimes quite an educational experience for the diners of global Japan.

GLOBALIZED ARCHITECTURE

In fact, there has been much influence from the wider world on the architecture of Japan over the centuries as well, and some of the buildings that are now shown off as quintessentially Japanese: for example, the Tōsho-gu complex at Nikko where the Tokugawa shoguns are memorialized shows a clear resemblance to architecture from mainland Asian countries such as China and Korea. There are even scholars who draw connections between so-called traditional Japanese housing and styles found widely in Polynesia and Micronesia. There is no doubt at all that much contemporary building in Japan has drawn on Euro-American styles and technologies in creating cities that in parts look little different from conurbations in any other part of the world, and Japanese homes have, from the outside at least, a remarkably international range of forms. In this section, however, I would like to examine again some examples of global influence in buildings and interiors that are used largely for leisure and entertainment.[3]

An interesting movement that took place in the 1980s, largely in rural Japan, was the building of a number of new forms of tourist accommodation known as *pensions*. These range in style from a Swiss-type chalet to a minimalist concrete structure with tall roofs somewhat reminiscent of the Shirakawa *gassho-tsukuri* houses of rural Gifu Prefecture. In direct contrast with the *tatami*-matted living of the Japanese style emphasized at the tried-and-tested but somewhat expensive *ryōkan*, and the homely family *minshuku*, however, these places provide beds for sleeping and tables and chairs for eating and drinking. They were modeled on the European idea of a cheap but comfortable form of lodging, providing separate rooms, some small enough for an individual traveler, others large enough to accommodate a whole family together.

Meals are usually offered too, and these are typically basic but nutritious dishes that are relatively inexpensive.

Within those overall constraints, some of the pensions sought to offer special features that aimed to draw visitors back to their particular type of atmosphere – an idea perhaps gleaned from the way that European travelers return again and again to a favorite family *pension* – but it seems that Japanese sojourners prefer novelty, and few seem to have succeeded in that aim. One example that I know was carefully designed and constructed with its creator's own hands, with only minimal professional help, and he studied European-style carpentry in order to make the furniture himself. He went into the business with a couple of friends, one an artist who took over the interior design, the other a chef with a penchant for European cookery. The owner was keen on jazz, and he offered a splendid selection of tapes and CDs for the consumption of the visitors, as well as regular live music on two or three evenings a week. Another, in Okinawa, preferred an American theme, although the owner also read avidly on local history and liked to engage his visitors in discussion. He also liked to play the piano, indulging in a broad selection of theme tunes from old films, especially favorite Westerns, many of which he also held on video to amuse his guests.

In my somewhat limited experience, the people who invested in these forms of holiday accommodation were responding to two relatively new patterns of travel: the first, youthful exploratory travel within Japan, and the second, short breaks for parents and children. However, they also sought a personal style of life that offered a fair amount of control over their surroundings, and at the same time allowed them to share their own interests with their visitors. Typically, the location was an attractive part of the country so that interesting daytime activities were assured, but evenings could be spent eating and drinking with other guests in a congenial environment offering some special feature, often of an international nature.

Another well-known global influence on the architecture of venues of entertainment is to be found in the "love hotels" that are scattered all over the country. Rooms are here available to hire for periods measured in hours as often as whole nights, and the accommodation usually comprises a large comfortable bed, bathing facilities, and a variety of cheerful, often themed, decorative accessories. Some of these buildings are quite extraordinary from the outside, perhaps depicting a huge fairytale castle, a gorgeous luxury palace, or even a giant reproduction of a brightly colored animal. According to a survey carried out by the architect Sarah Chaplin, the interiors of these buildings also often provide a selection of different themed environments, and those from different countries make a popular choice. In the lobby, a chart of the accommodation available includes photographs of the room interiors, lit up if they are free, and demonstrating a range of cultural fare.

Choose Italy, for example, and the room may devote whole walls to photographs of beautiful Italian scenery, perhaps mountains on one side, charming city streets on another, and a set of false windows to complete the impression of really being in an Italian room. The furniture will be of an Italianesque style, ornate high-backed chairs matching the headboard of the neatly prepared bed, and a table with carved legs to hold the bowls of pasta and fresh fruit available from room service. Soft, classical music – perhaps a Rossini opera – will fill the air, and a large television screen may well display costumed performers enacting the scenes, though a range of channels will probably also be available. Some such establishments will take care to provide jasmine, mimosa, or other appropriate perfume to linger in the air as well. Choose another venue for your lovemaking, and the backdrop can quickly become a Brazilian carnival, a Mayan temple, or a scene from the Serengeti game parks of East Africa.

Bathing may have a global theme as well, and a nine-story bathhouse in Osaka offers a whole bevy of bathing environments, ancient and modern. One can happily pass hours moving from the adorned tubs of ancient Greece and Rome through to the minimalist facilities and somewhat extreme temperatures of contemporary Finland, pausing to rest and dip beside an azure Aegean, or a slightly spartan German pool, and take a coffee on a Parisian boulevard. All this was on the "European floor," available on the day of my visit for female customers, but on another level, confined that day to the men, an "Asian section" offered baths in the style of China, Islam, India, and Persia and several varieties of Japanese ones. On other levels there were massage parlors, saunas with a range of herbal fragrances, different kinds of bubbling tubs, a large pool for swimming, rest areas with television, and restaurants serving abundant meals and snacks.

MUSIC AND SPORT IN THE GLOBAL VILLAGE

Areas of popular culture that seem best to cross national boundaries, such as sport and music, have also been examined by anthropologists of Japan; in this volume they are reported on by Elise Edwards and Shuhei Hosokawa, respectively (see chapters 3 and 19). However, one of the issues they address is precisely that of the extent to which the activities are localized. An early internal example of the consideration of the effects of the import of a sporting activity is a study which is well known in Japan by the anthropologist Nagashima Nobuhiro (1988) on the anthropology of horse-racing. In this case, the originally aristocratic associations of the British sport when first introduced in the 19th century were soon marred by prior negative Japanese attitudes to gambling. On the other hand, according to Yamaguchi Masao (1998:19), the success abroad of sumo wrestling, which increased its status and popularity in Japan, depended on different kinds of appeal in different foreign locations. In Spain, he reports, it was enjoyed as a fighting sport, whereas in Britain it was more the ceremonial and stylized aspects that people liked.

Japan's contribution to the global in terms of what is known as "classical music" is well known, and the names of Japanese composers, musicians, and dancers may be found on the programs of major concerts around the world. Even in Britain, one of the newest rising stars in the national ballet company is Japanese, one of the most recorded pianists is Japanese, and a young and successful Japanese violinist represents a second generation of Japanese musicianship in Europe as his family took him to Vienna for his early education. Within Japan, too, concerts of high-quality classical music may be heard regularly, and some of the productions are second to none. On New Year's Day, the Viennese Strauss concert was for many years apparently attended by more Japanese than any other nationality, and it is broadcast throughout the nation on Japanese television. Again, the essentially Japanese form of leisure known as *karaoke* has been taken up avidly around the world, very often with its own local manifestations, in Britain, for example, providing the backing for groups singing together, an activity long associated with public houses, particularly in the north (Kelly 1998; Mitsui and Hosokawa 1998).

Popular music derived from the rest of the world may also be found in Japan, but an interesting anthropological study by Ian Condry (2000, 2001) identified again this element of Japanese adaptation in his examination of Japanese versions of the music of black American ghettos. Hip-hop music provides the focus for his research, and his argument reiterates the idea that copying an outside art form by no means precludes a subsequent creativity, not only in the music, but also in the dance and the culture that go with them. This is masked somewhat by the clothes and even dreadlocks chosen by participants, but young people in turn-of-the-century Japan sport a huge variety of hairstyles and colors, and their apparel also expresses an apparently borderless range of inspiration and influence.

Soccer hit Japan as a sport a couple of decades ago, and, as in the case of baseball, it has been possible to identify interesting local differences. An article by Italian anthropologist Simone Dalla Chiesa (2002) titled "When the Goal Is Not a Goal" is a particularly poignant example of the almost diametrically opposed attitudes to the same game of players brought up in different cultural traditions. It is precisely in the area of soccer, however, that some of the best examples of a new and more sophisticated ability to make distinctions has been manifest amongst ordinary Japanese supporters. Over the period of increasing interest in the game, fans have moved their attention from different varieties of European soccer, including the expensive problems associated with hiring a famous British practitioner and a wider interest in other aspects of Spanish culture, to the more successful recent admiration of the exciting Latin American version. In 2002 the audiences at the World Cup championship expressed this new awareness of global distinctions while cheering on the champions, who in this case happened to be Brazil (see chapter 18 in this volume).

A Mature Global Village?

Views of the outside world have changed through time, as have views of the place of Japan within that world, and indeed the place of different peoples within Japan. In the glare of world attention that accompanied its extraordinary economic achievement, Japanese people sought to understand themselves as the "uniquely" successful Asian nation, and an emphasis was placed on the culture and history of a people who seemed quite homogeneous relative to the melting-pot that their biggest outside neighbor claimed to be. Since the so-called "lost years" of the 1990s economic recession, Japan has actually found a place within the wider group of Asian neighbors that have also come to succeed in that world of Western capitalism, and young people, in particular, are traveling in the area. At the same time, ordinary people living in Japan have had to recognize and come to terms with an increasingly diverse population of migrant workers, not only from other parts of Asia, but from more distant countries as well.

It seems that some mutually beneficial tourism in the last few years may have begun to soften the antagonism directed toward Japan and the Japanese by Asian and Pacific peoples, absorbed, often brutally, into the Japanese empire. And there has been a positive "boom" of interest in "Asian" goods from a variety of neighboring locations. An interest in local cultural differences would also seem to have reawakened an interest in Japan's internal diversity, and parks representing cultural features of the Ainu and the Okinawans have also enjoyed some success (see chapters 6 and 7 in this volume). In 1910, at the Great Britain–Japan Exhibition, the Ainu people were put on display by Japan, but the international mood of the time was to discourage indigenous diversity, and like the Gaelic people of the Scottish islands and Native Americans, the Ainu were expected to abandon their cultural roots and integrate with wider Japan. In even earlier centuries, when Chinese dynasties had been a predominant influence for Japan, China's view of itself as the Middle Kingdom surrounded by colorful lesser peoples who paid tribute to the center was also adopted in Japan.

Japan now leads the world in significant ways, and its contribution to the global village of fun and leisure was until recently almost unrivaled. I have even found a powerful Sony speaker booming out contemporary music in the middle of the Kizelkum desert, and this and other Japanese names dominate the electronic sections of music stores around the world, as do the advances in mobile telephone technology. Foreign restaurants are of course found in cities around the world, and architecture is often quite international, but I contend that, in the case of parks that offer the simulated experience of visiting a foreign country for a day, Japan again has a definite edge. There are some huge ones in China, for example at Shenzhen, but they combine many different influences in the same park, and have nowhere near the level of sophistication found in the Japanese parks. Visitors claim to go to the parks for fun, and that, it seems, is what they find there – just as if they were taking a mini-foreign holiday; but foreign holidays can also broaden horizons and encourage an understanding of other peoples and their ways.

At the start of the 20th century, the view many Japanese seem to have had of the "outside" world would seem to have been rather a mature one, based on a series of different perspectives that can now be represented without rancor in parks of recreation. The peoples on display are essentially on an equal footing with the visitors, and the range of cultural variety available to the visitors is quite impressive. When Japanese people travel abroad these days, they are, in my view, much better informed about the places they are going to than are some of their counterparts from many other technologically highly developed countries, and they display a willingness to learn and understand that only a generation ago was rare. At the same time, ordinary people in Japan maintain their own local versions of the culture they have taken for their own use, and they celebrate the diversity with little danger of being overwhelmed by outside influences. If powerful people in the political and economic spheres could learn from their playful counterparts, and exercise confidence in the broad view of the world they seem to have adopted, they might have an even greater contribution to make to the future of the presently somewhat threatened global village.

ACKNOWLEDGMENTS

The material for this chapter has been gathered over several years' work in Japan, and I am indebted, as always, to the many kind people who gave up time to talk to me. Specifically for this project I would like to thank Hirose Yoko for introducing me to "global dining" and for hospitality during the investigation of the same, Noda Hiroyuki for introducing me to the world of "pensions," Laura Inoue for taking me to the one I describe in Okinawa, my son James for involving me directly at an early stage of the burgeoning Japanese interest in soccer, and Jennifer Robertson for inviting me to write about all these fun activities. The research on which much of the chapter is based was made possible during a trip to Japan funded by the Japan Foundation Endowment Committee (UK).

NOTES

1   Editor's note: "Black Ships" (*kurofune*) refers to the fleet of Commodore Matthew Perry, who sailed into Uraga harbor on July 8, 1853 with a message from President Fillmore to the shogun Ieyoshi which precipitated the opening to Americans of the ports of Shimoda and Hakodate. "Black ships" today is a metaphor for "forced Americanization" (see Raz 1999).
2   Editor's note: Since at least the mid-1980s, non-(mainstream) Japanese Asian cuisine – and particularly the cuisine of areas formerly part of the Japanese empire, and including Okinawan and Ainu dishes – is referred to and advertised as "ethnic" (*esunikku*) food. In this case, "ethnic" would seem to be a label redolent of the us-versus-them mentality camouflaged by the pan-Asianism of the Japanese state's Great East Asia Co-Prosperity Sphere rhetoric.
3   See Cybriwsky (chapter 14) in this volume.

REFERENCES

Atkins, A. Taylor. 2002. Blue Nippon: Authenticating Jazz in Japan. Durham, NC, and London: Duke University Press.

Awata, F., and T. Takanarita. 1987. Dizuniirando no keizaigaku (The Economics of Disneyland). Tokyo: Asahi Bunko.

Condry, Ian. 2000. The Social Production of Difference: Imitation and Authenticity in Japanese Rap Music. *In* Transactions, Transgressions, Transformations: American Culture in Western Europe and Japan. Uta Poiger and Heide Fehrenbach, eds. pp. 166–184. Oxford and New York: Berghahn Books.

——2001. Japanese Hip-Hop and the Globalization of Popular Culture. *In* Urban Life: Readings in the Anthropology of the City. George Gmelch and Walter Zenner, eds. pp. 357–387. Prospect Heights, IL: Waveland Press.

Cox, Rupert. 2002. The Zen Arts. London: RoutledgeCurzon.

Cwiertka, Katarzyna. 1998. How Cooking Became a Hobby: Changes in Attitude toward Cooking in Early Twentieth-Century Japan. *In* The Culture of Japan as Seen through its Leisure. Sepp Linhart and Sabine Frühstück, eds. pp. 41–58. New York: State University of New York Press.

Dalla Chiesa, Simone. 2002. When the Goal Is Not a Goal: Japanese School Football Players Working Hard at their Game. *In* Japan at Play: The Ludic and the Logic of Power. Joy Hendry and Massimo Raveri, eds. pp.186–198. London: Routledge.

Hendry, Joy. 1993. Wrapping Culture: Politeness, Presentation, and Power in Japan and Other Societies. Oxford: Clarendon Press.

——2000. The Orient Strikes Back: A Global View of Cultural Display. Oxford: Berg.

Horne, John, and Wolfram Manzenreiter, eds. 2002. Japan, Korea and the 2002 World Cup. London: Routledge.

Itō, Masami. 1994. Hito ga atsumaru tēma pāku no himitsu (The Secret of Theme Parks where People Gather). Tokyo: Nihon Keizai Shinbunsha.

Ivy, Marilyn. 1995. Discourses of the Vanishing: Modernity, Phantasm, Japan. Chicago: Chicago University Press.

Kelly, William H. 1998. The Adaptability of Karaoke in the United Kingdom. *In* Karaoke around the World. Mitsui Tōru and Shūhei Hosokawa, eds. London: Routledge.

Martinez, D. P. 1998. The Worlds of Japanese Popular Culture: Gender, Shifting Boundaries and Global Cultures. Cambridge: Cambridge University Press.

Mitsui, Tōru, and Shūhei Hosokawa, eds. 1998. Karaoke around the World. London: Routledge.

Nagashima, Nobuhiro. 1988. Keiba no jinruigaku (The Anthropology of Horse Racing). Tokyo: Iwanami Shōten.

—— 1998. Gambling and Changing Japanese Attitudes Toward it. *In* The Culture of Japan as Seen through its Leisure. Sepp Linhart and Sabine Frühstück, eds. pp. 345–358. New York: State University of New York Press.

Notoji, Masako. 1990. Dizuniirando to iu seichi (The Sacred Place Called Disneyland). Tokyo: Iwanami Shinsho.

Ohnuki-Tierney, Emiko. 1997. McDonald's in Japan: Changing Manners and Etiquette. *In* Golden Arches East: McDonald's in East Asia. James L. Watson, ed. Stanford, CA: Stanford University Press.

Raz, Aviad. 1999. Riding the Black Ships: Japan and Tokyo Disneyland. Cambridge, MA and London: Harvard University Press.

Robertson, Jennifer. 1997. Empire of Nostalgia: Rethinking "Internationalization" in Japan Today. Theory, Culture & Society 14(4):97–122.

Tsu, Timothy. 1999. From Ethnic Group to "Gourmet Republic": The Changing Image of Kobe's Chinatown in Modern Japan. Japanese Studies 19(1):17–32.

Yamaguchi, Masao. 1998. Sumo in the Popular Culture of Contemporary Japan. *In* The Worlds of Japanese Popular Culture: Gender, Shifting Boundaries and Global Cultures. D. P. Martinez, ed. pp. 19–29. Cambridge: Cambridge University Press.

PART IV

Socialization, Assimilation, and Identification

CHAPTER 16 Formal Caring Alternatives: Kindergartens and Day-Care Centers

Eyal Ben-Ari

INTRODUCTION

In this chapter I chart the main characteristics of Japan's preschool systems and inquire about changes that they are undergoing. Enrolling over 95 percent of Japanese children before they enter the first grade (a rate that far surpasses that of the United States or Britain), these institutions are central in preparing children for the educational system and (later) for participation in the labor force. After introducing the main contours of the preschool systems, I sketch out three issues that are crucial to their dynamics: the cultural assumptions underlying care and education provided for children, the diversity and homogeneity that mark early childhood institutions, and the social and cultural reproduction and innovation that characterize them.

CARING ALTERNATIVES: THE TWO SYSTEMS

Historically, the first preschools were established by American missionaries and by Japanese educators who had been on study tours in Europe and the United States at the end of the 1800s (Wollons 2000). The real enlargement of the system, however, came after World War II and, since the end of the 1960s, basically any parent who wants to send their children to such an institution can do so (Hendry 1986:62). In Japan, institutions of early childhood education are differentiated into *yōchien* (kindergartens) that are under the control of the Ministry of Education, Culture, Sports, Science, and Technology (Monbukagakusho), and *hoikuen* (day-care centers) that are the responsibility of the Ministry of Health, Labor, and Welfare (Kōseirōdōshō). Except for a handful of institutions attached to prestigious universities, preschools are not academically oriented. Both *yōchien* and *hoikuen* are structured to develop the social skills of the children while teaching the importance of group identity and group skills. The aim is usually defined as developing the minds and health of children and introducing them to group life in preparation for primary school (Hendry 1986:61). For many children the move is from the highly dependent atmosphere and lavish attention bestowed on them at home to membership in the rather large preschool groupings (sometimes reaching 40 children per class) (Ben-Ari 1997b). As Hendry (1986:64) notes, the aim is not to turn the children into little robots but rather to impress on them the idea that the world is full of people like them with their own needs and desires.

The two types of institution are similar with respect to physical facilities, curricula, teaching styles, and classroom activities. However, they do differ in some major respects. Kindergartens are usually open half-days (about four or five hours) with a minimum of 39 school weeks per year. They cater for children aged 3, 4, and 5. In 2002 nearly 1.8 million children attended about 14,000 institutions, with private ones comprising 58 per cent of the total (Ministry of Education, Culture, Sports, Science, and Technology 2002). The number of children attending kindergartens has steadily fallen since the peak of about 2 million children reached during the mid-1990s. Whether private or government-run, most institutions are subsidized by the government. In contrast to stereotypical images of Japanese kindergartens, the curriculum is primarily nonacademic, and although constructed by each individual institution, it must meet standards dictated by the national Ministry (Frasz and Kato 2002). Over the years the ministry has disseminated various guidelines to kindergartens. The latest (issued at the beginning of the 1990s) emphasizes developing and expressing personal thoughts and feelings as part of a more individualistic accent (Holloway 2000:175; Morigami 1999), the encouragement of independent activities within a group structure, the attainment of education mainly by instruction through play, and providing guidance in accordance with the characteristics of each individual child (Frasz and Kato 2002).

In the past two decades, however, the type of institution that has shown the greatest rate of growth has been the day-care center (Hoiku Hakusho 2000). In the first years after the war most care-taking institutions in the country were operated privately, very often as what were called "baby hotels." Throughout the 1960s and 1970s considerable attention – on the part of the media, politicians, and welfare officials – was directed at the conditions found in these "baby hotels" and at their unregulated and profit-seeking babysitting facilities. It was during these two decades that the number of government-run or government-regulated day-care centers grew considerably. Alongside these institutions are found some special day-care programs attached to large organizations such as hospitals or department stores. Today there are over 22,000 public or private (but publicly recognized) day-care centers that cater to over 2 million children (Kōseisho 2002). Day-care centers cater to children of working mothers between the ages of a few months and 6 years (in reality most of the children attend only after the age of 2) and normally operate for a whole day (often from 7 in the morning until 6 at night – to accommodate the various schedules of employed mothers) (Tobin et al. 1989). The fact that children attend day-care centers for whole days involves a much more complex set of tasks which are to be provided for: not only educational activities and play, but also such things as eating, sleeping, dressing, and the longer hours over which the children must be monitored.

The social processes leading to the formation and current maintenance of day-care centers in Japan are related to older government policies of social welfare (Uno 1999) and (as in other countries [O'Connor 1992]) to the movement of women into and out of the labor market. Japan has always had a population of mothers working outside the home, but it was only in the late 1950s that it saw a significant growth in their employment. The reasons for these trends are varied and include the development of a full-employment economy in which labor is short; the increased impact of higher education; a decrease in the size of families and improvement in home facilities which have partly freed women from housework; the decline of housework as a meaningful activity; and the need, in many families, for women to supplement household incomes. Women now represent over 40 percent of the Japanese workforce, and almost half of all females beyond the age of 15 are working either as salaried employees or as family workers (Carney and O'Kelly 1987:127–128). As more and more women have entered the labor force they have encountered difficulties in providing care for their children. The nuclearization of the family, coupled with high rates of mobility, have led to a situation in which fewer and fewer households have grandparents to fulfill the traditional role of caring for preschoolers. Moreover, whereas in the United States a large part of care-taking is undertaken by babysitters, such an alternative is still very rare in Japan (Boocock 1989:57). In these circumstances, Japanese working mothers have increasingly come to depend on the support of day-care centers.

The vast majority of teachers at both kinds of institutions – kindergartens and day-care centers – are graduates of at least two years of junior college (or its equivalent), and many hold first degrees from four-year universities. Comparatively speaking, this situation implies that on the whole the educational level of teaching staff at Japanese preschools is one of the world's highest. The young age of the majority of teachers serves to keep Japanese preschools affordable (Ben-Ari 1997a; Tobin et.al. 1989:216–217). As salaries in preschools (like salaries in most Japanese organizations) are linked to years of service, the short careers of most teachers (three to six years) keep down personnel costs, which are the biggest outlay in most preschool budgets. Staffing patterns thus reflect notions of sex and gender differences: this is a relatively low-paid job which is often seen – by men and women – as suitable to the "natural" inclinations of women. Where one does find men in the preschool systems, they are usually heads of institutions: either leaders of religious bodies to which the preschools are attached (overwhelmingly Buddhist or Christian) or bureaucrats assigned to government sections dealing with childcare.

ASSUMPTIONS AND PRACTICES

Boocock (1978:71) notes that "[how] a society treats its children depends upon its views of what children are like, as well as upon what is perceived as necessary for the smooth functioning of the society itself." Two basic premises shape the official state view of institutional care in Japan: one about the "natural" needs of children, and the other about the proper loci for their fulfillment. According to this perspective, the child's natural place until the age of 3 or 4 is in the home with its mother. Indeed, it is only in close physical contact with the mother and the large amounts of affection that she bestows that the child can develop normally (Ben-Ari 1987:204–205). Espoused by teachers, educational specialists, and governmental officials, this idea is the one that is most widely accepted among the urban middle class of today's Japan. The view is, in turn, related to the broader social definitions of the role of married women in Japanese culture and the juxtaposition of three principles which bear upon how mothering and childcare are perceived: first, that the woman's natural place is in the home; second, that the mother/wife role is primary and that all other activities be subordinated to it; and third, that ideally a child should be in its own home surrounded by her or his family and in close proximity to the mother (Fujita 1989:77; Hendry 1984:106). Indeed, so crucial are these conditions for "natural" development, it is held, that their lack is seen to eventuate in pathologies like juvenile delinquency later on in life. The continued acceptance of this view is attested to in a survey carried out by the Ministry of Health and Welfare in 1991:

> Among the female respondents, 52% thought that women should leave their jobs after giving birth and resume work when the children were older, an increase of 10 percentage points over the 1982 survey. Only 18% felt that women should continue working even after they gave birth, a slight rise of 3 points. . . . The results indicate that many women continue to hold a traditional image of the family, one that centers on children. (Embassy of Japan 1992)

It is on the basis of these maxims that government policies for institutional childcare rest. Thus the governing idea is that it is only once the children are safely dependent on mothers that preschools should grant them something that they cannot find at home. It is in this light that the heavy stress on group life in Japanese preschools should be seen. The experience in kindergartens is aimed at providing children with familiarity with the skills needed to function in the wider social world beyond the family. In day-care centers the issue is more complex. Here the idea is that day-care centers develop certain skills and characteristics that are related to the independent functioning of children (dressing, eating, or talking, for example), as well as developing certain sentiments of belonging and social relations.

It is this perspective, moreover, that governs views of day-care centers. The idea here is that it is only when there is no alternative that the child should be allowed to attend a day-care center. In other words, it is only when there are no other options that the state must take over for the mother and the family. A number of administrative arrangements underscore these notions. One has to do with the ways in which the children are classified bureaucratically. Children attending day-care facilities are not categorized along with the children who attend the "normal" kindergartens but are consistently catalogued – along with orphans and the physically and mentally handicapped – within the framework of the Ministry of Health, Labor, and Welfare (Kōseisho 2002). The assumption here is that day-care centers are institutions that cater for neglected or deprived children. Thus, officially, day-care centers are not enabling institutions in the sense of enabling women to go out to work to fulfill themselves as a matter of course, but rather compensatory facilities turned to only as a matter of last resort. Next, consider the fees for centers that are based on ability to pay. For married women whose husbands provide "adequate" incomes, the fees are usually the major proportion of any income they can earn. The assumptions behind this arrangement are that a mother's place is in the home, and that only economic necessity justifies sending a child to a center. In order to place children in day-care centers, parents must provide proof such as letters from employers or the tax office that the mother is working or ill, or that there are no grandparents at home who can act as care-takers.

These circumstances form the background for the perceived differences between kindergartens and day-care centers. Tobin and his associates (1989:45) discuss the unspoken yet clear class and status distinctions between these two types of institutions. These distinctions are based on the different groups they were historically established to serve: upper- and middle-class children and the children of poor people. Today, however, "the class distinction is...muddled by growing presence of children of dual-career, high-status professional parents (such as physicians) in *hoikuen*" (Tobin et al. 1989:47). My observations are close to Fujita's (1989:77) who notes that *hoikuen* are less prestigious than *yōchien* and some people still express strong reservations about sending children to day-care. Nevertheless, as we shall presently see, the image of day-care centers is fast changing and they have come to provide what is considered a legitimate and worthy caring alternative for increasing numbers of families.

TEACHING AND CARE-TAKING ROLES

It is against this background that the teaching and care-taking roles may be understood. In a word, nursery teachers are seen by themselves and by others not in a custodial role but as comprising two other interrelated roles. Up until about the age of 3 they are (in a sense) mother substitutes, or women acting in place of the children's mothers. Substitution is predicated on somehow overcoming the artificial separation between mothers and their children. That this is a "substitutional" rather than a "custodial" emphasis is illustrated through a stress – not taken for granted in other care-taking systems such as those in America or Israel – on providing all-round care. This means that care in Japanese day-care centers involves a constant accent on the moral, educational, and emotional dimensions not only of "hard" curricula, but also of eating, going to the bathroom, keeping clean, and sleeping. These notions are not unlike the ones held by elementary school teachers in Japan, who emphasize educating "whole-persons." The idea is not one of promoting only cognitive skills in a child's development but of having a strong future orientation with stress on shaping the whole child. The stress on substitution is perhaps even clearer in the "mother-like" prescriptions that are given to teachers. The following passage is taken from a guide to nursing infants:

> The best thing for the development of emotion at the infant stage is close skin contact with the warm-hearted mother or substitute....One teacher should take care of one infant as long as possible, and try to have body contact such as hugging. Not only teachers but also parents should show affection directly. (Early Childhood Education Association 1979:57)

To reiterate, because of assumptions about the "proper" place of children at home, caretakers see themselves (and are often seen by others) as substituting for the mothers in the context of *hoikuen*.

But from the time the children are 3 a new set of role components emerges. From this age, teachers in day-care centers begin to systematically disengage themselves from the children and to increasingly take on a role of educators. As in kindergartens, the primary aim of this separation is to foster independence in the children and to get them used to group life. Accordingly, from this stage and onwards much effort is devoted to peer interaction and cooperation within the larger group, without which parents and teachers feel that children would become selfish and over-indulged. In putting the goals of group life into effect, institutions of early childhood education are seen as organizations that grant children something that is missing at home. Most parents, educators, and government representatives in contemporary Japan believe that to cultivate a "true" Japanese character is only possible if, in addition to the family, children undergo experiences within the framework of formal institutions of education: preschools and schools (Tobin et. al. 1989:58). To develop only within the confines of the nuclear family involves the danger of becoming selfish. More generally, this view is related to the attempt at granting children institutional versions of the "traditional" extended family, or the village or neighborhood communities of yesteryear.

These various educational emphases, however, are actualized in the context of organizations that are predicated on intervention in children's lives. In kindergartens, for example, the official encroachment upon the lives of children is effected through a plethora of mechanisms such as talks and lectures to parents, home visits, phone calls or personal meetings with teachers, personal message books or class letters sent home, the use of message boards at preschools, and the participation of parents in PTAs, parents' days, and various parties and ceremonies. In day-care centers this intervention is taken even further: first, direct regulation is extended and carried out in relation to the lives of children who are below the age of 3 or 4; second, it takes place over longer hours, and in regard to many of the activities not covered by regular half-day kindergartens (sleeping, eating, toilet training); third, it is taken within the framework of organizations run or inspected by a welfare bureaucracy and not by the local Board of Education. Indeed, Boocock suggests that though no systematic empirical comparisons have been carried out, there are indications that control at *hoikuen* is greater than at *yōchien* (1989:46). Moreover, in Japan certain cultural concepts tend both to legitimate and to amplify a stress on official involvement in children's lives. As the mainstream view would have it, teachers – and still to a great, if contested, measure bureaucrats – are representatives of the Japanese state. As such, they possess certain duties and prerogatives to intervene in and control the private sphere in the name of furthering communal and societal aims. As Dore eloquently puts it, "No Confucian has recognized the validity of the distinction between public and private morality. No homes are castles in the sense that one can be allowed to do what one likes within them. All moral conduct is of concern to society" (1978:193).

These ideas are actualized in institutions of early childhood education in terms of teachers functioning as overseers of mothers and children for the children's sake. The assumption of the staff at many facilities is that it is their social obligation to intervene in families on behalf of the children if they are neglected and to bestow something on them in day-care centers that will compensate for what is missing at home. Moreover, the general idea is that it is the role of the teachers to control mothers and the way in which they fulfill their motherly roles (Allison 1991). A number of observers have noted that day-care teachers continually try to get mothers to fulfill their role (Fujita 1989:78; Sano 1989:128).

DIVERSITY, HOMOGENEITY, AND COMPETITION

There are certainly some differences between preschools in Japan. The main axes of differentiation are class, government-run versus privately run institutions, and religious affiliation. While there is a general dearth of studies about the class divide, there do appear to be dissimilarities between preschools serving wealthier children and those serving poorer – working-class – children. These differences are expressed in such phenomena as class size, space for play, and materials used by the children (Holloway 2000:25). On the other hand, however, because some of the historically more progressive local governments (such as Kyoto's) have established preschools in poorer areas, several institutions in the poorer areas of the country actually have quite good conditions that are high by national standards. In terms of the government/private divide, private institutions tend, on the whole, to be bigger than government-run ones. For example, private kindergartens often have classes for 3-year-old children as well as for the top two years. The reasons for this situation lie in the needs of private preschools to assure high enrollment in order to survive. Conversely, because many government-run institutions are somewhat more protected from market pressures they can have smaller classes (for instance, in very rural areas or for special groups, like the outcaste Burakumin), which means that more attention can be devoted to children as individuals. Many preschools in Japan are affiliated to religious institutions such as Christian churches or Buddhist temples – a very small number are associated with Shinto shrines. Many parents find these institutions (and especially the Christian ones) attractive because they have a good reputation for reliable and conscientious education and care (Ishigaki 1987:161). The overwhelming majority of parents, however, are not themselves – and do not want their children to become – Christians.

The biggest factor in creating diversity, however, is that demographic trends of shrinking numbers of children have led to a situation in which there is heightened competition between preschools. While this competition was at first limited to kindergartens, today many day-care centers also compete for dwindling numbers of children. Much of this competition is centered on attracting children to institutions on the basis of their distinctive characteristics. Thus one finds centers offering such activities as English conversation, music education, sports and swimming, drawing and painting, "free play," or other mixed-age-group education. But as Tobin and his associates (1989:209) observe, with the falling birth rate "some Japanese preschools will have to close, and a gradual shift in women's life-styles from full-time mothering toward a more job- or career-centered orientation seems to favor survival of *hoikuen* over *yōchien* in the long run."

Indeed, according to Uno, "[d]espite a conventional wisdom that extols female domesticity, especially motherhood, and expresses misgivings about women's permanent, full time wage work, day-care continues to thrive in post-war Japan" (1999:155). One unintended consequence of setting up good day-care facilities to compensate for the "deficiencies" of mothers has been to turn them into very attractive institutions. It may be ironic that as teachers provide excellent care in the guise of maintaining conservative assumptions, they have in effect changed the very image of day-care centers. In this way they have made these establishments a more acceptable alternative for working mothers, those very mothers who – according to such assumptions – cannot fulfill a mother's role.

Yet despite the factors generating diversity, when placed in a comparative perspective, it seems that preschool education in contemporary Japan still tends to be rather uniform in terms of caring standards, the level and content of teacher training, and a large variety of administrative arrangements. The primary reason for the high level of standardization of preschool practices is the role of government. In this respect Japan is similar to France and Sweden in that centralized bureaucracies regulate preschools. The Japanese situation contrasts with the case of Germany or England and the United States, where local municipalities and churches run institutions of early childhood education and where a greater variety is to be found. Thus, despite the celebration of diversity in Japanese preschools propagated by some American scholars (e.g., Holloway 2000), when placed in a comparative perspective, the Japanese case shows how centralized preschool systems and their attendant mechanisms of bureaucratic control, and the more centralized systems through which caretakers are trained, lead to a rather uniform system of childcare.

In this respect, preschools figure in a much wider (and more pervasive) set of procedures that the Japanese state (like any state) has undertaken in the name of enhancing unity, stability, and economic progress (Lock 1993:43). From the point of view of the state, this set of procedures is undertaken so that individuals (and families) are "normalized." Practices carried out in preschools are related to the preoccupation of the state (central, prefectural, and local government bureaucracies and teacher-training schools) with the kind of education and care given to children. The discipline of children, the control of teachers, and the national standardization of preschool education all form part of the means by which the state works toward the coordinated and efficient use of people and resources. A penetration into individuals' lives (parents, children, and teachers) is done in terms of national aims.

But what are these national aims? If we understand that a primary prerequisite for any social system is the replacement of its members then we must relate two sets of demographic and educational processes:

> The first step is the production of the right quantity and desired quality of children. This process is usually referred to in theory as "patterns of fertility", and in practice as "family planning" or "fertility policy." ... The second step is the attempt to transform the children into desirable future citizens. (Shamgar-Handelman 1993:7)

In this approach, the state's regulation of childhood is seen as one step – along with the administration of demographics – enabling the state to assure the best social replacements. The implication of this approach for the study of preschools is that the focus should not be limited to either an examination of how children "become Japanese" or how cultural models of "good children" are employed in preschools.

Lea Shamgar-Handelman's analysis of childhood in Israel aptly describes the case in Japan. Only by realizing that these two steps, becoming Japanese and becoming good children, "are part of the same process can the full meaning of patterns of state supervision and control of the process of physical and social replacement be comprehended" (Shamgar-Handelman 1993:8). Recognizing this point necessitates relating biomedicine and fertility policy in Japan to aspects of its early childhood education.

The decision on the part of almost all Japanese families to limit family size is connected directly to the fertility policy of the government (Coleman 1983) and indirectly to enveloping policies regarding the price of homes and education, and the hazards of divorce. These specific and background conditions influence the perceptions of families of what is affordable and acceptable and therefore relevant to the number and spacing of children. In Japan abortion is legalized and (comparatively speaking) widely used. But from the state's point of view, administrative procedures related to abortion are aimed at culling those cases where handicapped children may be born. While no explicit fertility policy has been explicated in Japan since the late 1950s, family-planning clinics have been receiving increased government funding since 1977. A stated objective of these clinics is to provide genetic counseling and screening devices, but in reality genetic screening is their primary function (Norgren 2001).

At first glance, the similarity between preschools and institutions dealing with fertility seems striking. The instruments available to the state are regulations and laws, various types of fiscal policies, and the provision of services. In both areas planning for the future is carried out by controlling the institutional arrangements of large-scale systems: abortion clinics, hospitals, and medical associations on the one hand, and kindergartens, day-care centers, and teacher-training colleges on the other. In both areas a major part of state effort is expended to assure the quality of social replacements. And in both cases a central underlying interest is keeping down the future social costs of treating members who are not defined as "normal" (whether they be handicapped individuals or social deviants). But such similarities should not be taken too far, for both empirical and theoretical reasons. Empirically, the realm of early childhood education seems to be much more "normalized." Compared with the existence and accessibility of alternative medical systems (Lock 1980; Ohnuki-Tierney 1984), Japanese individuals have far fewer real options in regard to preschools. Moreover, the policies directly regulating early childhood education are much more explicit and pervasive than those administering fertility policy (Goodman 2000).

The regulation of preschools, however, is not only the outcome of mechanisms internal to Japan but also the result of what has been termed the "globalization of childhood" (Rogers and Rogers 1992; Wollons 2000). Historically speaking, at the level of assumptions regarding "normal" childhood and the expectations of preschools, the basic similarity between Japan and other industrial societies is striking. These commonalities are related to the global flow of ideas and the creation of a widespread global consensus about childhood and its social and organizational prerequisites. The governing conception which originated in Europe and North America, and which is now accepted around the world, justifies schooling, the differentiated culture of childhood, and the distinct patterns of institutional treatment given to children on the basis of an assumption that the state has the authority to create and hasten modern technical development through the creation of more productive individuals (Boli-Bennett and Meyer 1978:799). Contemporary institutional rules of childhood "assume a theory of socialization and of childhood as a period in which biological and social forces interact to generate the competent and effective person" (Boli-Bennett and Meyer 1978:799). Against this background, it may be clear that many of the assumptions which we tend to attribute to the Japanese state are historically situated premises that to a large degree originated in European countries and the United States.

CONCLUSION: PRESCHOOLS, REPRODUCTION, AND INNOVATION

Among the most prominent stereotypes of Japan found in many Euro-American countries is that of robotic and highly disciplined preschoolers. At first blush, this image may have some substance to it. As Holloway (2000:2) suggests, because the idea of preschool is to "enable young children to obtain social and intellectual skills needed to function successfully in Japanese society. . . it serves a conservative function – both preserving and transmitting Japanese values to the younger generation." This kind of stress has marked almost all studies of Japanese preschools that portray them as social mechanisms that prepare youngsters for an assortment of future roles such as school pupils or company employees. In reality, however, most preschools in Japan are far from static: "rather, each preschool is a vibrant, dynamic system whose participants engage in an ongoing, active process of perceiving, interpreting, and synthesizing beliefs and practices available in their cultural milieu" (Holloway 2000:2).

   This vibrancy and liveliness often ends up in noisy, messy, and frenzied activity. But when scholars have attempted to explain the relatively chaotic nature of Japanese kindergartens and day-care centers they have done so in terms of how such disorder contributes to the children's development. Sano, for example, suggests that underlying the apparent chaos of day-care centers is good classroom management that utilizes both the resources of teachers and the children to make day-care goals more effective (1989:127–128). Tobin (1992:30) notes that periods of apparent disorder and silly and uninhibited play are coupled with periods of order so that the children learn to distinguish contexts and the behaviors appropriate to them. Indeed, Tobin, in an essay with Wu and Davidson, uses the term "developmentally appropriate chaos" to characterize the period of preschool as mediating the sheltered life of home and the tumult of the real world (Tobin et al. 1991:30).

   But what of "developmentally inappropriate behavior" such as irony, jokes, satire, and subversion? How do they fit the order and disorder of Japanese preschools? An approach, which integrates ideas of negotiation, choice, and agency into a model of social life, is by now quite commonplace within the social sciences. But I would posit that it has become a standard one primarily in regard to adults, to the grown-up members of societies. The problem is that many of the models related to childhood practices still proceed from an assumption of the relative passivity, immaturity, and dependency of children. I suggest that we may benefit from treating children as political actors with at least some power to resist and change the circumstances within which they live. Such a model would help us examine such issues related to childhood as bargaining and coalition-building, the power of the weak, collective goals, creating factions, and rehearsals for leadership.

Consider, for instance, the criticisms, irony, obscenity, and name-calling that I and other ethnographers encountered during fieldwork in Japanese preschools (Ben-Ari 1997b; Kotloff 1988). Such behaviors may violate certain academic and stereotyped notions of Japanese children, but their sheer ubiquity and dynamism underscore how central they are to the ways in which youngsters relate to their lives. To paraphrase Helen Schwartzman (1978:12), teachers and educators (and most of the "experts" they depend on) tend to view such play behavior in terms of what it is not: not work, not real, not serious, not productive, and not contributive (for a related example, see Kishima 1991). My contention is that much of our social scientific understanding of socialization in general, and in Japan in particular, has adopted this view of critical play. Indeed, these assumptions underscore the idea that both the preschool and the workplace are essentially similar sites where serious and productive work is undertaken. In contrast, my argument is that acts of caprice and questioning should be seen as constitutive of preschools to the same degree as their formal organizational hierarchy, division of labor, and curriculum. Corsaro (1997:4) suggests that "children are active, creative social agents who produce their own unique children's cultures while simultaneously contributing to the production of adult society." It is Holloway (2000:2) who has most explicitly phrased this in regard to Japan with her contention is that preschools do not merely reproduce a uniform cultural script.

A political model of preschools has another implication that is not always associated with politics. My proposition is that such a model intimates a different conceptualization of the socialization of selves in Japan. Take the long-term effects of "mischief." By these effects I do not mean the standard view that sees early childhood education as preparing children for the rigors of school and the workplace. Nor do I refer to Tobin, Wu, and Davidson's stress on "developmentally appropriate chaos" through which the children learn to differentiate between the behaviors suitable to different situations. Rather, I would argue that the long-term effect of critical play can be understood in terms of the capacity an individual develops to distance herself or himself from highly committed social situations; to develop what Erving Goffman terms "role distance." In discussing the "typical" worker in Japanese organizations, Plath notes:

> He may be loyal to the organization, he may serve it with diligence. This does not mean he deposits his mind in the company safe. He must maintain a healthy detachment, sustain a sense of personal continuity among what he is likely, in his organizational role, to experience as a planless tangle of reassignment and delays. (1983:9)

I suggest that the ability to disengage oneself from ongoing organizational (or, more generally, social) life that is found among many Japanese workers begins to be acquired in preschool through a variety of playful behaviors. The capacity for detachment – not always fully conscious, often mixed with humor – seems to be no less important for survival in companies and bureaucracies than other traits such as perseverance, powers of concentration, and the ability to work in a group.

My last point is related to another assumption that marks many studies of socialization in Japan. The goal of most such studies is to explain how social systems maintain sameness (Schwartzman 1978:99). This assumption is evident in the questions we ask. How is a culture transmitted from one generation to the next? In asking such a question, we assume that Japanese culture is a kind of static entity that can be transferred wholesale from one point in time to another. Newer approaches (e.g., Bachnik 1994) stress the constant negotiability that marks Japanese (as any other) culture. In these approaches, however, the basic parameters are given and people negotiate about how to actualize them in specific situations. But if our goal is also to explain how social systems generate difference, then a focus on other aspects of behavior – such as clowning, mischief, or make-believe play – may be useful. In other words, because the power of critical play to recreate reality, and to reinvent culture, lies in the novelty of forms it gives rise to, this may ultimately be its most significant role. It may well be that future studies of early childhood socialization will turn to these sources of cultural innovation.

REFERENCES

Allison, Anne. 1991. Japanese Mothers and *Obentoos*: The Lunch-Box as Ideological State Apparatus. Anthropological Quarterly 64(4):195–208.

Bachnik, Jane M. 1994. Introduction. *Uchi/soto*: Challenging our Conceptualizations of Self, Social Order, and Language. *In* Situated Meanings: Inside and Outside in Japanese Self, Society, and Language. Jane M. Bachnik and Charles J. Quinn Jr. eds. pp. 3–37. Princeton: Princeton University Press.

Ben-Ari, Eyal. 1987. Disputing about Day-Care: Care-Taking Roles in a Japanese Day Nursery. International Journal of Sociology of the Family 17:197–216.

—— 1997a. Japanese Childcare: An Interpretive Study of Culture and Organization. London: Kegan Paul International.

—— 1997b. Projects in Japanese Childcare: Culture, Organization and Emotions in a Preschool. London: Curzon.

Boli-Bennet, John, and John W. Meyer. 1978. The Ideology of Childhood and the State: Rules Distinguishing Children in National Constitutions. American Sociological Review 43:797–812.

Boocock, Saranne S. 1978. A Crosscultural Analysis of the Childcare System. *In* Current Topics in Early Childhood Education. L. G. Katz et al. eds. pp. 71–103. Norwood, NJ: Ablex.

—— 1989. Controlled Diversity: An Overview of the Japanese Preschool System. Journal of Japanese Studies 15(1):41–68.

Carney, Larry S., and Charlotte G. O'Kelly. 1987. Barriers and Constraints to the Recruitment and Mobility of Female Managers in the Japanese Labor Force. Human Resource Management 26(2):193–216.

Coleman, Samuel. 1983. Family Planning in Japanese Society: Traditional Birth Control in a Modern Urban Culture. Princeton: Princeton University Press.

Corsaro, William A. 1997. The Sociology of Childhood. Thousand Oaks: Pine Forge Press.

Dore, Ronald. 1978. Shinohata: A Portrait of a Japanese Village. London: Allen Lane.

Early Childhood Education Association of Japan. 1979. Childhood Education and Care in Japan. Tokyo: Child Honsha.

Embassy of Japan in Singapore. 1992. Japan Topics. Embassy of Japan in Singapore.

Frasz, Chris, and Kazuo Kato. 2002. The Educational Structure of the Japanese School System. www.ed.gov/pubs/Research5/Japan,structure_j.html.

Fujita, Mariko. 1989. "It's all Mother's Fault": Childcare and Socialization of Working Mothers in Japan. Journal of Japanese Studies 15(1):67–92.

Goodman, Roger. 2000. Children of the Japanese State: The Changing Role of Child Protection Institutions in Contemporary Japan. Oxford: Oxford University Press.

Hendry, Joy. 1984. Becoming Japanese: A Social Anthropological View of Childrearing. Journal of the Anthropological Society of Oxford 15:101–118.

—— 1986. Becoming Japanese: The World of the Pre-School Child. Manchester: Manchester University Press.

Hoiku Hakusho. 2000. Hoiku Hakusho 2000. Tokyo: Zenkoku Hoikuen Dantai Rengokai.

Holloway, Susan D. 2000. Contested Childhood: Diversity and Change in Japanese Preschools. London: Routledge.

Ishigaki, Emiko H. 1987. A Comparison of Young Children's Environments and Parental Expectations in Japan and Israel. Early Child Development and Care 27:139–168.

Kishima, Takako. 1991. Political Life in Japan: Democracy in a Reversible World. Princeton: Princeton University Press.

Kōseishō. 2002. Kōsei hakusho. Tokyo: Kōseishō.

Kotloff, Lauren J. 1988. Dai-Ichi Preschool: Fostering Individuality and Cooperative Group Life in a Progressive Japanese Preschool. Ph.D. dissertation, Cornell University.

Lock, Margaret M. 1980. East Asian Medicine in Urban Japan. Berkeley: University of California Press.

—— 1993. Ideology, Female Midlife, and the Greying of Japan. Journal of Japanese Studies 19(1):43–78.

Ministry of Education, Culture, Sports, Science, and Technology. 2002. Home page www.mext.go.jp/english/statist/gif/44agif.

Morigami, Shiro. 1999. Yoochien kyoiku. Tokyo: Fureberu-kan.

Norgren, Tiana. 2001. Abortion Before Birth Control: The Politics of Reproduction in Postwar Japan. Princeton: Princeton University Press.

O'Connor, Sorca. 1992. Legitimating the State's Involvement in Early Childhood Programs. In The Political Construction of Education. Bruce Fuller and Richard Robinson, eds. pp. 89–98. New York: Praeger.

Ohnuki-Tierney, Emiko. 1984. Illness and Culture in Contemporary Japan. Cambridge: Cambridge University Press.

Plath, David. 1983. Introduction: Life is Just a Job Resume? In Work and Lifecourse in Japan. David Plath ed. pp. 1–13. Albany: State University of New York Press.

Rogers, Rex Stainton, and Wendy Stainton Rogers. 1992. Stories of Childhood: Shifting Agendas of Child Concern. New York. Harvester.

Sano, Toshiyuki. 1989. Methods of Social Control and Socialization in Japanese Day-Care Centers. Journal of Japanese Studies 15(1):125–138.

Schwartzman, Helen B. 1978. Transformations: The Anthropology of Children's Play. New York: Plenum.

Shamgar-Handelman, Lea. 1993. To Whom Does Childhood Belong? The Hebrew University of Jerusalem unpublished MS.

Tobin, Joseph. 1992. Japanese Preschools and the Pedagogy of Selfhood. In Japanese Sense of Self. Nancy R. Rosenberger ed. pp. 1–39. Cambridge: Cambridge University Press.

Tobin, Joseph J., David Y. H. Wu, and Dana H. Davidson. 1989. Preschool in Three Cultures: Japan, China, and the United States. New Haven: Yale University Press.

Uno, Kathleen S. 1999. Passages to Modernity: Motherhood, Childhood and Social Reform in Early Twentieth-Century Japan. Honolulu: University of Hawaii Press.

Wollons, Roberta. 2000. The Missionary Kindergarten in Japan. In Kindergartens and Cultures: The Global Diffusion of an Idea. Roberta Wollons, ed. pp. 113–136. New Haven: Yale University Press.

SUGGESTED READING

Hendry, Joy. 1986. Becoming Japanese: The World of the Pre-School Child. Manchester: Manchester University Press.

Holloway, Susan D. 2000. Contested Childhood: Diversity and Change in Japanese Preschools. London: Routledge.

Peak, Lois. 1991. Learning to Go to School in Japan: The Transition from Home to Preschool Life. Berkeley: University of California Press.

Tobin, Joseph J., David Y. H. Wu, and Dana H. Davidson. 1989. Preschool in Three Cultures: Japan, China, and the United States. New Haven: Yale University Press.

Uno, Kathleen S. 1999. Passages to Modernity: Motherhood, Childhood and Social Reform in Early Twentieth-Century Japan. Honolulu: University of Hawaii Press.

17 Post-Compulsory Schooling and the Legacy of Imperialism

CHAPTER

Brian J. McVeigh

If it is true that empires never die, but only fade away, then as we enter the new millennium Japan cannot be understood unless we acknowledge its postwar imperial remnants. In this chapter I will explore how Japan's imperialism – more generally Japan's encounter with modernity – has configured an array of postwar educational institutions that, while not compulsory, nevertheless perform a key role in segregating, shunting, and positioning individuals throughout the socioeconomic system.

"Modernity" is a slippery, contested term, but for my present purposes we may broadly define it as the emergence (in the 19th century) and consolidation (during the early 20th century) of mass/mobilized political participation, industrialization, mass affluence, modern techno-science, centralized states, and nationalist ideologies (which were either deployed or suppressed by political centers for empire-building or national state unification). Universal education has been absolutely essential for these projects, particularly at the "compulsory" stage of educatio-socialization. Indeed, the preindustrial state is "interested in extracting taxes, maintaining the peace, and not much else, and has no interest in promoting lateral communication between its subject communities" (Gellner 1983:10). All this changed with the rise of the modern state, which not only promoted lateral communication between its citizens, but ensured that formalized schooling inculcated within them the same knowledge of and sentiments about national identity. In fact, it is remarkable that, although modern states have failed to keep many of their pledges, they have generally made good on one promise: to educate their citizenry (Gellner 1983:28). In this regard, Japan is quite ordinary if compared to other democratic (post)industrialized societies.

Though (post)industrialized societies cannot be appreciated without looking at compulsory education, "non-compulsory" – or, to be more exact, "post-compulsory" – education is just as important during the final stages of being integrated into the employment system. All the educational institutions I will discuss have one thing in common: they are "officially" not compulsory (in Japan, compulsory education designates primary school, or the first to sixth grades, and middle school, or the seventh to ninth grades; see Table 17.1[1]). Nevertheless, for many individuals they have become de facto compulsory, granting the necessary credentials for aspiring to middle-class life.

IDEOLOGICAL AND INSTITUTIONAL VESTIGES OF IMPERIALISM

The year 1945 is usually considered the dividing-line between an expansionist, highly nationalistic Japan, and an inward-looking, pacifist Japan. This division is in many ways artificial, because though there were certainly momentous changes and reforms after the war, there were also significant ideological and institutional continuities. The point to bear in mind is that, whether by military or economic means, Japan's elites (like elites everywhere) have pursued the strengthening of their politico-economic system, both before and after 1945.

How can we come to terms with Japan's trans-war continuities? At the risk of oversimplifying complex historical developments, for the sake of argument we can speak of two ideological currents that motivated the thinking of imperial Japan. Admittedly, these currents overlap in many ways and are not always easy to separate. Be that as it may, the first current may be termed "colonial Japan": Japan was an inclusive, "tolerant" civilization expressing itself via an imperial mandate that embraced and incorporated the diverse peoples of Asia who are culturally and "racially" related to the Japanese. These peoples, Koreans, Chinese, Southeast Asians, and South Asians, needed liberation and protection from Western expansionism. The second current may be termed "superior Japan": due to their highly advanced culture and inherent moral superiority, the Japanese people should take an exclusive stance vis-à-vis their subject peoples.

Table 17.1   Types and number of non-compulsory schools

School Type	Total	State	Public	Private
High schools	5,478	15	4,145	1,318
	(113)[a]	–	(69)[a]	(44)[a]
Special education schools[b]	992	45	932	15
Colleges of technology	62	54	5	3
Vocational schools	3,551	139	217	3,195
Junior colleges	572	20	55	497
	(10)[a]	–	–	(10)[a]
Universities	649	99	72	478
	(26)[a]	(1)[a]	–	(25)[a]
	(479)[c]	(99)[c]	(50)[c]	(330)[c]
Miscellaneous schools	2,278	2	40	2,236

[a] Schools offering correspondence programs, including graduate schools.
[b] Includes all levels.
[c] Of which universities with graduate schools.

Both these currents played a part in shaping modern Japan. However, because of the sudden and complete implosion of imperial ideology in 1945, Japan's borders abruptly contracted to form a national state, highlighting the "superior Japan" ideological current and reinforcing a 19th-century vision of an exclusive "one state for one nation." At the same time, "imperial Japan," now associated with defeat, humiliation, and fanatical militarism, was for the most part historically submerged. The ideological makeover that Japan underwent after 1945 was in no small part assisted by US hegemonic policies that, in order to use Japan to check the spread of communism, had a great stake in bolstering an economically sound ("capitalist"), politically stable ("democratic"), and militarily reliable ("US ally") state in Northeast Asia.

Seemingly overnight, then, Japan went from a *taminzoku* ("many peoples") empire that – at least at the official level – encouraged racial and cultural diversity, to a *tanitsu minzoku* ("single people") national state that advocated cultural and "racial" homogeneity. Added to this was a general watering down of wartime atrocities and injustices that sullied Japan's new identity as pacifist. Though it is debatable to what degree Japanese leaders and ordinary people took the rhetoric of a multi-ethnic empire seriously, the fact still stands that about one-third of Japanese subjects were not ethnoculturally Japanese.

How does Japan's imperial legacy, as contested as it is, relate to post-compulsory schooling? There are numerous ways to respond to this question, but for my present purposes I will limit my discussion and introduce the following five themes which I weave throughout my analysis: the trans-war continuity of state structures; an educatio-examination system driven by economic nationalism; the myth of a "homogeneous" Japan; confronting the wartime era; and a patriarchal capitalist system.

The state and institutional lineage

As in other (post)industrialized national states, Japan's formal school system is sanctioned and monitored by the state. More specifically, it is the Ministry of Education, Culture, Sports, Science and Technology (Monbukagaku-shō; referred to below as the Education Ministry) that is the main administrative arm overseeing education. Under the Education Ministry, there are three types of schools: state (or "national"), public (prefectural or municipal), and private. Most post-compulsory schooling is private (while most compulsory schooling is public, indicating the state's primary concern with the early stages of educatio-socialization). Here it should be noted that, regardless of the appellation "private," the state exerts considerable sway over such schools through subsidies, accreditation, and, most significantly, informal but influential "administrative guidance" (*gyōsei shidō*). Currently, the Education Ministry forms the apex of a nationwide three-tiered organization which implements elite-guided "strategic schooling" (the educational counterpart of what Huber (1994) calls Japan's "strategic economy"):

1 *strategic*: executive bodies that design comprehensive plans (the Education Ministry's secretariat, state officials, advisory councils, political circles, business associations, conservative pressure groups);

2   *intermediate*: mediating levels of implementation, composed of ministerial bur-
    eaus, their divisions, and prefectural and municipal education commissions
    (*kyōiku iin-kai*) that link strategic and tactical levels;
3   *tactical*: schools and other sites administered and monitored by the Education
    Ministry.

Sakamoto writes that, though the military and the infamous Ministry of Home
Affairs were discredited and dismantled, the Education Ministry's wartime responsibility has never been adequately acknowledged (Sakamoto 1992:14). Horio notes
another legacy of the imperial period: "The argument that there is no difference at
the level of compulsory education between the State's and the People's control
reveals a shocking lack of understanding of the historical significance of the consti-
tutional provision for the right to receive an education, and demonstrates precisely
how prewar education thought governs conditions even today" (Horio 1988:
141–142). None of this should be surprising, given the fact that there was remarkable
institutional continuity from pre-1945 times in terms of personnel, bureaucratic
structures, and, most significantly, ideological outlook.

Economic nationalism and the educatio-examination system

Though the educational bureaucracy has displayed remarkable institutional innovation and flexibility since the Meiji period (1868–1912) and in spite of the 1945
collapse of imperial institutions, Japan's leaders have safeguarded the continuity of
ideologies of nationalist identity and ensured that schools have instilled knowledge
forms underpinning Japan's version of economic nationalism (i.e., a capitalist developmental state) within the citizenry.

How does economic nationalism manifest itself in schools? The answer lies in how,
over the decades, capitalist developmentalism has driven an integration, indeed
unification, of educational and economic aims. The empire demanded obedient
subjects, and the postwar national state now demands hardworking citizens; however,
a trans-war commonality can be found in how state-guided capitalism and structures
have contoured schooling, producing an "educatio-examination" system motivated
by economic nationalism. Though after the war American authorities criticized the
examination system, Japanese officials saw no need to alter it in any significant way,
and postwar "examination hell" is a continuation, intensification, and expansion of
prewar educatio-examination practices.

The link between academic achievement and job placement, then, is a ladder of
tests that becomes harder to climb between the primary and secondary levels,
especially for those students aiming for university (here it is worth noting that, as
of 2000, 25.2 percent of students who are in post-compulsory education are *not* in
universities or two-year colleges). In Japan (perhaps more than in most industrialized
societies), learning is conceived as a means for passing examinations.

The stress caused by examination preparation (at the expense of less focused but
more spontaneous forms of learning) is perhaps the most obvious outcome of
economic nationalism. But there are other manifestations. Consider the emphasis
on "egalitarianism," which is premised on the belief that all children are endowed

with an equal amount of ability, and that those who do well in examinations are simply more motivated and have put more effort into their learning endeavors. Whatever benefits such a pedagogical philosophy has, it often mutates into "bad egalitarianism" (*aku byōdō*), or mere standardization, which measures learning by an impartial but unforgiving objectivity that often ignores individual learning styles and strengths. "Egalitarianism," seemingly fair and effective, is convenient from a corporate perspective, which is concerned with strictly grading and positioning all students in an economic hierarchy. From the official perspective, any differentiation or distinction among students not related to test-taking, such as streaming or tracking, easily becomes regarded as a form of "discrimination." A practical consequence of this schooling ideology is that even the most gifted children cannot skip a grade, and all students must (ideally) learn the same content. If neither gifted children nor slow achievers are furnished with the proper opportunity for appropriate education, an atmosphere is created which breeds frustration, resentment, and even aggressiveness. This takes its toll on students: falling behind (some of whom end up dropping out of school altogether), refusing to attend school, bullying, and students who, once they enter post-secondary education, simply have learned to dislike being in the classroom.

The postwar myth of a homogeneous Japan

If economic nationalism expects egalitarianism – not in the sense of leveling social inequalities, but rather of putting everyone on the same starting line in a meritocratic race – then ideologies of homogeneity are useful for bolstering a sense that "though we're running against each other, we're being treated fairly since we're all in this race together." The ideologies of egalitarianism and homogeneity, in fact, legitimate – or to go one step further, disguise – socioeconomic differences. Indeed, there is considerable evidence that, as in other places, education is geared toward the reproduction of socioeconomic classes, and that Japan's schooling system is not more meritocratic than others (Ishida 1993). Thus, middle-class life has been made to look like a reward for academic success while anything less looks like a punishment for laziness. Notions of egalitarianism and homogeneity, then, are linked. Here it might also be noted that in Japan the subtext underlying "homogeneity" has sometimes been that "because we're homogeneous, we are somehow a cut above other peoples" (i.e., a relic of the imperial era's "superior Japan").

How is homogeneity conceptualized? One key term would be *nihonjin* ("Japanese person") whose meaning, for the average person, is often ambiguous: it may mean citizenship, ethnocultural identity, or perceived physical traits. A shifting definition allows it to be used for different purposes depending on political expediency. Another important term is *minzoku*, a word used to describe the various peoples under imperial Japan's purview and now often conceptualized as "ethnic group." Basically meaning "nation" in the German sense of *Volk*, it is sometimes a difficult word to translate since its definition may oscillate between "cultural group" (a people united by an *acquired* common heritage), and "race" (a people united by perceived physical traits and/or appearance). Yoshino notes the pseudo-scientific racialist definition of *minzoku* when he explains its three aspects that shape postwar "Japaneseness": the belief among many Japanese that they belong to a distinct "racial group" due to their possession of "Japanese blood"; the belief in the "mono-racial" (*tanitsu minzoku*) and "homogeneous" composition of the Japanese, who are a "pure-blooded people" (*junketsu no minzoku*); and the denial or de-emphasis of other groups in Japan (e.g., Koreans, Chinese, Ainu) (Yoshino 1992:24–26; see also chapter 21 in this volume).

It should be noted, as mentioned above, that, for the most part, the denial of the Korean and Chinese residents in Japan occurred after 1945. Under the empire, Korean subjects came to Japan as forced labor. After 1945, most returned to their homeland, but those who had lost property in Korea as a result of Japanese colonialization stayed on. After the division of Korea in 1948, repatriation became even more difficult, and when Japan became a sovereign state in 1952, Koreans suddenly became foreign nationals. There are now approximately 700,000, though if naturalized Koreans and Japanese with a Korean parent are included, the figure reaches over 1.2 million.

In spite of recent assaults on the homogeneity myth, ideological obscurantism that denies diversity and complexity can still be found in the academic literature and media representations of Japan. For example, the notion that Japan, as a geographical unit, Japan as a nation, and Japan as a state naturally correspond is a powerful misconception (after all, Japan's present boundaries are recent, and in some places still disputed). Below a political scientist reiterates all the clichéd myths in his description of the Japanese:

> Japan has always been a country relatively self-confident about its own nationality and culture. With a long cultural history and lacking in the social divisions of religion, ethnicity, and language that split so many other countries, Japan's inhabitants rarely have been confused about who they are: clearly they are Japanese. Nationality, citizenship, ethnicity, and cultural identity are largely meaningless distinctions for most Japanese. Being a Japanese means identifying similarly with all such terms. (Pempel 1998:115)

Besides being historically inaccurate, the above quote seems to assume that "nationality, citizenship, ethnicity, and cultural identity" are universal, ahistorical concepts (they are, in fact, in their modern senses, relatively recent 19th-century inventions). Moreover, Japanese are not born confused about such concepts; rather, they are socialized, within educational institutions, to believe in – or at least acknowledge – their role in identity formation.

Confronting the wartime past

The most obvious and controversial legacy of Japan's imperial past is war atrocities and brutal colonization. The manner in which Japanese society and the educational authorities have dealt with these events has called into question the meaning of Japan's postwar "pacifism," as well as polarizing public debate and provoking outrage among Japan's international neighbors.

Since the mid-1950s, certain elements within the Liberal Democratic Party have been concerned with "undoing the excesses" of the occupation reforms and restoring "Japanese values." Nationalist and conservative circles have been critical of Japan's post-1945 educational system, claiming that reforms have not been suited to the Japanese heritage and were forced on Japan by the American occupation (though it should be pointed out that many reforms were implemented with strong Japanese support and cooperation). Their main target for nationalist revisionism has been the Fundamental Law of Education, which for some was a foreign imposition that does not accord with Japanese culture. A number of education ministers have publicly expressed reservations about postwar arrangements, for example, Kiyose Ichirō's criticisms of occupation reforms (1955–56); Araki Masuo's arguments for revising the Fundamental Law of Education (1960–63); and Sunada Shigetami's regret that the highly conservative Imperial Rescript had been abandoned after the war (1977–78).

More recently, a Japanese leader will occasionally let slip a comment that reveals sentiments for what may be termed nostalgic nationalism, or a longing for a time when the Japanese empire was the leading player on the Asian stage. In 1986, Prime Minister Nakasone Yasuhiro dismissed Education Minister Fujio Masayuki over imperio-nationalistic comments on past Japanese–Korean relations. Two years later, Okuno Seisuke, director-general of the National Land Agency, resigned over similar comments concerning Japanese–Chinese relations. In 1995 Eto Takami, director-general of the Management and Coordination Agency, was forced to resign for his statement that "Japan did some good things for Korea during its colonial rule"; that same year, former vice-premier, Watanabe Michio, was told to apologize for saying that "The 1910 treaty that handed Korea's sovereignty to Japan was formed peacefully." Education Minister Shimamura Yoshinobu (1995–96) publicly questioned the need of Japan to apologize for its war atrocities, leading to international criticism from China and South Korea. In 1997 Nakasone wrote that the Fundamental Law of Education "contains such words as 'mankind,' 'peace,' 'freedom,' and 'democracy' but does not have such words as 'nation,' 'race,' 'culture,' 'history' or 'households',", the latter notions being what are, presumably in his opinion, the essentials of "Japaneseness." After all, the Law is "based on musty classical modernism and is not a law tailored to suit the ethos of Japan." Being like "distilled water, it has no Japanese 'flavor',", and "it is very doubtful that the blood of democracy runs through the veins of Japanese in postwar Japan." He also noted, not surprisingly, "errors in school education that were committed during the early postwar years" (Nakasone 1997). In 2000 Tokyo Governor Ishihara Shintarō used the term *sangokujin* – "third-country people" – a derogatory term used for Koreans and Chinese in the immediate postwar period, as well as the insulting "Shina" to refer to China. That same year Prime Minister Mori Yoshirō stated that "Japan is a divine nation centered on the Emperor" and used *kokutai*, a pre-1945 word meaning the "national polity" but conveying the sense of the mystical unity of the emperor and the Japanese people.

Nostalgic nationalists have not necessarily attempted to deny Japan's wartime deeds, but rather to glorify its imperial past. Middle-school history textbooks have been severely criticized both in and outside Japan for glossing over atrocities, as well as denying the realities of Japan's imperial past. Fujioka Nobukatsu, a professor at the University of Tokyo, has said that bringing up the issue of wartime "comfort women" (i.e. sex slaves) is an attempt by "left-wingers" and "foreign elements" to disparage the Japanese state. He is a member of the nationalistic Japanese Society for

Textbook Reform, which has published textbooks that have passed (though with some mandated revisions) the Education Ministry's screening process.

More recently, there have been moves that some hail as progressive (though each move seems to be counterbalanced by eruptions, indicating that nostalgic nationalism runs deep). For example, there has been more coverage of Japan's colonial rule of Korea and an acknowledgment that not all issues of war compensation have been resolved. Some instructors, in spite of pressures to follow authorized textbooks for examination purposes, teach as they please. Other progressive moves have included more treatment of Japan's minorities: for example, in 1997 the Education Ministry ordered the publisher of a textbook to delete remarks made by Prime Minister Nakasone in 1986 that Japan is a "homogeneous nation." Education Minister Machimura Nobutaka stated in 1997 that Japan should make a forthright admission that its colonialism and wartime aggression inflicted tremendous pain on Asians.

Gendering education

Gendering, or the socializing of males and females to accept culture-specific sexual and occupational roles, is configured (though not determined) by politico-economic forces. Japan, like other industrializing societies, employed and sharpened gender distinctions for capitalist production in the late 19th century, conceptualizing females as the "marked" gender/sex. In other words, being female means requiring special attention from the authorities. It appears that, if men are regarded as the base, women are thought of as derivative; if men are regarded as standard, women are thought of as somehow out of the ordinary (for example there are no special schools or administrative offices for men).

Though gendering has always existed in Japan, gender definitions vary according to historical period. Since Meiji, two powerful ideological themes have been implicated in the reproduction of women's gender and sexual identities as they relate to nationalist definitions and economic production: *the cultivation of character*: a moral refinement that should ideally permeate all spheres of daily life and bring out a woman's innate "femininity," "womanly virtues," and "maternal instinct"; and *practical, non-professional training*: an education oriented toward producing comforting wives/nurturing mothers, and, more recently, workers skilled at "woman's work," or, at best, semi-professional employees.

Historically, the two themes cited above have intertwined, mutually legitimizing and supporting one another, so that they are difficult to disentangle. But whatever the particular period, political interests and economic pressures have utilized these two pedagogical themes, gendered notions that have been used over time for a variety of purposes: educating guardians of "Japanese tradition"; instilling nationalism in mothers who in turn educate patriotic sons and dutiful daughters for Japan's empire-building and war machine; cultivating "good wives/wise mothers" (*ryōsai kenbo*) who provide comforting homes for work-weary husbands and well-educated young for Japan's labor force; or training cheap and temporary female labor for periods of high economic growth who, used as an economic "safety-valve," are the first to be let go during recession.

PARA-OFFICIAL SCHOOLS

Any credit that Japan's formal schooling receives for educating students should be shared by what may be called the "para-official schooling" system, comprising *yobikō* (preparatory schools), *juku* (cram schools; literally, "private schools"), and home tutors. These are all components of the educatio-examination industry and key aids in *shingaku* (academic advancement) which describes the screening and selection mechanism driven by economic nationalism.

Yobikō teach university-bound students how to answer the maximum number of frequently asked questions in the minimum amount of time. The first *yobikō* was founded in 1894, indicating the early roots of Japan's educatio-examination industry. These schools can be divided into three types: by 1991, one type enrolled fewer than 500 students each (67.7 percent); another type had about 10,000 students each in different branches; a third type specialized in running medical universities (Tsukada 1991:6).

Juku, of which there are probably 50,000, absorb the need for the additional schooling to pass examinations that the formal sector – at least from the parents' and their children's viewpoint – does not provide. They are sometimes called "secondary schools" (regular schools being "first schools"), and they illustrate the effects of strategic schooling. The educational authorities have periodically criticized *juku*. Recently, however, the Education Ministry admitted defeat to the embedded forces of the unofficial educatio-examination industry and decided to officially "acknowledge" them. In 1999 the Education Ministry-affiliated Council on Lifelong Learning concluded that, though certain *juku* practices (holding classes late at night and at weekends) needed to be curbed, these schools actually supplemented regular schools and should be recognized since "lessons at cram schools are said to be easier for students to understand" and regular schools "need to improve their teaching methods" (*Daily yomiuri* 1999).

Juku range from small schools conducted in houses with just a few students, to chains of *juku* run by large companies for profit. They can be divided into two main types: non-academic (hobbies, sports, arts) and academic, which usually teach math, science, and English. Academic *juku* can be further divided into *shingaku juku* (literally, "*juku* for academic advancement") for better students; supplementary *juku* in which "catch-up" is the main concern; "remedial *juku*" for those who have difficulty keeping up with others; and "comprehensive *juku*" which have both classes for examination preparation and supplementary lessons. *Juku*, then, serve the needs of two types of students who, in an important sense, are not well served by the typical school policy of satisfying the average student: quick learners and those who fall behind.

The attendance rate at *juku* has increased since the mid-1970s, with most percentages being particularly high for middle school students (Table 17.2). *Juku* attendance is probably much larger than any survey might indicate, because some students only attend for a short period of time.

Despite negative media portrayals of the role of *juku* in Japanese society, some students seem to enjoy studying there. It is commonly heard that many *juku* (which are not under the jurisdiction of the Education Ministry but under that of the

Table 17.2   Elementary and middle-school students attending *juku*

	Elementary-school students (%)	Middle-school students (%)
1976	12.0	38.0
1985	16.5	44.5
1993	23.6	59.5

Source: Jiji 1996:108.

Economy, Trade and Industry Ministry) employ teachers disillusioned with regular schools and attracted by better pay and the freedom to design their own curricula.

HIGH SCHOOLS: STANDARDIZATION OR "EGALITARIANISM"?

Practically all middle-school graduates advance to higher-level schooling, though most go on to high school, making the latter a de facto compulsory educational institution. There are three basic types of high schools: "academic"(*futsū*; literally "general"), in which 73.2 percent of students are enrolled; vocational (25 percent of students); and those with an "integrated curriculum" (*sōgō gakka*), combining academic and vocational courses, and enrolling 1.7 percent of students. Okano and Tsuchiya offer another way to classify high schools: elite academic (feeding top universities); non-elite academic (enrolling most students; this constitutes the mainstream); vocational (most graduates are not university-bound); evening (for working students or those who missed out on places at regular high schools); correspondence (for those who for a variety of reasons cannot or could not attend regular schools); and "special education" high schools (for students with disabilities) (Okano and Tsuchiya 1999:63–67).

   High schools are quite gendered, as can be seen from Table 17.3, which shows that only about a quarter of teachers are female (in contrast to lower-level schools). Table 17.4 shows that the top three positions in high schools are disproportionately male, while Table 17.5 (vocational schools) illustrates the gendered nature of vocational high-school curricula.

   Though some overseas observers have admired Japanese high schools (and Japanese education in general), many Japanese are extremely critical of their own schooling system. The most common complaints concern too many rules, rigidity, examination-centered teaching, bullying (*ijime*), truancy, and "school refusal" (*tōkōkyohi*), though some overseas observers have considered these problems "to be merely a few negatives in a generally very positive, successful system" (Yoneyama 1999:19). Though Japanese high schools do not necessarily compare unfavorably if viewed in international perspective in matters of violence and truancy, statistics do not tell the entire story: in Japan, many students "attend" school but are not attentive (and many do not even necessarily sit in class, but frequent the nurse's or principal's office). This lack of academic interest is blamed on an educatio-examination system which limits learning styles, is suspicious of individual differences, and standardizes in the name of "egalitarianism," so that not a few students become "apathetic, passive, bored, low in energy, unwilling to think or make decisions or initiate any action" (Yoneyama

Table 17.3 High schools in 2000

Number of students	Female students (%)	Full-time female teachers (%)	Private schools (%)
4,165,434	49.8	25.6	24.1
(181,877)[a]	(43.8)[a]	(29.6)[a]	(22.1)[a]

[a] Correspondence programs.

Table 17.4 Male and female teaching staff at high schools in 2000

	Number of male teaching staff	Number of female teaching staff	Female staff (%)
Principals	5,224	181	3.5
Vice-principals	7,545	312	4.1
Teachers	236,576	56,278	23.8
Assistant teachers	1,027	567	55.2
School nurses	6,103	6,009	99.9
Part-time instructors	12,552	5,140	43.1

Table 17.5 Female students in vocational high-school programs in 2000 (%)

Agriculture	Industry	Commerce	Fishery	Home Economics	Nursing	Other
40.0	9.1	66.0	25.4	92.1	97.7	60.1

1999:9). Indeed, "regular day high schools are not adequately equipped to accommodate youths with 'differences'" (Okano and Tsuchiya 1999:101). Moreover, according to one observer, "the biggest crime committed against teachers is the act of asking a question, presenting a counter-argument, explaining one's position or situation, all of which are taken to be 'talking back' and acts of rebellion" (Yoneyama 1999:113).

In spite of criticisms, recent reform efforts have attempted to introduce diversity into the high-school curriculum. Also, special schools and programs for "returnees" – students of parents posted overseas who, because they have not been educated in Japanese schools, have not been adequately socialized to be "Japanese" – have been established (Goodman 1993). There are also schools that combine middle and high schools (*chūtō kyōiku gakkō*) in an attempt to minimize examination pressures. However, in 2000 there were only four such schools (two state, one public, and one private), with 1,702 students.

Japan's imperial legacy is clearly visible in how minorities are treated by the schooling system: how should former subjects who are no longer part of the post-1945 nationalist community be treated by the educating arm of the state? And how should groups which, for whatever reason, do not appear to be adequately "Japanese" be regarded? Key minorities include third-generation Korean and Chinese residents, *buraku* (descendants of an outcaste group), Ainu, Okinawans, and, since the mid-1980s, South Americans of Japanese ancestry and other groups. Here I will limit my discussion to Korean residents in Japan.

In addition to facing discrimination, Koreans "have benefited less from mainstream schooling than their Japanese counterparts" (Okano and Tsuchiya 1999:113). Presently, most Koreans are in Japanese schools, though not a small number are in North Korea-affiliated schools and a very small minority are in South Korea-affiliated schools (numbering 101 and collectively called "ethnic schools," *minzoku gakkō*; these are classified as "miscellaneous schools"). Students from ethnic schools have typically not been allowed to participate in sporting events organized by the National High School Athletic Association. However, since 1996 this organization has allowed soccer teams from Korean schools to participate, and since 1992 students from these schools have been allowed to participate in the biannual high-school baseball tournament, but they cannot participate in the annual National Athletic Meet.

On the more positive side, it should be pointed out that, since 1953, *dōwa* education for *buraku* (an egalitarian or assimilation program) has been implemented, and in some schools teachers make efforts to dismantle discriminatory practices and discuss human rights, focusing on Korean and Chinese residents, Ainu, other minorities, and the disabled.

VOCATIONAL AND OTHER SCHOOLS

Vocational schools

Officially translated as "specialist training schools" but broadly known as "vocational schools," *senshū gakkō* were established in their current form under the amended 1976 School Education Law (Table 17.6). These schools, not as prestigious as universities, offer programs in a wide range of professional, vocational, and technical subjects, as well as in general education. Their programs last for one year (800 class hours per year). Vocational schools, 90 percent of which are private, can be divided into three types:

1   "upper-secondary specialist training schools" (*kōtō senshū gakkō*), which require middle-school graduation for admission. Students who have completed an upper-secondary program of a specialist training school may apply to a university;

Table 17.6   Vocational schools in 2000

Types of vocational schools	Number of students	Female students (%)	Full-time female teachers (%)
Upper-secondary specialist training schools	68,877	57.3	58.8
Professional training schools	637,308	55.3	51.2
General programs	44,639	31.4	32.7
Total	**750,824**	**54.1**	**51.3**

2   "professional training schools" (*senmon gakkō*), which require high-school gradu-
    ation, or completion of upper-secondary courses of specialist training schools, for
    admission. Beginning in 1995, professional training schools have awarded the
    "technical associate degree" (*senmonshi*);
3   schools offering "general programs" (*ippan katei*).

Colleges of technology

Hardly known outside Japan, "colleges of technology" (*kōtō senmon gakkō*) are a type
of vocational school established in 1961 by a revision of the School Education Law.
Only a small percentage of students attend them. They have curricula that last five
years, specifically designed for "industrial education," for example engineering (57
schools) and mercantile marine studies (five schools). Unlike university, they only
require the completion of middle school for admission. These schools are almost all
central-state-administered, and, as Tables 17.7 and 17.8 indicate, are strikingly
gendered. After graduation students receive an associate degree. However, graduates
of colleges of technology may apply to the upper division of a university, and indeed,
in 2000 33.6 percent of graduates went on to university.

Miscellaneous schools

Miscellaneous schools (*kakushu gakkō*) have various admission requirements
depending on the school. Their programs last for one year or more (680 class
hours), though some have programs that last for only three months. They teach a
whole range of subjects, ranging from dressmaking, computers, automobile driving,
typing, word-processing, and cooking to bookkeeping. Most require completion of
middle school (Table 17.9).

Table 17.7   Colleges of technology in 2000

	Number of students	Female students (%)	Full-time female teachers (%)	Private schools (%)
Colleges of technology	56,714	18.7	4.0	4.8

Table 17.8   Male and female staff at colleges of technology in 2000

	Number of male teaching staff	Number of female teaching staff	Female staff (%)
Principal	62	0	0.0
Professor	1,714	13	0.8
Associate professor	1,559	52	3.3
Assistant professor	630	67	10.6
Assistant	494	48	9.7

Table 17.9 Miscellaneous schools in 2000

	Number of students	Female students (%)	Full-time female teachers (%)	Private schools (%)
Miscellaneous schools	222,961	51.4	37.7	98.2

HIGHER EDUCATION

Universities: "Moratorium before regular employment"

Of all the links in the Japanese educational system, higher education is the most criticized. Educational authorities and media routinely and severely criticize universities and colleges as "playgrounds," "kindergartens for adults," "resorts," or a place where there is "cessation of thinking after high-school graduation." Despite the failings of higher education, families devote considerable emotional effort and financial resources to climbing the last rung in the educatio-examination ladder. In 2000, 55.6 percent of high-school graduates attempted to enter universities or colleges; 49.1 percent were successful.

If education in Japan is geared toward disciplining students (or "silencing them," as more vocal critics assert), the consequences are most obvious in the university classroom (though, of course, there are exceptions). Though Yoneyama is discussing high schools, what she says applies to tertiary education, where alienation "is more likely to appear in negative forms – as absence, silence, default. For Japanese students, to be vocal and to be able to attend school are contradictory propositions" (Yoneyama 1999:86). Furthermore, critically considering social issues while they are at university shapes in no small way the opinions, hopes, and outlook of individuals on a wide range of social, economic, and political issues which confront them later in life. Such issues might involve gender, attitudes toward labor, environmental problems, racial and ethnic discrimination, immigration policies, and Japan's wartime history and place within the international community.

Despite a steady rise in the number of female students attending university (from 27.4 percent in 1990 to 36.2 percent in 2000), an examination of what women actually study reveals salient gendering: among students who majored in science and engineering, only 25.3 percent and 9.9 percent, respectively, were women. In domestic science, only 4.8 percent of students were male. The figures are just as telling at the graduate level. In science, women constituted 20.6 percent of students in Master's programs while in engineering, females made up 8.6 percent of all students. At the Ph.D. level, 15.3 percent of science students were female, and 9.5 percent of engineering students were female. Moreover, an examination of female faculty also reveals gendered structures (Tables 17.10 and 17.11).

How are non-Japanese treated in higher education? The guiding premise here is the School Education Law, which states that only graduates of Education Ministry-sanctioned schools are allowed to sit for university examinations (though there are provisions for those who have not graduated from an officially sanctioned school). Thus, as a rule, state universities do not allow graduates from ethnic high schools in

Table 17.10   Universities in 2000

Students/schools	Number of students	Female students (%)	Full-time female teachers (%)	Private schools (%)
Regular	2,740,023	36.2	13.5	73.2
Graduate	205,311	26.4	7.5	50.8
Correspondence	220,747	0.26	13.0	96.1

Table 17.11   Male and female faculty at universities in 2000

	Number of male faculty	Number of female faculty	Female faculty (%)
President	639	47	7.4
Vice-president	244	14	4.1
Professors	58,137	4,595	7.9
Associate professors	34,872	4,575	13.1
Assistant professors	19,112	3,594	18.8
Assistants	37,459	7,489	20.0

Japan to sit entrance tests. The result is that "being Japanese," state-recognized schools, and the educatio-examination system are all tightly interlinked. However, there is some resistance to the system: currently, 57 public and 220 private universities do accept graduates of ethnic high schools. Also, the Japan Federation of Bar Associations has urged that central state universities be opened to all high schools in Japan in order to avoid human rights violations.

Though the state has attempted to attract foreign students in order to "internationalize" Japan ("100,000 students by 2000"), this program has not been as successful as was hoped, and in 2000 there were 48,246 students from abroad (if permanent residents are included, the total rises to 59,092 non-Japanese students) (Table 17.12).

As for non-Japanese faculty, severe restrictions on their employment have created a discriminatory, two-tiered system that has parallels with the way imported "foreign experts" were treated during Meiji. Only 3.3 percent of full-time faculty at universities and colleges are non-Japanese, mostly at private schools (5,534 full-time, 10,534 part-time). Non-Japanese staff "are best seen as the equivalent of foreign technical advisors ... as transitory, disposable transmitters of foreign knowledge or techniques – rather than as fellow laborers in the ongoing quest of human knowledge" (Hall 1998:93).

Women's junior colleges as the apex of a gendered education system

Junior colleges (*tanki daigaku*; literally "short-term colleges") are two- (sometimes three-) year schools. They are the most clearly gendered academic institution in Japan (Tables 17.13 and 17.14): most are "women's schools" and at their peak of student enrollment in 1993, 92.5 percent of their students were female. The next year the number fell to 520,638, and by 2000 it had fallen to 327,680. Between 1996 and 2000 26 junior colleges closed or were upgraded to four-year universities because of declining student numbers. While the combined number of university and junior college students has fallen, the number of university students has risen during the last few years and the number of universities has increased, from 507 in 1990 to 649 in 2000.

For the most part, women's junior colleges may be broadly classified into *kyōyō* (general education with connotations of refinement) and practical, semi-professional training (often teaching or home-related). Senju, in fact, goes so far as to state that modern Japan's system of higher education for women still reflects pre-Meiji insti-

Table 17.12   Origins of non-Japanese students in 2000

	Total	University	Graduate school	Junior college
China	22,915	11,385	10,572	958
South Korea	9,172	4,910	3,959	303
Taiwan	3,446	2,213	1,042	191
Malaysia	1,664	1,347	311	6
Indonesia	1,122	232	876	14
Other Asian	4,344	1,369	2,916	59
Oceania	478	334	139	5
North America	1,194	898	287	9
Central and South America	821	199	614	8
Europe	2,008	896	1,096	16
Middle East	433	129	300	4
Africa	649	81	567	1
Total	**48,246**	**23,993**	**22,679**	**1,574**

Table 17.13   Junior colleges in 2001

Students/schools	Number of students	Female students (%)	Full-time female faculty (%)	Private schools (%)
Regular	327,680	89.6	43.8	91.2
Correspondence	28,711	67.5	9.3	100.0

Table 17.14   Male and female faculty at junior colleges in 2001

	Number of male faculty	Number of female faculty	Female faculty (%)
President	370	42	11.4
Vice-president	119	21	17.6
Professors	6,660	2,089	31.4
Associate professors	4,637	2,035	43.9
Assistant professors	3,497	1,926	55.1
Assistants	1,469	1,226	83.5

tutions of female learning, with four-year women's universities corresponding to *terakoya* (temple schools) and women's junior colleges to *ohariya* (sewing schools): the former produce "well-educated housewives" and the latter "practical housewives with little professional knowledge" (Senju 1971:45).

A sampling of typical school mottoes provides an idea of the educational philosophy advocated at many women's junior colleges. The theme of cultivation is common, some schools promising to bring out an essential, inborn "woman-ness": "An Educational Philosophy that Cultivates and Improves the True Nature of Women"; "An Education for Maternity, Intellect, Compassion, and a Desire for Harmony"; "An Academic Program that Utilizes a Woman's Special Qualities." A related aspect of the cultivation theme is refinement through "traditional womanly" arts: "An Education Enriched in Sentiment through Tea Ceremony and Flower Arrangement"; "Become Licensed to Teach Flower Arrangement and Tea Ceremony." Some schools attempt to combine ladylike training with more practical skills: "Training Good Professionals and Members of the Home"; "Traditional Commerce and Economics – Up-to-Date Domestic Science."

CONCLUSION

Japan, like other societies, confronts the problem of deciding on the definition of "assimilation": does it mean to dilute diversity in order to maintain an ethnocratic system (remnants of "superior Japan"), or does it mean promoting a common civic protocol that encourages communication while enthusiastically accepting differences? In other words, Japanese society must decide if its educatio-socializing system is either "nationalist" – the Japanese state articulates an idealized and monolithic Japanese "nation" and consequently, schools should subsume diversity within an exclusive national community; or "national" – the state oversees schooling that accepts a public composed of differences (whether conceptualized as "Japanese," "Korean," "Chinese," "Ainu," or other) and encourages their incorporation into an inclusive civic community. Such determinations, of course, are related to how Japan defines itself as a polity: is it fundamentally a progressivist "social democracy" along western European lines, or an obdurate "nationalist democracy" (contrary to any US pretensions, Japan is not a "liberal democracy" along Anglo-American lines)? At a deeper level, such determinations are shaped by how "Japaneseness" itself is defined: is it political (citizenship), ethnocultural (customs and heritage), "racial" (perceived physical traits), or some combination thereof?

NOTE

1   Unless otherwise indicated, all figures in the tables in this chapter are from Ministry of Finance 2001.

REFERENCES

Daily yomiuri. 1999. Panel welcomes role of cram schools. *Daily yomiuri*, June 10.
Gellner, Ernest. 1983. Nations and Nationalism. Oxford: Basil Blackwell.

Goodman, Roger. 1993. Japan's "International Youth": The Emergence of a New Class of Schoolchildren. Oxford: Clarendon Press.

Hall, Ivan Parker. 1998. Cartels of the Mind: Japan's Intellectual Closed Shop. New York: W. W. Norton.

Horio, Teruhisa. 1988. Educational Thought and Ideology in Modern Japan: State Authority and Intellectual Freedom. Steven Platzer, ed. and trans. Tokyo: University of Tokyo Press.

Huber, Thomas M. 1994. Strategic Economy in Japan. Boulder, CO: Westview Press.

Ishida, Hiroshi. 1993. Social Mobility in Contemporary Japan: Educational Credentials, Class and the Labour Market in a Cross-National Perspective. London: Macmillan.

Jiji, Tsūshinsha. 1996. Kyōiku dētarando 1996–1997 (Databook of Educational Statistics 1996–1997). Tokyo: Jiji Tsūshinsha.

Ministry of Finance. 2001. Monbu tōkei yōran (Statistical Abstract of Education, Culture, Sports, Science and Technology). Tokyo: Ministry of Finance.

Nakasone, Yasuhiro. 1997. Re-examine Fundamental Education Law. Daily Yomiuri, April 21.

Okano, Kaori, and Motonori Tsuchiya, eds. 1999. Education in Contemporary Japan: Inequality and Diversity. Cambridge: Cambridge University Press.

Pempel, T. J. 1998. Contemporary Japanese Athletics: Windows on the Cultural Roots of Nationalism-Internationalism. In The Culture of Japan as Seen through its Leisure. Sepp Linhart and Sabine Frühstück, eds. pp. 113–137. Albany: State University of New York Press.

Sakamoto, H. 1992. Monbushō no jikkan wa naze mienikui no ka (Why Is the Real State of the Ministry of Education Difficult to See?). In Monbushō no kenkyū: kyōiku no jiyū to kenri o kangaeru (Research on the Education Ministry: Thinking about the Freedom and Rights of Education). H. Sakamoto and H. Yamamoto, eds. pp. 13–25. Tokyo: Sanichi Shobō.

Senju, Katsumi. 1971. The Development of Female Education in Private School. Education in Japan 6:37–46.

Tsukada, Mamoru. 1991. Yobiko Life: A Study of the Legitimation Process of Social Stratification in Japan. Berkeley: Institute of East Asian Studies, University of California.

Yoneyama, Shoko. 1999. The Japanese High School: Silence and Resistance. London: Routledge.

Yoshino, Kosaku. 1992. Cultural Nationalism in Contemporary Japan: A Sociological Inquiry. London: Routledge.

SUGGESTED READING

Kihara, Takahiro, Takasuke Mutō, Kazunori Kumagai, and Hidenori Fujita, eds. 1983. Gakkō bunka no shakaigaku (The Sociology of School Culture). Tokyo: Fukumura Shuppan.

Matsui, Michiko. 1997. Tandai wa doko iku ka, jendā to kyōiku (Where are Junior Colleges Going? Gender and Education). Tokyo: Keisō Shobō.

McVeigh, Brian J. 1997. Life in a Japanese Women's College: Learning To Be Ladylike. London: Routledge.

—— 2002. Japanese Higher Education as Myth. New York: M. E. Sharpe.

Rohlen, Thomas. 1983. Japan's High Schools. Berkeley: University of California Press.

Sakamoto H. 1986. Kōsoku no kenkyū (Research on School Regulations). Tokyo: Sanichi Shobō.

Shimizu, Yoshihiro. 1992. Tandai ni ashita wa aru ka (Is There a Future for Junior Colleges?). Tokyo: Gakubunsha.

Toyoda, Toshio, ed. 1987. Vocational Education in the Industrialization of Japan. Tokyo: The United Nations University.

CHAPTER 18

Theorizing the Cultural Importance of Play: Anthropological Approaches to Sports and Recreation of Japan

Elise Edwards

In the last decade of the 19th century, Stewart Culin, an American-born businessman turned anthropologist, decided to expand upon his research on play and games among Native Americans in the United States and turned his anthropological gaze to playful pursuits in Japan, Korea, and China. Culin's research was influenced by the prominent and highly respected Sir Edward Burnett Tylor, one of the first social scientists to recognize games and "primitive sports" as worthy subjects of scholarly investigation. Tylor's interests in sports and games reflected the dominant British anthropological approach to cultural artifacts and practices at the time. He and other researchers looked for common characteristics among sports and games across geographical distances to prove paths of cultural diffusion. They also construed forms of play as "technologies" that supported evolutionary theories about stages of cultural development popular at the time. Unlike his contemporaries, Culin was not particularly interested in diffusion, but rather viewed games as keys to understanding the universal "primitive mind" of humans. For Culin, games were not "conscious inventions," but rather "survivals from primitive conditions" originating in magical and divinatory rites (Culin 1958 [1895]:xviii). They were "the most perfect existing evidence of the underlying foundation of mythic concepts upon which so much of the fabric of our culture is built" (Culin 1958 [1895]:xviii). As he explained in the forward to his book,

Games of the Orient (1895), Culin turned to Asia because, in his opinion, games had "nearly lost their original meaning" in the more "civilized" locales of America and Europe. Japan and its neighbors, on the other hand, retained a level of "primitiveness" that held great promise as he searched for the underlying structures and patterns of human consciousness that he believed remained embedded in forms of games and play. In *Games of the Orient*, a book filled with beautiful prints, drawings, and diagrams, Culin documented the magnificent variety of games, from shuttlecock to backgammon, and forms of children's play, including jump rope, see-saw, and tug-o'-war. The similarities and often exact duplication of gaming devices and forms of play between the three countries, Culin argued, was less a sign of diffusion and more proof of the existence of a universal underlying structure of human consciousness, traces of which remained in the more "primitive" regions of the world.

Thus, the first Euro-American anthropological inquiry into sporting and recreational activities in Japan was inspired less by a desire to understand Japan and more by the ambition of proving a grand theory of human evolution. Nevertheless, *Games of the Orient* provides a wonderful glimpse of the amazing range of games, sports, and pastimes pursued in fin-de-siècle Japan. However, Culin mentions nothing of the sports imported from Europe and the United States, such as baseball, tennis, and rugby, which, although not as popular as they would become in later decades, were already enjoyed in communities across Japan by the 1890s. Perhaps because he associated these sports with the more advanced stages of civilization in Europe and the United States, an acknowledgment of their enjoyment in Japan would undermine his assertion that Japan and its Asian neighbors were the perfect places to observe "primitive survivals."

Culin's work provides a provocative opening to a larger examination of anthropological approaches to sports and recreation in modern Japan. The fact that Culin posed Japan as a site of "traditional" practices at a time when the country was several decades into importing and incorporating a range of "modern" sports and physical practices from Europe and the United States points to the representational politics that inform all ethnographic writing. I will highlight the concerns and questions that have compelled commentators of various disciplinary affiliations and political stripes to consider sports in Japan, and to describe it in a diversity of ways. I will examine how political concerns, disciplinary trends, and a desire to document new or shifting cultural forms have influenced critical interest in sports from the late 19th century to the present. I have used a liberally inclusive definition of anthropology in order to recognize the contributions of individuals working outside either the academy or departments of anthropology, who have provided ethnographic documentation and theoretical insights that have both prefigured and contributed to contemporary pursuits on sports by professional anthropologists and sociologists. I also refer to biological anthropology in this exploration since it has, as I will explain, played such a critical role in the development of modern sports in Japan and elsewhere.

ETHNOGRAPHY OF MODERNITY AND NEW SPORTS CULTURE

While Stewart Culin elided mention of sports and games that did not support his evolutionary scheme, he had numerous contemporaries within Japan, including journalists, educators, social critics, and writers actively documenting and in various ways commenting on new forms of sports and exercise introduced from the United States and Europe, and on the new forms of social behavior and interaction occasioned by the rapidly changing sports environment. Gonda Yasunosuke (1887–1951), an ethnographer of modernity, was just one of a diverse group of commentators in the early 1900s who felt compelled to document and discuss the importance and meanings of the interactions of Japan's modern citizens with sports. Devoting themselves to the observation, survey, and recording of "mass play" (*minshū goraku*), Gonda and his small cadre of students spent countless hours pursuing in-depth fieldwork. They distributed questionnaires to movie- and theater-goers, observed patrons in cafés, bars, and the shopping streets of Ginza, and carefully documented every other type of behavior they deemed "playful." In Gonda's opinion, human pastimes and amusements, although seemingly trivial and overlooked by many, were important social acts full of ethnographic insights. Nothing seemed beyond his interest or notation: young students' penchant for playing cards, changing fads in musical instruments, and popular meeting spots. Gonda was also a keen observer of sports. He commented on seeing factory workers playing baseball in their lunch breaks, and described the "strange phenomenon" (*fushigi na genshō*) of hundreds of men and women standing still for hours outside of theaters in Asakusa to catch every innings of college baseball games broadcast from speakers positioned outside the entrances (Gonda 1933:3 cited in Kōzu 1995:253). For Gonda, the realm of play was not something separable from work and certainly not apolitical. Play, he declared, was a realm of creative, productive, and historically grounded social practice. As Miriam Silverberg has eloquently described, Gonda and many of his contemporaries were "constructivist" in the sense that they saw forms of human consumption and play as "constructive" practices that had the ability to create new forms of social interaction and meaning, as well as opportunities for resistance and empowering social connections (Silverberg 1992).

Beginning in the 1910s, Gonda's essays and studies appeared in a wide array of newspapers and magazines. However, his essays were certainly not the only works dedicated to documenting and understanding the plethora of new leisure pursuits and pastimes emerging in the lively Taishō and early Shōwa eras. When it came to the specific issue of sports, there were numerous commentators of diverse political persuasions and disciplinary backgrounds who joined passionate debates about the role of sports in society. Some of Gonda's contemporaries, while sharing his opinion that forms of play and sports were changing the rhythmic dynamics of everyday life, disagreed radically with regard to their effects. While some framed play and sports as means of positive self-actualization with emancipatory potential, other commentators expressed the fear that play and sports were party to the construction of new means of repression and exploitation. Writers of different political leanings found common ground in their recognition of sports as a social form particular to modernity that was creating new relationships between individuals and institutions (such as the military, schools, and other manifestations of the state), and new forms of interpersonal socialization and communication, such as fan associations and school rivalries, which suddenly took on new importance. Working several decades before the realization of a formal discipline of sports sociology, and certainly sports anthropology, these writers raised issues and made observations that prefigured many projects pursued in formal academic departments decades later.

Fiction writers of the 1920s and 1930s were among the most observant field-workers of modern sports in Japan. They produced numerous creative and colorful works that introduced characters and storylines that captured the emotions and scenes of sports at the time. Much of their work was inspired by actual sporting events, and included specific data from historic games and sports spectacles. The quality of the descriptions of the practical and affective aspects of sports captured in much of this fiction makes it arguably some of the richest ethnographic data that we have about Japanese sports in the early 20th century. Novelists, such as Abe Tomoji, included carefully integrated ethnographic data in his docufiction in order to capture the atmosphere of sporting events and the diverse political debates that were swirling around them. His short story, "A Competition Between Japan and Germany," which appeared in *Shinchō* (New Tide) in 1930, provides perceptive and accurate documentation of the events of an actual track meet that occurred between Japan and Germany in Tokyo in the fall of 1929. Attendance figures, the names of competitors, and race and event results are among the ethnographic details that Abe used to both ground and enliven his narrative about contemporary sports debates. As illustrated in Abe's story, these debates included voices from the right and the left, and from those who celebrated and those who demonized sport. It also provided an opportunity for him to express his own view of the liberating potential of sports.

Abe's fictional recreation of the track meet was just one of seven short stories about sports that he wrote that year. The famed fiction writer Nagai Kafū was also interested in the new cultural developments, including sports, emerging from the ruins of the Tokyo earthquake. However, Nagai was more skeptical about sports than many of his contemporaries, and saw modern sports as a manifestation of the anxiety and social upheaval that he felt marked the 1920s and 1930s. He outlined the connections that he believed existed between sports and a contemporary culture inured to increasing levels of violence in the epilogue of one of his most famous novels, *Bokutōkidan* (A Strange Tale from East of the River; 1937). These connections, Nagai suggested, were reflected in the behavior and lack of public censure of rowdy and sometimes even violent college baseball fans. He described the behavior of groups of Keiō University students and alumni he had witnessed the previous year joined together in the Ginza district of Tokyo after a game with their arch rival, Waseda. The fans strutted around in groups of four and five with their arms wrapped around each other's shoulders; they proceeded to get drunk and wreaked havoc on the area by disrupting café-goers and vandalizing houses and shops. Nagai was dismayed by this violent conduct, but even more confused and alarmed about the fact that this destructive group behavior seemed to be accepted and treated as commonplace by most Tokyoites (Sakaue 1998:82–3). Nagai's piece was unquestionably partly meta-phorical: it was a commentary on Japan's growing militarism and what he sensed as public complacency about that trend. But, like the work of many of his contemporaries, Nagai's writing also reflects a recognition of the relationships between sports and other pastimes – dismissed by many as frivolous – and larger cultural forces and ideologies.

In the 1920s and 1930s, newspapers and liberal magazines, such as *Chūo kōron* (Central Review) and *Kaizō* (Reconstruction), became lively sites of debate about sports in modern Japan and their connection to issues of class, nationalism, and political consciousness. Marxist intellectuals such as Hayashi Kaname, Sawada Toshio, Kaneko Yōbun, Murayama Tomoyoshi, and Yamakawa Tokio tried to account for the growing popularity of sports participation and spectatorship, and contemplated its political implications in articles and special magazine issues with titles such as "Classism and Sports," "Fan Psychology," and "Sports, Marx, and Cinema." The majority of writers, echoing the concerns of their Frankfurt School counterparts, viewed sport – as Hayashi put it – as part of the "smoke screen of modernity" (Sakaue 1998:148). They argued that the almost ravenous consumption of sports, particularly by students and intelligentsia, reflected the insecurity of the present moment. In their view, sports fostered passivity among the masses, masked class conflicts, and served as a means of ideological control by the state that effectively derailed the possibility of a socialist revolution. In 1931 Sawada elaborated on these arguments, together with a vision of a more empowering form of sports practice designed by the laboring masses for the masses, in his *Puroretaria supōtsu hikkei* (Proletarian Sports Handbook) (Sakaue 1998:150). Socialist critic Yamakawa Hitoshi's anxious contemplations in a 1936 article on the significance of Japan's winning the right to host the 1944 summer Olympics (which were later canceled due to the war), anticipated scholarly analyses produced in the late 20th century about the symbolic strength of sports in constructing dominant visions of national identity, and, by extension, jingoistic sentiments (Sakaue 1998:221–225).

A number of writers also explored the relationships between sports and modern subjectivity and wrestled with questions that interest sport scholars today. In his contribution to a *Chūo kōron* feature on "Fan Psychology" (1928), writer and literary critic Kataoka Teppei drew on his personal experiences attending baseball games to discuss fan subjectivity. He wrote about the seemingly inexplicable yet intense feelings of connection that fans feel for their team's players. These feelings could be so intense at times, he argued, that one could imagine being out on the field with the team. Kataoka explored these and other emotions – from severe stress to pure elation – that could be experienced in the new modern setting of fan bleachers. He and others also explored the influence of sport on the media and vice versa. They were intrigued by the rapidly growing number of sports pages in national dailies and by radio broadcasts of baseball games, as well as by the new nationwide phenomenon, beginning in 1930, of early-morning broadcasts of "radio gymnastics" (*rajio taisō*) (cf. Ochi 1930). These writers recognized the strong connections between sports and mass media developments, and contemplated the influence of sports media on social behavior and identity.

Individuals involved in planning sports and physical education policy also joined in ongoing debates about the purpose and effects of exercise and recreation. They often reiterated the arguments made by leftist commentators, albeit with a different political twist. For instance, in 1926, the head of the physical education division at the Ministry of Education, Kita Toyokichi, wrote about the positive relationship between sport and ideology in an article for a publication entitled *Asurechikusu* (Athletics) (Sakaue 1998:94). Like some of his leftist contemporaries, he too saw sports as a means of human escape. However, whereas Marxist critics portrayed this escape as a form of false consciousness that masked social inequalities and pacified the masses, Kita and others, interested in educating citizens to better serve the interests of the state, regarded the escape provided by sports as a positive "safety valve" (*anzenben*) that maintained social harmony. Like their leftist counterparts, these government officials acknowledged the ability of sport to forge group solidarity and national identity, and serve as a means of producing a disciplined citizenry. They grouped these potentials under the rubrics of "ideological guidance" (*shisō zendō*) and "national training" (*kokuminteki kunren*).

BUILDING BETTER BODIES: THE DEVELOPMENT OF "SPORTS SCIENCE"

The earliest vestiges of multiple disciplines that today fit under the rubric of "sports science" in Japan developed in departments of physical education and gymnastics newly formed in the late 19th century that were intertwined with medical science and anthropology. Consistent with the general trend of modern sports development in Europe and the United States, the earliest forms of Japanese physical education were firmly rooted in theories of racial physiology, the science of anthropometry, and notions of physical energy and fatigue that were central to the fields of physical anthropology and eugenics at the time. It is important to note that scientific research aimed at improving the human organism was not created to serve human interests in sports and play. Rather, it was the Enlightenment-inspired scientific interest in human measurement and calibration that *gave rise to* physical education – a discipline specifically designed to use physical movement and exercise to improve the physical constitution of individuals as well as to raise the quality of the "racial stock."

Mori Arinori (1847–89), the first Minister of Education, an influential Meiji intellectual, and the father of Japan's modern physical education system, serves as a powerful example of the co-constituting relationships between early Victorian anthropology, racial science, and sports. Mori's revolutionary promotion of physical education in Japan was greatly influenced by the theories of racial hygiene and eugenics coming from Europe and from within Japan as well. A personal friend and avid follower of Herbert Spencer, Mori rearticulated in his own writing the British scholar's arguments about the importance of physical exercise for human and social development. It is also interesting to note that one of Mori's protégés, Takahashi Yoshio, was the author of one of the first treatises on eugenics in Japan (Robertson 2001:4–5). The work and pursuits of Mori's European contemporary Erwin von Baelz also highlight the close connections between anthropology, eugenics, and sport in Japan at the turn of the century. Trained as a medical doctor, von Baelz spent 30 years (1876–1906) in Japan researching racial origins, and was very influential in shaping the Japanese discourse of eugenics at the time (Robertson 2001:4). In addition to medicine, von Baelz's interests included anthropology, folklore, and physical exercise and sport. He avidly studied *jūjitsu* and the modern derivative, *jūdō*, invented by Kanō Jigorō, another prominent proponent of physical education in fin-de-siècle Japan. Von Baelz published a book in Germany entitled *Kanō Jūjutsu* to promote Kano's new martial art of *jūdō*, and to share stories of his experiences furthering health education in Japan (Inagaki and Tanigama 1995:200).

Von Baelz made manifest his intersecting interests in Japanese racial biology and eugenics by promoting sports and exercise in Japan. Besides promoting *jūdō* in Germany, von Baelz was instrumental in popularizing the sport in Japan and out-spoken about his concerns about the unhealthy lifestyle of Japanese students. In fact, in 1896 he served as an advisor to the Japanese government's first "School Hygiene Advisory Group." Unquestionably, von Baelz's vision of sports differed considerably from that of his contemporary Stewart Culin. For von Baelz, Japan was not primitive but rather a key site of scientific research and invention. Despite his slightly Oriental-izing fascination with the martial arts, von Baelz also regarded Kanō's invention of *jūdō* as a form of physical exercise that rivaled the various forms of gymnastics being developed in Europe. He portrayed Japan as a country with a modern education system and programs of national hygiene, as well as the home of a modern type of exercise that he believed should be adopted in Germany and elsewhere.

Although the deep connections between physical education, social hygiene, and eugenics are too numerous to cover here, a few more snapshots of key pundits and their activities will help to provide a sense of the nature and range of the relationship of these mutually constitutive realms. Naruse Jinzō was an early and outspoken proponent of women's education – including physical education – for the purpose of training strong and able "good wives and good mothers" necessary for the success of a modern Japanese nation. Having studied for many years in the United States, Naruse was heavily influenced by Dudley Sargent, Harvard's famous women's phys-ical education pioneer. Naruse acknowledged his indebtedness to Sargent in the opening pages of his influential book, *Joshi kyōiku* (Women's Education; 1896). Dudley Sargent was a leader in applying anthropometric and physiological testing in the development of physical education curricula for women that would ostensibly improve their childbearing capabilities, restore nervous energy lost through mental activity, and bring them physically closer to "natural feminine perfection" (Cahn 1994:13, 19; Park 1987). Other physical educators trained in the United States and Europe, such as Iguchi Akuri, Nagai Michiaki, and Fujimura Toyo, were equally influenced by physical education traditions enmeshed in racial science and eugenics. They continued similar research, employing anthropometry and other physiological measures as they worked to develop and promote rational and scientifically based curricula aimed at improving the health of Japanese women, and, by extension, the health of yet unborn Japanese citizens. The three educators mentioned here were all centrally involved in both formulating national physical education policies and training young teachers who disseminated their ideas and education philosophies and techniques throughout Japan.

Beyond noting the linkages between physical education, physical anthropology, and eugenics in the late 19th and early 20th centuries, it is important to recognize the inherently anthropological character of the debates, research projects, and political struggles that swirled around the topics of sport and recreation from the final decades of the 19th century through to the end of World War II. Pedagogues, government officials, social commentators, and early ethnographers wrestled with questions regarding sport as a site of human activity, cultural production, and political practice. Although physical educators were mainly looking to use exercise and sport practically to train physically strong citizens, they also were concerned with creating a desired type of mind and disposition. Thus, they too, like contemporary politicians and social critics, were conceptualizing sport (as many anthropologists think about sport today) as spectacle, ritual, and disciplining practice. Central to their debates and ideas about sport and recreation were deeper questions about what it means to be a human being, mind–body connections, and the relationship between physical movement and thought, human production and social transformation. In addition, sports and recreation became a salient site for physical educators and social critics alike to contemplate citizens' relationships with the modern state, and pose politically informed arguments about desired social worlds. These debates, of course, became more charged and critical for everyone involved in an environment of rapidly escalating militarism.

Sports Sociology as a Formal Discipline

While physical educators continued to theorize about the physiological and psychological effects of different training regimes and education styles after the end of World War II, a formal discipline devoted to the social scientific study of sports and recreation also took shape in the 1960s. Japanese sports sociology developed alongside of, and was greatly influenced by, developments in sports sociology in the United States. Early articles and texts written by American scholars Gerald Kenyon (1965) and John Loy (1969) greatly shaped the character and course of the development of sports scholarship in the social sciences through the 1980s, and continue to exert considerable influence to this day in Japan and elsewhere. Kenyon, and those who followed in his footsteps, pursued a form of sports inquiry rooted in Comtian positivism and functionalist analysis. Japanese sports sociologists working within this tradition focused on the accumulation of social facts using empirical techniques, such as surveys and statistical analyses. Their methods were rooted in a belief in the objectivity and value-neutrality of the collected data – a position which, although untenable, was not significantly criticized until the 1990s. Social scientists working from this idealist or positivist perspective have been typically most interested in the functional relationship between sports and the outside world, and see sports as providing social cohesion and mechanisms for proper individual (usually male) socialization. Despite the problems, early functionalist studies represented an important step in the history of sports studies since they reflected a recognition of the importance of athletic and recreational practices in everyday life and their impact on social relationships and processes.

A frequently cited study that reflects the influence of the "Kenyon school" of sports scholarship and one of the earliest of countless other similar studies was a longitudinal survey project pursued by Arai Sadamitsu and Esaji Shōgo in Fukuoka Prefecture in the late 1960s and early 1970s. These two scholars distributed duplicate surveys in 1965 and again in 1971 to residents of Maebaru City located in western Fukuoka. The researchers were interested in how larger socio-structural changes, specifically the community's transition from agriculture to industry, were influencing residents' involvement in and enjoyment of local recreation and sports opportunities. In addition to recording the specifics of local citizens' employment histories, Arai and Esaji inquired about their general feelings of life satisfaction, their forms of class consciousness, and their involvement in sports-related activities. This one study is representative of a social-scientific approach to sports and recreation that continues to dominate sports sociology in Japan. Focused on the collection of quantifiable data and statistically informed conclusions, the studies are typically interested in identifying and evaluating variables that influence the degree of recreational and athletic involvement. Questions about different degrees and types of participation according to sex, age, class, and even "personality," just to name a few common variables, are standard among these studies. This genre of research takes a very policy-oriented and practical approach to the study of sports. Unlike earlier commentators, who were somewhat dubious about the social worth and political implications of sports participation, sociological studies of sport in the postwar era have been marked by an unfailing faith in the positive influence of sports. Sports sociologists research questions and draw conclusions that are based on the assumption that participation in sports inherently is a good thing. Researchers have also often assumed the task of evaluating the efficacy of government-led sports programs or charting general trends in sports and recreation practices that help to shape future government policies or actions. Arai and Esaji's study, for instance, was in many ways an effort to assess the effects of government initiatives enacted as part of 1961 Sports Promotion Law (Shimizu 1999:323). The Ministry of Education's push to develop "community sports" in the 1970s coincided with various studies focused on examining participation patterns in newly organized local sports programs. Similarly, the ministry's efforts to promote "lifetime sports" (*shōgai supōtsu*) in the 1980s spurred efforts to collect data on sports participation among senior citizens and other age groups (Shimizu 1999:324).

A dominant feature of sociological approaches to sport in Japan is the portrayal of sports as socially beneficial if implemented properly. The strong historical and institutional ties between sports sociology and physical education – effectively evinced by the number of sports sociologists working within departments of physical education – have unquestionably contributed to the programmatic and relatively unreflective pro-sports bias of sports sociological work. Although issues of meaning do enter these sociological projects, with some scholars inquiring about the factors shaping individual attitudes toward sports (for example studies that find that only small numbers of female college students participate in activities they perceive to be "masculine"), they usually do not examine sports events and participation as sites and processes of cultural production informing and informed by the larger social worlds in which they exist. Despite their lack of analytical or political sophistication, however, these studies have succeeded in furthering scholars' collection of a large amount of data, which provides useful documentation of sports development and participation in Japan and remains available for use and application in future projects.

Sociological studies of women's participation in sports were at first only an outgrowth of the larger discipline, and focused mainly on the variables affecting girls' and women's rates of participation. However, following the intellectual trajectory of other realms of women's studies, as data were accumulated on the characteristics of women's participation and patterns of inequality were realized some scholars began to ask new questions about the political significance of sport in informing and supporting dominant sex-role divisions and notions of gender. For instance, significant decreases in women's participation after marriage and childbirth, and the low rates of female participation in sports that were described by surveyed students as "masculine" led to new questions about sport as a site of knowledge production that shaped women's opportunities and social identities. Feminist approaches to sport in Japan have also been greatly influenced by a parallel interrogation of social-scientific approaches to sport by feminists in the United States and Britain that began in the 1970s, in addition to the broader influence of Japanese feminist activism emerging in the late 1960s. As was true elsewhere, feminist investigations into unequal opportunities in sports have been central to a gradual intellectual shift in Japan away from conceptualizing sport as an autonomous sphere disconnected from systems of power and toward a new understanding of sport as a realm of cultural practices that shape and are shaped by the larger social world. In some of the most outstanding work, scholars have looked at the ways that, despite a policy goal of entirely equal and gender neutral co-education in public school gym classes, teachers instruct their students in sports in ways that emphasize and teach gender difference according to their own notions of "natural" sex difference (Nagatsu 1995; Tada and Kuroki 1993). Despite the substantial inroads made by feminist scholars, there is still a considerable amount of sports research in which scholars fail to recognize the historically specific and culturally constructed nature of categories such as "masculinity" and "femininity." They continue to use these and other terms unreflectively rather than interrogating their use and the manner in which their formulations are constructed and reaffirmed by the sporting realm.

Physical Exercise and "Japanese Uniqueness"

Various Japanese actors have turned their attention to sports and recreation motivated by the intrigue of new cultural formations and practices, interests and concerns on the left and the right about the political power of sports, new scientifically and state-guided interests in shaping human minds and bodies, and recognition by the growing science of sociology of the importance of sport as a form of social practice. English-language literature about sports in Japan, however, has been dominated by work reflecting the prevalent tone of the postwar anthropology of Japan. Just as Stewart Culin bracketed his vision (and the vision of his readers) of games and sports in Japan to further his efforts to portray the country as a more "primitive" locale and thus a great site to find "survivals" of the psychological and spiritual structures underlying Western civilization, so foreign commentators three-quarters of a century later also have turned to sports to promote and reaffirm a particular vision of Japan. As we will see, this vision is evident in the kinds of sport practices they chose to research, and the ways in which they conceptualized sport as a realm of human practice.

   The majority of English-language material on sport in Japan is about the "traditional" martial arts, or *budō*, such as *jūdō* and *sumō* (e.g., Draeger 1981; Harrison 1950; Kushner 1988; Sargeant 1959; Turnbull 1990). Many of these works provide a wealth of information about the various terminologies, practices, and famous names connected to the martial arts. However, the writers frequently treat martial arts in a reified manner, as embodiments and proof of the persistence of a unique and transhistorical Japanese identity. Rather than exploring the ways in which martial arts have been constructed and appropriated in various processes of social and national identi-fication, scholars have frequently held them up as a mirror and a timeless and treasured cultural vessel that simultaneously reflects and continues to hold indomit-able truths of "Japan" and "Japaneseness." One of the most prominent authors of this martial arts genre is British scholar Stephen Turnbull, who has written over half a dozen books on the martial arts. In all of his work, Turnbull situates the martial arts first and foremost as a critical aspect of "samurai culture." Beyond the problematic fact that his notion of samurai history is culled from an amalgam of several literary sources, historical fragments, and classical myths, Turnbull presents this "history" as a relatively continuous and cohesive whole, with the unifying theme of *bushido* "the way of the warrior" threaded throughout. The visual images in Turnbull's book *The Lone Samurai* effectively reproduce the conflated history and image of a perduring Japanese essence. He combines undated woodblock prints, images from modern comics (*manga*), and movies, and pictures of contemporary martial arts practitioners in a haphazard montage with no historical or social context.

In one respect, we can read much of the Anglophone work on the martial arts in Japan as part of a much larger body of Japan scholarship that represents Japanese esthetic culture and its institutions, such as the tea ceremony and calligraphy, as perduring despite the disintegrating forces of modernity, as repositories of a timeless and unique Japanese essence. The martial arts and the "samurai ethos" they cultivate, like other aspects of esthetic culture, are imagined as a realm free from the influence of social and political forces and redolent of "the" true Japanese spirit. The writing of Turnbull and others also reflects the influence of Ruth Benedict's *The Chrysanthe-mum and the Sword* (1974 [1946]), which epitomizes the "national character stud-ies" approach to cultural analysis. Benedict's creation of a reified, psychologically reductionistic, and overly essentialized image of Japan and "the Japanese" produced an easy, enticing, and influential paradigm that has greatly shaped the course of Japan anthropology in the United States, along with the production of *nihonjinron* (dis-courses of Japaneseness) in Japan (Kelly 1991; Robertson 1998). Turnbull, for instance, marks his allegiance to Benedict by echoing her portrayal of the Japanese as embodying paradox and contradiction: he describes the "samurai spirit" as a binary entity with a "light" and a "dark" side, a force that is exemplified in contem-porary Japan by the coexistence of "right-wing extremism" and cities with streets that are "the safest to walk in after dark" (Turnbull 1990:55).

Robert Whiting (1977, 1990) similarly invokes a Benedictian image of the Japan-ese as inherently inscrutable and paradoxical in his cutely titled *The Chrysanthemum and the Bat* (1977). In explaining what makes Japanese baseball fundamentally different from the American "original," Whiting pushes Turnbull's ahistorical argu-ment about the samurai ethos one step further. He argues that, in Japan, the baseball diamond is a modern version of a medieval battlefield, and the players are modern samurai holding bats rather than swords. Focusing on the problems faced by talented American "Big League" players drafted by Japanese teams, Whiting positions the United States and Japan in a series of irreconcilable contrasts reminiscent of Benedict's list of cultural oppositions. America, the home of the World Series, advanced sports medicine, scientifically developed training techniques, and the best players in the world, contrasts with Japan, a country that despite its economic success reveals its cultural backwardness through the medium of baseball. Whiting presents Japan as "strange and fascinating," a site of a variety of anachronistic practices, where ballplayers seek cures for sore shoulders at austere Buddhist temples, where marathon training regimens flout scientific rationality, and where an indefatigable "fighting spirit" persists in the modern day (Whiting 1977:1). Whiting's approach is consistent with much of postwar writing about Japan in which Japan is oversimplified as the mirror-image of the United States: "Japanese character [is] rendered intelligible as American national character the other way around" (Robertson 1998:304).

The Chrysanthemum and the Bat, which has been translated into Japanese along with a second book, *You Gotta Have Wa* (1990), are among the sources most frequently cited by American and Japanese social scientists alike working on sports and recreation in Japan. Despite the somewhat glib nature of his writing, Whiting is to be commended for bringing the vibrant world of Japanese baseball to the attention of non-Japanese audiences, and for creating an interest among anthropologists for more careful research on the history and cultural dynamics of that sport. William Kelly (1998), for instance, critiques the image of "samurai ethic" in Japanese baseball by exploring how portrayals of baseball – specifically media treatments of the Yomiuri Giants of the late 1960s and the 1970s – actively produced culturally salient images of Japanese citizenship, including ideals of dedication to one's company and diligence at work, during Japan's period of dramatic economic growth. Shimizu Satoshi (1998) explores the history and present circumstances of high-school baseball in the context of Japan's most famous sporting event, Kōshien, the national high-school baseball championships. Using archival records documenting the creation of the national event, analyses of televised games, and interviews with players, parents, and community members, Shimizu produces an intricate picture of the "narratives" (*monogatari*) of high-school baseball in Japan in the 20th century. He indicates the centrality of baseball and the Kōshien tournaments to cultural understandings of "adolescence" (*seishun*) and "youth" (*seinen*), and to the production of both local and national discourses of identity. Whiting approaches sport as an apolitical and structurally inert phenomenon that, due to its commonality across cultures (i.e., same equipment, similar rules) was an ideal site for elucidating cultural difference. For Whiting, baseball is a mirror that reflects the personality and spirit of the people playing. Kelly and Shimizu, on the other hand, envision sport as a realm where notions of difference (national, racial, gendered, and so forth) are *created*, reproduced, reaffirmed, imprinted on the bodies of players and transmitted to and reformulated by spectators.

In recent years, a handful of scholars have problematized depictions of the martial arts as practices reflecting a timeless Japanese cultural essence. Several have worked to explain that, rather than a physical form virtually unchanged from its ancient origins, *jūdō* is in fact a modern invention that was promoted as a "national sport" (*kokugi*) in the 1920s and 1930s, and utilized as a nostalgia-laced repository of a culturally authentic Japanese national identity during the country's mobilization for total war (Inoue 1998a, 1998b; Sakaue 1998). Lee Thompson (Thompson 1990, 1998) has written about the *sumō* community's efforts at the turn of the 20th century to modernize the rules and structure of *sumō* while simultaneously trying to establish it as a quintessentially "traditional" practice. His work represents a more productive and stimulating approach to sport that underscores the importance of "play" in processes of cultural signification and the role of sport in negotiations of power and social transformations.

HISTORICAL CONTRIBUTIONS AND PROMISING BEGINNINGS

Since the 1980s, social scientists have turned their theoretical attention to the centrality of bodily regimes and discourses of hygiene to the construction of modern states and modern identities, a trend that has focused attention on the political content of sporting and recreational practices. Feminist scholars have pointed to the role of sport in producing and reaffirming sex and gender constructions, underscoring the impossibility of studying sport without addressing the attendant issue of power. The layered histories of sport also figure in recent research in Japan and elsewhere. While earlier histories of sport contained a confusing welter of dates, names, places, and other statistics, over the past 30 years historians have delved into a variety of topics and archival spaces and produced rich narratives documenting the central role of sports in the creation of the modern Japanese state and modern Japanese consciousness. This work documents the roles of physical education, exercise, sports performance, and spectatorship as ideological tools of the state and as sites of contestation over desired forms of daily life and political futures. Scholars have colorfully documented the proliferation of sporting practices in the final decades of the 19th century through 1945, noting variations in urban and rural experiences, the role of sports in the development of class identities, and the centrality of sports to a range of other forms and moments of political contestation (e.g. Kōzu 1995; Roden 1980). Much ink has been spilt revisiting the ideas and pursuits of early physical educators along with government policies which early on shaped the form, direction, and underlying ideology of school-based physical education (e.g., Inagaki and Tanigama 1995; Josei 1981; Kinoshita 1971; Kishino and Takenoshita 1983). Several scholars point to the great interest among pedagogues and bureaucrats in the newly modernizing Japan in developing special exercise and sports opportunities for girls. The Meiji government's pro-natalist policies and desire to strengthen the citizenry in pursuit of imperialist projects translated in practice to the development of a national physical education program designed specifically for girls and women (Josei 1981; Kaminuma 1967). Additionally, some historians have explored the ways in which gender difference, and femininity specifically, was conceptualized and constructed in and through physical education and sports in the early years of their development (Kaimizu 1988; Oie 1995). Scholars have paid considerable attention to the numerous intersections between physical education and militarism during Japan's wartime period, and recognize the importance of sports events and competitions as sites for the creation of new public rituals in the service of nationalism (Irie 1986; Sakaue 1998; Yoshimi et al. 1999).

Although there has been significantly less historical research conducted on sports in postwar Japan, examinations of narratives of the 1964 Tokyo Olympics as a genre of postwar memory (Igarashi 2000), and the popular myths linking Japan's postwar economic growth to Japanese-style professional baseball (Kelly 1998), point to the rich material in need of critical analysis. The Japanese sports historian Seki Harunami (1997) has produced a comprehensive and detailed review of postwar government sports policy, pointing to its connections with broader political and ideological currents in Japan. Although many political goals and methods have shifted over time, Seki's work also points to continuities between the first and second halves of the 20th century: physical education and competitive sports continue to be sites manipulated by the state in the hopes of stirring nationalist sentiment and creating productive (and consumptive) citizens.

However, in my view, a good deal of the most recent sports scholarship is theoretically rich yet ethnographically thin, which suggests deeper problems insofar as theories should be developed from empirical evidence. Japanese scholars have spent considerable time displaying their facility with the new theoretical perspectives that have emerged from the Euro-American academy since the 1980s. Consequently, there is a large literature on such topics as the relationship between viewership and performance, the inculcation of ideologies through bodily practice, the connection between the rationalization of sports and the creation of modern identities, and sports as symbolic display and ritualized experience (e.g., Inoue and Kameyama 1999; Kameyama 1990).

Unfortunately, however, only a fraction of this theoretically inclined literature is informed by actual empirical data collected in the course of ethnographic fieldwork. Few researchers have pursued full, book-length ethnographic projects. Instead, edited volumes and short articles, which do not provide adequate space for the full and careful treatment of topics, are the most popular publishing venues for new social scientific sports scholarship. Moreover, along with applying new theoretical perspectives from abroad, Japanese scholars also (re)present numerous case studies from foreign locales and give short shrift to Japanese sports and their histories. Ironically perhaps, theoretical problems concerning representation and historical specificity arise when the theories and the evidence used to substantiate them are recast as universally relevant. Articles on women in sports that carelessly vacillate between salient issues faced by Japanese women athletes, on the one hand, and their American counterparts, on the other, can have the effect of reinforcing, rather than dismantling, the erroneous assumption that sex and gender – as well as the ways in which they intersect with issues class and "race" – are universally consistent across cultures. Similarly, the notion of sports as a "common language" can deflect scholarship focused on historical and cultural specificities in favor of grand theories and the illusion of transnational commonalties.

The "soccer boom" of the 1990s sparked several ethnographic studies of Japanese sports. Although this "boom" is most frequently associated with the stratospheric success of the new professional men's J-League, a parallel women's L-League has also garnered attention as the only women's professional league of its kind in the world in the early and mid-1990s (Edwards 2003). The rapid growth of youth soccer and the coalescing of local fan groups and communities around J-League teams are among the associated phenomena worthy of ethnographic study. In addition, Japan's co-hosting of the 2002 Men's World Cup with South Korea offers an exciting and critical site for exploring the intersections of sporting practices and the constitution of Japanese and Korean identities. Some of the most recent sports scholarship has focused on the role of J-League teams in boosting local economies and rejuvenating local-place consciousness. Team sponsors, municipal governments, and local volunteers work together to create new forms of community consciousness for which sports teams function as an affective core (Koiwai 1994; Takahashi 1994). Researchers have also been intrigued by the new forms of social interaction, volunteerism, and local activism that emerged in combination with the popularization of soccer in the 1990s (Nakajima 1998; Yamashita and Saka 2002). In a related vein, the J-League and the growth of soccer more generally has occasioned interesting ethnographic investigations focused on J-League fans and their modes of performance at games and forms of socializing away from the pitch, and the meanings individuals attach to being fans (Shimizu 2000; Takahashi 1994).

The popularity of the internet has prompted scholars to consider the mutually constitutive relationship between sports and technology. Internet technology is facilitating new modes of communication between fans and soccer stars. Some players have even created their own independent websites in efforts to usurp more traditional media channels, tell their "own stories," and create more direct links with their fans (Sugimoto 1999). In turn, the internet has increased "connectivity" between "virtual fans" (*bāchuaru fuan*) and expanded the possible constituencies of and interactions between "imagined communities" beyond those provided by print and televisual technologies (Hashimoto 2000). Satellite broadcasts of European league matches beamed into Japanese households, the increasing visibility of top Japanese athletes in American and European teams, and the rapidly developing industry of sports tourism are also motivating researchers to think in new ways about the influence of sport on modern subjectivity and its role in the creation of new social networks, including diasporic communities linked through sport (Hirai 1999).

Most researchers today regard sports as "constructive" practices capable of producing new forms of social interaction and meaning. Significantly, these new and exciting areas of recent scholarship on sports and related playful practices are surprisingly reminiscent of the everyday ethnography conducted by the aforementioned Gonda Yasunosuke and others almost a century ago. Those of us who study sports should not forget the legacy of earlier intellectual approaches to the subject, or to the specific phenomena that captured the interests and imaginations of earlier generations of writers in and outside the academy. We must stay attuned to the complex intermixing of persisting or recurring patterns in sporting practices and events, as well as to their transformations across time and space. We also need to better understand the attitudes and identifications of sports fans and athletes, and to research the history of sporting spectacles and bodily practices, whose beginnings lie in activities that may seem far removed from the world of sport.

REFERENCES

Benedict, Ruth. 1974 [1946]. The Chrysanthemum and the Sword. Boston: Houghton Mifflin.

Cahn, Susan K. 1994. Coming On Strong: Gender and Sexuality in Twentieth-Century Women's Sport. New York: The Free Press.

Culin, Stewart. 1958 [1895]. Games of the Orient: Korean, China, Japan. Rutland, VT: Charles E. Tuttle.

Draeger, Donn F. 1981. The Martial Arts and Ways of Japan. New York: Weatherhill.

Edwards, Elise. 2003. The "Ladies League": Gender Politics, National Identity, and Professional Sports in Japan. Ph.D. dissertation, University of Michigan.

Gonda, Yasunosuke. 1933. Rajio gorakuron (Discussions of Radio Play). Chōsa jihō 3(9):3.

Harrison, E. J. 1950. The Fighting Spirit of Japan: The Esoteric Study of the Martial Arts and Way of Life in Japan. New York: Foulsham.

Hashimoto, Junko. 2000. Intānetto ue no sakkā (Soccer on the Internet). *In* Gendai supōtsuron. Nakamura Toshio, ed. pp. 118–123. Tokyo: Sōbun Kikaku.

Hirai, Hajime. 1999. Supōtsu no gurōbaraizēshon (The Globalization of Sports). *In* Supōtsu o manabu hito no tame ni. Inoue Shun and Kameyama Yoshiaki, eds. pp. 210–228. Kyoto: Sekai Shisōsha.

Igarashi, Yoshikuni. 2000. Bodies of Memory: Narratives of War in Postwar Japanese Culture, 1945–1970. Princeton: Princeton University Press.

Inagaki, Masahiro, and Tanigama Ryōshō, eds. 1995. Supōtsushi kōgi (Sports History Lectures). Tokyo: Taishukan Shoten.

Inoue, Shun. 1998a. The Invention of the Martial Arts: Kanō Jigorō and Kōdōkan Judo. *In* Mirror of Modernity: Invented Traditions of Modern Japan. Stephen Vlastos, ed. pp. 163–173. Berkeley: University of California Press.

—— 1998b. Kindai nihon ni okeru supōtsu to bushidō (Sports and the Martial Arts in Modern Japan). *In* Henyō suru gendai shakai to supōtsu. Nihon Supōtsu Shakaigakkai, ed. pp. 225–235. Kyoto: Sekai Ahisōsha.

Inoue, Shun, and Kameyama Yoshiaki, eds. 1999. Supōtsu bunka o manabu hito no tame ni (For People who Study Sports Culture). Kyoto: Sekai Shisōsha.

Irie, Katsumi. 1986. Nihon fuashizumuka no taiiku shisō (Ideology of Physical Education under Japanese Fascism). Tokyo: Fumidō Shuppan.

Josei, Taiikushi Kenkyūkai, ed. 1981. Kindai nihon josei taiikushi: josei taiiku no paioniatachi (The History of Women's Physical Education in Modern Japan: Pioneers of Women's Physical Education). Tokyo: Nihon Taiikusha.

Kaimizu, Kayoko. 1988. Senzen no gakkō taiiku seido ni okeru joshi no tokusei ni tsuite (References to Girls' Special Qualities in Prewar Physical Education Policy). Fujimura gakuin tōkyō joshi taiiku daigaku kiyō 23(3):1–8.

Kameyama, Yoshiaki. 1990. Supōtsu no shakaigaku (Sociology of Sports). Kyoto: Sekai Shisōsha.

Kaminuma, Hachirō. 1967. Kindai nihon joshi taiikushi josetsu (Introduction to Modern Japanese Women's Physical Education History). Tokyo: Kokusai Bunken Insatsusha.

Kelly, William. 1991. Directions in the Anthropology of Contemporary Japan. Annual Review of Anthropology 20:395–431.

—— 1998. Blood and Guts in Japanese Professional Baseball. *In* The Culture of Japan as Seen through its Leisure. Sepp Linhart and Sabine Frühstück, eds. pp. 95–111. Albany: SUNY Press.

Kenyon, Gerald S., and John W. Loy. 1965. Toward a Sociology of Sport. Journal of Health–Physical Education–Recreation 36:24–5, 68–9.

Kinoshita, Hideaki. 1971. Nihon taiikushi kenkyū josetsu (An Introduction to Japan Sports History Research). Tokyo: Fumidō.

Kishino, Yūzō, and Takenoshita Kyūzō. 1983. Kindai nihon taiikushi (History of Modern Physical Education in Japan). Tokyo: Nihon Toshō Sentā.

Koiwai, Zenichi. 1994. Sakkaa ni yoru machizukuri: "kōgyō no machi" kara "wakamono ga teichaku suru tanoshii machi e" (Town-Making Through Soccer: from "Industrial Towns" to "Fun Towns Established by Young People"). Toshi mondai 85(12): 59–69.

Kōzu, Masaru. 1995. Nihon supōtsushi no teiryū (Undercurrents of Japan Sports History). Tokyo: Sōbun kikaku.

Kushner, Kenneth P. 1988. One Arrow, One Life: Zen, Archery, and Daily Life. New York: Arkana.

Loy, John W., and Gerald S. Kenyon. 1969. Sport, Culture, and Society: A Reader on the Sociology of Sport. New York: Macmillan.

Nagatsu, Yoshi. 1995. Danjo no tokusei o ikashita shidō: yūkō na kadairei (Instruction that Brings Out Male and Female Characteristics: Effective Examples). Joshi taiiku 37(4):20–23.

Nakajima, Nobuhiro. 1998. Chiiki shakai kara mita j-rīgu: shimin reberu de no kōryū no kanōsei (The J-League from the Perspective of Local Society: The Potential for Exchange at the Level of Citizens). In Henyō suru gendai supōtsu shakai to supōtsu. Nihon Supōtsu Shakaigakkai, ed. pp. 148–156. Kyoto: Sekai Shisōsha.

Ochi, K. 1930. Supōtsu ga rajio ni naru made (Sports Have Made It To Radio). Rajio no nihon 11(4):2.

Oie, Chieko. 1995. Meijiki ni okeru kōtō jogakkō no taiiku no jissai ni kan suru shiteki kōsatsu (A Historical Investigation of the Realities of Meiji Era Girls' High School Physical Education). Nihon Taiiku Daigaku Kiyō 25(1):1–13.

Park, Roberta J. 1987. Sport, Gender and Society in a Transatlantic Perspective. In From "Fair Sex" to Feminism: Sport and the Socialization of Women in the Industrial and Post-industrial Eras. J. A. Mangan and Roberta. J. Park, eds. pp. 58–96. London: Frank Cass.

Robertson, Jennifer. 1998. When and Where Japan Enters: American Anthropology Since 1945. In The Postwar Developments of Japanese Studies in the United States. Helen Hardacre, ed. pp. 294–335. Boston: Brill.

——2001. Japan's First Cyborg? Miss Nippon, Eugenics, and Wartime Technologies of Beauty, Body and Blood. Body & Society 7(1):1–34.

Roden, Donald F. 1980. Schooldays in Imperial Japan: A Study in the Culture of a Student Elite. Berkeley: University of California Press.

Sakaue, Yasuhiro. 1998. Kenryoku sōchi to shite no supōtsu (Sports as an Apparatus of Power). Tokyo: Kōdansha.

Sargeant, J. A. 1959. Sumo: The Sport and the Tradition. Rutland, VT: C. E. Tuttle.

Seki, Harunami. 1997. Sengo nihon no supōtsu seisaku: sono kōzō to tenkai (Sports Policy in Postwar Japan: Structure and Development). Tokyo: Taishūkan Shōten.

Shimizu, S. 1998. Koshien yakyū no arukeorogii: supōtsu no "monogatari," medeia, shintai-bunka (The Archaeology of Koshien Baseball: Sports "Legend," Media, and Body Culture). Tokyo.

——1999. Jisshōteki apurōchi (Empirical Approaches). In Supōtsu bunka o manabu hito no tame ni (For People who Study Sports Culture). Inoue Shun and Kameyama Yoshiaki, eds. pp. 321–340.Tokyo: Sekai Shisōsha.

——2000. Sapōtā: sono hyōshō to kioku, soshite ima tsukareteiku mono toshite (Supporters: Symbol, Memory, and that Created in the Moment). In Gendai supōtsu hyōron. Nakamura Toshio, ed. pp. 75–90. Tokyo: Sōbun Kikaku.

Silverberg, Miriam. 1992. Constructing the Japanese Ethnography of Modernity. The Journal of Asian Studies 51(1):30–54.

Sugimoto, Atsuo. 1999. Supōtsu fuan no bunka (Culture of Sports Fans). In Supōtsu bunka o manabu hito no tame ni. Inoue Shun and Kameyama Yoshiaki, eds. pp. 150–167. Tokyo: Sekai Shisōsha.

Tada, Ryōichi, and Kuroki Kei. 1993. Hajimete torikumu danjo kyoshū no dansu shidō: supōtsu bamen o toraete (Tackling Co-educational Dance Instruction for the First Time: Capturing the Sports Scene). Joshi taiiku 35(9):28–31.

Takahashi, Yoshio. 1994. Sakkā no shakaigaku (Sociology of Soccer). Tokyo: Nihon hōsō shuppan Kyōkai.

Thompson, Lee. 1990. Supōtsu kindairon kara mita sumō (Sumo from the Perspective of Modern Theories of Sport). *In* Supōtsu no shakaigaku. Kameyama Yoshiaki, ed. pp. 71–94. Kyoto: Sekai Shisōsha.

——1998. The Invention of the *Yokozuna* and the Championship System. *In* Mirror of Modernity. Stephen Vlastos, ed. pp. 174–190. Berkeley: University of California Press.

Turnbull, Stephen R. 1990. The Lone Samurai and the Martial Arts. London: Arvis & Armour Press.

Whiting, Robert. 1977. The Chrysanthemum and the Bat: Baseball Samurai Style. New York: Avalon.

——1990. You Gotta Have Wa. New York: Vintage Books.

Yamashita, Takayuki, and Saka Natsuko. 2002. Another Kick Off: The 2002 World Cup and Soccer Voluntary Groups as a New Social Movement. *In* Japan, Korea and the 2002 World Cup. John Horne and Wolfram Manzenreiter, eds. London: Routledge.

Yoshimi, Shunya, Shirahata Yōzaburō, Hirata Munefumi, Kimura Kichiji, Irie Katsumi, and Kamisuki Masako. 1999. Undōkai to nihon kindai (Sports Festivals and Japanese Modernity). Tokyo: Seikyusha.

SUGGESTED READING

Horne, John, and Wolfram Manzenreiter. 2002. Japan, Korea and the 2002 World Cup. London: Routledge.

Sugimoto, Atsuo. 1997. Supōtsu fuan no shakaigaku (Sociology of Sports Fans). Kyoto: Sekai Shisōsha.

CHAPTER 19 Popular Entertainment and the Music Industry

Shuhei Hosokawa

INTRODUCTION

"Popular entertainment" is difficult to define as a scholarly subject. Can feasts, gambling, hobbies, games, sports, and play in general be considered as entertainment? What does "popular" mean in this case, and would its opposite be something like "aristocratic entertainment"? Instead of delving into the terminological debates, I will loosely apply the term "popular entertainment" to refer to forms of mass-oriented performance – whether staged or not, live or not – produced and mediated mainly by the professionals. (I will use "popular entertainment" and "entertainment" interchangeably.) As a theatrical practice, entertainment consists of sounds, images, and/or spectacles. Anthropologists who study entertainment are especially interested in the interconnection between industry, audience, and technology. How has professionalism been established, and how does the audience interpret the performance, performer, and the other spectators? Does or can technology determine the condition of production and reception, and to what degree? What do the elite consider entertainment and how have censorship, Enlightenment ideologies, and social reform intervened in the politics of entertainment? These are some of the issues I will address in this brief review of the history of popular (musical) entertainment in Japan. I will focus specifically on popular music: it is increasingly omnipresent in our daily life and has become a catalyst generating distinctive moods in a variety of settings; it also connects different sections of the entertainment industry. But I shall begin with an overview of the scholarship on popular entertainment.

Entertainment as a cultural institution minimally comprises a production team, a product (work, performance, program, text), and an audience group. The production is collectively organized by artists, performers, publishers, managers, patrons, sponsors, publicity agents/agencies, and many other auxiliary players. The resulting collective product usually has a title and author(s), and more or less standardized and predictable contents. To reach an audience, the product has to be mediated by a number of intermediaries and technologies, and together these agents build up an industry. The entertainment business intends to make the largest profit from the product, using various types of technology available for amplifying, distributing (transmitting), and receiving the sounds and images. Today no "live" performance would be conceivable without electronic equipment. The enlargement of the industry, and the greater extent of technological intervention in the processes of production, mediation, and reception, inevitably involves the audience.

The audience is of course heterogeneous in terms of age, gender, sexuality, locality, class, ethnicity, race, and other attributes. How a large production team manages to create an artifact is as complicated as how a given audience interprets it, depending on the individual members' social and cultural backgrounds. Audience interpretation is also contingent upon how each momentary experience of an artifact or performance is linked to other ones.

Distinction (1979), Pierre Bourdieu's groundbreaking work on taste and social judgment, spurred social scientists to recognize taste formation as a key to understanding social stratification and positioning. Anthropology treats the audience as an agent that interprets a given product or performance according to its members' relationship to global and local circumstances. This relationship is not always anticipated or predicted by the production side, which addresses how and where the performance and program are produced and received, how the producers and audience intend and interpret the products, and how and why people engage in seemingly unproductive activities. The sociological view of media audiences has shifted from an image of passive and manipulated subjects to a recognition of active agents who "read" the text – not necessarily according to the intention of the author(s). Recently, the theory of an active audience has been challenged by scholars who insist that, for the most part though with some exceptions, audience responses are shaped by the embedded intentions of media producers. Active audience theory without ethnographic depth ends in the celebration of "the audience" conceived ideologically as merely the reversal of the pessimistic typology of the popular culture industry advanced by Theodor Adorno.

But the difficulty of studying audiences lies in how we obtain the data on their experiences, ideas, and interpretations. Interviews of course provide anthropologists with useful sources; however, the results are difficult to systematize. Written materials (fanzines, reviews, mailing lists, etc.) tell us about so-called "deep audiences," or those fans who are emotionally engaged enough to write about their experience for other readers. Probably the most difficult subject to study is the capricious majority who are interested in many products simultaneously and momentarily, and who do not display their passion overtly. They are also accustomed to multi-tasking, often distractedly, in domestic or public settings. Some sociologists rightly believe that analysis of the "flow" of disparate experience is more important than that of the reception of particular "works." As much as the product (or "text" as some define it) is usually a composite of the visual and the audio, the verbal and the non-verbal, the spoken and the sung, audience experiences are heterogeneous. Some spectators tend to pay close attention to the star, for example, and others prefer to interpret the narrative or listen to a song.

STUDIES OF ENTERTAINMENT IN JAPAN

Entertainment was not regarded as worthy of in-depth research by Japanese scholars until the 1920s when the first systematic studies of popular entertainment were undertaken. It was during this decade that radio, electric recording, and film developed rapidly on a global scale. Since then, the entertainment industry has been consolidating a worldwide network of sound and image, humans and goods, information and communication. The early researchers of popular entertainment were all conscious of the radical transformation in people's way of living, feeling, and thinking encouraged by the new cultural industry and technology. The Frankfurt School and the Chicago School are representative of new intellectual trends in the study of popular culture, the former drawing inspiration from Marxism, the latter from urban subcultures.

In Japan, Gonda Yasunosuke (1887–1951), probably without knowledge of these intellectual trends overseas, started conducting quantitative research in the early 1920s on the audiences for popular film and theater. His motive was to collect data as a first step toward the "reform" of messy urban spaces and people's lives. Gonda focused on the Asakusa area, "Tokyo's Montmartre" before the great Kantō earthquake (1923), a veritable melting-pot of lower-class workers, bohemians, and anarchists. Using interviews and inquiries, he discerned the patterns of behavior and taste preferences displayed by film and theater audiences, the relationship of class and profession to those patterns, and the industrial background of entertainment. Gonda treated audiences collectively as agents of new cultural formations, and regarded entertainment as an urban institution that made the masses visible (Gonda 1974; see also Silverberg 1992). Following him, Kon Wajirō (1888–1973), an industrial designer by training, charted the behavior of crowds through close and statistically quantifiable observations, and called attention to the new lifestyle after the 1923 earthquake. Directly or indirectly, both Gonda and Kon were sensitive to the radical changes in progress that they observed in the mode of cultural production, distribution, reproduction, and consumption occasioned by the emergence of new entertainment technologies.

The democratic milieu of postwar Japan facilitated the ability of intellectuals to refer to "mass culture" since, for Marxists and liberals alike, the "masses" had become potential agents to be liberated from the feudal-military system. The authors of the liberal journal *Shisō no kagaku* (Science of Thoughts), founded in 1946, represented the first wave in the study of entertainment after the war. Drawing in part on social reformists and American social psychologists, they discussed, among other things, how the seemingly banal contents of popular songs and novels reflected both the unspoken fantasies and the conservatism of the populace. Taking popular culture seriously was already a radical gesture that was detached from elitism. In general, contributors to *Shisō no kagaku* advocated the popular and the democratic – these two concepts were often used synonymously – rejecting the authoritarian and the "feudalistic." In retrospect, they tended to be naively populist and must be understood in the intellectual context of the Cold War era (see Yoshimi 1994).

Among those affiliated with *Shisō no kagaku*, Tsurumi Shunsuke is especially important for his influential concepts of *kōkūyu geijutsu* (high art), *taishū geijutsu* (mass or popular art) and *genkai geijutsu* (marginal art). Popular entertainment, as I have defined it, falls into the category of "mass art," or the expression produced by professionals for the service of a large, anonymous collective (Tsurumi 1982). Another influential scholar connected with this journal is Minami Hiroshi (1987), the "founder" of social psychology in Japan and mentor of scholars such as Mita Minesuke, author of *Social Psychology of Modern Japan* (1992). These scholars have pursued the analysis of the Japanese national *mentalité* and sensibility through popular culture. Implicitly, they have presupposed a unified history that embraced the nation as a homogenous whole. To counter such a simplified narrative became a task for scholars in later decades (cf. Robertson 2001 [1998]: 28–37).

In the 1960s the terms "mass communication" (abbreviated as *masukomi*), "information," and "media" gained currency through the Japanese translations of Marshall McLuhan, David Riesmann, and other North American authors. The burgeoning GNP and the concomitant rise in the quality of material life effectively ensured the popularity of these scholars. Television became a focal point for many commentators, whether they treated it as a tool for democratic entertainment or for vulgar passions. In 1976 Kansai-based scholars and dilettantes, including Kuwabara Takeo, Tada Michitarō and Tsurumi Shunsuke, founded the Gendai Fūzoku Kenkyūkai (Research Group on Contemporary Popular/Everyday Culture) in order to look into the details of quotidian life that had mostly been neglected by academics. Scholars and non-scholars alike have sought out curious objects that are too banal to be noticed, usually relying on empirical methods over high theory. The sociologists of popular entertainment such as Inoue Shun (leisure), Ogawa Hiroshi (popular music), Nagai Yoshikazu (social dancing) and Ukai Masaki (popular theater) are affiliated to this circle (Ivy 1995).

The number of translations of European authors increased in the 1970s and 1980s, and the works of Adorno, Benjamin, Enzensberger, Barthes, Baudrillard, and many others were perused for their critical and theoretical insights. So-called "semiotic" readings of television, advertisements, sports, walkman, pop music, *manga*, animation, and other mass products became abundant. Popular entertainment was acknowledged as a legitimate subject worthy of systematic and critical research. Toward the end of the 20th century, such a tendency was further encouraged by the rise of Anglophone cultural studies in Japan. Today, a growing number of scholars and students are conscious of the importance of studying popular culture and entertainment.

MODERNIZATION OF THE MUSIC ENTERTAINMENT INDUSTRY

It is important to realize that Japan's entertainment industry was not the exclusive result of Western contact in Meiji. Show business has been developing in Japan since the 17th century along with sophisticated production teams, distribution and information networks, and organized and unorganized audiences. The prototype of today's multi-mediated entertainment industry can be found in the popular *kabuki* theater and various *shamisen* genres thriving in the licensed "pleasure quarters" during the Edo period (1603–1868), especially after the 18th century.

The nascent show business was the fruit of economic and artistic collaboration among *kabuki* directors, managers, patrons, the public, and the artists. Top actors had their fan clubs organized on a neighborhood basis aimed at monopolizing the patronage and personal acquaintance with the stars. Club members had first choice in tickets for a good seat; these club functions are essentially the same as those operative today. Famous actors authorized woodcut portraits and patented kimono designs and sweet cakes named after them. Review articles were influential on the reception of the performance and the reputation of the actors, and gossipy leaflets amplified rumors about actors and courtesans/singers. Many such cases were related to the commercial alliance of the theater world with patronage, the print media, censorship, commodities, fashion, food, and the fan community (Hattori 2003).

One of the new developments in Meiji music was the emergence of "authorship." The concept of "author" had been mostly alien to the performance practices of Edo period music, and was occasioned by the modernization of the print media. Unlike the anonymous songs diffused from the "pleasure quarters" from the 18th to the mid-19th centuries, Meiji period street singers began the practice of selling leaflets with the name of the lyricist as part of their street performance. Similar to the "broadside balladeers" in Victorian England, these singers usually rearranged the melody of existing songs and added political, romantic, comical, satirical, erotic, and other types of lyrics (Nishizawa 1990; Soeda and Soeda 1982). Though musically unrefined, their performance, a mixture of calling and singing in pairs, attracted the attention of passers-by. The introduction of the violin in 1910 seems to have inspired the composition of sentimental – even tear-jerking – songs, the lyrics of which were drawn from best-selling novels and *shinpa* dramas. Such narratives usually dealt empathetically with the moral conflict between the feudalistic family code and modern womanhood. Although they were not yet systematic, the links in show business between popular songs, journalism, and drama were beginning to be forged.

The connection of songs with the stage arts was clinched when the Geijutsuza (Art Theater) troupe incorporated the popular hit "Kachūsha no uta" (Katyusha's Song) into their première performance of Tolstoy's *Resurrection* in 1914. Nakayama Shinpei (1887–1952) was the first composer to make a living by selling his melodies. He thus established the concept of authorship in song-writing. The principal performer of his songs was the provocative actress Matsui Sumako, who interpreted Nakayama's songs in her stage shows. Such a close connection of songs with a particular singer was unprecedented at that time. Recordings and the sheet music, which were available in fin-de-siècle Japan, also accounted for the nationwide reputation enjoyed by both individuals.

Throughout the 1910s and 1920s, a period characterized by a political atmosphere of détente and middle-class activism, the record and music publishing industries alike were growing and, consequently, the pursuit of a hit song became quite intense. Record companies strove to discover new and trendy songs while the print media produced elaborate artwork and established a distribution network. Nakayama's early songs were recorded by Geijutsuza actresses accompanied by a piano, a luxury item symbolic of the education received by a typical upper-middle-class woman. The new kind of sheet music, in turn, followed a Western format featuring pentagrams (or numeric notations), lyrics and, most importantly, beautiful covers designed by commercial artists. These artists were especially popular among middle-class schoolgirls, a new target audience within a consumer-oriented society, who purchased and collected sheet music for both the notations and for the artwork. These handsome sheets were a prominent aspect of print capitalism and were graphically distinct from the coarsely made leaflets sold by the aforementioned street singers, who, along with geisha, were nevertheless indispensable agents in the circulation of Nakayama's songs. Popular songs of the Taisho period (1912–26), represented by Nakayama's hit tunes, marked an important shift in the production site of popular music from the pleasure quarter to the recording studio. Songwriting became as professionalized as the print media and recording. Popular songs were rapidly parlayed into commodities, and Western instruments came to prevail as the new tastes of the growing middle class created an unbridgeable distance from music and musical sensibility the Edo period.

INTO THE ELECTRIC AGE

The industrialization of music production and consumption quickened after the 1923 earthquake. The decade of that catastrophic event was witness to the emergence of a modern lifestyle characterized by the new electric media such as radio and talkie films, the commodity economy, Americanism, and so forth. The zeitgeist was signified by the loanword *modan* (modern). To define a new concept of "the people" formed by the social force of new cultural technologies and capitalism, the word *taishū* was replaced with *minshū*, a notion connoting a grassroots collective active since the 1910s. *Taishū*, by contrast, usually implies the people administered "from above," manipulated by industry. Of course, neither term is free from cultural ideology (Ivy 1995:ch. 1; see also Kawazoe 1980; Robertson 2001 [1998]:33–34).

A major auditory change was associated with the omnipresence of electrically produced sound. "Modernites" were, willingly or not, exposed to this sound from radios, talkies, phonographs, and public address systems in public halls, train stations, on the streets, and in other spaces. The word "jazz" was often used synonymously with these new sound sources; it was also used as a euphemism for moral decadence and cultural contamination. The 1920s have been nicknamed the Jazz Age. It is rare for a musical term to evoke such a wide range of values and feelings. Jazz, for example, became a metaphor for the noise generated by cities. What the use of this terminology reveals is how people's acoustic experience underwent a radical transformation in the 1920s.

In popular music, too, the introduction of microphones and electric recording systems was crucial. While the former brought the vocal technique of crooning to Japanese popular music, the latter clinched the dominance of major labels backed by foreign capital, such as Victor, Columbia, and Polydor. Their monopoly affected the entire domain of popular music production. These labels were closely linked with the publication and publicity sectors, and they signed exclusive contracts with composers, lyricists, and singers, which occasioned an assembly-line approach to song production. This system also fostered a new and active role in song production on the part of record companies. Whereas, by the end of the 1920s, local companies had recorded pieces written or popularized by street singers, geishas, and others, the major labels made it a rule to release a certain number of new songs every month, even though only a few of them became commercial successes. Thus, the major companies began to take the initiative in creating musical fads (Komota et al. 1994–95).

Despite the general economic depression, the entertainment industry continued to grow in the 1930s, as is attested by the construction of large theaters, record sales, significant production costs, huge audiences, and other factors. The major labels, and show business in general, intensified their relationship to commodity culture, the mass media, fan organizations and other informational and commercial networks. This strategy, known as the "tie-up," paralleled the enormous growth of the entertainment industry, along with the development of available technologies and the education of audiences. A notable example of this new business practice was the film *Tokyo kōshinkyoku* (Tokyo March), which was shown in movie theaters in 1929. A massive public relations campaign included the novel of the same name serialized in *Kingu* (King), a popular magazine, and Nakayama's song in the film. All three of the identically titled works became the best-selling items that year in their respective categories.

The "tie-up" strategy was immediately applied to patriotic campaigns orchestrated in the wake of Japan's imperialistic encroachments into China in 1931, beginning in 1932 with the saga of the "three brave men," the name for the suicide attackers who helped the Japanese army secure Shanghai. Within several weeks of the appearance of their "heroic" story in the mass media, all the "culture industries" had joined to fuel their popularity cult. The major newspapers organized a nationwide campaign for lyrics and music eulogizing the three men: over 200,000 readers responded. Radio stations broadcast real and fictitious stories and songs about the heroes, and movie theaters were crowded with audiences eager to watch newsreels and "documentaries" on the attacks. Modern and traditional theaters were used, along with various story-telling genres, to present dramatic works on the heroes, and new fashions and foods were created in their honor and sold at department stores (Akazawa and Kitagawa 1993).

The "three brave men" boom attested to the media's loyalty to state policies and paved the path for the culture industry to profit from war by fomenting mass enthusiasm for things military. For example, all the "military gods," or soldiers who died in a dramatic way, as well as the successful battles, were eulogized in songs, novelized "true stories," and films. Newspapers and magazines regularly solicited new lyrics (and sometimes melodies) with specific themes. "March of the Pacific" and "Song of Gratitude to Imperial Soldiers" were two such songs recorded by famous singers. Other solicited songs were typically debuted in stage shows that included newsreels, patriotic speeches and other musical fare. Radio shows and films based on the songs followed. The wartime mobilization of the entertainment industry became more obvious when the military situation worsened for Japan and censorship became more strict (Kasza 1988; Robertson 2001 [1998]:ch. 3; Tsuganesawa and Ariyama 1998).

The establishment of music authorship entailed the consolidation of copyright practices. By the 1930s, royalties had become a primary source of income for composers, lyricists, and singers, enabling them to live as "professional" authors or artists in their own right and, consequently, to establish an identity as "author" or "artist." Their professional activities were subject to the commercial demands of standardization and the division of work. The establishment of authorship prevented record companies from recording extant melodies to which they added new, parodic lyrics (*kaeuta*) as had been done in previous decades. The copyright law of the 1930s protected the rights of Japanese artists but not those of foreign works, which were performed and adapted quite freely in theaters, concert halls, films, and broadcasts. During the 1930s, a German agent representing European copyright law filed numerous lawsuits against the illegal use of foreign works but met only with xenophobic refusals. Japanese entrepreneurs tried to avoid international legal stipulations for paying permissions and royalties by arguing that their use of foreign works was not motivated by profit-mongering, but that Western (copyrighted) art was needed for the purposes of enlightening the nation. The ensuing legal conflicts alerted the music industry to the urgent need for an internationally sanctioned organization, resulting in the establishment of Japan's own organization for copyright control. After World War II this organization was restructured and named the Japanese Association for the Rights of Authors, Composers and Publishers (JASRAC).

Ironically in light of the above, Japanese artists and entertainment businesses discovered in the 1980s that entrepreneurs in various East Asian countries had appropriated Japanese popular cultural forms without permission, including unauthorized cover versions of popular songs, translations of novels, and pirated cassette tapes and cartoons. Backed by the principles of the protection of artists' rights and international trust, JASRAC initiated an intra-Asia campaign to ban the illegal use of Japanese products. Perhaps it might be said that Japan, which boasts the largest music industry in Asia, is "civilizing" its neighbors in the way that some Japanese claimed Western products "enlightened" early 20th century Japan! The copyright lawsuits thus reveal how cultural flow can often be premised on an asymmetrical relationship between the powerful and the powerless; how some popular products can travel beyond national and geographical boundaries; and how the international cultural industry uses copyright not only as a financial tool but also as a "civilizing" agent (Mitsui 1993).

AUDIOVISUAL EXPERIENCE AND THE EMERGENCE OF YOUTH CULTURE

The outbreak of the Fifteen-Year War (also known as the Pacific War) coincided with the beginning of Japanese talkie films (1931). This audiovisual technology exerted a strong influence on popular music, as many hit songs from the mid-1930s onward preceded or followed the so-called "song film," a feature film with a few singing sequences in which songs were sung either diegetically (that is, the sound source is present in the narrative world) or non-diegetically. Narratives of this genre are usually formulaic and predictable. The cooperation of two reproductive technologies – phonograph and film – was thus consolidated in the talkie genre.

Japan's defeat in 1945 had little effect on the overall structure of the popular music industry; that is, the fact of defeat did not interfere with the hegemony of major labels, the tie-up strategy, and audiovisual media cooperation. Probably what impacted most on postwar Japanese popular music was the real and imagined presence of the United States, which dominated the Allied occupation of Japan from

1945 to 1952. Not only were American military bases an important site and work-place for many Country & Western (C&W), jazz, and rock musicians, but the image of America was synonymous with advanced novelty and progressiveness, in contrast to a "backward" Japan. It is likely that the trope of "America" influenced the emergence of Japan's postwar nationalism. The label "Made in America," so distinctive in one period, disappeared and was later remade and naturalized in Japan. The boundary between "Americanness" and "Japaneseness" is always changing. For example, the idioms of rockabilly music became part of a Japanese generic pop sound in the 1960s, and West Coast rock, dominant in the US in the late 1960s, influenced many singer-songwriters in the 1970s. Japanese cover versions of American songs popular until the 1960s basically involved translating lyrics and altering part of the arrangement while retaining an overall "Americanness." Many pop tunes dating from the 1970s have effaced that "Americanness," a development that parallels diminishing sound structures and quality (Atkins 2000).

The end of World War II did not have an immediate impact on popular music except for a rush of new sounds such as C&W and bebop; after the Allied occupation, however, the introduction of electric guitars and television spurred a radical change in the entertainment industry. The electric guitar became a symbolic object representing a new teenage culture around 1957. Of course, the electric steel guitar had already been introduced by a Hawaiian Japanese musician in the mid-1930s and was included in the standard instrumentation of C&W bands after the war. In the mid-1950s some younger C&W bands played rockabilly music on electric guitars, causing an instant sensation, probably because of the energetic beat and big sound in addition to the musicians' Presley-like movements and flamboyant attire. The electric guitar was strongly associated with a "rebel" image. Teenage girls were among the most numerous fans, and their "hysterical" behavior was negatively interpreted by some critics as a vulgar display of Americanism and a decadent sign of postwar "democracy," including co-education. Rockabilly (rock 'n' roll) was the first popular music that specifically targeted teenagers (and especially girls) in Japan, marking an important step in the formation of a postwar youth culture influenced by America. Significantly, the performative style of, but also audience reactions to, rockabilly were "learned" and adapted from American films and graphic magazines.

Many contemporary novels and films depicted teenagers in post-occupation Japan as dangerous and lascivious "heroes" who defied the moral establishment. Among the most eloquent works that epitomized this new generation were Ishihara Shin-tarō's novel *Taiyō no kisetsu* (The Season of the Sun; 1956) and his late brother Yūjirō's film *Kurutta kajitsu* (The Crazed Fruit; 1956).[1] The novel and the movie both glorified the pleasures and conflicts of well-to-do youth, who are preoccupied with cars, marine sports, beach parties, rockabilly music, fights, prostitution, and sex. Youths who emulated them were labeled the Sun Tribe (*taiyōzoku*), the first of a succession of youth "tribes," or sub-cultural collectives characterized by a distinctive look and a defiant attitude, as well as by conspicuous materialism. The succession of youth tribes is related to the cycle of fashion through which the establishment appropriates and neutralizes those who may be (or become) dangerous.

It is an irrefutable fact that television – launched publicly in 1953 – radically altered the terms of spectatorship and audiovisual experience for audiences. The living room became a privileged zone for viewing musical performance, and music programs on

television gradually replaced the "song film." Television thus reinforced the techno-
logized intimacy between the vocalist and the listener. Recently, the imaginary
proximity of artists and audiences has been exploited by the entertainment industry
in the form of the *aidoru* (idol), a veritable assembly-line for generating money and
the subject of the next section.

FABRICATING *Aidoru* (IDOLS)

The loanword *aidoru* entered into parlance around the late 1960s and began to be
used to refer specifically to the teenage singers in the early 1970s. Older teenage
singers were not especially novel, even in the 1960s, but from the 1970s onward
younger teen singers began to be recruited. New faces, with the exception of adult-
oriented *enka* (nostalgic ballad) singers (see Yano 2002), now have to be under 16.
Most appear on television almost daily when at the peak of their popularity, assuming
the roles of interviewee, interviewer, actor/actress, game player, quiz competitor,
food taster, judge, and so forth. This is matched by their heavy exposure in commer-
cials and frequent, obligatory meetings with fans.

Aidoru are not merely singers, although all *aidoru* sing. They embody a "communication port" through which flow sound and images, finances, and emotions. They
are usually obsolete by the age of 20 unless they can actually sing well or possess other
redeeming talents – the more resilient *aidoru* can survive for more than two decades.
The relatively short life of *aidoru* is related as much to the rapid cycles of show
business as to the image of fleeting puberty that they embody. Their "infantilism,"
some (adult) detractors claim, is more a sign of calculated irresponsibility and innocence than an absence of talent per se. The production agencies of each *aidoru*
orchestrate their media exposure, and the *aidoru* themselves are quite conscious of
their own commodity value.

The rise of *aidoru*dom coincided with the expansion of the entertainment market,
and especially the market among youth for domestic popular music. Record sales of
domestic music surpassed those of imported music in 1967, indicating important
changes in the music industry. This is not to say that Japanese music became more
popular than foreign music; rather, it points to an unprecedented growth in domestic
record sales owing, I believe, to the postwar babyboomers in their teens and early
twenties. The growing national economy allowed them to spend more money on
leisure items than was possible for previous generations. Show business soon realized
the economic potential of this sector and began to promote music targeted specifically at them. Since then, the consumption patterns of youth between 14 and 24 years
of age, and of others in general, have become diversified.

Another factor insuring the commercial prominence of domestic artists is related to
the dependence of hit songs on visual media – formerly film, now television. Ever
since the television set became an indispensable household appliance in the 1960s, no
song can make it into the Top Twenty without continuous play on television.[2]
Foreign singers, even those who are successful internationally, are almost automatic-
ally excluded from television programs unless their concert tours in Japan are televised. The principal vehicles for non-chart-oriented music include radio, recordings,
special coffeehouse gigs, and clubs. These are mainly addressed to self-selected

listeners and viewers among a relatively small sector of television viewers. The majority of listeners and viewers tend to ignore foreign artists, even American and British superstars. This situation has changed somewhat since the 1990s in the wake of a flood of music videos featuring foreign singers and groups, although very few foreign artists have been able to rival the popularity of Japan's own megastars in the long run. In terms of music (and fashion), the *aidoru*, or more precisely their support staff, are keenly aware of international trends and combine every possible sound in their own performances – R&B, heavy metal, hip-hop, disco, and so forth. Ambitious composers and arrangers, who are usually knowledgeable in many styles, be they faddish or nostalgic, use their skills to enhance the feeble voices of the typical *aidoru* and to hold the attention of their fickle audiences.

*Aidoru*dom was born of, and is inseparable from, television. In 1971 an audition program aptly called *Sutā tanjō* (A Star Is Born) debuted, marking a shift, in the history of musical variety shows, from 1960s programs featuring professionals to programs highlighting amateurs (Stevens and Hosokawa 2001). What distinguished it from previous audition programs was that talent agencies actually "bid" for the competitors – mostly girls – by announcing the price they would pay for a contract. The program not only exposed the backstage of showbiz but also encouraged the audience to participate in the "Cinderella story" from the outset. The journalistic media followed up with sentimental stories and "secret" pictures of the competitors, informing the audience of how a shy girl-next-door was transformed into a million-record-selling star, and how the entertainment machinery created her celebrity. The winners tended to be cute girls in their mid-teens who played to audiences with their "little-girl" style of speaking, casual gestures, bright smiles, and sparkling temperament; in fact, these aspects were emphasized over any talent for singing and acting. It could be said the first generation of *aidoru* were born from this show.

One important criterion for the "auctions" in "A Star is Born" was the matter of how the would-be idols interacted with the emcees. The ability to chit-chat is crucial for wannabe *aidoru* from even before their actual debut. If their musical performance is inadequate, then the girls must put on a good verbal (and gestural) performance. The chattiness of *aidoru*, and of pop singers in general, is demonstrated by the structure of music programs on Japanese television which emphasizes talk over music. Video clips of actual performances are usually played only fragmentarily in the countdown section of a "Top Twenty" type of television show, and MTV (and MTV-like programs) targets special fans and is broadcast only on a few cable channels and in the after-midnight time slot. The fresh and feel-good esthetic of *aidoru* is conveyed by the polysemic word *kawaii*, most often translated as "cute." *Kawaii* captures the gestalt of the ostensibly young, girl-like personality embodied by *aidoru* in a variety of modes: chatting, smiling, writing, acting, and so on (Kinsella 1995).

While female *aidoru* typically have been discovered on television programs or by (male) producers, their male counterparts typically have signed with Johnny's Jimusho (Johnny's Office), the largest "star factory" in Japan since the 1980s. Johnny's *aidoru* are always packaged in groups, such as SMAP, and are quite good at choreographed performance. Characteristically each member of such a group embodies a stock character, for example, leader, joker, and introvert. Hardly macho, they represent a gentle, good-humored, and, most importantly, woman-friendly (yet not womanish) type of adolescent. The vast majority of their fans are girls and women ranging in age from the low teens to adult. Boys and young men tend to emulate their fashion, but few males claim to be devoted fans.

It seems to be the case that female *aidoru* attract more male than female fans, and that male *aidoru* are fawned over by girls exclusively. This sexual division of fan labor has undergone changes since the late 1980s, when some female fans began to acknowledge not just the cuteness, but also the self-realization and professional fulfillment of some female *aidoru*. These fans regard the young women as "artists" rather than *aidoru*, and as exemplars of tough (and rich) women succeeding under and despite male-centric conditions of employment.[3] *Aidoru* thus "sell power" to girls and "sell cuteness" to boys. The girls know that cuteness is visual capital, both in the world of show business and in real life. Their success is interpreted by supportive fans as less the result of hype and luck, and more an outcome of their exercise of free will and the necessary perseverance to win the "rat race." The mass media effectively endorse this approach, and fans, conscious of the business machinery, seem willing to cooperate with the entertainment industry in order to promote as superior their favorite *aidoru*. Not coincidentally, the most frequent phrases *aidoru* utter in public are *gambattemasu* (I'm doing my best) or *gambatte* (Do your best). They have to show off their best professional performance as models of morality for an audience living in an industrious and industrialized society. Fantasy and reality both separate and overlap. *Aidoru* somehow transcend the ordinary and at the same time remain in it (Aoyagi 2000).

Fans of *aidoru* – predominantly high-school and college students – are kept at a distance not only by an *aidoru*'s bodyguards, but also as a result of fan-on-fan surveillance and a tacit agreement between the fans and an *aidoru*'s agent. Should a fan transgress a hidden line, he or she is usually regarded by other fans not with envy but antipathy. Good fans believe that it is their responsibility to protect the *aidoru* from harm wrought by disorderly fanatics. Fans of course try to outdo each other with displays of devotion to the *aidoru*, but at the same time they share a certain sense of egalitarianism. What might be called "differentiated egalitarianism" characterizes the affective identity of *aidoru* fan groups (Kelly 2004).

Some fans chase after the *aidoru* literally 24 hours a day, following them from their private apartments to the studio, restaurants, and other public places, all the while using their cellphones to take pictures, chat with their friends, and send text messages. In addition to, or instead of, money, these *okkake* ("chasers" or "stalkers") invest their time in demonstrating their devotion to their "co-fans." They make an emotional and financial investment in the entertainment industry on their own terms. In a sense, they "buy intimacy" (to use Carolyn Stevens' term) by paying for CDs, concert tickets and *aidoru*-licensed goods. Listening to music and going to concerts are still central, but are not the most privileged aspect of *aidoru* fandom.

Male fans of girl *aidoru* are stereotypically depicted as introverted, asocial (sometimes anti-social) and suffering from a "Lolita complex" (*rorikon*) or pedophilia. A common explanation for their veiled passion is substitution theory: *aidoru* are harmless substitutes for the girlfriends they hesitate to socialize with in real life. Some are attached more to the commercially unsuccessful girls than the popular ones, in part because "B-grade *aidoru*" are less protected by their production companies, allowing fans greater accessibility. Some commentators have offered explanations premised on a perceived dialectical relationship between the socially and commercially marginalized. In my view, such facile explanations overlook the heterogeneity of male fans of *aidoru*, and gloss the processes of fan group-formation through multi-mediated experiences, including the projection of heterosexual and patriarchal desire upon the vulnerable *aidoru*.

Out of the visibly and less obviously committed fan groups, there are a vast number of "passing" fans who are unmarked by any distinctive outlook, behavior, taste, fashion, or philosophy, in contrast to the more fanatic groupies. Historically, the latter range from male fans of *onna gidayū* (female singers of ballad-dramas) in the early 20th century and the "hysterical" female fans of the electric guitar bands of the 1960s, to the very recent "hikkies," the name for fans of pop singer Utada Hitaru. It is easy to find scornful or pathologizing descriptions of such fans; they are grist to the mill of gossipy tabloid journalism. Even such negative portrayals, however, can spell profits for the entertainment industry. Over the decades, the industry has had to come to terms with the various fan communities and has learned how to negotiate with them. It seems to me that the industry now knows how to both arouse and tame the collective impulses of audience. There are too few ethnographies of *aidoru* fans to understand fully how they are grouped by age, sex and gender, class and so forth; how their attachment to idols is socially and sexually mediated and channeled; and how they regard their peers.[4]

LIVE AND MEDIATED EXPERIENCE OF KARAOKE

One of the most influential media for Japanese contemporary pop songs is karaoke, which needs no English translation today (Mitsui and Hosokawa 1998). It is now common for record companies to include a karaoke track on a CD single and to make a song available immediately at "karaoke rooms" – basically, rooms rented by the hour which are kitted out with sing-along equipment. The popularity of a song is judged not only by CD sales, but also by the number of times it is requested by karaoke singers. To become popular in Japan, a song should not only be played frequently on radio and television; it should also be sung by anonymous people. Songs in foreign languages, even if listed in the wired, karaoke network, have little chance of competing with domestic tunes – which, perhaps ironically, often include (faux) English lyrics as a hook or refrain.

Singing along with prerecorded sounds – a "live and mediated performance" according to ethnomusicologist Charles Keil – is not in itself novel. Even in the early American talkies of the 1930s we can see the "jumping ball" following the lyrics as the melody plays. In the 1960s, some Japanese professional singers started using reel-to-reel tape recorders for their accompaniment if a band was unavailable. They called this set-up *karaoke*, or "empty (*kara*) orchestra (*oke*)." This neologism is clearly misleading because it is not the orchestra but rather the vocals that are absent. Early karaoke was essentially a variation on the "minus-one record," that is, a record with a missing part to be filled by a student of said instrument. In the early 1970s, a similar device was designed for the use in bars where previously male clients had often sung along with a strolling guitarist or accordionist. The prerecorded accompaniment was adopted in response to a decrease in the number of these street musicians and an increase in the number of requested melodies. The introduction of the cassette-tape recorder – cheap, handy, and easy to operate – was a decisive moment for the diffusion of karaoke. Because the device is technically quite simple, several self-styled inventors have claimed credit for karaoke.

In the mid-1970s the karaoke system was industrialized by makers of car stereos, coin-slot machines, and other devices that had been peripheral in the music industry, and it quickly became a feature in night spots. A typical image associated with karaoke in this decade was of tone-deaf, drunken *sarariiman* (salarymen, or white-collar workers) singing nostalgic ballads (*enka*). The users slowly established loose rules of socialization in karaoke bars. For example, the order of singers should be based on corporate hierarchies; status inferiors and younger people should not sing the favorite songs of their superiors and elders; women should sing when requested by men (especially in duets); the microphone should be turned over to anyone present; one should only sing one song per turn; good singers, especially status and age inferiors, should never show off their talents; and one should politely applaud any and every singer. These tacitly understood rules were based on a respect for hierarchy coupled with a certain egalitarianism, and are obviously related to the behavioral codes informing many Japanese drinking parties: namely, that every person present should participate in the event on equal terms even though he or she does not necessarily wish to do so. Thus, the apparent informality in karaoke bars is misleading as karaoke does not always suspend the social order shaping the business day, but rather extends it to "after-hours" entertainment. In other words, the atmosphere is as tense as it is easygoing. It is of course the job of hostesses in karaoke nightclubs to make clients "feel at home," as well as to confirm the gender, sexual, and social hierarchies operative in their clients' lives through their skillful conversation, singing, companionship, and other such services.[5]

An important change in the use of karaoke took place in the early 1980s when, following the privatization of the rail system, discarded rail cars began to be recycled as rental spaces for family and friendly gatherings. Karaoke equipment became indispensable, and these spaces quickly became known as "karaoke boxes." These boxes became so popular among the women and the young people who had been excluded from the bars that similar equipment was installed in leased rooms in multi-story buildings. They are regularly used by housewives, elderly people, and teenagers during the day and by office workers and college students at night. With a seating capacity of five to ten persons, the rooms have an obligatory small window, usually on the door, to assuage worries about their possible delinquent use by persons under 18 years of age.

The accessibility of karaoke singing was fostered by a series of audiovisual innovations in the 1980s. From still images to animated ones, from VHS to laser discs and VCD, the decade saw a significant transformation in the visual aspect of the karaoke experience. Many innovations were directed at quick cueing, quality of image, synchronized coloring of lyrics on the screen, and updating the musical repertoire. And, because the digitalization of sound has enabled a one-touch transposition of the key signature of a song, users need no longer worry about their vocal range. In the 1990s, in response to both the diversified tastes of demanding users and quickening cycles of faddishness, a system was introduced that transmitted audiovisual data from a computer to each terminal or karaoke room. It facilitated the replacement of unpopular tracks with some 20 or so songs a month. Another profitable aspect of wired karaoke involves the POS system for the record retailers, which counts the number of times a given song is played and which, therefore, is useful in devising marketing strategies.

Today, many low- and mid-teen girls use karaoke boxes not only for singing but also for dancing wildly as if they were in a makeshift disco. During the World Cup 2002, supporters of Japan's team congregated in karaoke boxes to make noise while watching the games on television. Housewives tend to get together in the early afternoon, while solitary men may rent a space in the early evening in order to practice for their nighttime performance. A mixed group of high-school dropouts may use the same space as an asylum or refuge of sorts. The karaoke rooms serve multiple purposes for diverse consumers. Moreover, each group may have a different set of rules of socialization governing its box.

The latest statistics suggest that the halcyon days of karaoke have ended, and that, according to some analysts, without further technological innovations or a constant stream of mega-hits, it will be difficult to sustain its popularity. As a form of entertainment, karaoke's short history provides evidence of the close connection between technology and the entertainment industry in Japan. This is much more obvious in the computer game parlors or game centers which are totally dependent on the installment of the latest machines and software in order to keep old clients and attract new ones. People's obsession with the latest technology has unquestionably been a driving force of the entertainment industry.

CONCLUSION

As a means of creation, recreation, and socialization, popular entertainment involves numerous issues for anthropologists. There are no overarching theories dealing with all those issues, nor are there integral points of view through which to examine them, mainly because the concept of entertainment is so broad. "Entertainment" signifies too many domains – from gambling and striptease to computer games – to be theorized in any coherent way. Perhaps our first step toward theorization is to sharpen semantically that seemingly unproblematic concept itself, "entertainment." Another intriguing question is whether there exist certain "Japanese" sensibilities and behavior patterns in entertainment. Is entertainment nationally bound, despite the continuous exchange of products, ideas, and artists from overseas? What is historically changing and, simultaneously, unchanging, and why? I have underscored the interplay of reproductive and audiovisual technology, industry and audiences, by tracing the historical transformations in the world of entertainment since the Meiji period, and by reviewing information about that world today. Obviously my cursory glance at popular music cannot grasp the entire domain of popular entertainment. In a way, what I have done is to question rather than to answer a variety of issues central to the anthropological understanding of key aspects of Japanese popular culture.

NOTES

1   Editor's note: Ishihara Shintarō, a pugnacious, nationalistic and relentlessly ethnocentric man, is the current governor of Tokyo.

2 This method of using sales statistics to stimulate consumption, another pivotal feature of *aidoru*dom, was applied to Japanese songs for the first time in the late 1960s.
3 Editor's note: The recognition by *aidoru* fans of the resilience and relative subversiveness of female *aidoru* is remarkably similar to the views of female fans of the all-female Takarazuka Revue (see Robertson 2001 [1998]).
4 Editor's note: Robertson (2001 [1998]:chs. 4 and 5) discusses female and male fans past and present of the Takarazuka Revue at length, including the subject of (homo)sexual desire.
5 Editor's note: For more information on the professional hostesses, see Allison (1994) and Jackson (1976).

REFERENCES

Akazawa, Shirō, and Kitagawa, Kenzō, eds. 1993. Bunka to fasizumu (Culture and Fascism). Tokyo: Nihon Keizai Hyōronsha.
Allison, Anne. 1994. Nightwork: Sexuality, Pleasure, and Corporate Masculinity in a Tokyo Hostess Club. Chicago: University of Chicago Press.
Aoyagi, Hiroshi. 2000. Pop Idols and the Asian Identity. *In* Japan Pop! Inside the World of Japanese Popular Culture. Tim Craig, ed. pp. 309–326. Armonk, NY: M. E. Sharpe.
Atkins, E. Taylor. 2000. Blue Nippon: Authenticating Jazz in Japan. Durham, NC: Duke University Press.
Gonda, Yasunosuke. 1974. Gonda Yasunosuke Chosakushū (Works of Gonda Yasunosuke), 4 vols. Tokyo: Bunwa Shobō.
Hattori, Yukio. 2003. Edo kabuki bunkaron (On the Culture of Edo Kabuki). Tokyo: Heibonsha.
Inoue, Shun. 1987. Fūzoku no shakaigaku (Sociology of Popular Culture). Kyoto: Sekai Shisōsha.
Ishikawa, Hiroyoshi, et al., eds. 1991. Taishū bunka jiten (Encyclopedia of Popular Culture). Tokyo: Kōbundō.
Ivy, Marilyn. 1995. Discourses of the Vanishing: Modernity, Phantasm Japan. Chicago: University of Chicago Press.
Iyoda, Yasuhiro. 1998. Terebisi handobukku (Handbook of the History of Television).Tokyo: Jiyū Kokuminsha.
Jackson, Laura. 1976. Bar Hostesses. *In* Women in Changing Japan. Joyce Lebra, Joy Paulson, and Elizabeth Powers, eds. pp. 133–157. Stanford: Stanford University Press.
Kasza, Gregory J. 1988. The State and the Mass Media in Japan, 1918–1945. Berkeley: University of California Press.
Kawazoe, Noboru. 1980. Nihon bunmei to taishū bunka (Japanese Enlightenment and Mass Culture). Jurisuto (Jurist) 20:6–12.
Kelly, William W., ed. 2004 (in press). Fanning the Flames. Fans and Consumer Culture in Contemporary Japan. Albany, NY: SUNY Press.
Kinsella, Sharon. 1995. Cuties in Japan. *In* Women, Media, and Consumption in Japan. Lise Skov and Brian Moeran, eds. pp. 220–254. Honolulu: University of Hawaii Press.
Komota, Nobuo, Shimada, Yoshifumi, Yazawa, Kan, and Yokozawa, Chiaki. 1994–95. Nihon ryūkōkashi (History of Popular Song in Japan). Tokyo: Shakai Shisōsha.
Kurata, Yoshihiro. 1979 [1992]. Nihon rekōdo bunkashi (Cultural History of Recordings in Japan). Tokyo: Tokyo Shoseki.
——1980. Meiji taishō no minshū goraku (Popular Entertainment in the Meiji and Taishō Eras). Tokyo: Iwanami Shoten.

Minami, Hiroshi. 1987. Shōwa bunka 1925–1945 (Shōwa Culture, 1925–1945). Tokyo: Keisō Shobō.

Mita, Minesuke. 1992. Social Psychology of Modern Japan. London: Kegan Paul International.

Mitsui, Tōru. 1993. Copyright and Music in Japan: A Forced Grafting and its Consequences. *In* Music and Copyright. Simon Frith, ed. pp. 125–145. Edinburgh: Edinburgh University Press.

Mitsui, Tōru, and Hosokawa, Shuhei, eds. 1998. Karaoke Around the World: Global Technology, Local Singing. London: Routledge.

Nagai, Yoshikazu. 1991. Shakō dansu to nihonjin (Social Dancing and Japanese). Tokyo: Shōbunsha.

Nishizawa, Sō. 1990. Nihon kindai kayōshi (History of Popular Song in Modern Japan). Tokyo: Ofūsha.

Ogawa, Hiroshi. 1993. Media jidai no ongaku to shakai (Music and Society in the Media Age). Tokyo: Ongaku No Tomosha.

Robertson, Jennifer. 2001 [1998]. Takarazuka: Sexual Politics and Popular Culture in Modern Japan. Berkeley: University of California Press.

Silverberg, Miriam. 1992. Constructing the Japanese Ethnography of Modernity. Journal of Asian Studies 51(1):30–54.

Soeda, Azenbō, and Soeda, Tomomichi. 1982. Chosakushū (Works), 5 vols. Tokyo: Tōsui Shobō.

Stevens, Carolyn, and Hosokawa, Shuhei, 2001, So Close and Yet So Far: Humanizing Celebrity in Japanese Music Variety Shows, 1960s–1990s. *In* Asian Media Productions. Brian Moeran, ed. pp. 223–246. Richmond: Curzon.

Tada, Michitarō. 1962. Fukusei geijutsu ron (On the Reproductive Arts). Tokyo: Keiso Shobō.

Tsuganesawa, Toshihiro, and Ariyama, Teruo, eds. 1998. Senjiki nihon no media ibento (Media Events in Wartime Japan). Kyoto: Sekai Shisōsha.

Tsurumi, Shunsuke. 1982. Genkai geijutsu ron (Marginal Arts). Tokyo: Keisō Shobō.

Ukai, Masaki. 1994. Taishū engeki eno tabi (Voyage to Popular Theater). Tokyo: Miraisha.

Yano, Christine. R. 2002. Tears of Longing: Nostalgia and the Nation in Japanese Popular Song. New York: Harvard University Press.

Yano, Christine, and Hosokawa, Shuhei. 2004. Popular Music in Modern Japan. *In* Japanese Music: History, Performance, Research. Alison M. Tokita and David W. Hughes, eds. Cambridge: Cambridge University Press.

Yoshimi, Shun'ya. 1994. Media jidai no bunka shakaigaku (The Sociology of Culture in the Media Age). Tokyo: Shinyōsha.

There's More Than *Manga*: Popular Nonfiction Books and Magazines

CHAPTER **20**

Laura Miller

Anthropologists who study societies with an ancient literary tradition know that print media have great power to shape and reflect cultural beliefs and memories. In place of oral performance by Senegalese griots or Tewa storytellers, written texts are the primary repository for group knowledge and preoccupations. For a modern society such as Japan, books, magazines, and other writings are important evidence of historically situated social anxieties, particularly debates over the modern versus the traditional, and the native versus the foreign. In 1997, when the Japan Anthropology Workshop (JAWS) met at the University of Melbourne with the theme "Mass Media and Popular Culture," members presented papers that illustrated ways in which media have engaged with changing ideas about social roles and identities. In their efforts to excavate print media for insights into Japanese culture, anthropologists have gained a deepened understanding of issues of production and consumption of popular culture. Regardless of whether or not the information and images contained in printed material start out as political propaganda, capitalistic bait, or idiosyncratic imagination, they may in time become routine banality that resides in mass consciousness. Print media alert us to the idealized models of society people are orienting to or challenging. They reflect the strains and concerns found in everyday social life. Two forms of cultural production in particular, nonfiction books and magazines, have played a powerful role in the socialization of individuals into productive workers, national subjects, and gendered reproducers.

Academic writers have shown intense scholarly interest in Japanese *manga* (comics), especially their representation of Japanese sexuality and fantasy. *Manga* is usually translated as "comics," although this term does not adequately describe the Japanese version, which accounts for approximately 20 percent of all publishing revenue. *Manga* are read by people of all ages and backgrounds, and have a powerful influence on Japanese culture, from fashion to language use. *Manga* are published weekly, biweekly, and monthly, and usually contain a number of different serialized story narratives, some of which can go on for decades. As a form of diversionary or comfort reading, they generally have fewer Chinese characters than other writing, so are easy to digest quickly. The translation and publishing of Japanese comics is a noteworthy business in China, Indonesia, Vietnam, Thailand, Europe, Australia, Canada, and the US. This globalization is also revealed by the release of at least two English-language books on how to draw Japanese-style comics. The ubiquity and global appeal of *manga* deserve analysis, and, understandably, scholars of popular culture have been engrossed in analyzing the images, themes, and storylines found in them (Allison 1996; Erino 1990; Kinsella 2000; Napier 1994; Schodt 1986 [1983], 1996; Suzuki 1999). Even so, *manga* are not the only type of text contemporary Japanese enjoy, and the study of other mass reading is equally productive for those interested in print media as an institution through which culture is produced, transmitted, and resisted.

The Japanese publishing industry is one of the largest in the world, with around 69,000 new book titles published in the year 2001 alone (Asahi shimbun 2003:245). This thirst for printed material has historical roots, and the Japanese have been avaricious readers for centuries. During the later part of the Tokugawa period (1603–1868), urban centers were home to commercial lending libraries which provisioned merchants, samurai, and literate farmers with romantic novels, satires, poetry, encyclopedias, and other things to read. People from different classes of society sought information on improving their fortunes in life, creating a niche for self-help books and other forms of practical information. Two significant historical events in Japan were the rise of mass literacy and the change to typeset printed books. Before a society can promote mass literacy, however, it needs to have a broad educational system coupled with the idea of a unified language. Prior to the major sociopolitical reforms undertaken during the Meiji period (1868–1912), a national consciousness of one unified language was weak, if not absent. The Meiji leaders instituted a campaign for the unity of the written and spoken language, for which they imposed one dialect (Tokyo) as the basis for the creation of a "standard" language for the nation. This oral and written standard as taught in schools and used in mass media coexists with a wide diversity of enduring regional and social dialects. New printing technologies such as moveable type were also adopted during the Meiji era, enabling mass production of newspapers, magazines, and informational books. Beginning with the publication of the first magazine in 1867, named *Seiyō zasshi* (the Western Magazine), hundreds of educational, humor, anti-government, and current affairs magazines were launched.

Book and magazine publishing escalated until the late 1990s, when it experienced significant change. During the early postwar years publishers began producing small paperbacks that would easily slide into pockets and bags. Their popularity has dramatically increased, and as many as 100 million *bunko* paperback versions of nonfiction bestsellers, comics, and literature are published each year. Economic recession continuing from the 1990s resulted in decreasing book and magazine sales, but not in the number of titles published. A new kind of bookstore that began to appear after 1995 (called *shinkoshoten*) sells inexpensive used books in good to mint condition, especially *manga* and *bunko* paperbacks. All of these changes indicate that publishing is increasingly driven by the tastes of the lowbrow mass consumer rather than of elite intellectuals, who had dominated publishing trends for most of the 20th century.

Anthropologists, sociologists, and other scholars of Japan have been especially intrigued by the pervasiveness and volume of a media domain called *nihonjinron* (theories of the Japanese), a distinct type of writing that emphasizes the unique aspects of Japanese language, biology, business, and culture. As documented by scholars such as Befu (2001), the *nihonjinron* folk model of Japaneseness is not a genre as much as a discourse that permeates books, newspaper articles, and journal writing about a variety of subjects. Although this type of writing is often lambasted, these ideas about Japanese typicality are important to scholars tracking the construction of ethnic and racial subjectivities. One aspect of *nihonjinron* that sometimes escaped the notice of critics is its representation of the average Japanese not only as a lifetime-employed, middle-class company worker, but as male. In recent years Japan's stagnated, male-centered economy and society have come under internal attack, and the formerly reified salaryman has lost his allure, a change seen in popular culture imaging that contains more diversity. It will be interesting to see if this shift in focus will be reflected in the gendered nature of *nihonjinron* writing in the future.

In addition to their presence in books that promote provocative theories about cultural uniqueness, ideas about Japanese cultural norms are also seamlessly embedded in books with explicit pragmatic objectives and themes. Self-help and how-to books, together with books on true crime, sex, divination, and the meaning of life, have dominated nonfiction bestseller lists since the postwar era. The belief that all Japanese could become company workers helped generate sales of practical books on how to improve language ability, etiquette, and manners to propel the reader into those desired ranks. Mass media attention to the unpolished woman and inept man targeted people between the ages of 18 and 30, and predominantly from lower-middle-class backgrounds. Women in particular bought books that taught them the cultural and linguistic skills needed for class advancement. Indeed, the descriptor OL, ''Office Ladies'' (generally young, unmarried clerical workers), was frequently used in the titles of this advice literature. *Fundamental Checklist of Office Lady Manners* (Nakamura 1993), and *Anthology of Office Lady Taboos* (Zennikkū Eigyōhonbu Kyōikukunrenbu 1991) are two examples of this enormous genre. It is odd that, although there are distilled folk notions about Japanese behavior as powerful as *nihonjinron* discourse, aside from a few exceptions, self-help literature is often ignored by Japan anthropologists. As explicit instruments of socialization, they contain idealized and codified notions about gender and class.

An example is the book entitled *Manual of Deportment and Manners* (Chiteki Seikatsu Kenkyūjo 1995), which provides female readers with instruction in such things as how to manage their bodies when sitting on floor cushions. It informs us that a woman who tilts too far forward, lets her head droop down in front, or leans too far back is exhibiting rather bad form. The book even provides a helpful diagram of these various improprieties. Guidelines such as this, which unambiguously enumerate what one should not do or say, are increasingly prevalent in Japanese advice literature. Unlike American counterparts, which some scholars characterize as rather simplistic, contemporary Japanese versions address the entire presentation of self in explicit detail, from speech to body movement, as one package which is painstakingly diagnosed and cataloged. These templates for femininity unveil the unconscious in lapidary commentary that addresses all aspects of interaction. Similar to self-help writing everywhere, they ostensibly hold out the promise of improving one's life through mastery of manners and speech necessary for inclusion in middle-class life. This new advice literature explicitly links linguistic ideology with body management through the use of visuals and graphics which illustrate exactly how ill-behaved women look when they say displeasing things. Readers are invited to condemn them with the help of drawings, photos, and comics that expose every nuance of the uncivil. Scholars usually describe this type of prescriptive literature as both elitist and conservatively resistant to social change. Yet this new wave of writings on women's conduct grapples with contemporary transformations in women's roles and identities, accommodating some changes without actually disrupting the fundamental gender hierarchy. The result is an enumeration of conflicting norms as well as contradictory advice on how to negotiate social life, a characteristic of other recent forms of women's popular writing (Miller 1998).

The science of language and body management for women includes some material identical to that also directed at the male white-collar worker in the salaryman's how-to book market. For instance, the same instructions are given for exchanging business cards, proper hierarchical seating arrangements in cars, reception areas, meeting rooms, and even where to stand while riding in an elevator. Self-help and inspirational books for men are usually found in the so-called "business" section of a typical Japanese bookstore, and will be shelved next to other selections a non-Japanese person might not think of in that context, but which make perfect sense to a Japanese office worker. There are books by and about corporate idols, especially Microsoft's Bill Gates, whose book *The Road Ahead* (1995), while not a great commercial success in the US, made it to the Top Twenty bestseller list in Japan soon after it was translated.

Many other translations of American self-improvement books have become best-sellers, including Carlson's *Don't Sweat the Small Stuff* (1998), a bestseller in 2001, and Johnson's *Who Moved My Cheese? An Amazing Way to Deal with Change in Your Work and in Your Life* (2000). Of course, there's always the durable *How to Stop Worrying and Start Living* by Carnegie (1984), originally published in 1948 but popular in Japan decades later. These translations augment domestically produced books such as Ōmae's *Salaryman Survival* (1999), the number one business book the year it was published, Suenaga's *Make Money!* (1999), and Takai's *Skillful Ways to Get Employees to Quit* (1996). Japan's inspirational literature possibly reached a pinnacle with the mega-hit *Unsatisfactory Limbs* (Ototake 1999, translated into English with the title *No One's Perfect*), the memoir of a man born without arms or legs who overcomes life's obstacles, which sold more than 4.5 million copies.

One form of self-help literature targets the use of the standard language. This commodification of the Japanese language is highly apparent in books on honorific speech. Because not all Japanese have command of this linguistic code (Miller 1989), both women and men see it as a critical component of their quest for success. Popular folklinguistic books on honorifics have been especially noticeable since the 1960s, with titles like *Correct Honorific Speech* (Ōishi 1971), *Dictionary of Errors in Honorific Speech* (Okuaki 1978), and *Reader in Modern Honorifics* (Sakagawa 1969). During the 1990s a new metalinguistic category was created which includes not only honorific usage, but also other ways of speaking combined with bowing, bodily demeanor, and affect. This new category of language and body co-occurrence rules is usually called either *manā* (manners), or *echiketto* (etiquette), and books with these words in their titles flooded bookstores. Many recent bestsellers are essentially language manuals, reflecting widespread insecurity about class status or cultural competence. The famed linguist Ōno (1999), once criticized as a *nihonjinron* writer by an American scholar, published a how-to language book that sold more than 1.6 million copies. Another bestseller was *Practical Japanese You Should Know*, by the well-known linguist Shibata (2001). Despite existing linguistic variation that reflects class, gender, occupational, generational, and other social diversity, only one regional and class-based version of the Japanese language is enshrined in these manuals of "correct" usage, indicating the cultural dominance of one segment of society. The enduring popularity of language manuals suggests that the Japanese continue to optimistically believe in self-transformation and class mobility.

Some observers have linked the popularity of self-help books to post-bubble economic and social malaise, but self-help and how-to books have always been desired by non-elite members of Japanese society. An optimistic philosophy of self-help was already present among late Tokugawa period peasantry. Members of the samurai class were also avid consumers of self-help literature. Kinmonth (1981) reports that young samurai waited all night for bookstores to open so they could purchase the first Japanese translation of Samuel Smiles' *Self-Help*. Self-improvement literature of that era aimed at moral and philosophical reformation of the self in order to better serve society. An example was the *shingaku* (heart-mind learning) religious and ethical movement founded by Ishida Baigan (1685–1746), who combined ideas from Zen Buddhism, Shinto, and Neo-Confucianism in his lessons for the merchant class on self-realization and service to society (Bellah 1957; Robertson 1979; Sawada 1993). The difference in the new forms of this genre is their emphasis on transformation of the individual for their own economic, hedonistic, and social benefit.

In addition to various forms of advice literature and *nihonjinron* speculation, there has been an increase in the number of nonfiction books published by and about women. During the 1990s, bookstores began to set aside areas for female fiction, confessionals, self-help, biographies, and exposés. These new areas for women's books are different from the prosaic and still intact housewife sections (where there are books on cooking, childcare, sewing, and hobbies). Popular books found in this new print arena include titles such as *Love is Fine, But I Like Books, Too* (Kishimoto 2000), *55 Ways to Have a Likeable Self* (Satō 2000), and *Learning to Fight under Ueno Chizuko at the University of Tokyo* (Haruka 2000). The expanded list of female-centered nonfiction books reflects shifts in women's postwar roles and identities. Women have been driving other consumer industries for decades, and books are another expression of their power in the marketplace. Scholars acknowledge that popular nonfiction writing about women does not need to be accurate or reflective of reality in order to be worthy of study. The representations of women found in print media manifest historically situated anxieties about gender through constructs which are widely promoted and debated, such as the Menopausal Housewife, the New Breed OL (Hirakawa 2000), and the Yellow Cab (Kelsky 1994). Social concern and anger over women's cultural independence was also evident in the publication of a bestselling book by sociologist Yamada (1999), who castigated young adults who continue to live in their parents' home. Ignoring the economic basis for the phenomenon, Yamada called them self-indulgent "parasite singles," a nasty term the media loved and came to apply mainly to live-at-home working women who reject marriage and reproduction. The popularity of the book and the label tell us that many Japanese are still uneasy or unaccepting of women's full emancipation from a patriarchal gender ideology. This is not to say that print media only support the status quo, since for each book that buttresses traditional norms there is a book to counter them with alternative views, such as Yamamoto's (2001) response to Yamada. There are many other instances of dueling books, such as *The Croissant Syndrome* (Matsubara 1988), a book that claimed women had been duped into making bad lifecourse decisions because of what their favorite magazines wrote, and *The Anti-Croissant Syndrome* (Wife Editors 1989), which opposed that view.

Japanese intellectuals, editors, and scholars are disturbed by the dominance of self-help and other humble books in their publishing world. They are losing a struggle for cultural authority, but they are not going away without a fight. Publishing their own works about the demise of "serious" books and small publishing firms, they worry that reading is a dying pastime; that young people only send email and look at computer screens, and they blame the educational system for the disappearance of the book. Yet, it seems that the debate is not really about books, but about the type of books being consumed. Fewer fiction or philosophical books now make it onto bestseller lists. Iijima Ai, a former adult video star whose autobiography was a Top Ten bestseller (Iijima 2001), has pushed aside widely read books by and about influential thinkers such as Maruyama Masao (Maruyama 1956; Miyamura 2001). What to critics signals the demise of civilization is really the expansion of publishing that is increasingly driven by vernacular interests. Critics seem particularly embarrassed that books by religious leaders of nontraditional postwar sects continue to have huge sales. Both Ikeda Daisaku, leader of Soka Gakkai, and Ōkawa Ryuho, founder of Kofuku no Kagaku, sell millions of books each year and are always present on bestseller lists. In *Who Would Kill Books?* Sano (2001) also describes the current crisis in the book publishing industry, yet he lays the blame for lagging sales on an outdated distribution and sales system rather than on a defective consumer. For anthropologists, the effect of economic, sociopolitical, and cultural change can be traced through these trends in book publishing and readership tastes. Print media have become more democratic, and previously excluded audiences, especially the female, young, and non-elite segments of society, have a larger role in establishing majority taste in these cultural products. The change in book publishing in which mass consumer tastes dictate what sells is also seen in the great diversification of magazine titles after 1980.

In 1995 a Japanese street magazine named *Egg* was hatched as a venue for schoolgirls to submit photos, essays, and drawings. It later changed publishers and came to resemble a traditional fashion magazine, but still publishes the unfiltered rants, email, letters, and photographs of its readers. Although the interaction between media producer and consumer is especially clear in this case, scholars have often recognized magazines as having a role in creating social communities or providing an outlet for subcultural identities. Hawkins (1999) examined how the magazine *Adonis* (1952–60) contributed to the creation of Japan's early postwar gay community, and Sakamoto (1999) found that, during the 1970s, young women's magazines such as *JJ* and *AnAn* reinforced changing attitudes held by its readers, and encouraged new and subversive identities. Magazines have also given scholars an opportunity to examine gendered language forms, including the type of script used or the preferred vocabulary items and syntactic structures (Frank 2000; Reynolds 1989). Scholars who look to magazines for insights into culture, society, and language have a lot to work with, given the immense range of Japanese magazine publishing.

Because of the extreme differentiation of readerships and the way target audiences are structured by class, region, age, and gender, magazines are especially useful for complicating the notion of Japanese cultural homogeneity. Each year approximately 4,000 different magazines are published, the majority of them monthly. The number of new titles fluctuates, as fresh magazines are introduced every year while others go out of business. Peak years were 1985, with 245 new magazines released, and 2000, with 209 new titles (Asahi shimbun 2003:245). Magazines focusing on cooking, hobbies, fashion, lifestyle, travel, gossip, entertainment, music, and other interests are sold according to several different age cohorts. Magazines cater to exclusive interests, such as *Hip Hop Style Bible* for those into hip-hop fashion, or *Fine Surf and Street Magazine* for surfing and skateboarding dudes. *GirlPop* is a specialized magazine devoted entirely to interviews and assessments of female musicians, singers, and songwriters. The availability of such diverse texts allows scholars many opportunities to call on contemporary theories of representation and cultural production in their analyses. Critics like to point to cosmetic and fashion trends and to the popularity of specific consumer goods as evidence of the power of global markets and the globalization of youth culture. Yet magazines targeting subcultural groups are global in more ways than simply appropriation or syncretism of world styles or music, because they also construct cross-border knowledge, language, and identities. For example, in *Fine Surf and Street Magazine*, female American surfing champions such as Lisa Anderson may be featured along with surfing contest winners and girls' idols Hirano Minako and Sugiyama Tomoyo. Readers of the magazine learn about not only surfing fashion and goods, but also the newest surfer language and ways of thinking. It is clear that magazines do more than simply reflect cultural or group identity. Despite what advertisers or editors claim, magazines play a role in cultural creation and modification.

It is women's magazines that have drawn the most interest from scholars in the past. Perhaps the best-known scholarship to use Japanese magazines is found in Skov and Moeran's (1995) edited collection. Topics as diverse as environmentalism (Skov 1995), reification, and the maintenance of traditional Japaneseness (Moeran 1995), marriage and lifecourse worries (Rosenberger 1995), teenage consumption (White 1995), and body display (Clammer 1995), as seen in women's magazines, are all found in that volume. Currently, over 100 publications directed specifically to Japanese women are available, with subcategories pegging readerships of various class statuses and age ranges. For married women there are magazines such as *Sutekina okusan* (Cool Housewife), *Katei gahō* (Household Graphics), *Shufu no tomo* (Housewives' Friend, first published in 1917), *Ohayō okusan* (Good Morning Mrs.), and *Madam*. Young women's magazines, such as *Frau*, *With*, *Can-cam*, *JJ*, *AnAn*, *Say*, *Non-no*, and *Olive*, are primarily concerned with fashion, cosmetics, dieting, and other beauty work, as well as personal and workplace relationships. There are also many specialty magazines for adolescents that focus on topics like music, entertainment, and celebrities, such as *Duet*, *Pretty Up*, *Live Magazine*, *Popolo*, *Junon*, and *Myōjō* (Venus).

A central concern for analysts has been to track the manner in which female gender has been represented in women's magazines, and to understand how such constructions are given vitality because of their wide media dispersal. One debate is whether or not magazines are simply vehicles for sanctioned gender models or manuals for capitalist consumption. In order to dispute the idea that magazine editors and advertisers are wickedly trying to force certain images and ideas onto readers, some scholars attend to the institutional and professional aspects of the production process (Moeran 1996; Sakamoto 1999). Regardless of how images and models of women actually get into magazines, or what the intentions of their producers were, they may nonetheless have detrimental effects on women's self-perception and lives. Because many magazines focus on everyday interaction codes and women's infringements of them, readers can't help but get a sense that they are the constant objects of social surveillance. Other people are always on the hunt for violations, which they may then pass on to readers through magazine polls, interviews, and forums. As the subject of continual evaluation and assessment, every aspect of one's person, from the most public to the most private, will be held up for appraisal, and any offense will be painstakingly diagnosed and cataloged. Magazines also have an impact on women because of their pervasive representation of contemporary beauty ideology (Miller 2000; Ochiai 1997). For example, unlike a century ago, visual images of beauty attributes are found in a broader array of media, especially magazines. Bombardment with normalizing images of selected types of women educate consumers about flaws and defects they may have been unaware of possessing, presenting them with often unattainable models for comparison.

A difference from a nonfiction book is that a magazine contains many voices and images, some opposing others. Depending on the magazine, images and text may either buttress or challenge prevailing social norms. Although magazines targeting women contain unrelenting advertising that promotes consumption of expensive clothing, cosmetics, and body transformation technologies and products, feature articles may nonetheless reflect a humorous, often sassy, in-your-face engagement with cultural ideology about proper personality and behavior (Miller 1997). One can find contradictory portraits and advice in any one issue. For instance, young women's magazines instruct readers to avoid being too playfully frivolous, or risk being labeled a phoney, yet if she's too serious and strict, the reader will be thought of as a wrangling scold. A woman is not liked if she's not smart enough to think deeply about anything, yet gets criticized for being intelligent enough to feel pessimistic and gloomy about the state of the world.

The content of some conduct articles in young women's magazines also illustrates ways in which Japanese society is changing. Magazines introduce novel labels and classification systems for good and bad women, and these reflect long-standing criteria and attributes thought to be significant in Japan's middle-class world view. In some cases they represent a specifically male or female perspective, and may also convey new assessments and reformulation of the social world. Articles that detail manners, behaviors, and modes of dress and speech tell us that knowledge of middle-class propriety is not fixed and unchanging, but is in a state of flux that requires constant monitoring by those trying to acquire it. We also see a shift away from traditional male-defined morality to acceptance of female selfhood and independence which still requires constant shaping and guidance, which the magazines, of course, helpfully provide. The vignettes, polls, and narratives found in magazines depict erring women who nevertheless have a strong sense of themselves and, almost always, are sexually active and knowledgeable. Magazine content therefore reflects an interplay between the forces of incorporation and resistance to culturally sanctioned and class-based ideals of femaleness.

Drawing theoretical insights from cultural studies and gender studies, scholars who study Japan acknowledge that the content and imaging in magazines need not be reflective of reality, and that there may not be a "true" meaning to measure these images against. Rather than their accuracy, they are concerned with the question of why some images occur when they do. What events or changes in cultural history account for the representations we find? For example, Bardsley (2000) examined the tensions about women's roles and aspirations, expressed through satire and debate, that appeared in a special 1956 issue of the popular women's magazine, *Fujin kōron*. Bardsley (2003) has also looked at the way six different magazines treated the royal wedding of 1959, which was lavishly promoted or else used as a wedge for criticism of the imperial institution. Media attention to the modern family, refracted though focus on the marriage of the Crown Prince, illustrated contentions and worries surrounding the future of women's role in a new democracy. These same anxieties and debates reappeared in magazines decades later during the marriage of the current Crown Prince to Owada Masako.

Scholars have found the gorgeous photography and quality paper of the middle-class and upper-middle-class magazines such as *More*, *With*, and *Katei gahō* more amenable to analysis than the grainy pages of women's tabloid magazines. On the list of bestselling magazines for 2000, we find two television magazines and a few young women's magazines, but the majority fall into a category called *shūkanshi*, "weekly magazines" (Shōgakukan 2001:492). The weeklies cover gossip about singers, actors, politicians, and sports figures, and range from the reputable to the unapologetically trashy. The scandal weeklies are gendered, with several targeting women readers, such as *Josei jishin* (Woman Herself, published since 1958), and *Josei seben* (Woman Seven, printed since 1963). These usually contain blurry shots of celebrities going into or out of love hotels, articles on corrupt politicians and true crime episodes, ads for breast enlargement products, and smarmy photos of the royal family. Anthropologists have not taken full advantage of what these magazines might tell us about the anxieties, preoccupations, and concerns of non-elite readers.

There are many other aspects of magazine culture that have yet to be fully explored by anthropologists. New in the publishing world are numerous periodicals targeting men, such as two recent lifestyle magazines for a mature audience, *Otoko no kakurega* (Men's Retreat), which came out in 2001, and *Obura*, which appeared in 2002. These contain articles on cooking, gourmet dining, fashion, travel, gardening, and interior design. Sakai (2002) links their inception to the recession, which has led men to reassess their personal lives, seeking improvement in quality of life through non-work-related activities and pastimes. Since the 1990s there have also been several new beauty work magazines for young men, such as *Bidan* (Beautiful Man), *Fine Boys*, and *Men's Non-no*. The study of these new men's magazines could be useful in understanding the role of print media in the negotiation of new forms of masculinity.

Notable in magazines targeting high-school and junior high-school girls published since 2000 is the attention given to sex. Changes in attitudes about sex are reflected in the explosion of published polls, call-in forums, and feature articles. It is expressed through the publication of responses to provocative questions posed to readers concerning their sexual experiences, proclivities, and fantasies. No attempt is made to be scientific or broad, and in some cases polls have fewer than 20 respondents. Most of the polls illustrate a full spectrum of sexual behavior and are not only focused on heterosexuality. In these pages young women openly talk about and critique sexuality. The subtext is that sex is part of self-expression and enjoyment, and is not tied to traditional reproductive roles. When young women write openly about sex, the dominant discourse of maidenly virtue is negated. As readers explore the variety of sexual experience reported by other readers, they gain an enhanced and critical awareness of what they share with other young women, leading to experimentation and the ability to generalize experience. The prevalence of sex in teen magazines awaits analysis by anthropologists and other scholars. Perhaps they will interpret this trend as a form of melioration of women's increased cultural power. The media's focus on individual pleasure and desire neutralizes dissent by redirecting attention away from sociopolitical issues such as sexist employment practices, environmental degradation, and political corruption.

In addition to heightened attention to sex, girls' magazines are manifesting another noteworthy vogue. Increasingly, *Cawaii*, *Seventeen*, and *Popteen* are emulating *Egg* magazine by publishing a new girls' art form called graffiti photos, which are photographs defaced with colored ink captions and iconic drawings. The idiosyncratic handwritten text on graffiti photos represents a rejection of the typeset orderliness and perfection characteristic of most male-dominated print media. An interesting outcome of this fad is that some magazines began replacing or augmenting typeset text with imitation girls' graffiti writing in feature articles and advertisements. In doing so they are reverting to a form of writing similar to that found in pre-Meiji woodblock printed books and magazines, which more closely approximated natural handwriting. Perhaps this girls' innovation will eventually have an influence on the direction of print media more generally.

Moveable type had been known in Japan at least since the Tokugawa era, but it was not until the Meiji era that typeset printing became popular. Although initially resistant, readers gradually came to prefer the efficiency and uniformity of typeset writing, thus transforming the way written language was consumed and appreciated. In a sense, non-elite readers, especially women, are taking back the publishing world from the intellectual class, creating or reinvigorating forms of cultural production. In an earlier century Ihara Saikaku (1642–93) produced one of the first bestselling books in Japan when he wrote *The Life of an Amorous Man* (Ihara 1964 [1682]), a story centering on the mentality and everyday life of a member of the rising merchant class. The common people are once again driving the publishing industry, and it is their reading tastes which are dominating bestseller lists and magazine sales.

Because print media are a cultural product, they offer a fertile domain for anthropological study. Print media go beyond the role of simply remembering and recording social and cultural life. The magnitude and salience of nonfiction book and magazine publishing make them pivotal to understanding contemporary cultural processes. They are obvious instruments for the dissemination of culture, particularly in the case of how-to and self-help books or magazine articles that provide content about how to negotiate everyday social life. Print media may be used to trace changing representations of ethnic selves, ethnic others, gender, and other subjectivities. Print media have a mutually constitutive relationship to cultural formation and change, offering an avenue for the expression of nontraditional norms, subcultural identities, and social change even as they participate in the construction and maintenance of culture and society. In print media we detect complex patterns of domination and resistance, and shifts in the display and exercise of cultural authority. Trends in Japanese print media offer anthropologists a unique, yet often overlooked, opportunity for learning about the debates, desires, and thinking of diverse members of Japanese society.

REFERENCES

Allison, Anne. 1996. Permitted and Prohibited Desires: Mothers, Comics, and Censorship in Japan. Boulder: Westview–HarperCollins.

Asahi shimbun. 2003. Japan Almanac 2003. Tokyo: Asahi Shimbun.

Bardsley, Jan. 2000. What Women Want: Fujin kōron Tells All in 1956. US–Japan Women's Journal 19:7–48.

——2003. Fashioning the People's Princess: Women's Magazines, Shōda Michiko, and the Royal Wedding of 1959. US–Japan Women's Journal 23:57–91.

Befu, Harumi. 2001. Hegemony of Homogeneity: An Anthropological Analysis of *Nihonjin-ron*. Melbourne: Trans Pacific Press.

Bellah, Robert N. 1957. Tokugawa Religion. New York: Free Press.

Carlson, Richard. 1998 [1997]. Chiisai koto ni kuyokuyo surunai (Don't Sweat the Small Stuff). M. Ozawa, trans. Tokyo: Sanmaku Shuppan.

Carnegie, Dale. 1984 [1948]. Michi wa hirakeru (How to Stop Worrying and Start Living). A. Kayama, trans. Osaka: Sōgensha.

Chiteki Seikatsu Kenkyūjo, ed. 1995. Gyōgi, sahō no benrichō (Manual of Deportment and Manners). Tokyo: Seishun Publishing.

Clammer, John. 1995. Consuming Bodies: Constructing and Representing the Female Body in Contemporary Japanese Print Media. *In* Women, Media and Consumption in Japan. L. Skov and B. Moeran, eds. pp. 197–219. Honolulu: University of Hawaii Press.

Erino, Miya. 1990. Redisu komikku no joseigaku (Women's Studies through Ladies' Comics). Tokyo: Seikyūsha.

Frank, Heidi. 2000. Japanese Lesbian and Housewife Letters: A Case for the Sociolinguistics of Orthographic Variation. MA thesis, Northwestern University.

Gates, Bill. 1995. Biru geitsu mirai o kataru (The Road Ahead). K. Nishi, trans. Tokyo: Asuki Shuppankyoku.

Haruka, Yōko. 2000. Tōdai de Ueno Chizuko ni kenka o manabu (Learning to Fight under Ueno Chizuko at the University of Tokyo). Tokyo: Chikuma Shobō.

Hawkins, Joseph R. 1999. An Ethnography of Same-Sexuality in Contemporary Japan. Ph.D. dissertation, University of Southern California.

Hirakawa, Hiroko. 2000. The Politics of Gender and Mass Media in Post-1975 Japan. US–Japan Women's Journal 19:49–82.

Ihara, Saikaku. 1964 [1682]. Koshoku ichidai otoko (The Life of an Amorous Man). K. Mamada, trans. Rutland, VT: C. E. Tuttle.

Iijima, Ai. 2001. Puratonikku sekkusu (Platonic Sex). Tokyo: Shōgakukan.

Johnson, Spencer. 2000 [1998]. Chiizu wa doko e kieta (Who Moved My Cheese? An Amazing Way to Deal with Change in Your Work and in Your Life). N. Kaneko, trans. Tokyo: Fusōsha.

Kelsky, Karen. 1994. Intimate Ideologies: Transnational Theory and Japan's "Yellow Cabs". Public Culture 6:465–478.

Kinmonth, Earl H. 1981. The Self-Made Man in Meiji Japanese Thought: From Samurai to Salaryman. Berkeley: University of California Press.

Kinsella, Sharon. 2000. Adult *Manga*: Culture and Power in Contemporary Japanese Society. Richmond, Surrey: Curzon Press.

Kishimoto, Yōko. 2000. Koi mo ii kedō, hon mo suki (Love is Fine, But I Like Books, Too). Tokyo: Kōdansha.

Maruyama, Masao. 1956. Gendai seiji no shisō to kōdō (Thought and Behavior in Modern Japanese Politics). Tokyo: Miraisha.

Matsubara, Junko. 1988. Kurowassan shōkōgun (The Croissant Syndrome). Tokyo: Bungei Shunjū.

Miller, Laura. 1989. The Japanese Language and Honorific Speech: Is There a Nihongo without Keigo? Penn Linguistics Review 13(3):8–46.

——1997. People Types: Personality Classification in Japanese Women's Magazines. Journal of Popular Culture 31:133–150.

——1998. Bad Girls: Representations of Unsuitable, Unfit, and Unsatisfactory Women in Magazines. US–Japan Women's Journal 15:31–51.

——2000. Media Typifications and Hip Bijin. US–Japan Women's Journal 9:176–205.

Miyamura, Haruo. 2001. Maruyama Masao, nihon no shisō seidoku (An Explication of Japanese Thought by Maruyama Masao). Tokyo: Iwanami Gendai Bunko.

Moeran, Brian. 1995. Reading Japanese in *Katei gahō*: The Art of Being an Upperclass Woman. *In* Women, Media and Consumption in Japan. L. Skov and B. Moeran, eds. pp. 111–142. Honolulu: University of Hawaii Press.

——1996. A Japanese Advertising Agency: An Anthropology of Media and Markets. Honolulu: University of Hawaii Press.

Nakamura, Yoichirō. 1993. OL manā kihon chiekku (Fundamental Checklist of Office Lady Manners). Tokyo: Isetan.

Napier, Susan. 1994. Redisu komikku o yomu (Reading Ladies' Comics). Chūō kōron 109:33–35.

Ochiai, Emiko. 1997. Decent Housewives and Sensual White Women: Representations of Women in Postwar Japanese Magazines. Japan Review 9:151–168.

Ōishi, Hatsutarō. 1971. Tadashi keigo (Correct Honorific Speech). Tokyo: Ōizumi Shoten.

Okuaki, Yoshinobu. 1978. Keigo no goten (Dictionary of Errors in Honorific Speech). Tokyo: Jiyū Kokuminsha.

Ōmae, Ken'ichi. 1999. Sararīman sabaibaru (Salaryman Survival). Tokyo: Shōgakukan.

Ōno, Susumu. 1999. Nihongo renshucho (Japanese Language Workbook). Tokyo: Iwanami Shoten.

Ototake, Hirotada. 1999. Gotai fumanzoku (Unsatisfactory Limbs). Tokyo: Kōdansha.

Reynolds, Katsue Akiba. 1989. Josei zasshi no kotoba (Language in Women's Magazines). *In* Josei zasshi o kaidoku-suru (Decoding Women's Magazines). T. Inoue, ed. pp. 209–227. Tokyo: Kakiuchi Shuppan.

Robertson, Jennifer. 1979. Rooting the Pine: Shingaku Methods of Organization. Monumenta Nipponica 34(3):311–332.

Rosenberger, Nancy. 1995. Antiphonal Performances? Japanese Women's Magazines and Women's Voices. *In* Women, Media and Consumption in Japan. L. Skov and B. Moeran, eds. pp. 143–169. Honolulu: University of Hawaii Press.

Sakagawa, Sakio. 1969. Shinjidai no keigo tokuhon (Reader in Modern Honorifics). Tokyo: Dōbunkan.

Sakai, Junko. 2002. The Emergence of "Men's" Magazines. Japanese Book News 38:4–5.

Sakamoto, Kazue. 1999. Reading Japanese Women's Magazines: The Construction of New Identities in the 1970s and 1980s. Media, Culture and Society 21:173–193.

Sano, Shin'ichi. 2001. Dare ga "hon" o korosu no ka (Who Would Kill Books?). Tokyo: President sha.

Satō, Ayako. 2000. Sukina jibun ni naru 55 no hōhō (55 Ways to Have a Likeable Self). Tokyo: Kōdansha.

Sawada, Janine. 1993. Confucian Values and Popular Zen: Sekimon Shingaku in Eighteenth-Century Japan. Honolulu: University of Hawaii Press.

Schodt, Frederik. 1986 [1983]. *Manga! Manga!* The World of Japanese Comics. Tokyo: Kodansha International.

—— 1996. Dreamland Japan: Writings on Modern *Manga*. Berkeley, CA: Stone Bridge Press.

Shibata, Takeshi. 2001. Jōshiki toshite shitte okitai nihongo (Practical Japanese You Should Know). Tokyo: Gentōsha.

Shōgakukan. 2001. Dētaparu: saishin jōhō yōgo jiten (DataPal: Up-to-Date Information and Encyclopedia of Terms). Tokyo: Shōgakukan.

Skov, Lise. 1995. Environmentalism Seen through Japanese Women's Magazines. *In* Women, Media and Consumption in Japan. L. Skov and B. Moeran, eds., pp. 170–196. Honolulu: University of Hawaii Press.

Skov, Lise, and Brian Moeran. eds. 1995. Women, Media and Consumption in Japan. Honolulu: University of Hawaii Press.

Suenaga, Tōru. 1999. Meiku manē! (Make Money!). Tokyo: Bungei Shunjū.

Suzuki, Kazuko. 1999. Pornography or Therapy? Japanese Girls Creating the Yaoi Phenomenon. *In* Millennium Girls: Today's Girls Around the World. S. A. Inness, ed. pp. 243–268. London: Rowman & Littlefield.

Takai, Nobu. 1996. Jōzu ni hito o yamesasetai (Skillful Ways to Get Employees to Quit). Tokyo: Kōdansha.

White, Merry. 1995. The Marketing of Adolescence in Japan: Buying and Dreaming. *In* Women, Media and Consumption in Japan. L. Skov and B. Moeran, eds. pp. 255–273. Honolulu: University of Hawaii Press.

Wife Editors. 1989. Anchi-kurowassan shōkōgun (The Anti-Croissant Syndrome). Tokyo: Shakai Shisōsha.

Yamada, Masahiro. 1999. Parasaito shinguru no jidai (The Age of Parasite Singles). Tokyo: Chikuma Shinsho.

Yamamoto, Takayo. 2001. Nonpara: parasaito shinai onna tachi no "hontō" (Nonparasites: The Truth about Women who Are Not Parasites). Tokyo: Magazine House.

Zennikkū Eigyōhonbu Kyōikukunrenbu, ed. 1991. OL tabūshū (Anthology of Office Lady Taboos). Tokyo: Goma Seibo.

PART V

Body, Blood, Self, and Nation

CHAPTER 21

Biopower: Blood, Kinship, and Eugenic Marriage

Jennifer Robertson

"Blood" has been a familiar metaphor in Japan since the turn of the 19th century for "shared heredity" or "shared ancestry," and even for the essential material imagined to constitute *the* "Japanese race." In Japan and elsewhere in the industrializing world, race was conceptualized both as a mix of discrete biological and cultural characteristics and as the specific group, nation, or human type that possessed and manifested those characteristics. Moreover, it was at this time that the nascent "science" of eugenics provided a framework within which blood became a cipher for specifically modern ideas of "disciplinary bio-power."[1] Blood remains an organizing metaphor for profoundly significant, fundamental, and perduring assumptions about Japaneseness and otherness; it is invoked as a determining agent of kinship, *mentalité*, national identity, and cultural uniqueness. And blood type is the basis for a very popular "sanguine horoscopy," in addition to other systems of fortune-telling and personality analysis based on East Asian cosmology.

The link between blood and nationality is certainly not unique to Japan, but it is inflected in ways that distinguish the Japanese phenomenon from others. My most general objective in this chapter is to layer into a coherent and demystifying narrative the cacophonous popular debates and welter of folk and scientific assumptions specifically about "Japanese" – and the Japaneseness of – blood and bodies. I shall address two large themes that bleed into each other, so to speak: the application of eugenic principles and propositions in fusing kinship and biology, and the normalization through popular eugenics of "ethnic national endogamy" as a dominant and modern cultural ideal.[2]

I must emphasize at the outset that "the popular" and "the scientific" did not inhabit opposite ends of a continuum of credibility. In fin-de-siècle Japan, eugenics – the reproduction of the "fit" – constituted a synergism of theory, ideology, and practice that blurred and even fused any hypothetical boundary between the street and the laboratory. This blurring and fusion were symptomatic of "eugenic modernity," by which I mean the application of scientific concepts and methods as the primary means to constitute both the nation and its constituent subjects.[3] As my cited references attest, established scientists used the mass media to foster an appreciation of race betterment through regulated procreation, and impresarios organized traveling hygiene exhibitions and eugenic beauty contests (the judges for which included some of the same scientists). Through eugenics, science was popularized, and the public was prevailed upon to cultivate a modern attitude of scientific curiosity.[4]

The new scientific order in Japan was introduced under the aegis of nationalism and empire-building. Beginning with the colonization of Okinawa in 1874 followed by that of Taiwan in 1895, Korea in 1910, Micronesia in 1919, Manchuria in 1931, North China by 1937, and much of Southeast Asia by 1942, the state consolidated through military force a vast Asian-Pacific domain, the so-called Greater East Asia Co-Prosperity Sphere (*daitōa kyōeiken*), a rubric coined in August 1940. Although empire-building forms the backdrop of this chapter, my focus is on colonizing practices pursued and implemented *within* Japan among the Japanese people, who constituted a proving ground for such practices throughout Asia and the Pacific. If East Asian prosperity was the euphemistic metaphor for Japanese dominance abroad, "family" was the operable image at home. The concept of a family-state (*kazoku kokka*) system was invented by late 19th-century ideologues to create a familiar and modern community – the nation – where one had not existed before. Some ideologues stretched out the family metaphor and likened nationality to membership in an exceptional "bloodline" (*kettō*).[5]

BONES, FLESH, SEEDS, AND BLOOD

According to cultural historian Nishida Tomomi, it was during the 17th through 19th centuries that "blood" (*chi*, *ketsu*), equated in earlier periods with death and ritual pollution, gradually acquired a positive metaphorical meaning of "life force" and lineage. It also became the main criterion of nationality, which, ever since the promulgation of the first constitution in 1890, continues to be based on the principle of *jus sanguinus*.[6] Before the 17th century, the dominant symbolism of blood was negative, located as it was in the ritually polluted female body; menstruation and parturition were classified in Shinto and Buddhism as "dirty" and especially dangerous to males (Nishida 1995:18–19). In addition to banishing females from certain "sacred" sites and spaces, males could avoid "blood poisoning" by undertaking Shinto purification rituals.[7]

Nishida surmises that the terms *ketsuen* (blood relationship), *kettō* (blood line), and *ketsuzoku* (blood relatives), indicative of an affirmative meaning of blood, were coined around the mid-19th century when they began to appear in a wide range of literary sources. The Japanese dictionaries compiled by Jesuits in the late 16th and early 17th centuries did not define blood in terms of heredity or lineage (Nishida 1995: 206–209). Before blood acquired its new, positive meaning, heredity was denoted by the term *kotsuniku*, or bone-flesh, where "bone" (*kotsu*) referred to paternity, and "flesh" (*niku*) to maternity (Nishida 1995:32–35).[8] Another term in use since at least the 10th century to identify paternity specifically was *tane* (seed). From the late 19th century onward, the Japanese-style term *hitodane* (literally, "person [*hito*] seed [*t(d)ane*]") was used to denote heredity in the sense of "germ plasm," as then understood. Thus, the phrase *tane ga kawaru* ("seed changes") refers to children with the same mother and a different father (Nishida 1995:35).[9]

Nishida notes that in Japan, unlike in China, "blood relations" (qua heredity) were not privileged over other types of social intimacy, such as adoption, which continues to be widely practiced in Japan (Nishida 1995:18, 65, 76). Important to realize in this connection is the fact that adoptions were and are arranged for pragmatic reasons, most commonly to secure a male to occupy the *situs* of household (*ie*) successor. They were not undertaken for personal or emotional needs, objectives that can be realized without actual co-residence and even through *post mortem* adoption and ghost marriages (Lebra 1993:125; Van Bremen 1998).[10] An increasingly positive interpretation of "blood" was accompanied by the normalization of patrilineality as the dominant rule of household succession. Moreover, within the framework of the Meiji constitution, "blood" was the basis of and for a person's civic and legal provenance and attendant rights. Until its codification, patrilineality was especially characteristic of pre-modern samurai, or warrior, households in particular, which comprised less than 8 percent of the population of roughly 27 million persons during the Edo (or Tokugawa) period (1603–1868), and specifically the 1720s (Honjō 1936:21; see also chapter 22 in this volume). Although bona fide membership in the samurai class was determined by the paternal "seed," intra-class adoption was also widely practiced.[11] The Meiji Civil Code sanctioned both the patriarchal household as the smallest legal unit of society and father-to-son succession as the most general, normative pattern of household continuity – a pattern referred to as "samuraization." Today, by contrast, under the auspices of the postwar constitution individuals are legal entities in their own right and succession a subjective arrangement. Although equal inheritance is mandated in the postwar constitution, the majority of Japanese continue the earlier practice of male primogeniture. Furthermore, as in the pre-modern period, sons need not be the biological offspring of fathers; rather, the terms "father" and "son" denote gender roles and social (including adoptive) statuses and not necessarily a biological relationship (although they may *connote* one).

Despite the normalization of patrilineality as an extension of the Meiji state's authority, eugenicists were unanimous in stressing the importance of reckoning kinship bilineally in order to build what they believed to be a scientific foundation from which to launch their collective project of bettering the Japanese race and creating a foundational generation of New Japanese. They also critiqued sharply the deleterious consequences of patriarchy and patrilineal ideology on the health and hygiene of girls and women. For example, writing in January 1945, Tōgō Minoru, a eugenicist, bureaucrat, and colonial administrator, echoed his predecessors in declaring that the physical and mental health of females had been woefully neglected under the feudal and androcentric regime of the Tokugawa shogunate (Tōgō 1945:34). Although early feminists supported many aspects of the eugenics movement, such as birth control and modern, scientific approaches to pregnancy and childbirth (see Otsubo 1999 and chapter 28 in this volume), the eugenicists' critique of patriarchy and patrilineal ideology was not motivated by overtly feminist concerns.

The (non-feminist) gynocentric, maternalist bent of these early eugenics associations was reflected in the postwar Eugenic Protection Law of 1948, which, in addition to preventing "the birth of eugenically inferior offspring," aimed to "protect maternal health and life." The 1948 law was replaced with the Maternal

Protection Law of 1996, from which references to "eugenically inferior offspring" were omitted and a singular emphasis placed on the protection of motherhood and maternal health (Norgren 2001:145, 155). The historical debates about blood and recent legal developments concerning maternity help us to understand why in Japan (unlike in Germany, Israel, and the United States), "eugenics" is neither an avoided nor a negatively charged term.[12]

MIXED BLOOD VERSUS PURE BLOOD

The concept of "pure blood" as a criterion of authentic Japaneseness began circulating in public discourse by the 1880s in many venues and media. "Purity" referred metaphorically to a body – including the national body – free from symbolic pollution and disease-bearing pathogens, as well as to genealogical orthodoxy. As a newly dominant concept, "pure-bloodedness" also effectively tightened what historically had been a loose sense of consanguinity. Although intellectual and ideological rivals, the founders of eugenics associations were nevertheless alike in seeking to improve *the* Japanese race by making bloodline synonymous with household succession (cf. Lebra 1993:125). Their emphasis on the necessary bilineality of a national genealogy consisting of "pure bloods" was not represented in the Meiji Civil Code, which instead privileged male primogeniture and Japanese paternity, or the "male seed," as the sole criterion of nationality and citizenship. This criterion was retained in the postwar Civil Code until 1985, when the nationality law was changed as a result of legal pressure brought by feminists to have the "blood" of Japanese females recognized as an independent and authentic agent of Japanese nationality and citizenship.

In contrast, bilineal kinship continues to supersede all other modes of reckoning the familial, legal, social, and political status of Burakumin ("outcastes") and spirit-animal possessors, that is, persons or households thought to control, or to be controlled by, supernatural animals.[13] In the Tokugawa period, their symbolic pollution and marginality was imagined to be "infectious," and later, with the conflation in eugenic discourse of blood and heredity, inherited and inheritable. In these cases, the new "affirmative" meaning of blood as life force and lineage did not replace the earlier, "negative" meaning of blood as a polluting substance, but rather congealed as both a coeval and a mutually constitutive system of belief (or prejudice). These tenacious popular beliefs, including the dangers of "female blood," represent another or an alternate world of local practices revolving around the negative valences of blood.

By the same token, the blood type fads today represent both a continuation and a distortion of 19th-century scientific ideas about bodies and blood that were embraced by leading intellectuals and introduced to the public at the turn of the century through a centralized education system and burgeoning mass media. (Although many of these ideas are no longer perceived as "scientific" they nevertheless persist in various guises.) The specific field of science that took up the "positive" meaning of blood as its subject was eugenics and race science, and it fueled a discourse that had permeated all aspects of everyday life in Japan by 1900. The public sphere shaped by the discourse of eugenics and race science was premised on a future-oriented vision of a racially improved nation-state, one peopled by taller, heavier, healthier, and fertile men and women whose anthropometrically ideal bodies would serve as the caryatids of the expanding Japanese empire.

At this juncture it is necessary to backtrack in order to review the beginnings of the imperial New Japan. The defeat of the involuted shogunate and the restoration of the emperor Meiji in 1868 within a German-style parliamentary system ushered in unprecedented social reforms based on a policy of selective and controlled Westernization. Among these reforms was the creation of a nation informed by the utopian ideology of the family-state system, noted earlier. People who had had primarily identified themselves and who were identified by region, domain (*han*), locality, and fixed social and domestic status, had to imagine themselves first and foremost as "Japanese." These layers of identity were contained by the new, umbrella-like category of *kokumin*, or "citizen," in the sense of subject of the imperial nation-state, itself imagined as having an organic, corporeal form (*kokutai*). Eugenicists and nationalists believed that New Japan (*shin'nippon*) could "compete successfully with the West in international affairs" and pursue an imperialist agenda of expansion and colonization only if it were peopled with New Japanese. Just how New Japanese could and should be created was the subject of a heated and divisive debate among the ideologues of blood that has shaped the discourse of eugenics to this day.

Eugenics, a term coined by Francis Galton in 1883, was translated into Japanese as the romanized *yuzenikkusu* and as the neologisms *yūseigaku* (science of superior birth) and *jinshukaizengaku* (science of race betterment). These terms were used synonymously with two terms coined a little earlier: "race betterment" (*minzoku/ jinshu kairyō*) and "race hygiene" (*minzoku/jinshu eisei*).[14] *Minzoku* and *jinshu*, the two Japanese words for "race" in both the social and phenotypical senses, for the most part were used interchangeably, although *jinshu* remains the more clinical, social-scientific term (cf. *Rasse*) and *minzoku* the more popular and populist term (cf. *Volk*).[15] When prefixed with names, such as Nippon and Yamato, *minzoku* signified the conflation of phenotype, geography, culture, spirit, history, and nationhood. All of these semantic and semiotic inventions were part of the ideological agenda of the Meiji state and were incorporated into the postwar constitution of 1947, which retained the definition of nationality and citizenship as a matter of blood, or *jus sanguinus* (as opposed to *jus solis*).

Eugenics, in the sense of instrumental and selective procreation, was hardly a new concept in fin-de-siècle Japan. Historically and mytho-historically, as well as across classes and statuses of people, the maintenance of genealogical integrity was a key strategy of household succession. Integrity in this historical context was understood as continuity; that is, the successful augmentation or replacement of household members from one generation to the next through strategically arranged marriages and adoptions.[16] Eugenics, in contrast, was equated with broad societal and nationalist goals, such as the propagation of New Japanese and the rationalization of marriage, with respect to both partner choice and the betrothal ceremony. Introduced under the auspices of "eugenic" was a new national premium on "pure blood" and "wholesome" (*kenzen*) heredity as a necessary condition of race betterment and modern nation-building. Heredity (*iden*) was understood in a general sense as whatever one received from one's parents and ancestors, making them morally as well as medically culpable should their offspring be less than wholesome. Japanese race scientists thus also worked to reform marriage and sexual practices more generally because it was through sex, regulated by the institution of marriage – as well as licensed prostitution – that either positive or negative eugenic precepts, or both, were most effectively implemented.[17]

Positive eugenics refers to the improvement of circumstances of sexual reproduction and thus incorporates advances in sanitation, nutrition, and physical education into strategies to shape the reproductive choices and decisions of individuals and families. The effects of biology (genetics) and environment are conflated. In this connection, "eugenic" was often used in the early 20th-century Japanese literature as both an adjective meaning, and a euphemism for, "hygienic" and "scientific." Negative eugenics involves the prevention of sexual reproduction, through induced abortion or sterilization, among people deemed unfit. "Unfit" was an ambiguous term that included alcoholics, "lepers," the mentally ill, the criminal, the physically disabled, and the sexually alternative, among other categories of people. Some traditional or premodern categories of stigmatized alterity, such as the Burakumin, were recast in scientific terms and deemed uneugenic, while others, such as horoscopic identity, were dismantled as "superstitions and folk beliefs" (*meishin*) of no eugenic consequence, although they could impede the implementation of scientific practices.[18]

Eugenics provided an avenue for the application of science to social problems, including public health, education, and hygiene. The fields of eugenics and public health shared much jargon and many assumptions, attitudes, and aims, not only in Japan, but in other countries as well (cf. Wikler 1999:192). What Martin Pernick notes about early 20th-century America pertains equally well to Japan, namely, that "eugenic methods often were modeled on the infection control techniques of public health": "infections were caused by germs; inheritance was governed by germ plasm. In both cases, 'germs' meant microscopic seeds. Both types of germs enabled disease to propagate and grow, to spread contamination from the bodies of the diseased to the healthy" through the medium of blood, a metaphor for heredity and a vehicle for infection (Pernick 1997:1767, 1769). Like their international counterparts, Japanese eugenicists tended to collapse biology and culture, and, consequently, held either explicitly or implicitly Lamarckian views on race formation and racial temperament. Thus, even those who were environmentally inclined also assumed that complex phenomena, such as the "uniquely Japanese *ie* (household) system," were "carried in the 'blood,' if only as 'instincts' or 'temperamental proclivities'" (Ikeda 1927a, 1927b; Stocking 1968:25). The melding of biology and culture, nature and culture, is also evident in the interchangeability of *jinshu* (race) and *minzoku* (ethnic nation), and in the prescriptions for race betterment.

Through networks of modern institutions and industries, such as the army, schools, hygiene exhibitions, immigration training programs, the press, fashion, advertising, popular genealogies, and so forth, the Japanese people were encouraged to think in totally new and different ways about their bodies. They were to think of their bodies as plastic, in the sense of capable of being molded, and as adaptable, pliable, and transformable through new hygienic regimens of nutrition and physical exercise. For males, these regimens were part of their military training beginning in 1873, when a modern conscription army was established, replacing the hereditary warrior (samurai) class that epitomized the Tokugawa period. Females, exempt from military service, were exposed to these regimens at the many private-sector schools and academies that competed to enroll girls and women whose education was more or less neglected by the Meiji government, at least initially. Clothing also fell under the eugenic gaze. Whereas boys and men were encouraged to wear crewcuts and Western-style outfits to symbolize the modernity of New Japan, girls and women were to represent through costume and hairstyle a nostalgically re-imagined traditional Japanese culture, although they were urged to loosen the normally tightly cinched *obi*, or sash, of their kimono, and to simplify the traditional chignon to facilitate the regular cleaning and combing of their hair. All Japanese were advised by public health agents to learn how to walk properly, to use chairs whenever possible, and to avoid kneeling for long periods of time, which was thought to cause bowed legs and pigeon-toedness (Irizawa 1939 [1913]:17–21, 34, 61). The desirable corporeal results and aesthetic effects of these new hygienic practices were perceived as transmittable by blood through "eugenic marriages" (*yūsei kekkon*), as elaborated below.

In Japan, the discourse of eugenics clustered around two essentially incommensurable positions concerning blood: the "pure-blood," or *junketsu*, position, and the "mixed-blood," or *konketsu*, position. The proponents of each position acknowledged the "mixed-blooded," or multiethnic, ancient history of Japan, an idea developed in the late 19th century by the German physician and genealogist Erwin von Baelz, who had spent 30 years in Japan (1876–1906) studying the racial origins of the Japanese people. Von Baelz, applying the then dominant teleological evolutionist paradigm, proposed that the so-called Yamato stem-race, associated with the imperial household and its allegedly unbroken lineage stretching back over 2,500 years, had, by the sixth century, conquered and subjugated the different racial groups coexisting on the islands. These groups, he maintained, were assimilated selectively and slowly, so that by the 19th century, "Yamato blood" was a refined and superior substance (Hayashida 1976:24). Japanese pundits favoring the pure-blood position were keen on preserving the eugenic integrity of the pristine Yamato stem-race; those promoting the mixed-blood position, enumerated the eugenic benefits of hybrid vigor through the mixing of Japanese and non-Japanese blood (Robertson 2001a).[19]

The "mixed-blood" position was first articulated in an 1884 essay, *Nippon jinshu kairyōron* (A Treatise on the Betterment of the Japanese Race), penned by the Keio University-educated journalist Takahashi Yoshio. Invoking a Social Darwinist scenario, Takahashi argued that Japan was undergoing a transition from a "semicivilized" to a "civilized" status represented, in his view, by northern European countries and their taller, heavier, and stronger populations. This "civilized" status could be expedited through the marriage of Japanese males and Anglo females, or, as he phrased it, the "mixed marriage of yellows and whites" (*kōhaku zakkon*).[20] Mixedblood marriages, Takahashi hypothesized, would create a taller, heavier, and stronger, in short "a physically superior Japanese race, thereby making it possible for the Japanese to compete successfully with Europeans and Americans in international affairs" (Suzuki 1983:32–34, 39).

The "pure-blood" position was advocated by Katō Hiroyuki, a veteran politician, imperial advisor, and chancellor of Tokyo University. Katō's scathing critique of the mixed-marriage plan was published in 1886 in both an academic journal, *Tōyō gakugei* (Oriental Arts and Sciences) and the *Tōkyō nichinichi shinbun*, a leading daily newspaper. To summarize, Katō first of all objected to the notion that the Japanese were less civilized than Europeans.[21] Second, he argued that interbreeding "yellows" and "whites" would create a completely new hybrid category of person whose political and social "status" would be unclear and perplexing. Miscegenation, Katō concluded, would result in race *transformation* and not race betterment, and would, over the course of several generations, seriously dilute the pure blood – or racial and cultural essence – of the Japanese. He declared emphatically that whereas mixed-blood marriages between yellows and whites would insure the "complete defeat" (*zenpai*) of Japan by Westerners, pure-bloodedness would insure for eternity Japan's distinctive racial history, culture, and social system (Fujino 1998:385; Katō 1990 [1886]:33, 40–47; Suzuki 1983:35–38).[22]

Although the pure-blood position emerged fairly quickly as the dominant one, the pros and cons of both positions were hotly debated in the eugenics literature through 1945, and continue today in other guises. For example, in an article published in the May 1911 issue of *Jinsei–Der Mensch* (Human Life), the first eugenics journal published in Japan, zoologist Oka'asa Jirō scoffed at the proposal of "white–yellow marriages," dismissing it as one example of the "maniacal fascination with the West" (*seiyōshinsui*) that defined the early Meiji period (Oka'asa 1915:2).[23] Over 25 years later, in 1939, political theorist Ijichi Susumu published an article in *Kaizō* (Reconstruction), a popular, generally liberal, literary periodical, advocating the intermarriage of Japanese males and "carefully selected" Manchurian females. He referred to his proposal as a "racial blood transfusion" (*minzoku yūketsu*), and argued that "mixing superior Japanese blood with inferior Manchurian blood would stimulate the development and civilization of inferior peoples by producing hybrid offspring who would mature as natural political leaders" (Ijichi 1939:86).[24] Ijichi's ideas in turn were rebuffed by Tōgō Minoru, noted earlier, whose ideas about blood circulated widely during the 1920s through the 1940s. Tōgō reiterated Katō's objections to mixed-blood offspring, arguing that they constituted a "new race" (*shinminzoku*); miscegenation by definition could only fail to produce the cultural objective of colonial assimilation, namely Japanization (*nipponka*). Mixed marriages between Japanese and non-Japanese Asians, he asserted, would effectively corrupt and "dissolve the soul [*tamashii*] of the pure Japanese race and national body" and thwart the imperial expansion of the Japanese people (Tōgō 1936:142–144; 1945).[25]

I realized, in the course of my research on blood ideologies, that the central tenet of the "pure-blood" position was anchored in a centuries-old construction of radical otherness transposed into a new vocabulary. Although he used mathematical charts and invoked modern science, Katō Hiroyuki's argument for preserving blood purity was strikingly similar to the persistent "one-drop" folk theory regulating marriages between symbolically pure and polluted Japanese. Briefly, according to this theory, Burakumin and spirit-animal possessors are labeled "black stock" (*kurosuji*) and their opposites are labeled "white stock" (*shirosuji*). The term *suji* ("stock" or "line") is very close to the 19th-century meaning of blood as an inheritable biological *and* cultural substance, but its affective range is much broader and the transmission process analogous to infection and contamination. Miscegenation among black and white "stockholders" would turn both a "white stock" person and that person's entire household "black" (Ishizuka 1983 [1972]:75–77; 112–115; Yoshida 1977 [1972]:58–60, 87–91). Katō seemed to define the nation in terms of *shirosuji*, a "white stock" lineage that could be irrevocably sullied – or turned "black" – by the mixing of Japanese and non-Japanese blood.

BLOOD MARRIAGES

The central focus in the Japanese eugenics movement concentrated on the physiques and overall health of girls and women. Japanese eugenicists argued that the physical development of Japanese girls and women had been neglected for centuries, resulting in their physiological inferiority. The need to grow the population in order to generate the human capital with which to fund nation- and empire-building motivated agents of the Japanese state and private sectors alike to focus their undivided attention on improving the bodies of females, who were, after all, the biological reproducers of the nation (cf. Fujo shinbun 1935; McClintock 1994). This part of the nationalist and imperialist enterprise was supported by some of the leading Japanese feminists, whose agenda of popularizing methods of birth control and promoting maternal health was incorporated into the discourse of eugenics, as I noted earlier (see also Norgren 2001; Otsubo 1999). In this connection, note that the early 20th-century (1940) *and* postwar (1948 and 1996) eugenics legislation and laws alike have been understood as measures to protect the reproductive health of mothers. "Maternal protection" (*bosei hogo*), in fact, is one of the many euphemisms for eugenic practices today.

Generally speaking, the pronatalist state encouraged the improvement of the conditions surrounding female reproductivity instead of advocating sterilization as a way to reduce the reproduction of the unfit. The Welfare Ministry (Kōseishō), established in 1938, inaugurated a "propagate and multiply movement" (*umeyo fuyaseyo undō*), which included the staging of healthy-baby contests throughout the country. Especially fertile mothers were eulogized in the mass media as comprising a "fertile womb battalion" (*kodakara butai*). The ministry also organized awards ceremonies, many of which were staged at department stores, where such mothers, babies in tow, were presented with certificates honoring their reproductive success.[26] Already in 1930, the Education Ministry (Monbushō), together with the *Tōkyo* and *Ōsaka asahi* newspaper companies, had inaugurated an annual nationwide contest to identify the top ten – of 260,000 contestants – "most healthy, eugenically fit children in Japan" (*nippon'ichi no kenkō yūryōji*). Contestants were selected from elementary schools throughout Japan and underwent further screening at the prefectural level before the finalists were selected by a central committee. In addition to a female and male winner, four pairs of runners up were selected, along with five pairs of semifinalists. Photographs of the scantily clad winners were published in the daily press along with charts detailing their physical measurements, medical histories, educational backgrounds, and maternal and paternal genealogies (Tōkyo asahi shinbun 1930:8–9; see also Ōsaka asahi shinbun 1931:11).[27] Eugenicists referred to this contest as a new (*shin*) *nenjū gyōji*, a term for the "annual events" comprising the agricultural calendar. In doing so, they sought to naturalize and traditionalize the incorporation into everyday life of eugenic practices as central both to the persistence of historical cultural practices and to the corporeal development of Japanese children (Yūsei 1937:8–9).

Worries about the anthropometric status of women and children were equaled by and linked to worries among a majority of eugenicists about the "high rate" of consanguineous marriage in Japan. One of the most prevalent topics in the four eugenics journals that I have scrutinized – *Jinsei–Der Mensch*, *Yūsei undō* (Eugenic Exercise/Movement), *Yūsei* (Superior Birth), and *Yūseigaku* (Eugenics) – was the "detrimental consequences" of "marriages among blood relatives," or *ketsuzoku kekkon*.[28] Much was made of how consanguineous marriages, mostly between first cousins, amounted to 5 to 6 percent of all registered marriages (Furuya 1941:117; Yasui 1940:14). It is not always clear from the Japanese literature what was the standard in relation to which this percentage constituted a "high rate." The statistics provided by Ethel Elderton, a Galton Research Scholar writing in 1911 and much cited by her Japanese colleagues, may offer a useful cross-cultural comparison. Elderton concluded that the percentage of first-cousin marriages "among all classes in England" was around 3 percent, although she found a "very high percentage" of cousin marriages, 7 to 11 percent, in cases of deaf-mutism and albinoism (Elderton 1911:24–28).

Using population and registered-marriage statistics compiled by the Japanese government between 1933 and 1943, I calculated that 5 percent would amount to an annual average of somewhere between 24,000 and 33,000 registered marriages (Jinkō mondai kenkyūkai 1933–43). The actual percentage of consanguineous marriages is actually much higher since many – in some cases over a third or more – marriages were not registered. Unfortunately, the number of unregistered, common-law marriages, or *naien*, for this period is not available, much less information as to what percentage of them were among "blood relatives" (Civisca 1957). Some villages, such as Narata and Yūshima in the Minamikoma district of Yamanashi Prefecture, were known as "blood-marriage hamlets" (*ketsuzoku kekkon buraku*) because the vast majority of inhabitants had married their first cousins, half-cousins, second cousins (*hatoko*), uncles, or nieces. These two villages were the subjects of a survey initiated in September 1943 by the Welfare Ministry, the results of which were published in 1949 (Shinozaki 1949). Imaizumi Yoko, a demographer employed by the same ministry, notes that the proportion of consanguineous marriages in Japan averaged 16 percent in the 1920s (Imaizumi 1988:235). Curiously, the American anthropologist John Embree elected *not* to explore the phenomenon of the "frequent cousin marriages" that he encountered while conducting pioneering fieldwork in rural Kyushu during the late 1930s. He did, however, note that "missionaries" of the eugenic marriage campaign were active in the area, and that the practice of consanguineous marriage was "being discouraged by more educated people on the questionable theory that it is biologically harmful" (Embree 1939:88).

The countrywide practice of consanguineous marriage reflected the premium placed on what I call the "strategic endogamy" practiced during the 250 years of relative isolation maintained by the xenophobic Tokugawa shogunate. By "strategic endogamy" I am referring to the transaction of marriages exclusively among and within certain categories of people defined by social status and geographical location; in Japan, "blood marriages" were not limited to elites. Familiarity was another desirable criterion, as it was popularly assumed that marriages between blood relatives were more stable and diplomatic in that they were free from disruptive anxieties about unknown or hidden factors.

Eugenicists in Japan and elsewhere argued among themselves over the negative and positive benefits of inbreeding among blood relatives. A minority in Japan pointed to Galton's thesis of "hereditary genius" and other seemingly positive examples of consanguinity, including the ancient Athenians (cf. East and Jones 1919:226–244). Applying quasi-Mendelian logic, they argued that, in order for inbreeding to be risk-free, the blood of each party must be absolutely pure (Mizushima and Mitake 1942; Taguchi 1940:33–35). The catch, of course, was that pure-bloodedness, while good in theory, was never completely ascertainable. The majority of Japanese eugenicists believed that the transmission and manifestation of diseases and defects were expedited and multiplied through inbreeding. They echoed and cited their foreign counterparts, such as Ethel Elderton, in linking a host of disorders and diseases to the hereditary transmission of faulty germ plasm (*iden*) – the word "gene" was not coined until 1908. In Elderton's words,

> The real danger of cousin marriage lies not in the existence of patent defects in the stock. Nor can we recommend cousin marriage because the stock has certain patent valuable characteristics. Behind the obviously advantageous quality may exist the rare but latent defect. The danger of cousin marriage lies in the probability that the germ plasm of each individual contains numerous latent defects, each of which is rare in the community at large, and each of which is of small danger to the individual or the offspring unless the mating is with another individual whose germ plasm contains one or more of the same latent characters. (Elderton 1911:38)

These "latent defects" included sterility, mental illness, alcoholism, feeblemindedness, physical deformities, disabilities, dementia, deaf-mutism, myopia and blindness, "deviant" sexuality, and proneness to tuberculosis, syphilis, and criminal behavior. Obviously, not all of these conditions are inherited, and those that are may be hidden in "normal-looking" carriers.

The vocabulary and vectors of eugenics were also used to pathologize and contemporize historical constructions of radical otherness, as in the case of Burakumin and spirit-animal possessors. Their stigmatized status was eugenically respun as the consequence of defective germ plasm. Curiously, of the several articles I read by eugenicists dismantling superstitions surrounding marriage practices, not one made an argument *against* the systematic discrimination against Burakumin in all arenas of Japanese society. Moreover, eugenic discourse was instrumental in creating a caste-like category of "stigmatized other." Not only were those Japanese who exhibited a newly identified hereditary defect ostracized, but their households were also marked as eugenically unfit. Whereas historically, symbolically impure groups were allowed to marry and reproduce among themselves, persons and groups classified as eugenically unfit, such as persons with Hansen's disease (leprosy), were quarantined, exiled, and prevented from marrying (unless sterilized) and reproducing.[29] Eugenicists such as Taguchi Eitarō expressed alarm that, although "genetically defective" and "feeble-minded" individuals constituted only 2 percent of the population, they reproduced at two to three times the rate of "normal and ordinary" (*futsū*) individuals. Taguchi even invoked Gresham's Law in arguing for the passage of the 1940 National Eugenics Law (Taguchi 1940:35).[30]

The imperial state and its agencies chose early on to pursue a eugenics-dictated agenda that called for the eradication of the apparently widespread practice in Japan of consanguineous marriage. Beginning in 1883, numerous "hygiene exhibitions" (*eisei tenrankai*) were staged countrywide, sponsored first by a Buddhist temple, the Hongan-ji in the Tsukiji district of Tokyo, and subsequently by the Japanese Red Cross and, after 1938, by the Welfare Ministry. By the late 1920s, the theme and content of many of these exhibitions were based on public opinion polls; the relationship between heredity and marriage practices proved to be one of the most popular themes (Fujino 1998:140–141). The sensationalistic and sometimes grotesque exhibits – such as a realistic wax model of a man's face riddled with syphilitic lesions – along with numerous articles in the popular press, drummed home warnings about the deleterious effects of both unregulated sex and inbreeding. Schoolchildren, along with the general public, were encouraged to attend the lectures that accompanied the exhibitions. Presented by doctors and university professors, these "blood talks" greatly simplified eugenics for the lay public, who apparently attended by the thousands. The speakers harshly censured superstitions and folk customs related to marriage, such as matchmaking based on horoscopy, the sexegenary cycle, and the five elements (wood, fire, water, earth, metal). But their sometimes facile presentations of hereditary diseases helped to spawn new superstitions based on popularized science, such as the attribution to consanguinity of a host of non-hereditary conditions such as leprosy, tuberculosis, and symbolic pollution and marginality (Fujikawa 1929; Fujino 1998:141–142; Kōseisho eisei kekkon sōdansho 1941).

EUGENIC MARRIAGES

The tenacious persistence of "blood marriages" despite private and state efforts to condemn their transaction provoked intensified efforts to eliminate that tradition. One of the first lines of offense was the "eugenic-marriage counseling centers" (*yūsei kekkon sōdansho*) that were first opened in Tokyo and regional cities in 1927. The earliest centers were sponsored and staffed by Ikeda Shigenori's Japan Eugenic Exercise/Movement Association. A year earlier, Ikeda had founded the Legs and Feet Society (Ashi no kai) as a means of popularizing eugenic principles. Like the earlier German Wandervogel and Czech Sokol movements that inspired Ikeda, the Legs and Feet Society sponsored, through its Tokyo and regional branches, collective hygienic regimens, nutrition lessons, group hiking, and wholesome folk-dancing in the countryside as ways to improve the bodies and minds of young Japanese so that they could "properly oversee the nation's global expansion" (Fujino 1998:83–86; Ikeda 1927a; Okada 1933).[31]

Ikeda regarded the ostracism and sterilization of the unfit as a crude and simplistic approach to the project of race betterment. Citing the evolutionary categories proposed by Lewis Henry Morgan in *Systems of Consanguinity and Affinity* (1871), Ikeda argued that monogamous marriage practices, together with the systematization of physical education, was the golden key to improving the Japanese race and modernizing Japan (Ikeda 1925:31–38, 386). Article after article in his journal, *Yūsei undō*, emphasized that "monogamy was the foundation of eugenics" and that a eugenically sound marriage insured the development of a prosperous, physically fit, and moral society (e.g. Ikeda 1929:19; Miwata 1927). Ikeda and his colleagues followed Francis Galton in emphasizing the dialectical relationship between eugenics and marriage:

> Eugenic belief extends the function of philanthropy to future generations, it renders its actions more pervading than hitherto, by dealing with families and societies in their entirety, and it enforces the importance of the marriage covenant by directing serious attention to the probable quality of the future offspring ... [and] brings the tie of kinship into prominence ... (quoted in Pearson 1909:45)

Dismissing as bunk the folk belief that the familiarity shared by married blood relatives insured household diplomacy and stability, Ikeda lectured throughout Japan on the need to shift the basis of and for desirable familiarity between females and males from close kinship per se to the modern alternative of equal coeducation and shared hobbies. In his lectures and essays, Ikeda repeated the slogan of his association, "superior seeds, superior fields, superior cultivation" (*yoi tane, yoi hatake, yoi teire*) which, he explained, was a metaphor for "superior genes (or germ plasm), superior society, superior education" (*yoi iden, yoi shakai, yoi kyōiku*) (Ikeda 1927a). Civic and educational institutions, not consanguineous households, were promoted by him as ideal sites for revising the terms of interpersonal familiarity and ultimately insuring marital success among persons unrelated by blood. Ikeda argued that a desirable intimacy among strangers could be facilitated through educational programs and leisure activities, such as those offered by the Legs and Feet Society, that replaced pervasive folk beliefs about "shared blood" as a key criterion of and for affinity and harmony (Fujino 1998:88).

A number of the eugenic marriage-counseling centers, including Ikeda's, were opened in department stores – such as Shirokiya in the elegant Nihonbashi section of Tokyo – in order to make information about social and race hygiene, and associated behaviors and practices, easily available to consumers. Women especially were targeted, for "female citizenship" was defined not in terms of legal rights but in terms of procreation and consumption (Robertson 2001a and 2001b; Yūsei 1936c). Modern scientific – specifically hygienic and eugenic – knowledge was dispensed as a commodity. Because consumption was inextricably associated with the body and its cosmetic, nutritional, and sartorial enhancement, the link between women's consumer citizenship and eugenics was naturalized by the state and commercial sector alike.

The staff of the eugenic marriage counseling centers also provided matchmaking services, introducing potential spouses to each other based on the autobiographical health certificates they had completed and filed at the centers. According to the health profile (*shinshin kensahyō*) of a eugenic couple appearing in *Shashin shūhō* (Photograph Weekly) in April 1942, by which time the centers were well established throughout Japan, the ideal woman was 154 cm tall, weighed 51 kg, and had a chest size of 80 cm.[32] The ideal man was 165 cm tall, weighed 58 kg, and had a chest size of 84 cm. Both were free from disease and had "normal" genealogies. As the quintessential eugenic couple, they were committed to observing the "ten rules of marriage," which were: choose a lifetime partner; choose a partner healthy in body and mind; exchange health certificates; choose someone with normal "germ plasm" and wholesome heredity and ancestry; avoid marriage with blood relatives; marry as soon as possible; discard superstitions and quaint customs; obey your parents; have a simple and economical wedding; and, reproduce for the sake of the nation. The health profile was accompanied by photographs of the couple and their health certificates, scenes of a simplified, eugenic marriage ceremony, and a cartoon of the desired outcome of eugenic marriage counseling; namely, a family of eight children (Shashin shūhō 1942:8–9).

Not only were women the primary audience for eugenic marriage counseling, they were also encouraged early on to undertake meticulous hygienic and eugenic surveillance work in their official gender role of good wife, wise mother. Married women were recruited by eugenicists to undertake the ethnographic surveys of their marital and natal households necessary to establish genealogical, or blood, orthodoxies within families as a foundational step toward race betterment. In 1887 the hygiene section of the Home Ministry established the Greater Japan Women's Hygiene Association (Dai nippon fujin eiseikai) in Tokyo under whose auspices married women in particular were organized as blood-marriage whistleblowers. An Osaka branch was established three years later (Fujino 1998:388). Encouraged to regard themselves as amateur ethnographers, the women were instructed to collect as much information as possible on the life histories of living and deceased relatives. The households and relatives of prospective marriage partners and their extended families were to be similarly scrutinized in order to prevent inbreeding.

By the early 1930s, detailed "eugenic marriage" questionnaires were printed in or inserted into popular magazines for public consumption, and the accompanying instructions underscored the slippery nature of questionnaires in general. The amateur ethnographers were reminded that, because there was often a huge difference between what people say they do and what they actually do, they could not take anything at face value and were obliged to maintain a healthy skepticism (Takada 1986 [1937]:394, 401, 514). By and large, the questionnaires were designed to foster a modern, anti-traditional attitude of scientific-mindedness.[33]

Ikeda Shigenori was convinced that these marriage questionnaires would not only insure the eugenic fitness of spouses but also help avoid class differences that could disrupt and even destroy a marriage. Moreover, he explained, they would be augmented by information from a eugenic couple's children. Ultimately, the goal was to create a database of individuals and their entire households – and ultimately "all Japanese households" – which would enable eugenicists to conduct in-depth surveys of any given family's genealogy (*kakei*) (Ikeda 1928:61). Because, Ikeda declared, the government did not yet have an institutional framework for administering a comprehensive eugenic marriage counseling office – the Welfare Ministry was established in 1938 – the Japan Eugenic Exercise/Movement Association was prepared to undertake this service (Ikeda 1928:61).

Ikeda's eugenic marriage counseling activities, which included the "mixers" sponsored by the Legs and Feet Society, "blood purity"-testing clinics, the eugenic marriage questionnaires, and the public hygiene exhibitions among other things, illustrate the extent to which scientific culture was popularized and popular culture "scientized" by social engineers keen on modifying and modernizing the behavior of the Japanese people. Additionally, articles and advice columns on eugenic themes appeared frequently in national daily newspapers and popular magazines. Eugenicists contributed regularly to the media, and the eugenics journals *Jinsei–Der Mensch*,

Yūsei, *Yūsei undō*, and *Yūseigaku* all included columns and articles devoted to summarizing the coverage of eugenics themes in the daily press (e.g., Yūsei 1936a, 1936b).

EUGENIC MARRIAGES AS NATIONAL STRATEGY

In addition to concerns, real and imagined, about the negative consequences of inbreeding among blood relatives, it occurred to me that the state – that is, the repertoire of agencies and institutions that reinforces and reproduces dominant ideologies and normalizes everyday practices (cf. Corrigan and Sayer 1985) – had another investment in the eradication of consanguineous marriages. What eugenics offered was a motive and rationale for the imperial state to more closely engineer and orchestrate the sexual, gendered, marital, and reproductive practices of its subjects. Nation-states have always maintained a vested interest in the sexual and social reproduction of the population, and New Japan was no different in this regard. In fact, in some respects, the imperial state was following a powerful precedent set by the Tokugawa shogunate, which had brokered and controlled all marriages and adoptions among the vassal *daimyo* as one means of insuring their subordination.

The imperial state differed from this precedent in two major ways. First, the patrilineal orthodoxy undergirding the Tokugawa regime extended to the prevailing ethno-embryology, which is best described as male monogenesis, or the notion that the female body serves as a vessel to contain the active life-producing agent supplied by the male alone. With the popularization of eugenics came an explanation of sexual reproduction that emphasized the critical and equal contributions of females and males to heredity. The imperial state thus recognized the importance taking both maternity and paternity into account in promoting the creation of New Japanese, despite the persistence of patrilineality as the singular criterion of nationality and citizenship.

The second major difference between the Tokugawa regime and the imperial state was the global scope of the underlying ideological agenda of New Japan, which was informed by the utopian ideology of the family-state system that characterized Japanese nationalism. By promoting eugenic marriages, the imperial state and its agents aimed to redefine historical and traditional boundaries of endogamy (*dōzoku kekkon*) and exogamy (*zokugai kekkon*). The state sought to replace one type of kin group endogamy with another system that I shall call "eugenic endogamy," which basically amounted to the introduction of "universal exogamy" among theoretically pure-blooded Japanese. Eugenic endogamy, in short, was at the foundation of the family-state system, or state familism. In seeking to instill in its subjects an awareness of the New Japan and their Japanese nationality, the state aimed to dissolve the boundaries that engendered local affinities – boundaries that were intricately shaped by historical and traditional endogamous practices based on kin group, pedigree, class, region, and "superstitions and folk beliefs."

An article published in 1889, in the journal of the Great Japan Association for the Betterment of Public Customs and Morals (Dainippon fūzoku kairyōkai), is one of the earliest calls for the practice of universal exogamy in Japan. In it, the author drew attention to the allegedly higher percentage of deformities and mortality among the offspring of couples related by blood.[34] Citing and agreeing with Katō Hiroyuki's opposition to "mixed marriages," the author recommended what they termed both *shūshi kōkan*, or "exchange of seeds," and *man'en kekkon*, or "marriage between widely dispersed individuals":

> marriage partners should be selected not from the narrow parameters of blood relatives within a village or circumscribed regions, but from all over Japan. A man from Satsuma [in the south] should marry a woman from the north; a woman from Shikoku [in the south] should marry a man from Niigata [in the north]. (Sakamoto 1889:8)

Forty years later, Ikeda Shigenori reiterated the pressing need for a new geography of marriage in his arguments for the establishment of eugenic matchmaking centers, which would have the effect of "greatly expanding the circle [*han'i*] of eligible spouses" (Ikeda 1928:60).

From a perspective *inside* Japan, universal exogamy was advocated; from a vantage point *outside* of Japan, eugenic or national endogamy was promoted – that is, the principle that Japanese should marry other pure-blooded Japanese comprising the imaginary national family based on eugenic criteria that replaced traditional endogamous practices. Limited exceptions were also made for politically strategic purposes, such as arranged marriages between members of the Japanese aristocracy and their Korean, Manchurian, and Mongolian counterparts. Arguments in favor of so-called "mixed-blood marriages" and "hybrid vigor" continued as part of the public discourse of eugenics, and have remained a foil for assertions today about the cultural and racial uniqueness of *the* Japanese.

EPILOGUE

I have reviewed the Japanese ideologies of blood that came into prominence in the twinned contexts of nation-building and imperialism. The Japanese people themselves were the proving ground of colonialist schemes in Asia and the Pacific for the reason that they needed to be claimed and remolded as a national community and recruited into the imperial enterprise as a supporting cast. The popularization of eugenics, race hygiene, and eugenic endogamy as elements of quotidian life was a (bio)powerfully effective method of national mobilization. In Japan, ideologies of blood vacillated between the two incommensurable theoretical positions of pure-bloodedness and mixed-bloodedness. Scrutinized from another perspective, we can see that these positions themselves were premised on competing notions of either the vigor or the vulnerability of *the* Japanese as agents of cultural encounter and transformation.

These positions were also refracted in the condemnation of consanguineous marriages and the promotion of universal exogamy within Japan among pure-blooded Japanese. The tension between these positions persists today in many popular forums.[35] Manichean arguments are waged in the mass media about whether or not the Japanese were imperialist aggressors, anti-colonial liberators of Asia, or victims of Western imperialism – tautological and essentially moot arguments that, since 1945, have worked to erode memories and records alike of tangible historical events.

Scientists have been no less willfully amnesiac: Matsunaga Ei, a geneticist writing in 1968 on birth control policy in Japan, made the preposterous and fallacious claim that "no eugenic movement has ever existed in this country" (Matsunaga 1968:199; see also Robertson 2005). Similarly, postwar demographers and biologists writing on consanguineous marriages in Japan somehow overlook or ignore the active role of the state and eugenics associations in fostering a negative image of inbreeding and instead attribute the decline in such marriages to an agentless "loss of traditional values" (Schull and Neel 1965:19). Moreover, the journal *Minzoku eisei* (Race Hygiene), launched in 1931, continues to be published, despite the disturbingly fascist allusions of the title.

It is clear that eugenic formulations – "blood prints" – about Japanese nationality remain suspended in a *continuous present* where they shape and support political social, cultural, and esthetic perceptions of ethnic and racial identity.[36] Only by recognizing and researching historical patterns of social engineering and nation-building, and only by remaining alert to their contemporization and to the continuous presence of their past, can we begin to frame a critical discourse of first- and second-wave eugenics both relevant to Japan and possessing comparative potential.

NOTES

1   "Disciplinary bio-power," as elaborated by Michel Foucault (1978, 1979), refers to a state's or dominant institution's politicization of and control over biology and biological processes, including recreational and procreational sexual practices, as a powerful means of assimilating and claiming people as subjects. Although the applications of bio-power can be positive or negative, Foucault focuses especially on the misuses and perversions.

2   This chapter is a changed, abridged, and differently titled version of Robertson (2002), and is part of a much longer chapter in my book in progress, *Blood and Beauty: Eugenic Modernity and Empire in Japan* (Berkeley: University of California Press). That chapter includes material on imperial assimilation policy as a technology of "blood," which I do not include here.

3   Jennifer Terry makes a similar point about the relationship between science and (homo)-sexuality in the United States (Terry 1999:11–13).

4   See Robertson (2001a, 2001b) and Mizuno (2001). Beginning in the 1910s and blatantly obvious by 1940 was the prolific use of *kagaku* (science) in the titles of popular magazines, such as *Kagaku sekai* (Science World), *Kagaku gahō* (Science Illustrated), *Kodomo no kagaku* (Science for Children), *Kagaku no nippon* (Science Japan), and *Shashin kagaku* (Photography Science), to name but a few magazines.

5   As Tessa Morris-Suzuki notes, "the imagery of the family was particularly apposite because it created the ideal framework for asserting the paramount place of the emperor in Japanese society" as the head of the family-state. The familial conception of the nation-state profoundly influenced the nascent idea of the uniqueness of *the* Japanese as a distinct race (Morris-Suzuki 1998:84–85).

6   Until 1985, paternal "blood," or patrilineality, was the *de jure* condition of nationality and citizenship, which in Japan, as in Germany, is *jus sanguinus* (unlike in the United States, where it is *jus solis*). That year, maternal "blood" was legally recognized as an agent of nationality and citizenship.

7   Historically, in some regions of Japan females were required to spend the period of their menses in a menstrual hut located at some remove from the main house (Segawa 1963). Many Japanese today are reluctant to acknowledge the equation of blood and symbolic pollution as one factor influencing the widespread corporate practice of allowing (until a few years ago) monthly "menstruation leaves." Today, Shinto priests rationalize as a precautionary measure the banishment of all females, regardless of celebrity or political rank, from the sumo ring, certain sacred mountains, and road construction sites on account of their polluted and dangerous bodies that can provoke destructive forces.

8   Note that *niku*, as in *nikumanjū* (flesh bun), has been a slang word for female genitals since at least the early 17th century. There is no apparent vulgar equivalent for *tane*.

9   The history of "blood" symbolism in Japan runs contrary to Foucault's Eurocentric theory that an *"ancien régime* of blood" endured as a descent ideology forming the foundation of a modern racialist and racist system of heredity. Moreover, in modern Japan, "blood" symbolism was collapsed with, and was not replaced by, sexuality and race (Foucault 1978:147–148; see the discussion with respect to Germany in Linke 1999:36–37).

10 Although Lebra here is referring in particular to the adoption practices of the modern Japanese nobility (which she presents in terms somewhat timeless), adoption was deployed pragmatically by all classes and status groups since at least the fourth century, when Japan first appears in Chinese dynastic histories. The *ie*, or household, is a corporate group and an economic unit of production that perpetuates itself from generation to generation beyond the life span of any single member of the group. Prior to the postwar constitution, the *ie*, and not the individual, constituted the smallest legal unit of society. The *ie*, which is lead by a househead who is regarded as the caretaker of the group, may vary over time in composition from a childless couple to several generations, although only one married couple per generation may claim membership in an *ie*. As I note in the body of the article, succession tends to be on the model of male primogeniture; younger sons form branch *ie*, and daughters marry out.

11 Also, wealthy merchants, who controlled the de facto monetary economy during the Edo period, could purchase swords that only samurai could, theoretically, own and which, therefore, were akin to sartorial markers of samurai status.

12 The association of eugenics with maternal health has overshadowed its invocation as scientific grounds for the ostracism, exile, and even sterilization of persons suffering from Hansen's disease and other conditions erroneously assumed to be hereditary, who were thus treated as pariahs.

13 Early in the Edo period, the Tokugawa shogunate codified a status hierarchy that classified people into four endogamous groups – samurai (*shi*), farmers (*nō*), artisans (*kō*), and merchants (*shō*). Above these groups were the members of the imperial household and the Buddhist and Shinto clergy, and below the four groups were people grouped into two categories of sub-humanity, the "non-people" (*hinin*) and, at rock bottom, the "filthy" (non-)people (*eta*). The *hinin* constituted a heterogeneous group comprised of beggars, prostitutes, itinerant entertainers, fortunetellers, fugitives, and criminals. Among their ranks were also individuals who had fallen out of the "real people" categories for one reason or another. *Eta* is a word of uncertain origin. In the Edo period, it referred to families of outcastes who performed tasks considered to be ritually or symbolically polluting, including the slaughtering of animals and disposal of the dead. The *eta* were "quarantined" in specific, undesirable locations, such as dry river beds, and forced to wear special clothing to mark their outcaste status; in some localities were mandated to wear a patch of leather on their sleeves, whereas in others, they were tattooed, as were some *hinin*. In 1871, as part of its modernization programs, the new Meiji imperial

government, whose supporters overthrew the shogunate, passed an edict officially abolishing all status discrimination. The four-part status hierarchy was leveled and reconstituted under the rubric "commoners" (*heimin*) – although aristocrats remained such – and the non-people and *eta*, were recategorized as "new commoners" (*shinheimin*), whose creation marks the beginning of the Burakumin, or literally "village people," a Meiji period name that emphasized their endogamous constitution. Moreover, the prefix "new," in "new commoner," did not eradicate but rather contemporized the centuries long practice of discriminating against persons historically categorized as subhuman.

14 The blurred semantics of "eugenics" and "race hygiene" also typified debates about "applied biology" in Germany before and during the Third Reich; see Proctor (1988).

15 *Jinshu* is the Chinese-style (*onyomi*) pronunciation of this compound ideograph; the Japanese-style (*kunyomi*) pronunciation is *hitodane*, or "human seed." My perusal of the early eugenics literature suggests that *hitodane* was the pronunciation used (indicated by the frequent inclusion of syllables [*furigana*] printed alongside the ideographs in texts) for the English term "germ plasm." Also, whereas *jinshu* is used for "race" in the biological (phenotypic) sense, *minzoku* denotes social race, or ethnicity.

16 Embree (1939:81–88, 88–89) suggests that consanguineous marriages tended to involve patrilineal parallel-cousins while adoptions tended to involve brother's sons or the sons born by women before their marriage. In his words: "The family system is patrilineal in pattern but, through the customs of adoption, often matrilineal in practice" (ibid.:85).

17 For definitive research on the history of sexology in Japan, see Frühstück (2000 and 2003).

18 Among the most tenacious superstitions is that of the *hinoeuma*, or zodiacal sign of the fiery horse that cycles every 60 years. Females born in the year of the fiery horse are, according to this "superstition," headstrong and predestined to harm males, and thus are eschewed as marriage partners.

19 Having published already on the vicissitudes of the "pure-blood" and "mixed-blood" positions, I will only briefly summarize them here in order to reduce redundancy and to allow more room to explore related phenomena; see Robertson (2001a).

20 "Marriage" was used as a euphemism for "procreative sexual intercourse."

21 Michael Weiner (1997:7) states incorrectly that Takahashi's ideas were shared by Katō.

22 Incidentally, von Baelz himself did not support mixed-blood marriages, and proposed instead a "negative" eugenics approach to race betterment by segregating the fit from the unfit (Fujino 1998:388). He did not follow his own advice, however, and married a Japanese woman, Hana, with whom he had two children. Similar arguments about the pros and cons of the pure-blood and mixed-blood positions were waged in China, where one advocate of mixed marriages attempted to strengthen his case by claiming that the Japanese government had sanctioned the practice of intermarriage between "whites" and "yellow," which of course was not accurate (Dikötter 1992:88); see also Dikötter (1998) for additional general information about the discourse of race and eugenics in China. Although aware of their Chinese counterparts, a number of whom visited and studied in Japan, Japanese eugenicists did not cite their work, favoring in contrast the publications of Europeans and North and South Americans. Doubtless Japanese imperial aggression in China since the Sino-Japanese wars (1894–95) also had a negative effect on scholarly exchanges between Japanese and Chinese nationalists and eugenicists. See also Stefan Tanaka (1993) for an informative analysis of the status of China in Japanese scholarship during the late 19th and early 20th centuries. Ann Stoler's perceptive article on the cultural politics of "mixed bloods" in French Indochina and Netherlands East Indies offers useful comparative material. However, she neither mentions nor addresses the influence of the international discourse of eugenics and race hygiene on French and Dutch colonial administrators, and glosses specific and distinctive French and Dutch

colonial strategies as "European." Perhaps their eschewal of miscegenation justifies their melding here, but the notion of an internally coherent "Europe" is problematic. Where, for example, do Spain and Portugal fit within the rubric "Europe," two arguably "European" colonial powers that *did* pursue miscegenation as a means of assimilation? The argument against miscegenation made by the Dutch legalist J. A. Nederburgh in 1898 parallels Katō's argument, made 12 years earlier, for preserving the purity of Japanese blood. It would have been interesting to know from what body of literature and contemporary debate Nederburgh was drawing (Stoler 1995:138). As an aside, Japanese writers apparently enjoyed musing about the conceptual problems associated with and the fate of "Dutch mixed-bloods" (e.g., Kaizō 1942; Kitahara 1943; Ōya 1943).

23 One of the main vehicles for popularizing eugenics among the fin-de-siècle Japanese public was the journal *Jinsei* (Human Life), founded in 1905 by Fujikawa Yū, an internist and medical historian. It was discontinued in 1919. Fujikawa was among the dozens of Japanese medical students who studied in Germany at the turn of the century and who were keen on applying European ideas about eugenics and race hygiene to the general project of "improving the Japanese race." *Jinsei*, subtitled *Der Mensch* (The Human), was modeled after German eugenicist Alfred Ploetz's *Archiv für Rassen- und Gesellschafts-Biologie* (Journal for Racial and Social Biology), founded a year earlier. The contents were divided into 16 categories which reflected the prevailing synthesis of Darwinian and Lamarckian theories and assumptions: biology, social anthropology, historical anthropology, physical anthropology, legal anthropology, comparative psychology, psychology, national psychology, cultural history of medicine, social hygiene, race hygiene, law, sociology, education and pedagogy, religion, and statistics.

24 Years earlier, some colonial administrators had considered a similar policy with respect to Korea and Koreans under the tautological rubric *dōbun dōshu no minzoku*, or "people of the same culture and race" – "tautological" because the alleged sameness was proposed by Japanese colonial ideologues who supported assimilation, or *dōka*, literally "same-ization," that is, Japanization. Support for assimilation and pacification through intermarriage waned as Korean hostility toward the occupiers grew more intense, especially after the anti-Japanese uprising of 1919. The very few "mixed marriages" that were officially condoned were those strategically arranged between Japanese and Korean royalty (Duus 1995:413–423). Ijichi's views paralleled the dominant position of the state's assimilation policy toward the aboriginal Ainu of Hokkaido, who, since the Meiji Restoration of 1868, had been categorized as "proto-Japanese." Assimilation, it was believed, would accelerate their evolution as "civilized people" (e.g., Takakura 1942).

25 Although published in 1945, Tōgō here reiterates a eugenic argument first made in his books on colonial administration published two decades earlier (e.g., Tōgō 1922, 1925).

26 Similar events, such as "better baby contests" were staged in early 20th-century United States at state fairs and other public forums.

27 Females averaged 11.9 years of age, 156 cm in height, and 45 kg in weight. The respective statistics for males were 11.10 years, 158 cm, and 46.5 kg (Tōkyo asahi shinbun 1930:8–9).

28 Another term used for consanguineous marriage was *kinshin kekkon*, or "marriage between close relatives." Beardsley et al. (1959:323) and Embree (1939:84–85, 88–89) suggest that patrilineal parallel cousin marriages were typical, while Joy Hendry (1981:124–125) indicates that there was no preference for either parallel or cross cousins, noting that first-cousin marriages have been discouraged since the end of World War II. All suggest that consanguineous marriages likely forged easier and closer household ties.

29 The Leprosy Prevention Law was formulated and informally activated in 1907, formally adopted in 1953, and abolished in 1996. In the spring of 2001, the Kumamoto District Court ruled that the government should pay ¥1.82 billion in reparations to the plaintiffs.

For various reasons, the government of Prime Minister Koizumi decided not to appeal the ruling (Kakuchi 1998; Oba 1996; Schriner 2001), although it remains to be seen how the former exiles will be "repatriated."

30 Gresham's Law refers to an observation in economics that "when two coins are equal in debt-paying value but unequal in intrinsic value, the one having the lesser intrinsic value tends to remain in circulation and the other to be hoarded or exported as bullion" (Gresham's Law 1985:536). A brief word about blood type is useful here in connection with overlapping notions of blood and purity. Although today the pseudo-scientific fiction that the Japanese constitute a "blood type A race" is widely invoked in the mass media, knowledge about specific blood types was not deployed as a eugenic tool in the discourse of race betterment. There were competing attempts among Japanese scientists to classify the so-called races of the world on the basis of the pattern of distribution of the A, O, B, and AB blood types. However, unlike in Nazi Germany, a specific race was not singled out for isolation and extermination in a diabolical scheme to purify "Japanese blood." By the same token, comparatively few involuntary sterilizations were performed in Japan following the passage of the National Eugenics Law in 1940. Between 1941 and 1945, 15,219 persons (6,399 females and 8,820 males) were targeted for involuntary sterilization, of which 435 persons (243 females and 192 males), or about 29 percent, were actually sterilized, over half of whom were women (Suzuki 1983:166; Tanaka 1994:164). From 1955 through 1967 in Japan, about 9,500 persons, two-thirds of whom were female, were involuntarily sterilized; about 432,000 persons, 97 percent of whom were female, underwent voluntary sterilization during this time (Health and Welfare Statistics Association 1987:104). From 1907 through 1957, over 60,000 persons (more than half of them females) were sterilized in the United States. One ultranationalist critic of sterilization argued that the "divine origins" and purity of the "Yamato race" raised serious philosophical doubts about the validity of that procedure: "one must not," he asserted, "equate a divine people with livestock" (Makino 1938:18–21; see also Suzuki 1983:163; Takagi 1993:46). Moreover, the militarily strategic need to raise the population by one-third in twenty years, from 73 to 100 million persons, together with an emphasis on bigger, taller bodies over enhanced intellectual ability, effectively diminished support for sterilization as a eugenic strategy (Suzuki 1983:162–163; Takagi 1993:46). Other critics of sterilization, such as sexologist Yasuda Tokutarō, stressed instead the importance of the physical and social environment on human development and also the complexity of human motives to reproduce or not (Suzuki 1983:162–3).

31 Unlike the Wandervogel and Sokol movements that inspired it, the Legs and Feet Society was a coed organization from the start. The Wandervogel was later absorbed into the Hitlerjugend. Born in January 1892 in Nikaho town (Yuri District, Akita Prefecture), Ikeda Shigenori attended college in Tokyo. Following his graduation from Tokyo Foreign Language University (Tokyo Gaigodai), he was employed by Kōdansha, a prominent publishing house, to edit the magazine *Taikan* (Outlook). He later joined the *Hōchi shinbun*, a major daily newspaper, and served as a special correspondent to Germany from 1920 to 1924, where he earned doctorates in eugenics and women's history. He was transferred to Moscow in 1925 before returning to Japan and founding the Eugenic Exercise/Movement Association and a eugenics journal, both of which were aimed to foster among the general public an interest in incorporating hygienic and eugenic practices into everyday life practices. The journal ceased publication in January 1930. Ikeda rekindled his journalism career three years later by assuming the editorship of the *Keijō nippō* (Seoul Daily News) based in Seoul, Korea. He returned to the *Hōchi shinbun* as an editor in 1939, and from 1941 through the end of the war worked for Naval Intelligence (Kaigun hōdōbu). After the war he became a prominent "social commentator" (*hyōronka*), known for his entertaining essays on a wide array of topics.

32   This ideal female body was somewhere between the measurements of the 1931 Miss Nippon and her "average" counterpart. Miss Nippon was nearly 159 cm in height compared to the average female's 148.5 cm, her chest measured 79 cm compared to the average female's 74 cm, and she weighed 52.5 kg, compared to the average female's 46.5 kg (Robertson 2001a:23–24).

33   For a detailed description of these questionnaires, see Robertson (2002).

34   The author, Sakamoto Shunpū, was the Akita Prefecture correspondent for the Great Japan Association for the Betterment of Public Customs and Morals.

35   Space precludes me from discussing these here; they are included in my book in progress (see note 2 above).

36   Similarly, Uli Linke argues that in contemporary Germany, "a retrograde archaism of national state culture is continuously repositioned in the present" (Linke 1999:239).

REFERENCES

Beardsley, Richard, John Hall, and Robert Ward. 1959. Village Japan. Chicago: University of Chicago Press.

Civisca, Luigi. 1957. The Validity of Naien. Tokyo: Sophia University Press.

Cooper, Michael. 1965. They Came to Japan: An Anthology of European Reports on Japan, 1543–1640. Berkeley: University of California Press.

Corrigan, Philip, and Derek Sayer. 1985. The Great Arch: English State Formation as Cultural Revolution. London: Basil Blackwell.

Dikötter, Frank. 1992. The Discourse of Race in Modern China. London: C. Hurst/Stanford University Press.

—— 1998. Imperfect Conceptions: Medical Knowledge, Birth Defects, and Eugenics in China. New York: Columbia University Press.

Dower, John. 1986. War Without Mercy: Race and Power in the Pacific War. New York: Pantheon.

Duus, Peter. 1995. The Abacus and the Sword: The Japanese Penetration of Korea, 1895–1910. Berkeley: University of California Press.

East, Edward, and Donald Jones. 1919. Inbreeding and Outbreeding; Their Genetic and Sociological Significance. Philadelphia and London: J. B. Lippincott.

Elderton, Ethel. 1911. On the Marriage of First Cousins. London: Cambridge University Press.

Embree, John. 1939. Suye-mura: A Japanese Village. Chicago: University of Chicago Press.

Foucault, Michel. 1978. The History of Sexuality, vol. 1: An Introduction. Robert Hurley, trans. New York: Vintage Books.

—— 1979. Discipline and Punish: The Birth of the Prison. Alan Sheridan, trans. New York: Vintage Book.

Frühstück, Sabine. 2000. Managing the Truth of Sex in Imperial Japan. Journal of Asian Studies 59(2):332–358.

—— 2003. Colonizing Sex: Sexology and Social Control in Modern Japan. Berkeley: University of California Press.

Fujikawa, Yū. 1929 Meishin no hanashi (Discussion of Superstitions). In Katei kagaku taikei (Outline of Household Science), vol. 13. pp. 289–325. Tokyo: Katei Kagaku Taikei Hankōkai.

Fujino, Yutaka. 1998. Nihon fuashizumu to yūsei shisō (Japanese Fascism and Eugenic Thought). Kyoto: Kamogawa Shuppan.

Fujo shinbun. 1935. Kokumin to hansū jogai (Half the Citizens are Excluded). Fujo shinbun, January 27.

Furuya, Yoshio. 1941. Kokudo–jinkō–ketsueki (Homeland–Population–Blood). Tokyo: Asahi Shinbunsha.

Gresham's Law. 1985. *In* Webster's Ninth Collegiate Dictionary. p. 536. Springfield, MA: Merriam Webster.

Hayashida, Cullen. 1976. Identity, Race and Blood Ideology of Japan. Ph.D. dissertation. University of Washington.

Health and Welfare Statistics Association. 1987. Tokyo: Health and Welfare Statistics Association.

Hendry, Joy. 1981. Marriage in Changing Japan: Community and Society. London: Croom Helm.

Honjō, Eijirō. 1936. Tokugawa jidai no jinkō mondai (The Population Problem during the Tokugawa Period). Yūseigaku 147(May):21–26.

Ijichi, Susumu. 1939. Kōateki konketsuron (Treatise on Asian Mix-Bloodedness). Kaizō 3:82–88.

Ikeda, Shigenori. 1925. Bunmei no hōkai (The Collapse of Civilization). Tokyo: Hōbunkan.

—— 1927a. Yūsei nippon no teisho (Discourse on Eugenic Japan). Yūsei undō 2(1):2–3.

—— 1927b. Yūsei undō to chihō jichitai (Eugenic Exercise/Movement and Local Governments). Yūsei Undō 2(1):4–7.

—— 1928. Kekkonsha no mimoto chōsahyō (Background Survey of Marriage Candidates). Yūsei undō 3(9):58–61.

—— 1929. Yūseigakuteki shakai kairyō undō ni tsuite (On the Eugenic Social Reform Movement). Yūsei undō 4(10):19.

—— 1956. Ikite yakutatsu hanashi no mimibukuro (An Earful of Stories Useful for Living). Tokyo: Hokushindō.

—— 1957. Ikite yakutatsu hanashi no mimibukuro – Zoku (An Earful of Stories Useful for Living – Continuation). Tokyo: Hokushindō.

Imaizumi, Yoko. 1988. Parental Consanguinity in Two Generations in Japan. Journal of Biosocial Science 20:235–243.

Irizawa, Tatsuyoshi. 1939 [1913]. Ikaga ni shite nipponjin no taikaku o kaizen subeki ka (What Can Be Done in Order to Improve the Physiques of the Japanese People). Tokyo: Nisshin Shoin.

Ishizuka, Takatoshi. 1983 [1972]. Nihon no tsukimono (Possession in Japan). Tokyo: Miraisha.

Jinkō mondai kenkyūkai. 1933–43. Jinkō mondai (Population Problems). Tokyo: Jinkō Mondai Kenkyūkai.

Kaizō. 1942. Daitōaken no bunkateki shomondai (Various Cultural Problems Facing the Great East Asian Sphere). Kaizō 4:70–94.

Kakuchi, Suvendrini. 1998. Rights-Japan: Leprosy Patients Demand End to Isolation. www.oneworld.org/ips2/sept98/05_15_010.html.

Katō, Hiroyuki. 1990 [1886]. Nippon jinshu kairyō no ben (Discussion of the Betterment of the Japanese Race). *In* Katō hiroyuki bunsho (Collected Writings of Katō Hiroyuki), vol. 3. Ueda Katsumi et al., eds. pp. 33–47. Tokyo: Dōhōsha Shuppan.

Kitahara, Takeo. 1943. Uki kuru (Advent of the Rainy Season). Tokyo: Buntaisha.

Kōseisho eisei kekkon sōdansho. 1941. Kekkon to meishin (Marriage and Superstition). Kōshū eisei 59(9):14–26.

Lebra, Takie Sugiyama. 1993. Above the Clouds: Status Culture of the Japanese Nobility. Berkeley: University of California Press.

Linke, Uli. 1999. Blood and Nation: The European Aesthetics of Race. Philadelphia: University of Pennsylvania Press.

Makino, Chiyozō. 1938. Danshuhō hantairon (An Argument against a Sterilization Law). Yūseigaku 15(4):18–21.

Matsunaga, Ei. 1968. Birth Control Policy in Japan: A Review from Eugenic Standpoint [*sic*]. Japanese Journal of Human Genetics 13(3):189–200.

McClintock, Anne. 1994. Closing Remarks. Yale Journal of Criticism 7(1):239–243.

Minzuno, Hiromi, 2001. Science, Ideology, Empire: A History of the "Scientific" in Prewar and Wartime Japan. Ph.D. dissertation, University of California at Los Angeles.

Miwata, Motomichi. 1927. Atarashii kekkon kikan (A New Marriage System). Yūsei undō 2(6):29–32.

Mizushima, Naoso, and Mitake, Katuso. 1942. Naisen konketsu mondai (The Problem of Mixed-Bloods in Korea). *In* Jinkō seisaku to kokudo keikaku (Population Policy and a Strategic Plan for the Homeland). Nakayama Yoshio, ed. pp. 20–21.Tokyo: Jinkō Mondai Kenkyūkai.

Morris-Suzuki, Tessa. 1998. Reinventing Japan: Time, Space, Nation. Armonk, NY: M. E. Sharpe.

Nagai, Hisomu. 1936. Aisatsu (Greetings). Yūsei 1(10):unpaginated.

Nishida, Tomomi. 1995. "Chi" no shisō – Edo jidai no shiseikan (Philosophy of "Blood": Conceptions of Life and Death in the Edo Period). Tokyo: Kenseisha.

Norgren, Tiana. 2001. Abortion Before Birth Control: The Politics of Reproduction in Postwar Japan. Princeton: Princeton University Press.

Oba, Satsuki. 1996. Abandoned by Heaven. Time (international edn) February 5.

Oka'asa, Jirō. 1915. Jinshukairyō wa jikkō ga dekiru ka (Is It Possible to Implement Race Betterment?). Eisei sekai 2(3):2–4.

Okada, Sadako. 1933. Atarashii oyakusho (A New Government Office). Kaizō 6:86–91.

Ōsaka asahi shinbun. 1931. Risō no yūryōji (Ideal Superior Children). Ōsaka asahi shinbun, June 7:11.

—— 1932. Nippon'ichi yūryōji (The Most Superior Children in Japan). Ōsaka asahi shinbun, May 31.

Otsubo, Sumiko. 1999. Feminist Maternal Eugenics in Wartime Japan. US–Japan Women's Journal (English Supplement) 17:39–76.

Ōya, Sōichi. 1943. Jawa no senden katsudō (Javanese Youth Activities). Tokyo shinbun November:13–15.

Pearson, Karl. 1909. The Scope and Importance to the State of the Science of National Eugenics. 2nd edn. London: Dulau.

Pernick, Martin. 1997. Eugenics and Public Health in American History. American Journal of Public Health 87(1):1767–1772.

Proctor, Robert. 1988. Race Hygiene: Medicine Under the Nazis. Cambridge, MA: Harvard University Press.

Robertson, Jennifer. 2001a. Japan's First Cyborg? Miss Nippon, Eugenics, and Wartime Technologies of Beauty, Body, and Blood. Body and Society 7(1):1–34.

—— 2001b. Les "Bataillons fertiles": Sexe et la citoyenneté dans le Japon Impérial (Fertile-Womb Battalions: Sex and Citizenship in Imperial Japan). *In* New Critical Approaches to Twentieth-Century Japanese Thought. Livia Monnet, ed. pp. 275–301. Montreal: University of Montreal Press.

—— 2002. Blood Talks: Eugenic Modernity and the Creation of New Japanese. History and Anthropology 13(3):191–216.

—— 2005. Dehistoricizing History: The Ethical Dilemma of "East Asian Bioethics." Critical Asian Studies 37(2).

Sakamoto, Shunpū. 1889. Kon'in no chūi: ketsuzoku haigu (Marriage Advice: Blood Marriages). Dai nippon fūzoku kairyōkai kaishi 14:7–8.

Satō, Tadayoshi. 1943. Daitōa kyōikuron (Educational Treatise on Greater East Asia). Tokyo: Kyōiku Kagakusha.

Schriner, Kay. 2001. Leprosy Court Case Shakes Japan. www.disabilityworld.org/05–06_01/leprosy.html, September 18.

Schull, W. J., and J. V. Neel. 1965. The Effects of Inbreeding on Japanese Children. New York: Harper & Row.

Segawa, Kiyoko. 1963. Menstrual Taboos Imposed Upon Women. *In* Studies in Japanese Folklore, Richard Dorson, ed. pp. 239–250. Bloomington, IN: Indiana University Press.

Shashin shūhō. 1942. Kore kara no kekkon wa kono yōni (How Marriages Should Be Transacted Henceforth). Shashin shūhō 218(April 29):18–19.

Shinozaki, Nobuo. 1949. Ketsuzoku kekkon buraku no jinruigakuteki chōsa gaihō (Summary of an Anthropological Survey of Blood-Marriage Hamlets). Jinruigaku zasshi 60(3):97–100.

Stocking, George. 1968. Race, Culture, and Evolution: Essays in the History of Anthropology. New York: Free Press.

Stoler, Ann. 1995. "Mixed-Bloods" and the Cultural Politics of European Identity in Colonial Southeast Asia. *In* The Decolonization of Imagination: Culture, Knowledge and Power. Jan Nederveen Pieterse and Bhikhu Parekh, eds. pp. 128–148. London and New Jersey: Zed Press.

Suzuki, Zenji. 1983 Nihon no yūseigaku – sono shisō to undō no kiseki (Japanese Eugenics: The Legacy of Eugenic Thought and the Eugenics Movement). Tokyo: Sankyo Shuppan.

Taguchi, Eitarō. 1940. Kokumin yūseihō to jinkō seisaku (The National Eugenics Law and Population Policy) 58(5):33–35.

Takada, Tomekao. 1986 [1937]. Dare ni mo dekiru kekkon chōsa no himitsu (Secret Tips to Enable Everyone to Conduct a Marriage Survey). *In* Kinsei shomin seikatsushi: ren'ai, kekkon, katei (Life History of Premodern Commoners: Love, Marriage, Family), vol. 9. pp. 393–446. Tokyo: Zōichi Shobō.

Takagi, Masashi. 1993. Senzen Nihon ni okeru yūsei shisō no tenkai to nōryokukan, kyōikukan (Views on IQ and Education in the Development of Eugenic Thought in Prewar Japan). Nagoya daigaku kyōikugakubu kiyō 40(1):41–52.

Takakura, Shin'ichirō. 1942. Ainu seisakushi (History of Ainu Policy). Tokyo: Hyōronsha.

Tanaka, Satoshi. 1994. Eisei tenrankai no yokubō (The Ambition of Hygiene Exhibitions). Tokyo: Seikyūsha.

Tanaka, Stefan. 1993. Japan's Orient: Rendering Pasts into History. Berkeley: University of California Press.

Terry, Jennifer. 1999. An American Obsession: Science, Medicine, and Homosexuality in Modern Society. Chicago: Chicago University Press.

Tōgō, Minoru. 1922. Sekai kaizō to minzoku shinri (Global Reconstruction and Ethno-National Psychology). Taipei: Taihoku dōjin.

——1925. Shokumin seisaku to minzoku shinri (Colonial Strategy and Ethno-National Psychology). Tokyo: Iwanami Shoten.

——1936. Jinkō mondai to kaigai hatten (The Population Problem and Overseas Development). Tokyo: Nippon Seinenkan.

——1945. Dai tōa kensetsu to zakkon mondai (The Construction of Greater East Asia and the Problem of Miscegenation). Shin jawa 2(1):30–34.

Tōkyo asahi shinbun. 1930. Kenkō yūryōji (Healthy, Superior Children). Tōkyo asahi shinbun, May 6:7–9.

Van Bremen, Jan. 1998. Death Rites in Japan in the Twentieth Century. *In* Interpreting Japanese Society. Anthropological Approaches. 2nd edn. Joy Hendry, ed. pp. 131–144. London: Routledge.

Weiner, Michael. 1997. "Self" and "Other" in Prewar Japan. *In* Japan's Minorities: The Illusion of Homogeneity. Michael Weiner, ed. pp. 1–16. London: Routledge.

Wikler, Daniel. 1999. Can We Learn from Eugenics? Journal of Medical Ethics 25:183–194.

Yasui, Hiroshi. 1940. Rippa na kodomo wa kenzen na kekkon kara (Splendid Children Result from Healthy Marriages). Shashin shūhō 144(November 27):14–15.

Yoshida, Teigo. 1977 [1972]. Nihon no tsukimono (Possession in Japan). Tokyo: Chūō Kōronsha.

Yoshino, Kosaku. 1997. Bunka nashonarizumu no shakaigaku: gendai Nihon no aidentitei no yukue (The Sociology of Cultural Nationalism: the Direction of Modern Japanese Identity). Nagoya: Nagoya Daigaku Shuppankai.

Yūsei. 1936a. Shinbun ni arawareta yūsei mondai (Eugenics in the Daily Newspapers). Yūsei 1(5):18–22.

——1936b. Shinbun ni arawareta yūsei mondai (Eugenics in the Daily Newspapers). Yūsei 1(9):15–16.

——1936c. Yūsei kekkon sōdansho annai (Guided Tour of the Eugenic Marriage Counseling Office). Yūsei 1(1):20.

——1937. Nippon'ichi no yūryōji no hyōshō (Statistical Profile of Japan's Most Superior Children). Yūsei 2(5):8–9.

Yūsei undō. 1928. Shimin no junketsu dē ni tassū fujin no sanka (Women Turn out in Large Numbers for "Citizens' Blood Purity Day"). Yūsei undō 3(12):21.

22 The *Ie* (Family) in Global Perspective

Emiko Ochiai

THE *IE* AND THE STEM FAMILY: INVISIBLE COUNTERPARTS

"Live and die one after another, cultivating the rice field in turn."[1] No other words have described the essence of the *ie* or the traditional Japanese family so nicely as this well-known *haiku* (the shortest form of poetry) written by Kijo Murakami (1865–1938). *The Dictionary of Comparative Family History* defines the *ie* as "the physical house itself; a Japanese traditional familial group (sometimes including non-kin members); and the abstract concept of the familial group represented in family names." The dictionary continues that "[t]he *ie* maintains its collective identity through the transmission of headship. This custom generates the abstract concept of cross-generational *ie* and is reinforced by the concept at the same time. The concept of *ie* is announced in the family name, ancestor worship, family rank, family precepts and so forth" (Hikaku Kazoku-shi Gakkai 1996). The house and the farmland are the most important family property to be inherited across generations, as the *haiku* describes.

Ie is often translated as "stem family." A leading family sociologist, Kiyomi Morioka, referring to Conrad M. Arensberg, includes the Japanese family in the category of the stem family system (*chokkei kazoku sei*) in his popular textbook of family sociology (Morioka and Mochizuki 1983:14). Arensberg lists the Japanese family under the rubric "stem family" along with French, German, Irish, northern Italian, northern Spanish and Philippine stem families (Arensberg 1960). However, Morioka specifies that the *ie* is a regional pattern of the so-called stem family.

However, there is another line of discussion in Japan concerning the *ie*.[2] The *ie* has been regarded as the core of Japanese cultural identity since the Meiji period. Some background information is necessary at this juncture. The Meiji government commissioned a French jurist, Gustave Émile Boissonade de Fontarabie, to draft the first Japanese civil code based on the Napoleonic Civil Code. Consequently, many Japanese scholars and journalists criticized it as being based on a "Western" (i.e., French) idea of family. The objectors finally succeeded in replacing it with a totally new version centered upon the *ie* system. Since then, the *ie* has been regarded as the symbol of Japanese cultural identity despite continual changes in its perceived value in various social and political contexts. One result of the tradition is a belief that the *ie* is so uniquely Japanese that intercultural comparison is impossible, or, if possible at all, only to reveal how the Japanese *ie* is different from other families. Most attempts at intercultural comparison have been made to contrast the *ie* with the nuclear family in the United States and western Europe. It is striking how little attention Japanese family sociologists and historians have paid to stem families in Europe, in spite of their unquestionable importance in European family history. Thus, even the researchers who agree to call the *ie* a stem family usually take it for granted that the most typical stem family is the Japanese *ie* and that the others are a negligible minority (Ochiai 2000).

The debates around the stem family in Europe and America have also been complicated by problematical questions. The term "stem family" (*famille souche*) was originally used in an academic context by a French social engineer, Frederic Le Play, who appropriated the German word *Stammfamilie*. The concept of the stem family was introduced to theorize about family change in western Europe, and has been referred to as a symbol of criticism of modernization in the central countries of modern Europe, and of national and ethnic identity in relatively marginal areas (Douglas 1993). The ideological value of the *ie* in Japan is surprisingly like the latter case. However, similarities in ideology did not and do not serve as a common basis for comparing actual family structures. On the contrary, the common belief that the stem family is the core of traditional culture has largely prevented researchers from comparing stem families in different areas critically and seriously. This is partly why the *ie* and other Asian stem families have been invisible in European scholarship, just as the European stem families have not been taken into account by Asian scholars (Ochiai 2000).

The purpose of this chapter is to examine the features of the Japanese *ie* in comparison with those of European and other Asian stem families, and thus to place the *ie* in the context of global family history. There have been only a few scholarly attempts to do this. The first half of the chapter is devoted to a review of how the *ie* has been discussed in a global context; the second half shows empirical results from two areas in Edo period (1603–1868) Japan.[3] Regional diversity within Japan will be the main focus of the latter part.

The *Ie* in a Global Context

The *ie* as a prototype of Japanese organization: Chie Nakane

There have been several efforts to place the *ie* in the context of global family history. The first and probably still the most comprehensive effort to introduce the *ie* to the international academic community is Chie Nakane's *Kinship and Economic Organization in Rural Japan* (Nakane 1967a). She introduces the *ie* as follows: "[the] primary unit of social organization in Japan is the household. In an agrarian community a household has particularly important functions as a distinct body for economic management." Nakane goes on to emphasize that a "household is normally formed by, or around, the nucleus of an elementary family, and may include relatives and non-relatives other than these immediate family members" (Nakane 1967a:1), and points out definitional differences that may cause misunderstandings among non-Japanese scholars:

> The term *ie* is often used in sociological literature as an equivalent of family, but the English term *household* is closer to the conception since it includes all co-residents and is not necessarily restricted only to the members of a family. Further, the *ie* is not simply a contemporary household as its English counterpart suggests, but is conceptualized in the time continuum from past to future, including not only the actual residential members but also dead members, with some projection also towards those yet unborn. (Nakane 1967a:1–2)

The organizational principle of the *ie* is, according to Nakane, expressed in succession rules. "There are two important rules of succession to the headship common throughout Japan. One is that the head should be succeeded by the 'son', not by any other kind of kinsman. Another is that it should be by one son only; never by two or more sons jointly" (Nakane 1967a:4–5). The first rule means that the heir must be a real son or an adopted son of the head. These rules provide the theoretical and empirical bases for Nakane to classify Japanese society as a "vertical society" in her bestselling book *Tate shakai no ningen kankei* (Human Relations in a Vertical Society), now a classic in Japanese studies (Nakane 1967b, 1972).[4]

Nakane is reluctant to call the *ie* a "stem family" even though the three types of household she proposes in her book, *Kazoku no kozo* (Family Structure) are quite similar to nuclear, joint, and stem – she includes the *ie* in the third type (Nakane 1970:35–38). And when she does refer to the Japanese family as a "stem family," she nevertheless insists that Japan is different from other societies that have stem families. According to her, such societies usually develop stem families only under certain economic conditions during a certain period of history. For example, the need to avoid fragmentation of land to cope with the economic crisis of farming families played a decisive role in forming stem families both in 20th-century Ireland and in Germany since the 16th century (Nakane 1970:12). "This practice has never been crystallized as a social institution as the *ie* system in Japan" (Nakane 1970:113). Nakane then proceeds to examine the Tokugawa feudal system under which the *ie* was made the unit of tax payment, before reviewing the more basic anthropological features of Japanese society in making her case for "the conditions special to Japan, different from Ireland or Germany" (Nakane 1970:113). In short, although Nakane placed the Japanese *ie* in a global context, her motive was to emphasize the uniqueness of the Japanese stem family.

The *ie* as an exceptional stem family: Peter Laslett

The *ie* once played an important role in scholarly explorations of family history. Three chapters in *Household and Family in Past Time* (Laslett and Wall 1972), for example, are devoted to the analyses of Japanese households.[5] Peter Laslett's introduction to the volume explicitly addresses both the stem family and the *ie* many times, and the stem family is the main target of his historical sociology. Laslett summarizes Le Play's definition of the stem family as follows:

> Le Play himself certainly thought of *la famille souche* both as a domestic group and as a patriline. . . . As a domestic group it seems definitely to have consisted in an extended family of two married couples with their children, the head of the second being the child of the first, an arrangement to which we shall give the title multiple family household, disposed downwards. The resident heir chosen by the household head was usually a son, perhaps as often the youngest as the oldest, though for want of sons the carefully chosen husband of a daughter, a nephew or even a more distant male relative might be introduced: a successor's widow could also head a household. . . . As a patriline, or as patriline permitting female succession occasionally, Le Play's stem family closely resembles the Japanese *Ie.* . . . A succession of direct descendants is identified with a house, a piece of land, or even a particular handicraft, and each in turn holds it inalienably and in trust for the family name and for all members of the line. . . . The stem family patriline, then, was the stem family household perpetuated, which is presumably why Le Play does not seem to have wished to distinguish the two. (Laslett 1972:18–20)

Laslett states that Le Play's stem family closely resembles the Japanese *ie*. Although Laslett only refers to the stem family as "a patriline" in that context, Japanese researchers would also agree to calling the *ie* stem family a domestic group in both Le Play and Laslett's definition of the term. Laslett also points out that the Japanese sample shows distinctive characteristics among six populations, which data he analyzes.[6] Regarding household size, the Japanese households are almost as small as the English ones. However, concerning household structure, "it is obvious that the Serbian and Japanese communities were quite different in these respects from the English, the American colonial and the French communities" (Laslett 1972:60).[7]

Laslett concludes the introduction with his well-known remark that the "wish to believe in the large and extended household as the ordinary institution of an earlier England and an earlier Europe, or as a standard feature of an earlier non-industrial world, is indeed a matter of ideology" (Laslett 1972:73). However, he writes, the "Japanese system seems deliberately to have provided for something like the gathering under one roof of the extended kin group which has been so widely and so unjustifiably regarded as typical of all the traditional households of the past, wherever they may found" (Laslett 1972:69).

The *ie* as a non-stem family organized around an ancestral cult: Michel Verdon

The *ie* disappeared from the major scene of global family history for more than a decade partly because Laslett, Wall, and other family historians concentrated on pursuing the past of the European household, and partly because Japanese historical demographers focused on demography, and not on the family. Michel Verdon's exclusion of the Japanese household from the category of "stem family" is unrelated to these factors. Verdon explicitly excludes the Japanese family, along with the Korean and Vietnamese families, from the stem family as he defines it, for the reason that, "in those societies, co-residence was organized around an ancestral cult, and not around the transmission of property. . . . In Western Europe, on the contrary, it was not the line that continued, but the estate" (Verdon 1979:87–105). The only Asian family he included under the rubric "stem family" was the Thai family. There is room for debate about Verdon's reasoning. The transmission of property, especially the house and farmland, plays a central role for the continuation of the *ie*, as Nakane described it – this is emphasized in the *haiku* I quoted earlier. However, Verdon is right to pay attention to the significance of ancestor worship in the Japanese family as well as in other East Asian families, for it certainly is a major difference between the *ie* and the European stem families. Another peculiarity of the *ie* compared with the European stem families is the widespread practice of adoption, which Peter Laslett noted many times in his introduction to *Household and Family* (Laslett 1972).[8] The ideology of patrilineality points to the underlying logic of ancestor worship and adoption practices in Japan.

The *ie* as a stem system of the western European type: Arthur Wolf and Susan Hanley

New efforts were made in the mid-1980s to place the Japanese family in a global context. Arthur Wolf and Susan Hanley advanced a provocative hypothesis that "the contrast between western and eastern Europe may have an East Asian parallel . . . China is to Japan as eastern is to western Europe"; moreover, the "Japanese family system [is] a stem system of the western European type" (Wolf and Hanley 1985: 3–4). Needless to say, they had Hajnal's framework in mind. John Hajnal proposed a framework of household formation systems, in which he argued that the stem family system, with the retirement custom of the household head, was "compatible with the general north-west European household formation rules" (Hajnal 1983:486). Wolf and Hanley also observe that, "In sum, it appears that where western European families limited their fertility by a combination of late marriage and celibacy, the Japanese accomplished the same end by a combination of late marriage and deliberate birth control" (Wolf and Hanley 1985:6).[9] After reiterating Hajnal's argument on the effect of late marriage on the accumulation of savings, Wolf and Hanley proceed to a much bolder hypothesis: "Could it be that similar marriage patterns explain why northwestern Europe and Japan led their regions in economic development? And if this is so, might it not be that one of the preconditions for modern economic development is a stem family system?" (Wolf and Hanley 1985:12). Modern Japan's economic success has necessitated changing the old question about modernization from "Why Europe?" to "Why Europe and Japan?"

The *ie* as a stem household formation system, third category: Laurel Cornell

Taking a different approach from Wolf and Hanley, sociologist Laurel Cornell proposes a third category, "the stem household formation system," independent from either the northwest or the east in Hajnal's framework. The most central of the "household formation rules in stem household societies" is that "a household can contain any number of married couples, but it can have only one in each generation" (Cornell 1987:152). Cornell notes the theoretical consequences of this system: "this does not put a premium on high fertility," for "only one child is necessary. Other children are only burdens" (Cornell 1987:153). The relationship between age at marriage, household formation, and economic conditions only concerns the "excess persons" who "cannot stay in the natal household" (Cornell 1987:153) "Hence," she observes, "a pattern of departure from home in adolescence, life-cycle service, and an age at marriage as that in pre-industrial northwestern Europe will exist, but among a much smaller proportion of the population . . . the mean age at marriage is likely to fall between the ages posited for the other two systems, and to have a large variance [because] the population of those who marry includes both those who stay and are likely to marry earlier and those who leave and marry later" (Cornell 1987:154). Cornell also mentions retirement and adoption, which should be common in a stem system. She states that "the Japanese family seems to follow the outlines of the stem household formation system rather closely," showing some empirical evidence of life-cycle service, age at marriage, household composition and age at attaining headship (Cornell 1987:154–157).

The *ie* as a genuine stem family system different from the European type: Osamu Saito

Osamu Saito focuses on the differences between the European stem family and the *ie*. He quotes Michael Mitterauer's argument that "most of the three-generational families so far observed were not genuine stem families. They simply took the form of *Ausgedingefamilie*, under which headship was handed over to the heir at the time of his marriage" (Saito 1998:169; see also Mitterauer and Sieder 1982:33–34). Mitterauer was referring to the arrangement "spread all over central and western Europe – from Ireland to the Sudeten, from Norway to the Alps." Like Hajnal, Mitterauer interpreted the stem family "more akin to the simple, nuclear family" (Saito 1998:169). Saito compares the size and structure of co-resident kin in Europe and in Japan (see Table 22.1), using the calculations of Teizo Toda, the founder of family sociology in Japan, which were based on data from the 1920 census (Toda 1937:222–229). European data are taken from the figures provided by Richard Wall (Wall 1983:53), which include Iceland, Norway, and Austria, "where either genuine or *Ausgedingefamilie*-type stem forms should have existed in the past" (Saito 1998:170).

First, Saito points out, the size of the Japanese kin group is much larger than that in Europe in the past. Second, the parents and siblings had the largest shares in the kin group in European stem family areas, whereas parents and grandchildren were conspicuous in the Japanese case. Further, the sons/daughters-in-law found in Japanese data are virtually non-existent in European data. Households in the north-central Europe "rarely extended downwards," whereas the Japanese household "could expand both upwards and downwards" (Saito 1998:173–174). In Europe "it was unlikely for the elderly to live with [their] heir's wife and children without giving up the headship of their households" (Saito 1998:174). Saito concludes that

Table 22.1   Relation to head in Japan, 1920, and 18th–19th-century Europe

	Japan, 1920		Europe, 18th–19th century	
	Number per 100 households	Modified[a]	Number per 100 households	Modified[a]
Parent	26	5.2	10	2.0
Sibling	12	2.4	11	2.2
Child-in-law	12	2.4	0	0.0
Nephew/niece	3	0.6	1	0.2
Grandchild	24	4.8	3	0.6

Source: Modified from Saito 1998.
[a] Estimated number per 100 individuals, assuming average household size is 5.

"the Japanese stem-family was more conspicuously vertically structured. It is, there-fore, probably safe to assume that the concept of descent line carried more weight in traditional Japan than in the European past" (Saito 1998:174). According to Saito, the Japanese family pattern was neither a variant of the joint family nor compatible with the simple-family system; it represented a separate, third type of family system (Saito 1998:180).

Reviewing the discussions of the *ie* in a global context reveals the ambiguous position of both the *ie* and the stem family. The questions of whether the *ie* is a stem family and whether the stem family constitutes a third category different from the nuclear and the joint, are not completely resolved.

REGIONAL DIVERSITY WITHIN JAPAN

The focus of European family history gradually shifted from the changes (or the lack of them) that accompanied modernization to regional diversity within Europe. Laslett's work already showed this tendency – as in the introduction to *Household and Family* – and he developed it further with his four-region hypothesis influenced by Hajnal (Laslett 1983). The provocative diagram presented by Emmanuel Todd is, in essence, along the same lines (Todd 1990:ch. 1). Todd subdivides the geographic spread of the stem family into four areas or blocs: the German bloc, the northern Scandinavian bloc, the Celtic bloc, and the Occitan and northern Iberian bloc. (This scheme is influenced by Le Play's idea of distinguishing the stem family in the northern area and southern areas.) What Todd's diagram does is to demonstrate the implausibility of regarding *the* European family, or *the* European stem family, as a homogeneous entity.

Japanese researchers in the postwar period also discussed at great length the extent of regional diversity within Japan. Their political motivation is clear from the view-point of intellectual history: they wanted to find popular traditions that deviated from the ideal of the *ie* that ostensibly enabled and facilitated Japanese militarism. These researchers emphasized the imposition of a universal family system under the Meiji Civil Code, which standardized the *ie*, neglecting differences of region, class, and social group. (Of course, it is important to remember that the code did not invent the *ie* from nothing.)

There are two important examples the researchers of this group often mention as a deviation from the *ie* principle. One is the custom largely observed in the southwestern areas, of branching out following retirement. In this case, a retired household head and his wife form a branch family and live separately from the new household head and his wife (Omachi 1975). This custom is often accompanied by ultimogeniture, because the younger children repeat the same process when the eldest among them marries, and eventually the youngest son succeeds to the headship of his parents' household (Naito 1973). Another well-known custom, common in the northeast, is absolute primogeniture, whereby the eldest child, regardless of sex, becomes the heir. When the eldest daughter is the successor, her husband marries into the household as an adopted son-in-law whereupon he formally succeeds her to become the next househead (Maeda 1976).[10]

Both of these two cases deviate from the rule of male primogeniture codified in the Meiji Civil Code. Note that the practice of absolute primogeniture conforms to the two criteria of the stem family used by Le Play and Laslett and completely fulfills Nakane's criterion of the *ie*, namely, one-child succession. The case of branching out upon retirement is more marginal, because partial inheritance would thereby be institutionalized in each generation. Nevertheless, Nakane categorizes the absolute primogeniture model as a modified version of the *ie* because it is understood as a transmission of headship in the social unit comprising the *ie* (Nakane 1964:104). This is because the retirement house is often built in the same compound as the main house. It is interesting to note that a custom quite similar to branching out upon retirement is still practiced in some areas of Southeast Asia (Mizuno 1968:842–852), which brings to mind one hypothesis about the origin of the Japanese as a hybrid of Southeast Asian and Northeast Asian peoples (Hanihara 1991).

In summing up the research into and discussions about regional diversity in Japanese households historically, Masao Gamo identifies three different regional tendencies: the increase, the decrease, and the stabilization of household size (Gamo 1966). Gamo maintains that the predominant pattern nationwide is a stem family with the tendency to stabilize its size. However, he adds, northeastern households tend to increase in size, sometimes even forming joint families including younger brothers as a labor force even after their marriage, as a strategy to secure family labor and to reverse the tendency to low productivity in the cold season. In contrast, southwestern households tend to be smaller and do not feature multiple couples living together. Absolute primogeniture, a custom peculiar to northeastern Japan, seems to be a strategy to decrease the depth of generations and to enlarge the size of a household, while the ultimogeniture model combined with branching out upon retirement is a typical southwestern practice that effectively divides households (Gamo 1966).

Under the influence of Gamo and Tadashi Fukutake, a leading rural sociologist who contrasted the vertical social structures found in eastern villages with the more egalitarian structures in western villages (Fukutake 1949), many Japanese family sociologists continue to share an implicit assumption that the typical *ie*, large in size and complex in structure with patriarchal power centering on the head and the eldest son, existed and still exists in the northeast. They also regard households in western

Japan as closer to the nuclear family system.[11] These views seem to be supported by recent statistics that show distinct regional differences in household size and structural complexity. In 1985, the average size of a household was less than 3.5 persons in the western region and more than 3.5 in the eastern region (Somu-cho Tokei-kyoku 1990:123). The corresponding figures for 1881 are less than 4.9 in the western region and more than 5.5 in the eastern region (Hayami 1998:231; Hayami and Ochiai 2001).

Akira Hayami recently proposed a three-region hypothesis to replace the east–west model: northeast, central, and southwest. The northeast is self-evident. The central region covers the western half of Honshu island and the eastern parts of Kyushu; households in this region fit a stereotypical *ie* pattern. Southwest refers to the westernmost areas of the Kyushu island; this region is well known for the practice of ultimogeniture and branching out on retirement. The southwest region includes many fishing villages, and further research may show that coastal areas in other parts of Japan have similar practices. Hayami even suggests, but has not empirically verified, that this similarity may extend to the coastal areas of southern China and southern Korea (Hayami 1998:243–245).

In the following sections, I will examine the household systems in two sample areas: the northeast and the central regions, following Hayami's three-region hypothesis, with the caveat that I will not claim that they are representative of the region. The questions I address are:

1   Are the household systems in the two areas stem household systems, and if so are they different?
2   Are the household systems in the two areas different from European stem families?
3   What are the demographic backgrounds and outcomes of the household systems in the two areas?
4   In what kind of economic and social systems are these household systems embedded?

DATA AND RESEARCH AREAS: NOBI AND NIHONMATSU

My analysis employs data sets derived from population registers compiled in the Tokugawa period, to be precise in the 18th and the 19th centuries, of the two areas: one from the Nobi plain surrounding Nagoya, the other from the former Nihonmatsu domain in what is now Fukushima Prefecture. The Nobi area belongs to the central region according to Hayami's three-region hypothesis, whereas the Nihonmatsu area is obviously situated in the southernmost part of the northeast. Although it is too bold to assume that the sample populations are representative of the central and of the northeast respectively, they retain some features common to the regions.

The data from Nihonmatsu are the population registers, called *ninbetsu aratame cho* (NAC), of two farming villages, Shimomoriya and Niita. Most analyses of the northeastern region in this chapter are based on the Shimomoriya data, although I sometimes employ the Niita data to support the results from Shimomoriya and to enlarge the sample size. During the Edo period, these villages belonged to the former Nihonmatsu domain, which covered the central area of present Fukushima Prefecture. Both Shimomoriya and Niita are in the intramontane basin of the Abukuma river, which flows from south to north between the Ou and Abukuma mountains. Niita lies on the Ou road, which runs almost parallel to the Abukuma river, while Shimomoriya is located at the rim of the basin. The Shimomoriya data cover the period 1716–1869, with nine missing years, and the Niita data cover the period 1720–1870, with only five missing years. Since the quality of the data is quite high, the villages have been studied by historians and historical demographers, and are known to be high-mortality and low-fertility areas suffering from cold weather and economic backwardness (Narimatsu 1985, 1992; Tsuya and Kurosu 1999). The northeastern region suffered several famines and prolonged cold weather in the 18th century and the first few decades of the 19th century. The region was the northernmost border of rice production at the time. As a result of the famines and inclement weather, the total population of the northeastern region decreased during the 18th century, and Shimomoriya and Niita were no exceptions to this trend. The total population of the villages decreased in the latter half of the 18th century and only started to recover in 1830s (Table 22.2).

The Nobi data include only one village, Nishijo, a sub-village of nearby Niremata village in the Nobi plain in present-day Gifu Prefecture; it was directly administered by the Tokugawa shogunate. With its absolutely flat land, crossed by three large rivers, the landscape makes an arresting impression. The natural environment of the area provides the perfect conditions for growing rice, although floods pose a potential risk. The data on this village are derived from *shumon aratame cho* (SAC) which literally means "religious investigation." These surveys were initiated as a means of ensuring that all villagers were registered Buddhists and not Christians – the practice of Christianity was prohibited in the early 17th century. However, the survey gradually lost its original purpose and began to function as a population register. Thus, there is no methodological problem with treating the NAC and SAC as essentially the same kind of document. The data for Nishijo cover the period 1773–1869. The quality of data is also very good. Nishijo has been studied, together with other villages in the Nobi area, by Akira Hayami (Hayami 1992). Whereas the total population of western Japan increased slightly before the 1830s, the population of Nishijo showed a decrease until the 1840s (Table 22.2). It was not because the village suffered from economic difficulties but rather because of the frequent migration of villagers to urban centers, including Nagoya, Kyoto, and Osaka. Nishijo was situated in the economically most advanced area of the country, in contrast to Shimomoriya and Niita.

Both the NAC of Shimomoriya and Niita and the SAC of Nishijo include census-type information – such as name, age, relation to head of household members – and records of life events – such as birth, death, marriage, adoption, service, migration, headship transmission, name change, etc. – that occurred over the course of one year. The unit of registration was the household or *ie*, and the household head was registered as the first individual in most cases. Note that the household itself is referred to in the name of the household head.

Some readers may think that the use of data samples from only one or two villages to represent a given area is problematic. However, the representativeness of these

Table 22.2 Total population, number of households, and average household size by decade in Nishijo, Shimomoriya and Niita

Year	Population			No. of households			Household size		
	Nishijo	Shimo-moriya	Niita	Nishijo	Shimo-moriya	Niita	Nishijo	Shimo-moriya	Niita
1710		411			112			3.68	
1720		416	530		105	129		3.95	4.11
1730		434	533		97	132		4.48	4.05
1740		448	527		91	129		4.90	4.08
1750		429	531		95	123		4.52	4.32
1760		380	528		92	127		4.15	4.17
1770	371	352	483	94	85	126	3.94	4.13	3.83
1780	346	318	438	88	76	119	3.92	4.18	3.70
1790	312	320	440	85	75	113	3.69	4.28	3.91
1800	331	309	418	81	69	108	4.08	4.49	3.86
1810	314	284	391	78	63	106	4.05	4.50	3.70
1820	313	279	392	74	63	99	4.26	4.41	3.97
1830	311	277	410	74	64	92	4.19	4.36	4.44
1840	295	266	434	70	57	90	4.22	4.65	4.84
1850	331	319	489	76	61	88	4.35	5.27	5.54
1860	360	340	529	79	62	89	4.58	5.47	5.95
1870		555			87			6.38	
Whole period	328	347	471	80	78	111	4.13	4.43	4.24

villages has been verified by previous studies by Hayami and Narimatsu (Hayami 1992; Narimatsu 1985, 1992). Other villages in these areas show similar tendencies to the villages in the database. The representativeness of these areas for the wider regions, the northeast and central, is a separate question, which I will address.

ANALYSIS

Household size

First, let us examine household size: is there in fact a difference in household size between the two areas, as is often claimed about eastern and western households? As shown in Table 22.2, the total population size of three villages all declined at intervals between the 1810s and 1840s, and recovered after that. However, the actual number of households steadily declined. Monotonic decreases occurred in Shimomoriya and Niita, but a short recovery in accordance with population trends is observed in Nishijo. As a result, household size is almost stable for the whole period in Nishijo and, until the 1830s, in Shimomoriya and Niita, but an obvious increase occurs in the last decades in Shimomoriya and Niita. The household size before the last increase in the northeast begins is around four persons in both areas. Regional differences in household size are not found in our data for the mid-Edo period.

However, Table 22.3, which shows household size reported from different areas in Japan during the Edo period, indicates that our research area has the smallest size of households in the northeastern region. As I see it, this can be explained by the frequent migration of staff services from this area in addition to the practice of branching out upon retirement which is commonplace in the northeastern region, although more ethnographic data are needed in order to clinch my hypothesis (Ochiai 1999b). In general, the households in the northeast are larger by around one person than those in the central area. Interestingly, an increase in household size is reported from all the areas in the northeast. Masao Takagi, who studied Toge, Shimoyuta, Okago, and Niinuma in the eastern area of the northeast as well as in our research area, notes that an increase in household size after 1839 was common to these four villages. The effect of the Tenpo famine, in particular in 1837–38, and the recovery from it, are conspicuous (Takagi 1986:13). Yambe, in the western area of the northeast, in contrast, experienced a steady increase in household size (Kinoshita 1995:244). The difference in household size between the northeast and central areas in general existed in the mid-Edo period and became even greater towards the end of the period.[12]

Table 22.3   Mean household size in different areas

Area	Period	Mean household size
Shimomoriya (northeast)	1716–1839	4.35
Niita (northeast)	1720–1839	4.01
Nishijo (central)	1773–1839	4.02
Shimomoriya (northeast)	1840–69	5.08
Niita (northeast)	1840–70	5.47
Nishijo (central)	1840–69	4.38
Yambe (northeast)	1760–1870	5.35
Toge (northeast)	1790–1870	4.0 → 4.5
Shiomoyuta (northeast)	1790–1870	5.3 → 5.7
Okago (northeast)	1790–1870	5.5 → 6.5
Niinuma (northeast)	1790–1870	5.0 → 6.2
Yokouchi (central)	1675–1866	6.9 → 4.43

Household structure

Household size is not particularly helpful in understanding household structure. Table 22.4 shows proportions of households in particular years in Shimomoriya and Nishijo classified by the Hammel–Laslett household typology. The difference in household structure between the two areas is evident. Around 40 percent of households in Nihonmatsu, and only 10–20 percent of those in Nobi, belong to the multiple family household (Type 5). In contrast, over 40 percent of households in Nobi are simple family households (Type 3). The extended family household (Type 4) comprises about 20 percent in both areas. Although the majority of the multiple family households in both areas have a stem family structure where all the conjugal family units (CFUs) are on the vertical line (Type 5s), the Nihonmatsu

Table 22.4 Household structure in Shimomoriya and Nishijo by Hammel–Laslett type (%)

Types	Shimomoriya				Nishijo		
	1750	1800	1851	1869	1800	1850	1869
1 solitary	3.3	12.5	5.0	6.6	11.3	8.2	7.7
2 no family	3.3	2.8	1.7	0.0	0.0	2.7	9.0
3 simple[a]	26.4	22.2	28.3	21.3	41.3	57.5	43.6
4 extended[a]	24.2	19.4	21.7	26.2	36.3	21.9	20.5
5 multiple[a]	42.9	43.1	43.3	45.9	11.3	9.6	19.2
5s stem[a] [b]	38.5	41.7	36.7	41.0	10.0	9.6	16.7
No. of households	91	72	60	61	80	73	78

[a] Those who have no evidence of being divorced or widowed are regarded as unmarried, forming a CFU with parent(s).
[b] Includes multiple family households with all CFUs on vertical line.

sample includes a certain proportion (5-5s) of joint family households where more than two CFUs exist in the same generation. As we shall see, most of them involve cases where two young couples remained in the parental household under the father's headship. Interestingly, an increase in household complexity is evident in both areas in the 1860s, especially in Niita and Nishijo.

Proportions of individuals according to their relationship to the head of house are another informative measure of household structure. We have already seen Saito's remarks on the difference between Japanese and European stem families. However, Table 22.5 shows the considerable extent of diversity within Japan. The most conspicuous difference between Nobi and Nihonmatsu is in the proportion of persons identified as "parent." This is 13 percent in Shimomoriya and only 1 percent in Nishijo. It seems that men in Nobi would not give up their headship and retire, whereas men in Nihonmatsu quite often retired. Borrowing Saito's expression, the Nihonmatsu households extend vertically both downwards and upwards, while the Nobi households extend vertically only downwards. However, it is not appropriate to generalize this finding to the northeast/central contrast, because our sample area Nihonmatsu is known to be an exception in the northeast where the retirement was nearly non-existent.[13] Probably this is the most striking example of deviance from the general features of the regions in which these sample populations are located.

As a consequence of the difference in retirement practice, more men in Nishijo remain classified as "child" than in Shimomoriya. What is interesting here is the small proportion of females listed as "child-in-law" in Nishijo, which indicates that most of the males recorded as "child" are unmarried. On the other hand, the proportion registered as "grandchild+" (including grandchildren and great grandchildren and their spouses) in Nihonmatsu is almost the same or even larger than that in Nobi, in spite of the common practice of retirement in Nihonmatsu. As I will show, these proportions are due to the difference in marriage age.

Lateral expansion of households is partly shown in the proportions of "sibling" and "uncle/aunt." The proportion of "siblings" is larger in Nishijo; but this does not mean that they form joint family households, for the proportion of "siblings-in-law" is small. Joint family households in Nihonmatsu are formed mostly by the "child" generation, as the relatively large proportions of "child-in-law" indicate. The households expand laterally to some extent in both areas, but the effect on household structure differs. In short, the tendency in the northeast to form joint family households is verified, but it is by no means a strong tendency.

The proportion listed as "servant" is almost twice as large in Shimomoriya as in Nishijo. This is an unexpected finding since Nishijo is located in an economically more advanced area and the village is also well known for its frequent service migration (Hayami 1992). The households in Nihonmatsu recruited their labor force from among both kin and non-kin. This is a fact concealed by the practice in northeastern households of keeping younger brothers at home as a labor force. We should bear in mind, however, that the character of service and servants is not the same in the two regions, as I elaborate below. Another obvious difference between the two areas is in the proportion of female heads, which is four times larger in Nobi than in Nihonmatsu.

Living arrangements of the elderly

The difference in patterns of household formation appears most clearly in the living arrangements of elderly members. George Alter's study on the living arrangements of

Table 22.5 Proportions of individuals by relation to head in Shimomoriya and Nishijo (%)

Relation to head	Shimomoriya		Nishijo	
	Male	Female	Male	Female
Head	35.7	2.6	39.9	8.2
Spouse	0.7	31.8	0.0	30.4
Child[a]	31.6	24.6	45.0	35.6
Child-in-law	3.8	6.1	0.7	3.9
Grandchild[b]	3.7	4.3	3.7	3.5
Parent	13.3	18.3	1.4	9.6
Grandparent[c]	1.9	3.7	0.0	0.2
Sibling	2.8	1.8	5.2	4.1
Sibling-in-law	0.0	0.3	0.0	0.5
Uncle/aunt[d]	0.3	0.3	0.2	0.7
Nephew / niece	0.2	0.5	0.6	1.3
Cousin	0.1	0.0	0.3	0.3
Servant	5.4	5.1	3.1	1.7
Other[e]	0.5	0.7	0.0	0.2
N person year	25,407	24,840	15,326	15,918

[a] includes adopted and stepchildren as well as biological ones.
[b] Includes grandchildren, great-grandchildren, and their spouses.
[c] Includes grandparents, great-grandparents, and so on.
[d] Includes siblings of parents and their spouses.
[e] Includes distant kin and non-kin.

the elderly according to the marital status of both parents and children provides a typical example of the nuclear-family pattern (Alter 1996:123–138). His study reveals four characteristics of household formation. First, the proportion of members living with children declines when parents become older. Second, the majority of children living with parent(s) are unmarried. Third, the proportion living with children differs depending on the marital status of the parents; that is, widowed parents are more likely to live with their married children. Fourth, widows are more likely to live with their married children than are widowers.

What pattern do we find in Edo period Japan?[14] In Shimomoriya, Hideki Nakazato found no decline in the proportion of members living with children regardless of the parents' age. He also shows that the majority of children living with their parent(s) are married, and that the marital status and sex of a parent do not affect the co-residential pattern (Nakazato 1998:276). This is the pattern we expect in a stem family society, where the residence of the heir and his or her spouse with the parents is institutionalized. Note that cases where the parents are living with their adopted children or children-in-law are included in co-residence with their "children." My previous study based on data from Shimomoriya reveals that the proportion of men living with their biological sons in their fifties is around 40 percent, but that the proportion living with all "sons", including adopted sons and sons-in-law, is over 60 percent (Ochiai 1995, 1997b).

The pattern in Nishijo is different from that in Shimomoriya. The first finding in Nakazato on the irrelevance of parents' age is also found in Nishijo, although the percentage is different. The proportion living with children in Shimomoriya is around 70 percent, and 80–90 percent in Nishijo. Contrary to the image that the northeastern households are typical *ie*, the parents in Nihonmatsu are less likely to live with their children. Frequent migration in order to go into service among married men and women in the area is the cause of this contradiction.

The marital status of both parents and children matters in Nishijo. Older men are more likely to live with their married children. Aging has no effect on the proportion of parents living with their children, but in Nobi, it does affect the proportion living with *married* children. Widowed men are more likely to live with their married children than are married men, regardless of their age. This finding suggests that the people in this area have a tendency to avoid the co-residence of two couples.[15]

Marriage and fertility

In order to understand the relationship between household-formation strategies and household patterns in each area, we need to take into consideration people's behaviors. The age at marriage shown in Table 22.6 suggests totally different attitudes toward marriage in Nobi and Nihonmatsu. The age of males in Shimomoriya and Niita at the time of their first marriage is 9.9 years younger than that in Nishijo, and that of females is 6.5 years younger. The age at first marriage in Shimomoriya and Niita is one of the lowest ever observed for an Edo period peasant population; the only comparable ones are also all from the northeastern region, for example, 19.6 for males and 15.6 for females in Shimoyuta (Hamano 1999:131).[16] In contrast, the age at first marriage for males in Nishijo is comparable to "European"

Table 22.6   Age at first marriage by period

Year	Shimomoriya and Niita				Nishijo			
	Male[a]		Female[b]		Male[a]		Female[b]	
	%	N	%	N	%	N	%	N
1720–39	16.9	64	11.9	54				
1740–59	18.7	92	13.9	56				
1760–79	21.7	75	15.2	46				
1780–99	20.0	69	14.9	47	25.2	13	20.6	11
1800–19	20.3	59	15.7	43	29.7	23	20.7	11
1820–39	19.8	53	16.0	49	31.0	35	25.0	8
1840–59	20.6	33	17.7	39	29.3	32	20.4	15
Whole period	19.6	445	14.9	334	29.5	105	21.4	45

[a] Survived to 40.
[b] Survived to 30.

marriage patterns in that they wait for many years before getting married. The households in this area seem to have a tendency to avoid the co-residence of two couples. Also significant in Nishijo is the eight-year difference in age between the wife and husband, which is much wider than in Nihonmatsu or Europe. This fact at least partly explains the relatively high proportion of females recorded as "parent" or "head" in Nishijo as shown in Table 22.5: presumably they are widows who live long after their husbands have passed away.

Does the low age at marriage in the northeast result in high fertility, as is conventionally believed for Asian populations? James Lee and Cameron Campbell found a significant difference in the level of marital fertility between European and East Asian populations. The marital fertility in the preindustrial period was low in East Asia and high in Europe, contradicting the conventional image. One cause of low fertility in this area is proved to be deliberate birth control, including both abortion (Ota and Sawayama, in press) and sex selective infanticide (Tsuya and Kurosu 1999). A negative attitude toward abortion and infanticide only developed in the 19th century when population growth was promoted in the northeastern region (Ochiai 1999a). I also suspect that the custom that a couple stops having sex after a grandchild is born existed in this area, since they stopped having children as early as in their mid-thirties. The average birth interval is shorter in Nishijo and longer in Nihonmatsu (Hayami and Ochiai 2001). Women and men in northeastern Japan marry early but their fertility is extremely low. What, then, does marriage mean for them? To answer this question, we need to view the household as a work group.

Service

What do the women and men of Nishijo do during their lengthy period of unmarried life? Hayami studied the frequent service migration in the Nobi area (Hayami 1992:ch. 10); however, service migration is even more common in Nihonmatsu.

The people in Shimomoriya also leave their own households to go into service quite often, but mostly after marriage. This tendency is more conspicuous among females. Almost no unmarried women departed for service purposes until the 1800s. The majority of male servants are married (Nagata 1999; Ochiai 1997a, 1997b). Service is what *married* people in Nihonmatsu do, while it is what *unmarried* people in Nobi do. Table 22.7 shows the dramatic difference in service between the two areas. Other studies show that frequent service and the presence of married servants are not peculiar to the Nihonmatsu area but are also observed in other areas in the northeastern region. Masao Takagi reports the high incidence of pawn service in Shimoyuta village in northern part of the northeastern region (Takagi 2002). Futoshi Kinoshita observes that the majority of servants are married in Yambe village in present-day Yamagata Prefecture, in the western part of the region (Kinoshita 2002).

Frequent service after marriage explains various phenomena in this area. The low fertility that seems to contradict the low age at marriage is at least partly explained by the custom of going into service after marriage.[17] For example, a girl may be married while still in her early teens – even before she has reached sexual maturity – not for reproduction, but for her labor, which is put in pawn soon after the marriage. The major form of service in the northeast in the 18th century was "pawn service," in contrast to the wage-service system in the central region. After a few years in service, the young wife returned to her husband's household to bear a baby, and in a few years left the household for service again (Ochiai 1997a, 1997b).

Service after marriage also offers a clue to understanding household composition in Nihonmatsu, as I noted earlier. The lower proportion of elderly people living with children in this area is the result of the temporary absence of married children away in service. On the other hand, service after marriage is made possible by the stem family structure, in that a young mother can leave her baby behind because she can expect support from other adult members in the household. It is also possible that service after marriage might have a function in forestalling or reducing conflict within the stem family.

HEADSHIP AND RETIREMENT

The last issue to address is headship. Since the transmission of headship is an essential element in a stem family system, retirement customs have been a key issue in European debates on the stem family. As I have said, there is a considerable difference between Nihonmatsu and Nobi with respect to headship and retirement. The age at headship succession is not so different in the two areas, although men in Nihonmatsu marry ten years younger than men in Nobi. A young married man in Nihonmatsu spends some years as a "son" under his father's or father-in-law's headship. The most conspicuous difference between the areas lies in the headship rates after the age of 50. The heads of house in Nihonmatsu retire rather quickly, while most of the heads in Nobi retain headship until the ripe old age of 70, suggesting that retirement is not a life event that many Nobi men experience. We should note, however, that frequent retirement is a special feature of the Nihonmatsu area, which is a well-known exception to the rule of "no retirement" in the

Table 22.7 Marital status of servants, Shimomoriya and Nishijo, by decade and by sex[a]

Year	Shimomoriya						Nishijo					
	Female			Male			Female			Male		
	Unmarried (%)	Married (%)	N	Unmarried (%)	Married (%)	N	Unmarried (%)	Married (%)	N	Unmarried (%)	Married (%)	N
1710	0.0	100.0	2	25.0	25.0	4						
1720	0.0	95.5	22	14.3	57.1	7						
1730	0.0	100.0	23	20.7	72.4	29						
1740	0.0	100.0	39	15.2	67.4	46						
1750	0.0	98.0	51	26.5	51.5	68						
1760	0.0	100.0	19	42.9	21.4	14						
1770	0.0	92.9	14	11.8	79.4	34	85.0	0.0	20	63.2	15.8	19
1780	0.0	78.0	82	19.0	64.3	84	94.9	0.0	39	76.7	13.3	30
1790	0.0	92.0	88	20.5	68.2	44	95.7	0.0	23	85.7	4.8	21
1800	0.0	91.7	60	16.7	63.9	36	93.1	0.0	29	87.5	4.2	24
1810	18.4	60.5	38	64.7	32.4	34	100.0	0.0	38	86.7	3.3	30
1820	29.4	41.2	34	38.3	61.7	47	96.3	0.0	27	100.0	0.0	17
1830	53.7	26.8	41	19.7	70.5	61	90.5	4.8	21	94.4	5.6	18
1840	67.9	32.1	56	29.4	69.1	68	100.0	0.0	16	100.0	0.0	18
1850	54.5	45.5	44	43.8	56.3	48	93.3	6.7	15	94.4	5.6	18
1860	11.1	77.8	9	19.0	81.0	21	81.3	12.5	16	90.5	9.5	21
Whole period	17.8	74.0	622	26.5	62.5	645	93.9	1.6	244	87.0	6.5	216

a The proportions of divorced and widowed are omitted.

northeastern region (Ochiai 1999b; Takeda 1964). Such exceptions make generalizing between the northeast and the central region especially difficult, especially with respect to retirement.

What can we say about the rates of female headship and retirement proportions? The vast majority of female heads of house are the wives of former heads of house. Female headship rates are higher in Nishijo than in Nihonmatsu, as shown in Table 22.5. The age pattern, however, which peaks at a later stage of life is common to both areas. It means that the female heads only appear on the scene when their husbands die at a relatively young age. The proportion of retired women is not as small as that of men in Nishijo largely because the large age gap between spouses in the area results in a high incidence of women who are younger, becoming widowed heads of house.

TWO TYPES OF STEM HOUSEHOLD SYSTEM IN JAPAN

Having examined various aspects of the households in Nihonmatsu and Nobi, we are now ready to answer the questions raised at the outset, beginning with whether the household systems in Nihonmatsu and Nobi differ. If we define the stem family in the simplest way, as a household system where only one child remains at the parental household and brings his or her spouse into the household, we can conclude that the households in both areas follow the formation rule for stem family household.

Household structure and the composition of household members in Nihonmatsu suggest that households in the area follow the one-child succession rule. Analysis of the living arrangements of the elderly confirms this finding, because age and aging do not seem to have much effect on the marital status of parents. A few joint family households in this area are annually observed, but they are mostly cases where two young couples remain at the parental household under the father's headship – temporary arrangements before one of the couples forms a branch household.

The case of households in Nobi is less clear-cut. One might think that the high proportion of simple family households confirms the hypothesis that the southwestern system is close to the nuclear household system. However, the proportion of households (10–20 percent) with a multiple structure is too high to warrant that conclusion. The living arrangements of the elderly also indicate a different pattern from the nuclear system discussed by Alter. When one becomes older, the proportion of households with no children should increase in a society with a dominant nuclear household system. On the contrary, the proportion of households without children is not affected by aging in Nishijo, and the proportion of the elderly living with married children actually increases. The pattern of the living arrangements of the elderly in Nishijo is, however, not the same as that in Nihonmatsu. The marital status of the parent affects the proportion living with *married* children; a widowed parent is more likely to live with married children than is a currently married parent. There seems to be a tendency to avoid the co-residence of two couples in different generations in the Nobi area.

We have shown that the stem household system existed in both Nihonmatsu and Nobi in the Edo period. Does this mean that the same household system prevailed in both areas? The concept of household formation system proposed by Hajnal includes not only patterns of living arrangements but also patterns of marriage and labor. If we take into consideration the patterns of marriage and labor, it is hard to assert that the household systems in the two areas are the same. The patterns of headship succession and retirement are also different. In Nobi, unmarried men and women spend many years out of their parental households as servants, similar to life-cycle servants in Europe. Later, the heirs go back to the parental household to marry at the end of their twenties, probably when the father is on his deathbed. They produce relatively many children in a short interval. In Nihonmatsu, by contrast, people marry quite young with little experience of service. A considerable proportion of men and women leave to go into service soon after marrying. Partly as a consequence, they produce only a small number of children with very long birth intervals. The two household systems are very different, although both of them are stem household systems. In short, the stem household system is not homogeneous. Both the Nobi system and the Nihonmatsu system belong to the stem household system, but we should recognize that they represent different variants of that system. This, then, is our answer to the first question, which leads to the second one.

Are the stem household systems in Nobi and Nihonmatsu different from the European stem system? At first glance, the Nobi system looks like the European stem system, having in common life-cycle service, a high age at first marriage (at least for males), and a large proportion of simple family households. Recall that the retirement practice characteristic of the stem family in central and western Europe is not widespread in the Nobi area. If we compare the proportions of "parent" in Nobi and in Europe as shown in Tables 22.1 and 22.5, however, the difference is not distinctive at all. We cannot deny the similarity between the Nobi stem system and the central and western European stem system, at least with respect to the comparability between these systems, although we must collect more information on both systems before coming to a definitive conclusion.[18] In contrast, most aspects of the Nihonmatsu system are completely different from the European system, although they have retirement in common.

The most evident demographic consequence of the two Japanese systems is low fertility in both areas, as Cornell predicted, although the paths to this end are strikingly different: late marriage is a significant factor in Nobi, while extremely low marital fertility is decisive in Nihonmatsu. Late marriage in Nobi is related to the system of headship transmission and life-cycle service. Low marital fertility in Nihonmatsu is presumably caused by the low frequency of childbearing after marriage due to frequent service migration, along with deliberate abortion and infanticide. Much more discussion is needed as to the demographic and socioeconomic background of the two systems. Hayami tries to explain the northeastern household system as a strategy "to maximize the labor force in the family and to minimize the number of dependents" under the severe climatic and economic conditions of the region (Hayami and Ochiai 2001). In contrast, he holds, good economic conditions enable population growth and frequent household divisions in the central area. We need more scrutiny of both household systems and the economic and demographic conditions of the areas to fully answer the third and fourth questions.

CONCLUSION

In seeking to situate the *ie* in the context of global family history, I have tried to answer the questions raised by previous discussions on the *ie* and the stem family. Whether the Japanese *ie* is a stem family is the first question; whether the Japanese *ie* belongs to the same type of stem family as the European one is the second. To answer these questions, I focused on regional diversity within Japan. The analyses employing the data sets from two areas, one from the northeast and the other from the central region, lead us to the conclusion that the household systems in both areas are recognizable as stem household systems, although they are far from identical. My analysis strongly suggests that the Nobi household system and the Nihonmatsu household system are different variants of the stem household system. The Nobi system has similarities to the European stem system in some aspects, although more research is necessary before definitive conclusions can be reached. Low fertility in both areas in Japan is a demographic outcome of the stem household systems in these areas, but the demographic, economic, and social conditions that contributed to the creation these household systems needs further exploration.

NOTES

This chapter was written under the auspices of a research project on comparative historical demography headed by Professor Akira Hayami and funded by the Grants-in-Aid for Scientific Research from the Japanese government, 1995–2000.

1   The original *haiku* in Japanese is *Ikikawari shinikawari shite utsu ta kana*.
2   For the debates on the *ie* in Japan and the stem family in Europe, see Ochiai (2000).
3   The database I employ for the analysis in this chapter has constructed by the Eurasia Project Japanese research team. I am grateful to Akira Hayami, the leader of the Japanese team, who granted me the opportunity to work for the project. I am also grateful to Saeko Narimatsu and Nobuko Saito, who transcribed the information from the old documents to BDS (basic data sheet), and to Miyuki Yoshida and others, who entered the data.
4   Editor's note: For critiques of Nakane's "vertical society" thesis see Befu (1980); Mouer and Sugimoto (1990 [1986]); and Yoshino (1992).
5   The chapters on Japan are by Robert J. Smith, Akira Hayami and Nobuko Uchida, and Chie Nakane.
6   The six populations are the sample of 100 communities in England, 1574–1821; Ealing in Middlesex, England, 1599; Longuenesse in Pas-de-Calais, France, 1778; Belgrade in Serbia, 1733–34; Hama-issai-cho in Nishinomiya, Japan, 1713; Bristol in Rhode Island, an American colony.
7   The proportions of stem families and *frérèches* are the highest in Nishimomiya and the second highest in Belgrade. According to Peter Laslett, if no parent is present in the household and the conjugal family units of siblings within the household are connected to each other entirely through the filial linkage, then the household is given the title of *frérèche*, adopted from the French (Laslett, 1972:30).
8   For the details of adoption practice in Japan, see Kurosu and Ochiai (1995).
9   Recent researches in Japan reveal that the age at marriage and the level of fertility differed considerably by region, as shown in the latter half of this chapter.

10   The custom of primogeniture regardless of sex is called *ane-katoku* (eldest-daughter headship) in folk terms, because the succession through the female line attracts attention.

11   The border between the western region and the eastern region is drawn somewhere between the southern end of the northeast (the Tohoku district) and the eastern end of the Kinki district according to the viewpoint. The "west" tends to expand further on the areas facing the Pacific Ocean, and the "east" sometimes reaches the San'in area of Chugoku region facing the Japan Sea (Omoto 1999).

12   The long-term decrease in household size reported from Yokouchi and other villages in the Suwa area, a basin surrounded by mountains in the central Japan, needs different line of explanation. See Hayami (1973).

13   Akira Takeda called northeastern Japan a "no retirement area" in Takeda (1964). Ochiai confirmed Takeda's observation based on empirical evidence (Ochiai 1999b).

14   A preliminary analysis of regional differences in living arrangements of the elderly by age and marital status is shown in Hayami and Ochiai (2001).

15   Historians suggest that the tendency to avoid the co-residence of two couples in particular in the patriline existed among the aristocrats in the Heian period, i.e., from the 9th to 12th centuries. The rise of virilocal marriage is observed among them, but the co-residence of two couples of the same patriline was exceptional until the 12th century (Kurihara 1994).

16   Editor's note: One must also take into account the manner in which age is reckoned: from the moment of birth, or from conception, or from some other point in time.

17   Another cause of low fertility in this area is proved to be deliberate birth control including both abortion (Ota and Sawayama, in press) and sex-selective infanticide (Tsuya and Kurosu 1999). A negative attitude toward abortion and infanticide only developed in the 19th century when population growth started in the northeastern region (Ochiai 1999a). I also suspect that the custom that a couple stop having sex after a grandchild is born existed in this area, since they stopped having children as early as their mid-thirties.

18   For example, the European data shown in Table 22.1 are not divided by sex.

REFERENCES

Alter, George. 1996. The European Marriage Pattern as Solution and Problem: The Households of the Elderly in Verviers, Belgium, 1831. The History of the Family 1–2:123–138.

Arensberg, Conrad M. 1960. The American Family in the Perspective of Other Cultures: The Nation's Children, vol. 1. New York: Columbia University Press.

Befu, Harumi. 1980. A Critique of the Group Model of Japanese Society. Social Analysis 5(6):29–43.

Cornell, Laurel. 1987. Hajnal and the Household in Asia. Journal of Family History 12:143–162.

Douglas, William. 1993. The *Famille Souche* and its Interpreters. Continuity and Change 8.

Fukutake, Tadashi. 1949. Nihon nōson no shakaiteki seikaku (Social Characteristics of Japanese Villages). Tokyo: University of Tokyo Press.

Gamo, Masao. 1966. Sengo nihon shakai no kozoteki henka no shiron (An Essay on the Structural Change in Japanese Society after the Second World War). Seikei ronshu 34.6:611–636.

Hajnal, John. 1983. Two Kinds of Pre-Industrial Household Formation System. *In* Family Forms in Historic Europe. Richard Wall, Jean Robin, and Peter Laslett, eds. Cambridge: Cambridge University Press.

Hamano, Kiyoshi. 1999. Marriage Pattern and Demographic System in Tokugawa Japan. Japan Review 11:129–144.

Hanihara, Kazuo. 1991. Dual Structure Model for the Population History of the Japanese. Japan Review 2:1–33.

Hanley, Susan, and Arthur Wolf, eds. 1985. Family and Population in East Asian History. Stanford: Stanford University Press.

Hayami, Akira. 1973. Kinsei nōson no rekishi-jinkōgaku teki kenkyū (Historical Demography of Early-Modern Farm Villages). Tokyo: Tōyōkeizai Shinpō-sha.

—— 1992. Kinsei nobi chihō no jinkō, keizai, shakai (Population, Economy and Society in Early Modern Japan: A Study of the Nobi Region). Tokyo: Sobunsha.

—— 1998. Rekishi jinko-gaku no sekai (An Introduction to the Historical Demography of Japan). Tokyo: Iwanami Shoten.

—— 2001. The Historical Demography of Pre-Modern Japan. Tokyo: University of Tokyo Press.

Hayami, Akira, and Emiko Ochiai. 2001. Household Structure and Demographic Factors in Pre-industrial Japan. *In* Asian Population History. Ts'ui-jung Liu et al., eds. pp. 395–415. Oxford: Oxford University Press.

Hikaku Kazoku-shi Gakkai, ed. 1996. Jiten kazoku (The Dictionary of the Family). Tokyo: Kobundo.

Kinoshita, Futoshi. 1995. Household Size, Household Structure, and Developmental Cycle of a Japanese Village: Eighteenth and Nineteenth Centuries. Journal of Family History 20:239–260.

—— 2002. Kindaika izen no nihon no jinkō to kazoku (Population and Family in Pre-Modern Japan). Kyoto: Minerva Shobo.

Kurihara, Hiroshi. 1994. Takamure Itsue no kon'in-josei-shizō no kenkyū (The Study of Takamure Itsue's Theory on Marriage and Women's History). Tokyo: Takashina Shoten.

Kurosu, Satomi, and Emiko Ochiai. 1995. Adoption as an Heirship Strategy under Demographic Constraints: A Case from Nineteenth-Century Japan. Journal of Family History 20:261–287.

Laslett, Peter. 1972. Introduction. *In* Household and Family in Past Time. Peter Laslett and Richard Wall, eds. pp. 1–89. Cambridge: Cambridge University Press.

—— 1983. Family and Household as Work Group and Kin Group: Areas of Traditional Europe Compared. *In* Family Forms in Historic Europe. Richard Wall, Jean Robin, and Peter Laslett, eds. pp. 513–63. Cambridge: Cambridge University Press.

Laslett, Peter, and Richard Wall, eds. 1972. Household and Family in Past Time. Cambridge: Cambridge University Press.

Lee, James, and Cameron Campbell. 1997. Fate and Fortune in Rural China. Cambridge: Cambridge University Press.

Maeda, Takashi. 1976. Ane-katoku (Eldest Daughter Succession). Osaka: Kansai University Press.

Mitterauer, Michael, and Reinhald Sieder. 1982. The European Family: Patriarchy to Partnership from the Middle Ages to the Present. Oxford: Oxford University Press.

Mizuno, Koichi. 1968. Multihousehold Compounds in Northeast Thailand. Asian Survey 8:842–852.

Morioka, Kiyomi, and Takashi Mochizuki. 1983. Atarashii kazoku shakaigaku (New Family Sociology). Tokyo: Baifukan.

Mouer, Ross, and Yoshio Sugimoto. 1990 [1986]. Images of Japanese Society. London and New York: Kegan Paul International.

Nagata, Mary Loise. 1999. Balancing Family Strategies and Individual Choice: Name Changing in Early Modern Japan. Japan Review 11:145.

Naito, Kanji. 1973. Masshi sōzoku no kenkyū (The Study of Ultimogeniture). Tokyo: Kobundo.

Nakane, Chie. 1964. Ie no kōzō bunseki (Analyzing Family Structure). *In* Ishida Eiichirō kyōju kanreki kinen ronbunshū (Sixty-First Anniversary Anthology of Ishida Eiichiro's Essays). Tokyo: Kadokawa Shoten.

—— 1967a. Kinship and Economic Organization in Rural Japan. London School of Economics Monographs on Social Anthropology 32. London: Athlone Press.

—— 1967b. Tate shakai no ningen kankei (Human Relations in a Vertical Society). Tokyo: Kodansha.

—— 1970. Kazoku no kōzō (Family Structure). Tokyo: University of Tokyo Press.

—— 1972. Japanese Society. [Trans. of Nakane 1967b.] Berkeley: University of California Press.

Nakazato, Hideki. 1998. Living Arrangements of the Elderly in Early Modern Japan: Effects of Marital Status and Age. *In* House and the Stem Family in Eurasian Perspective. Antoinette Fauve-Chamoux and Emiko Ochiai, eds. Proceedings of the C18 Session, the 12th International Economic History Congress, Madrid.

Narimatsu, Saeko. 1985. Kinsei tōhoku nōson no hitobito (Villagers in the Early Modern Northeast). Kyoto: Mineruba Shobō.

—— 1992. Edo jidai no tōhoku nōson (A Northeastern Village in the Edo Period). Tokyo: Dobunkan.

Ochiai, Emiko. 1995. To be Heirless in a Stem Family Society. Paper presented to the 18th Congress of Historical Sciences, Montreal.

—— 1997a. Were Japanese Women Working Outside?: Female Labor and Marriage in Northeastern Japan, 1716–1869. Paper presented to the Conference on Women's Employment, Marriage Age and Population Change, Delhi.

—— 1997b. Ushinawareta kazoku wo motomete (In Search of the Family We Have Lost). *In* Kazoku to sei (Family and Sex). Hayao Kawai et al., eds. pp. 35–57. Tokyo: Iwanami Shoten.

—— 1999a. The Reproductive Revolution at the End of the Tokugawa Period. *In* Woman and Class in Japanese History. Hitomi Tonomura, Haruko Wakita, and Ann Walthol, eds. pp. 187–215. Ann Arbor: University of Michigan Press.

—— 1999b. Retirement in Tokugawa Japan. Paper presented to the Annual Meeting of the Social Science History Association, Fort Worth.

—— 2000. Debates Over the *Ie* and the Stem Family: Orientalism East and West. Japan Review 12:105–127.

Omachi, Tokuzo. 1975. Omachi tokuzō chosaku-shū (Corpus of Omachi Tokuzo), vol. 1. Tokyo: Miraisha.

Omoto, Keiichi. ed. 1999. Interdisciplinary Perspective on the Origins of the Japanese. Kyoto: International Research Center for Japanese Studies.

Ota, Motoko, and Mikako Sawayama. In press. From Infanticide to Abortion: Government, Women, and Reproductive Culture in Tokugawa Japan. *In* Abortion, Infanticide and Reproductive Culture in Asia: Past and Present. Osamu Saito and James Lee, eds. Oxford: Oxford University Press.

Saito, Osamu. 1998. Two Kinds of Stem Family System? Traditional Japan and Europe Compared. Continuity and Change 13(1):167–186.

Somu-cho, Tokei-kyoku, ed. 1990. Setai kōzō to sono chiiki-sei (Household Structure and its Regional Patterns). Tokyo: Nihon Tōkei Kyōkai.

Takagi, Masao. 1986. Ninzu aratame cho wo mochiita kinsei tōhoku chihō nōmin kazoku no kōsei oyobi shūkiteki ritsudū ni kansuru kenkyū (The Study on the Composition and Cyclic Change of the Peasant Family in Early Modern Northeast Based on Population Registers). Final Report of Grants-in-Aid for Scientific Research.

——2002. Juhasseiki chūki tōhoku nōson no shichimotsu hōkōnin (Pawn Servants in the Mid-Eighteenth-Century Farming Villages of the Northeast). *In* Kindai ikoki no kazoku to rekishi (Family and History in the Modernization Process). Akira Hayami, ed. Kyoto: Mineruba Shobō.

Takeda, Akira. 1964. Minzoku kankō toshite no inkyo no kenkyū (The Study of Retirement as a Folk Practice). Tokyo: Miraisha.

Toda, Teizo. 1937. Kazoku kōsei (Family Composition). Tokyo: Kōbundo Shobō.

Todd, Emmanuel. 1990. L'Invention de l'Europe. Paris: Seuil.

Tsuya, Noriko, and Satomi Kurosu. 1999. Reproduction and Family Building Strategies in Eighteenth- and Nineteenth-Century Rural Japan: Evidence from Two Northeastern Villages. Paper presented at the 1999 PAA annual meeting, New York, March 25–27.

Verdon, Michel. 1979. The Stem Family: Toward a General Theory. Journal of Interdisciplinary History 10(1):87–105.

Wall, Richard. 1983. Introduction. *In* Family Forms in Historic Europe. Richard Wall, Jean Robin, and Peter Laslett, eds. Cambridge: Cambridge University Press.

Wall, Richard, Jean Robin, and Peter Laslett, eds. 1983. Family Forms in Historic Europe. Cambridge: Cambridge University Press.

Wolf, Arthur, and Susan Hanley. 1985. Introduction. *In* Family and Population in East Asian History. Susan Hanley and Arthur Wolf, eds. Stanford: Stanford University Press.

Yoshino, Kosaku. 1992. Cultural Nationalism in Contemporary Japan: A Sociological Enquiry. London and New York: Routledge.

23 Constrained Person and Creative Agent: A Dying Student's Narrative of Self and Others

Susan Orpett Long

For more than half a century, academic work on Japan has debated the relevance of a concept of person which is derived from the specific context of the European philosophical tradition. Are the Japanese premodern or postmodern "selves," or are they differentially shaped by a different culture or history? Do "Western" notions of self, individual, agency, and autonomy have meaning in Japan? The answers both Japanese and non-Japanese scholars propose to these questions again depend on the ideologies (or theories) they bring to bear on the issue.

My own view is that contemporary Japanese clearly have selves, individuality, and personhood, and that these are co-constructed with social life. People make choices in their lives that they may experience as relatively free or largely constrained. What characterizes modern societies is a heightened awareness of options and belief that we make free choices as individuals. Indeed, Giddens (1991) argues that, in late modern societies, we *must* make choices to construct a "self" that is socially recognized. Yet the belief that a decision is autonomous may itself be part of the social system, as critics of consumption-oriented mass society point out. Among the options that are available in society, significant limitations on the choices open to a particular person may also be due to historically and culturally specific understandings of sex, gender, age, and race, which may or may not be recognized by the person making the decision. These understandings have to do with differences in prestige and power; they are politicized and may be resisted or contested as well as accepted. The ideologies as well as the economic circumstances may change over time, thus creating new constellations of options for various social groups. Ultimately the physical body, too, limits choices, through size, strength, illness, and even death, yet even these are ultimately inseparable from changing meanings attributed to them (Lock 1993).

As people make choices among culturally limited options, they are not always rational or consistent. In other words, a series of decisions does not in itself constitute a sense of self, but rather the decisions, taken together, constitute the ingredients from which narratives of self are tentatively created. Both the choices and the narratives, however, are played out in relationships with others and in institutional contexts which provide social consequences (some severe), but always including validation, rejection, or proposed modification of the person's understanding of him- or herself (Plath 1980). Those consequences then become incorporated into the experiential raw material for continued self-definition. Yet this understanding of self is not only a matter of internal awareness. Because choices and narrative construction are social processes, people must be recognized not as determined by their culture (that is, *a* Japanese self), but rather as social persons whose actions impact the lives of others and the social institutions of which they are a part (Bourdieu 1977).

In this chapter, I will look at some of the ideas of self and person that have been proposed to understand Japan, beginning with some historical notions of self based on Confucian, Buddhist, and samurai understandings of the world. Social scientists writing about Japan in more recent times have frequently posited selves that are multiple, de-centered, and in motion. Some have emphasized that selves are constructed through negotiation, reflecting personal strategies, but also shaped by the gender, class, age, and other characteristics of the participants. I then present an example of partial narratives of self, as verbalized by a 21-year-old Japanese college student suffering from a terminal illness. The self that she relates is shaped by her age, her sex and gender identity, her social class, her "Japaneseness," and experience of being ill. In reviewing her story, I found that, in voicing a strong sense of self, she also conveys something about social agency in Japan. Despite severe restrictions on her personhood due to her illness, through the creative telling of her experiences, she reminds us of who she is in interaction with others, and that she remains a person engaged in action in the world.

HISTORICAL DISCOURSES ON SELF AND PERSONHOOD

Although we cannot hear what narratives of selfhood or personhood ordinary people in premodern times constructed, literature reveals the existence of a sense of subjective agency (Dissanayake 1996; Maraldo 1994). Religious and moral texts from earlier historical periods provide evidence for several different understandings of what a self *should* be. One view is associated with Confucianism. Although differing versions of Confucianism have been developed over the centuries, they have consistently focused on a social definition of self. In this conception, a human becomes a person through properly fulfilling social roles, that is, a person exists only in relation to others. I can only become who I am by acting as a proper daughter, wife, and mother, showing obedience, performing the tasks of the role, and making it one with my own desires. In contrast to European Enlightenment views of self, Confucian personhood is not located within the individual, nor is it based on reflection or autonomy. A self that insists on separateness from human bonds is selfish, and thus not fully human in a moral sense (see Smith 1983).

A second discourse on personhood comes from Buddhism, especially the Zen understanding of humans. As in the Confucian notion, self is located beyond the body; in contrast to Confucianism, Buddhism expects that the essence of a person continues past the death of the body by being reborn into other bodies. Buddhism, moreover, claims that any mindful sense of self is a delusion of separateness, for the true self is the unity of all things. Zen, in particular, thus rejects selfhood based upon reflection about the relation between a person and the larger world. To be human means to experience suffering, and the escape from that condition requires the awareness of "no-self" (Miller 1997).

The final historical discourse on the nature of personhood that I will mention is the privileged prescription for self-development of the warrior class of premodern times. This was the honor code, drawn in part from Zen and Confucian ideas, which valued loyalty, discipline, and sincerity. The ideal self was a strong one, forged through severe physical and mental training. Such training resulted in a strong spirit, or *seishin*, which was capable of loyalty and self-sacrifice. Thus, self-discipline transcended the self. Sincerity of action reflected the spirit of the person-in-the-world.

These discourses continue to be relevant in contemporary Japan, but as Allen (1997:4) points out, "we do not simply incorporate those [textual] images of particular self-constructions in a passive, static, completely deterministic manner. There remains the complex question of how such self-images are mediated, context-ualized, and reinterpreted." These historical discourses coexist with those of late modernity, including Christian, Enlightenment, and recent philosophical ideas originating in "the West." The extent to which these discourses are applicable to Japanese society has been much debated there, and how they are understood and appropriated by individuals of different life circumstances and ideological persuasions is important to understanding Japanese intellectual history in the 20th century.

JAPAN AND WESTERN EUROPEAN IDEAS OF THE SELF

In Europe, Protestantism and the Enlightenment emphasized the values of liberty and autonomy. The modern concept of self valued the world of the mind over the mundane existence of the physical body, and thus esteemed rationality and reflection. To become a person meant to establish intellectual and emotional independence from others. It is interesting to read of late 19th- and 20th-century Japanese intellectuals' response when they came into contact with these ideas. Writer Shimazaki Toson claimed to have found a self (an inner life) in reading Rousseau, expressing that he had been missing something prior to this discovery (Maraldo 1994). But others reacted with concerns for the social and political effects of the discovery of such a free self. Early Meiji period thinkers Fukuzawa Yukichi and Nakamura Keiu, for example, perhaps influenced by other discourses in spite of their European learning, argued that liberty must be constrained because it is "selfish" (Howland 2002: 97–107). Decades later, Japan's best-known political philosopher, Maruyama Masao (1965), recognized different ways in which individuals might relate to political life, but clearly equated individuation with "modern." Philosopher Watsuji Tetsuro

(1961), in contrast, explained that European and Asian cultures defined self differently due to differences in climate. In particular, he thought that the humidity and heavy rains experienced in Japan led to a self immersed in nature.

However, alternative understandings among European and US philosophers of different religious and political backgrounds also stressed a social self that was more in accord with native ideas of the self as emerging from relationships with others. Solomon (1994) points to the ideas of Hegel, Rousseau, P. E. Strawson, and Mark Johnson as falling within that tradition. Austrian-born Jewish philosopher Martin Buber and American social psychologist George Herbert Mead developed explicit models of how self develops in interaction. In Japan, Watsuji, who was familiar with the ideas of European philosophers as well as with Confucianism, advocated the notion that the Japanese self was one of *aidagara*, or "the space between" individuals rather than located within an individual mind. Mori Arimasa held that Japanese do not perceive themselves as an autonomous self interacting with an other, but rather see themselves as the "other" of the person with whom they are in a relationship (Maynard 1997:38–39).

Parkes (1997) describes the work of Nishitani Keiji, a Japanese philosopher who specialized in European philosophy, especially the nihilism of Nietzsche, but who incorporated Buddhist influences into his understanding of the relation of self to tradition. According to Nishitani, things and people (including tradition) that have been rejected as "other" can ultimately be seen as necessary for one's "becoming what one is," as part of one's fate (1997:136). Another philosopher trained in the European phenomenological tradition, Kojima Hiroshi (1998), defines self as incorporating two levels, a "serial I" which can distinguish itself from the physical body and is defined in interaction with other, and a "primal I," which experiences the self as the center of the universe and cannot reflect upon itself. Building on Buber, Kojima argues that these two levels of experience of self must be mediated by a fully reciprocal relation with a "you."

These accounts of subjectivity come from Japanese scholars of European philosophy (which draws on Judeo-Christian and Graeco-Roman world views), as they reflect upon their own experiences and a variety of discourses derived from Confucianism, Buddhism, and the warrior ethic. Their work has influenced the understandings of Western academics. Another approach to an interactive self by Japanese and Western scholars draws upon social psychology, especially the work of George Herbert Mead. American-trained psychiatrist Doi Takeo (1986) perceived the Japanese self as two-sided, a front (*omote*), which is presented to and interacts in the public sphere, and a back (*ura*), which is private. Others have discussed similar distinctions in terms of a continuum of inner (*uchi*) and outer (*soto*), or movement between true core (*honne*) and public expectations (*tatemae*) (Bachnik 1992; Roland 1997; Rosenberger 1992). Some have been explicitly influenced by postmodern and poststructural critiques of the Enlightenment "self," describing the self as "de-centered" and as "disciplined" by the power relations inherent in society.

Lebra (1992) develops the most detailed model of a multidimensional self based in interactionist sociology. She posits three dimensions of self in Japan: a multiple and variable "interactional self" which is presented to a "public" and which engages in reciprocal interaction; a complementary "inner self" which "provides a fixed core for self-identity and subjectivity" (1992:112); and a "boundless self" which transcends dichotomies such as subject–object and self–other, and offers a strategy for disengaging from the external and the internal worlds. These dimensions of self are interrelated, but the boundless self is the least regulated by culture, and is thus seen as the "purer" self. In a similar vein, Tada (1991) distinguishes *hito* (the social person based on a set of roles and statuses at a given point in time), *kojin* (the individual, the private being with individuated desires), and *jibun* (the detached, psychological self that mediates between the social demands on *hito* and the desires of *kojin*, generally suppressing individual desire).

Ethnographic studies in Japan provide evidence both that people have strong senses of self and that these are negotiated in interaction with others. Mathews (1996) asks how people define themselves as having meaningful lives and finds a variety of responses, from relatively public definitions such as workplace affiliation to more "inner" spiritual definitions of self. Rosenberger (2001) describes how Japanese women make meaningful choices from among socially defined options, moving back and forth from the public "front stage" to more private "backstage" places. She also notes a variety of "folk" concepts of self, in phrases such as *jibun ga nai* ("I don't have a self") or in notions such as developing one's self by experiencing as much as possible of life's variety (2001:227, 231). Lifestyle choices not only help formulate personal identities, but constitute "a discursive site where shifting priorities in Japanese society were negotiated" (Nakano 2000:95; see also McVeigh 2000). Kondo (1990) most explicitly incorporates gender and social class into her analysis of "crafting selves," as she shows how meanings are created and strategically negotiated in workplace relationships of unequal power.

Ideas of self in Japan thus insist that a person cannot be considered as a set of individual characteristics, but rather is inseparable from the power and meanings of social relationships. Choices are limited and experiences framed by cultural understandings of age, gender, and class, and it is from these that personal narratives of self are constructed, tried out in intimate and public settings, and subsequently modified (Plath 1980). These narratives then become part of the way that people act in the world and constitute social relations. Attributing social agency to persons links self and society, individual interpretation and cultural meaning, and provides a mechanism for social change.

INTRODUCTION TO MAYUMI

Narratives of self that are verbalized in ethnographic exchange are of course only partial. They are limited by time, by unconscious selection, and by conscious construction for the purpose of explanation to an outside researcher with her own agenda. When I conducted fieldwork in Japan in 1996, I was studying end-of-life decisions by listening to patients, family members, and medical staff talk about experiences of life-threatening illnesses. It was in this context that I met Mayumi, who at the time was a seriously ill 21-year-old college student. Before I met her, the physician who introduced us explained to me that she had a disease called primary pulmonary hypertension. Patients usually die about three years after symptoms appear, and Mayumi had been sick for two and a half years.

Knowing that patients with this disease are sometimes considered for a heart-lung transplant (which before Japan's 1997 Brain Death Law meant having the procedure done overseas), I asked whether that option had been considered for her. The doctor replied that yes, there had been some discussion early on. But for now, she had been accepted at a university, and wanted more than anything to experience college life. She was hospitalized this time because of a cold. Aware that cancer patients and others with terminal illnesses are not always told their diagnoses (Long 1999), I also asked if the patient knew how serious her illness was. The doctor responded that her parents knew the prognosis but that Mayumi herself had not been told.

Over a period of three and a half months, I visited with Mayumi in her private hospital room on eight occasions for varying lengths of time. The formality of the interview and the "heaviness" of its content depended on her wishes, her physical condition, and on what examinations and treatments the medical staff had planned for her that day. After the initial introduction from a physician at her hospital, I explained to her that I was interested in hearing the experiences and thoughts about the illnesses and treatments of people who were seriously ill. Mayumi made it clear that she agreed to participate not only to be helpful, but to ease the boredom of the hospital routine.

What follows is not a coherent narrative, but rather fragments that give us clues to her sense of who she is in the world. She was extremely articulate and appeared anxious to tell me her story. In it, we see the importance to her of her closest relationships and her ambivalence about her dependency on her family and doctors. Mayumi also makes us aware of the influence of her physical illness, sex, gender identity, age, social class, and "Japaneseness" on her definition of self, which constrained who she *might* become. It is also clear that she saw the presentation of this narrative of self as a means to act on the world, to be perceived in particular ways and to create meaning for herself despite her severely compromised ability to express agency. Although you will be reading this through my translation and selection, I present excerpts from our discussions to allow you to hear what she said as directly as possible. My own questions and comments are in italics when needed to provide context; editorial notes are in brackets.

MAYUMI'S STORY

Mayumi introduced herself by telling me that she was a student at a prestigious private university in a nearby city, majoring in English literature. She should have been in her fourth year, but had missed a lot of class due to her illness, so was behind. I then began to ask her about her illness experience.

> *What illness do you have?* Primary pulmonary hypertension. *How long have you had it?* Since I was a second-year student at the university – that was my first hospitalization. But that was when I got symptoms. When they looked at all my old X-rays from middle school and high school, it looks like I had the problem from back then. At first, I went to a small clinic [near my university] – I was living alone [in that city] while I went to school. [The doctor] said it was just a cold. But I didn't get better, so I went to City Hospital, where they thought I had a hole in my heart. I thought I'd come home and be examined.

I went to [a private university hospital]. That was my first hospitalization. They made this diagnosis, but couldn't do treatment. They didn't have a specialist in this disease there. So they referred me here [a public specialty hospital].[1]

Are the hospitals very different? They're very different environments. The other one was private. They brought our food in; here you have to go get your own. They say, "It's lunchtime." And even if you're sick you're supposed to go and get it. But there you had to clean your own room. The nurses would come in with a bucket. They'd wring out the rag for you, but you had to wipe around your stand and the window ledge yourself. It was a six-patient room, so they'd just wring out the rags and pass them out, "here, here, here" – like that. And if you didn't do a good job, they'd make you clean other things. That was my first time in the hospital, so I just figured that's how it is. But here the nurses come in every morning and wipe around and fix the bedding. It's great. Of course the food is terrible since it's a public hospital. I guess wherever you have your first experience, that becomes your standard. Maybe this food is normal for hospitals. There's a rotation, so you don't even have to take the lids off to know what's for dinner. I've never seen anything but white rice. But at the other hospital, they brought plain bread for breakfast and you had to toast it yourself, and there was only one toaster for the whole floor. The people at the end of the line had nothing to do but stand around and talk; they were green in the face before they got their breakfast! They wouldn't let you watch TV, and there was no TV in the lobby either. There was only one private room on the ward with its own TV. Everyone stood around the door to that room trying to listen during the sumo tournament. So the days were long. There was nothing to do except read books.

Do families visit? No, only patients who are very sick or in private rooms. Otherwise, the family doesn't help provide care for the patient.[2] So there's really nothing to do . . .

It's easier to talk to younger doctors, closer to my age; they know about university life . . . There are more young doctors at the university hospital, in their first few years out of medical school. Here, they're more in their thirties, but still close enough in age to talk to easily. Grand rounds is different. It makes everyone anxious because the "great doctor" comes around. He just goes thump, thump with his stethoscope. You wonder if they really are doing anything . . .

This illness that I have is not common. They don't know the cause – that's why it's called "primary." Usually I'm on oral medications. I'll start, probably today, on experimental drugs that are IV. I've had them before when I'm here. *Do they have an informed consent procedure for experimental drugs?* Yes, they explained everything very thoroughly. There are papers to sign. Since I'm over 20, I sign them myself. You have to sign if anything bad happens, you won't complain. It's a little scary.

Do you recognize yourself when you need to be hospitalized? What are your symptoms? Yes, I can tell. I feel really exhausted, fatigued. And my heart pounds. Usually, if I'm feeling okay, it's fine, but when I get tired, the pounding gets really strong. Also, people get a cough. I don't cough much, but when the condition is worse, people cough lot and get phlegm, because it's a lung problem. When I feel like that, I know I'll be admitted, so I don't want to go to the hospital. This time, I was only out two months. I was in four months and then had to come back after being home only two months.

. . . in the city where I live, they have a card to certify physical disability [*shintai shōgaisha kādo*] [that entitles me to medical and social service benefits]; that [program] helped pay for remodeling of our house because it's a two-story house and the stairs are too tiring for me. We put in a lift so I can sit and be lifted up the stairs. It cost ¥800,000 [about $7000].

What about your family? I have one brother. He works; his job is with computers. He lives at home. My father is an employee of a company related to automobiles. My mother was a middle-school English teacher. She worked all the way, even after she had kids, until I got sick. I have been able to go to the US twice for about a month each time through that connection. Also, my mother's older sister lives in LA because of her husband's business. So I have cousins who have grown up there. They have US citizenship and are bilingual. I understand English a little, but mostly they talk to me in Japanese; it's funny to hear them fight with their mother in English! *Do you fight with your parents?* Not lately, but when I was younger, we fought all the time.

At this point a portable X-ray machine was brought into the room for Mayumi, so I left.

Several days later, I checked at the nursing station to see if was all right to talk with her again. The nurse went in to ask her and returned saying it was all right. When I went in to the room, Mayumi said,

> Oh, I'm glad it's you. When the nurse came in and said the doctor wanted to talk with me, I thought it was going to be my regular doctor who had bad news to tell me about the test results. I get pretty bored here. It's tiring to read, and sometimes even to watch TV. The best thing is to listen to music.

We returned to our conversation of the previous day regarding her family relationships.

> When I was in middle and high school I was really rebellious. My brother, he's two years older than I, when he was that age he rebelled against my mother. But I fought with everyone – my mother, my father, and you should've heard the sibling fights my brother and I used to have! *Have the relationships changed since you got sick?* Since I've been sick, my brother has become kind. When I was younger, I used to always wish I was an only child; I would ask why he had been born! But now I'm so glad. I don't know if it would be the same if it were a younger sibling, but I'm really glad now I have an older brother. I don't think my relationship with my parents has changed much. My mother comes almost every day. Well, it's pretty close, too – only about 30 minutes by car. I feel badly. She has hobbies and things she likes to do, and I tell her she should just enjoy, I'll be okay. Sometimes she'll take a day off [from coming to the hospital] to take care of something, but she feels better if she can come and see that I'm eating and doing all right. My brother and father come sometimes too. Last night my father came for five minutes. Why bother for just five minutes? But he says he feels better if he can see my face. He doesn't go golfing on his days off now. And they don't take vacation. I told them they should go, the nurses are here to take care of me. So they took a two-day trip. But they said they just worry about me. I feel badly that everyone adjusts their schedules, their lives, to my being in the hospital.

She had a central line and was getting medications to "make my heart better." While I was there, her attending physician came in and said something about not starting the PGI until next week, which she later explained to me is the medicine that is put directly into the lungs. She also had liver failure. I asked if this was a different problem or related to the lung problems. She explained that it was related in some detail. Also, the nurse came in while I was there and adjusted the IV, and added in another liquid. People came to clean while she was telling me her boyfriend story (below), so she asked them to come back later; when they came back in about 15 minutes, she was still telling me the story, so she told them, "It's okay, don't clean today."

The IV machine makes a lot of noise, doesn't it! It's hard to sleep. I've gotten used to sleeping with the IV. I'm really careful with this (central line). It took about three months to get used to sleeping even with the IV in my arm. One night I knocked it out of my arm, so it was bleeding, and the medicine squirted out all over – it was a mess.

In another conversation we were discussing medical technology. I commented about different kinds of artificial hearts I had seen in Japan and the US. She asked,

They don't do heart transplants in Japan, do they? [They did not at that time because brain death had not achieved legal status.] Maybe we don't have the skills. *No, I think it's a matter of the law – the brain death issue.* Oh, yes, and there's the question of whether people will donate organs even if they do transplants. There's some feeling of separateness from others. But they now have bloodmobiles. They even come to my university. I think it's a good thing. Of course, some of the students come because they get juice to drink afterwards. "I'm thirsty," they'll say. I would give blood – but then, I don't know if my blood is healthy enough for anyone to want. But what do you think about brain death? ... *What about you?* I think if you don't have a chance of recovery, or if you couldn't recover consciousness, it would be all right if the family says, "Please take his organs," even if the heart is beating. After all, it won't hurt the patient. But it depends. It's really different though if the family asks as opposed to if the doctors come and say, well, he's basically dead so this is the time to take the organs. If the doctors say it, you don't know whether to believe it or not.

Later I asked her what she thought about telling a patient a diagnosis of terminal cancer.

I guess it depends on the person, if the family thinks they would want to know. It's quite a shock to hear, you know, when I was at the university hospital, I had the experience of the doctors telling me I would die within the year. *Really? What did they say?* The nurse came in and said the doctors wanted to talk with me. The young doctor, whenever I had asked, or talked about going back to the university, he just said, "Uh huh" and agreed. But this time, it was the senior doctor and the regular younger one. ... At first, the senior doctor just explained the illness – I had heard all that before, so was wondering what the big deal was. Then he said, "And it's really a bad situation." I asked about going back to school, and he said, "No you'd better quit school. You probably won't live more than a year." I think he was trying to be considerate, but I was shocked. I had been to the US two times for short times, and I really wanted to go back for a year. So I was working really hard so that I would qualify for the top-level exchange programs. I was in my second year then and I wanted to go in my third year. So I had studied really, really hard. I looked at the young doctor who had been saying "Uh huh, uh huh," and he just looked down. He knew he had not treated me right. ... I started crying and crying. I wanted more than anything to go back to the university – I had worked so hard. At that hospital, I was in a six-person room, so I couldn't go back in there. There was a private room open, so the nurse said I could stay in there for a while. I was so upset, I just cried and cried. Everything became black, like someone had pulled down a shade. I went over and opened the window and looked out. I was up on about the 10th floor. I looked down and saw the train tracks and thought about jumping ... Then a train came along and I thought that was perfect – to jump on the tracks, but then I realized that it would delay the train and that would cost a lot of money. Like when people jump on the tracks at a station, they have to pay a lot of money afterwards. I can remember thinking that so clearly even now. If it weren't for that train coming by just then ...

How did the blackness lighten? That's really a long story. I was going with this guy – I really liked him, enough to think maybe we would get married. Because of his family background and experiences when he was young, he couldn't trust [*shinrai dekinai*] anyone. I really wanted him to trust me; I thought if he could just trust one person, then he would gradually learn to trust others, and I thought he could come to trust me....When I got sick the first time, it was he who went with me to City Hospital, when I was told I had heart disease. And he said that didn't matter, that we would stick together no matter what happened. But when I came to the university hospital here and was told I'd be in for three to six months, and there were no guarantees that it might not be even longer, he didn't want to wait. He put on a look of innocence [*shiran-kao*] that he had even said such a thing...I heard from friends that he was playing around with other girls...And after I heard that about only having another year to live, after I was discharged (I was out of the hospital for about a month before being admitted here), we went out and were sitting in the car talking about it. I was crying, and he was crying too. But I realized later that he was crying because he felt sorry for himself. It was like I was his mother and just there to take care of him. That's what he wants – girls to meet his needs. He doesn't really trust or like anyone except himself....He was such a jerk!...He worked part time in a disco. He was that type. That meant that he didn't get off work until 4 a.m. and then we'd go out. But I was a student, and wanted to do well, so I went to the university every day at 9 a.m. *Did you sleep at all?* Even if I went to sleep, he'd come over and wake me when he got off work....When I think of that now, I wonder if that lifestyle [of not eating and sleeping] had something to do with my getting sick....[My brother] didn't like him. None of my friends did....Now I get so angry when I think about him. I hear that he's used the story to get sympathy from other women: "I was in love with a woman who went into the hospital and then changed her mind about me..."

...After [he said he wouldn't wait], I was totally cold, flat emotionally. I was okay on the surface. I could say good morning to the nurses pleasantly. I could talk to my friends. But I didn't feel anything. I forgot how to laugh. I was like that for a year – it was a year ago February that one day I just realized how stupid I had been to have gotten involved with him. So I went through a period of rehabilitation of the heart [*kokoro no riha-biri*]...

On another day a few weeks later:

I'm not doing real well – it's a kind of wave [indicates wave with her arms and points to lowest point]. I watch TV a lot lately, because if I listen to music I can't hear when people come in. But my eyes get tired from the TV. So I watch for a while, then rest, then watch, then rest. I don't really sleep. It's pretty boring. And you can't really sleep either, because once an hour or so someone's coming in to bring lunch or do a test or clean the room.

My birthday is in a few weeks too, and it looks like I'll be spending another one in the hospital! I spent my twentieth birthday in the hospital too. I missed Adult Day [when people turning 20 visit shrines and/or participate in civil ceremonies]. My grandmother had bought me a kimono and everything. I felt badly I couldn't even wear it for her.

About a week later, I visited Mayumi and found her studying English. She claimed it was material she had known for her college entrance exams but that she has since forgotten. I asked her how things were going.

The treatment seems to be going well. I haven't had many tests lately, so I don't know what effect it's having. It's been about a month now, so I probably have another month, or six weeks.

Do you have side effects when you're on it for a long time? Not so much that it's for long time, but there are some. It depends on the person. My face breaks out, like an allergic reaction. And the seal [around the central line] makes my neck itch. But my side effects are on the light side, I think. Some people get headaches or their joints hurt – it makes mine hurt just to think about it. The IV is 24 hours a day. The first time I expected to just have it in like two hours at a time. When I found out it was all day and all night, I was really resistant. I hated it. But now I'm used to it. But I couldn't believe it had to go all night. It felt like I couldn't move.

Will you go home when the treatment ends? I'm not sure. I'll probably be here for a while. It's really lonely to be in the hospital [at New Year]! No one's here. Anyone who's not attached to one of these machines wants to go home then. But I have this IV, so I don't go anywhere. I hope I can go home by then.

We talked about the difference between Japan and the US in the length of a patient's stay in the hospital.[3] When I told her about how quickly Americans are discharged from the hospital, she asked, "Can't you decline?" I explained that you'd have to pay yourself and that would be very expensive. "In Japan, if anything, they encourage you to stay a little longer. It must be hard to be sent home while it still hurts."

Later, we spoke about a recent earthquake in the area. We had been discussing baths:

It's not the same just to be wiped off. I wish I could take a bath. It would feel so good.... I was in the hospital here when the earthquake occurred. I had just been admitted the day before and I didn't sleep well because I was nauseous, so I was awake when it happened. It was really frightening. The higher up you are the more you feel the swaying, right. The locker was rattling and glass bottles were falling and breaking all around. I couldn't do anything. I couldn't move because I was attached to all these tubes. The worst part was to hear the nurses running around.... You wonder if the doctors would come back for patients. Well, in any case, they could only carry one patient. What about the people hooked up to machines like this? If you cut the lines, what happens to them?

My parents' house had cracks, and broken dishes, but that was all . . . *They must have been worried since you weren't with them.* They couldn't check on me because there was no transportation and no phones. So they came and stayed here with me in my room. *Your older brother too?* He came and they took turns.... One funny story – at my brother's friend's house, they had to get out. In the quake, the sugar bowl had spilled and the grandfather was picking up the sugar. They said, "Come on, Grandpa, we have to go, come quickly." And he said "But the sugar spilled. First I have to clean up." [laugh] Can you imagine him having to clean up first!

As I was leaving, Mayumi apologized she hadn't told me anything helpful for my research. I jokingly responded, "No, I've learned about how boring life in the hospital is." Mayumi replied, "If the topic is how boring hospital life is, I could write a thesis!"

On another visit, we were conversing casually. She expressed how frustrating it was to be so fatigued. She said she envies people who can just go all over energetically. She can't even use a computer because she can't sit up long enough to type without getting too tired. In the morning, if she tries to sit in a chair and study, her energy lasts only about one hour.

She also spoke of her grandparents. She seemed to feel closer to her grandparents on her mother's side, who are 82 and 84 and healthy. Her father's father died when she was about a year old; her father's mother lives with her oldest son in a nearby city. She commented how ironic it was that her grandparents were so healthy; her grandmother walks 3 kilometers a day in the park, while she can only lie in her hospital bed.

Several weeks later, the physician who had introduced me to Mayumi and her attending physician independently suggested to me that I be sure to stop in to see her. Treatment was not going as well as they had hoped. To my untrained eyes, Mayumi did not seem very different, although she was obviously tired. Mostly Mayumi asked me questions that day, about the United States and about my family. She told me that she had spent some time on her birthday with friends; they had a party in her hospital room. The friends brought a cake for the occasion. Our conversation ended when a friend carrying a large bouquet of flowers arrived to visit her. Mayumi commented that I had just missed her mother; that was too bad because she had wanted to meet me.

When I was preparing to return to the US, I wanted to tell Mayumi that I was leaving and thank her again for talking with me. The doctor told me that Mayumi was gradually getting worse, and that she was having a bad day, but that it would be alright to go in for a few minutes to say goodbye. When I approached her, she could barely talk above a whisper.

> When the doctor asked me about your coming in at first I said I wasn't feeling well so could you come another time. But when he said you were going back to the US soon, I said in that case, for sure tell you to come for a few minutes anyway.
>
> I've had a fever, from this weekend. *Is that why you have the ice bag on your head?* Yes, I have a headache. *Is this an example of the kind of wave you talked about?* This seems to be at the nadir of a wave. I hope it'll be going back soon – usually a few weeks. I have so many more things I'd like to talk to you about. When I feel better [*chōshi ga yoku nattara*, which does not distinguish between "if" and "when"], I'll write to you.

She told me to take care, and to give her regards to my family. The doctor later told me he wondered if she would make it another three months. That was the last time that I saw Mayumi, but in fact, the doctor's estimate turned out to be overly pessimistic. Although she remained in the hospital another ten months, Mayumi rode out that wave and was able to return to her family's home for more than two years. In early 2000 she caught another bad cold, which worsened her lung and heart condition. She was readmitted to the hospital for another long stay in early 2000, but this time the medicines were not as effective. She died in the fall of that year.

MAYUMI'S SENSE OF SELF

In these narrative fragments Mayumi expressed a great deal about her values, her world view, and her sense of self. Two themes to which she often referred were the boredom of hospital life and the symbolic opposition between cleanliness and "mess." We will return to these later.

What is most striking to me is the ambivalence she expressed about her personal relationships. She seemed to be struggling to find the appropriate balance between dependence on and independence from her family and physicians. At times, this was expressed as an anti-authority attitude, as when she described grand rounds or told her parents to go on vacation, that she would be fine. But when no one visited, she was bored and lonely, even turning off her music so that she could hear when someone came into the room. Some of her ambivalence may have been continuing adolescent challenging of relationships of authority. Yet in her case, the ambivalence was heightened by her extreme dependency due to illness. She could no longer climb stairs, so her family had to remodel their house at significant expense. She wanted reassurance that she was not forgotten during a natural disaster. Her desire for support and medical treatment conflicted with her wish not to be a burden on those caring for her, feelings expressed by adult patients of all ages whom I have interviewed over the years in Japan and in the US.

Mayumi's ambivalence surely was not due to a weak sense of herself as a separate person. She talked about having been rebellious as a young teenager, and about her dreams for the future of completing college and of living abroad. At such times, we get glimpses into what Rosenberger calls the "backstage" area of self. Perhaps the strongest indication of this is her awareness of her prognosis, which she apparently did not discuss with her family and of which her doctors thought she remained ignorant. Mayumi expressed the emotions of resentment, anger, trust, fear, love, and frustration, distinguishing physical from mental pain. She described a blackness as though a shade had been drawn on her life, but retained the ability to interact while feeling emotionally flat. Her ability to reflect on what had happened to her and to articulate her thoughts so eloquently corresponds to the modern, Enlightenment understanding of self. Mayumi was unusual among the seriously ill people I interviewed in Japan in that she was so young and so articulate. Yet like Mayumi, most of the people with whom I spoke reflected in similar ways on their illness experiences, could separate their emotions from an objectified understanding of their situation, and analyzed behavior and relationships.

Mayumi's words also indicate elements of a relational or interactional self. In meeting me, she first defined herself as a university student, then as a daughter and sister, and as a friend. She demonstrated the shifting from inner to outer relationships when she acknowledged gaps between what she was experiencing and what she said, for example when the doctor was doing the tests and she was upset about her boyfriend, or when she wanted company but told her parents not to visit. In her period of blackness, she still said good morning to the nurses. At those times we see her adjusting what Lebra calls her "presentational self" to the circumstances in an attempt to negotiate relationships, in those cases, to gain a greater sense of independence.

At other points in our conversations, the distinction between self and those to whom she felt closest seemed more blurred, as when she said she supported family decisions about organ donations or when she did not question her boyfriend's right to wake her up when he got off work to go party in the middle of the night, despite her commitment to getting to school the next day. She decided not to jump onto the train tracks because of the cost to her family. In criticizing her former boyfriend and the students who give blood because they want the juice they receive, she expressed a distaste for "selfishness," and talked as though establishing relations of trust with some small number of others is necessary to be a full human being.

MAYUMI'S PERSONHOOD

Mayumi had a sense of herself as embedded in a set of relations, family, and friends that constitute the *uchi*, or inner circle. Relations with her boyfriend and with the medical staffs were more variable, moving closer in or more distant (*soto*) with time and circumstances, as Bachnik (1992) describes. She clearly tried to negotiate these, to control the movement in or out, as she talked her parents into taking a short vacation or tried to establish relationships with the younger doctors who she thought would be able to relate to her. Through her relationships with her grandparents, she also gained a sense of herself in historic time. She had a sense of herself as a person with a past, a present, and goals for the future.

The meanings of age, social class, gender, and "Japaneseness" also influenced who Mayumi was. Despite being unable to attend school, she defined herself as a university student first, the characteristic role of someone of her age and social class in contemporary Japan.[4] How would she see herself if she were still alive at 28 but had not yet completed her college education because of her illness? Social class is also implicated in the jobs her parents and brother hold, her mother's ability to stop working when Mayumi became ill, and her own dreams of studying and living abroad based on two short visits to the US. The universal health insurance system and catastrophic illness coverage by the government meant that most of the cost of her medical care would not be borne by her family. Mayumi assumed a high standard of living for herself, including multiple televisions on a hospital ward, variety in diet, cleaning services, a private university education, and a single family home, and complained when those were not forthcoming. Yet her family was not wealthy enough to take costs for granted completely, as she indicated at several points in our discussions about the status of her disease and treatments within the insurance and social services system and her concerns about the financial cost to her family if she had committed suicide. Socioeconomic status constituted both conscious and unconscious influences on her view of herself and her relations to society.

Her chronological and relative age also defined her view of herself and her relationships. Beyond the age-appropriateness of being a student, she clearly had concerns characteristic of her young adult age: relations with a boyfriend, determining her degree of independence from her parents, re-establishing adult relationships with her brother. She was forced to take her newly achieved legal adulthood seriously when she was required to sign informed consent forms for her experimental medication, but found it "a little scary." She made reference to relative age as well. She grew up feeling resentful of an older sibling, but was later glad that he was older than she. She found it easy to talk with the younger doctors because their experiences were close to her own. She noted the irony that despite her youth, her grandparents were more active and energetic than she, using cultural expectations of age-appropriate activity to perceive her own difference from other young people.

Her gender also contributed to who Mayumi was, although this was addressed only indirectly. She pointed out, but did not challenge, the gender gap in her parents' caregiving, that her mother was the one to quit her job and that her father came for five-minute visits. She felt supported by both, recognizing their sacrifices to be with her. We did not discuss her career goals beyond college, but she seemed accepting of her mother's decision to continue to teach while raising children and having personal hobbies. What she challenged was the assumption of her former boyfriend that women exist merely to take care of men. ("It was like I was his mother and just there to take care of him. That's what he wants is girls to meet his needs.") Her experiences in this relationship helped to shape her attitudes, future relationships, and ways of being in the world.

For Mayumi, being Japanese was also a part of her identity, defined in opposition to America. Her visits to the US, her English-teaching mother, and her bilingual cousins fueled her passion for studying abroad and mastering English, providing a channel for her curiosity about the wider world. In her comment about Japan not doing cadaver organ transplants because Japanese doctors lack the necessary skills, she expressed a valuation of the US as higher than Japan, an attitude not uncommon in the post-World War II period, but increasingly questioned in recent years. We might thus interpret her steps to become more cosmopolitan as actions to develop her self as well.

The final influence to consider is Mayumi's experience of illness. As she responded to my questions, she reflected on the illness as something external to her self, describing physical symptoms and treatments with objectivity, learning when she would have to be hospitalized, and accepting physical dependency on the hospital staff and others. Yet the meaning of serious illness went well beyond that, to influence her understanding of herself as a person.[5] The illness involved suffering as a person as well as physical pain. It clearly altered her daily life and obstructed her goals, large and small, for her future. Not only could she not attend school, but she could not even wear the kimono her grandmother had bought for her when she reached adulthood. What does it mean to know that you will never accomplish what had appeared to be a modest, realistic goal? Being ill redefined relationships with her brother, friends, and former boyfriend. It placed her into a new social category, that of "physically disabled person" (as indicated by the receipt of the *shintai shōgaisha* card which made her eligible for benefits). People with disabilities have become increasingly visible and outspoken in Japanese society in recent years. They have written bestselling books and have established support and lobbying groups, although I do not know that Mayumi was in contact with any of them. It appears that she gradually incorporated these aspects of the illness into her sense of who she was. Several times in our conversations, she referred to herself as me-plus-machine, for example when she described the hospital over the New Years' holiday, "Anyone who's not attached to one of these machines wants to go home then. But I have this IV, so I don't go anywhere." That this is not mere description is suggested in her later hypothetical comment about patients during a natural disaster: "What about the people hooked up to machines like this. If you cut the lines, what happens to them?"

CONSTRAINTS AND AGENCY

From Mayumi's narrative, her personhood is evident. She had a self that had been shaped by her experiences in particular social relationships and by the meanings of characteristics such as age, gender, class, and nationality. But this was not a passive self that had been formed by others. Rather, she interpreted these experiences and used them to define who she was. Her actions presented some aspect of that definition to others as she navigated her social world and reached compatible understandings with others of things and relationships, resulting in feedback to the self. Yet Mayumi was not fully free to act according to that sense of self. In particular, her agency was limited by the physical conditions of her illness and by her dependency on others for expert knowledge and for care she could no longer supply herself. In turn, this inability to act as she would wish constrained the person she became.

Yet even in these extreme circumstances, Mayumi continued to negotiate who she was and attempted to maintain agency. She signed informed consent forms, she was aware of her prognosis, she considered and rejected suicide, and she continued to compose narratives of self. I do not know whether she confided these things to others as well as to me, or whether perhaps she expressed different feelings and experiences to different people. Possibly my questions elicited her confidences. Yet the day she apologized for not telling me anything helpful for my research, I had to acknowledge that she was no longer (if she ever was) talking to me to answer *my* questions but rather to entertain herself and compose her story. She sent the cleaning staff away, preferring "dirt" in the physical environment to an extended interruption of her narrative presentation.

In particular, I see her relationship with me as attempting to do three things in these circumstances in which she had so little control. First, she established continued social existence by negotiating a new relationship that was mutually satisfying. This relates to the theme of trust, which was so important to her sense of personhood. Her continual comments on boredom I think referred not only to her inability to do the more exciting things young people enjoy in life, but also to a deeper loneliness. She did not want to burden her family further, and doctors were often the bearers of bad news, yet she did not want to play her music if it would make her unaware of someone coming into the room. My visits broke the routine and offered companionship, if only for short periods.

Secondly, talking with me allowed her to maintain a sense of continuity with the self that had dreamed of more international experiences. I was not only a visitor or a researcher, but importantly for Mayumi, I was American. The day near the end of my fieldwork when she asked me questions about life in the US enabled me to recognize my importance to her as a link to that wider world she had wanted to know first-hand. Sitting in a hospital room talking about America was a close as she could get to fulfilling that dream, as even the energy for reading became difficult to muster.

Thirdly, in talking with me Mayumi continued the project of creating her self. Her narratives insisted that she was a social person with agency, insight, and emotions. She was a person with an active past, a thoughtful and lonely present, and dreams of a future. In our conversations she could verbalize her attempts to construct order out of her life experiences in ways that might be inappropriate in more usual contexts. She might complain about the hospital food to her parents or express her anger at her former boyfriend to her good friends. But having an uncritical outsider to listen allowed her to construct a different type of narrative, one that was designed to engage me in an ultimate claim to continued agency. I wonder whether creating this order out of her own experiences was related to the apprehension she expressed of dirt and disorder – medicine and blood squirting from IV lines; sponge baths rather than soaking in a deep tub; the blackness in which she could no longer smile or laugh; the crashing of glass bottles falling during an earthquake. She seemed to want some order, some normalcy, but one rich enough to still allow laughter at the extreme image of a grandpa putting sugar back into the bowl before evacuating in an emergency. Perhaps putting her story together for a foreign anthropologist had the right combination of human work and fantasy.

Conclusion

But why focus the questions of self, personhood, and agency around someone who is dying? I would argue that in many ways, despite her illness, Mayumi was not atypical in the ways that someone of her gender, age, social class, and nationality experienced the world in the 1990s. She expressed many values that have been identified with Japanese culture, such as the importance of relationships with an inner circle and an emphasis on cleanliness. Like most young people in Japan, she framed her experiences in a totally secular idiom and like many of her social class, looked beyond national borders to define what is Japanese. In contemporary Japan, people assume women should be educated and possibly hold responsible jobs, while retaining their roles as caregivers and nurturers. Like many young women, Mayumi accepted some assumptions about gender while challenging others.

However, Mayumi was obviously not a typical 21-year-old because of her illness. Because she was limited in her physical activity, she had had more time to reflect on her values and relationships. To experience serious illness is to experience disorder of meaning as well as of the body's physical functioning, and to feel out of control at a time when one wants it most. I believe that this led Mayumi to a stronger desire to claim agency through her narratives of self, and a better ability to articulate them thoughtfully. Her words present convincing evidence of a strong sense of self, both as person interacting with others and at a more private, reflective level. Thinking about Mayumi as a person with the social agency she claimed helps to distinguish between the stereotype of Japanese having no self at all and the reality of constraints on her personhood by circumstances such as illness. Characteristics shaped and limited her, but also encouraged a negotiation of self that involved creative agency. In enacting the self that she constructed, she faced constraints on her personhood, but she could still create broader social meaning and alter the behavior of others as they responded to her. Through creative agency, she retains a claim on continuing social being despite her dying.

ACKNOWLEDGMENTS

The author gratefully acknowledges the support of an Abe Fellowship of the Social Science Research Council and the Japan Foundation for her project on culture and end-of-life decisions in Japan. Jennifer Robertson and Mariana Ortega provided helpful comments on an earlier draft of this chapter.

NOTES

1   The Japanese medical system has a complex mix of public and private facilities for both ambulatory (out-patient) and in-patient care. A universal insurance program establishes rates of reimbursement for hospitals and physicians under the public and private insurance schemes that cover virtually the entire population. Patients may either go directly to a clinic or hospital of their choice, or be referred by a physician. The hospital where I met Mayumi is an exception in that patients must have a referral to be seen at this government-run specialty hospital.

2   Before the development of modern hospitals, the ill and frail received care in their homes from co-residing family members. In the 20th century, hospital nurses were seen primarily as helpers to the physicians, and the family was expected to provide a great deal of the patient's simple nursing care, or to hire a private duty aide to do so. In more recent decades, staffing standards have been raised so that most hospitals now provide "full service nursing," and the continual presence of family or private duty aide is no longer required. The meaning of family presence has thus shifted from one of obligatory, task-oriented presence to that of personal visiting. Since Mayumi later tells us that her mother comes nearly daily, I think we should interpret this to mean that the hospital handles her nursing care and that family need not be continually present. But she is also suggesting an emotional benefit to the patient of that "old-fashioned" obligatory caregiving. Merely "being there" continues to be an important part of the definition of a caregiver's role (Long and Harris 2000).

3   In 1999, the mean length of stay was 30.8 days in Japan and 7.1 days in the US.

4   The proportion of Japanese women who continue their education beyond high school at a college or university was 48.5 percent in 2001, about the same as for men.

5   This may be related to Ohnuki-Tierney's (1984) explication of *jibyō*, "my very own illness." However, Mayumi spoke of her illness more as an external phenomenon that constrained her, and was only gradually and reluctantly coming to see herself as "me plus illness."

REFERENCES

Allen, D. 1997. Social Constructions of Self: Some Asian, Marxist, and Feminist Critiques of Dominant Western Views of Self, Culture and Self. *In* Philosophical and Religious Perspectives, East and West. D. Allen, ed. pp. 3–26. Boulder, CO: Westview Press.

Bachnik, J. M. 1992. Kejime: Defining a Shifting Self in Multiple Organizational Modes. *In* Japanese Sense of Self. N. R. Rosenberger ed. pp. 152–172. Cambridge: Cambridge University Press.

Bourdieu, P. 1977. Outline of a Theory of Practice. Cambridge: Cambridge University Press.

Dissanayake, W. 1996. Self, Agency, and Cultural Knowledge: Reflections on Three Japanese Films. *In* Narratives of Agency: Self-Making in China, India, and Japan. W. Dissanayake, ed. pp. 178–201. Minneapolis: University of Minnesota Press.

Doi, T. 1986. The Anatomy of Self. Tokyo: Kodansha.

Giddens, A. 1991 Modernity and Self-Identity: Self and Society in the Late Modern Age Stanford: Stanford University Press.

Howland, D. R. 2002. Translating the West: Language and Political Reason in Nineteenth-Century Japan. Honolulu: University of Hawaii Press.

Kojima, H. 1998. On the Semantic Duplicity of the First Person "I." *In* Phenomenology in Japan. A. J. Steinbock, ed. pp. 83–96. Dordrecht, The Netherlands: Kluwer Academic Publishers.

Kondo, D. K. 1990. Crafting Selves: Power, Gender, and Discourses of Identity in a Japanese Workplace. Chicago: University of Chicago Press.

Lebra, T. S. 1992. Self in Japanese Culture. *In* Japanese Sense of Self. N. R. Rosenberger, ed. pp. 105–120. Cambridge: Cambridge University Press.

Lock, M. 1993. Encounters with Aging: Myths of Menopause in Japan and North America. Berkeley: University of California Press.

Long, S. O. 1999. Family Surrogacy and Cancer Disclosure in Japan. Journal of Palliative Care 15:331–342.

Long, S. O., and Harris, P. B. 2000. Gender and Elder Care: Social Change and the Role of the Caregiver in Japan. Social Science Japan Journal 3:21–36.

Maraldo, J. C. 1994. Rousseau, Hakuseki, and Hakuin: Paradigms of Self in Three Autobiographers. *In* Self as Person in Asian Theory and Practice. R. T. Ames, ed. pp. 57–82. Albany: State University of New York Press.

Maruyama, M. 1965. Patterns of Individuation and the Case of Japan: A Conceptual Scheme. *In* Changing Japanese Attitudes Toward Modernization. M. B. Jansen, ed. pp. 489–531. Princeton, NJ: Princeton University Press.

Mathews, G. 1996. What Makes Life Worth Living? How Japanese and Americans Make Sense of their Worlds. Berkeley: University of California Press.

Maynard, S. K. 1997. Japanese Communication: Language and Thought in Context. Honolulu: University of Hawaii Press.

McVeigh, B. J. 2000. Wearing Ideology: State, Schooling, and Self-Presentation in Japan. Oxford: Berg.

Miller, M. 1997. Views of Japanese Selfhood: Japanese and Western Perspectives. *In* Culture and Self: Philosophical and Religious Perspectives, East and West. D. Allen, ed. pp. 145–162. Boulder, CO: Westview Press.

Nakano, L. Y. 2000. Volunteering as a Lifestyle Choice: Negotiating Self-Identities in Japan. Ethnology 39(2000):93–107.

Ohnuki-Tierney, E. 1984. Illness and Culture in Contemporary Japan. Cambridge: Cambridge University Press.

Parkes, G. 1997. Nietzsche and Nishitani on Nihilism and Tradition. *In* Culture and Self: Philosophical and Religious Perspectives, East and West. D. Allen, ed. pp. 131–144. Boulder, CO: Westview Press.

Plath, D. W. 1980. Long Engagements: Maturity in Modern Japan. Stanford: Stanford University Press.

Roland, A. 1997. How Universal is Psychoanalysis? The Self in India, Japan, and the United States. *In* Culture and Self: Philosophical and Religious Perspectives, East and West. D. Allen, ed. pp. 27–42. Boulder, CO: Westview Press.

Rosenberger, N. R. 1992. Introduction. *In* Japanese Sense of Self. N. R. Rosenberger, ed. pp. 1–20. Cambridge: Cambridge University Press.

——2001. Gambling with Virtue: Japanese Women and the Search for Self in a Changing Nation. Honolulu: University of Hawaii Press.

Smith, R. J. 1983. Japanese Society: Tradition, Self, and the Social Order. Cambridge: Cambridge University Press.

Solomon, R. C. 1994. Recapturing Personal Identity. *In* Self as Person in Asian Theory and Practice. R. T. Ames, ed. pp. 7–34. Albany: State University of New York Press.

Tada, E. 1991. Maintaining a Balance: Between *Hito* (Person) and *Kojin* (Individual) in a Japanese Farming Community. Ph.D. dissertation, University of California, San Diego.

Watsuji, T. 1961. Climate and Culture: A Philosophical Study. G. Bownas, trans. New York: Greenwood Press.

SUGGESTED READING

Allen, D., with A. Malhotra, eds. 1997. Culture and Self: Philosophical and Religious Perspectives, East and West. Boulder, CO: Westview Press.

Ames, R. T., with W. Dissanayake and T. P. Kasulis, eds. 1994. Self as Person in Asian Theory and Practice. Albany: State University of New York Press.

Bachnik, Jane M., and Charles J. Quinn Jr., eds. 1994. Situated Meaning: Inside and Outside in Japanese Self, Society, and Language. Princeton: Princeton University Press.

Dissanayake, W., ed. 1996. Narratives of Agency: Self-Making in China, India, and Japan. Minneapolis: University of Minnesota Press.

Kasulis, T. P. 1994. Researching the Strata of the Japanese Self. *In* Self as Person in Asian Theory and Practice. R. T. Ames, with W. Dissanayake and T. P. Kasulis, eds. pp. 89–106. Albany: State University of New York Press.

Moeran, B. 1986. Individual, Group and *Seishin*: Japan's Internal Cultural Debate. *In* Japanese Culture and Behavior, revised edn. T. S. Lebra and W. P. Lebra, eds. pp. 62–79. Honolulu: University of Hawaii Press.

Nakamura, H. 1964. Ways of Thinking of Eastern Peoples. P. P. Wiener, ed. Honolulu: University of Hawaii Press.

Suzuki, T. 1986. Language and Behavior in Japan: The Conceptualization of Personal Relations. *In* Japanese Culture and Behavior, revised edn. T. S. Lebra and W. P. Lebra, eds. pp. 142–157. Honolulu: University of Hawaii Press.

24 Nation, Citizenship, and Cinema

CHAPTER 24

Aaron Gerow

Scholars have grappled with many difficult terms in studying Japan – modernization, Westernization, feudalism – but "the one term which seldom appears to need discussion is the word 'Japan'" (Morris-Suzuki 1998:9). "Japan" is not only the name of a discipline, Japanese Studies, but refers to an entity that most take for granted. Japan is an island nation-state, its borders clearly delineated by ocean and sea, lacking the geographical porousness that characterizes other countries. This seclusion is thought to be a primary factor in fostering a people, language, and culture that, even with occasional influxes of foreign practices, has managed to develop an outward homogeneity, alleged to be unique in the world, by adopting external things on its own terms. The Tokugawa period (1603–1868) policy of seclusion (*sakoku*) and the fact that Japan has never been colonized are often cited as critical factors informing this apparent freedom to self-cultivate, just as the purportedly unbroken imperial line symbolizes the ancient continuity of things Japanese. When it comes to establishing who is Japanese, most people inside and outside Japan possess an unquestioned definition that combines race, language, and culture.

Although the image of a tall, blond, blue-eyed "white" person introducing himself in English as "Japanese" does not fit anyone's image of the typical Japanese citizen, there are such individuals. Early in 2002, Marutei Tsurunen, a Finn who acquired Japanese citizenship, became a member of the Japanese Diet. This is not merely an unprecedented exception to the rule of a (visually) homogeneous Japan. In an age of globalization where population flows are changing the ethnic map, even Japan is confronting the fact that other peoples and cultures are living within the nation's geographic domain and affecting Japanese culture(s). This is a problem that challenged the Japanese during the period of imperial expansion from the late 19th century through 1945. At that time, non-Japanese were hierarchically assimilated as Japanese imperial subjects under the ideology of the family-state, rendering them branches of the main "family" (Oguma 2002). Today's transnational flows threaten such clear-cut divisions. Global forces that transcend the borders of the nation-state (e.g., the European Union, multinational corporations, transnational media) are prompting many ethnic and other groups around the world to question accepted national and ethnic identities and to assert their difference(s) from the supposedly unified whole. In Japan, this is evident in the efforts of the Ainu of Hokkaido, Okinawans, resident Koreans and Chinese, peoples affected by environmental pollution and atomic radiation, and women in general to challenge and disturb dominant, masculinist, homogenizing definitions of collective identity.

Such assertions of heterogeneity have been accompanied by scholarly reappraisals of the nation. Many have come to question the long-held assertion that nations are the normal divisions of humankind, thus challenging the belief that the borders of a people, and the resulting sense of collective identity, are ancient and natural. Attention to the nation has also been sparked by examples of the violence of nationalism around the world. Yet, even these proofs that the nation is far from dead are taken by many as evidence that the nation is in crisis, in need of ever more violence to protect and maintain itself against global forces. If research up until the 1960s could still believe in the promise of the nation, since then most scholars have become disillusioned with that prospect. While recognizing the reality and materiality of nations, they seek to demystify and deconstruct the legends and premises of the nation.

In this chapter I will briefly outline the fundamental positions in recent studies of nation and citizenship and locate them with regard to contemporary discussions of the nation in Japan. Much of the new scholarship on the Japanese nation is deeply informed by the work of foreign scholars, which in turn has been adapted to the particular ideologies of the Japanese nation. To help focus the discussion, I will offer examples from my area of expertise, Japanese national cinema.

HISTORICIZING JAPAN

If the primary question of early studies of nation and citizenship was "*What* is a nation?" (Renan 1996), the query now is "*When* is a nation?" (Conner 1990). Far from assuming that national collectivities are ancient or natural, examinations of the nation have increasingly focused on the historical processes that created and naturalized the nation and its collective impressions. In most cases, this approach questions the histories nations themselves produce which locate the essence of the present in the past (establishing the continuity of the nation) while also arguing a temporal progression in which the present – the current nation – perfects that past. Historicizing the nation challenges such teleologies by countering continuities with ruptures and by examining how contemporary necessities, more than accounts of actual historical events, shape essential pasts and narratives of progress.

The nation is thus seen as a historical, not a trans-historical, construction. If one considers a nation to be a matter of consciousness (for example, believing oneself to be Japanese first, Okinawan second) of the majority (nations being a mass, not an elitist phenomenon), then even some European countries only became nations in the 20th century, if at all. This is an example of what Anthony D. Smith calls the "modernist" thesis: the argument that nations are not ancient phenomena, but are fundamentally products of modernity (Smith 1986). There are different versions of this thesis, but most agree that nations differ from earlier ethnic or religious communities in their degree of unified self-consciousness, political sovereignty, and secular authority. The modernist thesis has not been without its detractors, even among those sympathetic to it. Its Eurocentrism has prompted some to argue that the modernist thesis essentially closes off all the political possibilities of nationalism, deconstructing it before those without power in the world system have had the chance to use it against those who do. Others have charged that the modernist thesis, while intended as a critique of nationalism, nonetheless legitimizes the nation by linking it with industrial progress and development.

Much recent scholarship, however, by both Japanese and non-Japanese, has found a political imperative behind arguing for the modern, constructed character of the Japanese nation. Eric Hobsbawm's call for consciousness of the nationalist function of historiography, noting how, while ostensibly operating as a disinterested discipline, it has played an essential role in the construction of the nation (Hobsbawm 1983), resonates in Japan. Numerous fields of research, from linguistics to ethnology, and from philosophy to literary criticism, have not only fostered the imagination of an eternal, homogeneous Japan, but also quite literally have abetted domestic authoritarianism and the violent colonialist imperialism of militarist nationalism. There has been a surfeit of such scholarship on the nation over the last century or so, and it continues today, albeit in seemingly more benign forms. The 1970s boom in such *nihonjinron*, or theories of Japanese uniqueness, produced many works of dubious scholarly value, yet their commercial success testifies to the genre's widespread popularity and influence (both within and outside of Japan). While providing Japan, Inc., with the ideologies to mobilize corporate warriors and fend off foreign imports, *nihonjinron* is also a repressive device responding to social unease. Defining the essence of Japaneseness in, for instance, harmonious group behavior not only effaces the long history of social protest in Japan, but also dismisses protest as foreign to the national spirit, thereby rendering allegations of "un-Japaneseness" (*nihonjin-rashukunai*) a powerful force in preserving the status quo.

Deeply aware of this legacy, not a few present-day researchers have looked upon the modernist thesis as another powerful tool, both scholarly and political, in the struggle against essentialism and nationalism. Building on the earlier critiques of Japanist ideology by the philosopher Tosaka Jun, the intellectual historian Maruyama Masao, and other scholars, researchers are adapting the work of Eric Hobsbawm and Benedict Anderson to help dismantle the discourse of Japan as an ancient, homogeneous nation. While this scholarship is widespread, I will focus here on three primary arguments: the modernity of the Japanese language, the assertion of difference within Japan, and the deconstruction of the ideology of *kokutai* (organic national polity).

First is the argument that the creation of a national language was a primary means of shaping Japan as a nation. Within a larger emphasis on the discursive character of the nation, much European research on the modernity of nations focuses on the fabrication of national languages as a central part of nation-building. When Anderson (1983) wrote of the nation as an "imagined community," he was not referring to a "fake" or "fictional" community but both to the psychological dimension of nationhood (for instance, the willingness to die for people one has not met) and to the fact that the nation owes much of its existence to the words, signs, and symbols that constitute and shape its conceptualization. Individuals identify themselves with the national collective with flags and anthems as well as everyday patterns of speech, dress, and behavior that render nationalism so mundane an experience that it seems natural. Seeing the nation as discursive emboldens us to look at it in terms of the languages and signifying systems that represent it and shape people's thought and behavior. Many scholars stress the central role of elites, and especially intellectuals, in nation formation, either as model "citizens" or as government bureaucrats.

Perceiving the nation through language and discourse, however, reminds us how much it is "a deep, horizontal comradeship" (Anderson 1983:16) and not merely a false consciousness imposed from above. Anderson points out that the national expression of this linguistic comradeship only became possible in recent times. Earlier imagined communities, such as the Catholic Church, in which Latin was never the lingua franca, gave way to modern nations when vernacular languages were transformed into the lingua franca of the community, a process facilitated through print capitalism. The mass marketing of publications not only demands a mass audience that shares the same language, but also encourages and effects the creation of a new standardized, national language. Based in part on his research in and on Indonesia, Anderson further argues that what is experienced in these print-based languages is a new, modern sense of time. As is especially the case with newspapers, the citizenry develop a sense that they are reading the same texts simultaneously with others in the community, creating a shared but limited spatio-temporal discursive field.

The creation of a national language was also a serious matter addressed by the Meiji state. Significant linguistic differences exist between peoples in Japan, ranging from regional dialects to the entirely different languages spoken by Ainu and Okinawans. With respect to literacy, fin-de-siècle male elites often wrote in Chinese (*kanbun*), and even "Japanese"-style writing made use of archaic words, declensions, and set phrases no longer found in contemporary, everyday speech. The lack of a common language was an obstacle to nation formation, and created communication problems in the new national bureaucracy and conscript army, hampering the distribution of fresh symbols of unity. A standard language (*hyōjungo*) was a necessity, but the precise nature of this language was the subject of serious debate and involved tortuous selection procedures. "Tokyo Japanese" was eventually chosen as the linguistic model for the nation, and "unJapanese" languages, such as Okinawan, were suppressed, sometimes brutally. Historian Sakai Naoki (1996) has described this process as one in which difference and multiplicity were suppressed and labeled "foreign." Linguistic historian Lee Yeounsuk (1996) has argued that the act of creating a standard language was not simply a process of transforming Japanese into a national language (*kokugo*), but rather the reverse: a national language was established and "Japanese" was then molded to fit that.

Following Anderson, literary scholar Karatani Kôjin (1993) emphasizes the role of literature in nation-building, especially through the *genbun itchi* movement that attempted to unify (*itchi*) the spoken (*gen*) and written (*bun*) languages. The degree to which Japan was a modern invention is underlined by the fact that the proponents of this movement were members of the defeated People's Rights Movement (Jiyū minken undō). Standardized Japanese was less a matter of making writing conform to speech than of creating a new national language through writing. Important in the process, Karatani argues, is the way *genbun itchi* transformed language from an external play of signs into a form of internal expression, a metamorphosis that molded an internal subject through which the nation could be expressed. Ri Takanori (1996), a scholar of Japanese cultural history, expands on Karatani's thesis by showing how *genbun itchi* and other Meiji period transformations in representation created the anonymous landscape that was necessary for the generation of the deep, horizontal community of the nation.

A second argument about the Japanese nation focuses on the differences camouflaged by the hypothesis of an ancient national homogeneity. Influential in this project has been the work of the historian Amino Yoshihiko (1998), who has stressed differences, especially in ancient history, posed by marginal groups such as women, outcastes, the aged, and children, and by regional oppositions. Amino contests the unchanging meaning of even the terms "Japan" (*nihon*) and "emperor" (*tennō*): not only did they not exist before the late seventh century, but the elites of eastern and northern Japan did not even consider themselves part of "Japan" until much later. Few non-elites felt emotional loyalty to "Japan" up until the mid-Meiji period, as regional and class differences in culture and language took precedence over any "national" allegiance. The Meiji leaders were acutely aware of this and thus, seeking to fortify the nation against encroaching Western powers, used the media, education, the military, and the legal system to construct a unified nation under the central symbol of the emperor (Gluck 1985). What came to represent Japanese culture – the vertical, extended patriarchal familial structure of the *ie* system – was thus often unrepresentative of all elements of Japan at all times, and thus fundamentally a modern construction (see the essays in Vlastos 1998; see also chapter 22 in this volume). As Eric Hobsbawm and others have pointed out, one of the central paradoxes of nationalism is the use of the past to create a modern entity.

Inventing the new nation also involved changing its frontiers and ways of conceiving difference. Historian Tessa Morris-Suzuki (1998) has observed that, during the Tokugawa period, the capital Edo (now Tokyo) was at the center of concentric circles of geographic relationships: the further away from Edo, the more foreign people and places were. Thus, the Ainu of Hokkaido and Ryūkyūans (Okinawans) served to reinforce the integrity of the center or core (which may partly explain why the Ainu were prohibited from learning Japanese during that period) (see chapters 6 and 7 in this volume). The importation of modern ideas of nation and civilization in the Meiji period not only introduced the concept of clearly demarcated geopolitical borders (as opposed to concentric circles), but also reconstructed as temporal differences what had been thought of as spatial differences. Thus, the Ainu came to be viewed as an atavistic or prototypical kind of Japanese in need of civilizing. From the late 19th century onward, the Ainu and Okinawans were subjected to assimilation within a more totalizing vision of Japanese civilization that included language and lifestyle. Whereas – until Russia's defeat in the Russo-Japanese War (1904–05) – Euro-American states categorized Japan as a backward nation, the Japanese situated themselves at the center of a more local universe in which the Ainu and Okinawans were marked as primitive others.

As long as the Japanese defined themselves through such developmental differences, the distinctions remained intact; Ainu were compelled to catch up with the Japanese, thereby confirming Japan's modern and model status, but never to the point of actually *being* Japanese. The colonization of Hokkaido and the Ryūkyū Islands, together with the assimilation of Ainu and Okinawans was a proving ground and precedent for Japanese imperialist aggression in Asia and the Pacific. The subjugation of the Ainu and Ryūkyūans also served to clarify and unify Japanese national identity. The temporal definition of Japan as a modern nation coexisted with a spatial view of its eternal, ethnic foundation, a fundamental contradiction that was obfuscated by early Japanese ethnographers (see related chapters 2, 3, and 13 in this volume). By representing the Ainu and Okinawans as the timeless embodiment of what "original" Japanese were in the past, ethnographers such as Yanagita Kunio and Origuchi Shinobu effectively removed them from history. They did so in part as a critique of a rapidly modernizing Japan, but as a result also confirmed the popular perception of Okinawans and the Ainu as perpetually backward (Morris-Suzuki 1998; see also Christy 1993). Studies like those of Amino (1998) have not only shown how the Japanese nation by definition hides ethnic differences, but also how it needs and even reproduces the active discrimination of others as a key variable in national self-definition (cf. Robertson 2001 [1998]:91–111).

Third, the Japanese nation has been critiqued from within through a deconstructive analysis of its fundamental contradictions. Such work has been informed by scholars such as Homi Bhabha (1990) and others, who apply poststructuralist conceptions of discourse in approaching the nation as a text or narration. Smith (1986), for example, conceives of the historicity of the nation through the continuity of the "ethnie" of a people, or the shared meanings and experiences crystallized in the nation's myth-symbol complex that allegedly do not change fundamentally over time. Bhabha, however, sees such texts not as unified, but rather as interlaced by difference, contradiction, and indeterminacy. Just as the process of signification is never completed but endlessly deferred in a text, the nation is a fundamentally transitional entity, a Janus-faced sign ambivalently posed on the liminal border between such oppositions as public and private, rational and irrational, progression and regression. Literary analysis shows that texts *signify* – as opposed to presenting their own meaning – through intertextual relations of similarity and difference. Similarly, Bhabha locates the significance of nations in *inter*-nationality, or in the margins and spaces between nations. In this sense, nations are always global despite their pretensions to self-determination, for they are defined by relations of difference. Bhabha's conception of discourse allows him to deconstruct the nation by focusing on elements that are "other" to the community, either within or without that country's borders. Nations create themselves by declaring what they are not, and by marginalizing and excluding what does not fit. An examination of the excluded elements can tell us much about the core nature of the nation. Research on marginalized groups can illuminate the often contradictory logic of this exclusion; that is, the idea that a necessary exclusion nonetheless makes the excluded essential to the nation. Such research can also uncover the varied counter-narratives offered by marginalized peoples themselves.

Japanese scholars of intellectual history have focused their critical attention on the narrative of the nation, highlighting the contradictions and forms of exclusion it enables. Kang Sang-jung (2001), for instance, traces the contradictions of *kokutai*, from its use by the *kokugaku* (native/national learning) scholar Motoori Norinaga (1730–1801) and the Mito School nationalist Aizawa Seishisai (1781–1863), to its deployment in the postwar period. Norinaga located an original Japan in *yamato kotoba*, an ur-Japanese language that he thought pre-dated the importation of

Chinese writing, and in the sentiment known as *mono no aware* (the pathos of things) best expressed through *yamato kotoba*. In a sense, he was evoking an interiorized esthetic Japaneseness separate from the public world of politics. Following Maruyama, Kang sees this as a central duality in the Japanese *kokutai*, which operates as both a political entity demanding loyalty to the state and an esthetic realm of feeling. When the passive, esthetic appreciation of natural things is equated with the recognition of the work of Shinto *kami* (native spirits or gods who dwell in animate and inanimate things alike) and the emperor (a grand *kami*), the esthetic is thereby politicized. The *kokutai* demands a citizenry defined not as a "people" (*jinmin*) possessing natural rights, but as "subjects" (*shinmin*) whose rights issue from the grace of the emperor (Morris-Suzuki 1998). By the same token, *kokutai* logic renders every action taken by the state, including war, to be an esthetic and naturally occurring outcome. The circularity of this logic, which essentially treats any action as already given, inheres in the self-referentiality of *kokutai*, which defines itself by itself, through denying the necessity of the other. Thus, Norinaga's denial of Chinese script makes possible his discovery of "pure" Japanese words, even though that script was the means of expressing that discovery. Of course, as Kang emphasizes, such tautologies underscore just why *kokutai* is never (and can never be) fully defined; in some sense, *kokutai* epitomizes indefinability.

Kang's critical analysis aims at the possibility of rupturing the *kokutai* from either within or without, but he also warns that its emptiness makes *kokutai* an extremely flexible concept. *Kokutai no hongi* (Principles of the National Polity; 1937), one of the central texts of Japanese fascism, almost parasitically absorbs contradictions in promoting the universality of the emperor system (*tennōsei*). Similarly, historical anthropologist Jennifer Robertson emphasizes the illustrative homology between the practice of cross-dressing and "cross-ethnicking" in wartime theater, and *dōka*, the colonial policy of assimilating non-Japanese within a Japanist domain of pan-Asianism. She argues that, by "strategically assuming a protean or hybrid character itself, the Japanese nation neutralized the anxiety about hybridity that can accompany colonialism…in effect subverting the possibility of subversion (Robertson 2001 [1998]:93). Such an adaptable *kokutai* also explains how, even after Japan's defeat, the notion of the *kokutai* could continue up to the present time as a hybrid, Japanese–American model. Its very flexibility alludes to the difficulty of deconstructing the ambivalent and protean nation.

THE CONSTRUCTION OF "JAPANESE CINEMA"

Thus far I have provided a broad view of the scholarship on the (Japanese) nation. I now wish to elaborate on aspects of that scholarship in the context of Japanese cinema. Even when not specifically addressing the subject of nationalist cinema (e.g., wartime propaganda), there is a tendency for film scholars to connect Japanese cinema to the Japanese nation. In some ways, this is to be expected: Japanese films are made in Japan and feature Japanese people speaking Japanese. Yet the tendency to delimit a cinematic corpus on the basis of national boundaries, together with the use of films to highlight aspects of Japanese history, culture, *mentalité*, and/or religion indicates how tenaciously we read films through the nation and read the nation through films.

The relationship of film and nation is actually quite complex. For instance, does the cinema merely reflect the nation or does it actually help construct it? What follows is my exploration of how much the modernity, the indeterminacy, and/or the contradictions of the nation shape and are shaped by specifically cinematic issues.

Many histories of Japanese cinema begin with the technology's importation into Japan in the late 1890s; they then jump to the late 1910s and the emergence of the Pure Film Movement (Jun'eigageki undō), under whose auspices were produced what were termed the first truly cinematic films in Japan. In that sense, their histories begin less with the first films in Japan than with the first cinematic films. How do film historians as well as those filmmakers involved with the Pure Film Movement conceptualize cinema? At a time when state authorities regarded the new medium with suspicion, intellectual film critics dismissed earlier Japanese cinema as "uncinematic" for relying on theatrical conventions such as *onnagata* (males who perform as women in the Kabuki and other theaters) to act the parts of women, and *benshi* (narrators of silent films) to provide the storyline. Cinematic works, they said, should develop narratives independently through such visual devices as editing and the close-up. European and, especially, American cinema were cited as models of "pure film," against which Japanese films were harshly criticized. Crucial to understanding the early 20th-century zeitgeist is the fact that films featuring Japanese stories or casting Japanese actors, such as Hayakawa Sessue, were being produced by American and European companies at the time. The response of Japanese critics to these films was complex. On the one hand, while criticizing their often blatant Orientalism, critics could not help but admire their cinematicity when compared to domestic films. On the other hand, although they accused foreign filmmakers of stealing Japanese stories, they directed most of their rancor at Japanese film companies. The latter, according to the critics, only produced one print of their films instead of releasing them to a world market. What is more, the critics continued, Japanese film companies targeted mostly lower-class audiences who seemed incapable of understanding films without the aid of a *benshi*. They recommended exporting Japanese films that could represent the nation; however, as they argued, Japanese films could only be exported provided they were intelligible to foreign viewers, and provided they "spoke" the same cinematic language as American and European films, a language that most critics felt was universal and culturally neutral (Gerow 1998). Thus, the directors of some of the first truly "cinematic" Japanese films produced under the auspices of the Pure Film Movement described their efforts as the production of Japanese "translations" (*hon'an*) of American film.

Several patterns emerge here that would later come to dominate Japanese cinema history. First, Japanese cinema is often defined from without. Not only does true cinema supposedly exist outside Japan, but the "logic of exports" anoints the foreign spectator as the ultimate judge of what is acceptable or of what counts as Japanese cinema. According to this logic, Japan exists only in the mirror of Western knowledge, and, by extension, assertions of the uniqueness of the Japanese nation rely on Euro-American definitions. This tautology is a consequence of both the global nature of the nation and Japan's – and Japanese cinema's – subordinate position in a Eurocentric hierarchy of nations and the world film market, which is often homologous to that hierarchy. Even in the wartime period (1931–45), film critics such as Hazumi Tsuneo regarded the slow tempo of Japanese films as a manifestation of national character, but recommended that the tempo be speeded up, as if to render Japan itself more cinematic (Gerow 2002).

Second, Japanese cinema is both the product of and represents a break from the past. Far from being the outgrowth of historical esthetic and theatrical traditions as argued by Noël Burch and others (see Burch 1979), the origin of Japanese cinema is found in filmmakers' pointed rejection of certain dramaturgical practices, such as *onnagata* and *benshi*. While conventions from *kabuki* and other arts continue to be important in Japanese film history, we must understand that they are incorporated into Japanese cinema through the filter of this break with the past.

Third, the formation of Japanese cinema was contingent upon fundamental divisions within Japan. In the 1910s and 1920s, these were largely class divisions. Intellectual film critics such as Kaeriyama Norimasa, Mori Iwao (later vice-president of the Tōhō studio), and Shigeno Yukiyoshi blamed the "lower-class" spectators of Japanese films – laborers, women, and children – for preferring to watch movies that were a "national disgrace." The critics, in short, claimed the authority to arbitrate what was Japanese and what was cinema. The majority of Japanese spectators were placed in a subordinate position: they were constantly called on to reform themselves and to become more properly "Japanese." Embedded in the discourse on cinema was the implication that ordinary Japanese straddled the spatial and temporal definitions of the nation. While their "blood" guaranteed their Japaneseness, the temporality of the emperor system defined them as always needing to become more Japanese (see also Robertson 2002). Reformist critics writing in *Kinema record* and *Kinema junpō* maintained an ambivalent relationship to the nation, claiming to be representatives of both Japan and cinema, a medium external to Japan. Quite literally, they positioned themselves on the border between Japan and the world outside Japan, a border that, paradoxically, described the center of Japanese cinema.

Japanese cinema was thereby defined in a manner that involved both foreign audiences and internal processes of selection and exclusion, such as an attempt to eliminate any alternative definitions of cinema. While this definition informed the dominant way of discussing Japanese cinema for much of the 20th century, actual cinematic practices were much more complicated. Reforms associated with the Pure Film Movement drastically transformed Japanese cinema in the 1920s, eliminating *onnagata* and introducing many "Hollywood" elements, even though *benshi* and other aspects of early cinema continued to be employed, albeit in an altered form, for much of the 1930s. One could argue that the perdurability of such practices represented alternative conceptions of both cinema and modernity. They also represented a locally defined cinema, in the sense that to some audiences the local reception and experience of films took precedence over those shared by an imagined community of the nation.

Japanese cinema in the 1910s *was* essentially local. Film companies made only a single print of their films, and *benshi*, who sometimes added their own spin to a film, made the local theater an actual and viable site of the production of meaning. The films themselves, one might argue, did not dispense "national" meanings. This created a problem for government censors: how could they censor a text that was differently inflected and interpreted in every locale in which it was shown? Censorship had existed from the time cinema arrived in Japan, but from the late 1910s it was applied not just to eliminate content deemed unbefitting the nation, but also to forge a Japanese cinema, and a film audience, that were properly "national."

As film sociologist Hase Masato (1998) has argued, early cinema censorship concentrated on eliminating the local, "live performance" aspects of the medium in order to produce a universal text amenable to central censorship. The fact that, by 1925, the national government could centralize censorship reveals a certain conviction on the part of officials that the meaning of a movie was the same whenever and wherever it was shown. Censors did not ban the *benshi*, but rather chose to regulate them. A special seat was reserved for the police in every theater so that "unpatriotic" narratives of films by *benshi* could be silenced immediately. Moreover, *benshi* were required to pass licensing exams that tested their knowledge of such national agendas as the *kokutai*; if *benshi* were allowed to add meaning to a given film, it had to have the correct political "spin." *Benshi* were likened to "teachers" who instructed the mass movie audience; at the same time, they were envisioned as censors who, like the seated police officers, surveilled the audience and inserted national(ist) messages into viewers' more dream-like experience of a given film. Nationalist critics hoped that cinema spectatorship, the private and libidinal aspects of which unsettled them, could become an agency of the emperor system if viewers exercised self-censorship (Gerow 1994). Even after the disappearance of *benshi* by the mid-1930s, various dramaturgical conventions and textual devices were employed by directors to compel viewers to favor the official interpretation of a film story. These technologies were likely influenced by, as well as influencing, those utilized toward the same ends in popular theater (Robertson 2001 [1998]:117). A recent statement by the movie director Aoyama Shinji, in which he links the close-up photography to the emperor system, indicates how, even today, narrative devices that impose meaning(s) which both shape readers' perspectives and make those perspectives appear natural and normal are linked to the ideology of the nation.

From the late 1930s, the vision of the nation that authorities wanted to put across in the cinema was primarily the estheticized one that Kang (2001) has analyzed. Darrell Davis (1996) has identified in works such as Mizoguchi Kenji's *Genroku chûshingura* (The Loyal 47 Ronin; 1941–42), a "monumental style" of staid long shots and long takes which consciously operated to estheticize Japanese national values. In war films, this process of estheticization incorporated screen characters into the cinema's "machine esthetic" (Ueno 1994) and rendered violence part of an esthetic of sacrifice (e.g., *kamikaze*) that obfuscated the brutal realities of massacre in war (Nornes 1994). The tendency in wartime films to emphasize the rigors of military training and working on behalf of the nation as much as the evils of the enemy both pitted a "pure self" against the "demonic other" (Dower 1987), as well as expressed an esthetic of spirit over matter and a dissipation of identity into the national war machine.

Early 20th-century attempts to render cinema more national were not always successful. In the first place, the industry itself was not yet established on a national scale – the majority of Japanese did not have easy access to movie theaters, and those who did were confronted with a choice of about 500 films a year to view. It would be impossible under those circumstances to highlight and promote the "national (or citizens') films" (*kokumin eiga*) that the authorities wished Japanese citizens to watch. The 1939 Film Law and the government-led reorganization of the film industry reduced the number of film companies and their films, organized mobile projection teams, and advocated a more modern, national industry. Yet, even with this reorganization, the twofold problem of attendance and spectatorship remained. The fact that quite a number of *kokumin eiga*, such as *Genroku chûshin-gura*, were box office failures sparked debates in cinema journals over how to produce national films that the Japanese would actually watch. As film historian Peter High (2003) emphasizes, these debates were never resolved. The cooperation of audiences was essential in prosecuting the "film war" (*eigasen*); not only did people need to attend officially sanctioned films; they needed to learn how to view them properly. Bureaucrats such as Fuwa Suketoshi deliberated the possibility of "training" (*kunren*) spectators, and the psychologist Hatano Kanji elaborated on the notion of "correct spectators" (*tadashii kanshû*) (Gerow 1999; see also Robertson 2001 [1998]:125–127).

There was also the persistent issue of exporting films. Japanese movies were being shown abroad as part of the attempt to construct a "culture" of and for the Greater East Asia Co-Prosperity Sphere, but no one agreed on which films were best suited toward this end (see the essays in Goodman 1991). The historian Washitani Hana (2000) has shown how the controversy over Makino Masahiro's *Ahen sensō* (The Opium War; 1943) reveals contradictions in Japanese wartime film policy. A "national film" that was successful in areas of Asia under Japanese domination, Makino's film was criticized for being based on a D. W. Griffith movie and featuring Hollywood-style musical numbers. This film actually epitomized some of the contradictions of Japanese cinema itself, namely, the paradoxical attempt to represent Japan through a Hollywood film style and to create a Japanese national cinema in a foreign medium. The ceaseless debates on this paradox throughout the 1930s and 1940s suggest that even the flexible *kokutai* ideology had difficulty accommodating certain contradictions.

Efforts to define and make *kokumin eiga* ended with Japan's defeat, but film-makers' interest in developing a national or Japanese cinema continued. The restructuring of film corporations during the wartime period, which had aimed at creating a truly national film industry, provided a basic framework for the postwar movie business. Inflation sparked a nationwide boom in theater construction that finally brought the movies to the vast majority of Japanese. Japanese postwar films are often summarized as constituting a cinema of democratic humanism, but, as film scholar Yoshimoto Mitsuhiro notes, this characterization does not necessarily mark a change from the past. In order to claim a historical precedent for postwar films, film critics today have "discovered" a humanistic element in select prewar and wartime works. We can also point to thematic consistencies in the wartime and postwar works of directors such as Kurosawa Akira, among others. Universal humanism and its realist esthetic, both during and after the war, was compatible with nationalism to the extent that nation-building could be presented as part of universal human nature (Yoshimoto 2000). The success of Kurosawa Akira's *Rashōmon* (1950) at the Venice Film Festival confirmed that Japanese films embodied universal human values, and brought the Japanese film industry the level of foreign recognition that had been sought since the 1910s. Nagata Masaichi of the Daiei studios actually began producing Japanese films aimed at foreign consumer markets. Some of the classics of 1950s Japanese cinema, including Kinugasa Teinosuke's *Jigokumon* (Gate of Hell; 1953) and Mizoguchi Kenji's *Ugetsu monogatari* (Ugetsu; 1953), were consciously pack-aged for export as spectacles of Japanese exoticism.

Film historians usually treat the 1950s as the golden age of Japanese film. It was an age generated through interactions with foreign spectators and from the clash of contradictions pre-dating 1945. Many postwar films effectively denied Japan's war-time activity and responsibilities. Melodramatic genres, such as the *hahamono* (liter-ally, "mother films"), which featured the heroic suffering of self-sacrificing mothers, were employed to construct a narrative of Japanese victimization. By the same token, the victims of Japanese imperial aggression had all but disappeared in such films. It is important to acknowledge that the portrayal of such "others" was not at all a salient feature of Japanese cinema during its heyday; the absence of resident Koreans was especially obvious. Leftist, independent filmmakers did try to raise timely issues related to war and discrimination. Ironically, as the new wave director Ôshima Nagisa noted, they often opposed Japanese militarism by employing the very same stylistic politics as wartime cinema. By the late 1950s, films about World War II *kamikaze* fighters reproduced the wartime masculine ideology of young men sacrificing them-selves for the nation (Standish 2000). Blockbusters such as *Meiji Tennō to nichi-ro daisensō* (The Meiji Emperor and the Great Russo-Japanese War; 1957), and even Tōhō's special-effects films, such as *Kaitei gunkan* (Atragon; 1963), were providing audiences with openly nationalist narratives. Nationalism may have been a taboo subject in postwar intellectual circles, but it was thriving in Japanese popular culture.

By the mid-1960s, television had replaced cinema as Japan's prime form of enter-tainment, a situation that, perhaps ironically, allowed filmmakers the freedom to pursue themes that were not nationalistic. New wave directors such as Ôshima and Imamura Shôhei created a fresh, political – and politicized – cinema through which they critiqued postwar film narratives of humanism and Japanese sacrifice. Also at this time, a series of genre films coined "nationless" (*mukokuseki*) became popular at the theaters. Epitomized by Nikkatsu action movies, a typical "nationless" story featured male loners negotiating a foreign-like landscape within Japan. *Daisōgen no wataridori* (The Rambler Rides Again; 1960) is illustrative of this genre. *Rambler* starred a lone hero (played by Kobayashi Akira) venturing off to a scenic land (Hokkaido) and saving innocents (the Ainu) from unscrupulous gangsters. The location may have been Japan, but the "cowboy-and-Indian" narrative – Kobayashi as a gunslinger and the Ainu as the Indians – transformed Hokkaido into a landscape with little relation to the real Japan. Film critic Watanabe Takenobu (1981–82) argued that films like *Daisōgen no wataridori* showed how the independent individual could only exist in 1960s Japan in a space abstracted from the suffocating realities of the economically regenerating nation. At the same time, however, such films provided some of the first filmic narrations of a touristic discourse in which Japan itself was rendered an abstract, exotic object of consumption.

"Nationless" films were not actually nationless because, by the mid-1970s, Japan itself was becoming an exchangeable commodity and the Japanese were developing into traveling consumers, a trend capitalized on by the Japan National Railways' "Discover Japan" advertising campaign. It was therefore no coincidence that the primary cinematic representatives of the nation in the 1960s and 1970s were outlaw wanderers, of which there were two generic types. One was the gallant, itinerant yakuza of the Tōei studio's *ninkyō* (chivalry) genre, who wore kimono, observed a traditional code of honor, and killed off evil, pinstripe-suited gangsters. The other type was the nostalgia-steeped, good-natured yakuza peddler best exemplified by Tora-san of Shôchiku's *"Otoko wa tsurai yo"* ("It's Tough To Be a Man") series. Tora-san's hometown of Shibamata was redolent of traditional family values, even though he, in all his anachronistic innocence, could never settle down there.

From the late 1980s, the nation has been at the core of heated debates informing Japanese films. There has been a spate of films acknowledging marginal groups usually excluded from the imagination of the Japanese nation, including resident Koreans, illegal immigrants and undocumented workers, Okinawans and homosexuals. Globalization is helping to make the borders of the nation more open to contention. The best of these films, such as Sai Yôichi's *Buta no mukui* (Pig's Revenge; 1999), engage in a complex process of eschewing emotionality and countering the structures of power informing cinematic explanation. The film achieves this effect through a mode of stylistic detachment that refuses to impose feelings or meanings on what is viewed. Often refraining from resorting to close-ups and other conventional narrative devices, this and similar films strategically utilize long shots and long takes to create a distance from their non-Japanese subjects that renders them unknowable, and thus also recognizes and respects their alterity as "others." More than anything, this detachment attempts to acknowledge "the other" and to free "the other" from national appropriation.

The late 1980s also marked the revival of (neo)nationalism and the production of such unapologetic paeans to wartime nationalism as *Puraido: Unmei no toki* (Pride; 1998), about General Tōgō, and *Murudeka 17805* (Merdeka [Freedom]; 2001), about Japanese soldiers, and one charismatic soldier in particular, helping to free Indonesia from the Dutch who returned to their former colony following Japan's defeat in 1945. As I have argued elsewhere (Gerow 2000), even some films purportedly representing an ethnically diverse Japan, such as Iwai Shunji's *Suwaroteiru* (Swallowtail Butterfly; 1996), reveal that the globalization of consumerist spectacle can actually reinscribe the nation through a touristic spectacle of direct contact with, and national appropriation of, "the other." Globalism and nationalism thus operate here as two sides of the same coin.

Recent Japanese films, collectively engaged in a struggle between distance and proximity, detachment and appropriation, remind us of the complex space (and spatiality) of the postwar nation that juxtaposes global pressures with resurrected concerns for local autonomy. Perpetually negotiating its boundaries, the nation, through the mass media, including cinema, must repeatedly imagine and reimagine itself. I hope that, in this brief essay, I have shown how those same media can both reveal and contest the contradictions of that "glocal(izing)" project.

REFERENCES

Amino, Yoshihiko. 1998. "Tennō" to "nihon." ("Emperor" and "Japan"). *In* Nashonarisumu o yomu (Reading Nationalism). Jikkyô Shuppan Henshûbu, ed. pp. 117–130. Tokyo: Jikkyō Shuppan.

Anderson, Benedict. 1983. Imagined Communities. London: Verso.

Bhabha, Homi. 1990. Introduction: Narrating the Nation. *In* Nation and Narration. pp. 1–7. London: Routledge.

Burch, Noël. 1979. To the Distant Observer. Berkeley: University of California Press.

Christy, Alan. 1993. The Making of Imperial Subjects in Okinawa. Positions 1:607–639.

Conner, Walker. 1990. When Is a Nation? Ethnic and Racial Studies 13(1):92–100.

Davis, Darrell. 1996. Picturing Japaneseness. New York: Columbia University Press.

Dower, John. 1987. War Without Mercy. New York: Pantheon Books.

Gerow, Aaron. 1994. The Benshi's New Face. Iconics 3:69–86.

——1998. "Nihonjin" Kitano Takeshi (Japanese: Kitano Takeshi). Yuriika 30(3):42–51.

——1999. Miyamoto Musashi to senjichû no kankyaku (Miyamoto Musashi and Wartime Audiences). *In* Eiga kantoku Mizoguchi Kenji (Movie Director Mizoguchi Kenji). Yomota Inuhiko, ed. pp. 226–250. Tokyo: Shin'yôsha.

——2000. Consuming Asia, Consuming Japan. *In* Censoring History. Laura Hein and Mark Selden, eds. pp. 74–95. Armonk, NY: M. E. Sharpe.

——2002. Tatakau kankyaku: dai tōa kyōeiken no nihon eiga to juyō no mondai (Fighting Audiences: Japanese Films and the Problem of Reception within the Greater East Asia Co-Prosperity Sphere). Gendai shisō 30(9):139–149.

Gluck, Carol. 1985. Japan's Modern Myths. Princeton: Princeton University Press.

Goodman, Grant. ed. 1991. Japanese Cultural Policies in Southeast Asia During World War 2. New York: St. Martin's Press.

Hase, Masato. 1998. The Origins of Censorship. Review of Japanese Culture and Society 10:14–23.

High, Peter B. 2003. The Imperial Screen. Madison: University of Wisconsin Press.

Hobsbawm, Eric. 1983. Introduction: Inventing Traditions. *In* The Invention of Tradition. Eric Hobsbawm and Terence Ranger, eds. pp. 1–14. Cambridge: Cambridge University Press.

Kang Sang-jung. 2001. Nashonarizumu (Nationalism). Tokyo: Iwanami Shoten.

Karatani, Kôjin. 1993. Origins of Modern Japanese Literature. Durham, NC: Duke University Press.

Lee, Yeounsuk. 1996. "Kokugo" to iu shisō (The Idea Called "National Language"). Tokyo: Iwanami Shoten.

Morris-Suzuki, Tessa. 1998. Re-inventing Japan. Armonk, NY: M. E. Sharpe.

Nornes, Mark. 1994. Cherry Trees and Corpses. *In* The Japan/America Film Wars. Mark Nornes and Fukushima Yukio, eds. pp. 147–161. Chur: Harwood.

Oguma, Eiji. 2002. A Genealogy of "Japanese" Self Images. Melbourne: Trans Pacific Press.

Renan, Ernst. 1996. What Is a Nation? *In* Becoming National. Geoff Eley and Ronald Grigor Suny, eds. pp. 42–56. Oxford: Oxford University Press.

Ri, Takanori. 1996. Hyōshō kūkan no kindai (The Modernity of Symbolic Space). Tokyo: Shin'yôsha.

Robertson, Jennifer. 2001 [1998]. Takarazuka: Sexual Politics and Popular Culture in Modern Japan. Berkeley: University of California Press.

——2002. Blood Talks: Eugenic Modernity and the Creation of New Japanese. History and Anthropology 13(3):191–216.

Sakai, Naoki. 1996. Nashonariti to bo(koku)go no seiji (Nationality and the Politics of the Mother Tongue). *In* Nashonariti no datsukôchiku (Deconstructing Nationality). Sakai Naoki, Brett de Bary, and Iyotani Toshio, eds. pp. 9–53. Tokyo: Kashiwa Shobō.

Smith, Anthony D. 1986. The Ethnic Origins of Nations. Oxford: Basil Blackwell.

Standish, Isolde. 2000. Myth and Masculinity in the Japanese Cinema. Richmond: Curzon.

Ueno, Toshiya. 1994. The Other and the Machine. *In* The Japan/America Film Wars. Mark Nornes and Fukushima Yukio, eds. pp. 71–93. Chur: Harwood.

Vlastos, Steven, ed. 1998. Mirror of Modernity. Berkeley: University of California Press.

Washitani, Hana. 2000. The Opium War and the Cinema Wars. Inter-Asia Cultural Studies 4(1):63–76.

Watanabe, Takenobu. 1981–82. Nikkatsu akushon no kareina sekai (The Magnificent World of Nikkatsu Action), 3 vols. Tokyo: Miraisha.

Yoshimoto, Mitsuhiro. 2000. Kurosawa. Durham: Duke University Press.

25 Culinary Culture and the Making of a National Cuisine

Katarzyna Cwiertka

FOOD IN CONTEMPORARY JAPAN

Food pervades every aspect of life in Japan. A wide range of fresh and processed provisions is available in supermarkets, grocery stores, and through home-delivery services. In addition to fast-food outlets, 24-hour "convenience stores" (*konbini*) supply basic ingredients, a variety of snack foods, and ready-to-eat meals seven days a week. Moreover, Japan's ubiquitous vending machines dispense not only soft drinks, alcoholic beverages, candy and ice-cream, but also steaming noodles and grilled rice balls. Countless restaurants cater to diners of every age, sex, and degree of affluence, and provide an eclectic array of Japanese and foreign dishes. These are but the most obvious places where one encounters food in Japan. Long-distance train travellers can dine in buffet cars or purchase food from catering carts to eat in their seats. They can also eat at rail station cafés or purchase food to be taken on board. Food is also a typical and welcome gift in Japan: it is relatively cheap, easy to choose, can be shared, is easily disposed of, and is relatively neutral in symbolic implications (Daniels 2001:141, 219). Not surprisingly, rail station kiosks also stock a large variety of food souvenirs, usually locally grown fruit and vegetables, pickles, and confections for distributing the specialty consumables of the region from which one has come among colleagues, friends and family to mark the end of a journey and offer a vicarious sharing of the experience.

Edible souvenirs and gifts are just one example of food's role as an important means of communication in Japan. As sociologist Inoue Tadashi has pointedly observed, eating scenes are some of the most ubiquitous in Japanese soaps, because mealtimes are nowadays the only time when the always busy family members are actually able to meet (Inoue 1988:168). During these rare occasions family matters can be discussed, even if the attention of the diners is often disturbed by background noise from the television, which may be tuned to one of the ubiquitous cooking shows or food-focused talk or quiz shows – and many television dramas center around family meals.

Meals are very important components of family life. For many Japanese women, food preparation is a major part of the normative roles of wife and mother. Providing tasty and diverse meals for the family, while watching over the family's health and budget, is a domestic task that Japanese married women take very seriously. House-wives are generally receptive to culinary novelties if reasonably priced, possess an extensive knowledge of nutrition, and are demanding consumers in terms of the quality and safety of the food they buy. For younger and/or unmarried women who are not professional homemakers, food is an indicator of lifestyle aspirations. As anthropologist Merry White explains, nowadays, eating out with friends (as opposed to cooking together with friends, which their mothers enjoyed doing) and sharing information about food trends is a favorite form of recreation for young or unmarried women (White 2002:67). While constantly aware of the connections between diet and weight, these women choose their food for pleasure and self-expression – an attitude that is likely to affect family meals in the future. Recent surveys reveal that the new generation of homemakers who were born in the 1960s relies heavily on fast food and food from convenience stores to feed their families, and find everyday cooking boring (Iwamura 2003). Such accounts indicate the possibility that the 20th-century "family meal" is crumbling as an ideal.

Despite being caught in a complex web of commercial interests, food still retains strong spiritual and religious connotations in Japan, in large part due to its prominent role in Shinto and Buddhist rituals (Cobbi 1995). As in other societies, the connec-tion between food and religion is particularly pronounced on festive occasions, such as the New Year's celebration when a pyramid of pounded rice cakes (*kagamimochi*) is displayed in almost every household, or during the *obon* (autumn equinox) festival when the ancestors are worshiped with offers of fruit, vegetables, and rice wine (sake), in addition to the food they favored when they were alive. Gravestones covered with tangerines and small sake containers are familiar scenes in cemeteries throughout Japan. Food remains meaningful in daily ritual as well: many householders offer the day's first bowl of cooked rice – today very often the evening meal and not breakfast – to the Buddhist altar (*butsudan*) housing the memorial tablets (*ihai*) of deceased members (see Smith 1976).

The prominence of food in Japanese society is best reflected by its continual appearance in the media. Food is a regular feature, if not the centerpiece, of visual entertainment in Japan. Of course, the media-worthiness of food is not unique to Japan and is evident in postindustrial consumer cultures everywhere. Culinary fash-ions are constantly invented and reinvented in print and televisual media. The recreational and entertainment value of food is trumpeted in books and brochures dealing with food history, in recipes, in restaurant reviews in magazines, and in food-related quiz shows, contests, and documentaries. Even serious daily newspapers regularly include information related to the native and foreign culinary heritage. Serialized soaps and home dramas are often staged at restaurants or in traditional food workshops, and popular animated characters bear food-related names, such as the celebrated Anpan-man (Mr. Beanpaste Bun) and Sazae-san (Mrs. Top-shell). Travel programs invariably focus on cuisine. It seems as if no journey is considered complete without tasting local food, regardless of whether it is a refined meal at one of Japan's celebrated spas or a baguette in a Paris bistro. Cooking presentations belong to the most ubiquitous scenes. Moreover, each channel has several cooking shows targeted at specific audiences – housewives, children, and men for whom cooking is a hobby – and practically every talk show features a culinary segment where hosts and guests actually taste and comment on select dishes, often prepared live by an invited chef.

One of the reasons why cuisine rates so highly on Japanese television is the premium placed on the appearance or presentation of food. Japanese cuisine is best known abroad for its emphasis on the freshness and quality of ingredients, and beauty of presentation. This esthetic preoccupation is not limited to the native haute cuisine (*kaiseki*), but extends to daily meals and all culinary genres in Japan. However, the Japanese people's infatuation with food goes beyond taste, esthetics, communication, and entertainment. Food apparently occupies a meaningful place in people's consciousness and world view, as is evidenced by its enormous attraction as a topic of popular commentary. The purported origins of particular dishes and the appropriate methods and equipment for their preparation and consumption are debated in supermarkets, kitchens, restaurants, and on television. Many Japanese assume that food habits are fundamentally related to "national character" and that they reflect people's social and cultural values.

That the economic prosperity of the last few decades is largely responsible for the abundance of food choices in Japan seems quite obvious. The limited rations of the wartime and immediate postwar periods are a distant memory for the elderly alone, and gentrification of taste has progressed rapidly since the booming 1960s. Formerly expensive and exclusive types of food are now universally affordable, and for the first time in Japanese history, the daily menu of people of different social and economic status is basically the same. The recent recession has not altered this fact.

However, the question of how food came to occupy such an unquestionably prominent position in the life of the Japanese people requires a much more complex analysis that addresses issues far beyond greater disposable income and the influx of a multinational (fast) food industry in Japan. Generally speaking, two features characterize Japanese food culture. First is the emphasis on esthetic qualities in food preparation and presentation, together with a stress on the quality and freshness of the ingredients and harmony between the food, the vessel, the setting, and the season in which food is served. In pre-modern Japan, these characteristics were mostly limited to professionally catered *kaiseki* cuisine. The nationwide diffusion and standardization of the *kaiseki* esthetic accompanied the process of nation-state formation in the late 19th and early 20th centuries, a process that is virtually complete today. A second characteristic is the multicultural character of the Japanese food culture and an embracing of foreign ingredients and dishes, along with an impulse to domesticate them. Thus, an average Japanese daily menu may consist of a Western-style breakfast of toast, coffee, and fried eggs; a Chinese-style lunch of noodles or fried rice; and a Japanese-style dinner of white rice, soup, pickles, and a variety of side dishes. This culinary eclecticism was occasioned by encounters with Europeans: the Portuguese in the 16th century and the Dutch from the 17th to the mid-19th centuries, but mostly with a host of Euro-Americans from the late 19th century to the present; it was also influenced by the Japanese occupation of East Asian and Pacific Rim countries during the period of empire-building (roughly the 1870s to 1945).

Some scholars trace the strongly multicultural nature of contemporary Japanese food culture to the distant past, and argue that borrowing from abroad has been a recurring pattern of Japanese food history (see, e.g., Ashkenazi and Jacob 2000: 42–46). It is certainly true that rice, chopsticks, soybean products, and tea were imported (or exported, perhaps) from China by at least the sixth century, if not earlier, and that these and many other elements of Chinese culinary culture were incorporated into local Japanese contexts. But the same is true of other East Asian cultures whose cuisine was based on a foundation of Chinese cuisine. I suggest instead that the development of what I described earlier as the distinctive attitudes toward food on the part of the Japanese today was intertwined with social and political events from, mainly, the Meiji period onward. Rather than representing an ancient history, these attitudes and patterns of consumption accompanied Japan's transformation from a feudal type of society to a postindustrial nation-state.

PRE-MODERN REALITIES AND MODERN MYTHS

A standard Japanese meal centers on boiled rice accompanied by soup and side dishes, all served at the same time. Regardless of the type of side dishes, which nowadays may include a pork cutlet or potato salad, the Japanese character of the entire meal is secured by its "rice, soup and side dishes" structure. The foreignness of the side dishes may be "naturalized" by the addition of soy sauce (*shōyu*), eulogized today as the "soul of Japanese taste." Soy sauce is considered such a vital condiment that manufacturers have produced conveniently packaged, travel-size bottles so that Japanese travelers can venture forth into the world "armed with slippers and soy sauce" (Takagi 1988). For contemporary Japanese, rice and soy sauce are the ultimate symbols of Japaneseness: symbols more powerful than the cherry blossom, kimono, or the emperor in that they satisfy visceral cravings.

Yet it is only relatively recently that both rice and soy sauce have been consumed on a daily basis by the average citizen; previously they were luxuries enjoyed by commoners on special or festive occasions alone. Although the daily fare of farm householders, who until the postwar period comprised up to 80 percent of the population, varied depending on the region, millet, Deccan grass, and barley rather than rice were the staple grains, and soybean paste (*miso*) rather than soy sauce the primary flavoring agent. In the Edo period, farmers produced rice to supply the needs of the influential minority of military elites and urbanites. Despite the symbolic importance of rice (see Ohnuki-Tierney 1993) and its role as a form of currency in the pre-modern economy, a rice-based diet was not the Japanese norm until the postwar period. The consumption of soy sauce began to increase beyond the urban areas from the turn of the 20th century onwards, mainly due to the modernization of its production and the rising standard of living. Yet many farmers, who were basically self-sufficient in terms of food supply, continued to produce their own soy sauce substitute by squeezing out the juice from homemade *miso* or by clarifying its residue. Spending precious cash on a good-quality soy sauce manufactured at specialized workshops and factories remained for them a luxury.

Before the turn of the 20th century, polished white rice and soy sauce were primarily urban commodities. Documents from 1889 indicate that 16 million liters of soy sauce were consumed by the population of Tokyo during that year, which translates into approximately 10 liters of soy sauce per person. The average amount of rice consumed by urbanites was more or less half a kilogram per person per day – the equivalent of three to five bowls of rice per meal (Ehara 2000:37). Pre-modern cities, and especially Edo (present-day Tokyo) were both the setting in which the contemporary Japanese diet of rice and soy sauce emerged, and the locus of the development of a contemporary Japanese culinary "tradition." Dishes nowadays considered to represent *the* traditional Japanese cuisine, such as sushi, tempura, and buckwheat noodles (*soba*), are actually descendants of late 18th- and early 19th-century street or fast food. These and many other dishes developed during the halcyon days of pre-modern catering culture. Dishes turned out by professional cooks were patronized by wealthy urban gourmets and less affluent townspeople alike. Of course, the former dined at first-class restaurants and tea houses, while the latter ate at plebeian eateries and fast-food stalls. Food historian Ishige Naomichi calculated that, as of 1804, there was one restaurant per every 170 inhabitants of Edo, a figure that excludes the countless peddlers' stalls (Ishige 2000:1181).

Despite an apparent appreciation of good food, the home cooking practices of pre-modern Japanese urbanites were surprisingly simple and monotonous, regardless of a given household's wealth (Ehara 2000). The average urban citizen of pre-modern Japan subsisted mainly on rice and pickles. Breakfast was usually supplemented by *miso* soup and one side dish, and dinner by another side dish. A typical lunch consisted of a fish or vegetable dish accompanied by the customary rice and pickles; soup was usually not served at lunch. Not only were daily menus meager compared to what the Japanese consume on a daily basis today, but there was little variety in the types of side dishes that were served. Hot tofu in broth (*yudōfu*) or fresh tofu (*hiyayakkō*), different foods preserved by boiling in soy sauce (*tsukudani*), and simmered vegetables were served day after day.

Yanagita Kunio (1875–1962), a nativist ethnographer, noted that meals featuring a more varied array of ingredients marked a significant change in patterns of food consumption in the early 20th century (Kumakura 1993:29–30). The increased variety in diet was foremost a result of the rising standard of living, in conjunction with the introduction of new types of food from abroad and the development of new dishes inspired by foreign cuisine. The latter was particularly relevant for restaurant and catering services. Prompted by the modern state's promotion of an ideology of monogamous domesticity, married women gradually devoted more time and creative energy to home cooking. From the state's perspective, food preparation and consumption were critical performances through which the modern monogamous family could be properly staged (cf. Sand 1998:198–201). At first, urban middle-class households were targeted for resocialization under this new ideology. Such households ideally consisted of a male white-collar professional whose wife understood that homemaking was her (only) career, and who labored to make home meals a source of pleasure and relaxation. Such an ideal woman, known by the rubric "good wife, wise mother" (*ryōsai kenbo*), devoted herself to creating a broad and diverse range of dishes, often competing in this regard with her neighbors. Many middle-class housewives strove to make their home cooking distinctive by developing their own specialties and mode of presentation. By the 1960s, this exercise in distinction had become the national norm, and family meals were the central stage for the performance of "family."[1] Home cooking and a varied diet, along with the requisite official gender roles for females and males, were thus products of a modern ideology of domesticity first promoted in the late 19th century.

It should now come as no surprise to realize that many dishes and characteristic features regarded as hallmarks of "traditional" Japanese cuisine are actually modern introductions and inventions. This is not something that is unique to Japan. Wherever one looks, one realizes that food culture is always changing. New dishes, food-related habits, and culinary myths are daily created and transformed in most societies, and especially materially affluent ones such as Japan.

THE MAKING OF A NATIONAL CUISINE

The last decades of the 20th century marked the beginning of an era of a *common* culinary heritage for the majority of Japanese. By the 1960s, the sharp regional and class distinctions in dietary patterns characteristic of the 19th century and earlier had been homogenized, and differences between the sophisticated meals of the elite, the colorful eatery culture of the townsfolk, and the meager fare of peasants had all but disappeared. Despite recent media and local tourism-related efforts to revive and (re)invent local foodways, regional dishes and flavors are the exception rather than the rule in the dietary life of Japanese today.

The term "Japanese cuisine" (*nihon ryōri* or *washoku*) is a modern concept. It only began to be widely used after non-Japanese cuisines – Western cuisine (*seiyō ryōri* or *yōshoku*) and Chinese cuisine (*shina ryōri* or *chūka ryōri*)[2] – became established in Japan.

The making of a common or national food culture, and attendant customs and values, began in the late 19th century as part of the Meiji state's program to construct a national culture for Japan through the instruments of universal education, the mass media, and universal conscription (for males). This new consciousness of a national community – New Japan (*shin nippon*) – was to be built on two platforms: pre-modern samurai society and the Euro-American institutions selectively adopted by the Meiji state. Similarly, a Japanese national cuisine was assembled on a hybrid foundation of pre-modern urban culinary patterns integrated with dietary models selectively imported from European countries and the United States. It is important to realize, however, that the process of making a *Japanese* cuisine was by no means a seamless, top-down project. Rather, a national cuisine was given shape by both state initiatives and the cacophonous forces of industrialization, urbanization, and sundry modernizing reforms.

The most salient feature of the new Japanese national cuisine was its ability to bridge regional and class differences. This so-called democratization of taste was achieved through the gradual countrywide spread of regional foodways along with nationwide diffusion of newly introduced foreign dishes, and the popularization of the "rice, soup and side dishes" meal pattern among the rural population. And, as noted above, the modern ideal of domesticity with its emphasis on home cooking was an important impetus as well. The steady migration of rural folk to urban centers, an increased flow of information through nationally distributed newspapers and magazines, and an expanding railroad system greatly facilitated the blending of regional foodways in fin-de-siècle Japan. Improved preservation technologies, such as canning and freezing, along with rapid transport systems, played an equally important role in homogenizing the Japanese diet. Moreover, the introduction of home economics in schools and in magazines for girls and women was vital in creating a receptive public environment for a new, *Japanese* culinary culture. For example, the 1914 regulations concerning educational material for instructors in home economics at girls' schools still emphasized the necessity of adjusting the content of the nationally distributed manuals to the regional situation of each school. However, the standardization of home economics textbooks by the 1920s was accompanied by the homogenization of information about food and cooking techniques (Handa 1975:85).

The nationwide spread of foreign foodstuffs and dishes effectively reduced regional differences in foodways. Hybrid Japanese–Western dishes, such as the late 19th-century beef hotchpotch (*gyūnabe*, later known as *sukiyaki*), and early 20th-century creations such as curry on rice (*karēraisu*), deep-fried breaded pork (*katsuretsu*) and fish (*furai*), and potato croquettes (*korokke*), became edible national icons of a universal Japanese modernity. The great Tokyo earthquake of 1923 totally altered the character of dining-out culture in that city. The following excerpt from a newspaper article published in the early 1930s describes the new gastronomy:

> [G]one is that heyday when eating places had only to be exclusive in order to succeed. To be among the "surviving fittest" nowadays, the old houses for the elite with their big gates and spacious gardens are learning that they must have a popular appeal. With taxis honking and stocks, bonds, and exchange rates going up and down every minute, even the restaurant world has had to "step on the gas" and show speed....The modern requirement is to give all-round satisfaction, which means to be exclusive and popular at the same time. The age of speed is also producing a demand for quick service even at the table. That is why the old-time "odenya" ("kantodakiya" in Kansai) are growing in size and number, and why so many historical large restaurants are remodeling their places to add efficiency and speed to their erstwhile boasted comfort and distinction. (Osaka Mainichi 1932–33:65).

The popularization of *odenya* (eating houses [*ya*] serving a variety of ingredients simmered in hot stock [*oden*]) is a case in point. Whereas in pre-modern Japan *odenya* were a typical kind of lower-class eatery, their growing popularity in the 1920s among middle-class urban citizens is a barometer of the democratization of cuisine. The process of culinary democratization proceeded at an extraordinary speed during the next three decades, during which Japanese food culture as we know it today took its distinctive shape.

War, the Military, and the Democratization of Taste

Cultural transformations, including changes in diet, usually unfold over a long period of time. However, the exigencies of war often make it easier for people to abandon old habits and to quickly acquire new ones with less resistance than might be the case in peacetime. Economic recession and food shortages, typical features of protracted war, help to loosen dietary rules, trigger a reassessment of foods otherwise regarded as low in prestige, and accelerate the spread of new dishes and food customs. Perhaps the main impact of modern war on human food tastes may be that the thousands of individuals drafted into the armed forces are not free to choose the food they eat, and their food preferences come to be shaped by uniform military menus.

As I have written elsewhere, the imperial Japanese army and navy played a significant role in the homogenization of the modern-day Japanese diet (Cwiertka 2002). Universal conscription was instituted in 1873. It was a unprecedented social transformation, and, for the first time in Japanese history, opened up a military career to rank-and-file males. Military menus largely contributed to the nationwide adoption of rice as the centerpiece around which a meal was constructed, and of soy sauce as a key flavoring agent. By virtue of their conscription, the sons of farmers and other lower-class households, enjoyed the new "luxury" of having rice three times a day. (Actually, from the early 20th century onward, the military cooks mixed barley into the rice in order to provide enough B vitamins to prevent beriberi.) A fusion of Japanese, Western, and Chinese dishes were incorporated into military menus as side dishes. For thousands of Japanese men, a military canteen was the site of their first encounter with foreign culture in the form of curries, croquettes, and Chinese-style stir-fries.

The main reason for the armed forces to include non-traditional dishes was because they provided more nourishment. Serving nourishing and filling meals at the lowest possible cost was the general rule of military cookery, and the adoption of Western and Chinese recipes made this possible. A diet based on rice, vegetables, tofu, and seafood did not fulfill the caloric needs of the recruits. Meat, lard, potatoes, onions, cabbage, summer squash, and flour were the foreign foodstuffs that were most extensively used by the Japanese army. Non-Japanese cooking techniques, such as deep-frying, pan-frying and stewing, were also adopted by military cooks. High-calorie fried dishes were an inexpensive source of calories, and also a method of using up "ingredients of poor quality." Moreover, adding curry powder to Japanese-style simmered vegetables and noodles perked up the bland taste of ingredients of inferior quality. Curry powder also helped to mask the unpleasant smell of spoiled fish and meat. In short, the military's adoption of Chinese and Western dishes made a more nourishing, high-calorie diet economically possible.

Including non-Japanese dishes in military menus proved to be a perfect solution for dealing with regional differences in taste as well. Recruits hailed from all over the country, and the food they consumed in civilian life varied significantly. Military cooks would have faced intractable difficulties had they attempted to cater to all the regional taste preferences represented by the conscripted men – or, by the same token, if they had offered some regional dishes and not others. By serving foreign foods which were new to all of the recruits, army and navy cooks thereby not only helped level regional and social distinctions in the military, but also speeded up the process of nationalizing and homogenizing Japanese food tastes. Upon their discharge, the soldiers returned home and shared their newly acquired taste for Western and Chinese dishes with their families and neighbors, and encouraged them to visit eateries that served the novel food. At the same time, the military's ideas about a healthy and economical diet were disseminated among the public through popular publications and various educational activities that were especially actively coordinated in the war-ridden 1930s and 1940s. Wheat-based products, such as noodles and bread, for example, were actively promoted as less expensive, more plentiful, and more nutritious than rice. Innovations in catering to civilians in factories, schools, and hospitals were often initiated and even orchestrated by the military dieticians and accountants.

It is important to note that the dietary influence of the military continued long after the disappearance of the imperial Japanese army and navy from the political arena. The same people who under the auspices of the military were involved in activities geared toward the improvement of public nutrition continued their efforts after 1945. Westernized military menus were reproduced in restaurants and canteens where military cooks and dieticians found employment after Japan's surrender. Nutritional research continued in institutes with new names but unchanged personnel, and the food industry for decades thereafter marketed new products that had originally been designed for air squadrons and combat divisions. The association of the hybrid dishes with the military gradually disappeared as new dietary patterns were adopted and mainstreamed by civilians in the postwar period.

In addition to the influence of the military, the serious food shortages of the 1940s were a powerful motive for the democratization of the Japanese diet. During this harsh decade, the Japanese people as a whole were subjected to a subsistence diet, and the "one-pot" dishes typical of pre-modern peasant life became the temporary norm. Potatoes and bread were the primary staples, and dieticians provided culinary advice to help people make the most of the meager supply of ingredients. In 1949, for example, Higashi Sayoko (1892–1973), a graduate of the prestigious Cordon Bleu Institute in Paris and a renowned Japanese authority on French cuisine and Western dining etiquette, published a cookbook devoted entirely to potato dishes from all over the world.

During the largely American occupation of Japan (1945–52), the fact that food aid for the Japanese people consisted mainly of flour accelerated the popularization of bread in Japan, as did the school lunch system, introduced in 1947 by the occupation authorities as a means of improving the nutrition of Japanese children. School lunches differed markedly from the typical Japanese meal in the inclusion of bread and milk along with a cooked dish, often a stew or hearty soup. Interestingly, the first children's lunches were prepared from leftover military provisions (Ehara 2001:236). Bread remained the staple of school lunches until 1976, when it was partly replaced by rice. The postwar generations of children raised on American-style lunches are now adults whose daily fare includes flavors and foods distinctly different from those preferred by their parents and grandparents. The school lunch system has also been identified as an agent in the decline of regional variation in diet. Food historian Ehara Ayako argues that the lunch menus designed by the occupation authorities focused on nutritional aspects alone, without taking into consideration either local food habits or the culinary integrity of the assorted ingredients (Ehara 2001:238). It seems obvious that the tendency of contemporary Japanese to serve eclectic combinations of food in one meal was greatly influenced by long years of exposure to the hybrid dishes comprising school lunches in a 30-year period after World War II.

Chinese food was also introduced throughout Japan during the wartime period. Of course, Chinese innovations such as chopsticks, soybean products, and tea had been key components of Japanese food habits for centuries. But it was not until the 1920s and 1930s, when Japan expanded the boundaries of its Asian empire, that Chinese cuisine came to be widely consumed by civilian Japanese. Generally speaking, before this period and, with the exception of the exclusive Japanese–Chinese style of cooking (*shippoku ryōri*) that was developed in the 18th-century merchant enclave Nagasaki, ordinary Japanese had never really tasted Chinese food. Cheap Chinese-style eateries run by Chinese immigrants appeared in the 1910s, and military canteens began to serve Chinese–Japanese hybrids a decade later. At the same time, Chinese cuisine began to be served at the Japanese imperial court (Tanaka 1987:207), and swanky restaurants specializing in Chinese fare were opened with great fanfare in several Japanese cities. Cafés with Chinese-style decorations and waitresses dressed in Chinese costumes flourished, catering to the trendy middle class, and descriptions of Chinese dishes and food habits were regular features in popular magazines. Japanese imperialism fostered a culinary colonialism in Japan where things Chinese were consumed by civilians.

The colonial legacy continued to influence Japanese food culture after the collapse of the empire in 1945. The thousands of civil servants and employees of Japanese corporations who, along with the military personnel, had been dispatched to oversee the administration of Manchuria, had acquired a taste for Chinese food while abroad. Their repatriation after 1945 was another impetus behind the popularization of Chinese dishes in postwar Japan, such as the perennial favorite *gyōza*, known in English as "potstickers" (Tanaka 1987:224).

WHEN AFFLUENCE TOOK OVER

By the mid-1960s, when the Japanese economy had rebounded from the disastrous effects of war, the process of nationalizing Japanese foodways was complete. The "rice, soup and side dishes" formula became the national norm and Japanese–Western–Chinese hybrid menus reached even the most remote corners of the country. In a pattern reminiscent of Meiji ideological reforms, the family meal was transformed into a cult of domesticity, and an ability to cook was promoted as a key symbol of adult womanhood. The following decades witnessed the (re)invention of the Japanese culinary scene as we know it today: a "foodscape" saturated with local and international fast-food chains, ubiquitous vending machines, and culinary mass entertainment.

Economic affluence and a growing familiarity with foreign culinary trends fostered a concern among consumers about the safety of the food supply. The same factors have also occasioned an emerging pride in domestic produce and local specialties. Imported foods, which had been taken for granted as somehow superior, have gradually lost their attractive appeal. As anthropologist Jennifer Robertson noted in her study of the Japanese politics of nostalgia, advertisers from the 1980s onward began to capitalize on the notion that "future society is the flavor of *furusato*" (native place) (Robertson 1991:13). The term *kokusan* (domestically harvested or produced), became generally equated with goods of high quality, safety and perfection of form (Bestor 1999:169).

From the 1970s onwards, Japanese consumers became increasingly educated about the risks associated with pesticides and the connection between environmental pollution and mass food production (Jussaume et al. 2000). The notorious case of Minamata, where the living and unborn alike were seriously disabled and deformed by fish poisoned by the industrial mercury effluent dumped into the bay by the Chisso Corporation from the late 1940s onward, marked the beginning of a budding awareness in Japan of the need for a safe food supply. The Minamata case, first litigated in 1953, was finally settled in the late 1990s. The dangers of depending on other countries for food staples was brought home in 1973 when the United States temporarily suspended exports of soybeans to Japan in order to protect domestic supplies. Self-sufficiency was also a much-publicized matter in the late 1980s and early 1990s when the pressure from the United States and some European countries to force open Japan's rice market met with violent opposition (Ohnuki-Tierney 1993:26–28). Since then, Japanese politicians have made a regular practice of linking economic security with the integrity of cultural identity.

During the 1990s various consumer groups advocating organic farming and pledging a reduction in food imports gained public support all over Japan. There is near universal opposition on the part of Japanese consumers to genetically modified foods, despite the Koizumi government's insistence on their safety. The first case of "mad cow" disease, or BSE (bovine spongiform encephalopathy), reported in 2001, was traced to imported animal feed, further highlighting for many Japan's vulnerability as a food importer. Whether consumer pressure is enough to catalyze real structural changes in the corporatized food industry remains to be seen. However, the summers of 2000 and 2001, dubbed by the media as "summers of eating dangerously," which witnessed the Snow Brand milk poisoning scandal and culminated with the first BSE case, did result in actions by the government toward further revision of Japan's legislation concerning food production. Law specialist Luke Nottage argues that the enactment of the Product Liability Law in 1994 clearly reflected the growing power of consumers, and the events of 2000 and 2001 strengthened this trend (Nottage 2004).

Despite a decade-long recession, the Japanese still have a significant amount of disposable income which they tend to spend mostly on novelty foods, including regional products, which helps to "feed" the rural economy. Not a few urbanites elect to spend their holidays experiencing an ostensibly "traditional" and "more authentic" way of life at one of the numerous farm villages that are now part of the domestic tourist economy (Robertson 1991, 1997). The revival and outright invention of local foodways, largely stimulated by media attention, spices up the otherwise homogenized national cuisine.

Historian Eric Rath (2001) examined the connection between organic farming and so-called local traditions through a case study of the recent revival of heirloom vegetables in Kyoto. He focused on the exclusive brands of vegetables that, for the past decade, have been marketed under the label "Kyoto vegetables" (kyō yasai). This phrase refers to the varieties of vegetables produced by Kyoto farmers before World War II, that, until their recent revival, had been replaced by conventional varieties with their promise of higher yields and a greater resistance to disease. Using the history of vegetable farming in Kyoto as a backdrop, Rath methodically traces the process whereby "Kyoto vegetables" were reintroduced to the marketplace.

In the 1960s and 1970s, Kyoto city and prefectural authorities took the first steps toward preserving local vegetables threatened with extinction. Heirloom vegetables became a hit largely through the joint efforts of Kyoto-based restaurant owner-chefs who were dissatisfied with the taste of conventional vegetables and

Kyoto farmers eager to reclaim a market advantage. Greengrocers and restaurants specializing in heirloom vegetables opened, and "the taste of historical Kyoto" was shared throughout Japan via gift packs and souvenirs of eggplants, turnips, and yams. Most Kyoto heirloom vegetables are produced with no or very few chemical fertilizers and pesticides, and are usually available only seasonally, unlike conventional vegetables available at supermarkets throughout the year. By revitalizing the cultivation of seasonal vegetables, the image of Kyoto as the capital of Japanese culture and culinary heritage was greatly enhanced. However, as Rath's investigation revealed, claiming that a specific geographic site is a cultural and historical origin point, in this case for certain vegetables, is fraught with problems and contradictions. Cases like that of the "Kyoto vegetables" raise questions about both the historical authenticity of local culinary revivals and their effects on the future development of Japanese food culture and the Japanese food industry alike.

The trajectory of the Japanese culinary culture from its pre-modern to its contemporary form provides a useful framework for understanding the transformations experienced by Japanese society in the 20th century. Multiple forces, from industrialization and urbanization to colonialism and globalization, were responsible for the construction of the common culinary heritage shared by the majority of Japanese today. The careful analysis of the culinary transformation of modern Japan not only reveals food as an important medium for the understanding of the workings of society, but also confirms the importance of food and cuisine in social action.

ACKNOWLEDGMENTS

This chapter has greatly benefited from the comments, suggestions, and editorial work of Jennifer Robertson.

NOTES

1   Editor's note: The 1985 film *Kazoku gēmu* (Family Game) parodies the pathological aspects of family dinner performances by showing how fragile is the official ideology of domesticity. The family of four in question dines sitting on one side of a long rectangular table, and serve themselves from a cart that can be wheeled by hand back and forth along the front of the table. Their meals are orderly and banal affairs until the status quo is disrupted by their son's tutor, who, invited to dinner, starts a raucous food fight.
2   Editor's note: *shina*, used historically in reference to China, is now associated with Japanese imperialist aggression in China and regarded as a pejorative reference. *Chūka* derives from the Chinese name for the People's Republic and is therefore the preferable term today.

REFERENCES

Ashkenazi, Michael, and Jeanne Jacob. 2000. The Essence of Japanese Cuisine: An Essay on Food and Culture. Richmond: Curzon Press.
Bestor, Theodore C. 1999. Constructing *Sushi*: Food Culture, Trade, and Commodification in a Japanese Market. *In* Lives in Motion: Composing Circles of Self and Community in Japan. Susan Orpett Long, ed. pp. 151–190. Ithaca, NY: East Asia Program, Cornell University.

Cobbi, Jane. 1995. *Sonaemono*: Ritual Gifts to the Deities. *In* Ceremony and Ritual in Japan. J. van Bremen and Dolores P. Martinez, eds. pp. 201–209. Richmond: Curzon Press.

Cwiertka, Katarzyna J. 2002. Popularising a Military Diet in Wartime and Postwar Japan. Asian Anthropology 1(1):1–30.

Daniels, Inge Maria. 2001. The Fame of Miyajima: Spirituality, Commodification and the Tourist Trade of Souvenirs in Japan. Ph.D. dissertation, University College London.

Ehara, Ayako. 2000. Nichijō no shokuzai to ryōri (Everyday Ingredients and Dishes). *In* Rakugo ni miru edo no shoku bunka (Food Culture of Edo as Seen through Rakugo). Tabi No Bunka Kenkyūjo, ed. pp. 33–55. Tokyo: Kawade Shobō.

—— 2001. Sōkatsu: shoku no denshō, kyōiku, jōhō (Summary: Food Transmission, Education and Information). *In* Shoku to kyōiku (Food and Education). Ayako Ehara, ed. pp. 227–252. Tokyo: Domesu Shuppan.

Handa, Tatsuko. 1975. Taishōki no kateika kyōiku (Domestic Science Education during the Taishō Period). *In* Taishō no joshi kyōiku (Women's Education of the Taishō Period). Nihon Joshi Daigaku Joshi Kyōiku Kenkyūjo, ed. pp. 74–106. Tokyo: Kokudosha.

Inoue, Tadashi. 1988. Katei to iu fūkei: shakai shinrishi nōto (The Landscape Called "Home": Notes on Socio-Psychological History). Tokyo: Nihon Hōsō Shuppan Kyōkai.

Ishige, Naomichi. 2000. Japan. *In* The Cambridge World History of Food. Kenneth F. Kiple and Kriemhild C. Ornelas, eds. pp. 1175–1183. Cambridge: Cambridge University Press.

Iwamura, Nobuko. 2003. Kawaru kazoku, kawaru shokutaku: shinjitsu ni hakai sareru māketingu jōshiki (Changing Family, Changing Meals: Facts that Demolish Conventional Marketing Wisdom). Tokyo: Keisō Shobō.

Jussaume, Raymond, A. Jr., Shūji Hisano, and Yoshimitsu Taniguchi. 2000. Food Safety in Modern Japan. Japanstudien: Jahrbuch des Deutschen Instituts für Japanstudien der Philipp Franz von Siebold Stiftung 12:211–228.

Kumakura, Isao. 1993. Enkyō to shite no shokutaku (Dining Table as Happy Circle). *In* Shōwa no sesōshi (The History of Social Conditions during the Shōwa Period). Naomichi Ishige, ed. pp. 29–46. Tokyo: Domesu Shuppan.

Nottage, Luke. 2004. Product Safety and Liability Law in Japan: From Minamata to Mad Cows. London: Routledge.

Ohnuki-Tierney, Emiko. 1993. Rice as Self: Japanese Identities through Time. Princeton, NJ: Princeton University Press.

Osaka Mainichi. 1932–33. Lunch Counters à la Japonaise. The Osaka Mainichi 65–68.

Rath, Erik C. 2001. How Does a Vegetable Become "Traditional" in Kyoto? Paper presented at the Annual Meeting of the American Anthropological Association, Washington DC, November 29.

Robertson, Jennifer. 1991. Native and Newcomer: Making and Remaking a Japanese City. Berkeley: University of California Press.

—— 1997. Empire of Nostalgia: Rethinking "Internationalization" in Japan Today. Theory, Culture and Society 14(4):97–122.

Sand, Jordan. 1998. At Home in the Meiji Period: Inventing Japanese Domesticity. *In* Mirror of Modernity: Invented Traditions of Modern Japan. Stephen Vlastos, ed. pp. 191–207. Berkeley: University of California Press.

Smith, Robert J. 1976. Ancestor Worship in Contemporary Japan. Stanford: Stanford University Press.

Takagi, Nobuo. 1988. Japanese Abroad: Armed with Slippers and Soy Sauce. Japan Quarterly 35:432–436.

Tanaka, Seiichi. 1987. Ichii taisui: chūgoku ryōri denraishi (A Narrow Strait: The History of the Introduction of Chinese Cuisine). Tokyo: Shibata Shoten.

White, Merry I. 2002. Ladies Who Lunch: Young Women and Domestic Fallacy in Japan. *In* Asian Food: The Global and the Local. Katarzyna J. Cwiertka with Boudewijn C. A. Walraven, eds. pp. 63–75. Honolulu: University of Hawaii Press.

SUGGESTED READING

Bestor, Theodore C. 2004. *Tsukiji*: The Fish Market at the Center of the World. Berkeley: University of California Press.

Cwiertka, Katarzyna J. 2003. Eating the World: Restaurant Culture in Early Twentieth Century Japan. European Journal of East Asian Studies 2(1):89–116.

Ishige, Naomichi. 2001. The History and Culture of Japanese Food. London: Kegan Paul.

Noguchi, Paul. 1994. Savor Slowly: *Ekiben* – The Fast Food of High-Speed Japan. Ethnology 4:317–330.

PART VI

VI Religion and Science, Beliefs and Bioethics

CHAPTER 26 Historical, New, and "New" New Religions

Ian Reader

INTRODUCTION

Japan has a complex history of religious traditions, ranging from the numerous sects of established Buddhism, many of which drew initial inspiration from China and others of which developed in Japan, and which provide models of how world traditions may be adopted and transformed within particular cultural contexts, to an ethnically oriented historical tradition, Shinto, to numerous new religions of all sizes. Its contemporary significance for anthropologists and sociologists of religion is also evident through its position as a highly developed post-industrial society in which the various problems and vicissitudes of religion in modern societies (for example, questions of secularization, of the relationships of religion, state, and society, religious reactions to modernity, and globalization) are manifest and provide a pertinent comparative frame of reference with relation to the post-industrialized Western world.

Because of its complex religious culture (besides those traditions already mentioned, Confucianism, Christianity, and Taoism have all influenced the situation, as has the folk religious tradition, which is covered elsewhere in this volume) it would be impossible to cover them all in the scope of one chapter. Therefore, and because of the vast scope of the subject, this chapter is of necessity both generalized and selective. I will first make some very broad general comments on the field, and then will focus on some contemporary topics whose study contributes greatly to the field at large.

STUDIES OF RELIGION IN JAPAN: OVERVIEWS AND PERSPECTIVES

A first point to note concerns the developing terminological nuances in the field and the ways in which Japanese studies of religion were initially influenced by

Euro-American academic studies but have subsequently developed their own orientations and modes of interpretation. The early emergence of the discipline of the study of religion (*shūkyōgaku*) in Japan was not dissimilar to that of Europe, with a primary emphasis on philology, doctrine, text and belief structures within major traditions, while such things as practice and ritual were either ignored or were studied in other disciplinary areas such as anthropology and folk studies. Given Japan's Buddhist tradition, it is unsurprising that one of the first branches of the study of religion to develop academically there was Buddhist studies (*bukkyōgaku*), which was heavily influenced by the philological orientations of 19th-century European scholars such as Max Mueller. This orientation also privileged the Indic languages in which the early Buddhist sutras were written, and Buddhist studies in Japan (even when focused on China and Japan) are often still carried out under the rubric of *indogaku* (Indian studies). They have also in many areas had a confessional aspect, with much work being carried out within sectarian traditions in Japan, and focused on sect doctrines and founders.[1]

Such sectarian orientations have been enhanced also because of the institutions at which much of this research has been carried out. Many religious organizations in Japan have their own universities at which sectarian-focused studies are carried out and which often specialize in elucidating and interpreting the doctrinal formulations and histories of particular traditions. Such institutions include universities such as Ōtani and Ryūkoku (both of which are affiliated to the Jōdo Shin Buddhist sect), Kōya (Shingon Buddhism), and Komazawa and Tōhoku Fukushi (Sōtō Zen), as well as Shinto-affiliated institutions such as Kokugakuin University. While these produce much valuable research in many areas they also have a strong tradition of sectarian doctrinal interpretation and commentary. There are also a number of universities founded by Christian traditions (e.g. Sophia and Nanzan universities, both of which have Catholic affiliations), and which have been active in promoting and enhancing the study of religion in Japan. For a comprehensive view of these traditions in the context of their study and the academic traditions that have developed in Japan, readers are referred to Reader (in press) (the Nanzan Guidebook for the Study of Japanese Religions).

In many other areas, too, Euro-American influences conditioned both the development of academic studies and also any theoretical approaches. Thus, for example, as anthropologically oriented studies of religion – focused primarily on thematic issues such as rituals and festivals – developed, they drew heavily, for modes of theoretical interpretation, on Euro-American scholarship. The same has been true of sociological studies of religion, which developed in Japan very much under the shadow and influence of major European "gods" in the field such as Weber and Durkheim. Indeed, one of the cardinal "rites of passage" of Japanese sociologists of religion in establishing themselves in the field has been to translate one or other of the works of such European figures into Japanese. (On such issues and on some of the underlying perspectives in Japanese sociological studies of religion, see Reader 1989.)

The above comments imply that Japanese studies of religion have thus tended historically toward the descriptive and the theoretically derivative, and one point that should be made repeatedly is that traditionally such studies have tended toward insularity and a lack of comparisons (often fueled by underlying ideological notions of "uniqueness') rather than engaging in cross-cultural analysis. However, such criticisms are becoming increasingly less valid as new generations of Japanese scholars develop and engage in studies that are both cognisant of the wider field and under-pinned by a willingness to engage in comparative studies and to incorporate or challenge existing academic theories based on their readings of the Japanese situation. This, too, has led to various areas of theoretical development, in which Japanese scholarship – often interacting with new generations of non-Japanese scholars who have studied and worked in Japan – has developed increasingly sophisticated analytical accounts and studies of religion in Japan, and has provided valuable critiques of Western-derived theories along with studies of value for a wider understanding of religious phenomena.

This shift is in some ways also reflected by the changing Japanese interpretation and use of *shūkyō*, the word most widely used in Japanese to refer to the English term "religion," and which contains as many problematic meanings as does the English term. It has often, erroneously, been assumed by some Western scholars (notably anthropologists) that the term *shūkyō* (made up of the ideograms *shū*, sect/organiza-tion, and *kyō*, teachings) is a 19th-century invention designed to translate into Japanese the notion of "religion" as it was then understood in Western terms, and which equated "religion" with organized institutions, teachings, and doctrines.[2] This is not actually the case: *shūkyō* existed primarily as a Buddhist term indicating specific religious doctrinal systems well before the Meiji period, although it came into wider usage after Meiji because of such meanings.

Just as the term "religion" has been a contended category that has changed as academic studies have advanced in Euro-American contexts, to the degree that studies of religion nowadays incorporate studies of practice and ritual and utilize fieldwork (qualitative) and statistical/survey (quantitative) methodologies as much as they emphasize doctrine and text, so, too, has the term and understanding of *shūkyō* undergone reassessment and change in Japanese scholastic circles. Certainly confes-sional and doctrinally focused notions were central to early Japanese studies of religion, where early pioneers such as Anesaki Masaharu of Tokyo University were concerned with identifying what Anesaki saw as a common religious consciousness in all people, and, in his case, with viewing the role of religious studies as that of defending (rather than analyzing) religion (see Isomae 2002). However, much has changed since then, with the field and the term *shūkyō* undergoing modification as Japanese scholars (and, most strikingly, scholars with interests in the study of rituals and practices associated with "folk" religion) have developed them in the light of their own country's traditions (see chapter 27 in this volume). Notably, too, Japanese scholars, far from regarding terms such as "religion" and *shūkyō* as colonial impos-itions on the Japanese situation, emphasize their importance as valuable tools in comparative methodological studies (e.g., Miyake 1989; Reader, in press; Shinno 1991; and chapter 27 in this volume).

Thus scholars such as Miyake Hitoshi (1974, 1989), Gorai Shigeru (e.g., 1975, 1984, 1989), Sakurai Tokutarō (1982), Shinno Toshikazu (1991), and others, with interests in a variety of fields ranging from the study of Japanese mountain religion, to the relationship between Buddhism and folk practices, to studies of religious itiner-ants, came to interpret and understand *shūkyō* in ways that drew together doctrinal, folk, organizational, and other areas (such as studies of ritual and practice). Miyake (1974), for instance, has discussed the "structure of Japanese religion" (*nihon shūkyō no kōzō*) through an examination of such topics as calendrical festivals, prayers for worldly benefits, beliefs associated with spirit possession, and the like. Initially, in this volume, Miyake's work manifested the influence of European scholars such as Mircea Eliade and his emphasis on the relationship of the sacred and profane (Japanese: *sei to zoku*), ideas which remain of major interest in Japanese studies of religion. Subsequently his work, which has consistently used the mountain religious tradition and ritual practices of Shugendō – itself a blend of folk, Taoist, Buddhist, Shinto and ascetic elements – has sought to incorporate religion in Japan within a broader comparative context, discussing it in its popular, folk dimensions in Japan through an analytic framework applicable to any religious system and based in a linguistic/ structuralist interpretation of the language and structure of rituals (Miyake 1989).

Japanese sociologists of religion, too, have focused on issues of practice and on levels of engagement in a variety of events – many of them customary and associated with the social order – as indices of religiosity (see, e.g., Inoue 1994; Ōmura and Nishiyama 1988; Yanagawa 1988), and have consistently used statistical surveys on issues such as performing New Year worship rites (*hatsumōde*), worshiping ancestors, cleaning graves on specific Buddhist ritual occasions, visiting diviners and getting oracle lots and the like to this end. Yanagawa, one of Anesaki's successors as Professor of Religious Studies at Tokyo University (where he taught from 1960 until his retirement in 1986), trained and strongly influenced later generations of scholars in the sociology of religion, and played a leading role in emphasizing the importance of focusing on practice, and on seeing and developing an understanding of religion as an aspect of daily life (see Akaike and Swyngedouw 1986 for a fuller discussion of his work and influence). This focus on practice and behavior, besides challenging the older, doctrinally based, focus of the study of religion also provided a means through which Japanese scholars were able to challenge and critique some of the prevailing assumptions and theories emerging in Euro-American sociology of religion in the latter part of the 20th century, notably the notion of secularization, as I discuss below.

Overall, then, the concept of *shūkyō* (and the academic discipline of studying it, *shūkyōgaku*, normally translated as "religious studies") is one that continues to undergo rethinking in the present day. However, as the field has developed, the influence of those who have engaged with the study of where and how folk customs and practices intersect with the structures of organized and established traditions, and who have examined what people do (for example, in relation to festivals, and visits to shrines, temples, and other institutions affiliated to religious organization), has helped shape critical analysis and also open up the possibilities for engaged discussion of other cultures and practices in a variety of areas.

DEVELOPMENTS IN BUDDHIST STUDIES

These advances, and the growing turn toward critical analysis and away from earlier confessional modes, has been evident, too, in many other areas. Thus, while much Buddhist scholarship retains a sectarian orientation, it has also developed highly critical faculties that influence Buddhist studies beyond Japan. The critical investigations of Ch'an and Zen Buddhist texts and records that scholars such as Yanagida Seizan (see Faure 1991:390–391) have helped pioneer, have been part of a new wave of critical studies of Buddhism that have deconstructed the hitherto widely accepted, idealized constructs set forth by D. T. Suzuki and other early writers. It has led to a new wave of Euro-American scholarship that has paid close attention to the relationship between Buddhism and popular practices such as death rituals, relic worship, and the like, and that has altered our understandings of Buddhism in origin and development (e.g., Bodiford 1993; Faure 1991; Ruppert 2000). In addition to such developments, one can also note the important, yet highly controversial, modes of critical textual interpretation that have emerged out of sectarian universities in Japan – most notably through the "Critical Buddhism" (*hihan bukkyō*) developed by Hakamaya Noriaki (e.g., 1989, 1990) and Matsumoto Shirō (e.g., 1993), two scholars based at the Sōtō Zen sect's Komazawa University, which challenges the social and political implications of Buddhist thought in Japan, and suggests how doctrinal formulations such as the doctrine of *hongaku shisō* (original enlightenment) have led Japanese Buddhism to become highly conservative, socially moribund, and complicit with power structures in Japan, helping reinforce discrimination and negative views of women (for a full discussion of Critical Buddhism and further details of Hakamaya's and Matsumoto's work and responses to it see Hubbard and Swanson 1997). While Hakamaya's and Matsumoto's work has been highly contentious in Japan, it has helped open up scholastic debates over the relationship between Buddhism, the state, power structures, and society and led to a growing field of study of Buddhism in terms of sex and gender relations and issues related to social discrimination which are of much interest (e.g., Bodiford 1996; Josei to Bukkyō Tōkai Kantō Nettowāku 1999).

Equally significant, a theme that has been central to academic understandings of religion in Japan is the recognition that one cannot readily draw definitive lines of categorization between traditions, and that there is much that is shared between and across traditions, in terms of practices and commonly held beliefs. Early assumptions that "Shinto" and "Buddhism," while displaying much mutual interaction, were clearly separate traditions – with Shinto portrayed in nationalist discourse as having existed from the origins of the Japanese nation – have been repeatedly challenged by new waves of scholarship, which have indicated that Shinto and Buddhism were thoroughly intertwined until the forcible separation that occurred after the Meiji Restoration.[3]

INTERACTION AND MEANINGS

Thus, one of the primary themes within the study of religion in Japan relates to the interactions between traditions, and also to topics in which the evident lack of clear-cut divisions between different areas (for example, Buddhism and Shinto, folk practices and Buddhism) are evident. It is such areas that are perhaps of most interest for anthropological studies of religion, and here I will note just a sample of the many topics that have been studied by Japanese (and some Euro-American) scholars. I will also, in the concluding section of this chapter, draw attention to some areas that have, by comparison, been less well studied thus far. Areas that have seen some degree of study include rituals and festivals, particularly those centered on Shinto institutions and deities (e.g., Yanagawa 1987), the relationships of Buddhism, death rituals, ancestors, and households (e.g. Kōmoto 1988, 2001), the role of charismatic and ascetic figures who mediate between established religious institutions and the lives of ordinary people (e.g., Shūkyō Shakaigaku Kenkyū Kai 1987), the relationship between Buddhism and "folk" religion, especially as it centers on holy, liminal figures such as *hijiri* (a term that is often translated as "wandering ascetic" or "wandering holy figure"), and mountain religious practices and their role in bringing together Buddhist and folk themes (e.g., Gorai 1975; Shinno 1991), and the participation in seemingly "folk" practices by adherents of established religious organizations (e.g., Kaneko 1991).

In each of these fields there is a growing amount of research by Japanese and Western scholars. To cite just a sample, one could point to the interest that has been shown in festivals and shrine rituals – for example, in the context of their relationship to wider social and community structures, and as a means of developing community consciousness, as well as in terms of their symbolic meanings. These have long been studied by scholars such as Yanagawa Keiichi (1987), who has especially drawn on structuralist analyses to decipher the meanings of festivals, and Sonoda Minoru (1988a, 1988b), an academic and Shinto priest, who has sought to discuss Shinto in the context of, and as a manifestation of, the Japanese natural and social environment. More recently, textured studies integrating historical and anthropological work have been done by American scholars such as Schnell (1999) and (in terms of the working of shrines) Nelson (1999). The relationship between Buddhism, death rituals, the ancestors, and the household has been a theme discussed by both Japanese and Western scholars. This relationship is one of the deepest elements in Japanese religious structure, so much so that some have categorized Buddhism as primarily a funeral religion in Japan (e.g., Tamamuro 1963). Major studies on who the ancestors are, how they are venerated in familial contexts, and who is worshiped at family Buddhist altars have been conducted through fieldwork examinations by Robert J. Smith, whose 1974 study remains a key work for Japanese scholars, and more recently by Kōmoto Mitsugu (1988, 2001), who has examined the incidence and changing patterns of such practices in Buddhist and household contexts in contemporary Japan. It is also a topic area that has attracted much interest in recent times among Euro-American scholars, with a number of recent doctoral theses and research projects having been carried out into funeral practices since the Meiji era, the modernization of funerals, and the like (for an overview of such research and insights into the types of research in progress see Kenney and Gilday 2000).

The relationship between Buddhism and folk religious practices, and the ways in which wandering mendicants through much of Japanese history have served as links between temples and ordinary people, has been a topic of much interest in Japanese scholastic terms (e.g., Gorai 1984; Miyake 1974; Miyata 1993; Sakurai 1982). Arguing that too much emphasis had hitherto been placed on studies of organized and institutional religion, scholars such as Shinno Toshikazu have turned to detailed studies of figures such as the ascetic *hijiri* who, as Shinno (1991) shows, played a seminal role in the promotion of temple cults, pilgrimage, and the like, and who, as such, were central elements in the structure of Japanese religion and in the development of a dynamic creativity within Japanese religion. Shinno also draws attention to the charismatic, miracle-working powers of such figures, thereby linking them into wider Japanese studies of shamanic figures (e.g., Sakurai 1974, 1977) and to modern faith healers who also, he notes, manifest charismatic tendencies as well as mediating between ordinary people and the spirit world.

PILGRIMAGES

An area of study related very much to the aforementioned tradition of holy wanderers, which is particularly relevant to anthropological concerns and methods of study, and which has an extensive literature in Japanese, is the study of pilgrimage. This is an area in which the study of religion in Japan has much to add to wider studies, although as yet it has not attained the significance it ought to have. This is not just because of the Western-centric orientation evident within the broader study of pilgrimage (in which much of the literature claiming to make theoretical advances in the field has been almost wholly focused on the study of Christian pilgrimage), but also because virtually all the work that has been done on Japanese pilgrimage has been done in Japanese and hence has thus far been inaccessible to wider audiences.

This general ignorance of the Japanese situation in the context of pilgrimage is especially unfortunate in that, in terms of the scope of academic work that has been done on it, from the more historical to the anthropological, as well as of the complexity of its "pilgrimage culture" (Reader and Swanson 1997), Japan is almost unrivaled. Not only has Japan developed an extensive vocabulary of pilgrimage which relates to a multiplicity of forms and types of pilgrimage practice (Hoshino 1989; Reader and Swanson 1997) but these forms have been extensively studied and analytically and typologically delineated by Japanese scholars using methods ranging from the sociological (Maeda 1971; Satō 1989, 1990a, 1990b; Waseda Daigaku Dōkūkan Kenkyūkai 1997) to the anthropological (Hoshino 1980, 1981, 1986a, 1986b, 1989, 1999, 2001) to the historical (Shinno 1980, 1991, 1996) and the social-historical (Shinjō 1982).[4] What characterizes all such studies is that, while they may take a particular disciplinary approach, they generally also display a depth of historical consciousness and awareness that is not always evident in Euro-American anthropological studies, whether of pilgrimage or other topics. As such, much Japanese scholarship in this area serves to emphasize the critical importance of combining a variety of approaches (most particularly the historical and the anthropological) in order to study pilgrimage.

Some of the work prevalent in this field has already been mentioned above (e.g., Shinno's study of ascetics as a uniting point in religious structure, which also emphasizes the importance of pilgrimage as a core religious value and practice in Japan (1991:19). Others mentioned above provide some of the most detailed and comprehensive accounts of what pilgrimages were like in pre-modern times that can be found anywhere in the world. Thus Shinjō's work (e.g., 1982) illustrates how local and regional issues and economic factors may shape and affect pilgrimage practices, while Maeda Takashi's (1971) study of pilgrimage in the 17th–19th centuries, based on the calling cards left by pilgrims at temples on the Saikoku and Shikoku pilgrimages, represents one of the most detailed sociological accounts of pre-modern pilgrims anywhere in the world. Because of its bureaucratic and controlled nature, Tokugawa Japan has been especially valuable in providing materials – from pilgrims' journals to laws relating to pilgrims, to records of their travels as they passed through regional barriers – of value to the study of pre-modern pilgrimage (see, e.g., Kondō 1971, 1982). A major focus of such studies also has been the interaction between local people and pilgrims – an area that has thus far been little discussed in studies of pilgrimage elsewhere, but which has recently been augmented in the Japanese context by the work of the French scholar Nathalie Kouamé (2001), whose detailed study of the local laws governing pilgrims in Shikoku in the Tokugawa period, and of local customs of almsgiving to pilgrims, marks a new stage in the understanding of the influence of local populations on pilgrimages.

In anthropological terms mention should be made of the work of Hoshino Eiki (e.g., 1980, 1981, 1986a, 1986b, 1989, 1999, 2001), whose studies of the Shikoku pilgrimage make use of historical records and research into pilgrims' journals through the ages, along with fieldwork studies and interviews. While Hoshino, who makes use of the theories of Victor Turner, notably his concept of communitas, points to problematic aspects of Turner's work, he also provides salient counter-arguments to those who have critiqued Turner, by arguing that pilgrims, interacting with local people, create a specially structured religious environment around the island and the pilgrimage, and that they function within the framework of this special environment (Hoshino 2001).[5] Hoshino's studies of pilgrimage records from the earlier part of the 20th century also indicate that many Shikoku pilgrims were from the island itself (2001:258–309), a point that has been affirmed also by modern-day sociological studies of Shikoku residents (e.g., Kaneko 1991) and of Shikoku pilgrims (Waseda Daigaku Dōkūkan Kenkyūkai 1997, Osada et al. 2003; Reader 2005). These studies serve as valuable counter-arguments to the widely assumed notion that pilgrims do not visit sites within their locality, preferring to travel to distant places instead.

THE NEW RELIGIONS

While pilgrimage is an area where Japanese case studies and research could provide new insights for the wider field, the Japanese new religions are an example of an area in which Japan has already provided some insights and relevant theoretical materials for scholars in the wider field. Probably the most striking religious phenomenon of the modern (i.e., Meiji and after) era has been the development of waves of "new religions" (*shin shūkyō*) and "new" new religions, *shin shin shūkyō*, the latter a term used by Japanese scholars to refer to the more recent, post-1970s, new religions. Extensive studies have been conducted by Japanese scholars, who have tended primarily toward the historical and thematic, examining the new religions as a general phenomenon. The centerpiece of these studies is the extensive authoritative *Shinshū-kyō jiten* (Encyclopedia of New Religions: Inoue et al. 1991), which provides extensive details about these religions, their founders, organizations, use of media, and much else. Various other works by Japanese scholars, such as Shimazono (1992a), Inoue (1992), and Numata (1988), have been supplemented by a number of field-work and in-depth studies of particular new religions by Euro-American scholars (e.g., Davis 1980; Earhart 1988; Hardacre 1984, 1986; Reader 1993, 2000a). More recently, a number of more detailed, fieldwork-based studies have been conducted into particular new religions by teams of Japanese researchers, most notably the extensive study of the small new religion Hōseikai by Shimazono Susumu and a group of his Tokyo University graduate students (see Shimazono 1993, 1999).

It is widely agreed by scholars in the field that while the new religions manifest a variety of different guises and forms of teaching and practice, they can nonetheless be considered as a unitary phenomenon with a variety of common characteristics, ranging from commonalities in structure such as being centered around charismatic founders, having a lay focus, and proselytizing through family and personal connections; in teachings, including claims to the discovery of new truths (or the revival of hidden truths) that will spiritually transform the world, and affirmations that one needs to engage in spiritual practices in order to improve the self; and in their practices, which center on techniques that can be engaged in by all and which are often claimed to provide spiritual healing and to help members overcome problems and give new meaning to their lives. Equally, too, they have been widely seen as conservative in moral and political terms, affirming the value of traditional practices (e.g. ancestor worship) and a Confucian morality in which deference to seniors and affirmations of traditional gender relations are highly valued. They are also largely conceived of as urban movements or as movements that have emerged in response to, and in conditions of, social change and unrest, and as providing spiritual alternatives to the established religions, which are widely seen as failing to provide adequate support for people in times of rapid change.

The size of the Japanese new religions phenomenon, coupled with the extensive studies that have been made of them, have meant that Japanese new religions have much to contribute to the wider field of the study of new religions, a field that has really come into focus since the 1970s, when the term "new religion" really began to emerge in the writings of scholars studying religion in the industrialized countries of Europe and the United States. Indeed, there has been some inconclusive debate about whether the term "new religion" was in fact imported into non-Japanese scholarship because of its usage in Japanese contexts.[6] While the wider field has at times tended to marginalize or treat Japan as a "unique" situation (partly because of the linguistic problems involved in its study), there are some areas in which it has taken note of the findings of Japanese scholarship, and more recently in which it has become a critically important area of study (see below). Here I will flag up four main areas where studies of Japanese new religions have contributed to or can say much about the wider field, or where their study has led to challenges to wider sociological theories of religion.

One such area relates to the patterns of historical emergence of new movements. Japanese scholars have analyzed the new religions as an enduring historical phenomenon, in which new movements have consistently been generated over a period of a century and a half. Compared to studies of new movements in Europe and the United States (which have largely been focused on the post-1960s era) this has given the Japanese field a historic depth, and has enabled it to develop typologies of development, centered around eras of development and social conditions that as yet have not been widely discussed in non-Japanese contexts (see, e.g., Inoue 1992). Moreover, because many of the older "new religions" are primarily now centered on third- and fourth-generation members (and some of these older movements also appear to lose members who move on to newer, more dynamic movements), scope also exists for continuing discussions of one of the more interesting theoretical questions in this field relating to definitions about how long a movement can continue to be called "new," and whether one can use the framework of "new religions" to relate to movements of this type.

One major focus of studies of the Japanese new religions has been the role of founder figures, who are invariably charismatic figures who have often undergone extreme personal crises, who have found ways of overcoming these and who, in so doing, have made themselves into archetypal examples of the potential for self-transformation. The nature of religious charisma, as located within the person rather than in the office they hold, has been a theme that has come through in many Japanese accounts of such leaders (e.g. Shūkyō Shakaigaku Kenkyū Kai 1987; Shimazono 1999), and in this emphasis on charisma one can see links to the studies of ascetic mendicants of pre-modern times.

A related point, which comes through most compellingly in the writings of Shimazono Susumu, is the relationship that occurs in the new religions between concepts of magic and morality. While classic Weberian theory has suggested that modernization and educational advances in a society will produce a shift away from the magical and toward an emphasis on morality, in effect suggesting that magic and morality are at opposite ends of a spectrum, Shimazono has shown that the two can coexist and indeed mutually reinforce each other, and that often adherents of new religions may be attracted both by the emphasis these movements have on magic and spiritual healing and by their insistence on clearly set out moral codes. Indeed, magical healing may be predicated upon correct moral behavior (especially in the context of correct observance of obligations relating to the ancestors: see, e.g., Shimazono 1992a).

By the same token, while Weber considered magic to be a serious impediment to economic progress and to the development of rationality within society, Shimazono and others have challenged this view under the aegis of the Japanese new religions. It has, indeed, been one of the main achievements of the Japanese sociology of religion – notably by Shimazono (1992a), but also expressed in the works of non-Japanese specialists on Japan such as Davis (1980) – to demonstrate that, in (post)modern times, such paradigms do not operate well, and that, rather than impeding each other, magic and morality may well function together and mutually reinforce each other in modern society. This issue has come out, too, in studies both of the "new" new religions, which, as various scholars (e.g., Nishiyama 1988; Numata 1995; Shimazono 1992b, 1996) have noted, have flourished very much because they operate in modern, urban contexts, are at home with and use modern technologies, speak in ways that communicate directly with the modern youth of the cities, and affirm and are centered around notions of magic, mystery, miracles, and notions of supernatural power. It is in this fusion that their appeal and power lie, and it is in such contexts that Japanese scholars have thus provided countervailing arguments to Euro-American sociological theories.

Indeed, as recent scholarship has shown, there is much in Japan that can be related to the "New Age" phenomenon found in the West, and scholars such as Shimazono (1996, 2001) and Haga Manabu and Yumiyama Tatsuya (1994) have pointed to what they see as an increasing fragmentation of religious structures and an emergent individualization in which people "pick and mix" a variety of practices together in a form of personalized religion, but without specific adherence or affiliation.[7] While scholars in Japan have paid some attention to the work being done in Europe and the United States on New Age phenomena, and have used it as a comparative example through which to develop their theoretical frameworks, at present the reverse has not been the case, but it is evident that some consideration of the Japanese case and of the work being done by Japanese scholars will be increasingly critical for scholars seeking to understand the changing patterns of religion in (post)-industrial societies.

SECULARIZATION AND CHALLENGE

Another area in which Japanese sociologists of religion have questioned prevailing Western assumptions is over the issue of secularization, broadly taken to mean the decline of religious affiliation and adherence in the modern day. While, in the 1960s and early 1970s, there was some interest in such Western-based theories, by the early 1970s Japanese scholars had begun to question the validity and applicability of theories and ideas founded in a climate in which there was one overriding established religious tradition (mainstream Christianity) to an environment, Japan, where a more variegated and mixed religious structure existed. Moreover, as Japanese scholars were very aware, the apparent "decline" in religion central to the notion of secularization theory was nowhere near as apparent in Japan, where the continued vigor and growth of new religions as well as much evidence of the continuing popularity and strength of "folk" customs – ranging from consultations with shamanic mediums and diviners to the use of charms, amulets, and prayers for worldly benefits at temples and shrines – provided evidence to suggest that modernity and education need not be accompanied by religious decline. Here, of course, one can see how the studies of new religions which had challenged Weberian theories on rationality and magic were also valuable in the context of challenging secularization theory.

  Thus, while Japanese scholars initially questioned secularization theories because they felt that a Western-derived model might be inappropriate in Japanese contexts, they rapidly came to consider that the theory itself was flawed, in that it failed to allow for the potential resurgence – or rearticulation – of religious practices as a counter-vailing move against modernity. Since the 1970s, Japanese scholars have been far less concerned with secularization as a mode of analysis, and more focused on considering how – as the established religions have clearly declined in stature – new modes of practice and of religious articulation and association are coming to the fore to replace them.[8] In recent years, Euro-American sociologists have largely abandoned secularization theory as a viable model of analysis; it should be noted that in this they have been some way behind their Japanese counterparts.

AUM SHINRIKYŌ AND ITS IMPACT ON THE STUDY OF RELIGION

I have suggested that Japanese studies of new religions have opened up especially rich fields of discussion, and that the new religions continue to offer fertile scope for comparative analysis. This is nowhere more evident than in the case of Aum Shinri-kyō, the apocalyptic millennial movement led by the charismatic and blind Asahara Shōkō, which attained international notoriety because of its nerve gas attack on the

Tokyo subway in 1995. No other incident or case in the history of Japanese religions has attracted so much attention outside of Japan as this, as scholars studying new movements, millennialism, and the relationship between religion and conflict sought to learn about Aum and, in so doing, came to recognize that this Japanese movement manifested, albeit in extreme forms, signs and parallels with other cases of violence and destruction in small-scale religious movements that could be set alongside cases such as the Branch Davidians in Waco, Texas, and the People's Temple at Jonestown in Guyana. Yet, while this incident has opened up areas of the comparative study of religious movements through the use of Japanese examples, and has been the most prominent example of how studies of Japanese religion can shape and influence the theoretical perspectives of Euro-American scholarship at the same time, it has also, simultaneously, proved to be the single most damaging incident that the field of modern religious studies has faced in Japan, a point to which I will turn shortly.

When the Aum affair erupted in 1995, it attracted immense interest, especially from American scholars of new religions who were at the time grappling with the Waco affair and whose interpretations of the relationship between new religions and violence had been excessively colored by the spectacle of government intervention at Waco. Standard understandings of new religions – especially communal, introverted, millennial movements – had been heavily based on the notion that external pressures were the main contributory factor to such violence. When the Aum affair exploded, an initial reaction by some American (and Japanese) specialists was that Aum must have been pushed to violence by external pressures – a view that was rapidly undermined as Japanese analyses of Aum developed to show how violence originated inside the enclosed movement (independent of any external pressure on it) and spread outwards. Hence, the case of Aum challenged existing assumptions about the ways in which new movements became involved in violent confrontations, and as such became one of the "must study" cases of modern scholarship on religion, terrorism, violence, and millennialism. Thanks to studies by both Japanese and Western scholars (e.g., Reader 1996, 2000a; Shimada 2001a; Shimazono 1995, 1997), Aum has come to stand as a primary example of how new religions can, in certain contexts, generate violence from within.[9]

Studies of Aum have thus contributed extensively to understanding of the ways in which millennial movements can become violent, and has helped frame the understanding and world view of scholars of new religions across the world. However, although it clearly indicates the importance of scholarship on the new religions and the like in Japan, the Aum affair has simultaneously been an unmitigated disaster in scholarly terms in Japan, in that it has done untold damage to the reputation of scholars and has created immense barriers to the continuing study of religion. This has been partly because, at the time of the subway attack, a small number of scholars appeared to defend Aum. One prominent Japanese scholar had, prior to the subway attack, described Aum as peaceful and had denied that it was involved in wrongdoing, while two American scholars of new religions who were not cognisant of the Japanese situation visited Japan at Aum's invitation after the subway attack and initially declared – in line with standard post-Waco interpretations that new religions in conflict are generally victims – that Aum was not guilty of the crimes attributed to it.

These errors became rapidly apparent and caused public outrage. It became clear that severe methodological weaknesses underpinned such mistakes. The Japanese scholar had relied on the word of senior Aum officials, thereby pursuing a common Japanese scholarly methodology based on high-level interface with senior officials without conducting micro-empirical studies over extended periods of time. The Americans spoke no Japanese and were thus reliant on English-speaking Aum officials, who were able to mislead them, and they disregarded the voices of former Aum members and journalists. These methodological errors brought opprobrium upon the Japanese academic community in the field, and while the subsequent exposure of Aum was a salutary lesson to the wider field, it also had the impact of tarnishing the entire field of the study of religion in Japan. As a result, academics specializing in the study of religions have been attacked as a group in the press and by proponents of the "anti-cult" movement that has grown in Japan since the Aum affair, who have accused the field in general of either being Aum apologists (manifest in the acts of those mentioned above, who defended Aum) or for being complicit in its violence, by not speaking out or exposing it earlier. Equally, the mass media and anti-cult activists alike have issued demands that the role of scholars of religion should be to expose and denounce religious movements, rather than analyze them (see Kisala and Mullins 2001; Reader 2000b). At the same time, a rampant anti-cult movement has developed, and much of the recent rhetoric and discussion about religion in Japan has been framed in its terms, with less focus on the analysis of religion, and more on the assumption of judgmental attitudes toward religious groups.[10]

SUGGESTIONS FOR FUTURE INNOVATIVE RESEARCH AND TOPICS

I have only been able to touch on a small number of issues and topics relevant to a highly complex area with a long history. The areas that I have focused on are sufficient, however, to show how Japan provides a wealth of material and potential for analytical focus that can enrich wider studies of religion in numerous ways, ranging from the historical to the sociological and anthropological, and relating to issues as widespread as secularization theories, the dynamics of new religions and their historical appearance, pilgrimage practices, and millennialism. Studies of Japanese religion, conducted both by Japanese scholars and by European and American scholars fluent in Japanese and enjoying good working relationships with Japanese scholars, have been particularly influential in such areas, and have contributed to new understandings of such diverse topics as the relationship between Buddhism and death rituals, the patterns of development of new religions, and the behavior of enclosed and volatile millennial movements, and their potential for implosion and violence.

I will map out some areas where there remains massive scope for further empirically grounded, fieldwork-based qualitative and quantitative studies of contemporary religious issues. It is ironically the field of the study of contemporary religion that is least well represented in the Japanese and Western religious studies arena at present. One major reason for this at present is the Aum affair, whose repercussions have damaged the field in Japan, and made research into the new religions especially difficult. Another serious long-term problem remains the innate conservatism of the discipline of religious studies – especially in the United States – which continues to privilege the past over the present, and the study of doctrine, texts, and other manifestations of elite institutions (such as Buddhist statues and art) over religious practices carried out in the here and now by living people, and over the religions of the modern day.

While this situation is reprehensible, it also offers many opportunities for the keen researcher. There have, for example, been few studies of the established traditions (Buddhism and Shinto) as they interact, function, and operate in society in the present day, especially when compared with the energy that has been put into examining the relationship between Buddhism and Shinto in pre-Meiji Japan, the relationships between medieval Buddhism and society, and so on. There have been few doctoral dissertations examining the workings of contemporary Buddhist sects in Japan, or studies looking at how Buddhist sects are attempting to deal with the pressing problems of modernity.[11] It is a commonplace assumption of the sociology of religion in general that older, established traditions are losing support in modern society, and certainly this is the assumed situation also in Japan. Yet very little empirical work has been done in this area to determine if such assumptions are correct. Importantly, too, very little has been done to examine what, if any, strategies or activities have been undertaken by the established traditions, or by individual temples and shrines, to counteract this apparent decline in support. Jose Casanova's complaint that the sociology of religion has neglected the old historical religious traditions in favor of the new and the exotic is valid here (Casanova 1992:39). How such traditions have survived and to what degree is a relatively uncharted area in Japan, and while some suggestions have been made about how various practices and popular cults (from worldly benefits, to pilgrimage, to memorial services for aborted babies) have been used to such ends by Buddhist temples (see Hardacre 1998; Reader and Tanabe 1998), relatively little specific study of these issues has occurred.

Such issues may be of particular importance in rural Japan. It is widely accepted that rural temples and shrines are struggling because of the diminishing clienteles that result from depopulation. But, while these issues have attracted some general comment and discussion, relatively little detailed fieldwork has been done on such issues, and hence there is much scope in this respect for projects examining why rural temples may no longer be able to support priests, and what impact this is having on local communities and on the Buddhist sects in both local and national terms. Equally, given the critical importance of the relationship between Buddhism, the household, and the ancestors, it is over 30 years since Smith's (1974) seminal study, mentioned earlier, was published. A detailed scrutiny of family altars and the relationship *today* between temples, households, and ancestors are topics that are long overdue. Such studies, too, would be valuable in the wider context of the problems faced by established traditions in postmodern societies in general, and could contribute to comparative debates and theoretical discussions that are developing in societies where work is being carried out on the state (and/or decline) of established and mainstream traditions.

Similarly, little work has been done on Shinto in the present day. Although there are some fine studies of Shinto shrines (e.g., Nelson 1999) and of festivals (e.g. Schnell 1999) to be placed alongside the more general works of Japanese scholars, the study of Shinto remains largely locked into discussions over its pre-modern role and relationship with Buddhism, on the one hand, and its relationship with state, emperor, and identity (again, mainly in pre-modern terms) on the other. Very little has been done to question its support structures and levels of adherence in the present day, even though the same questions that need to be asked of established Buddhism in Japan (Is it dying at local levels? Are support structures crumbling in the face of modernization?) are equally if not more relevant for Shinto. There is thus vast scope for field research on Shinto, in terms of ritual practices, their meanings, the patterns and meanings of patronage in ritual contexts, and the relationship between local communities and shrines in such contexts. Little, too, has been made of the roles of ritual officiants in fields such as gender relations and the balance between the roles of shrine priests, who are almost all male, and female participants such as *miko*, shrine maidens, who often perform the more visual aspects of rituals, such as sacred dances and the like. Such officiants need to be studied in fieldwork contexts, to examine questions of authority and inheritance in terms of religious institutions (the priesthood of both Shinto shrines and Buddhist temples is nowadays usually an inherited position, but as yet little work has been done on the implications of this inheritance system on the nature and workings of these traditions), and to examine the lives of those who carry out such religious roles at shrines. This is an especially interesting issue given that the majority of Shinto priests and *miko* are not full-time religious specialists but have other jobs or social roles to play as well. Less than a quarter of all Shinto priests in Japan work full-time at shrines, while most *miko* are either part-time or travel between shrines and work for a number of them at once.

Politically, too, Shinto continues to raise questions, and its relationship with the state will remain a key area of research. Yet the recurrent question of Shinto has also obscured other possible areas of research in the context of religion, politics, and the state in Japan, an area where it is assumed (apart from the well-known links between Sōka Gakkai and the political party Kōmeitō) that there is very little interaction today between the secular state and religious groups. Such assumptions may only be able to exist because of a lack of empirical research. New religions, especially in urban areas, can mobilize supporters to act as powerful voting blocs and to assist politicians whose policies they support, and some – such as Risshō Kōseikai, with its commitment to nuclear disarmament – will support Diet members who publicly campaign on specific issues. The extent of political influence of such new religions is very unclear, and until detailed research has been done in this area, through the avenue of religious studies or by scholars of Japanese politics, it is likely that the common assumptions mentioned here will continue, perhaps mistakenly so.

The new religions themselves, not least because of their sheer number, continue to offer one of the most fruitful arenas for further research in numerous ways, such as how different new religions function, how they appeal to recruits, where their teachings come from (an area that has hardly been examined in English or Japanese), their healing techniques, the role of their founders, and the role and nature of charisma in the construction of new religions. While, as noted earlier, several examinations of specific new religions have been carried out in English, the vast majority of new religions have not been the focus of specific research projects, and relatively few thematic comparative analyses between new religions have as yet been carried out. Moreover, little has been done on the strategies or continuing development and/or survival of older new religions that may have turned, in institutional terms, into established traditions primarily dependent nowadays on retaining the support of third- and fourth-generation members. What evidence there is suggests that such older new religions (i.e., those formed in the 19th or early 20th centuries) are losing support and members, but this is an area that requires further study.

These are just a few of the many topical areas that offer scope for exciting research in the present day. Other areas that have been touched on in this general survey of the field, but which remain critical topics in the contemporary study of religion in Japan, include the continuing repercussions of the Aum affair and its impact on attitudes toward religious organizations, and the continuing growth of the "anti-cult" movement in Japan. The latter issue is significant, for it raises questions of the extent to which this reflects (or is an extension of) wider patterns of opposition to "cults" and alternative religious movements in places such as Europe and the United States, and, hence, whether this is a sign of a globally significant movement. In such contexts, too, one can see new challenges to the concept of "religion" as an organized and institutionalized entity in Japan which are of significance in considering the nature of religion in the (post)modern world. There are, in other words, many avenues and potential areas of study to interest anyone who wishes to conduct research on religion in contemporary Japan. If Japan, as noted at the outset, manifests a variegated and often extraordinarily complex religious culture, it also offers an extraordinarily rich field of potential research for those keen to engage in fieldwork and to examine questions of immense relevance for the study of religion in modern societies.

NOTES

1 For a comprehensive overview of academic studies of Buddhism in Japan see Stone (in press).
2 The most striking example of this error – which leads on to numerous further mistakes and presumptions – is found in Fitzgerald 2000: for a clear exposition of the errors in Fitzgerald's work see Shimada 2001b.
3 Here, particular mention must be made of Kuroda Toshio (on Kuroda's work, along with an extensive bibliography plus English translations of some seminal articles see Dobbins 1996), whose seminal studies of the relationship between Buddhism and Shinto in premodern times argued that esoteric Buddhist thought and practice deeply influenced and permeated the Shinto tradition, which was in effect largely a manifestation of the Buddhist tradition. Kuroda's influence has been immense, especially on Western scholars.
4 For a fuller bibliography and overview of Japanese studies of pilgrimage and of the emergent field of Western language materials in this field see Reader and Swanson 1997.
5 Re Hoshino 2001 see pp. 343 and 383–384 especially, where he most clearly draws parallels between the Shikoku pilgrimage environment and Turner's notions of communitas and anti-structure. For a fuller discussion of Hoshino's work see Reader 2003.
6 This discussion occurred on the new religions discussion list (now closed: www.nrms.hartsem).
7 See also Haga and Kisala 1995 for an overview of this field.
8 See, for general discussions of the issues raised by secularization theory and its repercussions, Morioka (1976), Reader (1990), Swyngedouw (1979), and Yanagawa and Abe (1978).
9 Aum, too, was seen as a "textbook case" of violence by millennial religious groups, in the eyes of Western intelligence agencies such as the FBI and others, concerned about the potential for religiously inspired problems in the run-up to the year 2000, and was the focus of intensive study and reports by such groups, in which the research of those who had studied Aum was used (see Reader 2002).

10 While the sorts of emotive accusation mentioned above that have been directed at scholars may have been based in misunderstandings of the scholar's role, they, along with the current hostile attitude to religion that has emerged since the Aum affair, have had a massive impact on the field. Media attacks on scholarly integrity have led many to question the value of continuing to work on new religions in the present day, especially since it has become more difficult to carry out research, because the new religions themselves in this post-Aum age have become deeply defensive and reluctant to open up to external probing. As a result, scholars have turned away from studying such movements and turned to more historical (and hence thematically "safer") subjects, while also reporting that the numbers of graduate students wishing to work on new religions has fallen sharply. Colleagues in Japan report that new religious movements have become more circumspect about talking to outsiders and answering researchers' questions since the affair. I, too, have had difficulties in obtaining interviews or information from some new religions since 1995. Given that relatively few non-Japanese scholars and graduates are at present working in the field, this represents a serious problem for at least the near future.

11 Among the few I am aware of in English are dissertations on Sōtō Zen Buddhism (by Ian Reader at the University of Leeds in 1983), Tendai Buddhism (by Steven Covell at Princeton in 2001), and on contemporary Rinzai Buddhism (by Jørn Borup at Aarhus, Denmark, in 2002). In Buddhist contexts, there is little material in Japanese apart from the surveys conducted by the sects and commentaries by the sectarian research offices of various Buddhist institutions.

REFERENCES

Akaike, Noriaki, and Jan Swyngedouw, eds. 1986. Religion and Society in Japan: A Tribute to Yanagawa Keiichi. Japanese Journal of Religious Studies special issue 13(2–3):119–240.

Bodiford, William. 1993. Soto Zen in Medieval Japan. Honolulu: University of Hawaii Press.

—— 1996. Zen and the Art of Religious Prejudice: Efforts to Reform a Tradition of Social Discrimination. Japanese Journal of Religious Studies 23(1–2):1–27.

Breen, John, and Mark Teeuwen, eds. 2000. Shinto in History. Richmond: Curzon Press.

Casanova, Jose. 1992. Private and Public Religions. Social Research 59(1):17–57.

Davis, Winston. 1980. Dojo: Magic and Exorcism in Modern Japan. Stanford, CA: Stanford University Press.

Dobbins, James C., ed. 1996. The Legacy of Kuroda Toshio. In Japanese Journal of Religious Studies special double edition 23(2–3).

Earhart, H. Byron. 1988. *Gedatsukai* and Religion in Contemporary Japan. Bloomington: Indiana University Press.

Faure, Bernard. 1991. The Rhetoric of Immediacy: A Cultural Critique of Ch'an/Zen Buddhism. Princeton, NJ: Princeton University Press.

Fitzgerald, Timothy. 2000. The Ideology of Religious Studies. Oxford: Oxford University Press.

Frey, Nancy Louise. 1998. Pilgrim Stories: On and Off the Road to Santiago. Berkeley: University of California Press.

Gorai, Shigeru. 1975. Kōya hijiri (The Wandering Ascetics of Mount Kōya). Tokyo: Kadokawa Sensho.

—— 1984. Bukkyō to minzoku (Buddhism and the Folk Tradition). Tokyo: Kadokawa Sensho.

—— 1989. Yugyō to junrei (Itinerancy and Pilgrimage). Tokyo: Kadokawa Sensho.

Haga, Manabu, and Robert Kisala, eds. 1995. The New Age in Japan. Japanese Journal of Religious Studies 22(3–4):235–461.

Haga, Manabu, and Yumiyama, Tatsuya. 1994. Inoru fureau kanjiru: jibun sashi no odesse (Praying, Touching, Feeling: Odysseys of Self-Discovery). Tokyo: IPC.

Hakamaya, Noriaki. 1989. Hongaku shisō hihan (A Critique of the Doctrine of Original Enlightenment). Tokyo: Daizō Shuppan.

—— 1990. Hihan bukkyō (Critical Buddhism). Tokyo: Daizō Shuppan.

Hardacre, Helen. 1984. Lay Buddhism in Contemporary Japan: *Reiyūkai Kyōdan*. Princeton, NJ: Princeton University Press.

—— 1986. *Kurozumikyō* and the New Religions of Japan. Princeton, NJ: Princeton University Press.

—— 1988. Shinto and the State. Princeton, NJ: Princeton University Press.

—— 1998. Marketing the Menacing Fetus in Japan. Berkeley and Los Angeles: University of California Press.

Hoshino, Eiki. 1979. Shikoku henro to sangakushinkō (The Shikoku Pilgrimage and Mountain-Centered Faith). *In* Daisen. Ishizuchi to saikoku shugendō (Sanshūkyōshi kenkyū 12). Miyake Hitoshi, ed. pp. 310–328. Tokyo: Meicho Shuppan.

—— 1980. Shikoku henro ni okeru seichisei no tokushitsu (The Characteristics of the Nature of Sacred Place in the Context of the Shikoku Pilgrimage). *In* Gendai shūkyō – 3 seichi (Religion in the Present Day, vol. 3: Sacred Places). Sasaki Kōkan et al., eds. pp. 89–102. Tokyo: Shunjūsha.

—— 1981. Junrei: sei to zoku no genshōgaku (Pilgrimage: The Phenomenology of the Sacred and Profane). Tokyo: Kōdansha Gendaishinsho.

—— 1986a. Kisei bukkyō kyōdan no kōzō to minshū bukkyō (Folk Buddhism and the Structure of Established Buddhist Organizations). Tōyō gakujitsu kenkyū 25(1):89–103.

—— 1986b. Aruki to mawari no shūkyōsei (The Religious Nature of Walking and Doing Pilgrimages). *In* Yugyō to hyōhaku (Taikei Bukkyō to Nihonjin, vol. 6). Yamaori Tetsuo, ed. pp. 231–271. Tokyo: Shunjūsha.

—— 1989. Junrei to seichi (Pilgrimage and Sacred Space). *In* Bukkyō bunka jiten (The Dictionary of Buddhist Culture). Kanaoka Shūyū and Yanagawa Keiichi, eds. pp. 731–740. Tokyo: Kōsensha.

—— 1999. Shikoku henro ni nyū eiji? Gendai aruki henro no taiken bunseki (A "New Age" in the Shikoku Pilgrimage? An Analysis of the Experiences of Contemporary Foot Pilgrims). *In* Shakaigaku nenshi (waseda shakaigakkai) 40(3):47–64.

—— 2001. Shikoku henro no shūkyōgakuteki kenkyū (Research in the Shikoku Pilgrimage from Religious Studies Perspectives). Kyoto: Hōzōkan.

Hubbard, Jamie, and Paul L. Swanson, eds. 1997. Pruning the Bodhi Tree: The Storm Over Critical Buddhism. Honolulu: University of Hawaii Press.

Inoue, Nobutaka. 1992. Shin shūkyō no kaidoku (Interpreting New Religions). Tokyo: Chikuma Shobō.

—— ed. 1994. Gendai nihon no shūkyōshakaigaku (The Sociology of Religion in Contemporary Japan). Tokyo: Sekai Shisōsha.

Inoue, Nobutaka et al., eds. 1991. Shin shūkyō jiten (Encyclopedia of New Religions).Tokyo: Kōbundō.

Isomae, Junichi. 2002. The Discursive Position of Religious Studies in Japan: Masahary Anesaki and the Origins of Religious Studies. Method and Theory in the Study of Religion 14:21–46.

Josei to Bukkyō Tōkai Kantō Nettowaaku, ed. 1999. Bukkyō to jendaa: onnatachi no nyozegamon (Buddhism and Gender: Female Testimonies). Osaka: Toki Shobō.

Kaneko, Satoru. 1991. Shinshū shinkō to minzoku shinkō (Pure Land Faith and Folk Religion). Kyoto: Nagata Bunshōdō.

Kenney, Elizabeth, and Edmund T. Gilday, eds. 2000. Mortuary Rites in Japan. Japanese Journal of Religious Studies 27(3–4):163–440.

Kisala, Robert J., and Mark R. Mullins, eds. 2001. Religion and Social Crisis in Japan: Understanding Japanese Society through the Aum Affair. Basingstoke and New York: Palgrave.

Kōmoto, Mitsugu. 1988. Gendai toshi no minzoku shūkyō: kakyō saiken to chinkon (Folk Religion in Modern Cities: Reconstructing Ancestral Homelands and the Repose of the Spirits). *In* Gendaijin no shūkyō. Ōmura Eishō and Nishiyama Shigeru, eds. Tokyo: Yuhikaku.

——2001. Gendai Nihon ni okeru senzo saishi (Ancestral Rites in Contemporary Japan). Tokyo: Meiji Daigaku.

Kondō, Yoshihiro. 1971. Shikoku henro (The Shikoku Pilgrimage). Tokyo: Ofūsha.

——1982. Shikoku henro kenkyū (Research into the Shikoku Pilgrimage). Tokyo: Miyai Shoten.

Kouamé, Nathalie. 2001. Pèlerinage et société dans le Japon des Tokugawa: Le Pèlerinage de Shikoku entre 1598 et 1868. Paris: École française d'Extrême-Orient.

Maeda, Takashi. 1971. Junrei no shakaigaku (The Sociology of Pilgrimage). Kyoto: Minerva Books.

Matsumoto, Shirō. 1993. Zen shisō no hihanteki kenkyū (Critical Research into Zen Thought). Tokyo: Daizō Shuppan.

Miyake, Hitoshi. 1974. Nihon shūkyō no kōzō (The Structure of Japanese Religion). Tokyo: Keiō Tsūshin.

——1989. Shūkyō minzokugaku (Folk Religious Studies). Tokyo: Tokyo Daigaku Shuppan.

Miyata, Noboru. 1993. Yama to sato no shinkōshi (The History of Faith in the Concept of Mountains and Villages). Tokyo: Yoshikawa kōbunkan.

Morioka, Kiyomi. 1976. Comments by a Japanese Sociologist. Japanese Journal of Religious Studies 3(4):279–281.

Nelson, John. 1999. Enduring Identities: The Guise of Shinto in Contemporary Japan. Honolulu: University of Hawaii Press.

Nishiyama, Shigeru. 1988. Gendai no shūkyō undō (Contemporary Religious Movements). *In* Gendaijin no shūkyō (The Religion of People in Contemporary Society). Ōmura Eishō and Nishiyama Shigeru, eds. pp. 169–210. Tokyo: Yuhikaku.

Numata, Ken'ya 1988. Gendai nihon no shinshūkyō (New Religions in Contemporary Japan). Osaka: Sōgensha.

——1995. Shūkyō to kagaku no neoparadaimu (The Paradigm of Science and Religion (in Japanese New Religions)). Osaka: Sōgensha.

Ōmura, Eishō, and Nishiyama Shigeru, eds. 1988. Gendaijin no shūkyō (The Religion of People in Contemporary Society). Tokyo: Yuhikaku.

Osada, Kōichi, Sakata Masaaki, and Seki Mitsuo. 2003. Gendai no shikoku henro: michi no shakaigaku no shiten kara (The Shioku Pilgrimage in the Present Day: From the Perspective of a Sociology of the Route). Tokyo: Gakubunsha.

Reader, Ian. 1989. Recent Japanese Publications on Religion. Japanese Journal of Religious Studies 16(4):299–315.

——1990. Returning to Respectability: A Religious Revival in Japan? Japan Forum 2:57–68.

——1993. Recent Japanese Publications on the New Religions: The Work of Shimazono Susumu. Japanese Journal of Religious Studies 20(2–3):101–120.

——1996. A Poisonous Cocktail? Aum Shinrikyō's Path to Violence. Copenhagen: NIAS Books.

——2000a. Religious Violence in Contemporary Japan: The Case of Aum Shinrikyō. Richmond and Honolulu: Curzon Press and University of Hawaii Press.

——2000b. Scholarship: Aum Shinrikyō and Integrity. Nova Religio 3(2):368–382.

Reader, Ian. 2002. Spectres and Shadows: Aum Shinrikyō and the Road to Megiddo Terrorism and Political Violence. *In* Millennial Violence. Theme issue. Past, Present and Future 14(1): 147–186.

——2003. Local Histories, Anthropological Interpretations, and the Study of a Japanese Pilgrimage (review article). Japanese Journal of Religious Studies 30(1–2):119–132.

——2005. Making Pilgrimages: Meaning and Practice in Shikoku. Honolulu: University of Hawaii Press.

——In press. Folk Religion. *In* Nanzan Guide to the Study of Japanese Religion. Clark Chilson et al., eds. Nanzan Institute for Religion and Culture. Honolulu: University of Hawaii Press.

Reader, Ian, and Paul L. Swanson. 1997. Introduction: Pilgrimage in Japan. *In* Pilgrimage in Japan. Ian Reader and Paul L. Swanson, eds. Japanese Journal of Religious Studies special double edition 24(3–4):225–270.

Reader, Ian, and George J. Tanabe. 1998. Practically Religious: Worldly Benefits and the Common Religion of Japan. Honolulu: University of Hawaii Press.

Ruppert, Brian D. 2000. Jewel in the Ashes: Buddha Relics and Power in Early Medieval Japan. Cambridge, MA: Harvard University Press.

Sakurai, Tokutarō. 1974 (vol. 1) and 1977 (vol. 2). Nihon no shamanizumu. Tokyo: Yoshi-kawa Kōbunkan.

——1982. Nihon minzoku shūkyōron. Tokyo: Kōbundō.

Satō, Hisamitsu. 1989. Gendai no junrei: saikoku junrei ni tsuite (Contemporary Pilgrimage: The Saikoku Pilgrimage). *In* Kazoku shakaigaku nōto (Notes on the Sociology of the Family). Maeda Takashi, ed. pp. 183–222. Kyoto: Kansai Daigaku.

——1990a. Shikoku henro no shakaigakuteki kōsatsu (Sociological Investigations into the Shikoku Pilgrimage). Mikkyōgaku 26:29–47.

——1990b. Osamefuda ni miru shikoku henro (The Shikoku Pilgrimage Seen through an Analysis of Pilgrims' Prayer Slips). *In* Bukkyō to shakai: Nakao Shunpaku sensei koki kinen (Buddhism and Society: A Festschrift in Honor of Professor Nakao Shunpaku). Nakao Shunpaku Sensei Koki Kinenkai, ed. pp. 437–459. Kyoto: Nagata Bunshōdō.

Schnell, Scott. 1999. The Rousing Drum: Ritual Practice in a Japanese Community. Honolulu: University of Hawaii Press.

Shimada, Hiromi. 2001a. Oumu: naze shūkyō wa terorizumu wo unda no ka (Aum: Why Did Religion Give Rise to Terrorism?). Tokyo: Transview.

Shimada, Katsumi. 2001b. Review of Fitzgerald, *The Ideology of Religious Studies*. Shūkyō kenkyū 328, vol. 75(1):175–181.

Shimazono, Susumu. 1992a. Gendai kyūsai shūkyōron (A Study of Contemporary Salvationist Religions). Tokyo: Seikyōsha.

——1992b. Shinshin shūkyō to shūkyō būmu (The "New" New Religions and the Religious Boom). Tokyo: Iwanami Booklets 237.

——ed. 1993. Sukui to toku: shin shūkyō shinkōsha no seikatsu to shisō (Salvation and Virtue: The Life and Thought of Believers in a New Religious Movement). Tokyo: Kōbundō.

——1995. Aum shinrikyō no kiseki (The Position of Aum). Tokyo: Iwanami Booklets 379.

——1996. Seishin sekai no yukue: gendai sekai to shinreisei undō (The Traces of a Spiritual Society: New Spiritualist Movements and the Contemporary World). Tokyo: Tōkyōdō.

——1997. Gendai shūkyō no kanōsei: oumu shinrikyō to bōryoku (The Potential of Contemporary Religion: Aum Shinrikyō and Violence). Tokyo: Iwanami Shoten.

——1999. Jidai no naka no shin shūkyō: Idei Seitarō no sekai 1899–1945 (New Religions in their Historical Context: The World of Idei Seitarō, 1899–1945). Tokyo: Kōbundō.

——2001. Posuto modan no shin shūkyō: gendai nihon no seishin jōtai no teiryū (Postmodern New Religions: Spiritual Undercurrents in Contemporary Japan). Tokyo: Tōkyōdō Shuppan.

Shinjō, Tsunezō. 1982. Shaji sankei no shakai keizaishiteki kenkyū (Social, Economic, and Historical Research into Pilgrimages to Shrines and Temples (in Japan)). Tokyo: Hanawa Shobō.

Shinno, Toshikazu. 1980. Tabi no naka no shūkyō (Religion in the Context of Travel). Tokyo: NHK Books.

——1991. Nihon yugyō shūkyōron (Essays on Japanese Pilgrimage and Religion). Tokyo: Yoshikawa Kōbunkan.

——ed. 1996. Nihon no junrei (Japanese Pilgrimage), vol. 1: Honzon junrei; vol. 2: Seiseki junrei; vol. 3: Junrei no kōzō to chihō junrei. Tokyo: Yūzankaku.

Shūkyō Shakaigaku Kenkyū Kai, ed. 1987. Kyōso to sono shuhen (Religious Founders and their Environments). Tokyo: Yūzankaku.

Smith, Robert J. 1974. Ancestor Worship in Contemporary Japan. Stanford: Stanford University Press.

Sonoda, Minoru. 1988a. Matsuri to seikatsu no kankaku (The Aesthetics of Festivals and Daily Life). In Shintō: Nihon no minzoku shūkyō (Shinto: Japan's Folk Religion). Minoru Sonoda, ed. pp. 355–362. Tokyo: Kōbundō.

——1988b. Shintō: nihon no minzoku shūkyō (Shinto: Japan's Folk Religion). Tokyo: Kōbundō.

Stone, Jacqueline I. In press. Japanese Buddhism. In Nanzan Guide to the Study of Japanese Religion. Clark Chilson et al., eds. Nanzan Institute for Religion and Culture. Honolulu: University of Hawaii Press.

Swyngedouw, Jan. 1979. Reflections on the Secularisation Thesis in the Sociology of Religion in Japan. Japanese Journal of Religious Studies 6(1–2):65–88.

Tamamuro, Taijō. 1963. Sōshiki bukkyō (Funeral Buddhism). Tokyo: Daihōrinkaku.

Waseda Daigaku Dōkūkan Kenkyūkai, ed. 1997. Shikoku henro to henro michi ni kansuru ishikichōsa (Fieldwork Studies into Understandings Related to the Shikoku Pilgrimage and the Pilgrimage Route). Tokyo: Waseda Daigaku Dōkūkan Kenkyūkai.

Yanagawa, Keiichi. 1987. Matsuri to girei no shūkyōgaku (Festivals and Rituals from a Religious Studies Perspective). Tokyo: Chikuma Shobō.

——ed. 1988. Seminaa shūkyōgaku kōgi (Lectures in Religious Studies). Tokyo: Hōzō Sensho.

Yanagawa, Keiichi, and Yoshiya Abe. 1978. Some Observations on the Sociology of Religion in Japan. Japanese Journal of Religious Studies 5(1):5–27.

CHAPTER 27 Folk Religion and its Contemporary Issues

Noriko Kawahashi

My central concern in this chapter is to identify the kinds of questions and issues that must be considered when dealing with folk religion today. As space is limited I will primarily emphasize those issues at the core of current debates on folk religion in Japanese scholarship, and suggest possibilities and approaches to innovative research for the benefit of those who are just beginning to study folk religion.

What are some of the changes that have transpired in recent years in the terminology and topical interests of folk religion? In addition to addressing this question I will discuss how folklore studies themselves have been re-examined as a subject of study, a subject that has attracted considerable scholarly attention. My own research has focused primarily on gender in religion, and I will review this topic from the perspective of folklore studies.

In his now classic *Japanese Religion*, Byron Earhart commented as follows about folk religion:

> Organized religion (Shinto, Buddhism, Taoism, and Confucianism) is conspicuous because of its writings, priests, liturgies, shrines, and temples. In Japan, however, much religion is practiced informally. Because of its informal character, folk religion does not lend itself to simple identification and historical tracing . . . (Earhart 1982:60)

Indeed, the manifestations of folk religion cover an immense and varied range. It encompasses fortune-telling, taboos, incantations, and other such folk knowledge and lore. It is engaged in by various different types of folk religion adherents and shamanic religious practitioners. It extends to annual rites and observances, folk practices and beliefs associated with death, and other such practices that have been transmitted in folk traditions and communal groups. It involves deities (*kami*) of the mountains, of fisherfolk, and of merchants, the *hayarigami* ("faddish deities") that become transient objects of devotion in urban areas, and multitudes of spirits (*mono*, *tama*) that exist in the natural world. Folk religion exhibits a truly extraordinary richness in its diversity.

One crucial point to remember is that the Japanese term used to refer to folk religion has changed since the coinage of *minkan shinkō* (folk beliefs) in the 1890s.[1] Beginning in the late 1970s this term was gradually replaced over the following decade by *minzoku shūkyō*, whose literal meaning corresponds more closely to the English term "folk religion." Shinno Toshikazu commented on the rationale behind this change:

> Recently Japanese scholars have stopped using the term *minkan shinkō* (folk beliefs) in favor of the term *minzoku shūkyō* (folk/popular religion). This modification signifies not merely a change in terminology, but also a major shift in the boundaries of what anthropologists and scholars of religion perceive as religious phenomena, i.e., in what is, or could be, the object of the study of folklore or folk religion. (Shinno 1993:187)

This innovation in terminology was described by Ian Reader as "less easy to explicate in English translations," though he also states that the shift has "opened up the way for greater comparative and cross-cultural studies that can place the study of Japanese religion in a more universal context" (Reader, in press).[2] Reader makes three important points in demonstrating this change.

First, the relationship between folk religion studies and Japanese folk studies (*nihon minzokugaku*) must be taken into consideration. As Shinno has also emphatically reiterated in a recent study (2000:98), folk religion was the most important topic in folk studies. According to Reader (in press), folk religion existed as a field of study largely because of the influence of Yanagita Kunio, the founder figure of Japanese folk studies, and the purpose of the discipline was to seek out the "unique religiosity that marked the Japanese out from other peoples and that provided the bedrock of native Japanese culture and of the lives of its people." This approach followed an "innately nationalistic agenda" which filtered out Buddhism and Confucianism as foreign elements in order to isolate the uniqueness of the Japanese people.

Second, it is clear that attempts to isolate folk religion by separating it from Buddhism, Shinto, or any other such religious tradition are founded in the binary logic that separates great from little, high from low, elite from popular, texts and doctrines from ritual practice, and so on. This narrow and static attitude has been criticized on methodological grounds. This point has also been addressed by Swearer (1987) and Long (1987). Reader himself, in a joint work with George Tanabe, has criticized conventional religious studies that are thoroughly caught up in such concepts of the elite versus the common people (Reader and Tanabe 1998), and focuses instead on the concept of the importance of "practical benefits" (*gense riyaku*) as a Japanese religious motif.

Third, in referring to an important study by Sakurai Tokutarō, Reader shows that, within its former framework, the field of folk religion is limited to the disappearing world of rural Japan.[3] In a society such as that of present-day Japan, where the rural world is rapidly passing out of existence, the study of popular religious phenomena will require "new understandings and frameworks for analysis" (Reader, in press). That is, given present post-industrial realities, it is meaningless to pursue research on the "unique religiosity" of Japan, which was rooted in an earlier folk society. In the aforementioned study, Shinno writes:

> In a sense folk religion is like grass with weak roots. In contrast to *minkan-shinkō* studies, however, *minzoku-shūkyō* studies offer the potential to examine religious phenomena as a part of folk society and as one aspect of religion in general. They provide the means to examine the breakdown of folk beliefs – the "secularization" of folk society. (Shinno 1993:189)

Let us look again at how changes in terminology have been implicated in the historical development of theory in this field. Hayashi Makoto, a historian of religion, wrote a historical overview of folk religion studies in postwar Japan in which he identified a number of important characteristics. First, during the 1950s and 1960s, scholars of folklore in Japan began to follow Yanagita in taking up questions of faith and the spirit. Hayashi explained that this was done in order to identify the subject matter of folk studies, as it overlapped with the study of history, and to demarcate it from the "intellectual territory" belonging to politics and economics.

Subsequently, during the 1970s and 1980s, there were a number of prominent studies of the adherents of folk religions, and research on shamanism flourished. A parallel phenomenon can be found in the growing participation by social anthropologists and scholars of religion in the genres where scholars of folklore were most active. Among the most significant achievements in this regard are Sasaki Kōkan's studies of shamanism (1980, 1984).

In other words, as Hayashi explains, the study of folk beliefs became interdisciplinary, and the participation by other disciplines was one reason that the term "folk belief" was necessarily replaced by "folk religion." According to Hayashi (1999), the topics of research became increasingly diffuse as that research grew – and as it continues to grow – increasingly interdisciplinary (e.g., Hayashi and Yoshihara 1988).

In 1998 research developed along these lines culminated in the *Nihon minzoku shūkyō jiten* (Dictionary of Japanese Folk Religion). About a decade earlier, a two-volume guide to methods of organizing surveys of folk beliefs had been compiled in an attempt to improve understanding of folk religion at a practical level (Tamamuro et al. 1987). The dictionary took a wide-ranging view of the many different manifestations of folk religion, defining this kind of religion as follows:

> In contradistinction to the scripture-oriented, institutional religions that have generally been denoted by such terms as established religion, existing religion, and organized religion, the present term refers comprehensively to the religious beliefs and practices that have become a close part of the ordinary daily lives of the people and which, though they contain elements of those more institutional religions, are not fully comprehended by the doctrinal canons of those religions. (Sasaki et al. 1998:547)

In other words, folk religions are religions that have their existence in the ordinary daily lives of the people in a society where institutional religions have become established to some extent. The above definition was written by Ikegami Yoshimasa, a scholar of religion. I consider him to be one of the most ingenious and imaginative scholars of folk religion, and will further introduce his work below.

Ikegami has stated that his research in folk religion contains, roughly speaking, two viewpoints. One is his focus on the complex, dynamic nature of folk religion. This constitutes a reassessment of earlier approaches which reified folk religion and situated it as a static object that is isolated from other traditions. This approach thus overlaps with Reader's views as described above. Ikegami further takes the stance, probably more emphatically than any previous scholar in the field, that folk religion possesses a religious quality. That is, he contends that folk religions "are not to be taken as epiphenomena that are incidental to established religion," but are, rather, "to be considered autonomous religious phenomena that actually sustain established religion at its very foundations" (Ikegami 1999a:15). This constitutes a protest against the conventional view of folk religion as nothing more than rituals embedded within a closed, traditional communal group, or as a transient processing of the desires and hopes of individual people, or as magical practices. Ikegami refutes both the notion that folk religion, although it proclaims salvation for the common folk, is ultimately concerned solely with the pursuit of practical, worldly benefit and the view that folk religions are simply scattered about on the fringes of authentic religion, and dismisses the doubt whether folk religions are actually anything more than agglomerations of folkways that have failed to be fully sublimated by authentic religions (Ikegami 1999b:129).

Ikegami's stance can be summed up, in short, as casting doubt on the view of religion that most modern people have accepted as self-evident. He attaches importance, instead, to the dimension of meaning and value that ordinary people find in their religious experience of the world. He also finds in their daily lives an autonomous realm of religious meaning, as well as the source of a creative power that can transform society. From a slightly different perspective, Araki Michio, who was a follower of Eliade in religious studies, also valued folk religion as the very fountainhead of energy in spontaneous religious creativity (Araki 1987).

Ikegami's singular position can be foregrounded by comparison, for example, with that of Hori Ichirō, who was the leading figure in Japanese studies of folk religion, and who is also noted for his works written in the English language. Hori, following Yanagita, made contact with his European and American counterparts with the aim of building an interdisciplinary, systematic framework for Japanese folk religion studies. Although he remained aware of the complex nature of folk religion, he also retained the oppositional contrast of folk with institutionalized religions. In one of his English-language studies, for instance, Hori equated folk religion with the "little tradition" (Hori 1968:50), remarking that people should be led from "folk beliefs onto a high level of religious experience, or from popular superstitions into right faith, as well as from magic to metaphysics" (Hori 1968:7).

The bias in Hori's study of folk religion, the result of its foundation in a particular hierarchy of values, eventually made it the focus of criticism. There is good reason to criticize it, especially for his assertion that folk religion is "*sein*, not *sollen*, its absolute value is slight, and no reason to feel any affection for it can be found whatsoever" (Hori 1951:14). For Hori, in other words, folk religion was a fragmented phenomenon that lacked intellectual depth. Hori's elitist, perceptive approach would, for Ikegami, come to represent a problem that had to be overcome.

In his latest study, Ikegami explains that, in one of its aspects, the discourse on folk religion is "a kind of cultural movement that seeks to redirect a certain positive light" on the process of meaning formation for ordinary members of society, a phenomenon that hitherto had never even been identified and named (Ikegami 2000:19). He tells us that the growing concern with such matters challenges the orthodoxy of those things called religion and faith, which have been shaped on a model of institutional systems, typically Christian, within the special historical context of the modern Euro-American world. Ikegami also suggests that this concern is related to the critique of Orientalism that has been taking place in recent years (Ikegami 1999a:18).

Ikegami's study of folk religion is thoroughly informed by his questioning of the authority of established religions that have been considered authentic and orthodox, and his doubts about Euro-American measures of value. His perspective appears to be linked with current postcolonial theorizing. The postcolonial condition refers to circumstances under which it has become possible to examine, critically and at a distance, the social knowledge and authority that were established within the modern framework. In the framework of orthodox doctrine conveyed by conventional scriptures and clergy, those religions that have been presented as legitimate have subjugated the religious practice and understanding of people who are dealing with the realities of life in the world. Surely it would be desirable for a theory of folk religion to open up perspectives that overturn distortions of this kind. If we view the postcolonial condition, as de Alva has said, not as "subjectivity after the colonial experience," but rather as "a subjectivity of oppositionality to imperializing/colonizing discourses and practices" (1995:245), then it also affords an appropriate occasion for recognizing value in the practices of those people who furnish the underlying impetus of folk religion.

Ikegami also refers to the work of James Clifford and Ōta Yoshinobu (a well-known Japanese anthropologist) in criticizing the authoritarian structure of relationships in folk religion fieldwork between informants and the researcher who usurps their voices and then presents their religious practices from a single, arbitrary perspective. He points out the necessity for listening modestly to what the people who serve as informants have to say, and being considerate of their historical and political context (Ikegami 2000:20–21). To the best of my knowledge, fieldwork in folk religion has very rarely been conducted consciously with this kind of attitude. Ikegami's major work, written from a similar perspective, is a study of various shamanic religious practitioners in the populace of Japan from its northern to its southern extremities, and it may well be the greatest achievement in this field (Ikegami 1999a).

This critique from a postcolonial perspective has recently come to be directed against Japanese folk studies themselves as a field of study. I stated earlier that the research in Japanese folk religion that was conducted within the framework of Japanese folk studies as proposed by Yanagita Kunio had its limitations, and this problem is related to the inherently ideological nature of Japanese folk studies, which have come under critical attack in recent years. Yanagita formulated a concept of the common folk, which in practice means farming people who practice settled rice cultivation, and the way that this notion has been used to deny the pluralistic, complex nature of Japanese culture is widely recognized (see chapter 13 in this volume). Even the realities of folk religion came to be simplified under the single central rubric of the common folk's faith (Ikegami 1999b:131–132).

Regarding Yanagita's fixation on Okinawa, Ikegami remarks on the irony that the elder's encounter with Okinawa, which ordinarily he was very likely to have contrasted with Japanese culture, instead reinforced Yanagita's belief in the uniqueness of a unitary Japanese people (Ikegami 1999a:42).[4]

The critiques leveled against folk studies in recent years attest to the criticism and self-questioning over the way that this discipline in Japan has constructed a unitary national culture which in turn has been appropriated, past and present, as a powerful ideology for unifying the nation-state. Self-critical examinations of this kind have, in recent years, spurred the beginnings of an attempt to transcend monocultural folk studies and to construct folk studies that are multicultural instead. A central figure in this attempt is Shimamura Takanori, who argued that

> Multicultural folk studies is a political dynamics that views the oral traditions (primarily unwritten folklore) of human culture with attention to all the differences and diversity involved, including differences of sex, class, group, region, individual, and so on. This is folk studies according to a new paradigm, one which attempts to make its examination with full awareness of the political nature of culture. This presupposes that, within this new paradigm, the various ideologies that have existed in folk studies up to this time, foremost among them the ideology of the modern nation-state, are deconstructed, and that scholarship is maximally self-aware of its implicitly political nature. (Shimamura 2001:323–324)

Shimamura is addressing this proposal to the next generation in the hopes that folk studies will experience a rebirth (Shimamura 2001:308). As chair of the joint project on Contemporary Cultural Research in Folk Studies (National Museum of Japanese History) – of which I am also a member – Shimamura practices what he proposes. He has suggested that such conventional research topics as nomadic entertainers, religious adherents, hunters, and fisherfolk be expanded to include groups traditionally subject to discrimination: long-term Korean or Chinese residents of Japan, Japanese emigrants to other countries, and illegal immigrants to Japan (Shimamura 2001:327).

There are likewise scholars, such as Iwatake Mikako, who are engaged in an intellectual and historical re-reading of Japanese folk studies from a postcolonial perspective. She observes that very few Japanese scholars of folk studies have bothered to reflect upon the possible political biases in their own work, much less attempted to redress folk studies in light of critical self-examination (Iwatake 1999a:14). (One well-known critical study of Yanagita in relation to colonialism is Murai [1995]. Iwatake is also a member of the joint project on Contemporary Cultural Research in Folk Studies mentioned above.) Iwatake, citing the strong resistance to Western scholarship felt by Yanagita and many other Japanese scholars of folk studies, asserted: "It is my contention that Japanese folklore studies needs to be situated within a wider historical and culture-political context of modernity in general, and to be reconsidered from the viewpoint of a 'postcolonial' critique in particular" (Iwatake 2000:210). Iwatake's valuation of Yanagita's work is instructive:

> Yanagita was a prolific author. . . . He did not conduct fieldwork in the anthropological sense but had contacts with numerous amateur folklorists across the country who faithfully provided him with materials. He made himself an authority and controlled what could be studied and written in folklore studies. His evaluation in recent years is varied. While some scholars praise him inordinately, others harshly criticize him, and there are those who fall between these two extremes. (Iwatake 2000:211)

This kind of colonialist division of intellectual labor between Yanagita and amateur folklorists can still be seen being enacted today in relationships between European and American scholars of Japan and native scholars in Japan. As Sakai has pointed out, there are European and American researchers who view local intellectuals in Japan as nothing more than convenient sources of information, and never treat them as colleagues on an equal footing (Harootunian and Sakai 1999). I myself have had the experience of providing considerable support to an American scholar of present-day Japanese Buddhism and women only to receive no acknowledgment at all in his published work.[5]

Yanagita's folk studies have also been criticized for being a "one-nation folklore." Akasaka, for example, points out that Yanagita severely cautioned against extending the comparative field to other parts of Asia. Akasaka goes so far as to say that those who conduct research on Asia at large are obliged to subject this "one-nation folklore" to radical criticism (Akasaka 1999:10). Iwatake, however, poses a somewhat different interpretation. She suggests that Yanagita's one-nation folklore could be understood as not merely focused on "Japanese folklore," but rather as seeking to establish a study of Japanese folklore by native Japanese scholars which was differentiated from ethnology, which he defined as the study of an alien culture by people from outside that culture (Iwatake 2000:218). Yanagita's various achievements are conscientiously examined within the framework of Japanese intellectual history by Kawada, the pre-eminent practitioner of folk belief studies after Yanagita (Kawada 1992).

As noted earlier, the stance taken by Japanese folk studies within its conventional framework plainly situated Japanese folk religion as a form of faith, unique to the Japanese people, that transcends class, region, and period. This was a search for a pure cultural essence that remained after every extraneous element had been removed. Narrow approaches of this kind have been criticized by Reader and others. Iwatake points out that, in his work on comparative folklore, Yanagita invariably took it for granted that the origin of a given folkloric theme was in Japan. Thus, if a certain type of oral literature existed in Japan, Yanagita would view any variations thereon that might be found in other cultures as being no more than permutations of the Japanese original (Iwatake 1999b:7).

Iwatake is also critical of Yanagita's use of a rhetoric that erases the authorship of anything that Yanagita believed to be an expression of essential folklore. In other words, the actual author of his "unsigned history by a resident of an unnamed outlying region of Japan" is none other than Yanagita himself, who is writing as a privileged individual from his position at the center while seeking to conceal his own authorship as though he were transparent (Iwatake 1999b:14). As an aside, since Yanagita utilized the work of amateur folklorists from the provinces without acknowledging them, the assumption of "authorship" on his part constitutes a betrayal, or an egregious omission, in two senses.

Viewed in this way from the perspective of a postcolonial critique, it becomes apparent that there are many problems with representation in Yanagita's folk studies. One is that diversity and difference are suppressed to build up a unitary image of the common folk. Another is that he has placed himself in a position of authority so that what he represents as the essence of Japanese culture is conveyed as though it were an authentic and transparent depiction of the everyday life of the common folk, totally free of any political bias. Tamanoi Mariko has questioned Yanagita's stance on this issue from a gendered perspective:

Folklorists as well as those interested in the history of folklore studies have conceptual-ized "various populations," whose knowledge was deemed essential to the formation of the new state, as gender-neutral populations. They have described them as the "common folk," "vulgar folk," "abiding folk," "simple peasants," or "rural population," but have rarely considered them as the populations in which men and women live interdepen-dently. (Tamanoi 1996:60)[6]

As noted earlier, this criticism is directed to Yanagita's practice of representing the lives (and particularly the spiritual lives) of the "common folk" in a unitary fashion. Tamanoi goes beyond that, however, to point out that, when Yanagita wrote about rural women, he did not acknowledge their subjectivities and he did not allow them to speak in their own voices. As Tamanoi puts it, Yanagita "deprived *jōmin* [common folk] women of their 'power' to transform their everyday life" (Tamanoi 1996:78).

This does not, of course, mean that Yanagita ignored the issue of women in folk studies. An examination of his writings will show clearly that women occupied an important position in his work. For example, his anthology *Yanagita Kunio zenshū* includes the essays and monographs *Josei to minkan denshō* (Women and Popular Oral Tradition) in volume 10, and *Imo no chikara* (Women's Power), *Fujo kō* (Study of the Female Shamanic Practitioner), and other works in volume 11. What does deserve criticism, however, is that Yanagita deals with women's history and culture as a unique and separate realm that is severed, so to speak, from the realm of men. He builds up a unitary image of women from his own perspective, and then presents it as though this were the universal experience of the entire female population of the "common folk." Thus, as pointed out in the *Dictionary of Japanese Folk Religion*, Yanagita possessed a

> view of women conveyed by folk studies that take gender differences as biologically fixed and treat women's capability to reproduce as some kind of divine power. The image of women that has been portrayed in such folk studies avoids recognizing discrimination as an issue, while positing a fixed division of roles according to [sex and] gender. (Sasaki et al. 1998:280)

The focal point of Yanagita's account of women is their religious or spiritual power, which is given fullest form in his monograph *Imo no chikara*. The remainder of this chapter will deal with the valuation accorded in recent years to Yanagita's theory of the religious power of the woman.

As I have noted, the core of Yanagita's theory of women is expressed in his *Imo no chikara*, which attributes to women a mystical, inborn spiritual power. Focusing on what he saw as the wisdom and nobility of women, he attributed these qualities to women's special physiology and emotional nature, by virtue of which women are innately possessed of an essential ability that properly makes them the supporting source of energy for indigenous faiths. In one well-known passage, Yanagita wrote:

> The vital portions of the religious actions of ritual and prayer all fell within the province of women. The shaman, among these people, was as a rule, a woman. . . . The reason that women were thought especially suited to this duty must at first have been because they have an emotional nature that is easily moved. Thus, whenever some incident occurred, women were the first among the people to enter abnormal psychological states, and the

first able to give voice to the mysterious. Sometimes gifted, sensitive children had an ability to see divinities and to declare oracles, but as they grew up, they quickly lost these special traits. Moreover, children like these were borne and raised by women, so women were constantly accorded esteem. The special physiology of women is a particular consideration, since it had a powerful influence on these kinds of mental states. (Yanagita 1990:25)

Yanagita's theory of "women's power," which attributes spiritual power to all the women in a particular population by virtue of their sex, has been the target of various critiques. Tanaka Takako, for example, a scholar of Japanese literature, points out that Yanagita's approach places excessive emphasis on women's ability to give birth, which is linked to the worship of women as goddesses. Used uncritically, she tells us, this approach runs the risk of generating the facile fantasy that all women today are worshiped as spiritual beings (Tanaka 1996:182).

It is easy to discern a kind of essentialism in Yanagita's work. From a feminist perspective, essentialism, as opposed to constructionism, is an unproductive ideology. An essentialist view of sex and gender approaches the differences between males and females, women and men, not as historical, cultural constructions, but rather as inherent and fixed differences that are "natural and universal." In other words, an essentialist view of gender promotes biological reductionism and biological determinism. Yanagita's notion of the spiritual power of females is essentialist because he attributes that power to women's reproductive capacities.

The most rigorous study of Yanagita's folk religion and women's power was made by folk studies scholar Kanda Yoriko, who introduces various critiques of Yanagita but also finds at the same time that the work done by Yanagita's followers, "supported as it was by the notion of women's power, has clearly shown that the lives women have led have not just been passages solely of prejudice and discrimination." Kanda also accords value to the fragmentary statements made about women's folk customs, finding there the intention to "situate them accurately in women's history" (Kanda 2000:78; see also Kamata 1990; Miyata 1983, 1995).

Among the most powerful criticisms of Yanagita's notion of "women's power" is that advanced by the historian Yoshie Akiko (1989). Whereas Yanagita claimed that ritual observances were originally and intrinsically the unique province of women, Yoshie points out that this cannot be verified historically, and finds rather that ancient ritual was performed by men and women acting together. Yoshie raises the possibility that the sexual union of men and women was considered an important aspect of ritual. Kanda concludes that the problem with Yanagita's folk studies is that he gave scant consideration to the specific contexts of folk phenomena because he analyzed individual cases by fitting them into the "specific frameworks" of "women's power," "the divine self," "spiritual power," and so on. Kanda instead suggests that we must (a) analyze how women were socialized as objects of worship and discriminated against in actual life situations, (b) identify the circumstances and course of events that underlay that treatment, and (c) understand how women's positions have been defined in the present as a result (Kanda 2000:80–84).

It should also be instructive to take a brief look here at how Yanagita describes the lives of women outside religion. Kuraishi Atsuko, whose work on Yanagita's notion of the housewife is outstanding, criticizes Yanagita and other male folk studies scholars for over-emphasizing the spiritual power of women. She suggests that female scholars of folk studies have turned their attention to women's lives at home and in society at large in part to counter this emphasis (Kuraishi 1995:21). According to Kuraishi, Yanagita's notion of the housewife conveys his image of the ideal housewife, who had authority over the running of the household, presided over memorial rituals for the ancestors, and managed the family food and fortune. She was the (only) one capable of skillfully managing all these operations, thus protecting and preserving the house-hold (Kuraishi 1995:90). Citing Yanagita's statement that "women must make it their first precept to do everything possible to take care of the home, bear and rear good children, and never fail in performance of the memorial rituals for the ancestors, or trouble will result," Kuraishi suggests that Yanagita's actual motive here was to make women understand that Japanese traditions must be preserved (Kuraishi 1995:94–97). On this point she agrees with Tamanoi's aforementioned criticism of Yanagita. Kuraishi also observes that Yanagita respected women to a degree that was anomalous among his contemporary male scholars, and surmises that this was related to his respect and love for his own mother (Kuraishi 1995:94, 100–101).

Finally, I should briefly discuss the subject of Yanagita's notion of women's spiritual power in connection with Okinawa, which is also my own research field. It is well known that Yanagita's encounter with Okinawa was an underlying factor in develop-ing his "women's power" thesis. Yanagita wrote in *Imo no chikara*, "In the past, the women in each household invariably served the deities, and it appears that the wisest among the women was the most superior priestess [*miko*]" (1990:25). Yanagita seems never to have actually discussed specifically how housewives performed the functions of a priestess in their households. In Okinawa, however, it is an everyday occurrence for housewives to act as priestesses, praying to the *hinukan* (hearth deity) enshrined in the kitchen to appeal for their family's well-being and happiness. The priest-like role in close-knit village communities, kin groups, and, long ago, even in the context of state ritual, was, with extremely few exceptions, limited in Okinawa to women.

Even more widely known is the Okinawan belief in *onarigami* (literally, "sister deity"). According to this belief, sisters become the spiritual guardians of their brothers and watch over them. This is considered one of the distinctive characteristics of Okinawan culture, and it has received considerable study (Higa 1987; Kawahashi 2000a; Lebra 1966; Mabuchi 1964; Røkkum 1998). Kanda asserts that Yanagita projected the *onarigami* faith and other phenomena of Okinawa on to the women of Japan's mainland:

> In his introduction to *Imo no chikara*, Yanagita wrote that we could prevent ourselves from arriving at forced conclusions by selecting and analyzing materials on phenomena that have been transmitted as a matter of everyday practice. Regardless of this statement, however, his encounter with *onarigami* belief led him to take the image of Okinawa, where the women in every household invariably served the deities, and apply it to the Japanese mainland, so that he in fact forced his conclusions. (Kanda 2000:85)

As Kanda also observed, many scholars have already noted the absence of any basis on the Japanese mainland for finding that every housewife was something of a shamanic practitioner and could take a role in ritual observances (Kanda 2000:85). Kuraishi has also criticized the Yanagita thesis:

> It would be easy to understand [Yanagita's "women's spiritual power" thesis] in a region where an actively functioning system of female ritual officiants existed and influenced life in village communities, such as we find in Okinawa. On the Japanese mainland, however, where such a system does not exist, Yanagita's thesis does not provide an immediately convincing rationale to support the notion of women's [spiritual] superiority in everyday life. (Kuraishi 1995:230)

Thus, Yanagita's notion of "women's power" as a key feature of distinctively Japanese beliefs was most likely borrowed from Okinawa. His thesis, moreover, fed and furthered the illusory notion that Japan's ancient past still survived in Okinawa. In imposing his ideas about female spiritual superiority, Yanagita overlooked or disregarded the distinct differences between Japanese mainland and Okinawan societies. In the former, women are frequently excluded as unclean, while in the latter there are almost no pollution beliefs associated with women who act as the primary officiants in religious observances.

Yanagita was not the only early ethnographer who promoted "women's power" as an essential attribute of Japanese women on the basis of female physiology. Orikuchi Shinobu, who is known for his efforts to excavate the essence of Japan's ancient past through folk studies, also advanced a similar notion. Orikuchi's interpretation of the link between women and religion was premised on the idea that the female shamanic practitioner was the wife of the deity; in other words, he viewed women actually and metaphorically as shrine maidens serving a male deity. This was Orikuchi's understanding of the role of women in folk religion (Orikuchi 1975). The theme of divine marriage, however, does not accord with the reality of women ritual officiants in Okinawa.

I will conclude with some observations deriving from my own particular field of study. The "women's power" that Yanagita went in search of definitely existed (and exists) in Okinawa. Although the official religious observances of almost all religions are dominated by men, it is a fact that the religious sphere in Okinawa is the domain of women, and it would be easy to dismiss Yanagita's thesis as the essentialist product of a patriarchalist project. In making such a maneuver, however, we must not thereby dismiss the rich reality of women's religious practices such as we find in Okinawa.[7] The effort to free oneself of essentialist thinking can be of great value. Such an effort, however, should not lead scholars to impose an arbitrary construction on actual women who practice the religion being studied, thereby misrepresenting their self-understanding and distorting their history.

How can we venture an analysis and explanation of the observed religious power of women in different cultures without falling, as did Yanagita, into the trap of essentialism? The intersecting topics of folk religion and women present us with an array of issues that address this problem; issues not just directed toward investigating women's spiritual power, but also those related to the perception of female "pollution," such as the *nyonin kinsei* (female forbidden) system for excluding women from certain religious sites.[8] These issues call out for ethnographic attention and for more complex and textured studies of women religious practitioners (for examples of such, see Blacker 1975; Kawamura 1991; Smyers 1999).

In closing, I would like to revisit Ikegami's theory of folk religion. According to Ikegami, studies in the Yanagita tradition dealing with questions of women in folk religion, proceeded almost entirely from a framing objective to search and recover the "unique" traditions of Japanese culture, such as women's allegedly superior "spiritual powers." Today, questions about women and religion are being recognized as key issues in the field of religious studies. Field studies of women shamanic religious practitioners need to be juxtaposed with studies of the actual, profound realities of those women's life experiences and religious activities. Only in this way can ethnographic research reveal that women have much to teach us about the creative power of religious human beings (Ikegami 1999b:142–143).

ACKNOWLEDGMENTS

I wish to thank Dr. Richard Peterson for the excellent suggestions and editorial expertise he provided during my writing of this chapter.

NOTES

1 *Minkan shinkō* was probably first used as a technical term by the religion scholar Anesaki Masaharu in 1897.
2 Reader's article is probably the most comprehensive and up-to-date study of folk religion in the English language. He provides a detailed bibliography that is particularly useful for texts in European languages.
3 For a summary of Sakurai's argument, see Shinno (1993:189–196).
4 *Yanagita Kunio zenshū* (Collected Writings of Yanagita Kunio) has been issued in 32 paperback volumes by Chikuma Shotō.
5 Editor's note: By the same token, as I and many of my Japan anthropology colleagues have discovered, the same pattern of behavior is also present on the part of some Japanese scholars who either dismiss the analyses of their non-Japanese counterparts or fail to cite the scholarship (even if in Japanese translation) of their non-Japanese counterparts even when "borrowing" liberally from their published works. Moreover, the same can be said about some (usually tenured) scholars in both countries who do not properly credit material and ideas drawn from the research, often unpublished, of "junior" colleagues or advanced graduate students – a problem exacerbated when sexism and gender ideology are factored into the equation. In short, the larger issue to be addressed here is the ethics of scholarship and collaboration.
6 Another critical reflection on Japanese folklore studies that Tamanoi also refers to is Ivy (1995).
7 An instructive example of the risks involved can be found in the study by Susan Sered (1999) of women religious practitioners in Okinawa. This is a problematic work in many respects, and one that has aroused a considerable reaction (see, e.g., Kawahashi 2000b; Wacker 2001). A "Declaration of Concern" signed by 14 scholars of Okinawa studies, including myself, has just appeared in number 54 of *The Ryukyuanist* (2001–02:5), summarizing many of the objections to Sered's work. Sered's project is a theoretically motivated attempt to deconstruct essentialism, but what she in fact does is to appropriate and negate virtually the whole of the immense body of scholarly results that has been achieved in Okinawa studies.
8 A clear discussion of *nyonin kinsei* can be found in Suzuki (2002).

REFERENCES

Akasaka, Norio. 1999. Minzokugaku ha mura to shinjū sureba ii (Folk Studies Should Die Together with the Traditional Village). Sōbun 415:10–13.

Araki, Michio. 1987. Shūkyō no sōzō (Creation of Religion). Tokyo: Hōzōkan.

Blacker, Carmen. 1975. The Catalpa Bow: A Study of Shamanistic Practices in Japan. Richmond: Curzon Press.

de Alva, J. Jorge Klor. 1995. The Postcolonization of the (Latin) American Experience: A Reconsideration of "Colonialism," "Postcolonialism," and *Mestizaje*. *In* After Colonialism. G. Prakash, ed. pp. 241–275. Princeton: Princeton University Press.

Earhart, Byron. 1982. Japanese Religion: Unity and Diversity, 3rd edn. Belmont: Wadsworth.

Harootunian, Harry, and Naoki Sakai. 1999. Dialogue: Japan Studies and Cultural Studies. Positions 7(2):593–642.

Hayashi, Makoto. 1999. Sengo minzokushūkyō kenkyū no saikentō (Re-evaluation of Postwar Studies in Folk Religion). Aichigakuindaigaku ningen bunka kenkyūjōhō 25:89–101.

Hayashi, Makoto, and Kazuo Yoshihara. 1988. Editors' Introduction. Japanese Journal of Religious Studies 15(2–3).

Higa, Masao. 1987. Josei yūi to dankei genri (Female Domination and the Principle of Male Lineage). Tokyo: Gaifūsha.

Hori, Ichirō. 1951. Minkanshinkō (Folk Beliefs). Tokyo: Iwanami.

——1968. Folk Religion in Japan. Chicago: University of Chicago Press.

Ikegami, Yoshimasa. 1999a. Minkan fusha shinkō no kenkyū (Study of Shamanic Religious Practitioner Beliefs in the General Population). Tokyo: Miraisha.

——1999b. Minzoku shūkyō no fukugōsei to reiiteki jigen (Complexity of Folk Religion and its Dimension of Divine or Spiritual Power). *In* Minzoku shūkyō o manabu (Studying Folk Religion). Yamaori Tetsuo and Kawamura Kunimitsu, eds. pp. 127–144. Kyoto: Sekai Shisōsha.

——2000. Shūkyōgaku no hōhō to shite no minkan shinkō, minzoku shūkyōron (Theory of Folk Beliefs and Folk Religion as a Method for Religious Studies). Shūkyō kenkyū 325:1–24.

Ivy, Marilyn. 1995. Discourses of the Vanishing: Modernity, Phantasm, Japan. Chicago: University of Chicago Press.

Iwatake, Mikako. 1999a. Jūshutsu risshōhō: hōgen shūiron saikō (Substantiation by Multiple Occurrence: Re-examination of the Theory of Dialects as Peripheral, 1). Mirai 396:13–21.

——1999b. Jūshutsu risshōhō: hōgen shūiron saikō (Substantiation by Multiple Occurrence: Reexamination of the Theory of Dialects as Peripheral, 2). Mirai 397:6–16.

——2000. A Postcolonial Look at Kunio Yanagita, the Founding Father of Japanese Folklore Studies, Folklore, Heritage Politics and Ethnic Diversity. *In* A Festschrift for Barbro Klein. Pertti J. Anttonen, et al., eds. pp. 206–229. Botkyrka: Multicultural Center.

Kamata, Hisako. 1990. Onna no chikara: josei minzoku gaku nyūmon (Power of Women: Introduction to Women's Folk Studies). Tokyo: Seiga Shobō.

Kanda, Yoriko. 2000. Minzoku shūkyō to imo no chikara (Folk Religion and Women's Power). Shūkyō kenkyū 325:75–96.

Kawada, Minoru. 1992. Yanagita Kunio: koyū shinkō no sekai (Yanagita Kunio: The Realm of a Unique Faith). Tokyo: Miraisha.

Kawahashi, Noriko. 2000a. Seven Hindrances of Women? A Popular Discourse on Okinawan Women and Religion. Japanese Journal of Religious Studies 27:85–98.

——2000b. Review article: Religion, Gender and Okinawan Studies. Asian Folklore Studies 59:301–311.

Kawamura, Kunimitsu. 1991. Miko no minzokugaku (Folk Studies of Shamanic Priestesses). Tokyo: Seikyūsha.

Kuraishi, Atsuko. 1995. Yanagita Kunio to joseikan (Yanagita Kunio and his Views on Women). Tokyo: Sanichi Shobō.

Lebra, William P. 1966. Okinawan Religion: Belief, Ritual and Social Structure. Honolulu: University of Hawaii Press.

Long, Charles. 1987. Popular Religion. *In* The Encyclopedia of Religion. Mircea Eliade ed. Vol. 11, pp. 442–449. New York: Macmillan.

Mabuchi, Toichi. 1964. Spiritual Predominance of the Sister. *In* Ryukyuan Culture and Society. A. Smith, ed. Honolulu: University of Hawaii Press.

Miyata, Noboru. 1983. Onna no reiryoku to ie no kami (Women's Spiritual Power and Household Deities). Kyoto: Jinbun Shoin.

——1995. Minzokushūkyō to "onna no chikara" (Folk Religion and "The Power of Women"). Kikan bukkyō 30:34–43.

Murai, Osamu. 1995. Nantō ideorogī no hassei (Birth of the Ideology of the Southern Islands). Tokyo: Ōta Shuppan.

Origuchi, Shinobu. 1975. Mizu no onna (Women of the Water). *In* Orikuchi Shinobu zenshū (Collected Writings of Orikuchi Shinobu), vol. 2, pp. 80–109. Tokyo: Chūō Ōronsha.

Reader, Ian. In press. Folk Religion: Nanzan Guide to the Study of Japanese Religion, Nanzan Institute for Religion and Culture. Honolulu: University of Hawaii Press.

Reader, Ian, and George Tanabe. 1998. Practically Religious: Worldly Benefits and the Common Religion of Japan. Honolulu: University of Hawaii Press.

Røkkum, Arne. 1998. Goddesses, Priestesses, and Sisters. Oslo: Scandinavian University Press.

Sakurai, Tokutarō. 1982. Nihon minzoku shūkyōron (Study of Japanese Folk Religions). Tokyo: Shunjūsha.

Sasaki, Kōkan. 1980. Shāmanizumu: ekusutashii to hyōrei no bunka (Shamanism: Culture of Ecstasy and Spirit Possession). Tokyo: Chūō Kōronsha.

——1984. Shāmanizumu no jinruigaku (Anthropology of Shamanism). Tokyo: Kōbundō.

——Noboru Miyata, and Tetsuo Yamaori. 1998. Nihon minzoku shūkyō jiten (Dictionary of Japanese Folk Religion). Tokyo: Tōkyōdō Shuppan.

Sered, Susan. 1999. Women of the Sacred Groves. Oxford: Oxford University Press.

Shimamura, Takanori. 2001. "Nihon minzokugaku" kara tabunkashugi minzokugaku e (From Japanese Folk Studies to Multicultural Folk Studies). *In* Kindai nihon no tashazō to jigazō (Portraits of the Other and the Self in Modern Japan). Shinohara Tōru, ed. pp. 307–344. Tokyo: Kashiwa Shobō.

Shinno, Toshikazu. 1993. From *Minkan-shinkō* to *Minzoku-shūkyō*: Reflections on the Study of Folk Buddhism. Japanese Journal of Religious Studies 20(2–3):187–206.

——2000. Minkan shinkō ha jitsuzai shita ka (Did Folk Beliefs Actually Exist?). Shūkyō kenkyū 325:97–120.

Smyers, Karen A. 1999. The Fox and the Jewel. Honolulu: University of Hawaii Press.

Suzuki, Masataka. 2002. Nyonin kinsei (System for Exclusion of Women). Tokyo: Yoshikawa Kōbunkan.

Swearer, Donald K. 1987. Folk Religion: Folk Buddhism. *In* Encyclopedia of Religion. Mircea Eliade, ed. vol. 5, pp. 374–378. New York: Macmillan.

Tamamuro, Fumio, Eiji Hirano, Hitoshi Miyake, and Noboru Miyata. 1987. Minkan shinkō chōsa seiri handobukku (jō), riron hen (Handbook on Organizing Folk Belief Surveys, vol. 1: Theory). Tokyo: Yūzankaku.

Tamanoi, Mariko A. 1996. Gender, Nationalism and Japanese Native Ethnology. Positions. 4(1):59–86.

Tanaka, Takako. 1996. Seinaru onna (Sacred Women). Kyoto: Jinbun Shoin.

Wacker, Monika. 2001. Review of *Women of the Sacred Groves*. Japanese Journal of Religious Studies 28(1–2):201–204.

Yanagita, Kunio. 1990. Yanagita Kunio zenshū (Collected Writings of Yanagita Kunio), vols. 10 and 11. Tokyo: Chikuma Shobō.

Yoshie, Akiko. 1989. Tamayorihime saikō (Reconsidering the Goddess Tamayorihime). *In* Miko to joshin (Shamanic Priestesses and Female Deities). Ōsumi Kazuo and Nishiguchi Junko, eds. pp. 52–90. Tokyo: Heibonsha.

28 Women Scientists and Gender Ideology

Sumiko Otsubo

INTRODUCTION

Modern Western science, which reduces natural phenomena to abstract principles and mathematical theories, is popularly imagined in Japan and elsewhere as universal, objective, value-neutral, and international. At the same time, however, concepts associated with science, such as reason and objectivity, are imagined as masculine, and much scientific research and development is conducted in male-dominated environments. For various, mostly unscientific, reasons, science has been instrumental in perpetuating the view that men alone are capable of abstract mathematical-physical reductionism and are thus intellectually superior to women. This view certainly prevails in Japan, where a centuries-long history of sex and gender differentiation and hierarchies allowed for the smooth adoption of an androcentric European model of modern science in the late 19th century.

Scholars have made the investigation of the gender politics of science a subject in its own right. Historian of science Morris Low uses the metaphor of "black boxes" to characterize the making of scientific and technical knowledge. He examines how these black boxes are gendered in the science- and technology-related workforce, and finds that they are used to justify the exploitation of women as a source of part-time labor. In the case of Japan, sex and gender hierarchies intersect with ethnicity as Asian workers are recruited by Japanese industries within and outside of Japan (Low 1999). In *Lifetimes and Beamtimes* (1988), anthropologist Sharon Traweek explores the differences between high-energy physicists in Japan and the United States, and briefly analyzes the sexual and gender politics operating within those communities. Using his technique of "participant observation," Samuel Coleman analyzes the organizational patterns – including the gender hierarchies – of the biosciences, which attract a larger proportion (20 percent–50 percent) of women researchers and technicians than other fields in science (1999). Other anthropologists and historians have analyzed the effect of the so-called "male/medical gaze" on the Japanese female body (Burns 1998; Lock 1993; Otsubo 1999).

Japanese-language biographies of female scientists – often written by the subjects themselves – and statistical analyses of women trained in science and engineering have appeared at intervals over the past 70 years (Endō et al. 1993; Muramatsu 1996; Nagashima 1937; Nihon Joishi Henshū Iinkai 1991; Ochanomizu Joshi Daigaku Rigakubu and Nichifutsu Rikōkakai 1998; Saruhashi 1999 [1981]; Yamashita 1970). An anthology of autobiographical accounts by 20 award-winning Japanese female scientists was recently translated into English (Kozai et al. 2001). Many of the essays were written with the explicit aim of encouraging young women to choose careers in science by documenting the careers of successful women scientists. These sorts of books are also aimed at changing the masculinist environment of scientific work, and, by extension, eliminating sexism and gender inequality in fields of science. Unlike some of their Euro-American counterparts, however, Japanese historians of science, male and female alike, tend not to advocate a "feminist science" (Fox Keller 1983, 1985; Harding 1991; Low 1989; Schiebinger 1992; Sugiyama 1994).

In this chapter, I examine the careers of women scientists before, during, and after the Asia–Pacific War (1937–45), and consider how they were influenced by education, family, employment, mentors, and social activism.

CAREERS OF WOMEN SCIENTISTS: EDUCATION

In her 1981 biography, geochemist Saruhashi Katsuko (b. 1920), an advocate for women in science, drew attention to the hierarchical practice in the Japanese academy of favoring both men over women and public over private higher education in Japan. Outside the laboratory to which she belonged, Saruhashi, who graduated from a private college, routinely experienced discrimination because of her sex and educational background (Saruhashi 1999 [1981]:30). Before and during the Asia–Pacific War, women's limited training did not necessarily reflect their lack of intelligence, aspiration, determination, and dedication. Rather, due to the androcentrism of the Japanese educational system, it was extremely hard for women to pursue an advanced education at public universities, where research facilities and financial support were available. Japan's pioneer woman scientist, Yasui Kono (1880–1971), for example, never received a university degree. Fin-de-siècle Japan was a patriarchal society based on the principle of *danson johi*, or "male superiority, female inferiority." Women were expected to be obedient and submissive to men. Schools beyond the primary level were not generally coeducational, loosely following the Confucian precept that "a boy and a girl should not sit together after the age of 7." The main objective of girls' schools was to produce "good wives and wise mothers" (*ryōsai kenbo*). The official gender ideology assigned females to a so-called private sphere of influence and to the mission of household management and childrearing. This contrasted with the mission of public universities, which was to produce men who would contribute to nation-building. Applicants to public universities needed to have graduated from a "higher school" (*kōtō gakko*), and such schools were open only to boys.

Yasui attended a prefectural normal school (in the girls' and women's division) for two years before majoring in science at the Tokyo Women's Higher Normal School

(TWHNS), which was established by the state in 1874 in order to train middle-school teachers. After completing a two-year extension program designed for candidates for professorship, Yasui began her career as an assistant professor at her alma mater. She also continued her cytological research on *algae prothallia*, and in 1911 published her study "On the Life History of *Salvinia Natans*" in the flagship journal *Annals of Botany*. When TWHNS requested the Ministry of Education to grant her an overseas study fellowship, bureaucrats were reluctant to approve it, for they assumed that women were not likely to be successful in scientific research.

Between 1875 and 1940, the ministry funded 3,170 men and only 39 women to further their training in Europe and the United States. It was easier for women who studied English or physical education to receive fellowships for overseas study, since these subjects were regarded as central to women's education (Tsugawa and Kanomi 1996:42). The ministry finally approved Yasui's application but added "domestic science" along with "science" as her key subjects of study. Her government fellowship was also rumored to be contingent on a tacit agreement that Yasui would never marry so that she could devote her full attention to scientific research upon her return to Japan. Despite her lack of a university degree, Yasui was regarded as a graduate student at the University of Chicago and Harvard University on account of her substantial publication record. In 1916 she both resumed her teaching at TWHNS and began her research at the department of botany, Tokyo Imperial University. Yasui has the distinction of being the first woman ever to receive a Ph.D. from a Japanese university. Her 1927 doctorate was awarded in recognition of her cytological analysis of Japanese coal, morning glories, and rose mosses. From 1929 to 1961, she also served as a business manager and editorial assistant for *Cytologia*, an international journal of cytogenetics founded by her Tokyo Imperial University advisor, Fujii Kenjirō (1866–1952).

Tokyo Imperial University was established by the Meiji state in 1877, followed by the founding of other well-funded and prestigious imperial universities in Kyoto (1897), Tōhoku (1907), and Kyūshū (1910). None of these universities, however, officially admitted women as undergraduate students until 1913, when Tōhoku Imperial University opened its doors to three women: Tange Ume (1873–1951), who studied chemistry, Kuroda Chika (1884–1968), who majored in chemistry, and Makita Raku (1888–1977), who pursued a degree in mathematics. Unlike Tokyo and Kyoto, Tōhoku admitted not only higher-school graduates, but also students with a middle-school teaching certificate, which was obtainable by women. Tange had majored in home economics at the Japan Women's College, a private school established in 1901, and Kuroda and Makita had studied in the Faculty of Sciences at TWHNS. Although Makita chose marriage over research after graduation, Tange and Kuroda remained unmarried and went on to receive advanced training overseas. Tange left for the United States in 1921 and received a Ph.D. in dietetic chemistry from Johns Hopkins University six years later. She returned home and began teaching food chemistry at her alma mater while continuing her research on Vitamin B-2 at the Research Institute for Physics and Chemistry (Riken) as an adjunct research associate. For this research, she obtained a Japanese doctoral degree in agriculture from Tokyo Imperial University in 1940. Kuroda studied organic chemistry at Oxford University in the early 1920s. Upon returning to Japan she too taught at her alma mater and engaged in research on the structural analysis of safflower pigments at Riken. Based on this research, Tōhoku Imperial University awarded her a doctoral degree in science in 1929 (Nagashima 1937; Nihon Joishi Henshū Iinkai 1991; Ochanomizu Joshi Daigaku Rigakubu and Nichifutsu Rikōkakai 1998; Tsugawa and Kanomi 1996; Yamashita 1970).

In addition to TWHNS, which focused on science education, Japan Women's College, Tokyo Medical College for Women, and Tokyo Women's Christian College were the major institutions of higher education for women in the early 20th century, specializing in home economics, medicine, and mathematics, respectively. Despite the efforts of their administrators to strengthen the caliber of the curriculum, however, the Ministry of Education declined to grant these colleges university status. Nevertheless, a university education became gradually more accessible to women, and by the mid-1930s six public universities had opened their doors to a small number of women who wanted to study in science or agriculture (Tsugawa and Kanomi 1996:187–8). By April 1937, there were 21 elite female scientists among the 12,356 students who had received doctoral degrees from Japanese universities. One of the women was Chinese. Three, including Yasui and Kuroda, were awarded doctorates in science, one in pharmacology, two, including Tange, in agriculture, and 14 in medicine. There were no women among the doctorates in humanities or social sciences (Nagashima 1937). Much of the scientific research by these female scientists dealt with subjects regarded at the time as "feminine," such as foodstuffs (green tea, wheat mold, sea bream, beefsteak plant, onion) and dyes (gromwell roots, safflower), perhaps because these women had studied and taught in departments of home economics and science education for women (Yamashita 1970:72–3, 217–9).

As in the United States and elsewhere, wartime shortages of men in academic circles expanded the opportunities for women to receive training in various scientific and technical fields. Between 1941 and 1944, four private women's colleges were established and offered programs in physics, chemistry, biology, and mathematics. Eight other existing colleges for women added science departments. By 1944, these new schools and departments enrolled as many as 700 women annually (Sugiyama 1994:168; Yamashita 1970:9). Geochemist Saruhashi Katsuko enrolled in one of these new schools, the Imperial Science College for Women. She completed the three-year curriculum in 1943 and took a job at the research division of the Central Meteorological Observatory. Most of her classmates chose to work at research institutions affiliated with the army or navy. Saruhashi later recalled that one professor had criticized her decision not to seek employment with the military (Saruhashi 1999 [1981]:13–14), although the state's mobilization of scientists was not limited to strictly military facilities. One of the first projects that Saruhashi participated in at the Observatory was wartime research on methods of dispersing the dense fog that occasionally compromised airport operations. In 1957 she received a doctoral degree in science from Tokyo University (the former Tokyo Imperial University) for her studies on the characteristics of carbonate. Her development of an effective method to gauge the density of radioactive elements in seawater brought her an invitation to participate in a collaborative project with the University of California's Scripps Institute of Oceanography in San Diego in 1962. Upon retiring in 1980, she co-founded the Association for the Bright Future of Women Scientists, which began awarding the newly created Saruhashi prize every year. The following year, she became the first female candidate for the Science Council of Japan and was subsequently elected as one of its 210 members (Saruhashi 1999 [1981]).

During the Allied occupation of Japan (1945–52), the Japanese education system was democratized and the former imperial universities were made coeducational. Many teacher training schools and colleges were upgraded to university status. For example, the Tokyo Women's Higher Normal School became Ochanomizu University for Women, the Japan Women's College became the Japan Women's University, and the Imperial Science College for Women became the coeducational Tōhō University. The percentage of women admitted to universities improved from 2.45 percent in 1955 to 22.94 percent in 1995; the corresponding percentages for men were 13.57 percent and 40.74 percent. The number of female students at Tokyo University, which had been closed to women prior to 1945, rose from 47 (1.2 percent) in 1950 to 2,790 (17.7 percent) in 2000. Recent statistical data show that women make up 26 percent of undergraduate science majors, 9 percent of engineering majors, 39 percent of agriculture majors, 52 percent of medical school majors (among which are included nursing and pharmacology, two fields dominated by women), and 96 percent of home economics majors. In doctoral degree programs, 14 percent of the graduate students in science are women, compared to 9 percent in engineering, 21 percent in agriculture, 22 percent in medicine, and 87 percent in home economics. Today, about 206,000 women at the undergraduate level and 6,700 women at the doctoral level are enrolled in programs in science and technology at Japanese universities (Kozai et al. 2001:307–308).

The greatly expanded and more egalitarian educational opportunities in postwar Japan are reflected in the ever-increasing numbers of women in prominent science and technology positions in recent years. For example, in the mid-1990s, four women were elected to preside over their respective academic societies, which had never before been headed by women. These four were Ishida Mizuho (Seismological Society of Japan), Kusama Tomoko (Health Physics Society of Japan), Ōi Misao (Spectroscopic Analysis Society of Japan), and Yonezawa Fumiko (Physics Society of Japan) (Muramatsu 1996:2). Both Yonezawa and Ishida were finalists for the Saruhashi prize.

Yonezawa (b. 1938), awarded the Saruhashi prize in 1984, studied physics in the Faculty of Science at Kyoto University, the only woman among 50 men. She began her theoretical research on various physical properties of disordered systems as a graduate student at Kyoto. After receiving her Ph.D. in physics in 1966, Yonezawa went on to refine her theory as a research associate at the Research Institute for Fundamental Physics (RIFP) at Kyoto University, the home of Japan's first Nobel laureate, physicist Yukawa Hideki (1907–81), who developed meson particle theory. Over a period of several years she published papers in which she formulated an internally consistent approximation for evaluating the electronic properties of disordered systems. She was one of four young physicists who independently came up with the same revolutionary theory of "coherent potential approximation" (CPA). Yonezawa recalls that Yukawa half-jokingly praised her as being productive both at work and at home because she gave birth to three daughters while writing important scientific papers. Between 1972 and 1975 she conducted research on liquid metals and disordered systems as a visiting scholar at Yeshiva University and the City College of New York.

Upon her return to RIFP, where she was promoted to Associate Professor, she assembled a group of physicists to collaborate on a study of amorphous semiconductors. She was very successful in securing funds from government and corporate sectors for various international and domestic symposia and large-scale projects. For example, in 1995 she won a ¥700 million ($US7 million) grant to organize research on complex liquids. This three-year project involved more than 100 physicists, who collectively published over 1,000 papers. Her discovery of a new mechanism of metal-nonmetal transitions was based on some of the experimental results of that project. In 1995 Yonezawa's peers elected her president of the Physics Society of Japan, one of the most prestigious – and androcentric – scientific societies in Japan. That year, only 3 percent of the society's 20,000 members were women. Yonezawa is currently a full professor at Keio University, a highly regarded private university in Tokyo (Kozai et al. 2001).

Ishida Mizuho (b. 1943), awarded the Saruhashi prize in 1989, is another female scientist with a distinguished career in postwar Japan. Instead of choosing a coeducational university like Yonezawa, Ishida majored in physics at Ochanomizu University for Women. As a graduate student at Tokyo University, she specialized in seismology within the geophysics program. Although she eventually got a Ph.D. in 1974, she encountered some difficulties in the course of her graduate studies. The student movement and campus disputes of the late 1960s disrupted her research at the Earthquake Research Institute, where she was conducting research on seismic wave travel-time anomalies in and around Japan. Professors were effectively barred from entering their laboratories. To complicate matters further, Ishida's advisor, Kanamori Hirō, accepted a job offer from the California Institute of Technology, and she was forced to complete her doctoral thesis without him.

Ishida was then appointed to the seismological division at the National Research Center for Disaster Prevention[1] as a researcher following her graduate studies. The Diet passed the Large-Scale Earthquake Countermeasures Act in 1978, which prompted geologists to focus their attention on seismic activity in the densely populated Kanto–Tōkai region, where a devastating earthquake had occurred in 1923. Ishida analyzed the configuration of the Philippine Sea and Pacific tectonic plates that lay beneath this region, which includes Tokyo. Her investigation focused on the interrelationship of earthquake mechanisms, velocity structures, and the pattern of distribution of earthquakes. Her work was instrumental in recalculating potential earthquake hypocenters based on three-dimensional models of velocity structures. Like Yonezawa, Ishida spent several years in the United States as a visiting researcher, initially with Kanamori at the California Institute of Technology in 1978, and later with Selwin Sacks at the Carnegie Institution during 1983. In the mid-1990s, she was the principal investigator in two major projects: Fundamental Research on Earthquakes and Earth's Interior Anomalies (FREESIA; 1994–96), and Superplume – Towards an Integrated View of Geophysics (1996). Her election to the presidency of the Seismological Society of Japan came only a few months after the destructive 1995 Kobe earthquake, in which 6,000 people lost their lives. As a result, Ishida became one of the most visible women scientists in the mass media. She heads the National Research Institute for Earth Science and Disaster Prevention (Kozai et al. 2001).

The careers of Yonezawa and Ishida illustrate the changes in women's education and career opportunities in postwar Japan, although significant biases regarding women in higher education and science remain, as Saruhashi Katsuko herself has remarked.

FAMILY

Although more women today have access to advanced scientific training, the enrollment of women in universities still lags behind that of male students, particularly in science and engineering. The relatively equal number of women and men in medicine dispels the notion that men and not women have an innate affinity for science. Maintaining a balance between research and housework was a challenge for many women scientists, who routinely needed to stay in their labs until late at night. Makita Raku was a promising mathematician who gave up her career for her painter husband, who was apparently unable to assist with household chores because they interrupted his studio time (Tsugawa and Kanomi 1996:110). Doubtless there was more than meets the eye to this marital drama, but it does reveal the tenacity of a gender-based double standard in the professions. Yonezawa, with a husband and three children, was an exception, although she also felt the social pressure to choose between marriage and physics. Virtually all the successful women scientists senior to her, including Yasui Kono, Tange Ume, Kuroda Chika, and Saruhashi Katsuko, were unmarried (Kozai et al. 2001:46). It should be noted that Yasui lived with her younger sister, whose role for 50 years was to care for her in a "wifely" way – a typical pattern for some successful Japanese women who remain unmarried (Tsugawa and Kanomi 1996:58–60).

Unlike their senior colleagues, half of the 20 women who were awarded the Saruhashi prize between 1981 and 2000 are married with at least one child, and one recipient lives with her male partner. Many women scientists with children have expressed frustration at the amount of time they have had to devote to childrearing instead of their scientific work. Some gave up career-advancing opportunities, including a chance to work with leading researchers outside Japan, because of family commitments (Kozai et al. 2001:27, 143–144, 208–209). Others, unable to handle alone dual responsibilities at work and home, had to solicit help from mothers or mothers-in-law with housework and especially childcare (Kozai et al. 2001:27, 294). Ironically, as the number of women who choose science as a career increases, and as more career options for women become available, more men and some women are voicing the opinion that married women with children should not devote themselves entirely to work outside the home. Regardless of their marital status, a woman's biological ability to bear children apparently makes prospective employers perceive hiring women, scientists or not, as a risky proposition.

EMPLOYMENT

It has been a challenge for women to land jobs that allow them to do scientific research. In the 1930s, talented women like Yasui, Tange, and Kuroda were all recruited by the women's schools from which they graduated. Although they were able to teach and earn a living, these schools more often than not lacked the facilities and funds to support their research. Thus, the women had to make special arrangements, such as using equipment at such institutions as Tokyo Imperial University and the Riken in the capacity of unpaid or poorly paid adjuncts. The wartime mobilization of men opened up opportunities for women, in both scientific education and other forms of employment. Saruhashi was hired by the Central Meteorological Observatory in this context. Yonezawa and Ishida found employment, but some of the other recipients of the Saruhashi prize were not as fortunate. For example, physicist Katō Takako (b. 1943), a recipient in 1992, received her Ph.D. in 1972, but she worked for another six years without salary before she was able to obtain a research associate position at the Institute of Plasma Physics, Nagoya University. Mathematician and mother of one Ishii Shihoko (b. 1950), a 1995 recipient, noted that it took her four long years to obtain a permanent position after she received a Ph.D., despite the fact that she had a sufficient number of important academic publications and presentations to her credit. Takabe Tetsuko (b. 1947), a 1997 recipient, recalled that she almost gave up trying to get a research job after earning an M.Sc. in agricultural science, when her applications to companies and national institutes went unanswered. While still a doctoral candidate, chemist Nishikawa Keiko (b. 1948), a 1998 recipient, took a research associate job at a private university assisting a professor, who was scheduled to retire in three years. A man would have likely hesitated to take such a temporary position, but Nishikawa had no choice since it was one of the few academic jobs available to female scientists. These women are now professors at the National Institute of Fusion Science, Tokyo Institute of Technology, Nagoya University, and Chiba University, respectively. Unfortunately, in the 1970s, graduate programs began producing more Ph.D.s than could be absorbed by academic and research institutions, and, while this situation affected men too, women suffered greater negative consequences (Kozai et al. 2001).

Despite the reality of a sexist double-standard in educational and employment opportunities, some women scientists, including Saruhashi and chemist Sōma Yoshie (b. 1942), a 1986 Saruhashi recipient, nevertheless insist that science as a field provides equal opportunities for women. Of course, they also admit to having mentors who treated men and women fairly and equally. Unfortunately, such mentors were, and are, few and far between.

MENTORS

Behind successful careers, there are usually understanding mentors. But it is particularly important for women scientists to have supportive thesis advisors, group project leaders, or supervisors because of social biases against them. Pharmacological chemist and discoverer of ephedrine, Nagai Nagayoshi (1845–1929), for instance, was instrumental in launching the careers of two pioneer women chemists, Tange Ume and Kuroda Chika. While teaching at the Tokyo Imperial University as a professor of medicine, he also agreed to teach chemistry at the Japan Women's College when its founder Naruse Jinzō asked him to do so. Nagai also taught at the Tokyo Women's Higher Normal School. Both Nagai and Naruse thought it was important to provide science education for women and used eugenics-inspired logic to promote higher education for women. When male university students at Tokyo complained that Nagai spent too much time and energy on women's education, Nagai, who had spent 13 years in Berlin and married a German woman, responded to the comment by arguing that well-educated German women reproduced mentally and physically fit Germans. Among them, there were great scientists, who were responsible for making Germany's medicine, pharmacology, and chemical industry the world's best. Japanese women should be educated so that they could be capable of giving birth to mentally and physically fit Japanese, which would help Japan catch up with advanced countries. Nagai underscored the public meaning of uniquely feminine reproductive ability. As soon as he heard the news that women were eligible to take the entrance examination of Tōhoku Imperial University, he encouraged Tange, whom he had taught at the Japan Women's College, and Kuroda, who was working as his assistant at the Tokyo Women's Higher Normal School, to apply. Nagai convinced others who were skeptical about the idea of female university students that it was necessary to have women applicants and to open the door of higher education to women.

Saruhashi Katsuko's mentor and geochemist Miyake Yasuo advocated better status for women scientists whenever he had the opportunity. After graduating from college, Saruhashi began working for Miyake at his laboratory in the Central Observatory. Saruhashi spent a year at the Scripps Institute of Oceanography in 1962. At one point, both Japan and the United States had projects to measure the levels of radioactive contamination of the oceans. Unfortunately, there was a discrepancy between US and Japanese calculations, and the US Atomic Energy Commission criticized the Japanese number as too high. Miyake, who believed in the accuracy of Saruhashi's measurement method, sent her to San Diego to prove it (Saruhashi 1999 [1981]:147). This was a major decision for him and an important task for her. Considering the unequal – some called it a "colonial" (Hiroshige 1965) – power relationship between US and Japanese scientists and the gender inequality in science, sending a woman scientist to represent Japan in proving the inadequacy of the American procedures challenged two establishments: male scientists and American science. When Saruhashi ran for the Science Council in 1981, as part of her campaign she was allowed to send postcards to 3,300 voters. Although he was 72 years old and had deteriorating eyesight, Miyake added a handwritten note to each postcard in support of her (Saruhashi 1999 [1981]:22–23). Like Nagai, Miyake was sometimes criticized by his male colleagues for being too nice to women. Miyake, however, maintained that he wanted to improve conditions for female researchers not because they were women or because he was sympathetic to the weaker sex. Apparently inspired by the socialist ideals of equality, he supported women scientists because in his view it was not acceptable to discriminate against women simply on the basis of their sex (Saruhashi 1999 [1981]:97).

In 1980 Saruhashi donated ¥5 million to establish the award named after her to recognize women scientists. By doing so she played the role of mentor not to a particular individual but to the entire community of women in science. Some of the Saruhashi prizewinners, like Sōma Yoshie and Takebe Tetsuko, emphasized how much the award helped them in their careers. Though they were virtually unknown at the time, the recognition that came with the award helped them to get promotions, research money, and other forms of support. Takebe commented that getting the award in 1997 shook up the larger field of agricultural science; suddenly other female researchers started to get permanent positions and promotions. While many women of science appreciated Saruhashi's initiatives, some found her "women only" approach problematic. For example, when Saruhashi asked for support for the Japan Society for Women Scientists in the late 1950s, Yasui Kono declined. She felt that women scientists' research was in no way inferior to that of men and that therefore there was no need to create a group segregating women from men (Saruhashi 1999 [1981]:79–80). Yasui insisted on equality between men and women in both research and teaching and strictly avoided special treatment for women (Tsugawa and Kanomi 1996:55).

Unlike Yasui, mentoring figures like Nagai and Saruhashi called attention to certain womanly characteristics in their efforts to correct poor conditions for women in science. Nagai stressed women's reproductive body and its potential utility for the state, and Saruhashi identified women scientists with the peace and environment movements. These are exactly the areas where social activism and science converged.

SOCIAL ACTIVISM

Hiratsuka Raichō (1886–1971), Japan's most prominent woman activist, made use of science in her pursuit of the wellbeing of women. She was involved in two seemingly contradictory campaigns: Before the war she led a nationalistic eugenics movement and after the war she promoted international peace (Sōgō Joseishi Kenkyūkai 2000:192–194).

Hiratsuka majored in home economics at Japan Women's College. Its founder, Naruse Jinzō, raised funds to create this private institution and upgrade the college to a university in the late 19th and early 20th centuries, when most others thought men's education should be the priority for building a nation, and that higher education would unsex women. To convince skeptical men of power and wealth to contribute and support his plans, Naruse underscored the significance for the state of women's role as reproducers and nurturers of the Japanese race. Toward this end, he recruited strong faculty members in home economics, including chemist Nagai Nagayoshi and physiologist Ōsawa Kenji from Tokyo Imperial University. Concerned with a possible decline of the race caused by the breakdown of natural selection and the spread of diseases such as tuberculosis, leprosy, syphilis, gonorrhea, and alcoholism within the family, Ōsawa proposed the prenuptial exchange of health certificates in 1904. Exposed to Ōsawa's view as a student and well-informed about the ideas of Swedish feminist and eugenics sympathizer Ellen Key, Hiratsuka put theory into action in 1920. To protect middle-class women who often fell victim to venereal diseases brought back by their sexually dissolute husbands, she submitted a eugenics bill to prohibit men with venereal diseases from getting married. She also called for women to voluntarily reject marriage to men infected with venereal diseases. To legitimate her effort, she asked Ōsawa to endorse her ideas and lend his scientific authority to the crusade. This was Japan's first eugenics legislation campaign, and after it eventually failed Hiratsuka withdrew from the movement. However, other women continued to use eugenics to gain concessions from the state such as marriage restrictions on VD patients, prenuptial exchange of health certificates, medical checks for pregnant women, health tests for newborn babies, research on sterility and stillbirths, and the abolition of state-sanctioned prostitution.

Female obstetrician and gynecologist Takeuchi Shigeyo (1881–1975) was one of these women. Takeuchi, the first graduate of Tokyo Medical College for Women, was one of 20 Japanese women who received a doctoral degree before 1937. Her 1933 thesis, "A Study on the Constitutions of Japanese Women," was supervised by Nagai Hisomu (1876–1957), professor of physiology at Tokyo (Ōsawa's successor) and president of the Japan Association of Race Hygiene. Takeuchi served as a medical advisor to the Eugenic Marriage Consultation Office and was vice-president of the Eugenics Marriage Popularization Society (EMPS). Both were established in the mid-1930s, as affiliates of the Association of Race Hygiene. The EMPS published a monthly journal, *Yūsei* (Well Born). In many *Yūsei* articles, medical experts like Nagai and Takeuchi popularized up-to-date genetic theories and other kinds of medical knowledge. They stressed that women's genes were as influential as men's and argued that women's infertility was often caused by men's sexual diseases and disputed the notion that women were just "borrowed wombs" that did not affect male bloodlines (see also chapter 21 in this volume).

In the late 1930s, Takeuchi represented middle-class women and participated in state health policymaking, including discussions that eventually led to eugenics legislation. The government enacted the Maternal and Child Protection Law in 1937 and the National Eugenics Law in 1940. In their vision of eugenic marriage, both Hiratsuka and Takeuchi encouraged women to take charge in choosing their future spouse carefully and scientifically for the health of themselves, their children, and the race (Otsubo 1999).

In the postwar years, Hiratsuka became the vice-president of the Women's International Democratic Federation (WIDF), which sought world peace. Having learned that Saruhashi Katsuko was an expert on radioactive isotope analysis, Hiratsuka asked Saruhashi in early 1958 to organize a women scientists' group and to act as its representative in the fourth WIDF meeting to be held in June. Saruhashi seized the opportunity to put Hiratsuka's plan into action, which she saw as a way to promote women scientists, in addition to contributing to world peace. In postwar Japan, women actively organized mass peace movements and anti-pollution campaigns. Their activism was an extension of their identities as mothers who cared about nature and children. There was also a certain feminization of Japanese men at this time as the result of the dropping of atomic bombs and the defeat and decolonization of Japan's once powerful Asian empire – events which emasculated Japanese men but at the same time gave them a new appreciation for "female" concerns such as peace and the environment.

The first nuclear bombs were dropped by the US onto the Japanese cities of Hiroshima and Nagasaki, killing more than 300,000 people. Many survivors of the explosions were affected by radiation and eventually died of so-called A-bomb disease. Nine years later, a Japanese fishing boat, "Lucky Dragon," was exposed to the deadly fallout of an American nuclear test, conducted near the Bikini atoll in the Pacific, and one of the crew died shortly afterwards. Scientists in Japan and around the world responded to these tragedies and participated in conferences against nuclear weapons in Hiroshima and Pugwash, Canada, in the mid-1950s. When the Japan Society of Women Scientists was established in April 1958, it sent a resolution against nuclear weapons to Vienna. The resolution was designed "to inform women in the world of radioactive contamination with scientific data on food pollution and human heredity, the issues which would be dear to women" (Saruhashi 1999 [1981]:139–140). The society also chose Saruhashi as a representative to be sent to Vienna, as Hiratsuka had hoped (Saruhashi 1999 [1981]:68–69, 76–79). This time Hiratsuka used not only Saruhashi's scientific authority, but also her image as a peace-loving woman.

In Vienna, Saruhashi gave a talk on the hazards of nuclear tests on human bodies as a Japanese, a woman, and a scientist. She explained the process of how radioactive fallout resulting from nuclear explosions contaminated soil and water, which then polluted plants and animals. Humans absorbed the most hazardous radioactive isotope, strontium 90, by eating vegetables, meat, dairy products, and seafood. Herbivorous animals ate contaminated plants and assimilated strontium 90, most of which would be deposited in the bones and not released into the body. Drinking milk or eating dairy products, therefore, resulted in an indirect exposure to the isotope that was safer than eating vegetables. Because their diet consisted of rice and vegetables, the Asian race (*ajia jinshu*) was thus more likely to assimilate strontium 90 than Americans and Europeans, for whom milk products were a significant source of nutrition. She also noted another dangerous isotope, cecium 133, which, once assimilated by humans and animals, would stay in the blood and gonads, with a pernicious impact on heredity. Saruhashi concluded that it was scientists' duty to use their knowledge for human wellbeing and peace and to prevent it from being used for mass murder and the destruction of civilization (Saruhashi 1999 [1981]:137–146).

Although Yasui intentionally distanced herself from the society and its "feminine" peace movement, her last paper in 1957 was a genetic study analyzing mutation and sterility among the descendants of a plant, spiderwort (*murasaki tsuyukusa*), exposed to the A-bomb radiation in Hiroshima (Tsugawa and Kanomi 1996:50). Saruhashi noted the effectiveness of the spiderwort mutation research as examples in the 1977 Anti-Nuclear Weapons World Congress (Saruhashi 1999 [1981]:159, 161), though Yasui was not the only researcher who had worked on this project.

IMPLICATIONS

Did Yasui Kono's spiderwort mutation research, with its focus on reproduction, heredity, and Hiroshima, express insights derived from her experience as a woman scientist? Rather than answering this question directly, let us consider what we can say about research themes. The majority of prewar women scientists' studies investigated problems associated with food and clothing (dyeing). These "feminine" subjects were related to the fact that, as students and teachers, all of these researchers came from a tradition of home economics and science education specifically designed for women. And we must not forget that the Ministry of Education, which controlled education-related monies, including study-abroad fellowships, insisted that Yasui study "domestic science" in the United States. Under constant social pressures like this, Yasui might have unconsciously chosen research themes that would simultaneously please her inquisitive mind and a conservative, patriarchal establishment.

As we have seen, the prewar educational system institutionalized official gender roles. The social assumption that men had superior minds became reality largely because of inequality in educational opportunities. Hierarchical gender roles fostered discrimination against prewar and wartime women scientists. Their research was often dismissed because they were women with lesser educational qualifications. Women had a hard time maintaining a balance between family and work, employment, promotions, and finding money for research and study abroad. Despite these obstacles, 20 women in science, agriculture, and medicine received doctoral degrees, while there were none in the humanities and social sciences.

Even after postwar reforms democratizing Japan's education system, female students continued to be underrepresented in science, and unequal opportunities were the norm even after 1945. But the most powerful mechanisms to sustain the prewar gender hierarchy ceased to function, and the last generation of men and women socialized within a traditional gender framework are being replaced by a new generation. The increase of female science majors and scientists, and diversified research topics – including contributions from CPA theory explaining disordered systems and work on the mechanisms of seismic activity, topics completely unrelated to domestic science – are signs of a delayed but tangible change.

In order to transcend gender barriers, women scientists have devised a number of different strategies. Tange Ume and Kuroda Chika challenged the educational system itself. Taking advantage of a small loophole in eligibility rules, they were able to gain entrance to a university system that had been monopolized by men. Biologist Yasui Kono and many others competed with male scientists by rejecting marriage and children. By contrast, Yonezawa Fumiko and others showed that women scientists had choices and were capable of handling research and family. Saruhashi Katsuko appealed to the public with the argument that women scientists were important since they could be the guardians of peace and the natural world. She also established organizations of women scientists that celebrated their colleagues' achievements. Though all these women scientists hoped to end subordination of women one way or another, their approaches were diverse. The tension between Yasui and Saruhashi paralleled those between feminists believing in the total equality of men and women and others who stressed women's motherly instinct to protect nature and children.

But how successful were these empowerment strategies in deconstructing women's subservient status in science? The goal of being exactly like men as university students and researchers separated women scientists as mere exceptions and did not really help change existing gender perceptions. Women giving up family strengthened the view that women were incapable of taking on dual responsibilities in and outside the home. Many women who married and had children were less productive, providing ammunition for those who preferred male scientists to female researchers. These women also helped to perpetuate the assumption that women should marry and have children. The idea that professional women with children could get help from other women (sisters, mothers, or mothers-in-law) was not completely convincing as a replacement for traditional sex roles. Emphasis on women's reproductive ability and their special affinity for issues of nonviolence and environmental protection bolstered existing gender dichotomies. As Yasui Kono implied, creating groups only for women scientists could be seen as an effort to share the misery of their underachievement. Can women scientists ever overcome gender inequality if empowerment strategies themselves reinforce the very hierarchical gender stereotypes that they wish to get rid of?

One possible way of unsettling the traditional gender order is an appeal to new scientific knowledge. The *Yūsei* articles based on recent genetics research had the unexpected effect of eroding existing orthodoxies on women's roles. These articles revealed that both men and women contributed to the genetic makeup of offspring, contrary to the popular and traditional notion that women were just "borrowed wombs" that did not affect male bloodlines. Underneath the emphasis on mother-hood and women's place at home, proponents of "male superiority, female inferiority" and eugenicists had fundamental disagreements on the role of women in society. Scientific discourse, with its built-in biases regarding the female body, has traditionally been one of the most important mechanisms perpetuating the gender dichotomies, as anthropologist Emily Martin has shown in her study of texts in reproductive medicine (1987). Stabilizing and destabilizing the effects of scientific theories on gender perceptions, and women's role in formulating, internalizing, and/ or disputing such theories, will be a fascinating topic for further investigation.

This chapter has demonstrated that various factors – including cultural and social values, the educational system, women scientists' empowerment strategies, and new scientific knowledge – have constructed, deconstructed, and reconstructed gender perceptions in scientific practices in a complex way.

ACKNOWLEDGMENTS

I wish to thank Jennifer Robertson, Susan O. Long, Laura Miller, and E. Taylor Atkins, who have kindly read earlier drafts of this chapter and given me various suggestions for possible improvements.

NOTE

1 This is the present-day National Research Institute for Earth Science and Disaster Prevention.

REFERENCES

Brinton, Mary C. 1993. Women and the Economic Miracle: Gender and Work in Postwar Japan. Berkeley: University of California Press.

Burns, Susan B. 1998. Bodies and Borders: Syphilis, Prostitution, and the Nation in Japan, 1860–1890. US–Japan Women's Journal, English Supplement 15:3–30.

Coleman, Samuel. 1999. Japanese Science: From the Inside. London: Routledge.

Endō, Hideki, Yukihiro Hirano, and Ryūji Shimoda. 1993. Josei kenkyūsha no genjō ni kansuru kiso chōsa (A Basic Study Regarding the Current Condition of Female Researchers). Tokyo: Kagaku Gijitsu-chō Kagaku Gijutsu Seisaku Kenkyūjo.

Fox Keller, Evelyn. 1983. A Feeling for the Organism: The Life and Work of Barbara McClin-tock. New York: W. H. Freeman.

——1985. Reflections on Gender and Science. New Haven: Yale University Press.

Harding, Sandra G. 1991. Whose Science? Whose Knowledge? Thinking from Women's Lives. Ithaca, NY: Cornell University Press.

Hiroshige, Tetsu. 1965. Kagaku to rekishi (Science and History). Tokyo: Misuzu Shobō.

Kozai, Yoshihide, Seiichirō Kawashima, Takeshi Tominaga, Tomoko Hisatome, and Katsuko Saruhashi, eds. 2001. My Life: Twenty Japanese Women Scientists. Tokyo: Uchida Rōka-kuho.

Lock, Margaret M. 1993. Encounters with Aging: Mythologies of Menopause in Japan and North America. Berkeley: University of California Press.

Low, Morris. 1989. The Butterfly and the Frigate: Social Studies of Science in Japan. Social Studies of Science 19:313–342.

——1999. Science, Technology and Gender. In Science, Technology and Society in Contemporary Japan. Morris Low, Shigeru Nakayama, and Hitoshi Yoshioka, eds. Cambridge: Cambridge University Press.

Martin, Emily. 1987. The Woman in the Body: A Cultural Analysis of Reproduction. Boston: Beacon Press.

Muramatsu, Yasuko, ed. 1996. Josei no rikei nōryoku o ikasu: senkō bun'ya no jendā bunseki to teigen (Making the Most of Women's Scientific Aptitude: A Gendered Analysis Based on Disciplines, and a Proposal). Tokyo: Nihon Hyōronsha.

Nagashima, Yuzuru. 1937. Onna hakushi retsuden (Biographies of Women with Doctoral Degrees). Tokyo: Kagaku Chishiki Fukyūkai.

Nihon Joishi Henshū Iinkai, ed. 1991. Nihon joishi (tsuiho) (A History of Female Doctors in Japan, Revised and Enlarged Edition). Tokyo: Nihon Joikai.

Ochanomizu Joshi Daigaku Rigakubu, Jendā Kenkyū Sentā, and Nichifutsu Rikōkakai. 1998. Josei kagakusha no genryū (Origins of Women Scientists). Tokyo: Rajiumu Hakken 100-nen Kinen Jigyō Jikkō Iinkai.

Otsubo, Sumiko. 1999. Feminist Maternal Eugenics in Wartime Japan. US–Japan Women's Journal, English Supplement 17:39–76.

Robertson, Jennifer 2002. Blood Talks: Eugenic Modernity and the Creation of New Japanese. History and Anthropology 13(3):191–216.

Saruhashi, Katsuko. 1999 [1981]. Saruhashi katsuko: josei to shite kagakusha to shite (Saruhashi Katsuko: As a Woman and a Scientist). Tokyo: Nihon Tosho Sentā.

Schiebinger, Londa L. 1992. Nature's Body: Gender in the Making of Modern Science. Boston: Beacon Press.

Sōgō, Joseishi Kenkyūkai, ed. 2000. Sekai heiwa e no negai to kōdō (Prayers and Actions for World Peace). In Shiryō ni miru nihon josei no ayumi (A History of Japanese Women Seen through Documents). Tokyo: Yoshikawa Kōbunkan.

Sugiyama, Shigeo. 1994. Josei to kagaku (Women and Science). In Nihon no kindai kagakushi (A History of Modern Science in Japan). Tokyo: Asakura Shoten.

Traweek, Sharon. 1988. Lifetimes and Beamtimes: The World of High Energy Physicists. Cambridge, MA: Harvard University Press.

Tsugawa, Akiko, and Satoko Kanomi. 1996. Hiraku: nihon no josei kagakusha no kiseki (To Open: A Trajectory of Women Scientists in Japan). Tokyo: Domesu Shuppan.

Yamashita, Aiko, ed. 1970. Kindai nihon joseishi (A History of Modern Japanese Women), vol. 4: Kagaku. Tokyo: Kashima Kenkyūjo Shuppankai.

SUGGESTED READING

Bartholomew, James R. 1989. The Formation of Science in Japan: Building a Research Tradition. New Haven: Yale University Press.

—— 1998. Japanese Nobel Candidates in the First Half of the Twentieth Century. Osiris 13:238–284.

Ishihara, Jun. 1942. Gendai nihon bunmeishi (A Contemporary History of Japanese Civilization), vol. 13: Kagakushi. Tokyo: Tōyō Keizai Shinpōsha.

Mizuno, Hiromi. 2001. Science, Ideology, Empire: A History of the "Scientific" in Japan from the 1920s to the 1940s. Ph.D. dissertation, University of California, Los Angeles.

Morris-Suzuki, Tessa. 1994. The Technological Transformation of Japan: From the Seventeenth to the Twenty-First Century. Cambridge: Cambridge University Press.

Nihon, Kagakushi Gakkai, ed. 1964. Nihon kagaku gijutsushi taikei (Compendia of A History of Japanese Science and Technology), vol. 1: Tsūshi 1. Tokyo: Dai-ichi Hōki Shuppan.

Ortner, Sherry B. 1997. Making Gender: The Politics and Erotics of Culture. Boston: Beacon Press.

Scott, Joan Wallach. 1988. Gender and the Politics of History. New York: Columbia University Press.

Warren, Karen J., and Nisvan Erkal. 1997. Ecofeminism: Women, Culture, Nature. Bloomington: Indiana University Press.

Watanabe, Masao. 1990. The Japanese and Western Science. Otto Theodor Benfey, trans. Philadelphia: University of Pennsylvania Press.

Yoshida, Mitsukuni. 1976 [1955]. Nihon kagakushi (A History of Science in Japan). Tokyo: Kōdansha.

Yuasa, Mitsutomo. 1983. Nihon no kagaku gijutsu 100-nenshi (A 100-year History of Japanese Science and Technology), vol. 2. Tokyo: Chūō Kōronsha.

CHAPTER **29** # Preserving Moral Order: Responses to Biomedical Technologies

Margaret Lock

Almost daily the media inform us about new developments in biomedical technologies, many of them billed as having the potential to save lives and cure disease. Cloning, stem cell research, organ transplants from animals into humans, or the discovery of specific genes associated with disease are often heralded as the way of the future. At the same time many of these technologies incite extensive social and political debate, frequently of a contentious nature. When boundaries assumed to be inviolable, particularly between what is assumed to be nature and culture and life and death, are threatened through technological tinkering, it quickly becomes evident that very many people believe that society is at risk; that we are "playing God," or at the very least endangering that which is assumed to be natural and timeless. Inevitably these debates take different forms depending upon their location. Examining the relationships among that which new biomedical technologies make possible and the discourse and biopolitics associated with how they are introduced and controlled, or alternatively rejected, provides a powerful lens onto contemporary social life.

Over the past four decades research that can be glossed as an anthropology of the body has shown clearly that what is understood as health, the experience of distress and disease, knowledge about the body (both public and professional), and the application of therapeutic practices and technologies of all kinds, including those of biomedicine, reveal a great deal about human social relations, hierarchies of power, and what is considered to be moral order (Kleinman et al. 1997; Lindenbaum and Lock 1993; Lock and Gordon 1988; Lock and Kaufert 1998; Nichter and Lock 2002). Among this research a great deal of that conducted in Japan has provided many enduring insights (Caudill 1962; Lebra 1974; Lock 1980, 1988, 1993; Long

2001; Long and Long 1982; Norbeck and Lock 1988; Nukaga 2002; Ohnuki-Tierney 1984; Robertson 2001, 2002; Rosenberger 1988; Tanaka-Matsumi 1979).

World-wide narratives about health and illness created by ordinary individuals, public commentators, people in distress, involved families, and by physicians and therapists, more often than not have assumptions embedded in them about a normative order and why certain people get sick while others apparently do not. Close examination of these narratives reveals fault lines and dissent that point to inequalities and divisions within societies that become particularly acute with modernity, in particular as a result of ruptures produced by the globalized economy. One tension often revealed by such narratives is between what is assumed to be traditional and what is taken to be modern, and therefore can be seen as a threat to moral order. Closely associated with this tension are worries, implicit or explicit, about Japan's place in the global order.

In this chapter I will elaborate on two specific biomedical technologies of current concern in Japan to illustrate the moral debate associated with them. The first is the implementation and governmentally orchestrated control of the application of reproductive technologies. The second is diagnosis of brain death in intensive care units and the possible procurement of organs from such patients.

THE POLITICS OF REPRODUCTION

Techniques for intervening in the procreation of children in unprecedented ways rapidly became routinized in the latter part of the 20th century in many parts of the world. As with so many biomedical technologies, these techniques were developed and put at once into practice, to be followed by a hasty post hoc consideration of the moral issues that are inevitably involved. Feminists in the West have been bitterly divided as to whether reproductive technologies and the genetic testing with which they are so closely allied have the potential to free women up from constraints imposed by biology, or whether, on the other hand, these techniques will permit yet more invasive control by those in positions of power over women (see Lock and Kaufert 1998 for a summary of this debate). This debate is grounded above all in issues of autonomy and the perceived right of individual women to make the choices believed to be in their own best interests with respect to reproduction. The response in Japan to these technologies has been rather different.

Throughout much of the 20th century the Japanese population was monitored with increasing rigor by the state through the systematic implementation of country-wide programs dedicated to the promotion of the health of all citizens (see chapters 21 and 28 in this volume). For their part the Japanese have, on the whole, cooperated with these programs, due to some extent to a strong, centuries-old ideal fundamental to East Asian medicine that requires individuals and families to take responsibility for the condition of their own bodies. From the outset, explicitly included in this monitoring, has been reproduction, in particular the creation of healthy families of the desired size. One aspect of this emphasis on the "ideal," normative family has been a stigmatization of those children labeled as socially or biologically "unfit" (Miyaji and Lock 1994). Although in recent years this stigma has abated to some extent, one might nevertheless predict that Japanese women and their partners would avail themselves very willingly of reproductive technologies, and especially of genetic testing and screening as they become more widely available.

There has been for many years now widespread lip-service to the "Western" notions of individual rights and choice, but it is evident that the extended family continues to play a major role in connection with reproduction, both as a normalized moral agent and also literally through direct intervention on the part of some potential grandparents in the activities of their children of reproductive age (see chapter 22 in this volume).

It is widely agreed that the dominant gender ideology in Japan today is one in which women are expected to enter into marriage and to produce two children, preferably one of each sex, for whose health and wellbeing their mother is held primarily responsible. It is also recognized by a good number of cultural commentators that this is a postwar ideology, a hardening of historically more flexible conceptions about women's roles in the family (Wakita and Hanley 1994). Until well into this century, the majority of Japanese women were valued above all for their economic contribution to the household. If no offspring were forthcoming from a marriage, or if the children were unable for whatever reason to carry on the family business, then a suitable substitute could be adopted quite easily into the extended family, either as a child or as an adult (Bachnik 1983; Lebra 1993). Prior to World War II economic pragmatism was the rule and, if blood ties (*chi no tsunagari*) were not effective in keeping the household competitive, then kin-related or even non-kin adoptees would do as substitutes. Of course, fertility was of concern; women were described at times as a "borrowed womb," or a "household utensil" until the end of the 19th century, and those who did not produce children within a year or little more after marriage were labeled "stone women." But, rather than fertility itself, it was the quality of the offspring that was of prime concern. Women could on occasion be sent back to their natal families if they failed to conceive; nevertheless, in many households their physical labor and management skills were as important as, if not more important than, fertility. After the Meiji Restoration of 1868, women were also valued highly as educators of their children, particularly in connection with morals, community, and national objectives. Motherhood and the raising of healthy, intelligent children, rather than fertility, were invested with prestige, so much so that Japanese feminists have described the Meiji government literature designed to invest worth in mothering as *boseiron* (treatises on motherhood) (Mitsuda 1984).

There is evidence that family size was to some extent controlled throughout Japanese history (see chapter 22 in this volume), but from the Meiji Restoration (1868), systematic planning of the population was nationally orchestrated, and a self-conscious attempt to encourage "human development" was part of this program (Garon 1993; Robertson 2002 and in this volume), in which planned families played a central role. Although abortion was tacitly accepted prior to the Meiji Restoration, after 1880 it was assumed that economic growth could not be sustained without population growth, and abortion was made a criminal act. By the late 19th century virtually all women received some schooling, and less emphasis was placed on the Confucian edicts of chastity, obedience, patience, and devotion – the essentials of "good wives and wise mothers." Women were educated more broadly, with a focus on moral education and hygiene. According to government tracts of the time, the masses were to be educated to rationalize their lives in the name of progress; Japan had to "catch up" with the West, and the "habits" of the people must therefore be reformed through "moral suasion" (*kyōka*) (Garon 1993; see also Frühstück 2003). Family units were explicitly likened to the family of the emperor, conflating the macrocosm of the nation-state with the microcosm of the family. Families, like the state, were in theory to be harmonious units in which, with the exception of certain ritual occasions, individual desire was suppressed for the sake of social and moral order.

The Taisho era of 1912 to 1926 saw the routinization of a systematic collection of vital statistics, and public health interventions were set in place throughout the country. By 1940, when human bodies were in great demand for military service, those couples who raised more than ten healthy children were given awards, a policy not unlike those pursued in Europe and North America at the time. Although a high birth rate was actively encouraged, at the same time, shortly before Germany introduced a similar ruling, the abortion law was amended and renamed the National Eugenic Law. Abortion was now legally permitted for eugenic and medical reasons, which meant in practice that those women designated as unfit to be mothers would forcibly undergo abortions (see Norgren 2001). Many Japanese women remain aware of these wartime policies, and a lingering resentment is evident at any effort on the part of contemporary Japanese governments to intrude into reproductive matters.

The formal extended family, the *ie*, with its national obligations and patriarchal power base, was officially abolished as a result of postwar reforms: 60 percent of Japanese now live in a nuclear family. However, in addition to those 40 percent officially designated as extended households, many people spend much of their lives in a loosely affiliated vertically extended family where elderly relatives live close by, and a sense of obligation and familial ties remain strong (Lock 1993).

Although there is evidence that many people actively uphold extended family ideals, albeit in modified form, a dominant perception exists that values commonly associated with nuclear households have swept through Japan. The rhetoric about family life, influenced by what are thought to be "modern" and "Western" ideals, has shifted markedly in the past 20 years to one of individual rights and choice, and independence for young couples. Nevertheless, implicit in this "modern" discourse remains the assumption that all women will "naturally" embrace the tasks of reproduction, together with the nurturing of family members.[1]

TECHNOLOGICALLY ASSISTED NATURAL FAMILIES

The majority of the 50 women whom I interviewed in the late 1990s who reside in Tokyo were cautious about all types of reproductive technologies deemed as invasive; nevertheless there was a widely shared sentiment that, if nature can be perfected through technology, then there is nothing inherently wrong with its use. Shirai found that infertile women feel more strongly about this than do others (1991; see also Norgren 2001). Even when reminded that powerful chemical stimulation is involved in all technologies used in connection with infertility, any fear of long-term side-effects is outweighed, it seems, by a desire to have children. This is a paradoxical response given that the pill is rejected by many Japanese women on grounds of iatrogenesis; nevertheless, 46 individuals responded that if a woman really desires a child, then IVF is acceptable. There was agreement that technology should be available as a service for judicious use in times of distress, notably once infertility is established. Those few interviewees completely opposed to IVF stated explicitly that women and their families should be educated into realizing that life can be fulfilled in many ways, and that childbearing should not be the unquestioned goal of every woman.

Although IVF is acceptable to most, the thought of its use by unmarried or gay couples made those women interviewed very uncomfortable, although lesbian couples are regarded more favorably. Nurturance of the child in a legally recognized family, and society's negative reaction to any child not raised appropriately, is uppermost in people's minds when they give these responses. And it is for these reasons too that neither the use of surrogate mothers nor AID is officially sanctioned in Japan, although a few people go outside the country to achieve their desires. These particular technologies were considered acceptable by only five of the 50 women I interviewed, and the majority showed concern that a child conceived by these means would not be loved or cared for adequately. Most are explicit that biological and social parenting should coincide, and that if they do not, then the child may suffer. Tsuge (1992) has found that Japanese gynecologists hold similar opinions.

All but six of the women I interviewed were opposed to adoption, and among those six only one would adopt a child of foreign parentage. Nearly everyone agreed that "blood ties" are important and, in effect, going outside the family is "risky," biologically speaking. Women also suggested that an adopted child might not be cared for as would genetically related offspring. However, several women stated that if their husbands wanted to adopt a child then they would acquiesce. Adoption is explicitly associated by most women with the outmoded patriarchal extended family and even with concubinage, and so is shunned. Nearly half of the women were clear that, if IVF failed (as they well know is often the case), they would rather not have a child at all than adopt one. Once again, the wellbeing of the child was stated as of prime concern, since without exception everyone agreed that children who are "different" have a hard time growing up in Japan.

Resort to IVF and other reproductive technologies is usually couched in the language of individual rights – the right of a woman to have a healthy child – but further questioning reveals that this rhetoric is quite superficial. All the women interviewed consulted with their husbands about reproductive decisions, and the majority indicated that the husband usually had the final word in most families. Despite the fact that everyone agreed that discussions about reproduction are no longer appropriate or necessary among the extended family, two young pregnant women whom I interviewed had been brought to the clinic by their mothers-in-law for genetic testing. It was quite evident, in spite of the doctor's efforts to keep the older women out of the clinical encounter, that it would be they who would make decisions on behalf of their daughters-in-law, both of whom had received very little education by Japanese standards.

In my previous work I have come across cases where women were forcefully urged to have abortions at the insistence of their mother-in-law, on the grounds that the older woman would not act as a baby minder as was anticipated, given the family circumstances, by the younger couple (Lock 1993). The ideal today is one of freedom from the extended family, but reality does not always bear this out, particularly when grandparents live in the same household.

REPRODUCING THE PAST

It has been argued that Japanese women are becoming increasingly autonomous (Iwao 1994), but I want to suggest that at the same time the majority participate fully in what has been described as a "community based family type" where the principles of authority and equality are both recognized (Todd 1985). Thus, even if residence is that of a nuclear family, individual rights and liberty do not necessarily take priority over extended family interests. On the contrary, fulfilling community and extended family values often takes precedence over individual desires. The senior generation may well expect to influence reproductive decisions made by young couples, and explicitly censure what are deemed to be inappropriate behaviors. Japanese feminists are concerned that these values, considered entirely outdated by the majority of women as a whole, drive some young women toward an uncritical acceptance of reproductive technologies, and increasingly to genetic testing, when demanded by the family, even when individual women may themselves be opposed to their use (Aoki and Marumoto 1992). At the same time many Japanese women, feminist or not, are equally critical of an unfettered individualism that they associate primarily with America.

The rigorous normalization of a planned family comprising two healthy offspring means that a heavy price is paid by those women and children who are socially marginalized. This is the case whether they be single women; women who are unable to bear children, whether it is they or their husbands who are infertile; or children who are perceived to be less than perfect in any way (Miyaji and Lock 1994; Shimazu 1994).

Perhaps because a good number of Japanese women are aware that they constitute the Other as seen from "the West," many are sensitive these days to cultural imperialisms arising not only from within but also outside of Japan. This situation helps to make some women exceedingly alert to the complexities and contradictions in the praxis of reproductive technologies. With this in mind one eminent research group in Japan composed largely of feminist social scientists has called for a re-examination of the idea that technological developments of all kinds possess uncontested "virtue" (Ochanomizu Jōshidaigaku Seimei Rinri Kenkyūkai 1990). At the same time this group extends a sympathetic understanding to those women who choose to use technology to bring nature onside with respect to individual aspirations and familial demands.

Whether the use of reproductive technologies is instigated primarily by individual women in their own interest, or by willing participation in familial objectives, or because individuals are actually coerced by family members or healthcare professionals, if the resultant children (when the technologies are successful) do not embody widely held societal values about appropriate kinship and "blood" relationships, their existence may well be judged as disruptive to the moral order. At present, the Japanese government can turn a blind eye to a small number of sex-selected pregnancies, and those few babies furtively produced through artificial insemination by donor or by means of surrogacy, provided that these behaviors are not openly institutional-ized. The state can apparently rest assured that the vast majority of Japanese citizens do not support such practices. At the same time the state actively supports those technological practices used to reproduce the ideal, healthy family in which biological and social parentage are one and the same. Such support is indirect, and mediated through the medicalization of reproduction. Creating the planned family of desired size has a long history in Japan. Formerly adoption was quite often the only way to achieve this end, but today reproductive technologies are understood as a highly desirable means to improve on the shortcomings of nature. The same conclusion cannot be drawn about the technology of organ transplantation and the procurement of organs for this purpose from brain-dead bodies.

WHEN PERSONS LINGER IN BRAIN-DEAD BODIES

The *Guardian Weekly* of August 4, 1996, reprinted an article originally published in the *Washington Post* under the headline, "Japanese are Dying for a Transplant." The article describes the case of 23-year-old Kiuchi Hirofumi, who would have died had he not been flown to Los Angeles for a heart transplant. The cost of $380,000 was raised through loans and by a fundraising campaign to which more than 10,000 Japanese, "many of whom had heart ailments," contributed (*Guardian Weekly* 1996). The article is unabashedly partisan in its stance and asserts that the situation in Japan has become a national embarrassment. Perhaps it is not at all surprising that an American journalist writing from Tokyo should summarize the problem as follows: "Citing tradition, culture and religious concerns, Japan has rejected medical advances that have given thousands of critically ill people around the world a second chance at life" (*Guardian Weekly* 1996).

What is surprising is the statement Mr. Kiuchi is reported to have made: "I feel that I was supposed to be killed by Japan, by the Japanese government, Japanese tradition, Japanese culture. If I had stayed there I would have died." It seems as though not only the journalist but also the patient is casting the problem as one of "technology versus tradition." What the journalist does not recognize is that, although Japanese patients have not been able to undergo transplants using organs from brain-dead donors in their own country for the past 25 years, in contrast to recipients living in many other technologically sophisticated societies, it is only in the past eight or nine years that recipients and potential recipients have become openly vocal in complain-ing about the situation in Japan. To cast Japanese culture in such a negative light, as does Mr. Kiuchi, has been very unusual, although the situation has recently changed to some extent.

It is tempting to start from the assumption that a wealthy society with the technological know-how would inevitably foster transplant technology and so to dismiss the Japanese situation as an anachronism – the result of the stubborn weight of "tradition." But can we rely on this journalist in Tokyo? Has she examined her own assumptions about this particular technology? What exactly does she mean by Japanese "culture" and "tradition"? Does she understand that the "brain death problem" (*nōshi no mondai*) has been the most contentious bioethical debate in Japan for over three decades, and that more than 1,000 monographs, journals, and magazine articles have been written in Japanese on the subject? And can we generalize from the words of one citizen, however much his physical condition moves our sympathies? Should we perhaps pay equal or greater attention to the argument of the Japanese sociologist Nudeshima Jirō when he concludes that Japanese "culture" is not at work, but that a lack of trust in doctors is the major reason why brain death remains unrecognized as the end of life (1989)? But then we must surely ask why Nudeshima does not consider Japanese attitudes toward the medical profession as part of culture. Clearly "culture" and "tradition" serve as interchangeable rhetorical devices and are used to signal the idea that culture works in opposition to the logic of modernity – to the hegemony of science and technology and their associated institutions.

BRAIN DEATH AND HUMAN DEATH

It is agreed by the vast majority of medical experts that the concept of brain death – the new death, located in the brain, that we created just over 30 years ago – was invented and routinized in medical practice in order that organs could be legally procured from patients diagnosed as brain-dead. From the outset the existence of brain-dead bodies has caused concern, resulting in extended debate as to whether or not such entities are "actually" alive or dead. In North America and much of Europe this debate was apparently settled by the early 1980s, but it is currently surfacing again (Lock 2002).

In 1969, less than a year after Christiaan Barnard carried out the first heart transplant in the world, the first such transplant was performed in Japan. Although it was at first greeted by a media accolade, the event turned sour when the recipient died shortly after the operation – this was the case virtually everywhere else in the world too. But in Japan criminal charges were laid against the surgeon, Wada, which were not dropped for several years. The diagnosis of brain death was formally recognized in the 1970s by the Japanese medical profession, but was not legally equated with the end of human life. Over the ensuing years, eight cases of organ retrieval from brain-dead bodies came to the attention of activists opposed to the recognition of brain death as the death of the patient, resulting in another two dozen murder charges being laid against the doctors who supposedly procured the organs. Several such cases took place in the United States in the 1970s, but with much less public fanfare, and all were relatively quickly resolved in favor of the doctors involved.

In the fall of 1997 the Organ Transplant Law was finally passed in Japan, making it legal for the first time to extract organs for transplant from patients diagnosed as brain-dead. The passing of the law took place in the wake of enormous media coverage and lively demonstrations against the recognition of brain death (in which many MDs participated). These demonstrations were countered by supporters of patients waiting for transplants and by political pressure by the Japan Medical Association. In contrast to virtually all other countries that carry out transplants, donor cards must be signed ahead of time in Japan, not only by potential donors themselves, but also by family representatives, before procurement can take place. Patients who become brain-dead and who have not signed donor cards are not counted as dead, and continue to be given life support until such time as the family is in agreement that further "treatment" is futile. After the law was passed the murder charges that had not already been thrown out of court for insufficient evidence were quietly dropped. However, in the four years since the enactment of the law, only 17 procurements have taken place that have made use of brain-dead donors. At the present time the subject has dropped out of sight in the media, and the situation persists unchanged, namely that most people in Japan who are hoping for an organ transplant never get one, with the result that a large number of people with heart, liver, and lung ailments die. The number of patients in Japan on kidney dialysis is proportionally the highest in the world.

When commenting on this situation, many outsiders assume, as did the reporter cited above, that religious beliefs or lingering superstition must be implicated in this impasse – that something fundamentally pre-modern remains at the core of Japanese society. However, representatives of the major Buddhist sects in Japan have at no time been particularly vocal in opposition to the recognition of brain death (Hardacre 1994).

When polled about attitudes toward brain death, many Japanese indicate that respect for their deceased relatives is of importance, and some agree that they are uncomfortable with the idea of organs being taken from the recently deceased, because they believe that this may inflict yet more pain and suffering (Lock 2002). However, research in Sweden and the United States suggests that numerous people in these countries feel exactly the same way and to the same extent, and Siminof and Chillag (1999) have recently shown that, of 400 families living in the United States who were approached about donation, more than half declined. In most countries it appears that the cut-off point for being comfortable about donation from brain-dead bodies hovers around 50 percent.

Given the ferocity with which the Japanese media have opposed recognition of brain death, questioned whether brain-dead patients are indeed dead, and exposed what are at times clearly unethical medical behaviors, the media have without doubt been more influential than has religious belief in making the recognition of brain death a contentious issue (Lock 2002). As noted above, Nudeshima Jirō and other Japanese commentators raise another possibility. They are emphatic that reluctance to recognize brain death is primarily associated with public concerns about corruption and greed in the Japanese medical profession. One reason why Nudeshima is reluctant to recognize an account based on cultural difference as valid is because he worries that such an explanation gives fuel to the fire of rhetoric about Japanese uniqueness.

Over and above tussles between cultural and politically based interpretations about continuing hesitancy on the part of the Japanese public to recognize brain death, it is important to pay attention to what actually takes place in intensive care units. It is widely recognized that death, even in ICUs, remains above all a familial event in Japan, and it is considered to be inappropriate for physicians to intrude on grieving family members to make direct inquiries about organ donation. A recent survey showed that nearly 70 percent of Japanese doctors would not take the initiative to approach families of brain-dead patients about possible donation. In my opinion it is this reluctance more than anything else that accounts for the remarkable difference in rates of organ procurement in Japan and North America; this, and the fact that proportionally fewer people become brain-dead in Japan than in America, because there are many fewer gunshot wounds and fewer car accidents involving fatalities.

WHEN PERSONS LINGER IN BODIES

It is virtually impossible and in any case unethical and tasteless to interview families in ICUs who are confronted with the possibility of donating the organs of their relatives. But one way to get at issues about organ procurement is to interview involved intensivists and emergency medicine doctors, for they too inevitably participate in everyday consciousness about the morality of a utilitarian approach to the bodies of those who are brain-dead. North American intensivists exhibit much more ambivalence than one might expect about organ procurement (Lock 2002), but I will focus here on the situation in Japan.

Tomoko Abe, recently elected to the Lower House of the Diet, and a pediatrician employed for many years in a hospital which specializes in neurological disorders, has spent considerable energy over the past 20 years working with the grassroots movement in Japan against the legalization of brain death as the end of life. In discussing her objections with me at one of our several meetings, she emphasized that the concept of brain death was created primarily for the purpose of facilitating organ transplants. She is emphatic that when a dying person is understood as the focus of both a concerned family and a caring medical team, then it is difficult to interpret brain death as the demise of the individual. Her opinion is derived, Abe states, from reflection on her own subjective feelings as a pediatrician, "The point is not whether the patient is conscious or unconscious, but whether one *intuitively* understands that the patient is dead. Someone whose color is good, who is still warm, bleeds when cut, and urinates and defecates, is not dead as far as I am concerned. Of course I know that cardiac arrest will follow some hours later – but I think even more significant is the transformation of the warm body into something that is cold and hard – only then do the Japanese really accept death." When asked why this is so, Abe replied, "It's something to do with Buddhism, I suppose. I'm not really a Buddhist but it's part of our tradition." Abe is completely opposed to organ transplants that are dependent on brain-dead donors, and also has strong reservations about living related organ donations (Lock 2000).

Among the 19 Japanese physicians who work in ICUs whom I interviewed in 1996, the majority of whom were neurosurgeons, I did not find anyone who took a position as extreme as Abe's. However, her sentiments and those of the many others (including other physicians) who think as she does are well known among the Japanese public because of their numerous television appearances and publications. The intensivists with whom I talked believe that brain death is an irreversible condition, provided that no errors have been made in diagnosis, and they also believe that a brain-dead body is not dead (as did every North American intensivist interviewed). But, in contrast to Tomoko Abe, they are not adamantly opposed to organ transplants, although none of them has ever actually been involved with procurement of organs for donation.

I conducted interviews in the year before the Organ Transplant Law was enacted. I returned briefly in 1998 and 1999, after the implementation of the law, to find that little had changed on the front line. The position of the majority of physicians working in intensive care remained as it always had been, that to declare brain death and then abruptly ask the family about donation is inappropriate. If the family does not raise the possibility independently, as they rarely do (although this is changing a little), then the matter will not be routinely discussed. The fact that it has been illegal to procure organs from the brain-dead, and that murder charges have been laid for doing so, has ensured that physicians have in the past been hesitant to approach families, and some concerns may remain about this eventuality. But, above all, it is the intrusion into the privacy of the family that holds doctors back.

The neurosurgeons interviewed all agreed that they "more or less" follow the Takeuchi criteria, that is, the standards set out by the Ministry of Health and Welfare in 1985 for determining brain death. However, several of them added comments to the effect, "We do not always make the diagnosis, even when we suspect brain death. We often guess, which is much easier for the patient and their family." What is meant here is that in cases that appear hopeless the attending neurosurgeon will do one or more simple clinical tests on the basis of which he concludes that the patient is either brain-dead or very close to it. He then informs the family that their relative is *hobo nōshi no jōtai* (almost brain-dead), or alternatively that the situation looks hopeless. The ventilator is not turned off at this juncture but is kept in place until the family requests that it be turned off, often several days after the diagnosis. One physician commented, "Perhaps this is unique to Japan, but we believe that it is most appropriate to tell the family that we are continuing to do our best for their relative even though brain death is 'approaching,' rather than to say as they do in America, 'the patient is brain-dead, here are the test results, we are going to terminate all care'."

Commenting on the actions of his colleagues, a neurosurgeon pointed out that "brain death is a kind of 'end stage,' in other words, there is nothing more that we can do for the patient, but we are ambivalent because brain death is not human death." He added:

> There was a case I had a while ago where a child stayed alive for six or seven days after a diagnosis of brain death, even after the ventilator had been turned right down. If the family had said early on that they wanted to donate organs it would have been different but there was no suggestion of this. As far as they were concerned, I would have been killing their child if I had turned off the ventilator – and in a way they were right. After all, we don't sign the death certificate until the heart stops beating. (cited in Lock 2002)

With the passing of the Organ Transplant Law, in those hospitals designated to procure organs there is now, of course, an enormous concern about precision in the determination of brain death, particularly so because the media expect to be fully informed about the most minute of medical procedures in an effort to make medical practices, especially those around organ procurement, fully "transparent" and open to public scrutiny.

Although many physicians and surgeons I interviewed stated clearly that, for them personally, once consciousness is permanently lost and a patient is unable to breathe independently, that patient is as good as dead, they do not believe that most families think as they do, and they do not think that for most people the location of "person" is firmly encased inside a brain, nor is it considered to be an autonomous entity without powerful social bonds that constrain independence.

As noted above, the idea of individual rights has apparently gained a strong foothold in Japan, and those in Japan who are actively opposed to the recognition of brain death as the end of human life argue for the "rights" of brain-dead patients. However, my research, together with that of Susan Long, shows rather clearly that when one is dealing with death and dying and with terminal care, the individual is most often conceptualized as residing at the center of a network of obligations, so that personhood is constructed out of mind, beyond body, in the space of ongoing human relationships (see chapter 23 in this volume).

Ironically, even though it is in Japan where the public has most clearly articulated fears that the lives of traumatized patients may be ended too soon in order that organs may be procured, in reality the chance of this happening is very slim as compared to North America or Europe. As Long's work shows in connection with matters that relate to the end of life, physicians today are less likely to behave paternalistically in Japan than they do in many other parts of the world because of this powerful constraining sensibility that the dead and dying body is above all social. This sensibility limits how much the medical profession can take over and make unqualified decisions. It also means that numerous patients who, in North America and most of Europe, would be quietly "let go" and taken off life support, remain on the ventilator in Japan.

While doing research on decisions about life-support and its withdrawal in Japan, Long gained the impression that a commonly held perception among doctors is that, since removal or discontinuance of treatment involving ventilators or feeding tubes would result in certain death, murder would in effect be committed by doctors who stopped the treatment. Doctors working in intensive care made similar statements to me. Long concludes that, unless families request that treatment be discontinued, or that the patient be allowed to die "peacefully" (sometimes to the great relief of doctors and nurses), aggressive treatment is continued (Fetters 1998; Long 2000). Ikegami Naoki makes a similar statement with respect to palliative care. His opinion is that doctors are reluctant to discuss palliative care with patients and families because the idea is conveyed that the doctor has given up on the patient (personal communication).

Many families, perhaps most of them, in part because they are not told without equivocation that their relative is dead, apparently keep hoping for a miracle. Even when families suspect the worst, they are not encouraged to think of brain death as human death and they too, like the physicians, are prone to interpret disconnecting the ventilator as equivalent to committing murder. A form of collusion sets in between doctors and families in which aggressive treatment is usually continued until the family gives up all hope. But, on the other hand, in North America, increasingly people are beginning to wonder if, with economic pressures and a pervasive ideology that severely damaged people are probably better off dead, we may indeed be giving up on some people much too soon (Lock 2002).

Public Commentary on the Brain Death Problem

Clinical activities in connection with brain death in Japan take place in the shadow of enormous, unrelenting media coverage on the subject. Numerous Japanese television programs, magazine articles, and books have repeatedly cast doubt on whether death can be understood as a clearly diagnosable event (see, e.g., Hirosawa 1992; Komatsu

1993). It is also stressed in books and the media for public consumption that irreversibility of brain damage is difficult to establish conclusively, and cases have been referred to (always outside of Japan) where mistakes have evidently been made.

Certain commentators question whether a lack of integrated brain function indicates death. One highly influential journalist, Tachibana Takeshi, author of several books and producer of more than one television program on the subject of brain death and organ transplants, emphasizes that brain cells continue to live even when the brain as a whole has no integrated function (1992). Tachibana dwells in all his media presentations on the "liveliness" of a brain-dead individual. A Saturday evening prime-time program, for example, aired in 1990 and hosted by him, started out with shots of a beautiful, active, 6-year-old child who was born, viewers were informed, from a brain-dead mother. "How *can* a brain-dead body not be living?" asked Tachibana rhetorically. There is agreement that it goes against "basic human feelings" to assume that a warm body is dead, and many commentators, like Tachibana, go on to assert that the average Japanese family could not in good conscience abandon a dying relative to a transplant team.

As Tomoko Abe the pediatrician made clear, the *presence* of death is not denied in arguments such as these, but what is being explicitly suggested is that the *process* of dying is arbitrarily transformed into a technologically determined point in time, as early as possible along the spectrum of biological demise. There is concern that family members cannot easily adjust to a medically determined diagnosis of irreversible brain damage, and that they are likely to assume that medicine has abandoned their relative much too early.

Other writers, taking a slightly different tack, stress that because brain death can only be determined by trained medical personnel – because it is *mienai shi* (death which cannot be seen) – it represents a radical departure from the usual situation where the family participates fully in the dawning recognition of an irrevocable process under way. Making integrated brain function the measure of death ensures that the family is pushed to the sidelines, rendered passive, and left entirely at the mercy of medical decision-making (Nakajima 1985).

Morioka Masahiro, a philosopher and bioethicist, has argued that the intensive care unit is in some ways similar to a modern prison, in that patients are monitored from a central nursing station (reminiscent of Bentham's panopticon, which inspired some of the writing of Michel Foucault) and are for the most part separated from family members (Morioka 1989). He suggests that brain death should be analyzed as more than a medical decision about the condition of the brain, and that the patient is best understood as existing at the loci of human relationships. This social unit should be the starting point for determining the acceptance or otherwise of brain death as the end of life.

Yanagida Kunio is well known in Japan as the son of the celebrated ethnologist of the same name who died some years ago. Recently, the younger Yanagida galvanized the Japanese public by publishing two widely distributed articles followed by a book about his own son, who tried to commit suicide and was taken to hospital, where he was diagnosed as brain-dead (Yanagida 1994, 1995). Yanagida writes that he started to think while seated at the bedside about organ donation because, together with his son, he had watched a television program on the subject, and his son had at the time expressed an interest in helping other people. Yanagida recalls that as he sat holding his son's hand and whispering his name, Yojiro's face was "bright and warm" and he "couldn't bear the idea" of someone putting a knife into his son's body and taking out the heart.

Yanagida reports that he became confused as to what brain death really signifies: was his son indeed a corpse or was he still suspended between life and death? Four days after the brain death diagnosis, upon reading his son's diaries in which he had expressed sadness at being of no use to anyone, Yanagida came to an understanding that it was his duty to "complete" his son's life. On the fifth day all treatment was stopped, and his son's kidneys and bone marrow were removed for transplant. Despite an expressed sensitivity on the part of Yanagida to those who are "waiting" for organs, there can be little doubt that his publications have consolidated the majority opinion in Japan, namely that families should not be rushed into accepting death the moment various tests reveal that a patient is brain-dead.

Doubts about misdiagnosis are also raised regularly by the Japanese media where it is argued that brain death and persistent vegetative state (PVS) cannot be easily distinguished (virtually no specialist in the neurosciences in Japan or elsewhere would agree with such claims). Such assertions are then usually followed by examples of patients who make partial, occasionally complete, recoveries from PVS. Three or four hospitals in Japan specialize in the treatment of PVS patients, and one such hospital, where intensive nursing care is employed as the prime treatment modality, has been the subject of a very moving national television program. This type of coverage, when coupled with media reporting emphasizing medical errors, means that those who would promote organ transplants in Japan have to constantly battle against a tide of media-manipulated popular opinion. Media commentary includes the opinions of a good number of very influential professionals and intellectuals opposed to the recognition of brain death as the end of life.

CONCLUSIONS

Whereas in North America a brain-dead body is biologically alive in the minds of those who work closely with it, it is nevertheless no longer a person, and therefore the majority believe that procurement of organs is acceptable, especially because those organs will go to save the lives of other dying patients. In Japan, in contrast, for the majority, including a good number of physicians, such an entity is biologically alive and is also a living person, at least for several days after brain death has been diagnosed. The identity of brain-dead individuals remains safely intact in Japan, constituted through family ties, and therefore a brain-dead body continues to be invested with "human rights." In contrast, in North America, a brain-dead body takes on cadaver status, retains only the respect given to the dead, and can, therefore, be commodified. It must be emphasized that these are the dominant positions in these two geographical areas and that in *both* locations they are contested and at times resisted. Those Japanese citizens who express fears that living cadavers may remain animated and could suffer further pain should their organs be taken for transplant are by no means alone. Such sentiments can be detected worldwide (Perkins and Tolle 1992; Sanner 1994).

It is the ambiguous status of the technologically produced living cadaver that permits the possibility of more than one calculation of its condition as alive or dead, but these differing conclusions are not determined by scientific practices in the ICUs. The conceptual space in which practitioners work, informed by discourse produced in courts of law, government documents, and the media and then disseminated as popular knowledge, allows scientific tests and measurements to be imbued with different meanings.

In Japan the plight of those individuals who have died for want of a spare part have until the past few years gone virtually unheeded. The passing of the Organ Transplant Law has not so far ensured that the number of organs donated in Japan is anywhere near comparable to donations in other countries. Will more Japanese permit themselves to think of the brain-dead as corpse-like rather than as a still living member of the family? Japan has more than proved itself utilitarian in connection with other aspects of technomedicine, including abortion, plastic surgery, and, as outlined above, reproductive technologies, and the country is moving rapidly ahead into genetic testing and screening. What this suggests is that the brain death and organ procurement debates have touched a particularly sensitive moral area in Japan, one in which a good number of citizens apparently believe that the interests of the medical profession and the needs of strangers are inappropriately taking precedence over those of the family.

ACKNOWLEDGMENTS

Funding for portions of this research was provided by the Social Sciences and Humanities Research Council of Canada (SSHRC) grant #205806.

NOTE

1   Editor's note: see Rousseau (1998) and the articles in the *US–Japan Women's Journal*, 24 (2003) for recent Japanese scholarship (in translation) on pregnancy and childbirth in the context of modernity.

REFERENCES

Aoki, Yayoi, and Marumoto, Yuriko. 1992. Watashi rashisa de uma: umanai (Being Myself: To Give Birth or Not). Tokyo: Nōsan Gyoson Bunka Kyōkai.
Bachnik, Jane. 1983. Recruitment Strategies for Household Succession: Rethinking Japanese Household Organization. Man (n.s.) 18:160–182.
Bethke, Elshtain J. 1987. Technology as Destiny. The Progressive 53(June):19–23.
Caudill, William. 1962. Patterns of Emotion in Modern Japan. *In* Japanese Culture. R. J. Smith and R. K. Beardsley eds. pp. 115–131. Chicago: Aldine.
Fetters, Michael D. 1998. The Family in Medical Decision Making: Japanese Perspectives. Journal of Clinical Ethics 9:143–157.
Frühstück, Sabine. 2003. Colonizing Sex: Sexology and Social Control in Modern Japan. Berkeley: University of California Press.

Garon, Sheldon. 1993. Women's Groups and the Japanese State: Contending Approaches to Political Integration, 1980–1945. Journal of Japanese Studies 19:5–41.

Guardian Weekly. 1996. Japanese are Dying for a Transplant. August 4.

Hardacre, Helen. 1994. The Response of Buddhism and Shintō to the Issue of Brain Death and Organ Transplants. Cambridge Quarterly of Healthcare Ethics 3:585–601.

Hirosawa, Kōshichirō. 1992. Junkanki senmon-i no tachiba kara mita nōshi to shinzō ishoku (Brain Death and Heart Transplants from the Point of View of a Circulatory System Specialist). *In* Nōshi to zoki-ishoku (Brain Death and Organ Transplants). Umehara Takeshi, ed. pp. 41–50. Tokyo: Asahi Shinbunsha.

Iwao, Sumiko. 1994. The Japanese Woman: Traditional Image and Changing Reality. New York: The Free Press.

Kleinman, Arthur, Margaret Lock, and Veena Das, eds. 1997. Social Suffering. Berkeley: University of California Press.

Komatsu, Yoshihiko. 1993. Sentaku gijutsu to nōshironsō no shikaku (Blind Spots in Advancing Technology and Brain Death Debates). Gendai shiso 21:198–212.

Lebra, Takie. 1974. Interactional Perspective on Suffering and Curing in a Japanese Cult. International Journal of Social Psychiatry 20:281–286.

—— 1993. Above the Clouds: Status Culture of the Modern Japanese Nobility. Berkeley: University of California Press.

Lindenbaum, Shirley, and Margaret Lock, eds. 1993. Knowledge, Power and Practice: The Anthropology of Medicine and Everyday Life. Berkeley: University of California Press.

Lock, Margaret. 1980. East Asian Medicine in Urban Japan. Berkeley: University of California Press.

—— 1988. A Nation at Risk: Interpretations of School Refusal in Japan. *In* Biomedicine Examined. M. Lock and D. Gordon, eds. pp. 377–414. Dordrecht: Kluwer Academic Publishers.

—— 1993. Encounters with Aging: Mythologies of Menopause in Japan and North America. Berkeley: University of California Press.

—— 2000. On Dying Twice: Culture, Technology and the Determination of Death. *In* Living and Working with the New Medical Technologies: Intersections of Inquiry. M. Lock, A. Young, and A. Cambrosio, eds. pp. 233–262. Cambridge: Cambridge University Press.

—— 2002. Twice Dead: Organ Transplants and the Reinvention of Death. Berkeley: University of California Press.

Lock, Margaret, and Deborah Gordon, eds. 1988. Biomedicine Examined. Dordrecht: Kluwer Academic Publishers.

Lock, Margaret, and Patricia Kaufert, eds. 1998. Pragmatic Women and Body Politics. Cambridge: Cambridge University Press.

Long, Susan O. 2000. Living Poorly or Dying Well: Decisions about Life Support and Treatment Termination for American and Japanese Patients. Journal of Clinical Ethics 11:27–41.

—— 2001. Negotiating the "Good Death": Japanese Ambivalence about New Ways to Die. Ethnology 40(4):271–289.

Long, Susan O, and B. Long. 1982. Curable Cancers and Fatal Ulcers. Social Science and Medicine 16:2101–2108.

Mitsuda, Kyōko. 1984. Kindaiteki boseikan no juyō to kenkei: kyōiku suru hahaoya kara ryōsai kenbo e (The Importance and Transformation of the Condition of Modern Motherhood: From Education Mother to Good Wife and Wise Mother). *In* Bosei o tou (What is Motherhood?). H. Wakita, ed. pp. 100–129. Kyoto: Jinbunshoin.

Miyaji, Naoko, and Margaret Lock. 1994. Social and Historical Aspects of Maternal and Child Health in Japan. Daedalus 123(4):87–112.

Morioka, Masahiro. 1989. Nōshi no hito (The Brain-Dead Person). Tokyo: Tokyo shoseki.

Nakajima Michi. 1985. Mienai shi: nōshi to zōki ishoku (Invisible Death: Brain Death and Organ Transplants). Tokyo: Bungei Shunju.

Nichter, Mark, and Margaret Lock, eds. 2002. New Horizons in Medical Anthropology: Essays in Honour of Charles Leslie. London: Routledge.

Norbeck, Edward, and Margaret Lock, eds. 1988. Health, Illness and Medical Care in Japan: Cultural and Social Dimensions. Honolulu: University of Hawaii Press.

Norgren, Tiana. 2001. Abortion Before Birth Control: The Politics of Reproduction in Postwar Japan. Princeton: Princeton University Press.

Nudeshima, Jirō. 1989. Nōshi, zōki ishoku to nihon shakai (Brain Death, Organ Transplants, and Japanese Society). Tokyo: Kōbundō.

Nukaga, Yoshio. 2002. Between Tradition and Innovation in New Genetics: The Continuity of Medical Pedigrees and the Development of Combination Work in the Case of Huntington's Disease. New Genetics and Society 21:39–64.

Ochanomizu Jōshidaigaku Seimei Rinri Kenkyūkai. 1990. Funin to yuseru onna tachi: seishoku gijūtsu no genzai to jōsei no seishokuken (Infertility and Women's Agony: The Current Situation in Connection with Reproductive Technologies and Women's Rights). Tokyo: Gakuyō Shobō.

Ohnuki-Tierney, E. 1984. Illness and Culture in Contemporary Japan. Cambridge: Cambridge University Press.

Perkins, Henry S. and Susan W. Tolle. 1992. Letter to the Editor [reporting American doubts about autopsies and organ procurement and the possiblity of people still being alive when such procedures are undertaken]. New England Journal of Medicine 326:1025.

Robertson, Jennifer. 2001. Japan's First Cyborg? Miss Nippon, Eugenics and Wartime Technologies of Beauty, Body and Blood. Body & Society 7(1):1–34.

—— 2002. Blood Talks: Eugenic Modernity and the Creation of New Japanese. History and Anthropology 13(3):191–216.

Rosenberger, Nancy R. 1988. Productivity, Sexuality, and Ideologies of Menopausal Problems in Japan. In Health, Illness and Medical Care in Japan: Cultural and Social Dimensions. E. Norbeck and M. Lock, eds. pp. 158–188. Honolulu: University of Hawaii Press.

Rousseau, Julie. 1998. Enduring Labors: The "New Midwife" and the Modern Culture of Childbearing in Early Twentieth Century Japan. Ph.D. dissertation, Columbia University.

Sanner, Margareta. 1994. A Comparison of Public Attitudes towards Autopsy, Organ Donation, and Anatomic Dissection. Journal of the American Medical Association 271:284–228.

Shimazu, Yoshiko. 1994. Unmarried Mothers and their Children in Japan. US–Japan Women's Journal 6:83–110.

Shirai, Yasuko. 1991. Japanese Attitudes Towards Assisted Procreation. The Journal of Law, Medicine and Ethics 21:43–52.

Siminof, L. A., and K. Chillag. 1999. The Fallacy of the "Gift of Life." Hastings Center Report 29:31–41.

Tachibana, Takashi. 1992. Nōshi rinchō hihan (Criticism of the Brain Death Special Committee). Chūō Kōronsha.

Tanaka-Matsumi, J. 1979. Taijin kyofushō. Culture, Medicine and Psychiatry 3:231–245.

Todd, Emmanuel. 1985. The Explanation of Ideology: Family Structures and Social Systems. Oxford: Basil Blackwell.

Tsuge, Azumi. 1992. Nihon ni okeru "funin chiri" gijutsu no kisei joki to sanfujinkai no taidō (The Situation of Restriction for Infertility Treatment and Gynecologists' Stance Towards the New Reproductive Technologies in Japan). Japan Journal for Science, Technology and Society 2:51–74.

Wakita, H., and S. Hanley, eds. 1994. Kindai to gendai nihon to josei (Women in Modern and Contemporary Japan). Tokyo: University of Tokyo Press.

Yanagida, Kunio. 1994. Sakurifaisu: waga musuko nōshi no 11 nichi (Sacrifice: Our Son and Eleven Days with Brain Death). Bungei shunjū 72:144–162.

—— 1995. Nōshi: watashi no teigen (Brain Death: My Proposal). Bungei shunjū 73:164–174.

Index

Page references in italics indicate tables.